Judy Foster is an artist and (retired) teacher of art. After studying at Monash University, a chance encounter with the book *The Language of the Goddess* by Marija Gimbutas in 1993 inspired her to begin researching the origin and meanings of visual symbolism. She has three daughters and lives in Melbourne.

Marlene Derlet taught at the Monash Centre for Indigenous Studies from 1989 to 1993. She co-authored, with poet Kristin Henry, *Talking Up a Storm* (1993). Born in Switzerland, Marlene is a linguist with a background in anthropology and sociology.

INVISIBLE WOMEN OF PREHISTORY

THREE MILLION YEARS OF PEACE, SIX THOUSAND YEARS OF WAR

JUDY FOSTER
WITH MARLENE DERLET

SPINIFEX

First published by Spinifex Press, 2013

Spinifex Press Pty Ltd
504 Queensberry St
North Melbourne, Victoria 3051
Australia
women@spinifexpress.com.au
www.spinifexpress.com.au

Editors: Maree Hawken and Susan Hawthorne
Cover design: Deb Snibson
Typesetting: Palmer Higgs
Index: Kath Harper

Front cover photo:
  Kabel, Matthias (14 January 2007) 'Venus of Willendorf', Wikimedia Commons <http://en.wikipedia.org/wiki/File:Venus_of_Willendorf_frontview_retouched_2.jpg>.
Back cover photos:
  1. Wikimedia Commons (September 2008) 'Venus of Laussel' <http://en.wikipedia.org/wiki/File:Venus-de-Laussel-vue-generale-noir.jpg>.
  2. Wikimedia Commons (December 2007) 'Tlatilco culture female figurines' <http://en.wikipedia.org/wiki/File:Tlatilco_culture_figurines.jpg>.

National Library of Australia
Cataloguing-in-Publication
Foster, Judy, 1934–
Invisible women of prehistory: three million years of peace, six thousand years of war / Judy Foster, Marlene Derlet
    978187675918 (pbk)
    9781742195483 (eBook: pdf)
    9781742197913 (eBook: ePub)
    9781742195513 (eBook: ePub USA)
    9781742197920 (eBook: ePub UK)
Includes bibliographical references and index
Women–History–to 500.
Women–Social conditions.
Prehistoric peoples.
Derlet, Marlene, 1936–
305.42

CONTENTS

List of Illustrations vii

A Timeline of Human Prehistory ix

PART ONE
The Prehistoric Female Principle: The Goddess of Old Europe 1

CHAPTER 1
The Theory of Marija Gimbutas 3

CHAPTER 2
Identifying Bias in Research 13

CHAPTER 3
Intangible Evidence: The Role of Language, Oral Transmission and Myth 27

CHAPTER 4
Tangible Evidence: Prehistoric Art, The Visual Image, Sign and Symbol 41

CHAPTER 5
Northern Hemisphere: The Prehistoric Goddess Figurines of Old Europe 53

CHAPTER 6
Hunter-Gathering, the First Horticulture and Agriculture 69

CHAPTER 7
Three Prehistoric Civilisations 83

PART TWO
The Indo-Europeans: 'Civilisation' and History Begin 113

CHAPTER 8
The First Indo-Europeans: The Beginning of 'Civilisation' and Written History 115

CHAPTER 9
The First Changes to Women's Status 129

CHAPTER 10
Indo-European Philosophies: Their Development and Effects 143

PART THREE
The Hidden and New Worlds: Prehistories, the Female Principle and Indo-European Influences 157

CHAPTER 11
Hidden Worlds: Africa 161

CHAPTER 12
Hidden Worlds: The Indian Subcontinent 179

CHAPTER 13
Hidden Worlds: China, Korea, Japan 203

CHAPTER 14
Hidden Worlds: Thailand and Indonesia 225

CHAPTER 15
New Worlds: Australia 243

CHAPTER 16
New Worlds: Oceania 265

CHAPTER 17
New Worlds: The Americas 285

CONCLUSION
Weaving the Threads 311

Acknowledgements 321

Notes 325

Bibliography 365

Index 393

LIST OF ILLUSTRATIONS

The Earliest Female Figurines xiv

Prehistoric Cave Paintings 2

Examples of Prehistoric Female Figurines 5

First Writing 21

Prehistoric Design Motifs which Led to Writing 22

Design Motifs Used in Oral Transmission 28

Old European Figurines and Spiral Designs 42

Chauvet Cave Paintings and Old European Figurines 54

Old Europe: Famous Goddess Figurines 60

Examples of the Few Early Male Figurines 66

Female Figurines of the Near East 73

Old European and Near Eastern Imagery 77

Gobekli Tepe 79

Saudi Arabian Rock Art 81

Anatolia: Wall Paintings and Figurines 84

Sculptures and Images Depicting Birth 87

Clay Stamp Seals and Painted Wall Motifs 91

Neolithic Newgrange 95

Neolithic Knowth 98

Irish Passage Tombs: Knowth and Newgrange 100

Hedgehog Goddess and Other Animal Imagery 104

Neolithic Minoan Crete: Knossos 107

Proto-Indo-European Sculptures, Pottery, and Rock Engravings 114

Earliest Warrior Equipment 121

Indo-European Weapons and Pottery 123

A Loulan Burial, Tokens 126

Early Warrior Goddesses 133

More Indo-European Imagery 137

Early Indo-European Goddesses 146

The Great Horned Goddess 158

Africa: Neolithic Images 160

Neolithic Egyptian Figurines 169

Africa: Goddess Figurines 171

The Great Horned Goddess 172

Figurines and Rock Art 183

India: Mehrgarh Figurines 186

India: Harappa Female Figurines 189

The Lady of the Spiked Throne 191

India: Traditional Women's Art 200

China: Hongshan Figurines 206

Symbolic Images from China 208

More Hongshan Female Figurines 211

Early Symbolic Korean Images 218

Early Dogu Figurines 220

Japan: Dogu Female Figurines 222

Thailand: Prehistoric Female Figurines 228

Traditional Arts of Thailand 232

Indonesia: Female Figurines 235

Early Indonesian Art 238

Australia: Rock, Body and Sand Art Forms 249

Australia: Various Symbolic Images 252

Endangered Burrup Peninsula Art 256

Oceania: Papua New Guinea Art 270

Solomon Islands and Papua New Guinea: Female Imagery 275

Torres Strait and Aotearoa/New Zealand: Female Imagery 278

North America: Designs and Sculptural Forms 289

North America: Female Figurines 294

Figurines of Mexico and South America 298

South America: Valdivia Figurines 304

Mesoamerica and South America: Female Figurines 307

Vulvas and Double Triangle Figurines 315

A Timeline of Human Prehistory

There are a number of landmarks indicating the emergence and development of human consciousness through the Palaeolithic era and Neolithic periods which lasted from before 2.8 million BP until after 6,000 BP. While tool-making commenced with the first hominids, *Homo habilis*, as far as is known at present the first symbol-making by *Homo erectus* did not occur until after 1 million BP. This is a largely hidden story of human societies before the advent of what is known as 'civilisation'. The modern human story did not begin 5,500 years ago with the first recorded history!

Contrary to popular belief, the discovery of agriculture 10,000 years ago did *not* change the communal, innovative and peaceful lifestyle of early societies. Instead, changes were due to the emergence of invading/infiltrating Indo-European pastoralists with their ever-increasing herd animals around 5,000–6,000 years later, who introduced male-dominant hierarchic social organisation, the acquisition of personal wealth, and violence, to the world.

A Timeline of Human Prehistory

Epoch	Stage	Tool Assemblages	Years BP	Developments
Pleistocene	Lower Palaeolithic	Oldowen	7,000,000–5,000,000	• Ethiopia: Earliest ape/human (January 1999) yet found*
			3,000,000	• Africa: *H. habilis* present
			2,500,000	• Ethiopia: *H. habilis* present
				• The earliest stone tools yet found date to this period
				• Jaw of *Homo* being (Hadar), oldest *Homo*
			2,000,000	• Africa and Asia: *H. erectus* present
				This suggests *H. erectus* evolved in a number of places, including Africa.
				• Collection of non-utilitarian objects
			1,800,000	• The Makapansgat hominid head carried 32 km to site
				• China, Russia, and Java: *H. erectus* present
				• Africa, Asia: Collection of red ochre pebbles, quartz crystals
			1,500,000	• Africa: First use of fire
		Lower Acheulian	1,300,000	• India: Collection of clear quartz crystals
			1,000,000	• Europe: *H. erectus* present
			800,000	• India: Red ochre 'crayons' with worn facets indicate ritual body or wall painting
		Acheulian		• India: First rock art, the cupules at Bhimbetka
				• South Africa, Spain, India, Russia and the Czech Republic: Red ochre in ritual burials
			700,000	• Java: First language, navigation and watercraft used by *H. erectus* implies use of woven fibres
			600,000	• Japan: First humans present
			500,000	• England: *H. erectus* present
				• France: Early controlled fire use by women
			300,000	• First intentional art images
				• Israel: The Berekhet Ram figurine
				• France: The meander engravings on the Pech de l'Azé ox bone
				• Germany, Spain, Crimea: First use of jewellery
				• Turkey, Germany: Finely crafted decorated tools
			200,000	• Europe and China: Archaic (early) *H. sapiens* arrives
				• Africa: Archaic *H. sapiens* present
			160,000–60,000	• Australia: Because of low sea levels at times during this period, humans could have come from either Java or Sulewasi.
		Upper Acheulian	140,000–120,000	• Australia: Core samples taken at Lake George indicate possible human interference with vegetation by the
			120,000–90,000	regular use of fire.
			100,000	• Israel: Earliest intentional burials
				• Java: Archaic *H. sapiens* present

Epoch	Stage	Tool Assemblages	Years BP	Developments
Pleistocene	Middle Palaeolithic	Micoquian	60,000	• South Africa and the Middle East: Modern *H. sapiens* present in a number of places, suggests they did not evolve solely in Africa but evolved multi-regionally • Australia: Red ochre 'crayon' and grindstone found in Malangangerr rock shelter in Arnhem Land was, until 1999, proof of the earliest presence of humans in Australia
		Moustarian	60,000–48,000	• Australia: Ritual cremation of Mungo Woman and Man, Lake Mungo
	Upper Palaeolithic		50,000–33,000	• Europe: Modern humans in eastern Europe spread to western Europe during this time
			48,000–42,000	• South Australia: Petroglyphs at Olary (open to revision)
			42,000–40,000	• South Australia: Engravings in Koonalda Cave, Nullarbor Plains • La Ferrassie, France: 18 cupules on limestone grave-marker
			40,000–35,000	• **The 'earliest' art first 'explodes' in Europe!** • Europe, Germany, and Siberia: Many female symbolic motifs; Schelklingen Woman, Hohles Fels cave • Europe: Shell and bone beads imply cord, thread • Australia: Polished, waisted stone axe at Cape York
		Aurignacian	32,000	• Austria: Galenberg figurine is earliest intentionally carved, three-dimensional female sculpture
			32,000–30,000	• Georgia: Earliest flax fibres = cord, Dzudzuana cave • Europe: Paintings in Cougnac and Cosquer Caves
			30,000	• France: Paintings in Chauvet-Pont-d'Arc Cave • Israel: Engraved limestone slab • Australia: Cuddie Springs – earliest use of mortar • Australia: Burrup Peninsula rock engravings, Western Australia
			30,000–17,000	• Australia: Kimberley Gwion Gwion paintings
			28,000	• Africa: Earliest portable paintings from Namibia • Australia: Paintings at Laura, Queensland • Australia: Petroglyphs at Hammersley, Pilbara, Western Australia
			27,000	• Java: *H. erectus* still living alongside Pleistocene archaic *H. sapiens* • Europe: Linen and hemp used for clothing
		Gravettian	26,000	• Czech Republic: Oldest clay modelled figurines of humans and animals • Australia: Lake Mungo footprints preserved
			25,000	• Russia: Pottery beads; burials of 3 people wearing thousands of ivory beads • France: Lespugne figurine with string apron
			22,000	• Australia: Human occupation at Drual rock shelter at Gariwerd (The Grampians), Victoria
			22,000–12,000	• Levant: Natufian settled culture, agriculture, permanent buildings, storage, etc.

Epoch	Stage	Tool Assemblages	Years BP	Developments
Pleistocene	Upper Palaeolithic	Solutrean	20,000	• Poland: Heavy carved ivory non-returning boomerang • Australia: Bone beads at Devil's Lair, Western Australia
			18,000	• Australia: Cave art (petroglyphs) at Cutta Cutta and Kintore, Northern Territory, and in Tasmania, Victoria and South Australia
			18,000–11,000	• Violent deaths in one place in northern Africa, only known evidence of violence in Palaeolithic apart from one instance in Italy • Japan: Pottery; Jomon culture – first pottery • Africa: Tassili, paintings similar in style to Lascaux and Altamira art
			17,000	• France: Lascaux cave paintings and rope
		Magdalenian	15,000	• Australia: Kow Swamp, ochre, tools • Japan: Two pebbles, engraved with women's torsos; perforated stone disc • China: Engraved antler with meander designs
			14,000	• Spain: Altamira Cave art
			13,000	• South America: Pigment ball with hole, perhaps an ornament; and polished, waisted stone axe • Italy: Two sites, arrow-like flint in woman's pelvis, arrow in child's vertebra, only evidence of violence in Upper Palaeolithic in Europe • Siberia: Amur site, early pottery
			12,500	• Southern Russia: People who were later to become the Indo-Europeans lived nomadic life
			11,500	• North America: Earliest agreed evidence of human occupation of the Americas; animal heads and a rhinoceros engraved on bone
Holocene	Neolithic		10,000	• Papua New Guinea and Middle East • Development of horticulture, agriculture • Anatolia: First sheep domesticated, used for meat • Australian mainland and Tasmania separate • Australia: Wyrie Swamp, wooden aerodynamic boomerangs, spears, etc. • Ireland: Humans arrive • Nile Valley: Agriculture
			9,500–5,500	• Sesklo and Vinca cultures in Europe
			9,000	• Southern Russia: The Yamna people of the Middle Volga Basin were pastoralists. • First sacrificial burials including horses in central Ukraine • Anatolia: Çatal Hüyük – a sophisticated settled civilisation • Turkey and Iran: Earliest metal work; linen used • India: Many paintings and engravings • Southern Russia: The Yamna people of the Middle Volga Steppe domesticate horses
			7,000	• Denmark: Naturalistic carved amber bear

Epoch	Stage	Tool Assemblages	Years BP	Developments
Holocene	Neolithic		6,400–6,300	• Australia: Lake Nitchie, unique tooth necklace • **Earliest invasions across Europe** by the early Yamna warrior peoples, now known as Proto-Indo-Europeans, from the Volga Steppe of Southern Russia
			6,300	• Vinča (Yugoslavia) culture ends
	Bronze Age		6,000	• Yugoslavia: Three clay tablets with first writing • Anatolia: Çatal Hüyük is abandoned • The first woolly sheep are selectively bred • Ireland: The passage tomb at Newgrange
		Period of written history	5,500	• Ireland: Knowth passage tomb • Sesklo (Thessaly) culture ends • **Second invasion of Old Europe** by Maikop warrior peoples from North Pontiac area • Sumeria: The 'first' writing – beginning of written history
			5,000	• Minoan period: The city of Knossos in Crete • England: Avebury Stones incl. Silbury Hill complex • America: Pyramid city of Caral; Neolithic • **Third invasion of Old Europe** by late Yamna warrior peoples; the end of Neolithic period
			4,500–3,000	• Ireland: Beaker people end Irish Neolithic period • Russia: Spoke-wheel chariot present • China: Caucasian Loulan people present • China: Caucasian Hami people present
			3,050	• End of the Minoan period in Crete
			CE	• Common Era begins

*These dates are not fixed – continuing new discoveries and updates frequently occur.

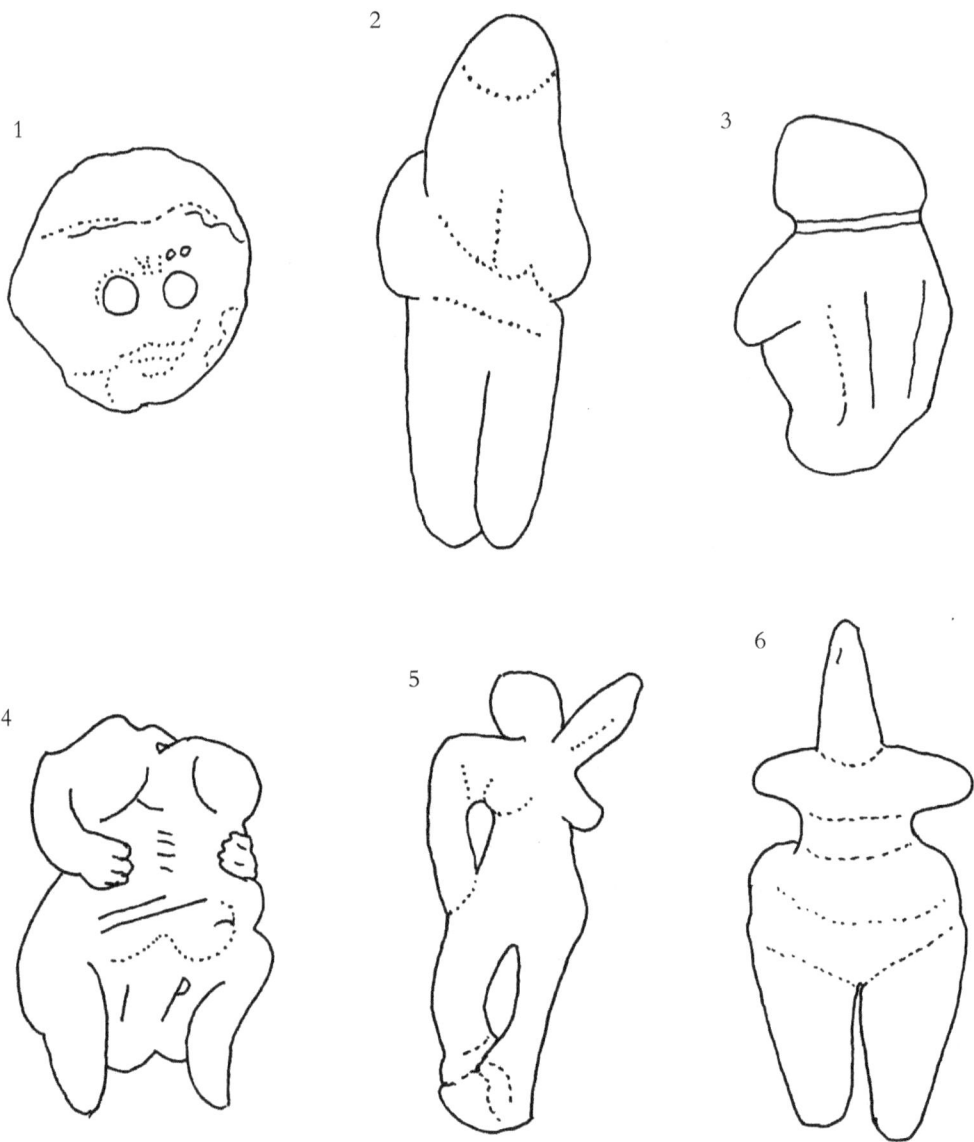

THE EARLIEST FEMALE FIGURINES

1. *Makapansgat hominid head*, Africa, 2,000,000 BP, a naturally formed pebble (Source: Bednarik, Robert, 1998)
2. *Tan Tan figurine*, Morocco, 400,000 BP
3. *Berekhat Ram figurine*, Israel, 300,000 BP (Source 2–3: Bednarik, Robert, 2001)
4. *Goddess from Hohle Fels*, the Scheklingen figurine, is 35,000 years old (Source: Jensen, H., 2009)
5. *Galenberg figurine*, Austria, 32,000 BP (Source: Bednarik, Robert, 1989)
6. *An early Cycladic figurine*, 7,000 BP (Source: Gimbutas, Marija, 1989)

All line drawings © Judy Foster, 2013

PART ONE

THE PREHISTORIC FEMALE PRINCIPLE: THE GODDESS OF OLD EUROPE

1

3

2

4

5

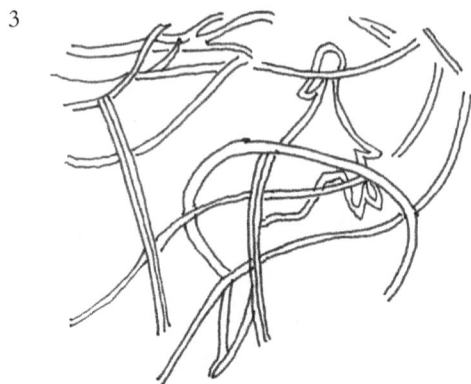

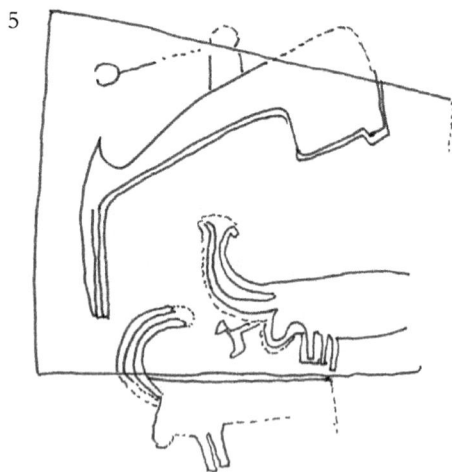

PREHISTORIC CAVE PAINTINGS

1. *Ariege cave painting*, France, 27,000-14,000 BP
2. *Cave paintings*, Altamira, Spain; Lascaux, France
3. *Pech Merle figure*, France, c. 20,000 BP
   (Source 1–3: Pericot-Garcia, Luis et al., 1967)
4. *Spanish cave art*, 8,000 BP
5. *Axe and bulls*, Gavrini, Brittany, 6,000 BP
   (Source 4–5: Gimbutas, Marija, 1989)
   All line drawings © Judy Foster, 2013

CHAPTER 1

THE THEORY OF MARIJA GIMBUTAS

Our search for the origins of visual symbolism led to the accidental discovery of *The Language of the Goddess* (1989), the first of three major works by Lithuanian archaeologist and mythologist Professor Marija Gimbutas. This impressive text illustrates the symbolism and records the underlying meaning of the prehistoric female figurines and associated objects belonging to a prominent female deity whom Marija Gimbutas named the 'great goddess'. In her second book, *The Civilization of the Goddess* (1991) she noted the presence of female figurines first appearing in the Upper Palaeolithic period. She recorded in great detail the habitations and cultures in the Neolithic world of Old Europe;[1] these were peace-loving and communal agricultural societies in which women were respected, even revered, and highly visible until as recently as 6,500 BP. Marija Gimbutas explained how these societies faded away or ended, often abruptly, as new horse-riding invaders proceeded to spread across Europe and Asia over the next thousand years, bringing with them new hierarchic and violent ideas and practices. So began the present patriarchal period.

In her third and final book, *The Living Goddesses* (2001), published after her death, Marija Gimbutas provided what has to be conclusive evidence of women-centred societies in prehistory, particularly in eastern Europe, reaching as far west as England and Ireland. She recorded thousands of female figurines and other artefacts reinforcing the powerful presence of the female principle. She followed the development of the multi-faceted goddess cultures from 9,000 years ago through the emergence of the Indo-Europeans and into the early historical period, observing the goddess's changing and diminishing role until recent times when the goddess has become almost invisible.

This unknown world before written history was revealed through the skills of archaeology, anthropology, linguistics, and mythology, combined disciplines which Marija Gimbutas named 'archaeomythology', and she used these to reinterpret the period in prehistory from 10,000 BP to 2,000 BP. It was not enough for her just to record the material culture of a society; she also found it essential to utilise other non-material research to discover the true picture of an archaeological site. Marija Gimbutas explained to Joan Marler that this different approach to the archaeology of Europe came about because of her background in Lithuania surrounded by folklore, mythology, and living goddess traditions, and her exposure to both Indo-European sky gods and earlier mythologies which were deeply connected

> with the Earth and its mysterious cycles that was still alive in the Lithuanian countryside ... The rivers were sacred, the forest and trees were sacred, the hills were sacred ... The people still followed traditional ways of working the land.[2]

3

She discovered that the great goddess who was to be found everywhere in Indo-European religions had been inherited from the earlier religions of Old Europe, and she came to recognise that there were two distinct systems: firstly, that of the peaceful Palaeolithic and Neolithic women-centred Old Europeans; and secondly, the aggressive male-dominant religious systems of the Indo-Europeans. It became necessary to study symbols through their context and association, and it was in this way that she discovered how the Old European cultures experienced long-term peaceful living with egalitarian social structures and non-material value systems of benefit to all. Until Indo-European contact these were, and where possible, still are, the values of most indigenous people around the world. Although Marija Gimbutas spent 25 years examining the visual symbolism of Old Europe, she felt she had only just begun the search, and her greatest wish was for succeeding scholars to discover the full story of the Old Europeans.

While a researcher at Harvard University, Marija Gimbutas led several excavations in Europe, Yugoslavia and Italy over 13 years. In her first report, *The Gods and Goddesses of Old Europe* (1974), she began to develop her hypothesis concerning a Palaeolithic and Neolithic multi-dimensional female deity, Indo-European origins and the beginning of the patriarchal period. She always read other excavation reports in their original language so that her overview of the general picture was as accurate as possible.

In her excavations Marija Gimbutas found many artefacts including female sculptures in household sites in positions which suggested they may have had religious significance. She began to notice certain often-repeated forms of symbolism, such as bird and snake imagery, associated with these female goddess forms which suggested a symbolic meaning. It was already known that from earliest times humans were aware of metaphysical forces such as spirits in various animal or other forms, or ancestral beings or deities, often manifested in ritual burial practices or incised rock art imagery that were concerned with some religious aspect. She found that metaphysical beings in the Neolithic context were female and noted not only for their birth-giving and nurturing aspects, but also for their guiding roles as carers of the community.

It also became clear to Marija Gimbutas that Palaeolithic and Neolithic (goddess) female sculptures expressed many more functions than those of fertility and motherhood. She defined the goddess as unifying all natural things, as a metaphor for earth's powers, and the expression of the power of nature through plant, animal and human life. In *The Language of the Goddess* (1989) she explains that the goddess religion was "a cohesive and persistent ideological system"[3] aspects of which live on into the present time despite being eroded away within the historic era.

Marija Gimbutas regarded as a serious ongoing problem the critical Western male association of female figurines with 'fertility' rites and cultic imagery when interpreting societies of the deep past. Such views are more likely to reflect pervasive masculinist and mainstream prejudices, and they assume prehistoric cultures to be similar to our own; it is still hard for most people to admit that a very different world could have existed.

Earlier women-centred earth/nature/goddess symbolic systems in which women and men each had their own role and their own power, were found to be very different to those in the warrior period, where all the gods were warriors. The most important gods in the new Indo-European era were the 'god of the shining sky', the 'god of the underworld', and the 'thunder god', while the goddesses were demoted to become powerless brides, wives

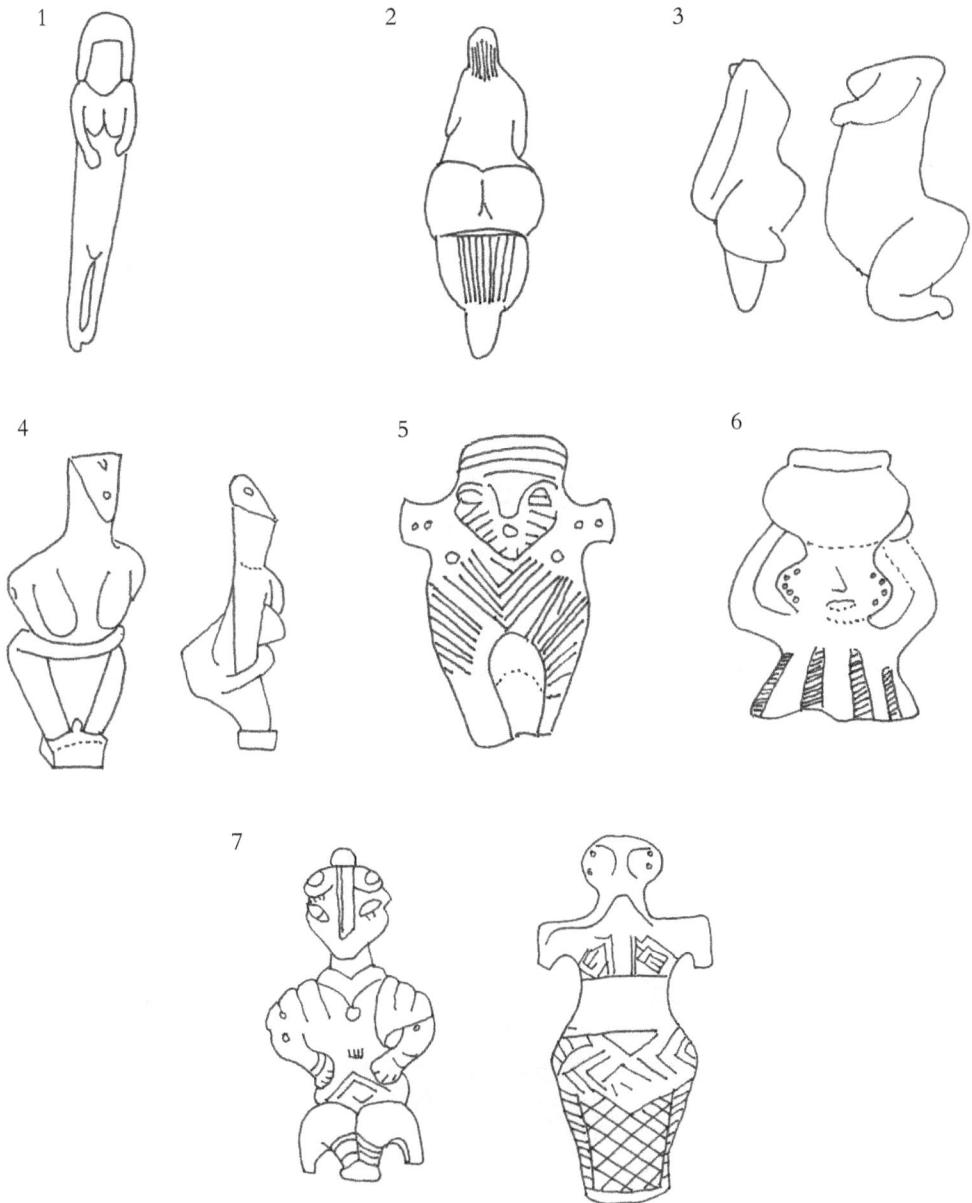

EXAMPLES OF PREHISTORIC FEMALE FIGURINES

1. *Figurine*, Malt'a, Siberia
2. *Lespunge figurine wearing her string apron*
3. *Two calcite figurines*, France, 23,000 BP
4. *Two views of a Malt'a figurine*, 7,500 BP
5. *Vinča bird goddess*, 7,000 BP
6. *Romanian ritual vase*, 7,000 BP
7. *Two Vinča figurines*, 6,500 BP
   (Source: Gimbutas, Marija, 1989)

All line drawings © Judy Foster, 2013

or maidens lacking any creative or social powers. These later Indo-European patriarchal cultures were found to be considerably less sophisticated than the earlier goddess culture, and this was clearly demonstrated by the disappearance of the refined and beautiful Neolithic artefacts which, evidence suggests, were replaced by the rather less sophisticated tools of the violent Bronze Age warriors.

Most (male) archaeologists also assume hierarchical interpretations for village layouts in the Neolithic period when the property of the peaceful agriculturalists had been communally owned; but it was the Proto-Indo-Europeans who introduced individual male ownership of people and goods. Social organisation became class-based, led by powerful wealthy kings or chieftains; women became male property and war victims were reduced to slavery. Villages now had to be surrounded by defensive fortifications in order to prevent unauthorised access or invasion. Agriculture and war did not start at the same time in the past: agriculture was developed over 4,000 years before the emergence of the pastoralist Proto-Indo-Europeans.

Since Marija Gimbutas completed recording her discoveries other evidence has emerged which supports her theory. For example, archaeologist David Anthony (1998), when studying horses' bit wear in the Russian steppe region, also identified the original Proto-Indo-European homelands in this area north of the Caucasus, a scenario similar to that described by Marija Gimbutas. He examined the jawbones of horses found in the earliest graves on the steppes and dated them to about 6,000 BP,[4] providing a date for the earliest horse riding, and for the homelands of the Proto-Indo-Europeans. His dates also align in every way with those of Marija Gimbutas.

In *The Mummies of Urumchi* (1999) Elizabeth Barber provides interesting and convincing textile evidence for the steppe homelands of the Proto-Indo-Europeans, and includes comparisons of looms and thread used in the Indo-European homelands and surrounds as against those used elsewhere in Eurasia. This research supports Marija Gimbutas's identification of the Proto-Indo-Europeans' homelands and their aggressive activities as they spread outward into the surrounding Neolithic European farming lands.

Geneticist Luigi Cavalli-Sforza (2000) has acknowledged the theories of Marija Gimbutas concerning the origins of Indo-European speakers. He also notes that genetic evidence supports David Anthony's more recent discoveries of the rise of horse riding in southern Russia. He is enthusiastic about the idea of multidisciplinarity (such as Marija Gimbutas's use of archaeomythology), and considers there are major benefits to be gained by involving many disciplines when examining a field of study.

The inspired scientific investigations of Marija Gimbutas have opened up to us new ways of seeing and understanding our past, but have upset many conservative (male) researchers, most of whom still refuse to recognise her discoveries, even as new evidence continues to support them. She has been greatly respected by European scholars for her meticulous body of work. In 1963, Marija Gimbutas became emeritus Professor of European Archaeology at the University of California, Los Angeles (UCLA) where she worked until she retired in 1989. Up until her death in 1994, she remained satisfied that her theories were soundly based, but anticipated that it would take 30 years or more for her theories to become generally recognised.

Achievements of Marija Gimbutas

A number of researchers have endorsed the greatest achievements of Marija Gimbutas.[5] Starhawk (1997)[6] argues that Marija Gimbutas's work has allowed acceptance of the antiquity, continuity and sacredness of immanence within Western cultures.[7] Researchers can disagree with Marija Gimbutas's interpretation of the goddess culture but they cannot ignore it without revealing their ignorance. Marija Gimbutas not only presents the evidence, but demonstrates how it had meanings which reflect spiritual values shared and understood by many peoples of the time.

Shortly before his death, noted mythologist and historian, Joseph Campbell told Maureen Barlow in 1998[8] that he profoundly regretted that Marija Gimbutas's research of Neolithic Old Europe was not available when he was writing *The Masks of God*. He compared the importance of the effect of her work to that of the deciphering of Egyptian hieroglyphics.

For Michael Dames (1997),[9] it was the subversive nature of Marija Gimbutas's approach, and her use of available techniques to examine the enormous variations between prehistoric cultures that allowed access to the individuality of those different worlds, which was so impressive. Marija Gimbutas set the format, leaving others to fill in the details later, and providing us with many stimulating questions to answer.

Charlene Spretnak (1997) feels that the basis for critics' attacks is the "anti-nature, anti-body orientation"[10] of Western philosophy. Indigenous cultures and prehistoric societies understood the *continuity* between humans and nature, and Marija Gimbutas's evidence shows it is entirely possible for humanity to again become whole with nature, just as we had been for a very long time in the past.

Carol Christ (1997a) points out that Marija Gimbutas's work unintentionally challenges patriarchy because it is implicitly feminist and radical. She would not have attracted so much criticism if she had not dared to challenge the "myth of progress"[11] which underlies Western 'civilisation' and condemns prehistory as inferior, primitive, and barbarian. Carol Christ warns that we must be continually aware that the critics of Marija still aim to discredit her carefully interpreted and developed theories.

Diarmuid O'Murchu (2000)[12] feels it would be unjust and very arrogant to ignore the many recent inspiring and visionary researchers who are also convinced of the presence of a single multidimensional female deity as Marija Gimbutas had envisaged.

While Marija Gimbutas was certain that prehistoric societies were predominantly peaceful from earliest times until contact with the emerging violent warlike Proto-Indo-Europeans, Elizabet Sahtouris (2000)[13] draws to our attention certain recent scientific theory which suggests that humans are indeed not innately violent, since our genes are closest to those of mainly peaceful orang-utans, chimpanzees and gorillas. She stresses that the occasional violence among these creatures is seized upon by patriarchal influences and emphasised to prove human violence as innate.[14] In recent years the research on the lesser-known primate, the bonobo, has led to the thesis that human society could model itself on the female-centric social patterning of bonobo interactions.[15] The chimpanzee turns out to be a very different model and there is no necessary connection between chimp behaviour and human behaviour as previously argued. Animals use ritual dances and fights to preserve their continuity in the natural world, providing they have adequate territory. These rituals of behaviour, formed in evolution, are a system of rules for living together in relative peace. (Humans, too, observed these rules until 6,000 BP). An obsession with violence (for example, the history of warfare) portrayed in the media and taught in schools and universities, perpetuates this myth of innate violence. Only in the past 6,000 years have humans been the only animal that stores more food and occupies more land than it needs. She warns that violent practices against other humans endanger us as a species and unless we return to living within peaceful cooperative communities, as have other successful long-surviving species, we may not have a future.

In an interview with Paula Harris in *Sonoma County Independent* (1997), Joan Marler describes Marija Gimbutas's work as a "radical retelling of the origins of Western civilization."[16] Marija Gimbutas had no feminist agenda but reported what she saw and discovered within a scientific framework. Joan Marler argues that her greatest legacy has implications reaching far beyond academic circles, and gives us hope and direction for the future in an uncertain world. Marija Gimbutas's dream was for us to share our discoveries of women's lives in prehistory and to always respect and remember our foremothers.

Critics

Marija Gimbutas has been most criticised for her identification of a single 'great goddess' who was worshipped all over Europe and beyond. This interpretation was based on her extensive study of the symbolic aspects of a wide-ranging collection of diverse female deities. For her, the great goddess "was one and many, a unity and a multiplicity."[17] People worshipped a goddess or goddesses in many forms; according to Marija, the great goddess "was the feminine force that pervaded existence."[18]

Most mainstream 'scientific' archaeologists consider it impossible to uncover the meanings of prehistoric symbols, or speak of religion because, in their opinion, there is no substantiating evidence. They argue that it was unlikely that one 'goddess' was recognised over such a large area when human groups were small and scattered and inter-communication limited. However, it is important to note that all 600 groups of Indigenous people in Australia, despite differences in language and culture, recognise the one Law, as well as the Earth Mother who had been known to most indigenous people prior to the historic period.

Despite the great respect that some European archaeologists have for the integrity and thorough investigations of Marija Gimbutas, her research has been considerably undermined by harsh and unfounded criticism by processual[19] archaeologist, Colin Renfrew, Professor of Archaeology at Cambridge University, and his followers. He has disagreed with every aspect of the Gimbutas theories ever since 1974, when he first proclaimed that it was impossible for agricultural practices to take place before the emergence of pastoral activities and the domestication of animals. However, linguists reject this view, as the earliest words for 'agriculture', and the names of most cultivated grains, are pre-Indo-European; furthermore, Old Anatolians and Old European Neolithic people would have been non-Indo-Europeans. Colin Renfrew also argues that horse riding could only have occurred between 4,000 and 3,200 BP despite all evidence to the contrary.[20]

A more recent aspect of the new processual archaeology is cognitive archaeology which examines earlier ways of thinking shown in prehistoric material remains, although this method is also limited to empirical testing. As non-material evidence cannot be scientifically tested it is ignored. For example, Norwegian Professor Gro Mandt (1997) argues that rock art holds much non-material information about human interrelations, and mediates "ideas and beliefs important in maintenance of gender ideology and relations of their society."[21]

She draws on the work of Julie Drew, one of the few Australian archaeologists who has analysed women and gender relations in Australian rock art in her (unpublished) 1991 thesis 'Depictions of women and gender relations in rock art of Australia'. Based on (unprovable) art symbolism, the subject is considered non-scientific by Australian processual and cognitive archaeologists. According to linguist Martin Huld in a letter to Joan Marler, Marija Gimbutas considered that the 'New Archaeology' was sterile, and laboratory techniques alone were not sufficient to provide the full picture. Martin Huld agreed that the multidisciplinary approach taken by Marija "was the only sound way to deal with the problems of prehistory."[22]

Among Colin Renfrew's followers are two other influential critics, one of whom is Paul Bahn. In *Prehistoric Art: Cambridge illustrated history* (1998), he upholds a sexist view of Palaeolithic figurines and symbols as he concentrates on relatively rare examples of the phallus and other prehistoric male images and ignores the multitude of female imagery Marija Gimbutas and other Eastern European archaeologists have found.

The second critic is Brian Fagan (1991)[23] who grudgingly admits that it is now generally accepted that all hunter-gatherer societies were peaceful, non-hierarchic and communal, although in his prehistory of the Americas (a university archaeological textbook) he carefully ignores any mention of the prominent female principle in Native American pre-contact societies. According to Joan Marler, Brian Fagan described Marija Gimbutas's work as 'sexist', a view which suggests that he does not understand the meaning of the word and has never properly read her reports. However, many prominent scholars have since firmly rejected his criticism.

In a letter to the editor of *Scientific American* (March, 2004) Joan Marler points out that Ian Hodder's recent archaeological exploration at Çatal Hüyük reinforces James Mellaart's and Marija Gimbutas's interpretations of their findings. Ian Hodder admits that the goddess cultures might have been "symbolic of the importance of women"[24] as he could not find any evidence which disproved their theories. In his 2006 report, *The Leopard's Tale: Revealing the mysteries of Çatal Hoyuk*, his research was firmly based within the conservative cognitive archaeological tradition where most non-material evidence is ignored. By examining only the material which could be scientifically tested, he exposed the limitations of this form of archaeology. Joan Marler observes that "innovation never comes from repetition of accepted formulas"[25] and Ian Hodder's report demonstrates the lack of courage and vision needed to build on James Mellaart's picture of Neolithic Anatolia. She adds that Marija Gimbutas "extended the methodological framework of her discipline to include ideological investigation ... within a multidimensional context"[26] and thus was judged 'non-scientific' and 'lacking methodology' by her critics.

For those who ignore or demean Marija Gimbutas's research, or claim it is just a hypothesis or speculation (such as Paul Bahn and Brian Fagan), Maureen Barlow reminds them that their own research can also be considered speculative. However, she recognises the threatening nature of such a view for most men since it means they can no longer dominate in a 'man's world'.

It is not only biased conservative male critics who reject Marija Gimbutas's views of European prehistory. Liberal feminists[27] such as processual archaeologists Lucy Goodison and Christine Morris (1998)[28] argue that earlier researchers including Marija Gimbutas did not record and interpret the artefacts they discovered 'in place', a practice which could greatly affect the meaning of the imagery, and was not 'scientific'. While most of the researchers found strong evidence for female 'divinities', they could not necessarily be assumed to be deities. Female figurines and pottery vessels featuring possible symbolic female functions, for example, might suggest various ritual and religious concerns, none of which would necessarily have been associated with a single female deity. Consequently they say there is no apparent (scientific) archaeological foundation for the presence of a single monotheistic dominant 'goddess' in the Upper Palaeolithic period (from 30,000 to 6,000 BP).

Marija Gimbutas's careful methodology is not recognised by the narrow focus of these conservative archaeologists because science cannot 'measure', 'interpret' or 'prove' the symbolic dimension of culture. Despite the fact that Marija Gimbutas's discoveries concerning the origins of the Proto-Indo-Europeans (or Kurgans, as Marija named them) have been fully supported by more recent genetic, linguistic and archaeological evidence, her Kurgan theory is not necessarily accepted either, as most prefer to believe that patriarchy has always been with us.

They dislike Marija Gimbutas's references to a goddess in her meticulous, multidisciplinary interpretation of an earth/nature female deity with many similar aspects found in many cultures across Europe and beyond. Rather, for these conservative scientific archaeologists the prominent female principle is represented by many female 'divinities' which are identified by some aspect which may suggest 'otherness', for example, large size, non-human features such as wings, or by non-personified forms such as the sun, animals, plants, etc. (the basis of symbolic designs). There is not one deity but many, with diverse meanings, a proposal never denied by Marija Gimbutas.[29]

Margaret Conkey and Ruth Tringham (1996) also attack Marija Gimbutas for speaking with "questionable authority" and "speculation" about "true facts"[30] concerning the archaeological evidence and interpretation of Neolithic symbolic images, so that their ambiguity and multiplicity of interpretations are lost. Nor do they accept her apparent focus on the "fashionable" goddess theory or accept a female emphasis without dominance in Palaeolithic and Neolithic societies. For these biased liberal feminist critics, women can never regain real power (power-over?) because they have never had it in the first place.[31] According to Joan Marler, processual feminist critics also do not understand that women's spirituality is not about revenge or power politics but is concerned with gaining power-within rather than embracing new systems of domination or power-over.

In a critique, Joan Marler (2003)[32] records that Cynthia Eller (like the other liberal feminists) argues that if past societies were not patriarchal then they must have been matriarchal, dominated by women. Under this form of 'matriarchy', women are considered equal or superior to men, and their culture is based on so-called powerful dangerous feminine values and life events. However, Marija Gimbutas rejected this description of women-centred prehistoric cultures because it implies social structures which reflect patriarchy.

Whether there were many deities, spirits or ancestral beings, or one goddess with many aspects as Marija Gimbutas asserted, it is important that we recognise a prominent female principle in those communal societies and the possible return to a focus on the equality of women and men. And while some researchers are critical of the way in which the female deity is presented as 'the one goddess' for all of Europe, arguing that this cannot be proved, others ignore the implications altogether, preferring not to make *any* interpretations of the rich non-material female symbolic imagery of the Palaeolithic and Neolithic periods.

The new awareness of women-centred earth-based spirituality and ecology which emerged in the 1970s and 1980s with the work and insights of Marija Gimbutas, and radical feminists Diane Bell, Mary Daly, Heide Göttner-Abendroth, Susan Griffin, Carolyn Merchant, Patricia Monaghan, Vandana Shiva, Charlene Spretnak, Starhawk, Merlin Stone, and others, allowed rejection of deeply held beliefs of universal male dominance and introduced the possibility that women could once again lead as 'creators of culture'.

Ethnographical studies of 150 indigenous societies by Peggy Reeves Sanday (2002) reveal male–female relationships which are "matrilineal, egalitarian, [and] democratic"[33] rather than male-dominant, according to Joan Marler (2003). To ignore such data and assume that women have always been subservient is to ignore considerable evidence to the contrary. She notes the assumption that prehistoric women had a lower status due to their major role of childbearing and nurturing. Denial and over-simplification of the part played by women in the past has resulted in a significant limitation and downplaying of the economic and social importance of women.

The Gimbutas theory of a prominent female principle present in prehistory has enormous implications for the current status of women, considering that Palaeolithic and Neolithic women had played such an important social and cultural role in the long period before the Warrior Age. It is this fact which male-dominant mainstream archaeological research considers threatening because it could render invalid the current long-standing, strongly-held beliefs about male superiority.

While some aspects of the 'one goddess' concept proposed by Marija Gimbutas do not convince some researchers, her theories about the earth-centred female principle have been clearly substantiated. In a number of sources, some of which have been adduced throughout this text, there are comments about the peaceful nature of Palaeolithic and Neolithic societies.

At the end of her 1992 interview with David Brown and Rebecca McLlen Novik, Marija Gimbutas expressed that although she may have made some mistakes in deciphering the goddess symbols, for her the process of understanding was ongoing, and criticism was not important because "[w]hat is true is true, and what is true will remain."[34]

CHAPTER 2

IDENTIFYING BIAS IN RESEARCH

Bias in archaeology affects the way we view the past and it also has a history. There is bias, firstly, in the representation of prehistoric societies before written history as 'primitive' or 'barbaric' when compared with historical 'civilisations'; secondly, in the way the term 'matriarchy' is used when reporting and interpreting archaeological discoveries, artefacts and prehistoric social relationships and hierarchies; and thirdly, in the understanding of the meaning of the term 'civilisation'.

Women's innovations since the earliest times, although critical to the development of human societies, have seldom been recognised or recorded as female inventions. Archaeological recording of any new evidence and its interpretation remains largely the realm of certain white Western male researchers who ensure that men remain the dominant force in society and in history. Only in recent times have female researchers drawn our attention to these obvious deficiencies in this picture of prehistory.

Sex, gender and bias[1]

As we have seen in the previous chapter, Marija Gimbutas was the archetypal victim of bias, a woman who dared to emphasise a predominant prehistoric female aspect in an historically male-dominated discipline. Many other women have also experienced such bias, and often have recorded the difficulties they faced in researching, recording and publishing their discoveries. In her 1973 preface to *Beyond God the Father*,[2] Mary Daly notes that women's reasoning and intuition have led to many discoveries which are rarely acknowledged; they have had unequal access to the printed word to publish their research, and have had their ideas stolen from them.

According to Elizabeth Twohig and Margaret Ronayne (1993),[3] and Gerda Lerner (1986),[4] bias continues to remain a problem when interpreting the past. Our understanding of sex and gender roles can bias us as we view the evidence from our own selective viewpoint. Also, the influence of previous (Western white male) researchers over several centuries of archeological practice has meant that there is a great need for women's perspectives to be incorporated in order to provide a balanced historical vision. Furthermore, since patriarchy is a historical system with a *beginning*, it can also have an *end*.

Joan Gero (1996)[5] notes that men record history from their point of view: they decide what is recorded and how. Male researchers are considered to be 'objective' and 'neutral', but 'subjective' female researchers tend to look for the unusual, the intimate and the unique aspects. Women in general are less inclined to emphasise technological and scientific aspects, and pay greater attention to the complexity and ambiguity of the subject.[6] Carol Christ (1980)[7] gives an example: if women want their writing to be taken seriously they have to conform to 'objective' male standards of format and presentation (a view accepted by liberal feminists). Providing accessibility for *all* readers is thus considered to be 'subjective' and therefore not 'scholarly'. According to Michael Dames (1997),[8] since the 17th century we have been living in the age of Scientific Rationalism, in which there is also a bias against supernatural influences or events which cannot be considered as 'objective reality', rather everything must be explained in abstract terms.

On archaeological sites, men and women are affected by the prevailing view of sex and gender which comprises the gender-based organisation of allocated 'local tasks' and data collection. Joan Gero (1996) reports an example of this at an Argentinian site: a female and a male crew member were assigned to document the position of certain freshly excavated artefacts. This procedure involved scraping the soil away carefully from the objects in situ. The resulting 'pedestal' supporting the object created by the female crew member was small and exact, while the pedestal created by the male crew member was larger than necessary, but therefore more impressive. The site director ignored the woman's more precise work, and took a feature photograph and recorded the data of the man's large pedestal. Joan Gero comments that such instances are apparently quite common.

Usually archaeological evidence provides a record of settlement lifestyles, such as the variety of houses present, the economic situation, and the foods eaten; in fact many details of everyone's daily life. But female roles and relations have not often been studied: what women might have done throughout prehistory has been considered quite irrelevant or even frivolous and impertinent! The early (male only) writings recorded unusual events exclusive to the lives of higher-class men and neglected the everyday lives of ordinary women and men, which is why details about women's social and political status in prehistoric societies are largely absent. Margaret Ehrenberg (1989)[9] records that there were very few studies of prehistory and none of prehistoric women before the 1970s.

According to Judith McGaw (1996),[10] when recording past societies there is a need to include the gendered and technological aspects of archaeology in order to balance the male Western bias. For example, prehistoric women developed specific skills and knowledge, and utilised a greater variety of tools (woven or net carry bags, baskets and mats, grinding and cooking utensils and vessels, looms and weights, digging sticks), in comparison with the more limited tool kits of men (stone blades, axes, spears). Not until the innovations of prehistoric women are recorded can we understand just how much emphasis is placed on the presumed innovations of prehistoric men to the detriment of women.

Assumptions and ideologies underlie how men conceptualise technology. For example, metallurgy appears to be considered much more innovative and important than weaving and cooking in the archaeological hierarchy. Yet the preparation of food has always been a basic human requirement and woven textiles were used in prehistoric societies in all social, political, economic and religious contexts, by both men and women.

Another area of concern is the depiction of the religious aspects of a culture. For example, if the female rather than the male principle appears to be more prominent in excavated evidence from Palaeolithic and Neolithic societies, then the current patriarchal society might suppress the information, since it could upset their hierarchic cultural and religious systems. Indeed they might prevent further excavations which would support such views. According to James Mellaart (1970)[11] this is precisely what occurred at Haçilar, and this promising Neolithic archaeological site was closed down before the earliest and deepest levels were reached. The authorities claimed that there was nothing new of *scientific* value to be revealed by further work on the site. It was then opened to the public, and exploited and destroyed by treasure hunters, a most tragic outcome for archaeological history. But strictly 'scientific' cognitive archaeological boundaries observed by Ian Hodder in his reports (from 1995 until 2006) concerning the more recent excavations at Çatal Hüyük, indicate that Ian Hodder is likely to be able to continue working there until 2017. That the postprocessural method has been given preference and access to the sites over James Mellaart's contextual method has implications for how prehistory is interpreted.

There are also possible political reasons for the somewhat narrow Eurocentric viewpoint: everyone wants to be the first to find the earliest art and its use; and everyone wants the first discovery to be in their own country, as proof of their early cultural superiority.

The bias against the research of many female archaeologists continues to this day despite claims (by men) that the work of women and men receives equal consideration. Alice Beck Kehoe's acknowledgement to her 1998 text illustrates this point superbly:

> As a woman entering graduate school at Harvard at the end of the 1950s, a married woman with a CHILD yet! – I lived outside the social circle of promising young archaeologists and their mentors. Then and after, my marginalised status brought me into the company of a host of interesting people, women and men, avocational and professional researchers and those who lived what we researched. For the information, support, and stimulation you all have given me, I thank you. And to you bastards who are too important to engage with someone lacking a prestigious position, I thank you, too, for illuminating the social structure of American archaeology. Without you, I couldn't have written this book.[12]

Bias in archaeology

Colin Renfrew and Paul Bahn's 1991 *Archaeology: Theories, method and practice*[13] (widely used in universities until the 2000s), presented a typical review of 'primitive' (male) prehistoric peoples and their societies, which not surprisingly, had ignored indigenous women's contributions.[14] They record that in the late 1850s (male) French and English scholars decided that cultural artefacts and skeletal remains which they had excavated could be classified as coming from different eras. Gradually it was realised that human evolution did not begin with the biblical idea of creation, but rather at a time long before recorded history, known as 'prehistory'.

An important example of historical bias is reflected in the influential and controversial theory of human beginnings developed by Charles Darwin who, in 1859, applied himself to the study of (male) 'native' inhabitants in different parts of the world. It was agreed that human societies had undergone three stages of evolution in a world of natural selection where only the fittest survived. Humans, as the highest form of evolution, were at the top of the evolutionary 'tree', and the oldest most 'primitive' (single-cell) life forms were to be found at the bottom.

In the human story, the first and lowest stage of this view of evolution was that of 'primitive hunting and gathering', and the so-called primitive indigenous peoples of the world were categorised as being on different levels of 'savagery' (men were always placed higher than women). Australian Indigenous people were considered the lowest 'savages' as apparently they were only intelligent enough to acquire the most basic tools, and to live in the most temporary of dwellings. The second, somewhat 'higher', stage of evolution was 'simple farming', or 'barbarism', while the 'highest form of society', the pinnacle of (male) human development, was known as 'civilisation'. Today this view is known as 'social Darwinism'.

According to Elizabet Sahtouris (2000), before Charles Darwin presented his theory, biologist Jean-Baptiste Lamarck (1801) had already proposed that all living things were able to change themselves during their lifetime in order to take advantage of their environment with the best known example being the giraffe, which began to stretch its neck to reach the high branches of trees, passing this ability on to its progeny, a theory that "was ridiculed, while Darwin's was adopted in the West". Elizabet Sahtouris says scientists of the time did not yet know how "larger multi-celled creatures could reorganise their genes" according to their environment, and some researchers still do not accept the evidence from epigenetics which proves Jean-Baptiste Lamarck's theory.[15] Darwin's theory prevailed, perhaps because it did not involve changing our perception of ourselves as being superior to the creatures of the natural world, and the human male as superior to the female.

In 1915, the French archaeologist, Abbé Henri Breuil, was the first person to carefully describe and classify the art found in locations such as the famous caves of Lascaux and Altamira in Spain. According to M. Lorblanchet (1977), Abbé Breuil took an ethnographical approach to his comparison of the art of the different contemporary indigenous cultures and societies in order to find the meanings of, and the purposes for, these early images. He saw many of these 'primitive' images as *men's* "early intuitive random scribbles"[16] within which recognisable images may have been discerned, and out of which emerged attempts at representations of animals or humans, which illustrated their reality.

In the 1920s, there were further attempts to account for the origins of cultures, which were thought to have occurred in the Near East. While some researchers argued that innovations such as stone architecture and metal weapons were the attributes of 'civilisation' and had been brought to Europe from the Near East by traders and immigrants, others maintained that some cultural development did occur in Europe. The idea of a Neolithic or early agricultural revolution leading to the development of farming was first proposed at this time (see timeline pp. x–xiii). But nobody considered for a moment that similar developments might also have been taking place in the Hidden Worlds of the Northern and Southern Hemispheres.

In the 1930s and 1940s, living cultures and their (male) lifestyles, occupations and environments, were studied in order to understand the stages of human evolution. The notion arose that cultures interacted within a particular environment, as well as with one another. Adapting to new environments naturally affected (male) cultural practices. These ideas were thought to have opened up new and deeper understandings of earlier societies. But cultures other than those in the Northern Hemisphere were considered too 'primitive' to be of much interest.[17]

In the late 1940s, radiocarbon dating was first used and archaeology became a science. Artefacts were now able to be more accurately dated and slotted into a timeframe and this data described, explained and interpreted in order to build up a picture of the object and the culture to which it belonged. Like Abbé Breuil, the (male) scholars who studied the art of the Upper Palaeolithic era not only described the (male) images but also tried to deduce from the art how and why it was used. This meant that there had to be a starting point for the time frame within which the date of an object falls, either BC (before Christ) or AD (after Christ).

In the 1950s, archaeologists such as Grahame Clark took the study of the past a step further by examining the interaction and adaptation of (male) human populations to their environments in order to understand earlier peoples. To find the origins of art and culture, it was now thought necessary to look at the whole of a culture and its environment.[18]

In the 1960s, what Colin Renfrew and Paul Bahn described as 'the New Archaeology' emerged with the 'process' of technology now considered a central component. American archaeologists, such as Lewis Binford, argued that the process of any archaeological theory should be made explicit. No longer was it enough that the results of a hypothesis could be presented; rather, the process by which this conclusion was reached should be made public so it could be debated by the (male) archaeological confraternity. Alice Beck Kehoe (1998) points out that the new archaeologists did not feel the need to look beyond the scientific and statistical evidence of artefacts. Therefore it was considered unnecessary to exhaustively explore a site, since just a few artefacts could reveal enough information about past societies.

In the 1970s and 1980s, proponents of the new processual archaeology decided that religion could not be effectively studied using only archaeological methods. This view was a response to the rise of research which concentrated on the artefacts suggesting cultures and symbolism which indicated a prominent female presence in prehistory. James Mellaart's groundbreaking discoveries of a predominant women's presence at Çatal Hüyük (in the 1960s), and Marija Gimbutas's more recent monumental interdisciplinary studies of Old European female deities and their symbolism, have influenced the research of other women in this and related areas, but their views have usually been considered by most (male) archaeologists to be too subjective, and therefore too unscientific to be of value. As Riane Eisler explained in 1990,[19] it is only in recent times, when women's half of history has begun to be taken seriously, that a new theory of history and cultural evolution has included the presence of both women and men in early societies. Just as Marija Gimbutas recorded her discoveries in situ, today everything (including non-material aspects) in an archaeological dig should be recorded in context with its immediate surroundings in order to identify it and interpret its purpose.

In the 1990s, archaeology seemed to have split into two understandings of the evolution of human culture: the mainstream (male) conservative position which holds that human (male) cultural evolution began in the Upper Palaeolithic period, thus reflecting a bias against the many invisible (female as well as male) innovators of earlier cultures; and the more progressive position where it is thought that the beginnings of human culture originated with the first appearance of what researcher Robert Bednarik (1995) calls 'scientific' "concept-mediated markings"[20] in the early to mid-Palaeolithic period.[21]

Also in the 1990s came the realisation that Darwin's theory of natural selection and survival of the fittest might only be part of the story since increasing scientific knowledge, including advances in epigenetics and DNA processes, had transformed the way we understood evolution. For example, microbiologist Elizabet Sahtouris (2000) explained that bacteria and multi-celled creatures have been able to rearrange their genetic material in response to any change in their environment since earliest times when, for example, ultraviolet radiation and poisonous oxygen might have killed them. They change *from inside*, at the same time triggering changes in other creatures in their vicinity in response to a constantly evolving environment. This forms a circular evolutionary pattern of behaviour: unity → individuation → negotiation → cooperation → unity which is common to all of nature, including humanity.

In the 2000s and up to the present, archaeology continues to be dismissive of any evidence other than that which can be tested and empirically proved by increasingly narrow scientific methods, and ignores any other evidence. (Is it possible that the post-processual school of archaeology has become fearful that their version of prehistory may be undermined if too much evidence of prehistoric women's considerable influence comes to light?)

However, archaeology in the 21st century is also now confronted with a growing number of female researchers who are redefining archaeological technologies in order to rectify that bias which omitted prehistoric women's contributions, and thus widen the picture of prehistory. Sex and gender roles are now considered an important component when defining social relationships in archaeological sites; technologies that were formerly ignored by male researchers, such as weaving, are now being included, and are proving very informative when considered as part of the archaeological picture of a prehistoric culture. With the considerable male bias underlying history it is not surprising that, until recent times, prehistoric women have seemed invisible.

Defining 'matriarchy'

The term 'matriarchy' can cause a lot of confusion when researching invisible women of prehistory. The original 19th century meaning referred to women-centred societies, but in the 20th century it was used to describe female dominance as opposed to male dominance or patriarchy. Today the word 'matriarchy' is correct and relevant terminology when describing societies in which a founding ancestress, mother goddess or queen influences the metaphysical and social spheres of the lives of both women and men. Women are involved as healers, peacemakers, wise women or mothers with a nurturing role within the group. Matriarchy in this context is not power over others or "power to subjugate"[22] (as in political power), but rather power to forge and regenerate present and future social ties, according to Peggy Reeves Sanday (1998). Joan Marler (2003) records her as saying that for over 20 years she investigated more than 150 different indigenous societies in which she found no evidence of universal male dominance, and Joan Marler concludes that "matrilineal, egalitarian, democratic relationships between men and women"[23] were the norm within these groups.

A more correct term for the patriarchal interpretation of matriarchy would be 'gynocracy' ('rule by women', from the Greek *gyne* – woman; and *kratos* – rule). Johann Jakob Bachofen (1967)[24] was one of the first theorists to argue for *Das Mutterrecht* ('Mother Right', meaning the rights of the mother over the child), an idea which came about by analogy with 'father-right' (and which had nothing to do with ethnographic field studies of women).[25]

Marija Gimbutas (1991) prefers the term 'matristic' in order to avoid the use of matriarchy, with the understanding that it incorporates 'matriliny'. A matristic society focused on women, but women did not dominate others as in patriarchy. The early 'goddess' civilisations of China, Tibet, Egypt, Near East and Europe were most likely matrilineal because women had developed agriculture. In a matrilineal system a man's property is passed down to his sister's children, while his children belong to his wife's matrilineage. The Neolithic period provided the best conditions for continuing matrilinear, endogamous systems. Marija Gimbutas argues that the layouts of settlements, together with the distinctive ritual burials, implied a matrilineal social structure, while economic equality was suggested by the particular variety of goods found in grave sites. There were no traces of hierarchic societies led by a king, queen or chieftain, or of royal graves, in any regions of the Old World and she points out that Çatal Hüyük, for example, contained evidence of a matrilineal culture where social structure was based on equality. Archaeological evidence suggests that this mode of living lasted in Eastern Europe from 6,500 BP until about 4,500 BP, and in the Mediterranean islands, such as Crete and Thera, until 3,500 BP.

Another term proposed by Riane Eisler (1990) is 'matrifocality', where there is equality and consensus between men and women, while Paula Gunn Allen (1986)[26] uses 'matricentric' or 'women-centred'. Margaret Ehrenberg (1989) notes another alternative, 'matrilocality', where married people live in the home of the wife's family, although in each situation, men are the leaders. In *Icons of the Matrix* (2004a)[27] Max Dashu uses the term 'matrix' for cultures based on 'mother-right', which are matrilineal, matrilocal and egalitarian, and "are life-support networks, with circles of exchange that reach beyond them."[28] She tells us that the word 'matrix' has an Indo-European root, and originally meant 'womb'[29] and she gives the first meaning of matrix as: "uterus or womb" (from Latin *matrix,* related to the word for mother which in Sanskrit is *matri*).[30]

Peggy Reeves Sanday (2002)[31] provides an example of matriarchy in its correct sense: that of a West Sumatran group, the Indonesian Minangkabau matrilineal people, where the male and female spheres of influence are separate and the sexes complement each other. Thus the terms to describe women-centred social systems, such as 'matricentred' or 'matrifocal', are insufficient to correctly describe complex societies such as the Minangkabau, because these categorisations describe women's activities within a patriarchal context. In the Minangkabau social system:

- under Minangkabau law the mother–child bond is sacred
- matrilineal descent customs are an inalienable right and the foundation of their identity
- rules of social conduct are linked through women to a common ancestress
- although men can be public leaders, their titles are inherited through the female line, and their political activities are governed by matrilineal principle and women's ceremonies
- women are public leaders due to traditional life cycle ceremonies which govern political action; ceremonies bring different clans together
- women lead men in tradition (*adat*) and work together to preserve their social order despite the tremendous temptations that exist within the nation-state and from outside. (For more on *adat*, see pp. 239–242.)

Defining 'civilisation'

The idea of being 'civilised' is a form of bias in itself – implying that if one is not 'civilised' then one must be 'barbaric' or 'primitive'.[32] Today this terminology is used to distinguish two very different types of societies:

- prehistoric earth-based societies, with their emphasis on a close relationship with the natural world
- so-called modern civilisation, the historical patriarchal period with its focus on human disconnection from earthly considerations and an emphasis on 'the higher world' which Plato and his followers have promoted so strongly.

But what then does being 'civilised' mean? We are said to live in a civilised world which began with the rise of the patriarchal Proto-Indo-Europeans in Europe, yet constant, increasingly violent wars, domestic and sexual violence, ever greater poverty and degraded environments suggest that today we are anything but civilised. There are many (Western) notions of civilisation which are more or less unchanged from the original idea, so perhaps it is time to clarify just what is meant by 'civilisation' today.

According to the *Australian Concise Oxford Dictionary* (2009), "to civilise [is] to bring out of a barbarous or primitive stage of society; [to] enlighten, refine, and educate …"; while civilisation is "an advanced stage or system of social development." Civilisation has also been defined more broadly as the ability to live in a medium-sized, permanent community, which was built using complex tools; in this context, being civilised means being a town-dweller, able to socially and culturally interact with others in a town environment.

Marija Gimbutas proposes the challenging view that 'civilisation' is readily applied to cultures before 7,000 BP because they were sophisticated, developing systems in keeping with their environment and the knowedge of their day.

Tim Flannery (1994)[33] explains that the ability of the first humans to adopt a more complex lifestyle in some countries, and not in others, was greatly influenced by the geographic position of the land in question, its fertility and its climatic conditions, and the ways in which these aspects affected small groups as they spread out across the land. The countryside in Europe has been a continually renewable resource because of periods of past glaciations.[34] Fertile soils, together with regular climatic conditions, meant thousands of generations of agriculturists have been able to continually till the soil to feed increasingly larger populations.

In addition, the presence of animals suited to domestication has allowed the collection, portage and storage of a food surplus, and the ability to live in settlements. Thus, large towns and, over time, cities, were able to emerge in the Northern Hemisphere, in Europe, India, and the Middle East (and are now gradually being rediscovered in the Southern Hemisphere in countries such as Peru in South America).

In so-called primitive countries such as Australia, the situation for the first people was very different. The land was a non-renewable resource because of poor soils, and they were subject to unpredictable climatic conditions due to what is now known as the 'Southern Oscillation effect', an irregular climatic change causing long droughts which results from variations in Pacific Ocean water temperatures (El Niño events). The Indigenous people usually could not build permanent habitations but instead had to adapt to this fickle climate by moving, often considerable distances, from one seasonal food source to another.[35]

The lack of suitable domestic pack animals meant that tool kits and utensils had to be lightweight, highly portable and very efficient. For the same reasons, the European style of agriculture could not occur in Australia even though, for over 10,000 years, near-neighbours in Papua New Guinea, like people in the Middle East, were living in villages and cultivating their gardens.

Australian Indigenous people concentrated on the few practices open to them in their difficult environment and continually refined their tool kits and utensils while still maintaining their portability. They developed forms of agriculture utilising fire, cultivated yam crops, and harvested such resources as grass seeds, fish, turtles, dugongs and eels where conditions permitted. Most importantly, both men and women spent much time building up complex communal ritual and cultural activities through knowledge and practice of story-telling, dance, song and the visual arts. In this way, Australian Indigenous people perfected a non-material lifestyle in which personal ownership of goods was considered of far less value than the acquisition of knowledge.

War was not on any indigenous agenda since all human safety and well-being was dependent upon good social relations with one another, and with neighbours, from whom they might have to seek help in hard times. As a result these were balanced societies without wars, hierarchy, or emphasis on materiality: they were true civilisations of the sort Marija Gimbutas describes when she envisages the civilisations which existed long before recorded history, as early as the Upper Palaeolithic (and perhaps well back into the deep past). She emphasises that Neolithic Europe was not a time 'before civilisation'; it was instead "*a true civilization* in the best meaning of the word."[36] The same could be said of Australian Indigenous societies until Indo-European contact.

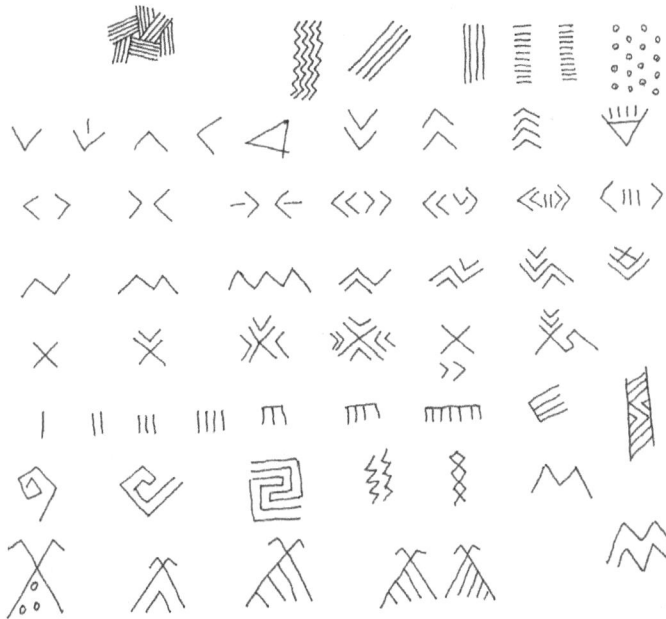

FIRST WRITING

Examples of *chevrons and other symbols* found on figurines and other related objects dating from 9,000 BP which Marija Gimbutas (1989) identifies as an early form of an Old European language not yet deciphered.

All line drawings © Judy Foster, 2013

21

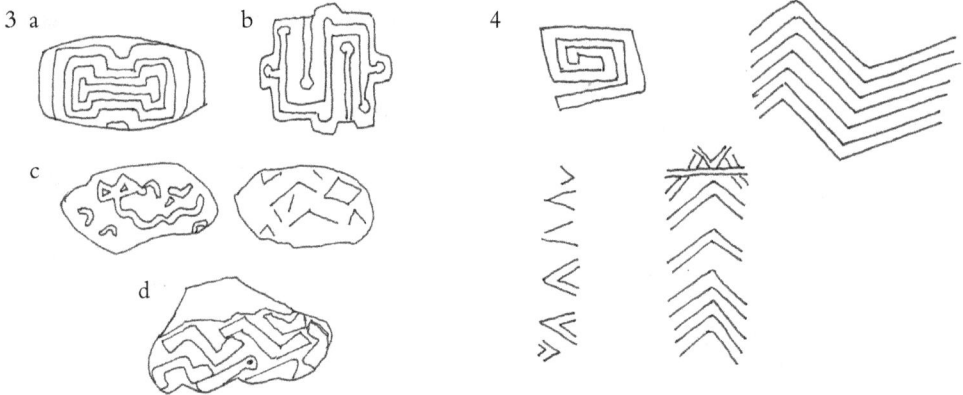

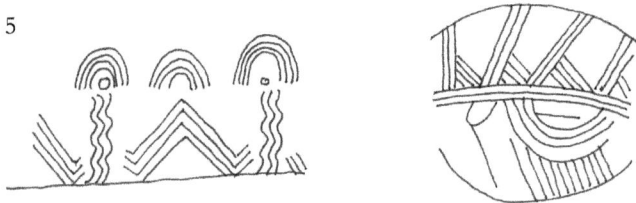

PREHISTORIC DESIGN MOTIFS WHICH LED TO WRITING

(Source: Gimbutas, Marija, 1989)
All line drawings © Judy Foster, 2013

Civilisation and the first writing

Researchers argue that the invention of writing and written history in Sumeria 5,500 years ago is widely accepted as marking the beginning of civilisation, and it is worth noting that this date coincides with the first Indo-European incursions into Europe. Yet Marija Gimbutas describes an Old European script as already emerging 2,000 years earlier in Yugoslavia, firmly located within the Neolithic period. She found that this as yet undeciphered script had been inscribed only on sacred items such as female figurines, pots, clay masks, temple models, and clay stamps, in the form of sacred hieroglyphs.

Marija Gimbutas (1999)[37] states that we are accustomed to seeing familiar Upper Palaeolithic and Neolithic sculptures, paintings and other artefacts, but few of us notice the many varied (decorative) signs and symbols either inscribed or painted on them, or beside them. These signs may take the form of letters, such as V, Y, M, and P; symbols, such as eggs, dots, seeds and arrows, or groups of two, three or more lines; branching configurations; or squares divided into four or more sections. Common motifs such as these had never been fully examined in context until Marija Gimbutas studied them. She considered that their meanings could relate to actual objects, or to certain activities within the images, such as the killing or wounding of animals. These signs and symbols were widely used for about 2,000 years by east-central European societies which, during that period, created metal objects, sophisticated architecture, and specialised crafts, traded widely, and practised complex religious rites. She found that the script disappeared with the arrival of the Proto-Indo-Europeans. This Old European script, now known as the Vinča script, contained 100 modified signs, whereas the English alphabet contains only 26 letters which are able to produce hundreds of syllables. As yet, nothing has been found which could provide the code for reading the script.

In 1996, Denise Schmandt-Besserat[38] was the first researcher to identify small geometric-shaped clay tokens dated to 9,500 BP, as the earliest tools used in accounting by Neolithic farmers in Syria, Mesopotamia, and Western Iran. Each geometric-shaped token represented a particular unit of goods. After 8,500 BP seals were used together with the tokens to identify the owner of the goods, thus allowing the recording or exchange of merchandise. Soon, round hollow clay 'envelopes', with stamped or incised signs denoting the contents, allowed certain tokens to be kept together as a form of accounting, and held in an archive. The signs on the seals and envelopes gradually evolved into an early form of writing by 5,303 BP. In fact, the early historic cuneiform script, so prominent in the Near East, was actually an earlier Neolithic invention "derived from an archaic counting device [the prehistoric clay tokens] dating to between 6,500 and 6,000 years ago ... [making it] the world's oldest known system of writing", argues Denise Schmandt-Besserat.[39] She specialises in art and archaeology of the Near and Middle East, and emphasises that these small impressed clay tablets had generally been ignored by archaeologists and, although mentioned in archaeological reports, were merely dismissed as 'numerical tablets' of no further interest.[40]

She maintains that there were no narrative designs on Neolithic Near Eastern pottery, or in cave paintings until after 5,500 BP. Instead, geometric or animal images were juxtaposed or informally arranged with symbolic meaning. Denise Schmandt-Besserat examines in some detail the 10,000 to 9,000-year-old wall imagery in paintings and reliefs recorded and described by James Mellaart at Çatal Hüyük, and demonstrates the way in which the human and animal figures in these wonderful symbolic mythic wall paintings, while arranged in relation to one another, are also individually aloof and disconnected from one another.

Richard Rudgley (1998)[41] considers that there is a bias against the recognition of this first writing, and the search for the tool to decipher it, because it would deny the 'superiority' of present day 'civilised' Western peoples. He considers the period of written history as a somewhat busy afterword to the long and interesting human story. He found that most of the key innovations in technology and science have their roots in the Palaeolithic and Neolithic periods, and he emphasises that the period we call civilisation is *not* civilised. There is an increase in cruel and barbaric actions in the historic period, in which technology and society have inflicted massive pain and suffering, most particularly on the very indigenous people who have been considered to be the most 'savage'. Today mainstream society remains paternalistic, imposing 'development' and Western social and cultural values on those regarded as uncivilised.[42]

Palaeolithic and Neolithic people lived long before feudalism and therefore, Richard Rudgley says, it is presumed they had no social and cultural rights whatever; yet most indigenous people, prior to Western invasion or integration, lived within communal systems governed by consensus. He summarises the many other early innovations also enjoyed by these early people, including scale and proportions in art, the use of numbers and lunar notation, an elementary form of mathematics using clay tokens, the first surgery and dentistry, the practice of medicine, and underground mining using shafts and underground galleries.

So we must conclude that those people in Northern Hemisphere Old Europe who lived comfortably in large towns or complex cities, practised elaborate agricultural pursuits (and fought ever larger and more lethal wars), should not be the only people considered 'civilised'; the term should also be applied to those prehistoric indigenous societies who led simpler lives, possessed few material benefits, but treasured peaceful values and a richly complex social and cultural life.

The 'Invisible' Hidden Worlds, New Worlds of the Northern and Southern Hemispheres

Recorded evidence for human culture in prehistory existed only in the north-western part of the world. This is where civilisation was considered to have begun and remained! Yet, during the northern Palaeolithic and Neolithic periods, remarkable innovations were taking place in the Hidden Worlds (Africa, India, and China) for as long as anywhere else in the world; and more recently in the New Worlds (East Asia, South-East Asia, Australia, the Americas and the Pacific regions); and a great many of these inventions were created by women.

There has been little information about lifestyles and symbolic art of earlier periods in certain northern and southern regions because European specialists have either chosen to ignore information provided by people of these regions, or doubted its authenticity. Robert Bednarik (1997)[43] provides the example of the Dutch archaeologist T. Verhoeven who, in the 1950s, published proof of *Homo erectus* having sailed to the island of Flores over 700,000 years ago. This discovery was not accepted by European researchers. However, in 1997, Australian archaeologist, Michael Morwood re-examined the evidence in situ and proved it to be true.

More evidence exists within the origins of languages and language 'trees' since this is where we find words gradually appearing which define societies and cultures. Prehistoric records of creation and human experiences were passed down orally, in the form of myths (universal truths), and stories (information and entertainment) to traditional indigenous people. Rock art (petroglyphs and paintings) and other non-utilitarian artefacts were created for many reasons, and they are a tangible record of human beliefs and activities since earliest times. How these forms of evidence came about, and something of their function, follows in the next chapter.

CHAPTER 3

Intangible Evidence: The Role of Language, Oral Transmission and Myth

Marija Gimbutas used two kinds of important evidence in her search for the prehistoric women of Old Europe: *intangible* evidence which includes the role of language, oral transmission and myth; and *tangible* evidence consisting of prehistoric tools, non-utilitarian objects, artefacts and visual symbols. Both forms are interconnected and have implications for women's invisibility and the female principle.

The ability to form concepts underlies the telling of stories and the making of art. According to theoretical physicist David Bohm and Mark Edwards (1991),[1] the ability to think has always been necessary to create, express and apply knowledge. Early humans collected knowledge through their good or bad experiences, and the most useful information and practices became the basis for tradition. It requires *thinking* to lift something out of its context and make it abstract. Early human communities selected the part of a context which had value and was relevant to their circumstances, and assigned to it an image and a purpose. Commonly held goals and values were achieved by the cooperation of all in the community, and complex social, cultural and religious systems began to emerge. For example, everyone would have been aware of the moon, existing beyond human control, which waxed and waned in regular cycles, imposing order in nature and continually dividing day from night, month by month. Early humans also regarded caves not only as shelter but as mysterious places relating to the metaphysical world, a world with natural forces raging beyond their control, and began to transform engraved or painted images of natural phenomena, such as the mysterious moon, into abstract symbols on their walls. For early humans the moon may have represented a supernatural force, so the act of engraving its shape a number of times as part of cyclic rituals could transfer its power into the cave. Markings on the earliest non-utilitarian incised artefacts are not only conscious and intentional acts, but are also proof of the early development of the human brain.

Alexander Marshack (1977)[2] explains that despite the fact that *Homo erectus* had a rather smaller brain capacity than later archaic *Homo sapiens*, these earlier humans not only had the ability to make symbols and create art, but also the ability to use some form of language to explain their meanings to others. Richard Leakey and Roger Lewin (1992)[3]

27

DESIGN MOTIFS USED IN ORAL TRANSMISSION

1a–c. *Traditional Australian Indigenous design elements*, Central Australia
 a. *painted on women's breasts*
 b. and c. *used in ritual ground art*
   (Source: Layton, Robert 1992)
2. *Seed/vulva symbols*, Old Europe
3a. and b. *Snake designs*
   (Source: Gimbutas, Marija, 1992)

4. *Hand prints in African cave*, prehistoric decorated hands prints, painting on rock wall by Khoi herders, Eland Bay, Western Cape, South Africa (Source: Department of Arts of Africa, Oceania, and the Americas, 2001)
   All line drawings © Judy Foster, 2013

note that it has now been proved that the early human brain (and vocal tract) was advanced enough for speech, and had the capacity to invent more complex tools, conceptualise abstract art images, and conduct rituals.

Prehistoric art: Tangible evidence for the early origin of language?

Robert Bednarik (1997b)[4] has identified three forms of possible material evidence for the early origin of language:

- the development of prehistoric art, which involves non-utilitarian practices and artefacts, such as painting and engraving
- the ability of early humans to build watercraft and navigate the seas (seafaring)
- evidence of underground mining activities.

All of these require concept making, some form of verbal communication and technological skills.

Prehistoric art

The 800,000-year-old collections of natural objects, such as red ochre pebbles (associated with body painting) and quartz crystals, and the creation of early prehistoric art and non-utilitarian artefacts, point to complex technological processes, and societies which utilised symbolic artefacts and ritual practices, such as those used in burials. These often include very early portable art, rock art, perforated beads and pendants and other objects, perhaps used as personal ornaments; and non-utilitarian incised or engraved objects, suggesting a reflective communication value system and a sophisticated social and cultural society. These are indirect evidence of cord, thread, string and the like, as some form of knotted, twined vegetable fibre would have been needed to make bead necklaces, to display pendants, and to create rope or net carry bags. Robert Bednarik notes that hominids would have needed the ability to convey complex information through language to achieve the quality and quantity of technically well-designed beads.

The 2 million-year-old African Makapansgat cobblestone, naturally shaped in a form resembling a hominid head, with 'eyes' and 'mouth', is thought to have been carried some distance to the cave in which it was found lying alongside stone tools. This symbolic unmodified natural object points to early recognition of its iconic properties.

Seafaring and underground mining

According to Robert Bednarik (1994b)[5] these activities involved risk-taking in alien environments, and skills including complex thought and forward planning which would have required some form of language use. Although very early humans (*H. erectus*) had existed in Java for nearly 2 million years, current archaeological evidence indicates that the earliest navigation occurred about 700,000 BP. (See next chapter.)

Stone tools on Flores Island, Timor, Sulawesi and Cerain point to early humans with a predominantly coastal economy who settled some coastal regions of Indonesia (and also very probably, Australia, although no direct evidence of this has been found as yet). Their ability to exploit the rich coastal and marine environment allowed them to harvest larger fish. Specific skills and technologies would have been required to enable extended travel by sea: obtaining, storing and carrying supplies; processing and cooking foods; portage of water; and various survival strategies.

It is thought that the vessels used for these early voyages were most likely to have been bamboo rafts, comprising a row of bamboo trunks lashed together, perhaps with twisted vines as a form of rope, with a cross-layer of bamboo above the water line forming a platform on which a shelter, stores and a dried-mud hearth would have been constructed. Reconstructions of similar water craft have proved to be relatively successful.

Language origins and the search for a universal proto-language

Forms of evidence which shed light upon the invisibility of women are, firstly, the presence of an early common language of the hunter-gatherers; secondly, finding the origin of Indo-European languages, when and where they spread; and thirdly, the first appearance of certain words in a language which may support other material evidence of, for example, the presence of the European Bronze Age Warriors. In this section and the next, linguist and co-author, Marlene Derlet, examines these topics in more detail.

In 1922, the Danish linguist Otto Jespersen[6] identified five main theories on how language might have originated. Speech and language arose through:
- imitation of sounds
- instinctive sounds and grunts made in response to pain and various emotions
- instinctive oral responses or gestures produced in consonance with environmental events
- the need to communicate with each other while working together, or
- language emerging from the sounds made in response to love, play and other socio-affective states, then developed into song and poetic feeling – the proto form of language.

However there is no concrete evidence to support these theories. Today linguists have a more scientific approach, incorporating research and knowledge from other disciplines such as archaeology and anthropology.[7]

It seems that the evolution of language was a slow and lengthy process. According to Jean Aitchison (1996)[8] human language may have occurred as early as 250,000 BP, or as late as 50,000 BP, with the average guess at 100,000 BP.[9]

Language: A common source?

The search for a common single source from which all present languages are derived is difficult, as the writing system is generally considered to have developed only about 5,000 years ago. Merritt Ruhlen (1994)[10] explains that there is no written evidence of any language before that time, however, there are still many languages spoken today which have no written form. Also, some languages may have evolved independently, but then later died out. These languages may have been spoken by *H. sapiens* or by earlier hominids. One thing seems certain: all normal humans have developed remarkably similar linguistic abilities, even though there are currently about 5,000 different languages spoken throughout the world.

For languages to be related, they must have evolved from a single original language, either recently or long ago. For example, Romanian, Italian, French and Spanish are related, and their mother language is Latin, originally spoken in Rome. They are daughter languages, all related and belonging to the Romance family. It is more difficult to find a relationship amongst languages with no written history, as with, for example, Proto-Germanic, the mother language of the Germanic family. We can only guess at relationships by researching daughter languages, such as English, Dutch, Danish, or Norwegian, etc. Both Latin and Germanic belong to the Indo-European family,[11] a language spoken at least 6,000 years ago, and it is without a written history. This family includes such languages as: Sanskrit, spoken during the first millennium BCE in Northern India and still used today in the Hindu religion; Old Iranian, Persian, Hindi, Bengali; and also European languages such as Gaelic, Greek, and Slavic.

How do languages change and how do we reconstruct a proto-language? Merritt Ruhlen lists three general factors that bring about language change:
- simplification to make pronunciation easier
- psychological reasons such as peer group pressure or what is fashionable
- the creation of new words, often due to reason of invention or specification.[12]

An example of the latter is the Proto-Indo European word *kuon* meaning 'hound' in Modern English. During the Old English period the word *docga* replaced the original word (hound) and today 'dog' is the general term and 'hound' has a specialised meaning. Steven Pinker (1994)[13] lists learning, innovation and migration as the main factors of difference in language between peoples. In general, language change over the generations is slight, mainly due to conservatism. Vocabulary and sounds may survive for millennia.

Another important factor in language change is invasion. Groups of people may be invaded by other groups who impose their language on the conquered people. As an example, we can look at the roots of English. They lie in northern Germany, near Denmark, where the Angles, the Saxons, and the Jutes lived in the first millennium. In the fifth century, these tribes invaded what is now England ('Angle-land') after the Roman Empire collapsed and its army left Britain.[14] These tribes also displaced the indigenous Gaelic-speaking peoples in Scotland, Ireland, Wales, and Cornwall. Linguistically, this was devastating. There are virtually no traces of Gaelic left in English.

Steven Pinker notes that although we have no written history, or much archaeological record, the similarities in vocabulary and grammar that exist between languages such as Germanic, Greek, Romance, Slavic, Celtic and Indo-Iranian[15] suggest a common source of these languages – that of the Proto-Indo Europeans.[16] He goes on to state that the language similarities suggest that the Indo-Europeans must have occupied most of Europe, Turkey, Iran, Afghanistan, Pakistan, northern India, western Russia and part of China. The reconstructed vocabulary indicates that they must have been the first Bronze Age people from southern Russia who had displaced those who spoke the language from inland northern Europe. It includes words for metals, wheeled vehicles, farm implements, and domesticated animals and plants. These words, and others such as 'patriarch', 'fort', 'horse', and 'weapons', conjure up "an image of a powerful conquering tribe spilling out of an ancestral homeland in chariots to overrun most of Europe and Asia."[17]

Not all European languages are classified as Indo-European. Finnish, Hungarian and Estonian are considered Uralic languages, as are Lappish, Samoyed and others, but all originated from central Russia about 7,000 BP. Basque, spoken in northern Spain and south-western France, is the odd one out. It may have originated from an island of Aboriginal Europeans (or Neolithic people?) who resisted the invasion of the Indo-Europeans.

One could also ask: what were the languages spoken by the hunter-gatherers? Scholars, such as Merritt Ruhlen and some other Russian linguists, have researched this question. There are some similarities among proto-languages of Indo-European, Afro-Asiatic, Dravidian, Altaic, Uralic and Eskimo-Aleut, Japanese and Korean and other groups. The 800 languages of New Guinea, and the approximately 200 of Australia, belong to a family of their own, or perhaps to a number of families, especially those of New Guinea.[18]

Having found similarities between languages, Steven Pinker and others have suggested that they all evolved from a common source. Approximately 1,600 words have been reconstructed. As no words for domesticated species have been found, it can be assumed that the speakers of Nostratic, a common ancestor proto-proto-language, were hunter-gatherers who originated in the Middle East and occupied Europe, Africa, and parts of Asia about 15,000 BP.

Language as oral transmission

Another aspect of language which provides clues to life in the distant past is that of oral transmission of myths (the passing down of accepted truths of a society), although researchers in archaeology and associated disciplines do not consider them to be a reliable source of information about the past. However, indigenous people have always regarded myths as an invaluable guide to the social and cultural rules of the clan or community, and the dispenser of ancestral knowledge. It is through accurately remembering their myths that they can share their past with us today. Indigenous myths and associated visual images may record geological happenings, such as volcanic eruptions, the flooding of river flats which later become inland seas, and the creation of islands due to rising seas at the end of ice ages. They should not be summarily dismissed simply on the basis that they cannot be scientifically proved.

Oral transmission and myth as fiction (European regions)

While in Palaeolithic and Neolithic times myths would have been understood to contain knowledge of accepted truths, the invading Indo-Europeans began the process which eventually led to the contemporary Western belief in myth as fiction. *The Australian Concise Oxford Dictionary* (2009) defines myth as:

1. a traditional narrative [usually] involving supernatural or imaginary persons and embodying popular ideas on natural or social phenomena
2. such narratives collectively
3. a widely held but false notion
4. a fictitious person, thing, or idea.

Mythologist Joseph Campbell (1969) defines myth "as a metaphor for what lies behind the visible world." Myths in traditional systems communicate directly from one inward world to another, in such a way that [they become] an effective form of communication across the void of space and time from one centre of consciousness to another [... through] words, images, motions, rhythms, colours, and perfumes, sensations of all kinds[19]

carrying past relevant associations into the present. Nineteenth century researchers described myth, ritual and magic as attempts by earlier cultures to control nature; for example, the bible is "a socially oriented mythology",[20] which focuses on the importance of people and the inferiority of nature.

Merlin Stone (1991)[21] explains the bias behind the point of view that myth involves imagination rather than truth. Mythologies, or creation stories, when contrasted especially with Christian theology by Western researchers, are usually regarded as reflecting a 'primitive' view of the world. Christian theology, which includes Western creation stories, is deemed to be 'true', and thus all other religious traditions are not true; therefore mythology should be understood as the stories, the truths, of 'others'. The Palaeolithic and Neolithic 'others' are the religions of the earth-centred deities before the Warrior invasions/infiltrations. Even today, those 'others', such as Australian Indigenous people, those outside Western religions, who do not worship the male god, are not considered 'town dwellers' and are therefore not 'civilised', but are labelled 'heathens' or 'pagans'.[22] This view enhances the exclusivity of established patriarchal religions; the earlier female-focused religions were communal, non-hierarchic and *inclusive*.

Merlin Stone explains that the religions of the female deity/deities were not considered sacred but 'mythological'. Although creation stories which were recorded on clay tablets or papyri are similar to Hebrew scripture in that they reveal spiritual contemplation and religious concepts, they are regarded as fictional mythologies rather than true religious concepts. Michael Dames (1996) maintains that contrary to popular opinion, mythology is alive and well today in predominantly agricultural places, such as Ireland. He is convinced that impressive sites such as Newgrange and Knowth originated with the Neolithic peoples who worshipped the European Neolithic goddess. He defines myth as one part of "three interrelated aspects of religious expression":[23] word, story and sacred rites; and it includes the need for sacred objects and a sacred space which could be part of the landscape.

Michael Dames identifies four 'canons' of mythology in the Northern Hemisphere which developed after the earliest occupation of Ireland, at least 9,000 years ago. These canons are relevant to our argument since they clarify the way in which we understand prehistory from a contemporary viewpoint, and help us recognise the specific bias against the idea of an important female principle existing at any time in the past. They form a dividing line between that ideology and the dominant male principle of today.

The four canons include:

1. the myths of the Mesolithic (Middle Palaeolithic) hunter-gatherers and the Neolithic agriculturalists (Old European myths focusing on the matrilineal female goddess of birth, death and regeneration appeared from 6,700 until 5,500 BP)
2. the myths of the male-dominant Indo-European warrior cultures, with their male sky god, including Celtic-speaking invaders who arrived about 5,000 BP
3. Christian mythology, with its previously unknown concepts of 'original sin' and a dualistic division between body and soul, world and spirit; this mythology arrived about 500 CE

4. Scientific Rationalism, which appeared in urban England about 1700 CE and remains with us today. Michael Dames says there are recent suggestions that scientific discovery is similar to explanatory story-telling originating in the field of myth, and its presumed objectivity is but one of many story-telling techniques.[24]

Elizabeth Barber (2004)[25] is best known for her investigations into prehistoric textiles, however she is also a linguist who specialises in mythology. Although she (together with Paul T. Barber) mainly looks at early historic mythology, she has identified certain rules to be followed which apply to all myths, including those of indigenous peoples. Formal oral mythologies record very important and relevant instructions and warnings on the clans' social and cultural laws, and often are the result of experiencing actual events. They are remembered more easily when the information is compressed as much as possible. All myths relate to 'the linguistic process' and it is possible for archaeologists to gain some knowledge of the late prehistoric world by decoding myths of a region.

The key rules for the transmission of myths include: firstly, any information must be regarded as very important; secondly, the information must be considered relevant and relate to objects or places still visible to the contemporary viewers; and thirdly, the information must be encoded in a simple but interesting manner so it will be remembered. If the story is repeated in several different mediums such as dance, song, painting or acting out, it becomes reinforced in the minds of the observers and is less likely to be forgotten. It is essential that the key information is not changed in any way, although the non-central details may be 'embroidered'.

There are instances where bias operates against the meaning of 'myth as truth'. An example is provided by Estella Lauter (1984)[26] who defines myths as powerful 'fictitious' stories or symbols, which have been repeated so often that they are finally believed to be true.[27] She maintains that, regardless of their original purpose, myths often reach sacred status; and when they are accepted as true they become almost impossible to disprove, and continue to exist until replaced by another equally powerful story. (One example of this line of thought is the myth that in prehistoric periods people were 'primitive', violent, ignorant, unskilled, male-dominant cave dwellers. Even a brief look at prehistory shows that this myth is clearly untrue, yet it is widely believed to this day). Elizabeth Barber (2004) emphasises that "heavily literate cultures tend to disregard the truth of the earlier events reported in myths and legends"[28] because they don't like or understand the events/truths which have been recorded.

Estella Lauter describes myths as a dynamic 'body of beliefs' which possess functions to mediate between language and the unknown, both recording the past and constructing a liveable new world. How they are interpreted depends on our ability to identify them, an easy task when they are very old myths, more difficult when they are modern. Modern myths can be so pervasive they may not always be recognised for what they are. Scientific myths are even more invisible. She points out that a story cannot be made a myth by one person, but must be validated by the group. Myths inform present-day traditional indigenous people about their ancestors and their way of life.

On language as oral transmission: Attitudes and problems of interpretation

In order to deal competently with the question of accuracy and truth in regard to oral transmission as a guide to past history, Marlene Derlet maintains that it is important to analyse in detail its working process, its problems and the prejudice involved in documentation. Material for the following discussion is mostly taken from examples of the Indigenous Australian and African situations, where oral transmission is still very much practised and relied upon in regard to describing the creation of the universe, history and the transmission of knowledge.

Margaret Clunies-Ross (1983) describes pre-contact Australian Indigenous society as one which did not use writing in its strict sense to pass on history, information, and knowledge, with the term 'strict sense' meaning "that of the employment of individual written signs or combinations of signs to correspond to discrete speech sounds."[29] Instead, they developed a very complex system of symbols to communicate, including sign languages, message sticks, sand pictures, ground sculptures, rock paintings, bark and earth paintings.

Many Australian Indigenous people, and other indigenous people around the world, still employ this complex system of communication without using writing in its strict sense. However, today they may:

- have an intact system of "orally transmitted standardised forms"[30] which has not been influenced by Western written tradition, culture or education
- have absorbed some aspects of Western tradition into their own communication system
- maintain one system which includes many cultural concepts, but where the conventional form of expression is largely lost, or where very little of culture with respect to both form and content, is inherited.[31]

Marlene Derlet explains that Indigenous Australians still have a very vibrant tradition of oral literacy, both in rural and urban settings, and many of the stories and themes have now been translated into written form. However, the conversion of oral narrative into written text is fraught with problems and difficulties. A short discussion of some of these difficulties may give us an understanding of what occurred when prehistoric stories were first textualised.[32]

According to Isidore Okpewho in *African Oral Literature* (1992),[33] Western evolutionist scholars could not recognise or accept the creativity of earlier societies and considered that these people would not have understood the material knowledge they were passing on because of their 'primitiveness'. Evolutionists were convinced that people basically thought alike throughout the world and therefore if two stories from two societies exhibited similarity in element and pattern, then these societies were at the same stage of cultural development.

On the other hand, some (Western) scholars, such as the German brothers Jacob and Wilhelm Grimm, thought that having similar stories indicated that the people or groups had been in contact at some stage and had borrowed cultural ideas from one another. These scholars mapped out the world into cultural areas on the basis of similarity of language, belief systems, customs, and so forth. They were in search of "the origins and paths of movements of European languages, customs and other forms of culture."[34] Isidore Okpewho calls these scholars 'diffusionists'. These evolutionist and diffusionist scholars did considerable work in comparative studies of folklore. They came to the conclusion that the origin of European forms of culture was India and they wanted to know more about the Indo-European spread of culture. The Grimm brothers, like many other scholars of that time, conducted their research with the prejudice that only superior people could distribute culture to their inferiors.

Furthermore, the ethnological research in Africa, Australia and other parts of the world occurred at the same time as European colonisation of these countries was at its peak. Many of the people who collected the ethnographical material were also colonial administrators. Their aim was to introduce 'superior' European culture to the culture of the country they were colonising. They also brought Christianity, with its code of morality which most likely would have been completely different from that of the indigenous peoples. The aim was to Christianise the colonies and eliminate the indigenous beliefs. Linguists eagerly studied the indigenous languages, and the Bible and hymns were translated into these local languages. In her observation in regard to the African situation, Isidore Okpewho notes that only the oral literature which upheld good conduct and Western morals was given credit.

The main difficulty really lay with the seemingly insurmountable incapability of the analysers and translators of the time to recognise the value and merit of indigenous oral literature due to cultural, ideological, political, or religious differences. Isidore Okpewho maintains that this has been the problem all along, especially when history is analysed by those in power. This has been the case not only in regard to ethnic/cultural background but also in regard to gender. It reaches right back to the first transmissions and translations of oral literature, the stories, myths, tales, and fables of pre-Indo-European societies.[35]

Indigenes sharing their past: Myth as universal truth (Hidden and New Worlds)

We have looked at Australian Indigenous oral tradition in some detail as it is the oldest existing today, and therefore may be similar in some ways to prehistoric European oral traditions. Concerning oral language linked with art imagery, Heather Goodall (1992),[36] and Eric Michaels (1987)[37] speak of the accuracy of Australian Indigenous myths/creation stories; while Diane Bell (1998)[38] provides a picture of past and present Indigenous women's oral traditions which, until recently, were unknown to outsiders. Australian Indigenous mythology, 'the Dreaming', as the longest standing set of living oral traditions, is of great importance in revealing aspects of the past.

Heather Goodall speaks of three processes in the development of the rich and complex oral sources of myth: the original emotional view of events; ways of finding meaning through their individual or group observations; and the "process of remembering"[39] in the retelling. The teller has to keep in mind that the myth has to be authorised by its owner and only told to certain people who are entitled to hear it.

Heather Goodall stresses that "in any culture there are conventions and accepted genres for what amounts to a performance of remembering."[40] For cultures which do not have written records there are complex methods for the holding and analysis of memory, some of which are very formal with strict codes for remembering and performance, as well as much less formal procedures for minor matters. She emphasises the vital use of rote learning and repetition devices which aid memory retention. Learning by doing is also critical. It is crucial that mistakes are not made in the telling of important myths since they are often a guide to practical living, for example, for physical survival in the sometimes harsh conditions of the Australian bush.

Diane Bell includes the use of inherited objects, such as portable artefacts or rock paintings and engravings, together with their histories, as aids in developing precise memories and accurate oral transmissions. Josephine Flood and Bruno David (1994)[41] give as an example the significance of rock art and its association and continuity with myth and oral traditions for the Victoria River in Northern Territory, people whose elders they consulted. (Contrary to popular opinion, Indigenous beliefs and customs are *not* uniform throughout Australia.) The function of rock art in the Victoria River region in this instance is to preserve cultural and economic continuity in the ways that land is used. It is a device to assist in the telling of important myths holding both sacred and secular information about the past. Sacred art as a form of communication and an expression of the Dreaming[42] is closely linked with oral transmission for both men and women. For example, art images upon a rock which depict the subjects of a creation story, might prompt the telling of that story. They could be said to be a 'written' record of the myth to which they relate. Images can be educational, a means of passing on traditional beliefs and laws to the next generation, and they also strengthen clan identity and relationships between people and their land.

Eric Michaels notes another aspect of oral traditions changing over time to absorb new experiences, making the original story relevant to the present generation. He describes the dangers of inventing new Indigenous stories. Myths are inherited, owned by, and identified with, certain people, and the responsibility for their accuracy rests upon those individuals. A story can only be altered or a new story made under strict conditions since any new or invented story may undermine the Law. Too many inventions are not encouraged.

Diane Bell's work with women in Central Australian clans including the Warlpiri, Warumungu/Warlmanpa, Kaytej and Alyawarra, and the Ngarrindjeri peoples of South Australia, reveal a number of interesting aspects of oral traditions and their transmission which include the areas of knowledge, feeling, continuity and the effects of Western interference. In Indigenous societies knowledge is a powerful resource for women and men; it is not a commodity to be openly traded or given to unsuitable people. Knowledge is the basis of social relationships, while sacred knowledge is restricted to those women and men who demonstrate the ability to use it properly, and who obey and accept the rules for its transmission. Oral culture does not rely solely on individual memories, but also on objects passed down from one generation to the next. Objects carry their own histories of the people who made them and why.[43] Stories, sites and ceremonies have a men's side and a women's side; men do not speak about women's knowledge, and women do not speak about men's knowledge.

Because Western men were most often the researchers and recorders of information until recent times, it was the Indigenous men's world which was recorded in depth. The researcher's interests were usually reflected in the kind of questions asked about different versions of a story and this could affect the way the story was recorded. Indigenous women's culture is only recently being recorded, and because of the way in which men's knowledge has been abused at times by white male researchers, Indigenous women are increasingly wary of imparting their knowledge to outsiders. Only the men's view of female ancestors has been noted. As in the Christian Bible, the wives of ancestral heroes are not identified, and the actions of the women who were present now have to be 'read' into the text. But Diane Bell shows evidence that women's versions would have not only named the women but also presented them as independent, spirited, capable women with their own active role to play.

Both the Ngarrindjeri of the south and the people of the north have spoken about a special aspect of cultural tradition connected with oral transmission which the Ngarrindjeri call *miwi,* or 'feeling'. Miriam Rose Ungurmarr-Baumann (1998) of Daly River in the Northern Territory refers to it as *dadirri,* which means 'listening to one another', "a deep inner listening and quiet, still awareness."[44] Judy Atkinson (2002) records that this process of "profound, non-judgemental watching and listening" allows "insight and recognition of the responsibility to act with fidelity in relationship to what has been heard, observed and learnt."[45]

Similarly, *miwi* relates to wisdom and deep feelings in the individual. It can be developed through training over time and the older a person is, the greater his/her wisdom – *miwi.* It is both sacred and practical, as Diane Bell explains. *Miwi* wisdom is at once "profoundly spiritual" and "disarmingly pragmatic" fusing "the emotional and intellectual into true knowledge."[46] *Miwi* in oral transmission acts to make the stories relevant to present listeners and warns of the consequences of wrongdoing. Rationalist Westerners have problems with the idea of 'feeling' as a means of knowing, since such 'feeling' cannot be proved or disproved.

Like the land within which they took place, oral traditions and stories were never static. For example, it is well known that the course of the Murray River has changed over time, and this is allowed for in the telling of the stories belonging to it. In addition, proof of continuity of oral transmission of stories is often to be found in their content. Diane Bell cites stories which record prehistoric physical changes to the landscape, and the migration of people from one area to another. At the end of the last ice age, waters rose and there were gradual but dramatic changes to plants and animals. For example, Kangaroo Island had separated from the mainland by 10,000 BP, and by 6,000 BP the sea reached its present levels around Australia. After this time Indigenous populations increased and their economy became more complex. This historical information can be found in traditional stories of the Dreaming.

Indigenous Australian people have used various ways of passing down knowledge to the next generation, and one such method, used by the Central Desert people is the 'sand story', as visiting American researcher, Nancy Munn (1973), explains.[47] This technique involves story telling while images are drawn in the sand illustrating the characters, and the region in which each part of the story takes place. Drawing in the sand is accompanied by sung or spoken words; the images utilising a basic range of motifs such as circles, lines or arcs, each of which may have a number of meanings depending on the context and content of the story. Both men and women draw motifs in the sand as they tell a story, or during general conversation, but for women it is a particular genre to do with many public aspects of women's law, *yawulyu.*

Women sing and use 'gesture signs' or *raga* as they make stylised hand and finger drawings. The motifs include circles, single or multiple arches, scalloped lines (denoting hilltops or treetops), half circles and ovals; and when these elements are combined during the telling of a story they can form rich designs. To non-Indigenous people the elements might look like geometric or abstract forms but for the tellers they are representations of people, places or objects. There are a number of design/motif categories used in different contexts.

Women's designs, to which only they have rights, are called *yawulyu.* Zohl dé Ishtar (1994) records Tjama Napanangka of the Ngardi-Kukatja clan who says: "women's culture, *yawulyu*, really strong."[48] She speaks of women's ceremonies for their sons; and women have many ceremonies that are always separate from those of the men. According to Nancy Munn, *yawulyu* women are ancestral women and can be represented in stories told in women's ceremonies, able to be seen by everyone.[49]

However, as Zohl dé Ishtar (2005) discovered during a period of time she spent living with the senior women (elders) of Wirrimanu (Balgo, Western Australia), *yawulyu* can have rather different, deeper and more complex meanings, such as to work with the elders to "protect, maintain, and teach" Women's Law. She says: "[T]hey intentionally set out to raise my awareness of the Tjukurrpa [Dreaming], and to teach me 'culture', their customs and some of their deep Law."[50] In order to learn she had to listen, observe, participate and, in the case of the Law, learn through touch, in order to absorb knowledge expressed in song, dance and rituals. *Yawulyu* took place in a special women's camp or *Tjilimi*, where women could live, create, pass on and enjoy a living culture, "a code, an instruction, a discipline, a moral authority."[51]

Diane Bell (1983)[52] notes that there could also be categories of secret-sacred *yawulyu* which only certain women are permitted to know. *Yawulyu* impart women's wisdom; they are used in healing, to produce happiness and well-being in the group, to teach young girls how to become women, and to pass down traditional knowledge. Children learn how to make sand stories by observation from an early age.

Paula Gunn Allen (1986)[53] speaks of her Native American view of myth which is also a living tradition; through her explanation we see that the passing down of myths from one generation to the next is not taken lightly. Although some minor changes might sometimes be made, there are special 'owners/inheritors' of the knowledge contained in any myth who make sure the myth is always told correctly (just as in Australian Indigenous societies). It is through the accurate remembering and retelling of myths that Native Americans can share their past.

In earlier times myth was defined as being similar to fables (stories which have a moral) while today in the West myth is defined as a story not to be taken seriously. Symbols are used in the telling of the stories which may feature supernatural heroes whose exploits are inspiring and may reflect social and cultural beliefs. Myths and rituals are passed down through visions deliberately sought by certain wise people who can instruct and guide others in relation to the universal mysteries or "other orders of reality and experience"[54] and positioning of people within the universe. (There is more on Native American oral tradition in chapter 17.)

Language, in the form of storytelling, dancing and image making, such as visual symbolic rock engravings, paintings and portable sacred objects, contains many clues which aid remembering the myth or story, and these aspects are our next focus.

CHAPTER 4

TANGIBLE EVIDENCE: PREHISTORIC ART, THE VISUAL IMAGE, SIGN AND SYMBOL

It is often argued today that the world no longer recognises symbols, just as it is said that most people do not believe in the metaphysical world. The terms 'sign' (such as 'road sign'), and 'symbol' (multiple meanings) are often confused. So-called Westerners, whose symbols have become so secularised, are challenged to rediscover the metaphysical dimension within basic symbols, which along with oral traditions and transmission of 'myths', continue to convey metaphysical meanings for the world's indigenous peoples. There is a need to understand what symbols are, and how they have worked in the past.

Prehistoric art evidence

There is little doubt that a consciousness of metaphysical forces and their control over all life forms was present very early in human prehistory. Physical evidence, such as the early collections of clear quartz crystals and red ochre pellets found among tools at various sites, suggests that religious ritual activity may have taken place as early as 2.5 million years ago. According to Robert Bednarik (1997a),[1] there is little else other than later engraved and painted symbolic art imagery, to provide clues as to what form these rituals might have taken. Visual images have always been subject to interpretation, whether by the people of the time in which they were created, or by the generations of people who have followed. Certain basic images reappear throughout prehistory/history and are found across the world, and these include the circle, parallel lines, the meanders and the arch or rainbow.

Because there is not necessarily any visual connection between the symbol and the object or idea it represents, its meaning may only be known to a limited number of people, even though its image may have some meaning for non-indigenous Western cultures today. Symbolic images might have innumerable meanings but these can differ across cultures. For example, when oral traditions and recorded mythology used by contemporary Australian Indigenous people today are taken into account, we may gain some idea of the meaning of early symbols, since they are often motifs which have been used for a very long time. While the meaning of early art will never be known for certain, it is possible that it performed functions not unlike the role of contemporary Indigenous art, the oldest art tradition still extant.

1 a   b   c

2   3 a   b   c

3 d

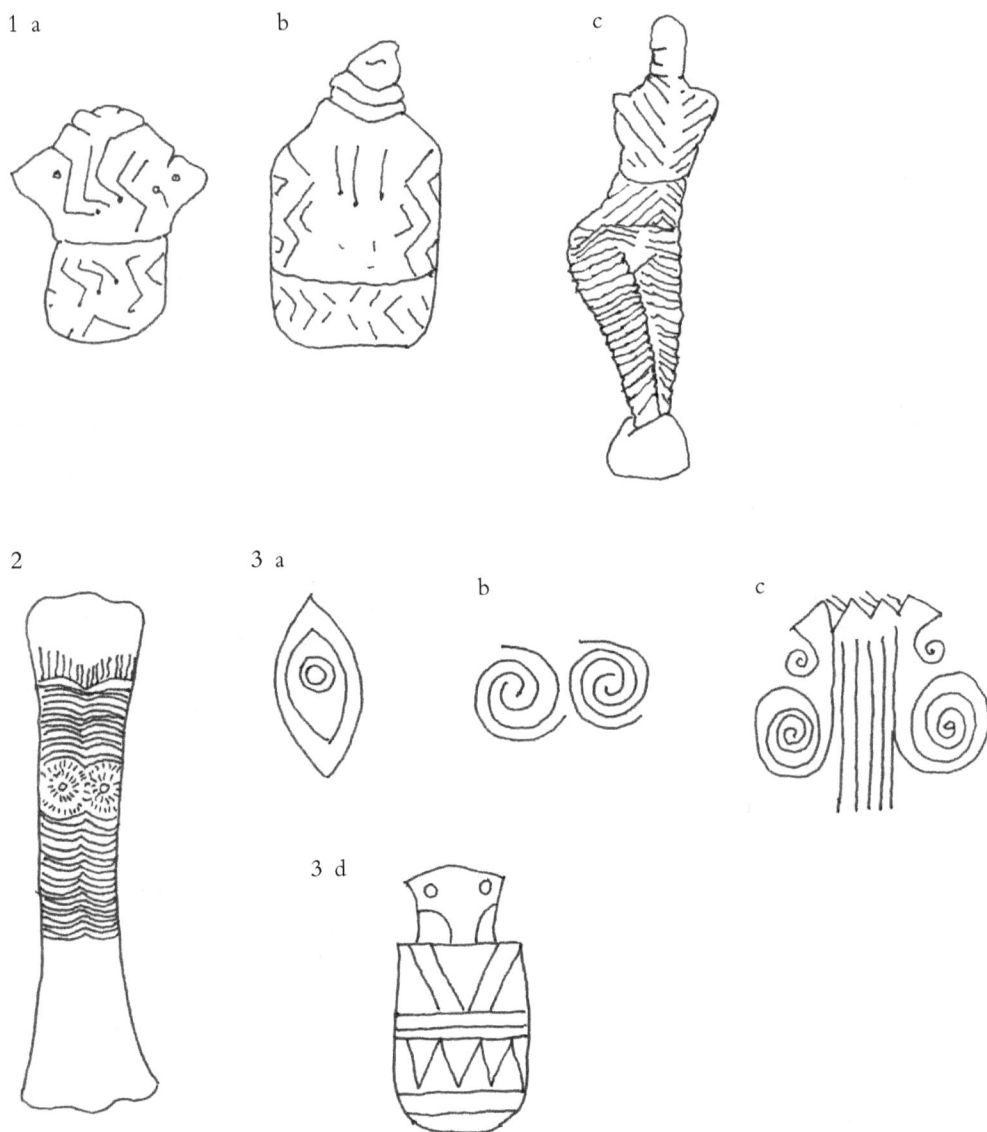

OLD EUROPEAN FIGURINES AND SPIRAL DESIGNS

1. *Three figurines*, 6,800–6,600 BP
2. *Owl goddess*, Spain, engraved bone 5,000 BP

3a–c. *Examples of spiral designs*
3d. *'V' design on Old European pottery*
(Source: Gimbutas, Marija, 1989)
All line drawings © Judy Foster, 2013

According to Marija Gimbutas (1989),[2] symbols and images form the basis of a different kind of language, transmitting multiple meanings, revealing the basic world view of our earliest ancestors. Symbols are almost always tangible, and linked to nature, thus some of their meanings may be revealed through study of their context and association. Mythical thought is the reason for, and basis of, symbolic art. Symbols are part of an interlocking system where an understanding of any one part allows an understanding of the whole which, in turn, opens up knowledge of further aspects. This is certainly the case in Australian Indigenous symbolism. Archaeological evidence in the form of symbolic images was the source of knowledge for an understanding of the spirituality of early civilisations.

Marija Gimbutas focuses on the period after 10,000 BP in Europe when the finds of prehistoric art and its symbolic images have been significant. Most of the symbols used at that time had their origins many hundreds of thousands of years previously, with the earliest appearances of art engravings and other non-utilitarian objects occurring over 1 million years ago. During this time the many and varied images of women's mysterious creative power underlay the experiences of the earliest religions.

Cupmarks (or cupules) which were formed by engraving cup-shaped hollows into stones of different kinds, and were sometimes surrounded by rings or concentric circles, were thought to be symbols relating to the life-giving Old European goddess. Triangular stones, possibly representing her birth-giving aspect, were placed over graves between 100,000 and 40,000 BP. This important interpretation necessarily takes into account the postures, gestures and headwear of the figures, and their context, as well as any other symbolic objects found in association with them. Marija Gimbutas considers it was the female ability to give birth and nourish offspring which was most sacred. She argues that it was a metaphor for the Great Mystery.[3]

According to Joseph Campbell (1969), all humans are united through symbol. Humans create symbolic art forms from lived experience, and throughout history – and prehistory – humans have always been united through "one fund of mythological beliefs, variously selected, organised, interpreted, and ritualised"[4] according to local need, but revered by every person on earth. A common cross-cultural theme is the transformation or changing of spiritual beings from an unseen presence into an earthly form. This is seen in the Indo-European Christian belief in the transformation of bread and wine into Christ's body and blood; the Australian Indigenous belief in the changing of the ancestral spirits into natural features of the land, such as hills or rocks; and the Indian belief in the goddesses who appeared in rock form in prehistoric times, or the historic gods who came down from the sky to merge within temple images, transforming them into their throne or seat. An example of this is the rock known as 'the seat of Bhima' at Bhimbetka in India which, at 800,000 years old, is the earliest symbolic art as yet discovered.

In 1968, Andre Leroi-Gourhan studied the images and symbols of French and Spanish caves in association with each other, according to their relative positions within their surroundings. These relations were based on oppositions where female or male images or symbols were either centrally based within the picture space, or placed in primary or secondary positions. He classified the images into two categories of symbols. The first group consisted of solid forms: triangles, ovals, rectangles, and circles; while the second contained linear motifs: lines of dots, dashes, or 'branches'. Any round forms were labelled 'female', and the linear forms, 'male'. Cave art was symbolic, the animals and figures not portraits, "not animals but images of animals";[5] while the rounded shapes of women or 'big-bellied' animals were not pregnant, but stylistic convention.

Alexander Marshack (1977)[6] based his theory on the internal processes involved in the making of the images and their use in ritual. He argued that such art was an essential part of ritual, with many of the forms repeated or added with each ritual use. This approach involved trying to understand the cultural system which lay behind the making and use of the images, and the reasons for their creation. Such art could not have been created without some form of language to explain the concepts behind it.

'Scientific' views of rock art

There are many definitions of 'art' as it is understood today in contemporary society. Scientists, including archaeologists and rock art specialists, seek to define the creation of art as a scientific phenomenon, yet as art historian H.W. Janson (1986) tells us, art is a means of transmitting concepts which cannot be explained in any other way. The symbolic image expresses ideas in a new way, opening up new experiences to us. Art is a word "which acknowledges both the idea of art and the fact that art exists." Art is "an aesthetic object" for us to look at and appreciate "for its intrinsic value."[7]

Robert Bednarik (1994c)[8] uses the term 'symbol' to refer to any early visual image; a motif which represents or stands for something else, perhaps a tangible image of an intangible concept accessible only to the creating culture. Today's scientific rock art specialists argue that such imagery cannot be interpreted because the meanings cannot be proved, thus disregarding numerous basic and timeless meanings of many symbols which are still relevant today. Marija Gimbutas, through her careful observations of prehistoric imagery in Europe, has clearly shown that this is not the case.

Another term for imagery is 'icon'. In the original sense, this referred to images of metaphysical, rather than real, religious subjects. Robert Bednarik (1994c) argues that the term 'iconic' refers to the depiction of a specific object, what artists would refer to as 'naturalistic' or 'figurative'. Iconic images appearing in Australian Indigenous rock art include portraits of metaphysical spirit beings (icons in the religious sense) as well as real people and other creatures. Engraved symbols such as figurative images of bird and animal tracks, or outlines of the sun, moon, and star images, should be included as iconic subjects under Robert Bednarik's definition although, curiously, he considers them to be non-iconic and abstract because of their unproven nature. While Paul Bahn (1998)[9] includes stencils of hands, feet and tools in the category of rock art, contemporary (scientific) researchers consider them to be mechanically reproduced impressions which do not represent anything.

H.W. Janson attributes the origin of symbols to the expression of universally experienced everyday occurrences with any number of specific meanings, but Robert Bednarik (1995),[10] and J.D. Lewis-Williams and T.A. Dowson (1988),[11] argue that such images are the result of internal experiences common to all humans. These last challenging contemporary scientific hypotheses as to the origins of art are known as the Entoptic/Shamanistic and the Phosphene theories.

The Entoptic/Shamanistic theory relates to individual mental attitudes and states of mind, involving mental images experienced in stages of altered consciousness, such as hallucinations, which may be experienced by both humans and animals. There are other aspects or internal causes of the non-iconic images of early prehistoric art, and these are phosphenes, which can be brought about by physical stimulation, such as pressure on the eyeball, and are present within the eye; they form constants, which derive from the optic system, probably beyond the eyeball itself. Lewis-Williams and Dowson argue that it is the individual medicine-man or shaman who, under the influence of any of the above altered states, creates external images. They suggest individual rather than community-based origins for early symbols, such as grids, zigzags, dots, spirals, and arcs, circles and concentric circles, parallel lines, and so forth.

Robert Bednarik argues that phosphenes are the basis of the art of young children and early humans (and even the subconscious doodling we modern humans sometimes practise today) and have a physiological cause. No one in this debate considers that the so-called entoptic images or phosphene images might have been the result of accurate observation of external natural phenomena by the artists and their communities. Non-representational images have no meaning other than patterning, unrelated in any way to natural forms, according to Paul Bahn (1998).[12] Yet these patterns clearly are aspects of natural objects; such patterns can be recognised everywhere in the natural environment by discerning eyes, as other researchers suggest.[13]

In 1998, John Feliks[14] pointed out that all basic entoptic forms can be seen in fossils which are complete representations of living plants and animals. Fossils found on the surface of rocks could have inspired early people to reproduce similar shapes on rocks. He remains critical of the entoptic and phosphene theories claiming that, while they have some merit, they do not give the full picture. He argues that attempting to force all purportedly 'abstract' images into the realm of entoptic phenomena and unconscious creation ignores entirely an artist's freedom to create from imagination, or to create deliberate representations of whatever he or she might choose.[15]

In 2006, John Feliks[16] reaffirmed that human awareness and experience of plant and other natural shapes on fossilised rocks, as collected by *Homo erectus*, reaches back into the Lower Palaeolithic. For example, those early deliberately incised parallel or fan shapes on bone or rock faces reveal keen human observation and understanding of simple geometric forms, an understanding gained from unique knowledge of their environment. Furthermore, John Feliks stresses that from the Lower Palaeolithic onwards, early humans were very much more intelligent than is commonly believed, although few researchers today would acknowledge this assertion.

The human ability to create iconic visual representations is shared by no other species. However, humans need to be exposed to already present natural imagery in order to learn how to make their own visual representations. Creating images on rock was a natural consequence of such observations. John Feliks points out the importance of fossil images for Australian Indigenous people who, in their creation stories, were very aware of the process of living things becoming fossilised. Indigenous people often tell of ancestral beings resting on the rocks while they 'were still wet', leaving behind their images as rock paintings.

Prehistoric visual imagery: Interpretation, art or accidental markings?

Although some experts consider engraved markings to have been made deliberately (as does John Feliks), others are similarly convinced that they have been accidentally formed as a result of natural forces. While it is true that some markings on ancient bones look very much like intentionally incised art motifs, a careful comparison between art and accidental conditions shows that there are differences between the resulting images. Alexander Marshack (1977) used these methods to establish the truth of the claim that the 300,000-year-old Pech de l'Azé ox bone was deliberately engraved. He argues that such objects suggest cognitive powers involving the ability to abstract, model, and construct works which were very different from manufactured tools.

Kalyan Chakravarty and Robert Bednarik (1997)[17] claim that the imposition of modern Western scientific constructs of reality onto the records of prehistoric people is a kind of 'cognitive colonialism'. On the other hand, John Feliks, whose 'natural representations' and 'fossil depiction' theories have been criticised as speculative by some rock art specialists, emphasises his belief in the value of insights which cannot be tested, and questions whether archaeologists and rock art specialists should attempt to apply a scientific approach as, in doing so, they diminish themselves by insisting on testable evaluations.

Paul Bahn (1998) suggests that prehistoric art is important because it demonstrates that humans have dimensions other than the purely utilitarian. He maintains that art has always been present in every society since the appearance of the first humans. The use of a wide variety of media, and the integration of art images into all aspects of the cultures of many societies, make art hard to define. Australian Indigenous cultures have never had a specific word for 'art' because it is a fundamental aspect of life and ritual, along with song, dance, and storytelling. But few art definitions fit the prehistoric models because the aims of the artists and their communities can never be known. He considers that the only possible definition of prehistoric art is intentional visual communication, expressing the artist's inner vision in a lasting meaningful way.

The earliest symbols: Line arrangements

The earliest *images* of which we know were linear, consisting of single and parallel lines often found in large panels, lines in fan arrangements, or in groups of notches incised on small portable objects made of stone, bone or ivory. Markings such as these may have been of practical use, for example, as representing ideas rather than objects, or the recording of numbers of animals hunted. Non-figurative or abstract motifs including groups of parallel lines (made by running the fingers of one hand along the soft surface found in some Australian caves such as Koonalda) and cup shapes, rings and spirals, geometric shapes and incised grids, are considered to be basic motifs as they are found everywhere. Paul Bahn (1998) notes that non-figurative imagery seems to have been even more important to early people than the first figurative or representational motifs, as they appear at least two or three times more often than figurative imagery.

Symbolism of the circle

The earliest symbol known to date is that of the 800,000-year-old engraved circle found at Bhimbetka in India. The heavenly bodies in the night sky are likely to have had great significance for early humans, so it is not surprising that their circular forms became the first symbolic shape. In those early uncertain times the well-being of the community depended upon the cooperation of all members. No one would have been able to invest so much time and effort in the making or decorating of an object, for example, the hammering of controlled marks onto a hard rock surface of a wall or object, unless it was of very great meaning and importance to the community, that is, its use value was its meaningfulness.

Marija Gimbutas (1989) defines the circle as "a transmitter of the concentrated divine energy of the centre."[18] During the period after 10,000 BP the circle and its aspects (dot in circle and concentric circles) was associated with the European seasonal spring and summer rites celebrating the sun as the "radiant divine eye"[19] of the female deity. In the 5,000-year-old Irish megalithic temple mounds, often the juxtaposing of the two symbols, concentric circles and cupmarks, were a ritual act which ensured continuity of the life forces. On menhirs surrounding the Irish mounds circular images appeared in groups of three: left crescent, full moon, and right crescent; or as three larger circles, a fourth smaller circle representing the dark moon apparently symbolised the lunar cycle.

For Marija Gimbutas and other researchers, lunar symbols such as those at Newgrange and Knowth in Ireland, connected the regenerative role of the female deity with cyclical lunar time. These wonderful Neolithic images combined circles of various kinds with other motifs, such as spirals, zigzags and meanders, forming what could have been a kind of symbolic language, such as the Vinča script, or a calendar recording the seasonal movements of the sun and moon. It is of considerable interest that the strong visual resemblance of the imagery (although perhaps not their meanings) to the symbols represented in the remarkable and very old petroglyphs created by Indigenous Australians (at Olary and Karolta in South Australia perhaps 80,000 years ago), strongly supports the notion that the circle in its various forms and associations is used worldwide, and is a very early symbol indeed. Australian symbols relating to the circle have both secular (public) and spiritual (sacred) meanings. Evidence in world mythology suggests that the circle remains an important symbol to this day.

Joseph Campbell (1969) equates the light and darkness phases of the moon to the cyclic re-entering into a dream world. Dawn and awakening from this world of dreams must always have been associated with the sun and sunrise. For example, the 'death' and 'resurrection' of the moon each month must have seemed miraculous to early people. While humans have always been entranced by the wonder of the night sky, the moon in particular has physical effects upon the earth, the tides and all living creatures; the menstrual cycle of women, and some human behaviours (such as what was known as 'moon madness') are also related to the cyclic phases of the moon. Other meanings of moon symbolism include fecundity, the cyclic period of gestation and birth of a new being. Rites of passage often associated with the moon, such as initiation, also released new life energies for new tasks, the initiate entered a new phase in life.

Marija Gimbutas notes that the circle also represents the sun, relating it to the regenerative female deity according to some interpreters. Not until the arrival of male-dominant cultures 6,000 years ago did it become a symbol of the male sky god. The images of the "birth of the sun, the young sun (spring) the triumphant sun (summer) and the old sun (autumn)"[20] all point to the power of the new patriarchal god. According to Joseph Campbell, for the Indo-Europeans the 'dark' of the old mythology contrasted with the 'light' of their new religion.

The circle as used by Indigenous Australian women

According to Diane Bell (1998a),[21] Indigenous Australian women today practise the very old traditional skill of circular weaving[22] along with numerous other arts, such as painting, engraving and carving. She records that Milerum, an early male Indigenous informant, stated that both men and women worked with fibres, although they created different objects, and each made their own specialised tools, for example, fishing lines, nets, or baskets. It should also be noted that people observed a year-long circular pattern of following seasonal food resources. Today, the weaving of baskets, mats and other objects is still widely practised around Australia by Indigenous women and men, and often includes the symbolism of the circle.

Ngarrindjeri woman, Doreen Kartinyeri, explains what the circle means in her clan where the weavings

> all start the same way ... the way we do everything in a circle ... a circle that's tying us all together. It's binding us together. The tightness of the stitches is like the closeness of the family ... [W]hen you finish and you're on the last strand of the rush, that is the filling, and when we do it that way, you can't see where it ends. And that is the *miwi* because there is no end to the *miwi* ... it's the life line.[23]

Daisy Rankine further explains that weaving is about the Indigenous historical past from the inside outwards "like our *miwi*" and "not cut in little boxes."[24]

Not only are there many symbolic meanings embedded in woven objects, but there are gendered meanings to particular weavings (just as there are in painted designs and on other objects). Ngarrindjeri women make distinctive mats upon which 'the coiled design' is similar to the radiating design found in South America, which for Diane Bell "is a window on the world that inspired and continues to inspire weaving."[25] The recurring, radiating, circular design of the mat is intimately connected to women's lives, rituals and work. The circle has always been commonly associated with Australian Indigenous women, and is their special symbol; it is painted on young women's breasts to make them appear bigger. Women sit in circles to prepare for rituals, and form circles to dance symbolic whirlwinds. Ngarrindjeri Ellen Trevorrow tells us that the time spent weaving circular mats leads to the sharing of a great many of the old stories. Starting in the centre

> you're creating loops to weave into, then you move into the circle, you keep going round and round creating the loops and once the children do these stages they're talking ... just like our old people lived, sharing time.[26]

The status of Indigenous Australian women was long assumed to be subordinate to that of the men. Yet through the accounts of the above individuals we find women engaged in activities that connect them to the land and the stories of the ancestors who created the land. We see individual men and women demonstrating equality and complementarity in both the cultural and ritual life of Indigenous people.

The circle as symbol of time

Until the arrival of Indo-European ideas and practices 6,000 years ago, the passage of time appears to have mostly been understood to be cyclic, its passing marked by seasonal changes in Nature. Many peoples (in the past, and today in traditional societies) have regarded time as simultaneously cyclic and linear, with death understood as merely a transformation from one state of being to another, a constant cyclic regeneration of life. It is interesting that some of today's scientists are now beginning to recognise this view. Sidney Liebes, Elizabet Sahtouris and Brian Swimme (1998) explain that Warrior Age people find it hard to accept death despite knowing that it is necessary. 'Recycling' is fundamental to continuing life, from the renewal of the tectonic plates in the earth's crust to the cyclic birth–death drama of the "living biomass." The human body is continually recycled "cell by cell, molecule by molecule, atom by atom"[27] so that around every seven years it has completely renewed itself.

Symbolism of the stars: The Pleiades

Munya Andrews (2004)[28] draws our attention to one very early subject of symbolism, that of the night sky and the stars. Anyone who has ever camped out on the Nullarbor Plain (South Australia) would be overwhelmed by the sheer scope and majesty of the sky which can be viewed to the horizon in every direction with such clarity that apparently there is no part of it which is not covered by thousands of bright or faint stars. The Milky Way forms a wide arch across the heavens like a river (or rainbow) while certain star formations appear here and there just as Indigenous people (and ancient mariners) would have recorded them over thousands of years. So it is not unexpected that there are many myths about the stars from all parts of the world, and those creation stories of the Indigenous Australian people are among the earliest known today, their telling preserved and handed down to each succeeding generation.

Munya Andrews gives us one example, that of the Pleiades, a particular star formation known in Australia as the 'Seven Sisters'. When she was told the story of the Seven Sisters by her grandmother (who came from the West Kimberley in Western Australia), it was with great affection for the Sisters: six bright stars, and one faint one who is the seventh sister "who is running trying to catch up with her older sisters."[29]

The symbolism of the Pleiades is to be found in many other countries, with many variations in the story. There are always seven young women pursued by an old man or men, although in some South American versions the 'sisters' are young boys. The Bandaiyan (Indigenous Australian) people regard them as 'close kin' promoting security in staying together, sharing land rights and responsibilities. Diane Bell notes with interest that they are usually portrayed as young women and that these stars (actually open galactic structures) are younger than the sun and other older stars. She says that this constellation is linked with seasonal changes in terms of when it is visible in the Southern Hemisphere.

The Pleiades is also associated with water, according to Munya Andrews, and this "symbolism [is] used to represent women or femaleness in Aboriginal Australia."[30] For the South Australian Ngarrindjeri people, the Murray River mouth, where fresh and salt water mix, "is the centre of Ngarrindjeri creation",[31] a women's place because it is connected with conception, reproduction and fertility, and the Dreaming of the Seven Sisters. The Pleiades may also be associated with hills, weather, birds and animals, navigation and sailing.

Munya Andrews became intrigued by the "profound similarities … that are quite literally, if not culturally worlds apart"[32] of many Indigenous Australian creation stories featuring the Pleiades when compared with those myths with similar meanings around the world. For example, the connection with: water, and water or ice maidens (Europe); the seven hills (Australia, Southern China); nets, cords, or knots (Australia, Europe, North Africa,

Greece, Japan, Polynesia); honey, bees, honeycombs, etc. (Australia, Greece, Italy). Not only are these basic symbols but they are also symbolic of the goddess/deity or female principle as recognised by Marija Gimbutas.

Symbolism of the meander

The earliest symbols – the circle and meander – and any other symbols with rounded shapes are usually considered to be symbols indicating the female principle. Angular symbols such as the square, rectangle, and so forth, on the other hand, refer to the male principle. While both forms were present during the Palaeolithic and Neolithic eras and in the following Warrior Age, female symbols were more prominent in the two earlier periods, while male symbols quickly become predominant in the latter period.

According to Marija Gimbutas, the meander was associated with water, and the water snake, with water birds, and the female bird deity. The meander (zigzag or serpentine line) is the symbol for water which was used as such both in the Palaeolithic and Neolithic periods. It was an important symbol associated with the Old European goddess.

A secondary unit in the composition of cupules in the cave at Bhimbetka is an engraved curving line. This must be one of the earliest uses of the meander symbol. Alexander Marshack describes the meander as being composed of double arcs or any number of parallel lines roaming across a surface.[33]

The early meander image on a Pech de l'Azé ox bone raised a number of questions for Alexander Marshack (1977). For example, the image could be iconic, perhaps representing something like a rainbow; or a map, showing directions. It might or might not explain or communicate a meaning. Perhaps its meaning was only known to the artist, or was just part of an art tradition. Maybe the sequence of the motifs was more important than the whole image. He eventually concluded that the art was definitely intentional and sequential, section by section building up to form an image, part of an evolving and complex tradition, since it appeared again frequently in cave art throughout the Palaeolithic era, and was not necessarily connected with a spiritual purpose. Other examples are to be found at Parpello in Spain, and Romanelli in Italy which are dated between 180,000 and 30,000 BP, as well as the Altamira and Lascaux cave sites of 17,000 to 14,000 BP.

Until recently, these random abstract designs were assumed to be early attempts at representational art, with little or no real meaning (and still are by the 'scientific' processual archaeologists). However it is now increasingly recognised that such engravings formed part of a system combining naming, language, and iconographic images, according to Alexander Marshack (1977). The meander is not related to the hunting and killing of animals, nor does it carry sexual connotations; rather it relates to cyclic representational images of animals used in some way in ritual. The meander ranges in form from the simple to the complex and remains stylistically similar, although never quite the same, in any two prehistoric cave sites.

Kalyan Chakravarty and Robert Bednarik (1997) identify the meander (snake), the single meander (arch), and the spiral images as very early symbols (an early example dated to 800,000 BP has been found in an Indian cave). Marija Gimbutas (1989) says the 20,000-year-old meander image represented the snake's energy which is drawn from water and the sun, hence its association with these aspects of the female deity. Symbolism of the snake includes benevolence and life force when appearing as spirals or coils. Snakes' coils representing the goddess's 'divine eyes' is a later symbolism used by Neolithic people.

The meander remains one of the most significant and interesting images not only because of its great antiquity, but because it remains a living symbol for Indigenous artists and others today.

Other symbols emerging in the Palaeolithic period

Various symbolic motifs described by Marija Gimbutas appeared in the more recent (Upper) Palaeolithic period and later gradually became more numerous in the Neolithic period. These motifs were associated with the female deity and illustrate a variety of her aspects. They were inscribed on walls, altars, on ritual objects made of pottery, stone, bone and wood as well as on the thousands of figurines representing the female deity throughout Old Europe. The symbols mentioned here originated in or before the Upper Palaeolithic period.[34]

- The 'V' shape and chevrons which are connected with the female bird deity are dated to between 20,000 and 17,000 BP, and the earliest examples are from eastern Russia. Some bone bird sculptures from Mal'ta in Siberia are tentatively dated to 26,000 BP. They were widely associated with the birth-giving properties of the Old European goddess, as are all the following symbols.

- The vulva symbol, part oval, part 'V' shape, either engraved or painted, is another very old symbol appearing around the world. There are many examples in Europe, but also in India (300,000 BP), the Americas (c. 8,000 BP) and particularly in Australia at Carnarvon Gorge (Queensland) and Lawn Hill (Northern Territory) where they are at least 10,000 years old and probably very much older. Marija Gimbutas relates the vulva to the seed in nature; both vulva and seed are birth symbols.

- Marija Gimbutas identifies the earliest known example of the zigzag and 'M' sign which was used by Neanderthal people around 42,000 BP, or even earlier, as a symbol of water, along with the meander. A French example first appeared engraved on a reindeer rib within an image of the female deity. This symbolic object was 32,000 years old. Zigzags also appear in association with bird, fish, anthropomorphic, and phallic images.

- Richard Rudgley mentions several other basic symbols, such as the cross and the spiral. The cross signifies the four corners of the world as well as the yearly cycle relating to such activities as the planting and harvesting of crops. It represents "wholeness, cyclical time and the renewal of life."[35]

- The spiral symbolises life force and is often associated with the lunar cycle (crescents, snake coils, winding snakes), the measuring of time, and the seasons. The best known examples are engraved on the orthostats at Newgrange and Knowth temple tombs in Ireand. The spiral is also symbolic of the snake, the "embodiment of the *dynamism, life force, and regenerative* powers of nature"[36] according to Marija Gimbutas.

- The powers of the snake are closely associated with water and rain and the snake has always been of great symbolic and ritual significance to the Australian Indigenous people, for whom it symbolises The Rainbow Serpent. Zohl dé Ishtar explains that the rainbow (single or double arch) signifies the equal but different aspects of the Law as it applies to the lives of women and to men: there is women's (business) Law, and men's (business) Law, represented by the rainbow where "the woman is on top and the man underneath, and in joining together, they made all the colours of the rainbow."[37] For Pacific people also, the sea snake is both feared and respected. The spiral appears as a basic unit in much Pacific visual imagery.

- The 'eyes of the deity' was sometimes associated with water streaming down the breasts of a female bird deity, and symbolised the eyes as a divine source when used with chevrons and 'V's. They also represent the all-seeing aspect of the deity. Owl eyes are also symbols of the divine eyes of the deity and first date to 25,000 BP.
- The net motif, first appeared in the Lower Palaeolithic, and infers the early use of cord/thread and is symbolic of the water of life. It is a basic symbol since it also appears in other cultures such as the art of Australian Indigenous people.
- Tri lines, or lines in groups of three, symbolise the three aspects of the deity: birth, death, and regeneration, according to Marija Gimbutas.
- She also describes the earliest symbolism of the egg; forms such as circles, ovals (lozenges), and ellipses symbolise birth as a type of rebirth or recreation of life. An early example is 14,000 years old and depicted on the image of a bull which was painted onto a cave floor in southern France. Egg and seed symbolise new life. The womb of the deity was understood as egg-shaped: from this "life would re-emerge." It is also associated with spirals, crescents, crosses, snakes, and sprouting plants, all of which are "symbols of becoming."[38]

The archaeological record points to a predominantly gentle metaphysical female or principle as demonstrated in the profusion of female figurines with their associated symbolic designs which include curved elements such as the egg, bird, snake and spiral. This symbolism contrasts sharply with the fierce angular symbolic images of powerful and angry gods with their destructive weapons which appeared from the beginning of the Bronze Age.

Having discovered the importance of language as oral transmission of myth, and visual symbolic imagery as the source of much evidence which Indigenous people may share with us about prehistoric cultures and societies, it is now time to see how they provide information about a number of early civilisations, not only in the European region, but also in the Hidden and New Worlds. As will be seen through art and artefact evidence, we find prehistoric cultures have been as sophisticated as circumstances allowed, that women were highly visible, responsible for many important innovations; and that the female principle was clearly paramount in Europe, and was apparently equally prominent with the male principle in the Southern Hemisphere until about 4,000 BP when contact with Indo-European ideas and practices first appeared.

CHAPTER 5

Northern Hemisphere: The Prehistoric Goddess Figurines of Old Europe

Lower (earliest) Palaeolithic figurines

Paintings, sculptures, engraved art imagery, and the like have been discovered over a long period of time, and during the historical era, have caused much conjecture as to their meaning. The concept of metaphysical beings as female and earth-based evidently originated very early in Northern Hemisphere prehistory. The first example of archaeological evidence is the earliest known naturally shaped stone sculpture, originally covered in red pigment, of the Moroccan 'Tan Tan' quartzite anthropomorphic figurine described by Robert Bednarik (2001)[1] as being 400,000 years old. The figurine has legs separated by naturally engraved lines and a head delineated by deliberately pecked lines (percussion marks) hammered into the rock. The second example is that of the sculpture of the female 'Berekhat Ram' figure from Israel which Robert Bednarik says is 300,000 years old. This small stone image is naturally shaped to resemble a woman's head and torso, and features incised markings to delineate her neck and arms. Why these sculptures were made and what they might have signified becomes a little clearer with a brief summary of prehistoric rock art discoveries and interpretations.

Rock art imagery and the metaphysical world

The art of the caves and rock shelters which included symbolic animal and anthropomorphic imagery are noted by Richard Rudgley (1998),[2] who mentions one example which was an early inscribed 30,000-year-old incised image of an animal found in Israel on a limestone slab. Paul Bahn (1992)[3] describes other engravings on the underside of a limestone slab found in a rock shelter in France at La Ferrassie, on which 18 cupmarks (engraved cuplike depressions) were found being used as a marker for a Neanderthal child's grave. He suggests this means that these humans were advanced enough to bury their dead in ritual fashion and possibly had some 'primitive' form of metaphysical belief.

Until recent times the most famous Upper Palaeolithic artworks had been the 17,000-year-old paintings found at Lascaux in France; and those at Altamira in Spain, which are 14,000 years old. Generally, European rock art of the late Upper Palaeolithic features

CHAUVET CAVE PAINTINGS AND OLD EUROPEAN FIGURINES

1. *Goddess figure*, Chauvet-Pont-d'Arc Cave, France (Source: Whitaker, Alex, n.d.)
2. *Lions*, Chauvet-Pont-d'Arc Cave, France (Source: Clottes, Jean, 2003)
3. *Two stiff white goddess figurines*, Moldavia, 5,500 BP and Sardinia, 6,000 BP
4. *Engraved bone figurine*, 10,000 BP
5. *Clay figurine with net and parallel linear design motifs*
6. *A double-headed Vinča figurine*, 7,000–6,800 BP
7. *A painted double-triangle figurine*
8. *A Minoan snake goddess*, 4,100–3,800 BP
   (Source 3–8: Gimbutas, Marija, 1989)
   All line drawings © Judy Foster, 2013

54

expressive well-proportioned, carefully observed images and symbols of (often female) animals including deer, cattle, horses as well as the occasional anthropomorphic figure. The animals seem to move across the walls just as freely as they did in reality. Human figures are often featured, or evidence of the hunt including weapons, spears and darts tell the story. Technical aspects such as the application of colour and the movement and style of the images indicate that accomplished artists were responsible for their creation. There has been much conjecture as to the meaning and purpose of the images, and there are few descriptions of the paintings which do not include some kind of interpretation.

At present the earliest known cave artworks are in Chauvet-Pont-d'Arc Cave in France, dated to 32,000 BP, and discovered in 1994.[4] These include wonderful red ochre or black charcoal drawings of the living animals in flowing movement, as if chasing or being chased across the red, yellow or white rock walls. Within the cave complex there are over 13 different varieties of animals, including not only hunted animals (bison, horses, deer, etc.), but also predatory animals such as lions, panthers, bears, rhinoceros, hyenas and owls. These paintings are magnificent, surpassing those at Lascaux and Altamira by far, despite being so much older.

Chauvet cave is unusual in that it has a rare partial goddess figurine in the deepest, and perhaps the most secret part of the cave complex, a space which French historian Jean Clottes has concluded was used for sacred rituals. The figurine, featured on a pale yellow ochre coloured rock wall, consists of a lower body and legs, drawn in long sure black charcoal strokes in a style similar to the small sculpted female figurines of the period. She is the earliest image in a prominent position within the space, and is placed in association with "two felines, a mammoth and a small musk ox"[5] according to Jean Clottes.

Recent discoveries include an anthropomorphic image in Fumane Cave in Italy; and Cougnac and Cosquer caves, also in France, hold paintings dated to 32,000–30,000 BP. Other early paintings are the 28,000-year-old stone plaques or portable paintings from Namibia (Africa); and wall paintings at Laura in Queensland (Australia), which are dated to 25,000 BP. Australian Indigenous engraved rock art in South Australia is believed to be as old as 45,000 years, but in general current techniques are not always reliable when dating rock art.

In the 1960s and 1970s, interpretations of the 30,000-year-old origins of art and culture often involved a comparative analysis of different images. As part of their search for the origins of art and culture, interpreters have argued for a metaphysical explanation for the images in Upper Palaeolithic art. A typical view in 1967 was that of P.M. Grand[6] who considered that the cave paintings were based on powerful long-standing traditional and religious concepts of the origins of the universe, a view upheld by Marija Gimbutas.

Because the art works are usually hidden deep in the caves away from accidental discovery by unauthorised people, H.W Janson (1986)[7] thought that they must have been produced as part of secret 'magic' ritual, perhaps to ensure a successful hunt. Most interpretations naturally assumed that the art motifs and their accompanying rituals were created solely by men for all-male purposes. It would have been unthinkable to biased Western male experts that women may have played a central role in religious rituals associated with the art and taken part in their creation. Nor was it thought possible that animals might have shared a sacred status similar to that of humans at that time. This is of course the patriarchal view.

Symbols associated with metaphysical female attributes such as the vulva, breasts and uterus are common, and are found not only in the caves but also in engravings on various other portable surfaces. Any male figures which are included seem to be of secondary importance.

It is significant that Upper Palaeolithic rock art and artefacts do not include any images of war; there are no large battle scenes, nor are there any images relating to the lives and deaths of kings and queens. Any weapons illustrated are those associated with ritual ceremonies or the hunting of animals. Due to the ever-enlarging world view of prehistoric rock art available to us since the late 1990s, we now realise that these early societies were predominantly peaceful. Even Paul Bahn admits that "interhuman violence is surprisingly rare in prehistoric art as a whole"[8] as there are only a couple of human-like figures in all of Eurasian art which might suggest they were speared. He notes that apparent battle scenes featured in Arnhem Land (Australia) Indigenous paintings depicting bows shooting at people are not necessarily angry clashes, but might be scenes of aspects of the creative activities of ancestral spirit beings. Threats and insults, and ritual fighting similar to mediaeval jousting, are devices used to relieve angry tensions among some Indigenous groups even today. (Fights stop with the first shedding of blood, when honour is considered to be restored.) Instead, the emphasis seemed to focus upon the human female and, in many instances, upon female animals.

The prominence of large animals and the inclusion of the occasional anthropomorphic figure in the paintings suggest to processual archaeologists that these animals were regarded not just as an important food source, but also as objects of fear because of their size, and therefore needed to be controlled by so-called magic shamans' ritual practices. Since Upper Palaeolithic men are considered 'uncivilised' this usually means that their 'primitive' hunting 'magic' practices associated with the worship of natural creatures or objects are never considered as a religious belief in supernatural forces belonging to the non-physical world. Their rituals were, and still are, almost always considered part of a 'magic cult' where control over people, creatures and objects is sought through strange 'pagan' ritual practices which are considered to have nothing to do with any Western notion of religion. Apparently only 'civilised' Western societies may experience religious worship.

Upper Palaeolithic figurines (50,000–10,000 BP)

One early example appearing late in the Upper Palaeolithic period is a recently discovered (2008) 35,000-year-old mammoth-ivory female figurine from a cave near Ulm in south-western Germany. Her discoverer, Nicholas Conard, from the University of Tubingen, named her the 'Venus' of Schelklingen, also known as the 'Hohle Fels Venus'.

Described in the journal *Nature*,[9] she apparently is the oldest known fully carved female figurine ever found. The figurine was probably a pendant as she lacks a head and has a hole in her neck for a cord. She has small arms and legs, generous body proportions and an enlarged vulva. Marija Gimbutas would most likely have interpreted her as symbolising the goddess of birth and new life, a woman perhaps about to give birth. Instead, she was lamentably identified by archaeologist Paul Mellars of Cambridge University, in an article in *The Age*, as a Venus figurine which "by 21st century standards could be seen as bordering on the pornographic."[10] Statuettes such as these were, and still are, commonly labelled 'Venus' figurines by their male discoverers because they display prominent breasts, stomachs, hips and pubic features, characteristics considered 'erotic' by many men.[11]

Another example is the 32,000-year-old female deity of Galenberg in Austria, the earliest known carved female figurine depicted in movement (perhaps dancing). The shape of her body and the thoughtfully planned movement of her limbs were dictated by the limitations of the brittle green stone from which she was carved. The sculptor solved these problems by folding back one arm and supporting both legs on a stand. Robert Bednarik considers that this indicates considerable skill which would have been part of a long tradition of sculpting fine figurines.

A low relief sculpture of the 24,000-year-old female deity of Laussel found in a French cave is another example. Her image was carved into a stone slab which includes three other figures. Emphasis was placed on the shape and function of her body; her breasts and hips were generous in size, her left hand placed over her pregnant stomach. Luis Pericot-Garcia (1967)[12] describes the Laussel figurine as being nearly 18 inches (46 centimetres) high. Of the three other less complete images which accompany her, one holds a curved object, perhaps a lamp, in her hand, while another is possibly a rare male figure wearing a belt. Graham Clark (1961)[13] considered her merely a featureless, obese, and naked woman, the horn in her hand marking her value as a 'fertility' symbol. Unfortunately he (and Paul Mellars more recently), like other biased conservative researchers, continues to consider that prehistoric female figurines were symbols of continuity and female 'cultic' sculptures deliberately created to incite male passions.

However, some other historians have been more discerning. P.M. Grand (1967), who regarded such images as sophisticated works of art, was much more conscious of a serious metaphysical meaning for the figurines since he described the female figurine of Laussel and her companions as an important work with considerable authority. In comparison with the female images, the accompanying male image appears almost static and expressionless without any of the distinction of the female deity holding the horn.

Among the numerous female images present in the Upper Palaeolithic period, there are other well-known examples, such as a 25,000-year-old mammoth-ivory figure from Lespugne in France, and a fired clay figure from Dolni Vestonice in Czechoslovakia. While many people think there were no cultures before the historic period, art historian H.W. Janson (1986) recognised these beautifully crafted little sculptures, with their generous curves and stylised features, as having emerged from traditions that were thousands of years old.

A somewhat later limestone figurine from Austria, the 22,000-year-old female deity of Willendorf, was more accurately considered by Alexander Marshack[14] to represent female maturity and fertility. She was originally covered with red ochre suggesting she was probably used in ritual.

Female figurines: Evolution of a female deity

Only 3,000 Upper Palaeolithic female figurines have been discovered so far, unfortunately often without context, in an area known as Old Europe, a term used by Marija Gimbutas (1999). But there are over 100,000 small figurines from the Neolithic period (10,000–5,000 BP) found in the same area (in settlements, graves, tombs, and temples) made from clay, marble, copper and gold. There are also numerous shrines, altars, ritual vessels, sacrificial implements, painted vases, inscribed objects, clay models of temples and temple life, which centred around an Old European female deity. This large range of Neolithic figurines, together with the Palaeolithic imagery, suggests a long-lasting emphasis on female forms and their relationship to the powers of nature and the cycle of birth/life, death and renewal of all living things.

Marija Gimbutas uses the term 'goddess' to suggest that the one goddess, and/or her many aspects, was common to all of the Old World.[15] Max Dashu more recently has made the point that 'goddess' is a term used by many cultures when referring to "ancestral mother/mothers, forces of nature, lawgivers, primordial creators"[16] and that the word 'deity' has Proto-Indo-European origins: *deiwa* (feminine), *deiwo* (masculine), ('day' or 'Diana'), and means 'shining'. The word 'goddess' is from the Germanic root *guda* or *gudhan* which has ritual associations. Max Dashu points out that many linguists favour *ghau*, 'to call on' or 'invoke'.[17] This does not mean that prehistoric deities should be worshipped today – rather they should be recognised and respected, not denigrated and labelled 'idols', 'cultic' or 'fertility' figurines.[18]

Because there are few artefacts from the Upper Palaeolithic period other than the figurines, it is difficult to form a picture of very early religions, and so the female figurines remain controversial. Belief in a female deity is thought by some researchers to have evolved in different ways. According to Gerda Lerner (1986)[19] it was concerned with the dependence of the child upon the mother for food, warmth and shelter, and for the passing down of survival skills. She says it was therefore not surprising that everyone experiencing the drama and mystery of female power, recognised the role of a 'Mother-Goddess'.

Alexander Marshack (1977)[20] suggests that the European Upper Palaeolithic female sculptures, together with the cave paintings of animals and occasional male figures, might have had their origin in early stories and myths. The animal cave art may have been associated with shamanic rituals, while the female sculptures could have been linked with women's mysteries.

Some 'goddess' categories

While female figurines were prominent from 800,000 until 6,000 BP (and longer in some instances) around the world, there are several styles of European Palaeolithic female figurines covering a time span from around 40,000 to 10,000 BP with many variations on a theme. Firstly, there are a series of small, delicate figurines. The Lespugne figurine is such an example, being about 16 centimetres high, and made from clay. Her head droops down above pendulous breasts, and she has large buttocks and abdomen. Her tapered legs narrow to a point as if she was meant to be standing upright. Secondly, there are images such as the less graceful, short and well-rounded figure of the 22,000-year-old 'Woman of Willendorf', carved so well in limestone that such an image must have been part of a long, highly skilled craft tradition. Yet another style includes flat stone or marble shapes representing the goddess, for example, the later highly stylised Cycladic figurines from Crete which Marija Gimbutas has interpreted as representing the goddess of transition from death to rebirth.

The well-rounded female figurines found from 37,000 BP are considered by Elizabeth Barber (1994)[21] to represent the essence of female beauty for women at these times. For practical reasons plump women could survive longer and breastfeed their babies during seasonal famine, so being stout obviously had its advantages for the well-being of the whole community. Marija Gimbutas recommends caution when using modern Western concepts about women and beauty to interpret these past images.

The goddesses of the Palaeolithic Period

The 'goddess' with a skirt – an ancient clothing code?

The earliest solid evidence of the use of string, cord, or thread to be found so far is that of flax fibres[22] dated to 34,000 BP, discovered in Dzudzuana Cave in the foothills of the Causasus Mountains in Georgia. The finders claim that this suggests the weaving of clothing, string bags and carry packs, mats, baskets and other domestic products, implying weaving as the work of women, although they are not mentioned.[23]

In April 2000, Olga Soffer announced her discovery of new evidence of woven textiles made 27,000 years ago, which shows that clothing is featured on many of the Upper Palaeolithic female figurines found in central and western Europe.[24] Until recently these markings had been ignored by all but Marija Gimbutas. Olga Soffer says the clothing includes basket hats and caps (such as the basket hat worn by the Willendorf figurine). Bandeaus (straps of cloth wrapped around the body above the breasts) and belts were worn at the waist or low-slung on the hips with string skirts attached (as worn by the Lespugne figurine). The evidence also consists of textile impressions made by someone accidentally leaning against a newly finished wet clay wall and sitting on a floor. Other impressions include clay fragments which may have lined baskets. There are many kinds of weaving techniques among the samples, including open and closed twines and plain weave which indicate the use of looms, as well as basketry and nets.

The 25,000-year-old Lespugne female figurine was described as being made from greenish coloured mammoth-ivory with her hair flowing over her shoulders. P.M. Grand (1967) was one of the few to notice that she seemed to be leaning against a seat or pedestal of some kind indicated by engraved lines behind her upper legs. More recently, Elizabeth Barber (1994) has interpreted these markings to represent a garment, a string apron worn hanging from the figurine's hips. She considers this to be the earliest known example of clothing worn as a code which provided information about the wearer. The coded meaning conveyed by clothing (only worn by women) has apparently been in use since Upper Palaeolithic times. Similar garments are still worn by women in parts of Europe today as part of traditional folk costumes.

The string apron worn by the Lespugne female figurine consists of twisted cords hung (behind her back) from a wide corded belt around the hips. The hanging cords usually had beads or knotted ends, or sometimes as in the Lespugne apron, the ends were frayed like tassels causing the skirt to sway as the woman walked along.[25] These skirts were not intended to cover up but to draw attention to women's sexual areas by framing them, and probably indicated an aspect such as their childbearing ability or perhaps their readiness to bear children. Marija Gimbutas has interpreted the symbolic role of the skirt as being intended to draw attention to their reproductive powers.

OLD EUROPE: FAMOUS GODDESS FIGURINES

1. *Weeping goddess* from Moravia
2. *Lespugne goddess* wearing a string apron, France, 25,000 BP
3. The *Laussel female figurine*, France, (with rare male figure) 24,000 BP
4. *Willendorf goddess*, Germany, 22,000 BP
5. A *pregnant female figurine* from France, 23,000 BP
6. and 7. *Two Cycladic goddesses* from Europe, 5,000 BP
(Source: Gimbutas, Marija, 1989)
All line drawings © Judy Foster, 2013

The 'calendar' goddess of the moon

Hilda Davidson[26] speaks of the connection of the female deity with the moon which had many implications: not only was she present in the sky, but at the same time was linked with the earth, water, caves, clefts, rivers, lakes and the sea. The significance of the moon, its connection with the female deity in the Palaeolithic and Neolithic periods, and its influence upon the measuring of time, movement of the tides, women's menstruation, and the nine-month gestation period, could have corresponded with the three aspects of the female deity: virgin, mother, and old woman; or in later mythology: bride, mother, layer-out of the dead.

There is evidence on the figurines which points to both symbolic and practical meanings. So it is not surprising that the 25,000-year-old goddess of Laussel, for example, may have been linked to the cyclic patterns of the moon since she holds a horn which is marked with 13 incised lines representing the 13 days of the waxing moon or the 13 lunar months. Dorothy Cameron (1997)[27] also relates the horn to women's menstrual cycles, and also to woman/moon/bull symbolism (which is described later in the overview of Çatal Hüyük). The horn could well have been used to call people together for ritual and ceremony (horns are still used in remote areas for this purpose) while its eerie sound echoing through the caves would have added an out-of-this-world dimension to any gathering.

Alexander Marshack[28] has recorded a system of lunar notation used by people at least 40,000 years ago. He observes that these signs, engraved on bone, stone, antler, and goddess figurines, could have facilitated the early development of agriculture, the calendar, astronomy, mathematics and writing. Denise Schmandt-Besserat (1992/1996)[29] argues that these incised notations were the first method of numbering which eventually led to the invention of writing. It may come as a surprise to many that clay seals, or tokens, which demonstrate an early form of accountancy, have appeared in many archaeological sites including Çatal Hüyük, Knossos, and centres in the Middle East, at least since 10,000 BP, although archaeologists have usually ignored them as meaningless lumps of clay.

The earliest clay tokens were plain but shaped in various geometric forms, while later tokens were often circular featuring different incised designs. Some were very small and enclosed in round clay 'envelopes', the numbers of tokens corresponding to the goods being recorded. Denise Schmandt-Besserat argues that clay tokens marked with incised symbols were most likely used by women in the Neolithic period to record 'economic data', where each token represented one exact unit of goods.[30] Over a period of time during the Neolithic period, tokens were developed to record more complex information and this involved new symbolic images representing different information, such as amounts of certain goods, and who collected them.

The Neolithic goddess figurines

Marija Gimbutas[31] lists two sets of Neolithic female figurines:
- the life-giving images, including mother and child, bear and deer, birds and the bird goddess, vegetation goddesses and gods, the pregnant vegetation goddess, the vegetation year god, and the conjoined female and male symbolising the sacred marriage
- images of death, and death/regeneration, including birds of prey, the stiff white goddess, the Gorgon masks with serpent-like characteristics, and many other masks featuring decorative symbolic imagery.

A third group contains symbols specific to regeneration and new life, including frogs and frog goddesses, the hedgehog, dogs and goats, bucrania and cattle horns, the phallus, the triangle, and the double triangle or hourglass figure. Animal and bird symbols include birds of prey such as vultures, which symbolised the transition from life through death to regeneration.

Tracing a goddess myth into the past

Some of the symbolic imagery Marija Gimbutas has interpreted may still be found today in parts of Europe, represented by seasonal rituals, and told in stories associated with goddess mythology. It is interesting that some different aspects and meanings of the Neolithic goddess images from 10,000 BP mentioned here, are also to be found in India, China, South-East Asia and the Pacific region, in particular the double triangle (hourglass) female deity, the spiral (snake), circle, zigzag, and animal and bird masks.

Hilda Davidson (1998) has traced the presence of a female deity concept back through recorded and oral mythologies and archaeological evidence to the Upper Palaeolithic existing alongside the painted animals of the caves. Her study of 'goddess' mythology gives one example of an early concept of the goddess as 'Mistress of the Animals' which was possibly linked to an early shamanic religion. This goddess was connected with a male deity known as 'Ruler (or Guardian) of the Wild', who either helped or hindered hunters. There is the 'hunting goddess' who guarded the forests and protected the creatures within: hunters could kill the animals if they respected her rules, but she destroyed them if they offended her. The threads of this myth can be followed through the Neolithic period to the Bronze Age and beyond, and show that a hunting goddess is still present today in some historical cultures, for example, in the Caucasus where deer and mountain goats are still hunted; and in Japan where bears are still hunted in the mountains.

Unlike Marija Gimbutas, Hilda Davidson does not make the important distinction between the peaceful Palaeolithic and Neolithic communal societies and the hierarchic Bronze Age warrior societies, which so affected the status of the female deity/deities. The Bronze Age goddesses held an increasingly reduced status and performed rather different functions to those of the Neolithic goddess.

Sexual goddess or wise woman?

For Anne Baring and Jules Cashford (1991)[32] there were remarkable similarities and parallels between the myths and the imagery of the goddess across apparently unrelated cultures. The figurines were also much more than 'fertility idols', with many aspects and purposes besides the most important one, that of the fundamental force governing all life. All cultures, whether simple or complex in social organisation, experienced sacred dimensions. A belief in the presence of the sacred was not just a *stage* in the history of consciousness but a part of the *structure* of all human consciousness.

Marija Gimbutas explains that in sacred art "the human body symbolises myriad functions beyond the sexual, especially the procreative, nurturing and life-enhancing."[33] It may also represent wise mature women who were the repositories of communal knowledge about issues such as health, agriculture, and social relations. The figurines are tactile – meant to be hand-held, as well as seen in place, whether standing upright in the earth or lying on an altar. Photographs cannot adequately capture the warmth and vitality conveyed by the figurines.

Goddess of the home and hearth

Early rituals took place in the first homes and then in home-like temples scattered among the houses throughout villages in Old Europe. Marija Gimbutas records that many Neolithic figurines were found within these houses, as well as in public places of ritual, demonstrating the goddess as central to all of life. She refers to the homes as 'house temples', in which women's daily tasks such as bread-making, weaving of cloth and pottery-making became a part of sacred ritual. Domed bread ovens, querns, storage jars, ceramic loom weights, and spindle whorls were the evidence of the integration of women's secular and sacred lives: art, craft and ritual were integrated as one entity. The importance of baking bread is a tradition which is as old as the harvesting of grain, according to Beth Hensperger (1997).[34] The Anatolian Natufians of 12,000 BP, and the Old Europeans, used querns and smooth round grinding stones for the preparation of grain for flour. For at least 30,000 years Australian Indigenous people have been collecting certain grass seeds and plant roots for baking as cakes in the hot ash of their fires. Their grinding stones were left near the sources of seed in preparation for their return each year.[35]

Grain was regarded as sacred as it vanished into the earth in winter, and reappeared in spring. Many Indo-European goddesses were linked with bread making and sharing. The main ingredients of flour and yeast and the basic processes used today around the Western world are similar to those used in the deep past.

Hilda Davidson describes the female deity in this instance as 'Mistress of the Household'. The position of the hearth was very important within a house, usually in the centre where specified places were allocated for women. Men would have had their own sacred space, and there may have been a special door through which they passed when going out to hunt, and through which they returned with game for the household.

Michael Dames (2009)[36] explains the sacredness of the home in Ireland, for example, as having its roots in very early myths of the Neolithic fire goddess represented by Saint Brigid, and her rituals were associated with the centrally placed home hearth. He considers that the cave sanctuary and temple/home were the women's domains because women were the intermediaries between the female deity and humanity.

The birth-giving goddess

The frog, and its relationship with water and resemblance to the human foetus, symbolises the goddess and her regenerative powers. The stylised frog as depicted on Neolithic pottery formed an 'M'-shaped sign which was to become a hieroglyph. Fish imagery was accompanied by the fish net sign, and symbolised the goddess because of its association with water and moistness of the womb, and was used in the cyclic spring rituals.

In Neolithic village temples there were special rooms for giving birth. These birthing shrines were painted red (the colour of blood/life) and the walls had paintings of women giving birth. There were three of these in Çatal Hüyük, and other examples in Malta. They also featured meander and other water symbolism. Painted birthing figurines in the 9,000-year-old Red Shrine at Çatal Hüyük depicted childbirth treated as part of ritual.

The Parthenogenic goddess/creatrix

Marija Gimbutas[37] defines the Parthenogenic goddess as able to create life out of herself. Just as the female body represented the goddess creatrix, the world was thought of as the body of the goddess. In the matrilineal (mother-kinship) system which appeared to predominate during the Palaeolithic and Neolithic periods in Old Europe, mother and mother–daughter imagery were always prominent. Prehistorian James Harrod (1997) describes two versions of Upper Palaeolithic double-headed female figurines: one, a woman with two heads; and another which has two heads and four breasts but only two arms. He asserts that these are meant to represent "archetypical spiritual transformation processes" relating to "the intergenerational flow of powers from mother to daughter."[38]

According to Marija Gimbutas there were no father images, perhaps because the father image was not always understood or as highly valued as the mother image. Evidence of the mother's role was easy to see through childbirth, but the father's role was far more nebulous. In these earlier cultures females had more than one sexual partner which meant paternity could not be proved (something which did not matter in matrilineal societies when property was passed through the female line, or communally owned). Not until the patriarchal period was paternity seen as essential, especially when controlling women's reproductive behaviour or with regard to the inheritance of (male-owned) property.

The stiff white goddess

There are a number of small mammoth-ivory figurines in a slender style from Mal'ta in Siberia which we now know to be about 35,000 years old. These and other sculptures from Mal'ta and Buret belonging to the Old European goddess tradition, extending from Spain to Siberia, have been interpreted by processual researchers as representing males or sexless people. Marija Gimbutas maintains that these white marble, alabaster or stone Cycladic sculptures represent the stiff white goddess of death and regeneration which often accompanied a person's burial, and symbolised transformation through death into the 'body' of the goddess to be reborn. The goddess lies stiffly in death, her life-sustaining attributes given little emphasis, often with arms positioned across her body, very small or no breasts, but well-defined pubic triangle. The images appear in graves from 9,000 BP, and are very common after 6,300 BP in the Cycladic Islands.

Other death goddesses wear masks featuring perforations into which gold or copper ring-shaped pendants could be fixed. Some masks may also have been decorated with snake symbols or shaped like raptors, or featured animal or snake characteristics. Marija Gimbutas says these suggest the combination of animal and human forces. Many of these symbolic masks are still made and used today, and feature in folklore rituals of the goddess.

The land as 'body' of the goddess

In *The Silbury Treasure* (1976), Michael Dames[39] describes land in the British Isles as being closely connected to the female deity, where her body forms the architectural shape of Neolithic earth constructions, for example, the Silbury Hill mound, Newgrange and Knowth passage tombs. The cruciform shape of the passages within Knowth and Newgrange represent her body, while the entrances (birth canal) lie between her 'legs'. Silbury Hill, which has no passage or chamber, was built by the Neolithic people, and is said to form the uterus of the deity, while the surrounding moat forms her body. More recently Michael Dames (2009) has discovered that ritually, Silbury Hill represented the Mother of the Universe, while the shape and position of aspects of the mound and surrounding moat at the time of the full moon symbolise birth and new life which in this case is nourishment of the harvest. Some agricultural rituals still practiced today have their roots in the Neolithic period.

Another interesting and inspiring source of little known information about land as body of the goddess is Cristina Biaggi's *Habitations of the Great Goddess* (1994). She examines the cultures of Malta (4,000–2,500 BP), the Orkneys (4,500–1,800 BP) and the Shetland Islands (4,000–2,500 BP) in detail "within the context of a theocratic society worshipping a female deity."[40] She discovered goddess symbolism on rock faces and on stone pillars (megaliths) forming the external and internal structure of both tombs and temples. These were in varied shapes that suggested earth as the body of the goddess, similar to those examples in Ireland and Europe. Cristina Biaggi suggests that the people of the time regarded these islands as sanctuaries, "remote places where life centred on religion and ritual."[41] Her report features many interesting illustrations and photographs of the female figurines, tombs and temples. It is a remarkable record of a previously missing part of the story of the goddess.[42]

Examples of 'henges' in southern England include Stonehenge[43] (begun 6,000 years ago) and the remarkable 5,000-year-old Avebury Stone Circle, and are Neolithic complexes dedicated to worship of the Neolithic female deity expressed through cyclic agricultural rituals centred on the sites. Marija Gimbutas says they were cooperatively developed by villagers and clan groups over several generations, and celebrated both the dead and the goddess of regeneration. Although archaeologists have labelled them as being used for military purposes, she stresses that they had social and religious uses only. The Avebury complex is huge, encircled by a large ditch 7–10 metres deep, the bank nearly 7 metres high. It covers over 11 hectares, with 98 upright stones, some as high as 5 metres.

Marija Gimbutas explains that the Old Europeans viewed death and transition processes very differently from later cultures. For Neolithic people life and death were positive and cyclical: birth (new life) emerged from the degeneration of the old; the womb (cave or grave) of the goddess took away in death and gave new life. Caves and rock cut tombs symbolised the birth canal and womb of the goddess, the narrow entrance, the vulva.[44]

Newgrange in Ireland features the most dramatic winter solstice alignment as the sun lights its internal passage only at that time, connecting the seasonal cycle to the ritual of regeneration. The many symbolic engravings in and around this venue include snake coils, zigzags, lozenges, and winding snakes, owl eyes, and three spirals forming a point-down triangle, all of which represent the goddess-given life/death/regeneration theme.

The triangle and double triangle symbol

The triangle represents the sacred female pubic triangle and is also a vulva symbol. It has been an important symbol of life-giving and regeneration from 300,000 BP until the present time. The double triangle represents the hourglass goddess who is often accompanied by spirals, chevrons, or meanders, all regenerative symbols, according to Marija Gimbutas (1999). She functions to bring about the new life of spring and the transition from death to regeneration of every living thing. In prehistory, triangular stones were placed at the entrances to megalithic tombs, or as back stones within a megalith. They were sometimes shaped as altars for ritual, or linked with symbols of energy such as hooks, horns and triangular axes. (Triangular rocks outside villages in India also represented the goddess.)

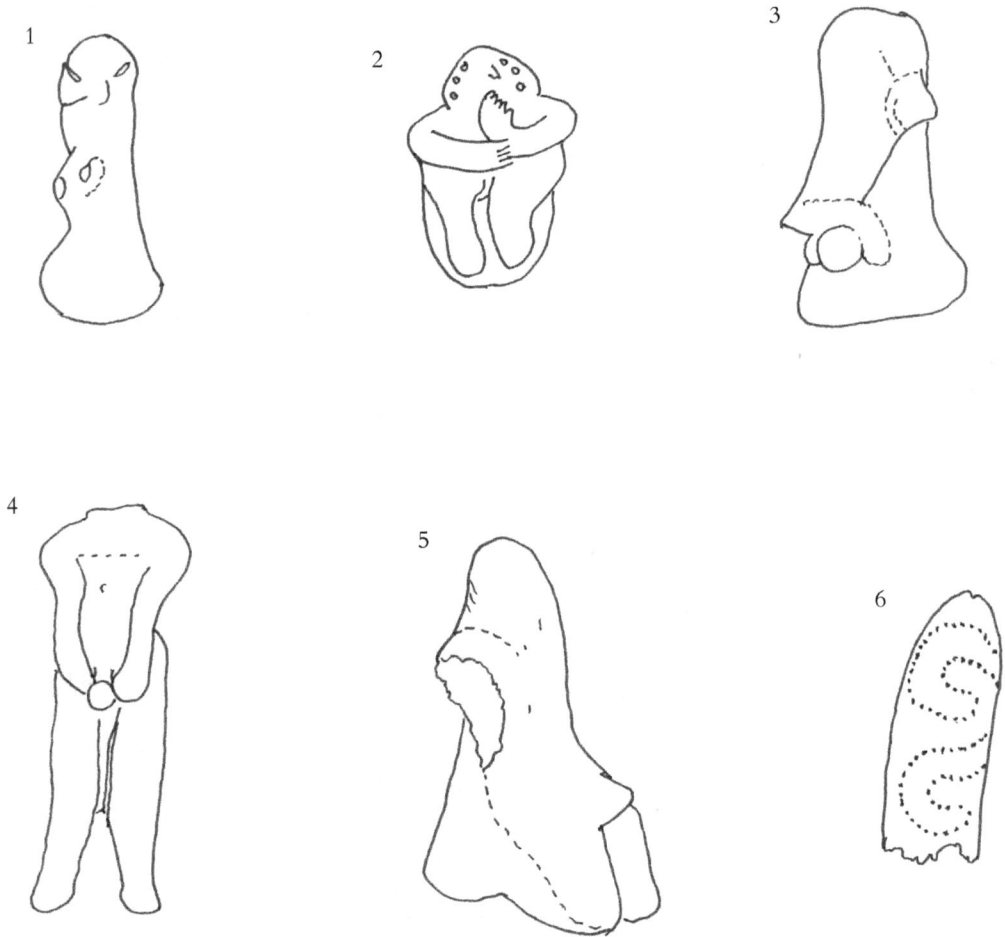

EXAMPLES OF THE FEW EARLY MALE FIGURINES

Clay male figurines
1. Yugoslavia
2. Lower Danube
3. Vinča, Moravia
4. Sesklo
5. Yugoslavia

6. *Bone phallus*, Moravia
   (Source: Gimbutas, Marija, 1982)
   All line drawings © Judy Foster, 2013

From 13,000 BP ritual buildings along the Danube River were constructed in the sacred triangular shape, with interior floors coloured in red ochre to symbolise the female reproductive system and the blood accompanying birth. Some of these buildings also included egg-shaped or round stones representing the womb. From around 11,000 BP in the Indian Palaeolithic period (long before the famous Indus civilisation), and still today in Indian country villages, triangular-shaped stones represent the Indian female principle or deity, known as Shakti (also known as Dhariti). She is "a mother who never dies"[45] according to Dilip Chakrabarti (1999).

In Christianity, for the past 2,000 years the triangle shape forms the symbol for the patriarchal trinity: 'God the Father, Son, and Holy Ghost/Spirit'. We suggest that the three spirals forming the female triangle representing the goddess in Newgrange passage tomb, placed at eye level on the wall deep in the passageway, are arranged point-down suggesting female reproductive organs (birth and new life); whereas the male triangle representing the Indo-European Christian god is placed point-up (male reproductive organs).[46]

No male 'gods'?

Margaret Ehrenberg claims that male figures in the Palaeolithic period have been ignored but this is not strictly accurate, as there was very little evidence of any gods present before the Northern Neolithic period. There are no father figures or female figurines with an accompanying man or men in Palaeolithic art and artefacts; they did not appear until the Neolithic period. Exceptions include: the half-human half-animal figures, depicted with animal heads, found in cave paintings; and one rare instance in a wall sculpture of a possible Upper Palaeolithic male figure wearing a belt but with no obvious sexual characteristics, placed in conjunction with three low-relief female figures which accompany the goddess of Laussel.

Marija Gimbutas (1989) has identified several categories of male gods in the Neolithic period, but they were rare in temples and houses because they were associated with wild nature, vegetation, and outdoor activities such as hunting. There was: the mature-year god, usually holding a sickle or crook, who represented the harvest; the vegetation god, consort of the pregnant year goddess symbolising the sacred marriage; the young, strong, and virile god who roused the world after the long winter; the sorrowful-year god, usually seated on a footstool or throne, leaning on his chin, pondering the end of his cycle; and the male guardian of animals/wild nature, who is still present in folklore in some countries today. These male gods complement the goddess/female deities, rather than filling a dominant role as did the Indo-European gods.

Male symbolism: The phallus

The phallic symbol associated with goddess figurines represents the male force, stimulating life energy, also associated with aquatic and other symbols of regeneration. It sometimes forms the body of the regenerative goddess with breasts and testicles combining both sexes, also decorated with chevrons, and including feet but no hands. The phallus symbol is significant but is not commonly associated with the goddess; when it is featured it is always secondary, as representing her partner or consort.

CHAPTER 6

HUNTER-GATHERING, THE FIRST HORTICULTURE AND AGRICULTURE

Human origins in Africa?

An exploration of the origins of humans in prehistory begins with a look at the ways in which human evolution is thought to have occurred. There are varied interpretations of the evidence, more of which is appearing every day. It is generally agreed that ancestors of the human species evolved from primates in Africa in a process of development lasting from 10 million years ago until about 5 million years ago. *Homo habilis*, a hominid species, was the forerunner of the earliest human species, *Homo erectus*. *H. habilis* possessed a well-developed brain and was light in build, similar to modern humans.[1]

The first of the human species from which modern humans were later to develop was *H. erectus*, according to Robert Bednarik (1996).[2] Evidence of these adventurous early people was first reported in 2006[3] describing the discovery of the 3.3 million-year-old bones of an Ethiopian hominid baby in the Rift Valley, belonging to the same species as the earlier find nearby of an African human, 'Lucy', who is 3.2 million years old. They appear to be linked in form to both *H. habilis* and *H. erectus*.

By 2 million BP early humans had moved across Europe and into Asia. Evidence discovered by Michael Morwood (2005)[4] has been found deep in a cave on Flores Island in Indonesia.[5] His discovery of the bones of an early form of a *H. erectus* woman dated to 18,000 BP shows that these early humans were still present in Flores as recently as 10,000 BP. Another discovery of similar bones dated to 1.8 million BP at Dmanisi (Georgia) in the Caucasus Mountains was announced in 2005.[6] Between 3 million and 1.5 million BP those first humans had evidently spread east to Mongolia and China, and through India in a southerly direction as far as Java in southern Asia or, as some scientists are now hypothesising, perhaps all along they had evolved separately in these regions rather than in Africa. The direct descendants of the first humans (*H. erectus*) seem to be the slightly more modern 'archaic' *Homo sapiens*; the first evidence in Africa dates to 600,000 BP. They, too, could have developed outside Africa.[7]

Remarkably, most of these movements took place during the Great Ice Age which lasted from 2 million BP until about 10,000 BP. Michael O'Kelly (1989)[8] explains that ice covered all of the land masses of Northern Europe and North America. During this Ice

69

Age there were four inter-glacial periods when warmer conditions prevailed which allowed new animals to emerge and migrate, and provided the right conditions for the growth and development of new varieties of vegetation thus allowing humans to continually move forward into new territory.

According to Robert Bednarik (1996),[9] by 200,000 BP both the early *H. erectus* and the later archaic *H. sapiens* had appeared in China; and around 100,000 BP archaic *H. sapiens* were living in Java. This was thought to be the time frame when modern humans (*H. sapiens*) first appeared in South Africa and the Middle East, and in other parts of the world. Some argue that modern humans also evolved around the same time from *H. erectus* in different parts of the world rather than spreading out of Africa. Australian Indigenous people say they have *always* been in Australia, at least for the last 120,000 years.[10]

Hunter-gatherer/horticulturalist women of Old Europe

Women were never invisible in prehistoric hunter-gatherer societies. This situation continued to be the norm well into the Neolithic period. Margaret Ehrenberg (1989)[11] describes the practicalities of life for hunter-gatherers and argues that the most important steps in the development of human societies were inspired by women who were central to their groups and innovators of various economic and technological practices, in direct contrast to the popular mythology of 'man the hunter, protector and provider' for his wife and children. In current non-Western hunter-gatherer communities, men do not follow such practices (nor do male primates), therefore it cannot be assumed that 'man the hunter' is the norm. This is typically the view upheld by today's 'scientific' researchers who do not take into account any metaphysical influences on hunter-gatherer societies which could have affected their sex roles.

Throughout the Palaeolithic period the typical lifestyle of hunter-gatherer communities was such that when food supplies became scarce in one area, they would move to set up new camps in another area where food was plentiful. Because they were nomadic they either built temporary shelters or lived in caves or under rock shelters. Tools and weapons for hunting and gathering were few, versatile, lightweight and efficient, and consisted of: those made of wood (spears, clubs, digging sticks, wooden bowls); fur skins for cloaks or hide (waterbags, slings for carrying babies or goods); plant fibre nets (for fishing and trapping animals); and bone and stone (tools for cutting, drilling and hammering). Cooperation between individuals was essential to group survival, leading to social equality between the sexes and different age groups. Such a lifestyle has been the way of Australian Indigenous people until European contact.

A very important aspect concerning the origins of sex-role behaviour involves the collection of food, and whether both women and men hunted and/or foraged. One argument, for example, focuses on the division of labour as occurring possibly quite late in human evolution because both sexes could physically have carried out either hunting or gathering. While men hunted large animals (not always successfully), women, children – and men – collected vegetable foods and some smaller meat supplies (lizards, birds and small mammals, fish). Diane Bell notes that women in Indigenous Australia in desert regions probably gathered around 80% of reliable diet, while in colder regions where there were fewer vegetables there was probably a higher protein diet, some of which comprised small animals hunted by women.[12]

Margaret Ehrenberg identifies three possible contexts for the origin of a division of labour:

- Hunting was dangerous and hunters could easily be killed in the process. Early societies could ill-afford to lose any of their members, especially women capable of bearing children.
- Hunting required a high degree of mobility. The elderly, and some women hampered by carrying babies or small children, would have problems moving quickly, and small children or infants could make a noise at the wrong time causing an unsuccessful hunt. Gathering was a different matter since it could quite easily be carried out while caring for young children.
- The increasing presence of small game and abundant plant life suitable for food, together with more elusive and scarcer big game during environmental changes meant that foraged food began to form a greater part of the human diet. Accordingly the more mobile male group concentrated on hunting while others, usually women, gathered.

Traditionalists have assumed that tools were used mostly (by men) for hunting, killing and butchering animals, but other tools would have also been vital. For example: the container was needed for carrying water and food when moving from place to place, and therefore was probably one of the earliest inventions – by women; the development of a sling for supporting the infant, found in almost all modern societies including foraging groups, would almost certainly have been invented by women.

Women not only contributed to the collection of food items, but were also concerned with food preparation and cooking, yet these latter activities, so critical to the well-being of all societies, are rarely recognised by researchers. Diane Bell (1998a)[13] tells us that Australian Indigenous women have also been responsible for the knowledge, collection and use of medicinal plants as part of their role in caring for the physical and mental health of their group, and the spiritual health of women. They also collected possum and other animal skins, and prepared them before stitching them together with bone awls and animal sinews to make warm winter cloaks. Elizabeth Barber (1994)[14] records that, later in the Upper Palaeolithic period, women invented the methods used in the making of clothing and created clothing codes which conveyed important information about the wearer. These home-based occupations facilitated the safe rearing of children, allowing women to play a significant role in those early communal societies.

A further very important invention she attributes to women is the twisting of plant fibres into string. Indirect evidence of string dated to 30,000 BP includes needles and beads pierced with increasingly smaller holes for threading. The discovery in 2008 of flax fibres in a Georgian cave dated to 34,000 BP indicates the earliest woven cloth. Previous solid evidence for this revolutionary innovation was depicted on the 22,000-year-old female figurine of Lespugne who wore a string apron behind her back, hanging from her hips. Also notable is Olga Soffer's[15] evidence of woven textile imprints on female figurines dated to 27,000 BP. Another early physical sample of string was a piece of rope found pushed into a crack in the walls of Lascaux Cave in France, dated to 15,000 BP. String was important because it could be used not only to make cloth, but also to secure the legs of captured animals to prevent escape; to tie up items, such as packages (made from large leaves holding foods or tools for portage); and to catch, hold, or carry via traps, fishing lines, fishing nets, tethers and ropes, carry baskets, and handles. String was also used to bind such objects as stone axe heads to their handles, or to make other complex tools. However, Robert Bednarik (1997a)[16] argues that it is far more likely that string or thongs, and the ability to tie knots, evolved much earlier since knowledge of these innovations would have been necessary in order to prepare watercraft for sailing to offshore islands over 700,000 years ago.

Elizabeth Barber (1994) mentions the time-consuming and complex making of pottery as another likely invention by women, since it could only be created at a more or less settled home base. Its early use would have been for domestic purposes, such as the carrying and storage of water (and the making of clay figurines). Thus the discovery of pottery at any site usually indicates the past presence of skilful female potters.

According to Margaret Ehrenberg, food sharing with children and other group members, and the exchange of foods from other environments was a precursor to living in regular social groups. Such food sharing would have taken place in groups with women as the main players. Provision of food is important in every society and may be an indicator of social position.

Elizabet Sahtouris (1999b)[17] says that for hunter-gatherer cultures in Europe and Asia nature was symbolised as a great mother goddess, who gave them life and everything needed to sustain them. They viewed nature as a deity/divinity. This helped to explain the natural abundance of food, and the birth of living things. Beautiful sunny weather suggested the 'good mood' of the goddess, while cold fierce storms or long droughts symbolised her 'bad moods'. Nature seemed to be both loving toward, and angry with, humanity, prompting life-affirming celebrations, as well as feelings of fear, awe and respect. The earth goddess cultures knew the goddess "as the creative force of nature", and not "the external creator of nature"[18] as was the Indo-European God of the Shining Sky.

The first agriculturist women: The European Neolithic period

There are two main aspects of the early European Agricultural (Neolithic) period:
* the discovery of archaeological and mythological evidence of the change from a semi-nomadic existence to a settled urban lifestyle, together with the development of agriculture and animal domestication
* the argument as to whether male-dominant cultures began within the Neolithic period or at its end. A major problem and the crux of this argument is the lack of official recognition of a discernable distinction between the peaceful Neolithic period and the warrior Bronze Age.

The comprehensive work of Marija Gimbutas (1991)[19] provides a wonderful picture of Old Europe. An important point she makes is that the Neolithic lifestyle was not nearly as 'primitive' as many would argue: they produced a plentiful variety of foods utilising careful agricultural practices; developed widespread domestication of animals, including new breeds of sheep which produced wool as we now know it; and developed higher-yielding crops aimed at production of more and better food, and fabrics for clothing, and so forth. The people built houses and temples; produced artistically carved stone, bone and wood objects, both aesthetic and useful; and made ceramics which were often decorated with complex symbolic imagery.

Marija Gimbutas found no evidence of hierarchy or violent deaths in any of the Neolithic settlements or villages, and no outstanding central buildings indicating a ruler

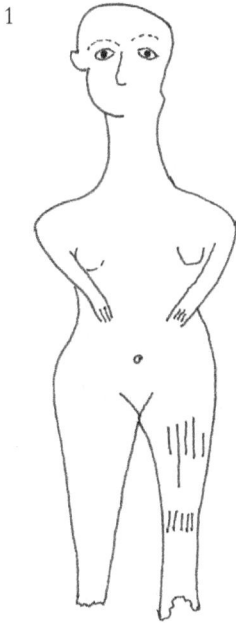

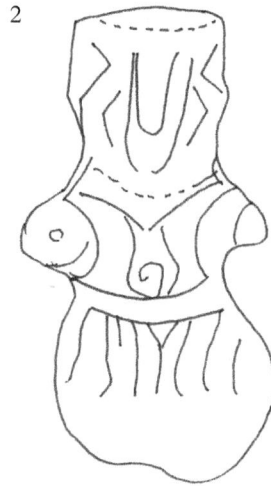

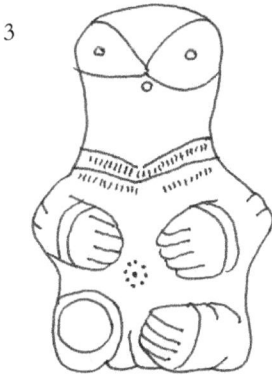

FEMALE FIGURINES OF THE NEAR EAST

1. *A Neolithic plaster figurine*, Jordan,
   8,750–8,250 BP
2. *Painted clay female figurine pot*, Hacilar,
   7,000 BP
3. *Clay female figurine*, Antalya, Turkey,
   7,000 BP

4. *Stone figurine*, Syrian–Turkish border,
   c. 6,500 BP
   (Source: Collon, Dominique, 1995)
   All line drawings © Judy Foster, 2013

of any kind. Nor were there any signs of acropolises or fortifications, except those which provided protection against wild animals. However, she did identify two- or five-room houses clustered in kinship groups, a central meeting house associated with clan gatherings, and a number of house temples in which ritual objects were found, indicating the importance of religious worship and ritual life to the inhabitants. Grave goods were sparse in comparison with the wealth in Indo-European graves: any artefacts accompanying Neolithic bodies were tools of trade and/or trade goods, including woodworking tools or stone axes for men, and querns, loom weights etc. for women. From 7,000 BP copper, shell and bone bead jewellery, ochre, pottery and palettes were included.

Processual archaeologist critics, including Ruth Tringham and Margaret Conkey (1996),[20] agree with this description of south-east Europe, but have considerable problems with Maria Gimbutas's interpretation of the artefacts. They argue that there are other reasons for the abrupt change from peaceful to violent hierarchic communities and, like Colin Renfrew, they prefer the notion that it was processes of urbanisation rather than pastoralism which changed women's status and brought Neolithic cultures to an end.

Another possible scenario, they argue, was change brought about by economic and technical development which may have included exchange networks combined with social and settlement changes including decentralisation, household fission, and increasing male control over village life. But they cannot say what might have triggered this change, nor provide strong evidence for it. Nor did they look at any linguistic or genetic evidence available at the time their report was produced. They ignored all the overwhelming evidence Marija Gimbutas and other European archaeologists had collected. Because the changes took place worldwide within a fairly close time frame, Marija Gimbutas's hypothesis provides the most logical explanation, and new evidence continues to support this theory.

Riane Eisler (1990)[21] points out matrilocal 'partnership' societies which were characteristically more peaceful, less hierarchical and non-authoritarian, according to anthropological evidence. Cultures as far removed in time and distance as Çatal Hüyük and Crete had the knowledge and skills to invent and make war weapons from copper, bronze, and gold, but instead chose to create artistic treasures, ritual objects, and useful implements for farming, and so forth. It was the invaders who were to exploit these durable materials. The earliest metal artefacts, dated about 8,000 BP, were found south of the Carpathian Mountains and in the Dinaric and Transylvanian Alps region, and consisted of jewellery, statuettes, and ritual objects. By 6,000–5,000 BP copper was used to make flat-axes and shaft-hoe axes (woodworking tools) wedge-shaped tools, fish hooks, awls, needles, and double-spiral pins.

Neolithic cultures were peaceful, artistic, agricultural societies with large towns in which women and men lived 'in partnership'. If the social rules in early societies were made by women then it is likely that these were based on equal treatment of girls and boys. Elizabet Sahtouris (2000)[22] says that boys are only given preferential treatment in certain more recent male-dominant cultures where men now make the rules which underlie all cultural activities.

Two early European Neolithic examples representative of the above societies studied by Marija Gimbutas are those of the Vinča culture of Yugoslavia, and the Sesklo culture of Thessaly in northern Greece. In these societies the female principle (along with women in general) must have been prominent as demonstrated by the presence of numerous clay female figurines and some architectural features of the buildings.

The Vinča culture

The Vinča culture of Yugoslavia dates from 8,000 BP. Marija Gimbutas (1991)[23] identifies as many as 650 sites and settlements found alongside rivers, some with as few as 200 people, and the largest with around 1,000–2,500 residents in the Belgrade and Hungarian Transylvania (Romania) region. The houses were built next to each other in the small settlements, and in the larger towns they formed streets. Early houses had two rooms, while later ones had up to five rooms, with some houses being up to 20 metres long. They were made of timber posts or split plank frames with walls of plaited twigs covered with clay plaster. Logs, stones filled in with scree, or stone slabs finished with smooth plaster, covered the floors. The architecture was very solid and refined.

Buildings which might have been temples had inside and outside walls painted and decorated with red, blue, and white designs. Ox skulls coated with a layer of clay, and the muzzles painted with motifs, were found attached to pillars or walls in these buildings. Other examples had altars, offering tables and hearths, and monumental statues of subjects such as double-headed and double-shouldered female figurines.

Copper mining began about 7,000 BP, and other mined materials included obsidian, alabaster, and marble, used for making tools and sculptures of zoomorphic, and anthropomorphic masked figures. Spondylus shell was used for making ornaments, cinabarite for colouring them. Women's pottery in varied shapes, painted and burnished, was very refined and delicate. The people farmed and raised cattle.

But Marija Gimbutas's greatest discovery was that of three clay tablets found in a ritual burial site, two of which featured a row of motifs suggesting a form of script. This script was arranged in the form of sets of abstract rather than pictorial signs in rows or clusters following one another, similar to all other scripts of the time. The Vinča script system is considered by Marija Gimbutas, Harald Haarmann and others to be a form of prewriting which emerged between 8,000 and 7,300 BP and disappeared with the invasion of Old Europe around 5,500 BP. The Vinča script is several thousand years older than the Mesopotamian script, and links between the two cultural traditions were broken with the emergence of the Indo-Europeans, so it cannot yet be deciphered.

The Vinča culture lasted until about 6,300 BP when the people apparently had to leave everything behind and move to live in caves hidden in uninhabited country in the north-west of the region.

The Sesklo culture of Thessaly

The Sesklo mounds, or tells, are described by Marija Gimbutas[24] as being composed of the remains of numerous earlier settlements which had occupied the sites from 9,500–5,500 BP. In 1976, Demetrios Theocharis discovered the remains of the pise walls of rectangular houses, which were found to be built separately and parallel with each other, the settlement being surrounded by a stone wall for protection against wild animals. Later houses had supporting timber posts. The houses were very orderly. Some had two rooms, one of which was possibly a temple, and the other, a workshop. Some houses were two-storey; many had special platforms on which symbolic sculptures of possibly female deities were found. Other artefacts included women's utensils such as hand-milling stones, pestles and pounders, grinding stones, grain, stone and bone tools, and clay spoons and pots. Tools for woodwork included chisels, adzes and axes, and those that women used for textiles included clay spindle whorls, clay spools and bone needles. Crops consisting of wheat, barley, millet, lentils, vetch and peas were harvested with obsidian and chert sickle blades. Sheep and goats, and later, cattle and pigs, were domesticated.

The Sesklo pottery, which women first made about 8,400 BP, became increasingly refined, varied and beautiful over time. Earlier versions were painted with geometric designs incorporating symbolic meanings relating to the goddess, while later pottery included decorated bird-shaped and anthropomorphic vases. Clay female figurines were very common: in one small area alone, over two hundred were found, most of them in temples, some in courtyards near a dais or oven; they were often found together with offering containers, lamps, ladles and seals with handles. Female figurines which Marija Gimbutas identifies as the "Bird Goddess, Snake Goddess, or Nurse"[25] were found in the houses or temples, while the 'Pregnant Goddess' was instead a focus on courtyard platforms near the bread ovens which had pits for offerings. Only two fragments of a seated male god were found. Without doubt this was a culture which was prosperous and comfortable, and one in which women held prominent positions.

According to Marija Gimbutas, by 6,000 BP the Sesklo culture was overcome or infiltrated by unknown pastoralists who were also hunters and fishermen, as shown by the change back to 'primitive' agricultural practices, rough unpainted pottery, and the use of antler and bone tools, such as hoes, grinding stones and sickle blades similar to those found in the steppes north of the Black Sea. Such roughly made pottery suggests Proto-Indo-European men may have taken over this activity, or women had become so overworked they no longer had time or interest to produce beautiful pots.

In the 1960s James Mellaart drew attention to older Neolithic cultures than those of the Vinča and Sesklo in the region known as the Near East which is situated near the birthplace of the Proto-Indo-Europeans between the Black Sea and the Caucasus Mountains.

The Near East: The Natufians

Since the 1950s a number of archaeologists have made remarkable discoveries in Turkey (Anatolia), north-west Syria, and the Palestine region. This area, known as the Fertile Crescent, was perhaps the source of the early agricultural practices, an idea still much debated. These discoveries suggest some continuity between cultures in this part of the world, one notable example being the culture of the Natufians.

James Mellaart (1975)[26] found that the Natufian cultures were present in Anatolia and Syria from 22,000–12,000 BP. The Natufians introduced flint microlith tools, often geometric in shape, set into bone or wooden handles used for many purposes. They also used the bow and arrow to hunt wild animals and birds. The early Natufians had originally lived in caves, rock shelters or small temporary huts, and later, built the earliest Neolithic settlements. Their houses were circular with a stone base, walls and roofs made of brush and reeds, floors covered with reed matting, and stone hearths. These Proto-Neolithic people were also among the first to gather wild grains, and by 9,000 BP, were planting small crops, as evidenced by numerous querns, mortars, pounders, grinders, storage pits and sickle blades. Pendants, animal carvings and small female figurines of bone have been found in the region, along with obsidian which is evidence of trade with other areas. James Mellaart also records Natufian cave art such as that of the fleeting deer with the bull painted on a rock wall in Antalya, Anatolia, dated to between 14,000 and 12,000 BP.[27] Discoveries of early settlements

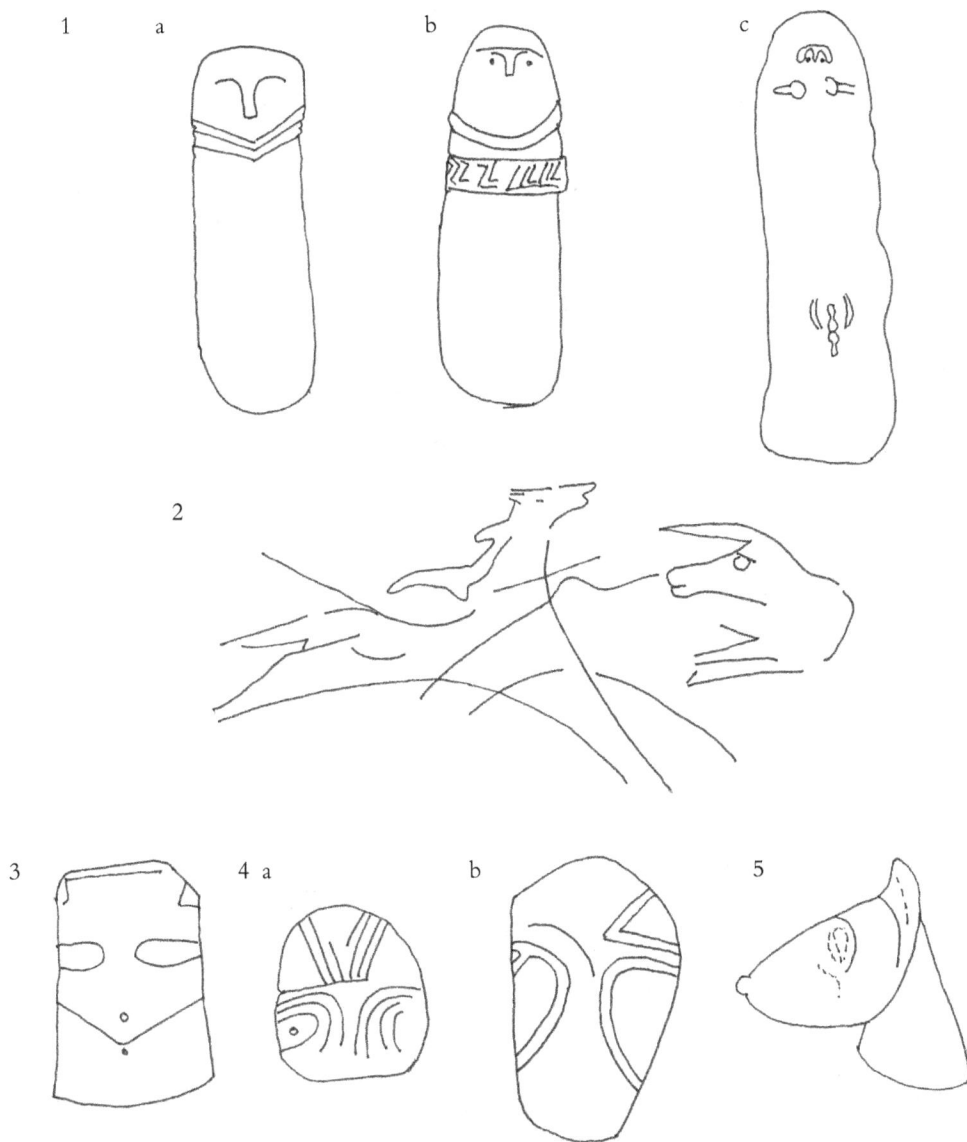

OLD EUROPEAN AND NEAR EASTERN IMAGERY

1a. *Owl figurine*, Spain
 b. *Bird goddess*, Sardinia, 7,500 BP
 c. *Owl goddess*, Spain, 6,000–4,000 BP
   (Source: Gimbutas, Marija, 1991)
2. *Deer and bull*, cave painting, Anatolia,
   c. 8,000 BP

3. *Carved stone head with incised features*, Hacilar,
   8,000 BP
4. *Two stone Natufian heads with engraved facial
   features*, 11,000 BP
5. *Stone gazelle's head*, Wadi Fallah, 8,000 BP
   (Source: Mellaart, James, 1965)

All line drawings © Judy Foster, 2013

are still being found in the region, including Nevali Cori, Tell Abu Hueyra, and Mureybet, to name a few.

The Nevali Cori settlement, was situated on the middle Euphrates in eastern Turkey, and excavated by Harald Hauptmann (1988)[28] from 1988–1993 shortly before being covered by the Ataturk Dam. The earliest level of (the Natufian?) occupation dates at this site from 12,000 BP, with the next level to 11,500 BP. From 11,500 BP, in Nevali Cori there were 23 long rectangular houses (with two or three parallel flights of rooms) which although larger, are also reminiscent of the small free-standing Sesklo houses. They feature stone slab floors supported by thick foundations of many layers of stones. Some houses contained possible graves with human skulls and partial skeletons.

At the north-west side of the village, part of the hillside had been levelled for a ritual centre or gathering place, and covered with a lime cement floor surrounded by dry-stone walls into which monumental limestone pillars were set. Two other large free-standing pillars, three metres high and featuring engraved animals, were set in the centre of the ritual space. The complex may have supported a flat brushwood/reed roof similar to the houses. A number of limestone statues, such as early level life-size anthropomorphic figurines were found, and also a life-size human head with snake topknot; smaller sculptures included one of a bird. Several hundred small (five-centimetre-high) baked clay human figurines were apparently ritual offerings.

Another site, Tell Abu Hueyra[29] in northern Syria, excavated in 1972–1973 by Andrew Moore et al before being flooded by the new Lake Assad, had been occupied by the Natufian hunter-gatherer settlers between 15,000–12,000 BP. (This discovery takes the time period of the Natufians back to a thousand years earlier than previously thought). The first settlement featured small circular huts cut into the sandstone terraced site, with wooden posts to hold up the brushwood/reed walls and roofs. The site is described as "a massive accumulation of collapsed houses, debris, and lost objects"[30] built up over a couple of thousand years of occupation, although the objects are not identified. The small population harvested wild grains and hunted animals. The Mureybet settlement nearby, also now under Lake Assad, was of a similar date to Tell Abu Hueyra. Its last phase included the discovery of eight figurines, seven of which were female, one of the few instances of such artefacts being recorded in the area.

However, the most spectacular find in recent times has to be the 12,000-year-old complex of stone-walled circles and standing pillars at Göbekli Tepe[31] which the excavator, Klaus Schmidt considers to be the earliest centre of religious worship in the world. Situated relatively close to Nevali Cori, the first circle of the many in the Göbekli Tepe complex to be excavated is 30 metres across, and surrounded by high stone walls within which stand monumental sandstone pillars up to 5.5 metres high and weighing 14.5 tonnes, some with T-shaped stones on top, others spike-shaped. Floors in the stone circle are made of polished burnt lime and clay to form a hard surface, and they are the earliest example of this process. Three other stone circles have been uncovered so far and around 20 more remain to be excavated in the 10 hectare site.

Many of the pillars feature engraved animals, including bulls, foxes, lions and crocodiles; there are scorpions, ants, spiders and snakes; and birds such as cranes and ducks. There is a carved boar, a lion, and a vulture's head on the pillars, as well as a free-standing carved human sculpture. However, there are no signs of graves or other artefacts, or indeed

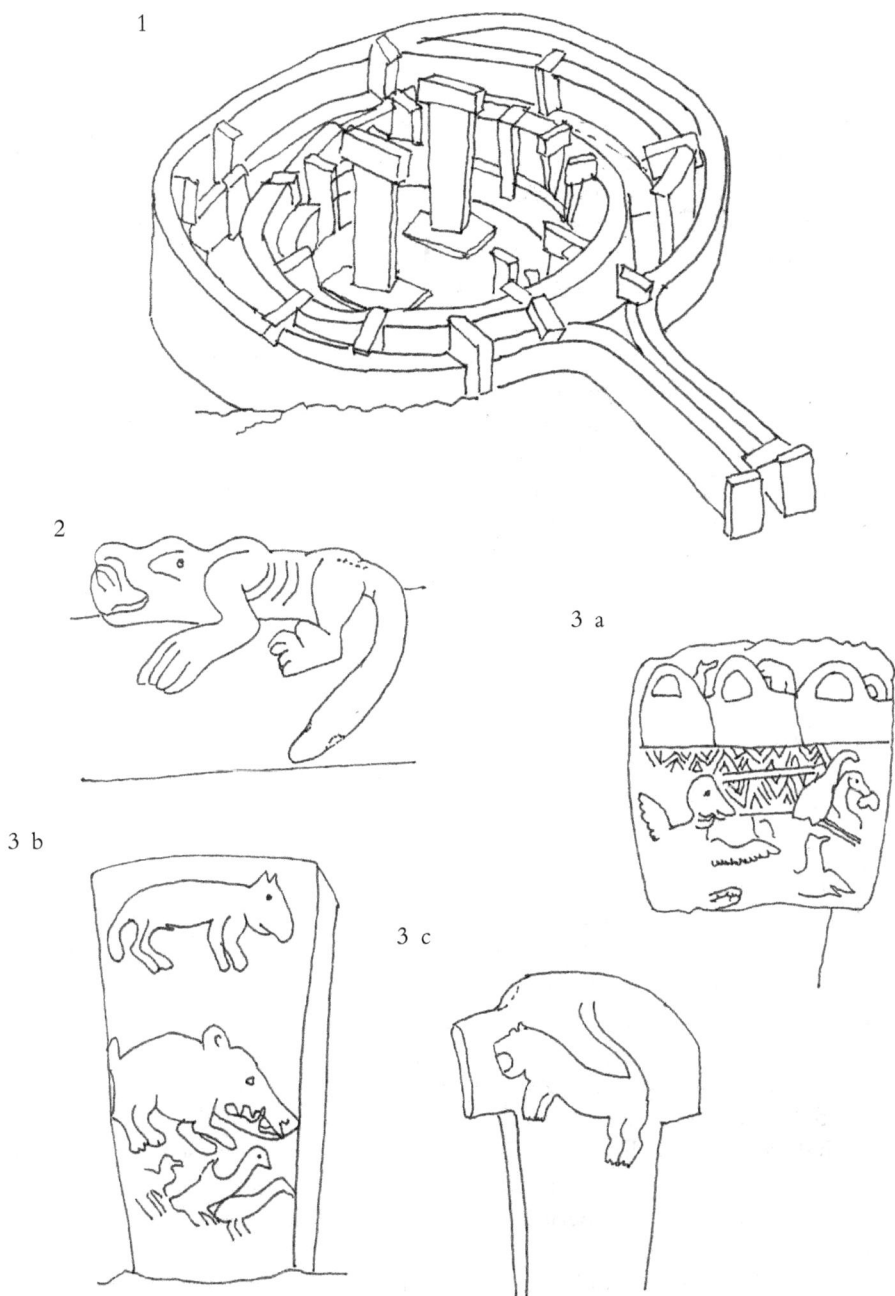

1

2

3 a

3 b

3 c

GOBEKLI TEPE

1. *Gobekli Tepe (model)* showing the layout of the first temple complex to be excavated

2. *A sculpted animal* on one of the tall sandstone pillars

3. *Animals and birds carved in low relief* on pillars (Source: *National Geographic,* June 2011)

All line drawings © Judy Foster, 2013

any evidence at all of people having lived in the complex, although evidence of habitation may still be found below the hard floors in the future. (Could it be that the builders and worshippers lived at Nevali Cori and established Göbekli Tepe for ritual purposes?)

There are two stages of the building at Göbekli Tepe:

- the earliest within the Pre-Pottery A period which ended by 11,000 BP, and is the more sophisticated. (Although it is not mentioned, these people could well have been late Natufians as Göbekli Tepe is in the same region as Nevali Cori and Abu Hureyra.)
- the second later period, Pre-Pottery B, featured circles with less well constructed lower walls, and without the engravings and so forth, and ended by 10,000 BP.

Klaus Schmidt argues that the site is critical to understanding the change from hunter-gathering to farming, and the change "from tribal to regional religion."[32]

Anthropologist Ted Banning[33] of the University of Toronto presents an interesting alternative interpretation to that of Klaus Schmidt for the use of the monumental buildings at Göbekli Tepe. Ted Banning records increasing evidence of regular flint-knapping and the preparation of food at the site which suggests there could have been a large group of people living within the circular 'temple' sites. The presence of decorative pillars does not necessarily mean that the sites were sacred places but they may have been large communal houses – 'house societies', as there were at nearby Nevali Cori. He says:

> Such societies often use house structures for competitive display, locations for rituals, and explicit symbols of social units … There is no reason to assume they were not also people's houses.[34]

In Ted Banning's recent paper in *Current Anthropology* he reports that on the lower Level 3 at Göbekli Tepe there are two buildings dated to 11,600 BP with "monumental stone entrances" and buildings "with U-shaped stone 'doorways' facing south or west."[35] He argues that rather than being temples, the buildings at Göbekli Tepe belong to an architectural style found at other sites in the region. Peter Akkermans, in his response to Ted Banning, gives the example of nearby Jerf el-Ahmar[36] which features "large round subterranean structures" provided with, among other objects, "wall paintings and stone benches with decorative friezes"[37] dated to before 10,000 BP. Nevali Cori (described earlier) is another example with some similar architecture.

Ted Banning says that on Level 2 (9,500 BP) the buildings are smaller, and many are rectangular, with "finely executed terrazzo floors, smaller undecorated T-shaped pillars, and sometimes including stone benches."[38] He suggests the buildings were used for both ritual and domestic purposes, since the sacred and the profane in prehistory were not separated as they are in the Western historic period, and suggests that those early south-west Asian peoples (like many other cultures today) recognised the spiritual aspects of their everyday lives. (For Australian Indigenous people the spiritual and everyday activities have never been separate – all of life has its sacred and profane aspect.)

Klaus Schmidt argues that the tall buildings may have had supporting wooden beams holding up a brush roof. Ted Banning agrees that the use of wooden roof beams is likely since the climate of the time was certainly moist enough for quite large trees to grow in the region. He also records that there were some artefacts found in connection with the buildings which were not mentioned by Klaus Schmidt. These included large bowls made of stone or lime plaster, along with hollows formed in the centre of the floors which suggested the use of hearths for cooking and heating. These were associated with basalt mortars, a basalt grinding stone, and stone tools such as scrapers, burins, and sickle blades. Ted Banning also mentions human and animal figurines, either whole or broken, present in rubbish heaps and among domestic contents, together with some other utensils (perhaps indicating ritual use?).

It is possible to see connections between the Sesklo culture, and the second occupation by the Natufian 'first farmers' which was from 11,000–9,000 BP, and included a much larger settlement with mudbrick houses built over a mound made from the remains of the earlier huts. An increasing variety of plants were grown, and animals domesticated. Women were weaving and making pottery from 9,300 BP, although there is no further information about these in this report.

No evidence of war weapons has been reported at any of the sites, so the people must have been peaceful, as were other cultures during these periods. The archaeologists assume that the high stone walls surrounding the settlements must have been for fortification, but as in Göbekli Tepe, they had other uses, such as protection from wild creatures, from strong winds or, in some instances, from flooding. There is little mention of women's activities, but the civilised nature of these early cultures is clearly demonstrated, and removes any notion of 'primitiveness'. These recent discoveries provide us with a more complete picture of Neolithic life which was apparently more complex, and occurred earlier here than elsewhere.

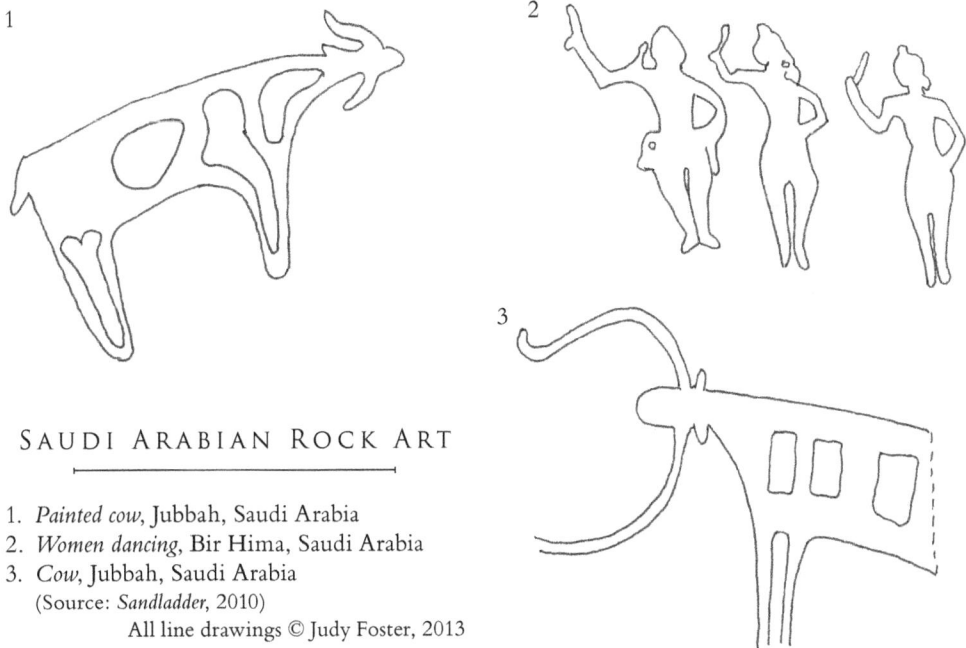

SAUDI ARABIAN ROCK ART

1. *Painted cow*, Jubbah, Saudi Arabia
2. *Women dancing*, Bir Hima, Saudi Arabia
3. *Cow*, Jubbah, Saudi Arabia
   (Source: *Sandladder*, 2010)
   All line drawings © Judy Foster, 2013

Saudi Arabian rock art

It should also be mentioned that, in the Middle East, Saudi Arabia has recently begun to explore its own hitherto largely unknown rock art sites. (This raises the fascinating possibility that all of the other Middle East Arab countries also have their own remarkable undiscovered art sites.)

In 'Art Rocks in Saudi Arabia' journalist Peter Harrigan[39] reports that rock art engravings covering the period from 9,000–6,000 BP were originally noted in 1879 by English travellers and deemed of little interest as the images did not include any form of writing. In the last ten years, continuing new discoveries of Lower Palaeolithic stone tools and Middle Palaeolithic rock art sites, and more accurate dating, reveals the growing importance of Saudi Arabian rock art, as it covers a long period of time, from the Middle Palaeolithic and into the historical period. Pecked, carved or engraved, the images reveal everyday or ritual events. Robert Bednarik (2005) considers Saudi Arabia as "one of the four richest regions in the world for rock art, along with South Africa, Australia and India."[40]

One example of the 2,000 known sites surveyed by Saudi Arabian specialists in 1976–1977 is a gallery at the site of Jubbah in the northern region of Saudi Arabia, which has come into prominence because of the wide variety of engraved animals. Other important evidence at Jubbah demonstrates the change from hunter-gathering to the early agricultural period. Early Neolithic rock art (9,500–8,500 BP) at Jubbah and other sites includes cupules, animals such as ibex, camels, oryx, gazelles, hyenas, ostriches, long- and short-horned bulls, cows, goats, and dogs. Horses were not featured until 3,000 BP (indicating the arrival of the Indo-Europeans?). Robert Bednarik mentions Shuwaymas, a newly discovered rock art site also situated in the north of Saudi Arabia, where there is evidence that suggests a great many Neolithic people were living in the region by 9,000–6,000 BP. Only in Shuwaymas rock art are there images of leopards and cheetahs, and more human than animal images represented in the petroglyphs.[41]

CHAPTER 7

THREE PREHISTORIC CIVILISATIONS

Three important early agricultural (Neolithic) civilisations provide information about the peaceful communities of Palaeolithic and Neolithic Europe before the Bronze Age upheaval:

Neolithic Anatolia:	Çatal Hüyük	9,000–6,000 BP
Neolithic Ireland:	Knowth/Newgrange	6,000–4,500 BP
Neolithic Crete:	The Minoan city of Knossos	5,000–3,050 BP[1]

Çatal Hüyük, Ireland's temple mound/passage tomb builders, and Minoan Crete show us how much more developed early agricultural societies were than is generally recognised, and dispel the 'myth' that all communities before the Bronze Age were undisciplined groups of 'ignorant savages'. A focus upon the female metaphysical principle is apparent in each society.

Neolithic Anatolia

The city of Çatal Hüyük (9,000–6,000 BP)

Anatolia (now known as Turkey), situated at the eastern end of the Mediterranean, was one of the earliest areas to take up agricultural pursuits and a more settled lifestyle (New Guinea is another example.) The ancient city of Çatal Hüyük (pronounced 'Setal Hoyok') is perhaps the best example of an Anatolian town of the period, since the dry climate has preserved many details of Neolithic culture seldom found in other places.

Evidence, including carved bone, ivory and antler artefacts, demonstrates a very long period of occupation in Anatolia and the Near East at least to 500,000 BP as reported in *The Artefact* (1994).[2] The Upper Palaeolithic people present from about 36,000 to 22,000 BP were hunter-gatherers who moved seasonally between bases and temporary camps in order to hunt large animals. They appear to have lived in small groups, as there were very few early communal burial sites.

First excavated in the 1960s by James Mellaart,[3] Çatal Hüyük (9,000–7,000 BP) consists of two mounds 13 hectares in size, beside an ancient river. It is situated on the Anatolian plateau 900 metres above sea level at the centre of a large plain. Another mound, occupied in the Late Neolithic/Early Bronze Age, lies on the opposite side of the river. The main eastern mound is oval-shaped and has the remains of 12 successive occupation levels. James Mellaart (1967)[4] identified the lowest level as belonging to the hunter-gatherer Natufians (see previous chapter) who had lived there between 22,000 and 10,000 BP. Çatal Hüyük is surrounded by irrigation channels which supplied early crops.[5]

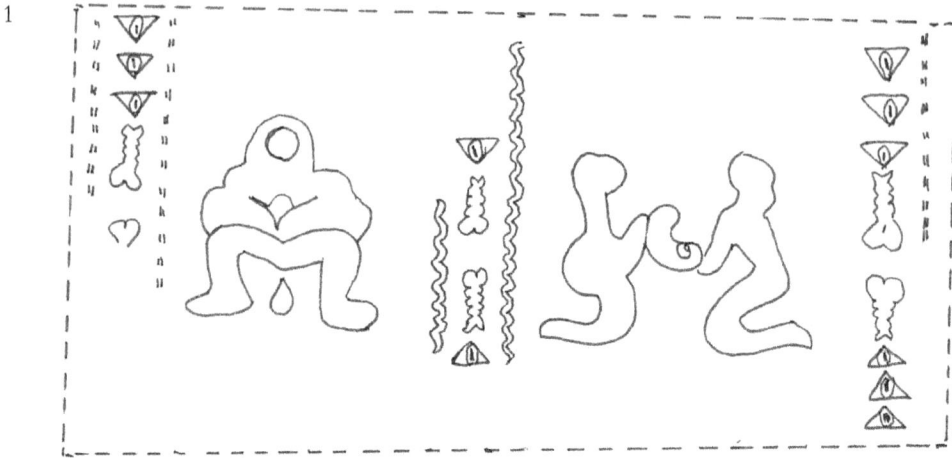

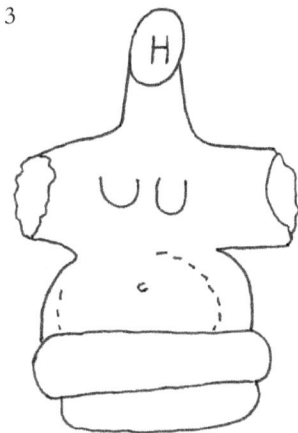

ANATOLIA: WALL PAINTINGS AND FIGURINES

1. *Painted mural depicting goddess/birth imagery,*
   Anatolia: Çatal Hüyük
2. *Wall mural: flowers and butterflies,* Anatolia:
   Çatal Hüyük

3. *Snake goddess,* Anatolia, 8,000–7,500 BP
4. *Marble dual goddess,* 8,000 BP
   (Source: Mellaart, James, 1967)
   All line drawings © Judy Foster, 2013

Ian Hodder of Cambridge University has headed new excavations at Çatal Hüyük since 1993 in another part of the city. Since the Mellaart excavations, scientific methods are being employed which provide more secure dating, and DNA samples are being collected but, as yet, the Mellaart and Gimbutas hypotheses still stand.[6]

The Neolithic agricultural people of Çatal Hüyük

According to James Mellaart, the Neolithic people of Çatal Hüyük (9,000–6,000 BP) were healthy, of average height, with a usual life span of 40 years; those who reached 60 years of age would have been highly respected. Evidence suggests that more women and children resided at Çatal Hüyük since there were far fewer burials of men. The clothing worn by the people, as shown in the wall paintings, did not suggest any difference in status between the sexes. Men, usually featured taking part in ritualised animal hunts, had bare torsos, wore white fabric loincloths or short robes underneath leopard-skin outer garments, which were caught at the waist with a belt. Sometimes the leopard skins appeared to be dyed pink, with black spots. In one painting there is a silhouetted figure, perhaps of a man, associated with vultures, who seems to be wearing a short flared skirt and a jacket or top with very short extended-shoulder sleeves.

Women's attire in the paintings was similar; they, too, wore white fabric under-robes and outer leopard-skin dress. Sometimes they wore necklaces and anklets. The female deities were sometimes clothed, apparently with leopard-skin scarves and outer dress over a fabric skirt, belted at the waist. They wore armlets, and sometimes a beret-like cap on their heads.

From the evidence found at the Mellaart site it seems certain that women were very important, just as they were in any Neolithic agricultural society with a female-focused religion. Perhaps there was some social inequality since some buildings were marginally bigger and better equipped than others, and burial goods were usually found only in association with probable priestesses in certain sites. As James Mellaart explains, the layout of the city was communal rather than hierarchic; there was no grand central building, and courtyards were randomly positioned throughout. There were no war weapons among the artefacts, no painted scenes of battles, and no fortified walls around the complex, although the unbroken outside walls of the houses (with roof entry only) would have afforded some protection against unwanted visitors and, even more likely, the strong winds of the Konya plains.

Buildings

In the Mellaart account each level of Neolithic Çatal Hüyük had numerous houses and some shrines and courtyards, but there were no streets as such. Instead, each house had its own walls but was built in conjunction with neighbouring buildings so as to provide greater wall strength than that of single dwellings. There were no doorways to the outside, or side windows; instead, people entered through roof holes using exterior and interior ladders, while light and air circulation were provided by staggered roof lines, and windows opening above the roof line of adjoining buildings (a detail not mentioned by Ian Hodder, 2006).[7]

James Mellaart describes the earliest occupation layers of Neolithic Çatal Hüyük as containing evidence of free-standing wooden houses with plaster panels. These dwellings were apparently not very durable, as they were replaced later by houses made of sun-dried rectangular mudbricks which were strengthened with straw, joined with black mortar then covered with cream or white plaster. There were no doors on the interior doorways which were low rectangular holes, through which people had to crouch or crawl. The walls, which were very straight, were supported in each corner by wooden pillars, which also supported the ceiling beams. Roofs were formed of two main wooden beams and many smaller beams, covered with bundles of reeds, topped by a layer of thick mud. Reed mats, placed between the beams and the reed bundles, gave the space clean lines.

There was built-in furniture, such as raised platforms for beds, chairs and tables. In the kitchens, ovens and a shelf for storage were set into the walls, and there were ventilation holes in the roof. Hearths with raised edges lay below the ovens to catch any loose coals and ash. It seems the houses were kept very clean and neat, with objects in situ and no rubbish found in them when excavated, and were apparently regularly replastered inside and out each spring after the rains, so they could dry out thoroughly over the summer.[8]

James Mellaart says that red paint was associated with ritual meanings, and painted on the doorways, posts, panels, niches and benches both inside and outside almost every house; it was also used on baskets and boxes. It may have been an important colour used in the clothes the people wore. The colour red is symbolic of blood and life, thus traditionally performing the protective function of keeping evil spirits away. Black was another symbolic colour often shown alternating with red, and used to great effect in wall paintings featuring vultures, cattle, or hands, and probably symbolised death and mourning. According to Marija Gimbutas,[9] these were symbols of the death and regenerative goddess to whom buildings such as these would have been dedicated.

In 1996, British archaeologist Ian Hodder found a greater number of ritual burials of children and young people than adults, at one new site in the houses. He found little difference between the number of men and women in the burials in this instance, but children and juveniles were buried on the east side of the room, adults on the west. Some wall paintings were noted, and many more bulls' horns. There were few figurines, and no ceramics, among the grave-goods. There was no evidence of any violent deaths reported in any of the Mellaart burial sites, nor at the Hodder site, apart from a few weapons and head wounds on skeletons found in one or two burial sites (although these could well date to the late Neolithic period).

In 2006, a full report, *The Leopard's Tale*, was published. Although Ian Hodder had completed excavating over 80 houses and investigated material remains of daily life, he restricted his information to only that which could be supported by scientific evidence and thus added little to the picture of Çatal Hüyük originally provided by James Mellaart. He failed to mention any important artefacts relating to women, but concentrated on emphasising a strong male hunter presence which he identified through reference to wild animal remains and images in the art. His constant comparisons of a remarkable 9,000-year-old Neolithic agricultural civilisation with the Polynesian island of Tikopia[10] horticultural culture less than 3,000 years old has done little to substantiate his argument, as they have such very different contexts.[11]

Religion, wall paintings and sculpture

In his first summary, *Çatal Hüyük: A Neolithic town in Anatolia* (1967), James Mellaart reported that there were wall paintings in one or more colours featuring obviously religious subject

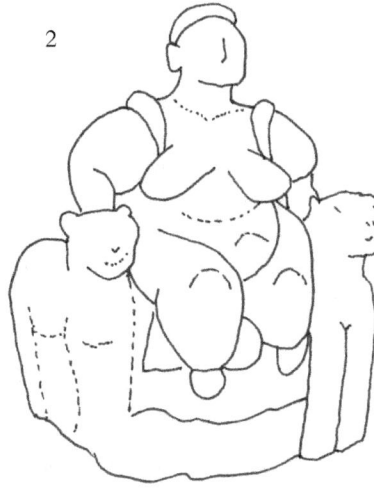

SCULPTURES AND IMAGES DEPICTING BIRTH

1. *A mother goddess*, 8,000-7,500 BP
   (Source: Gimbutas, Marija, 1989)
2. *The mother goddess giving birth, with leopards,* 7,000-7,500 BP
3. Painted wall relief of *the female deity giving birth*, 8,150 BP
   (Source 2–3: Mellaart, James, 1971)

4. A reconstruction by James Mellaart of *a kilim design* painted on a wall at Çatal Hüyük
   (Source: Mellaart, James, Udo Hirsch and Belkis Balpinar, 1989)

   All line drawings © Judy Foster, 2013

matter, incised plaster low relief sculptures of female deities, cattle horns, and modelled bovine heads attached to walls and set into the sides of benches. There were sculptures of male and female deities formed in a variety of stones or clay, often decorated with paint.

Marija Gimbutas was researching and excavating in Eastern Europe around the same time that James Mellaart was in Anatolia, and each respected the other's work. In 1989, James Mellaart, together with Belkis Balpinar (history), and Udo Hirsch (mythology, culture, economy, and environment) published *The Goddess from Anatolia*.[12] It featured many wall paintings of Çatal Hüyük, the imagery of which had been reconstructed from fragments found at the site. In her 1992 interview with David J. Brown and Rebecca McClen Novik in *Voices from the Edge*, Marija Gimbutas explained that Çatal Hüyük

> was such a great discovery in Anatolia. The wall paintings there were only published in 1989, 25 years after James Mellaart's excavation. 140 wall paintings – and archaeologists don't believe him because it's so sophisticated. And this is from the 7th millennium![13]

In this second and final report, James Mellaart provided more complete descriptions and interpretations of the wall paintings (and artefacts), many of which had to be carefully reconstructed from small fragments, a task which took many years. James Mellaart's team, which included scientists and other researchers, discovered that the state of the often burnt (and fallen) walls meant the painted images had to be recorded in situ as they were discoloured by smoke-stain leaving some patches of colour and frequently covered by packed rubble. The damaged paint literally fell off the fragments with the slightest touch, so artists were relied upon to record the imagery in drawings, always a difficult task on site because of climatic and other conditions. The individual drawings of each fragment of wall paintings had to be fitted together, a very long process, and so most of the material could not be incorporated in the early seasonal reports, or in the final report in 1967. As it was, it took James Mellaart and his co-authors 25 years to research the subject matter, including five years to write the 1989 text, yet every important detail was carefully recorded.

It seems likely that the inhabitants of Çatal Hüyük practised a peaceful religion which emphasised life and regeneration, rather than death and violence, because no ceremonial killing places were provided, nor bones of sacrificed creatures found. James Mellaart remarks that there was only one instance discovered of a sacrifice of preserved charred grain as ceremonial offerings at one shrine. Many other types of offerings were found: new and used tools; pots and bone utensils; cattle horns; eggshells; clay stamp-seals; beads; tubes and objects made of copper and lead; and small clay figures of animals and humans. There were also red ochre burials associated with the shrines. Some women (who would have been priestesses) were buried with obsidian mirrors and other items within some shrines. That the people firmly believed in an afterlife was proved by the ritual burial customs, and accompanying grave goods. There are other suggestions of ritual associated with death at both the Mellaart and Hodder sites, such as removal of heads on anthropomorphic figurines and in human burials.

James Mellaart recorded paintings at every level of occupation at Çatal Hüyük. Paint was used on plaster reliefs, figurines, skeletons, wooden vessels, baskets and pottery, and on the human body (as shown in the wall paintings). The full range of paint colours were derived from local and imported minerals including: iron oxides (for red, brown, and yellow ochres); copper ores (bright blue azurite, green malachite), mercury oxide (cinnabar for deep red); possibly haematite (red); manganese (mauve or purple); and galena (lead, for lead grey). The background wall colours of cream or white came from local Pleistocene lake beds, while black was made from soot. The minerals were finely ground but not necessarily mixed with any binding material, and were made into dry lumps, or formed into crayons. Sometimes the mineral mica was mixed with mauve paint to make a glitter finish. Flat stone palettes were used for mixing paint. The brushes used were fine while any broad stretches of paint on the walls were applied with a paint-soaked rag made of woven wool cloth or felt.[14]

In the shrines, large plaster panels featured magnificent paintings depicting symbolism of death. They usually appeared on the east and north walls, above the burial places. What were interpreted by Marija Gimbutas as birth scenes were on the western walls, and bulls on the north walls facing the Taurus Mountains. These paintings most likely had a ritual use since there were signs that later paintings were layered over earlier ones. Some walls had multiple layers of replastered paintings.

One particularly impressive painting features several huge dark red vultures flying across two pink walls, together with falling figures which are headless to indicate that these humans are no longer alive. Vultures could have symbolised death and regeneration: the flesh of the dead creating new life. It must have been quite an experience to enter such a room especially in dim light. The images of the birds and their outstretched wings are beautifully stylised and highly accomplished art, as are the numerous other wall paintings.

Only the goddess was portrayed in wall paintings, accompanied by partly anthropomorphic female deities in sculpted form. James Mellaart argues that the bull or ram represented male fertility and male powers, while leopards, boars or flocks of griffin vultures symbolised death and regeneration. He proposes that the power of the female deity was shown by her association with wild animals, suggesting her ancient role as the provider of game, while her power over all things agricultural was symbolised by the flower and vegetable images painted on her dress or on shrine walls, and in the small female figurines found among heaps of grain. (Ian Hodder says that most of the figurines are male and represent the importance of the male hunters.)

Paintings often featured bull hunts with running or dancing people surrounding the bull. At the time of James Mellaart's report on Çatal Hüyük in 1967, there was no mention of the ritualised game of bull-leaping in which both sexes took part, although there could have been a natural progression from dancing around the bull to leaping over it as was later depicted in the frescoes at the palace-temples of Crete. (Bison and cattle, particularly bulls, were also highly significant in other civilised societies, such as those of prehistoric India and the Americas.)

Twin female deities, or a female deity dressed in brightly coloured robes, were frequently featured in paintings alongside leopards and other animals. The images were usually naturalistic, although the colours were not always realistic. Other subject matter included: geometrically stylised birds, vultures, deer, and deer hunts, flowers, stars, butterflies and bees, plants, landscapes; symbols, such as circles; geometric patterns, some based on images of the goddess; and hand prints. One particularly interesting painting recorded by James Mellaart portrays a volcanic eruption.

Depictions of women – possibly deities, spirits or ancestors – and cattle heads and horns, first appeared about 7,700 BP. According to Marija Gimbutas (1989),[15] bull horns (or more likely, cow horns?)[16] had long been highly symbolic in the Northern Palaeolithic period, for example, the female deity of Laussel holds a horn thought to represent the crescent moon. In unpublished frescoes at Çatal Hüyük the bull/uterus motif is apparent where bovine heads and horns are "cleverly composed within the female figure."[17] At this time bovine heads were also shown in association with plants, seeds and nuts on engraved bone objects. Dorothy Cameron (1981)[18] argues that the link between cattle heads and the female deity originated in the similarity in appearance of the female uterus and fallopian tubes to the head and horns of a bull or cow.[19] This likeness was probably discovered through the Neolithic practice of excarnation of burials. James Mellaart in 1989 observed

> the pervasive central theme of a Goddess and bull's head – the latter almost the heraldic device of Çatal Hüyük – no two representations are the same ... [The majestic Goddess] is most often depicted with wide spread legs and uplifted arms, frequently pregnant, and equally often depicted in the act of childbirth.[20]

With the emergence of agriculture, the role of the goddess changed and she became the patroness of numerous and diverse activities such as weaving, pottery, bee keeping, irrigation, and the cultivation of fruit and nut trees. So, as Marija Gimbutas points out, the symbolism of the bull had not always represented the male principle but was also a symbol of regeneration, of becoming, associated "with life, water, moon, eggs and plants"[21] whether female or male.

In *The Goddess from Anatolia* (1989) James Mellaart notes the sophistication of the design elements in the lively Çatal Hüyük narrative paintings and the many repeated geometric forms based on goddess imagery painted on house walls which he argues Neolithic artists possibly copied from woven kilims of the time. Symbolism seemed to narrate aspects of the Anatolian goddess religion, with its cyclic agricultural themes of birth, maturity and death leading to rebirth and regeneration.

Interestingly, there is no emphasis on sexual characteristics of the female deity or other humans depicted: no reproductive organs are shown; nor are phallus and vulva images represented in the many wall designs noted by James Mellaart in 1967. This is unusual considering that sexual attributes of similar images were usually emphasised in the earlier Upper Palaeolithic period and in the Neolithic period in places other than Anatolia. For Ian Hodder (2006) these figures were obviously male hunters depicted in association with the wild animals they hunted, while the leopard was significant as a violent killer and the only wild creature not consumed when feasting. He also places emphasis on the baiting of bulls, leopards and other animals rather than the Mellaart interpretation of ritual games. Ian Hodder's narrow and prosaic interpretation of the cultures of Çatal Hüyük is typical of the processual approach to archaeology.

Trade and industry

Some information about the crafts of Çatal Hüyük has survived because fast-moving fires sometimes caused people to flee their homes leaving everything behind them, thus preserving any perishable goods which had been covered up in some way. Items such as cloth, fur, leather and wood were left after one fire which had occurred about 7,880 BP. Baskets, and textiles such as rush mats, vividly coloured woven wool or mohair kilims, and dyed fabrics, usually made by women, were commonly used in Çatal Hüyük.

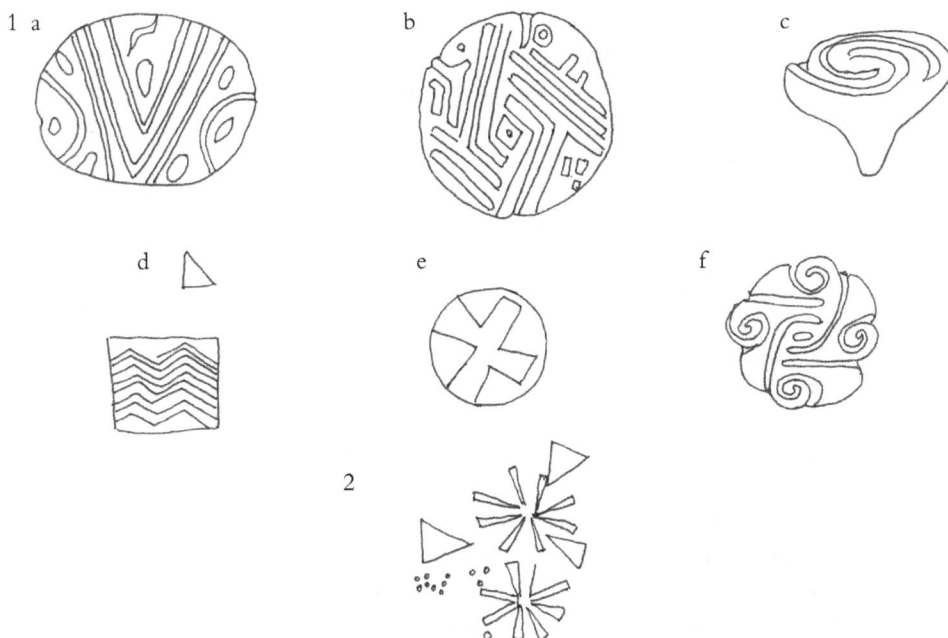

CLAY STAMP SEALS AND PAINTED WALL MOTIFS

1. Neolithic Çatal Hüyük: *Clay seals feature varied design elements*, 9,000–6,000 BP

2. *Painted wall motifs*, 7,000–7,500 BP (Source: Mellaart, James, 1967)

All line drawings © Judy Foster, 2013

James Mellaart discovered evidence of warp-weighted looms, such as the woven edges of fabric on some painted wall fragments. More than one scientist has postulated the use of a mixture of wool, hair and felt, fragments of which were also found (but not tested). Hans Helback[22] noted at least a dozen instances of impressions in wet plaster wall fragments of slit-tapestry weave, suggesting the use of complex tilted warp-weighted looms similar to those used today; and what were probably peg-holes, found high in the walls, suggested that woven wool kilims may have once hung there. James Mellaart notes that felt had been used for tents at least by 9,000 BP and so it is very likely kilim wall hangings were present.

Elizabeth Barber (1994)[23] reveals that sheep were first domesticated 10,000 years ago and selectively bred over about 4,000 years to produce usable wool; it is possible that this latter innovation could have taken place somewhat earlier in Anatolia. (Other examples are reported in her book *The Mummies of Urumchi*, 1999). Elizabeth Barber describes the Çatal Hüyük woven cloth textiles as consisting of several types of fabric with a variety of finishes featuring "both wide and narrow and plain-weave fabrics, weft twining of two sorts, fringed edges, rolled and whipped hems, and re-enforced selvedges."[24] She notes that such elaborate woven and constructed textiles indicate that women had the time to spend making them and, she argues, this suggests they had a high status. Textiles were dyed using plants, and the yarn which was used in the weaving of kilim mats was brightly coloured and formed into rich geometric designs. James Mellaart says the dyes were obtained from local cultivated and wild plants of the area. Ian Hodder makes no mention of woven artefacts in his report.

Some further items left after fires included beautifully shaped wooden bowls, dishes, platters, sauce boats, spoons, two-pronged forks, and even eggcups, as well as small wooden boxes carved in one piece with closely fitting lids. These finely crafted objects would have been trade items. Other trade goods could have been the oval, round or sub-rectangular incised clay seals which James Mellaart proposes were used to stamp images of spirals, meanders, and flower shapes in repeat designs on walls, textiles and other objects, since traces of such designs were found on some walls at the site.

Richard Rudgley (1998)[25] describes the paints as being made from mineral raw materials; minerals were also used for jewellery as well as craft items and utensils, and probably came from other groups in the Konya region. Obsidian and greenstone, from which art and utility items were made, would have been brought from the nearby volcanic mountains and traded for other items. The world's earliest mirrors, made from polished obsidian, have been found here.

Clay balls, some with incised designs, were also found. Such clay objects could fall into a recently interpreted category of artefacts labelled 'tokens', thought to be part of an early accounting system. We are reminded of the token theory proposed by archaeologist Denise Schmandt-Besserat (1992/1996),[26] who discovered an unexpected category of artefacts including miniature cones, spheres, tetrahedrons, cylinders, and other geometric shapes, all made in clay. She named these objects 'tokens' because they were not all geometric in shape; some were shaped like animals, vessels, tools, etc. Their size, shape, colour and other characteristics indicated to her that they formed some kind of system.

The earliest tokens were found in Syria, and Iran, dated to 10,000 BP. These are thought to have been used by a farming community to record numerous varieties of items where each different shape represented certain goods. This could also have been the purpose of some of the tokens at Çatal Hüyük. James Mellaart says that other unrelated objects included: clay figurines, beads, pendants, sling-stones, copper and lead beads; other trinkets were also made for trade to neighbours including gold and silver artefacts.

Textiles were found in graves, but not the spindle whorls or loom weights associated with them. In fact, James Mellaart found no evidence of industrial activity in this area, and concluded that craft industries and the like must have been carried out in another part of the town. The high quality and refinement of the artefacts indicated that the skills of weavers and woodworkers at Çatal Hüyük were valued above those of potters or bone-carvers. He was amazed by the craftspeople's ability to polish obsidian to a mirror finish, and drill through stone and obsidian beads to produce holes which are so fine that most modern needles cannot be passed through them.

Although evidence of the skills of bookkeeping and writing were not represented at Çatal Hüyük, we now know accounting was used for business records because of the presence of clay tokens. Music making can also be inferred because of the portrayal of dancing in the wall paintings – if only a rhythmic beat such as handclapping and singing.

Around 8,000 BP the people of Çatal Hüyük were cultivating and irrigating 14 species of food plants including barley, linseed, emmer, einkorn, peas and bread-wheat, according to James Mellaart. He also mentions fruits such as almonds, acorns, pistachios, apples, juniper berries and hackle berries from which a variety of wine was made. As well as hunting wild animals, the people kept sheep and goats for their fleeces, milk and meat. Insects depicted in connection with flowers suggest that honey may have been used as a food sweetener.

James Mellaart's investigations revealed a sophisticated culture at Çatal Hüyük that was present earlier than had previously been thought possible. It is still too early in the archaeological excavations at Göbekli Tepe to decide whether they are comparable civilisations, however it does indicate the growing sophistication of Near Eastern Neolithic cultures of the time. Although there is not nearly as much evidence left in Neolithic Ireland as has been found at Çatal Hüyük, what has survived suggests a civilisation which may have been just as sophisticated in its own way, as we are about to see in the next section.

Ireland

A second civilised society: Newgrange
(Neolithic Ireland 7,000–5,000 BP)

The second Neolithic civilised society is that of Knowth/Newgrange in Ireland. Recent dating places the Knowth, Dowth and Newgrange passage tombs within the period of 6,000–5,500 BP. Because the Irish tombs and their imagery are so similar to those in Brittany, it is thought the first people came from there and went on to Scotland. The impressive passage tombs and their wonderful petroglyphs suggest a civilisation which was rather more sophisticated than has been previously thought, although rather different from that of Çatal Hüyük both climatically and in resources and, as a result, more restricted in opportunity. The paucity of evidence of some aspects of Neolithic Irish life provides a somewhat unbalanced picture, and this is largely due to an environment which is not conducive to the preservation of many cultural items. Later zealous religious Indo-European groups were also likely to have been responsible for the destruction of other items. However, enough evidence remains to indicate an innovative and resourceful culture. And there are enough signs and symbols to suggest the Neolithic Irish religion was focused on a female nature-deity or spirit similar to the female deities of Çatal Hüyük and Knossos.

The sophistication of the Irish Neolithic culture is evident in the 300 known temple mounds (passage tombs) in Ireland, most of which are in the northern part of the country. Temple mounds are always built on the highest points of the land. Michael O'Kelly (1989)[27] describes three great 6,000-year-old mounds situated above a bend of the Boyne River, in an area measuring four by three kilometres. Situated on a high ridge, Newgrange, Knowth and Dowth are similar in size and would have been visible from a considerable distance. Newgrange has one passage, while Knowth has two: one running east-west, the other, west-east; and Dowth, not yet fully excavated, has two west passages.

Michael O'Kelly reports Newgrange in County Meath as the best known (and at the time of writing, it is the most impressive) of the Neolithic temple mounds, as it has been fully restored. It is as monumental and numinous for its time as any later European cathedral as it stands majestically on the top of the ridge. The building takes the form of a large kidney-shaped grass-covered mound over 100 metres in diameter and 13 metres high, with an interior featuring a cruciform-shaped chamber roofed by a high vaulted ceiling. It has 12 huge hewn stone columns standing outside the perimeters of the main mound, which itself features a frontal vertical 3-metre retaining wall. There are two cairns, the one on the north side is of plain rock, the southern one, located at the entrance, is built of white quartz and grey granite boulders. Nearby Knowth, fully restored in 2003, is a circular mound about 60 metres in diameter, and has a series of 18 smaller temple mounds, or 'satellite' tombs, around the base.[28] The third mound, Dowth, originally of similar size to the others, is the earliest mound in the Boyne complex.[29] Damaged during an earlier excavation in the 1800s, it has still not been fully excavated but perhaps will be restored sometime in the future.

According to Marija Gimbutas (1999/2001)[30] the female principle in this part of the world is symbolised by the 'pregnant' forms of the great temple mounds with their 'uterine-like' internal passages and their orientation towards the light of sun and moon at certain times of the cyclic year. She identifies the numerous predominantly circular and other rounded forms of engraved motifs, both inside and outside the mound, as owl's eyes and other imagery symbolising aspects of the Old European goddess of death, regeneration and new life. Both Marija Gimbutas and Michael Dames (1976)[31] agree that they were not only burial places, but would also have had a religious function similar to that of modern churches. Another view is provided by Martin Brennan (1994)[32] who is convinced that all aspects of the mounds, including the imagery, suggest they are calendars measuring time and marking special events in the cyclic year, a theory which does not contradict the Gimbutas interpretation.

The first people

Ireland has been occupied by humans only since the beginning of the melting of the ice sometime after 10,000 BP, and these were hunter-gatherers with sailing skills and distinct but limited tools, such as 'wave-rolled flints', stone axes, and small flint and chert blades, according to Michael O'Kelly (1989). They settled near the coast and inland along the rivers, building simple huts, digging storage pits, and collecting land and sea foods. The ice continued to melt, flooding low-lying land, and gradually removing much of the evidence of their activities. Acidic soils also contributed to the destruction of other traces of their lifestyle which lasted until about 8,000 BP. There is more evidence of arrivals after this date, people with a wider range of tools, and a semi-settled lifestyle in which men hunted and women kept some animals and increased their cultivation of crops. It is not known where they came from, although the tools they left behind are similar to those of the rest of Palaeolithic Europe.

Neolithic newcomers, possibly from Brittany or Iberia, arrived about 7,000 BP. The earliest direct signs of women's activities are noted by Marija Gimbutas (1991)[33] who describes one of the first houses in Ireland as marked by a hearth associated with pottery dated to about 6,500 BP. These solid early houses were rectangular in shape with split plank walls, while at one site several round houses have also been found. There is evidence that the later hunter-gatherer culture co-existed alongside the Neolithic way of life until about 5,000 BP.

According to George Eogan (1986)[34] the building of the temple mounds was related to the spread of agriculture into and across Ireland by a people who were not the 'primitive' people of popular myth but, like the earlier inhabitants of Çatal Hüyük, traders and travellers, farmers and fishers who exploited the fertile lands and the sea. They were creative artists and architects, living a comfortable, peaceful settled life practising complex spiritual rituals perhaps associated with a female deity or ancestral being.

There was probably a considerable population in the 50-square-kilometre Boyne valley, perhaps as many as 1,200 people; supporting such a population meant they must have

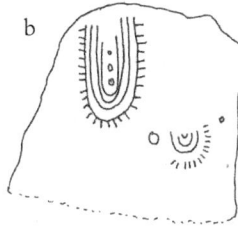

NEOLITHIC NEWGRANGE

1. Neolithic Newgrange: *Engraved entrance stone* features the female triple spiral motif, Ireland

2. Three examples of *engraved standing stones with spiral, meander and 'U'-shaped designs*, at Anglesey, Britain; Loughcrew, Ireland; and Orkney, Britain
(Source: Gimbutas, Marija, 1989)
All line drawings © Judy Foster, 2013

been materially wealthy, and efficient food producers. Evidence shows they grew wheat and barley, and kept oxen, sheep, goats and pigs. They also gathered plants, seeds and nuts, fruits, shellfish and fish.

Their building of the temple mounds suggests the people were religious. Marija Gimbutas argues that the mounds were reserved as ritual buildings which, according to the symbols engraved on their walls (both inside and out), were positive places dedicated to a life-giving and regenerative female deity, and constantly re-opened for ritual activities. Neolithic peoples in civilisations such as Çatal Hüyük and Crete celebrated life and regeneration rather than death; for people of the time death was not the negative process that it was to become with the later warrior societies, but merely a change from one aspect of life to another.

Buildings

George Eogan explains that since forests of large trees, such as oaks and elms, were readily available over much of Ireland, wood was the main material used for the construction of the people's houses. Because of the wet climate and acidic soils there is little trace of these today, apart from evidence of what had been post-holes and hearths. Wood was also used in combination with stone in the building of the temple mounds. While these were constructed near rock formations from which the building stones were obtained, wood was also used for the rollers upon which the large stones were moved to the site. Wooden props and levers were needed for the positioning of kerbs and stone pillars (orthostats).

The builders would have needed sophisticated engineering skills to plan the construction and design the stone ceilings (corbelled vaults), and for solving any stress-related problems of the materials used. Considerable geological knowledge was also involved in the selection of suitable stones. Michael O'Kelly adds that an important skill was that of organising the large workforce (both men and women) needed for the job. This would have demanded strong leadership and dedicated workers.

The temple mounds

Michael O'Kelly states that the earth mounds are known as 'passage' tombs by most archaeologists (who generally ignore any other connotations) because they feature passages of differing lengths; the walls are formed by orthostats which lead into rooms or chambers, some of which feature large circular carved stone basins, sometimes holding remains of human bones. The passages may be circular, oval, or polygonal, that is, they may open into smaller side rooms (or cells), thus forming a cruciform (cross). The passage within Newgrange finishes in a cruciform, as does the east-west passage in Knowth.

The large orthostats which form the walls to the passage tombs were engraved with symbolic imagery. Passages and rooms were divided into sections by sill stones. Underground roofs were composed of other lintel stones which were laid across the tops of the orthostats. The larger rooms usually featured curved ceiling stones forming corbelled vaults,[35] while the ceilings of smaller rooms on each side of the main room might sometimes be flat and finished with capstones.

Carefully placed large, beautifully carved, circular stone basins containing burnt human bones were placed at the end of certain passages. These basins could be as large as a metre across, and carved from a single stone. Specific varieties of rock were used for the orthostats lining the passages, since they provided a suitable surface upon which to engrave the many symbolic images decorating the tombs. George Eogan observes that the stones do not appear to have been specially prepared for the engravings, although the smoothest side was always placed outwards. (The outer kerbstones were usually massive orthostats made from glacial boulders, and were not suitable for engraving.) Elizabeth Shee Twohig (1993)[36] says these stones were sometimes reused, therefore could have earlier engravings upon them, not necessarily facing the front.

Although George Eogan suggests the temple mounds were probably family burial places, it is more likely that they contained the cremated remains of prominent people, as was the case in Western churches. But other smaller Irish grave sites around the countryside, such as court, portal and wedge tombs, were more likely to have been family burial places associated with prosperous farmers. Another likely use of the temple mounds of Knowth and Newgrange was to mark the passing of time (a form of calendar). Martin Brennan reports that all burial mounds have some similar architectural or astronomical characteristics, and preferences for certain cyclic solar times and events.

While Michael O'Kelly is wary of fixed interpretations of the engraved imagery associated with the mounds, he does agree that they record the winter solstice (21 December).

Then the sun's rays shine in a narrow shaft of light through a slit in the floor of the 'roof box' positioned above the tomb entrance, illuminating a carved basin within a stone recess for a week before and a week after the winter solstice. He has concluded that the south-east orientation of the mound is deliberate for this reason.[37]

Religion, the arts and grave goods

It is thought that Neolithic Irish people had originally come from Brittany or Iberia, bringing with them skills to create similar temple mounds in Ireland to those they left behind. Gavrinis in Brittany has one of the best examples, with a rich display of engraved abstract designs much like those at Knowth and Newgrange. It also has a capstone engraved with two naturalistic images, an axe and a bull (or cow) with part of the horns of a second bull, the rest of which has broken away. Marija Gimbutas (1991) records a passage grave at Carnac dated to 6,700 BP, with cupmarks, circles, concentric circles and an engraved hafted axe and an anthropomorphic female image.

The most stunning aspect of the mounds is their art. It is in harmonious relationship with the architecture of the buildings. While the art could be considered mere decoration, Martin Brennan (1994) argues that its main purpose was as a form of symbolic writing with a "limited, identifiable and relatively consistent range of symbols which appear in widely different places."[38] These were part of rituals dedicated to the sun and moon. He sorts the different images into groups including dots and cupmarks, lines, circles, quadrangles, arcs or crescents, zigzags, wavy lines, spirals and ovals (ellipses or lozenges). The rocks on which they are placed are always astronomically oriented. These images record the movement of sun, moon and stars and this can be verified by visual observation without using instruments. For Marija Gimbutas this imagery was similar in meaning to other imagery around Old Europe which symbolise the roles of the goddess, and are a form of early writing.

Michael O'Kelly (1989) observes that the artists were very highly skilled. Not only did they engrave the difficult circular images with a remarkable degree of technical skill, but they also used considerable imagination and good judgement in their placement. The rock features, their shape and degree of smoothness, were taken into account when placing the images. The method of engraving involved the initial marking of the position and shape of the images. Then the linear designs thus formed were deepened and widened as necessary. Sometimes these hammered lines and images show up as a motif in light relief according to the light source.[39]

For Marija Gimbutas it was clear that women served important religious functions associated with the temple mounds in Ireland, just as they did in other places which honoured female deities or ancestral beings, although there is little physical evidence left of their ritual activities beyond the circular engravings and a few small pieces of 'jewellery' as grave goods.[40]

There is some conjecture about Neolithic Irish religion. Neither women nor men are specifically identified as being associated with any of the Neolithic temple mounds although the predominance of circular imagery on the stones of Knowth and Newgrange relate to symbols of the female principle and female deities elsewhere. What *is* significant is the retention of the death/regeneration symbolism in the Irish passage tombs, and it is this symbolism which is an important connection between the three very different Neolithic cultures.

1 a

3

1 b

NEOLITHIC KNOWTH

1. *Knowth mace head*, front and back, 6,500 BP
2. *Knowth owl-faced goddess with central vulva symbol*
3. *Knowth standing stone*
   (Source: Gimbutas, Marija, 1989)

All line drawings © Judy Foster, 2013

2

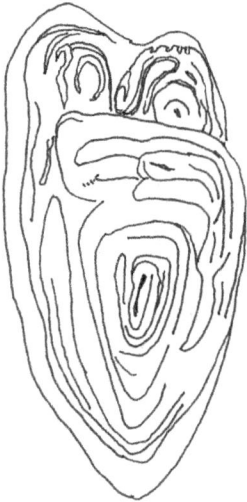

Marija Gimbutas puts forward a convincing argument for this interpretation. The late Neolithic tomb art indicates that people recognised and celebrated the cyclic risings of the sun and moon at specific times of the year and their connection with the cycles of all living things, especially of human birth, life, death and regeneration:

> The light that enters the megalithic tombs on winter solstice, illuminating their inner chambers, is also metaphoric. This is the sign of quickening – the womb of Death made fertile for new life ... Some megalithic tombs to this day are regarded as 'caves' of the Goddess.[41]

Marija Gimbutas suggests that some of the symbols at Knowth and Newgrange resemble the eyes of an owl. The owl as bringer of death (in those countries without vultures) was thus symbolic of the Neolithic female deity of death and regeneration in Ireland. The vulture carried this symbolism at Çatal Hüyük. The axe and the bovine, seen at Çatal Hüyük and Crete, held similar meanings for the temple mound people of Gavrinis in Brittany. Symbols are always part of lived experience and since there were no vultures or any wild cattle in Ireland, other more abstract images had to replace them.

Some decorated objects have been found inside the mounds. These include plain, smooth stone 'mace-heads', and one engraved example at Knowth which Muris O'Sullivan (1993) describes as featuring an anthropomorphic image which can be closely compared with "the famous cylinder [deities] of Iberia."[42] A drawing of the image in Muris O'Sullivan's text shows the unity and flow between the designs on all four sides of the mace-head. The 'mouth' of the image, the circular hole through which the wooden haft was placed, is delineated by elegant engraved flowing lines which connect with the spirals engraved on each side of the 'head'. The haft hole at the back of the head is enclosed within a circle. Engraved grooves extend like rays of the sun across the top and bottom edges of the 'face' and on the back of the head. These have been described as marking a beard, but when the image is seen as a whole it is possible they could also represent rays of light or perhaps tattoo lines. The beautiful and skilfully executed design of the Knowth mace-head demonstrates the presence of very cultured people.

Because Michael O'Kelly assumes the temple mounds were built for, and used by, kings or chieftains, he argues that the object, originally mounted on a wooden shaft or handle, was a symbol of hierarchic (male) authority, carried in ritual ceremonies. Yet kings and chieftains with their hierarchic societies did not first appear here until the arrival of the Indo-Europeans at 4,500 BP (that is, 3,000 years later, as was the case elsewhere in the world).

Other carved objects are in the shape of large 'pins', some 25 centimetres long and decorated with carved spirals around the shanks. Of the small bone and antler pins, some are very long with 'mushroom' and 'poppy' shaped heads, while others have a herringbone pattern on their shanks. There are also hammer-and-pestle shaped pendants, polished 'marbles' of chalk, and polished serpentine ornaments. These are thought to be ritual objects since they were found in very specific positions within the mounds.

The temple mound was considered the sole sacred representation of the all-important female deity in Ireland; as a whole it represented the womb of a female deity, her figure symbolised by the cruciform arrangement of passages within the mound, as described by Michael Dames in *The Silbury Treasure* (1976). It is also notable that there are no naturalistic or stylised images or figurines of a female spiritual being in the temple mounds, or indeed

1

2

3

4

5

6

7

8

IRISH PASSAGE TOMBS: KNOWTH AND NEWGRANGE

1. and 2. Two views of a *mammoth-ivory engraved tooth* (Source: Gimbutas, Marija, 1989)

3. *A ritual stone basin* at the end of one passage in Knowth Passage Tomb (temple-mound), Ireland, 5,500 BP

4. and 5. *Engraved orthostats* from Knowth Passage Tomb
(Source 3–5: Brennan, Martin, 1994)

6. *Open-mouth/beak sculpture* represents the Old European bird goddess, dated to 8,000 BP (Source: Gimbutas, Marija, 1989)

7. *Ritual mace head* from Newgrange Passage Tomb (Source: O'Sullivan, Muris, 1993)

8. *The goddess of regeneration,* Neolithic stone carving (Source: Dames, Michael, 1996)
All line drawings © Judy Foster, 2013

in any part of Ireland. Any female presence is confined to abstract symbols including double circles, triple spirals and triangles. In Britain, a rare example noted by Marija Gimbutas (1991) of a possible female deity associated with a Neolithic site is dated to about 5,000 BP. It is in the form of a granite menhir, carved into a human shape, featuring a headband and a necklace above circular breasts.

Pottery is tangible evidence of Irish Neolithic women's work and some of their pottery has been found in places where rituals might have taken place. Similar round-bottomed pottery was common in France and Iberia. Very fine and plain, technically well-finished and smooth pottery vessels were widely used domestically as well as ritually, and featured rounded bases, while later pots were flat-based. In some cases vessels were decorated around the rim and upper area.

Later pots reported by Michael O'Kelly were often coarse and decorated with incised or jabbed patterns, with a great variety of rim forms. Different areas produced distinctive styles of pottery; for example, at Knowth and Newgrange, Carrowkeel-style coarse pottery was associated with ritual. Distinctive Neolithic Sandhills and Carrowkeel pottery was roughly made and semi-globular in form, featuring all-over stab-and-drag incised linear designs. More common coarse domestic ware sometimes had a protruding base. (A decline in the refinement of pottery usually indicated it belonged to the beginning of the Indo-European Warrior Age.) Other pottery was decorated by wrapping thick string around the wet surface to create whipped-cord or cogwheel impressions; or by pressing other objects into the clay to form a linear design around the pots, and sometimes on the base. This is indirect evidence for the art of weaving in Ireland during the Neolithic period.

The pottery found in smaller single burial mounds and in stone enclosures of the time was usually decorated. It accompanied other grave goods, such as javelin heads, polished axes, and stone beads. In cist burial sites there were round-bottomed and highly decorated shouldered pots sometimes completely covered with geometric panels featuring oblique incised lines. A plain round-shouldered bowl was included in certain cist burials.

Trade

Trade with other centres can only be surmised since the evidence is not apparent beyond similarities between the mounds and engravings of Ireland and Brittany.

Neolithic Ireland, although only settled as recently as 10,000 BP, with its wet and difficult climate, left little evidence behind of a creative, civilised culture, with the exception of the great temple mounds, stone circles and stone burial sites. It contrasts starkly with Minoan Crete, with all its advantages including a better climate and the ability to support a larger population.

Crete

The Minoan civilised society of Knossos (5,000–3,050 BP)

Minoan Crete is thought to have been first settled by people from Anatolia. Until the excavation of Çatal Hüyük, it was not realised just how much of their culture the first Anatolian immigrants brought with them to Crete over 8,000 years ago. While the Minoan civilisation lies within the late Neolithic and early Bronze Age periods, it has the ideology and artefacts of the Neolithic era.

Marija Gimbutas (1991) describes the Minoan civilisation (thus named by its discoverer, Arthur Evans) as emerging when the population of Crete expanded and came into contact with other countries of the region. They refined their lifestyle and their cities, in particular, Knossos, which was built above a series of early settlements on a low mound. The Minoan culture lasted well into the Bronze Age yet retained its Neolithic outlook.

Like the Neolithic civilised societies of Çatal Hüyük and Knowth/Newgrange in Ireland, the story of Neolithic Crete is told in the considerable remains of the layers of the ancient buried cities of Knossos, in rather more detail than in Ireland. Here, evidence for the female principle, the importance of women, and the sophistication of the Minoan culture may be clearly discerned. Arthur Evans (1936)[43] first excavated Knossos in the early 1900s. He gave the name 'Minoan' to the sophisticated Neolithic civilised society of Crete, even though King Minos, after whom it was named, would not have appeared in Crete until towards the end of the Minoan civilisation.[44]

Crete was apparently not settled until about 8,000 BP. It is a highly fertile island, with a range of climates which allow successions of harvests and green pastures on the plains and up the hillsides. Snow on the mountain peaks melts and provides good spring water and streams which never dry out. In early Crete there were plenty of materials for building dwellings, including wood and stone. Fruit and nut trees were plentiful, and pastures grew abundantly.

The Minoan people

The Minoan people and their lifestyle were depicted in the wall paintings and frescoes of Knossos. Women were important in Minoan society, as they were at Çatal Hüyük, and active in every aspect of society alongside men. In fact, according to Nicholas Platon, "where men and women appear together in Minoan art it is as partners in relationship, most strikingly in the bull-vaulting seals and frescoes, where they trust their lives to each other."[45]

Dorothy Cameron (1997)[46] suggests that the high status of Minoan women was shown in their attire. Early dresses featured heavy gathered skirts, but these were replaced by skirts with narrow waists, fitted to the hips, and falling to the ground in layers of flounces, or flaring out to a decorative hem or embroidered edge. Sometimes a decorative double apron was worn which echoed the form of the bull's horns shape, and this is repeated in women's poses, where their arms are raised in the angular ritual gesture representing the form of stylised horns.

Jacquetta Hawkes (1968)[47] provides a picture of the clothing of the day: the jackets were frontless with short full sleeves; a tightly laced wide belt went around the waist below the breasts; colours included blues, yellows, soft reds and greens, and the most likely fabric used was linen. The women had various hairstyles, and sometimes wore hats. James Mellaart (1967) gives very little detail of the dress of the Anatolian women of Çatal Hüyük, but he does say that finely woven fabrics were available to them. It seems likely that they, too, had bare breasts, and wore skirts as depicted on the figurines. Anatolian men also wore loincloths but with animal skin outer robes. Jacquetta Hawkes describes the slim and elegant Minoan women as walking gracefully "among the flowers, birds and butterflies of the gardens"[48] with hair coiled and curled, and wearing form-fitting jackets supporting and displaying bare breasts. Their floor-length skirts featured rows of deep frills.

She notes that the men's waists were emphasised by wide belts, and they wore codpieces or penis sheaths, and also multi-coloured loincloths which reached to the knee in front, with a fringe, while at the back the robes were not as long. For sport they wore a shorter version, split each side to the hip. Men also wore gold necklaces, armlets, bracelets and anklets, with personal seals hung from wrist or neck. Their hair was long and, like the women, they sometimes positioned curls to hang in front of their ears. They were usually depicted in active, possibly ritual events, in occupations such as boxing and wrestling.

Buildings

The first people to arrive in Crete are considered to have come from the area of Çatal Hüyük about 8,100 years ago. James Mellaart explains that the first settlement they built was on the low mound where Knossos is located, was only half an acre in size, and housed about 100 people. The first houses were thought to have been made of mud, although they evidently did not last long, perhaps because of climatic problems. Jacquetta Hawkes (1968) notes that the builders also cut storage pits into the rock underneath. Over the next four building periods, the town doubled in size.

Later houses were rectangular and similar to buildings in Çatal Hüyük, but stones (sometimes old querns) were substituted for the less durable Anatolian mud bricks, and these were mortared and plastered inside with mud. The houses were clustered together just as they had been in Çatal Hüyük, and there were no streets. Villages in Crete at the time were communal settlements with no signs of hierarchy. There were no traces of pottery, although baked-clay female figurines testifying to the presence of the female principle were found and may have accompanied the early people. They used obsidian blades and crafted ground stone querns. This early Neolithic period (7,620 BP) lasted until 6,200 years ago, during which time several more layers of rectangular buildings were constructed. Then, dark coloured pottery suddenly appeared; it may have been a trade item, or perhaps new Anatolian migrants arrived, the women bringing pottery and weaving skills with them.

The palace-temples of Crete

By 4,000 BP the lands surrounding the island of Crete were all ruled by the Bronze Age warrior cultures. Jacquetta Hawkes describes the differences between these warlike people and the gentle Neolithic Cretans as being extreme. For the warriors, urban life was non-existent, their rulers not far removed from barbarism, their settlements surrounded with fortifications. But the peaceful Cretans became ever more refined and civilised in their ways.

She records the palace-temples of Knossos as having every amenity, while the surrounding people's homes were comfortable in well-made streets opening out into the countryside. Towns had paved and drained streets, while the spacious houses sometimes had more than one storey. Houses in the countryside were often quite large and comfortable. There were no fortified walls around the towns. Systems of roads ran over much of the island, with a paved highway from Knossos to the southern ports which passed over an impressive viaduct, but other minor roads were usually not much more than tracks. It is now generally accepted that the great palaces of Knossos were not built for kings or queens, but for priestesses and people, since no proof of rulers has ever been found. Carol Christ (1995)[49] argues they were in fact communal centres where celebratory agricultural rituals took place, where the fruit, vegetables and grains were stored, and farming and distribution of foods

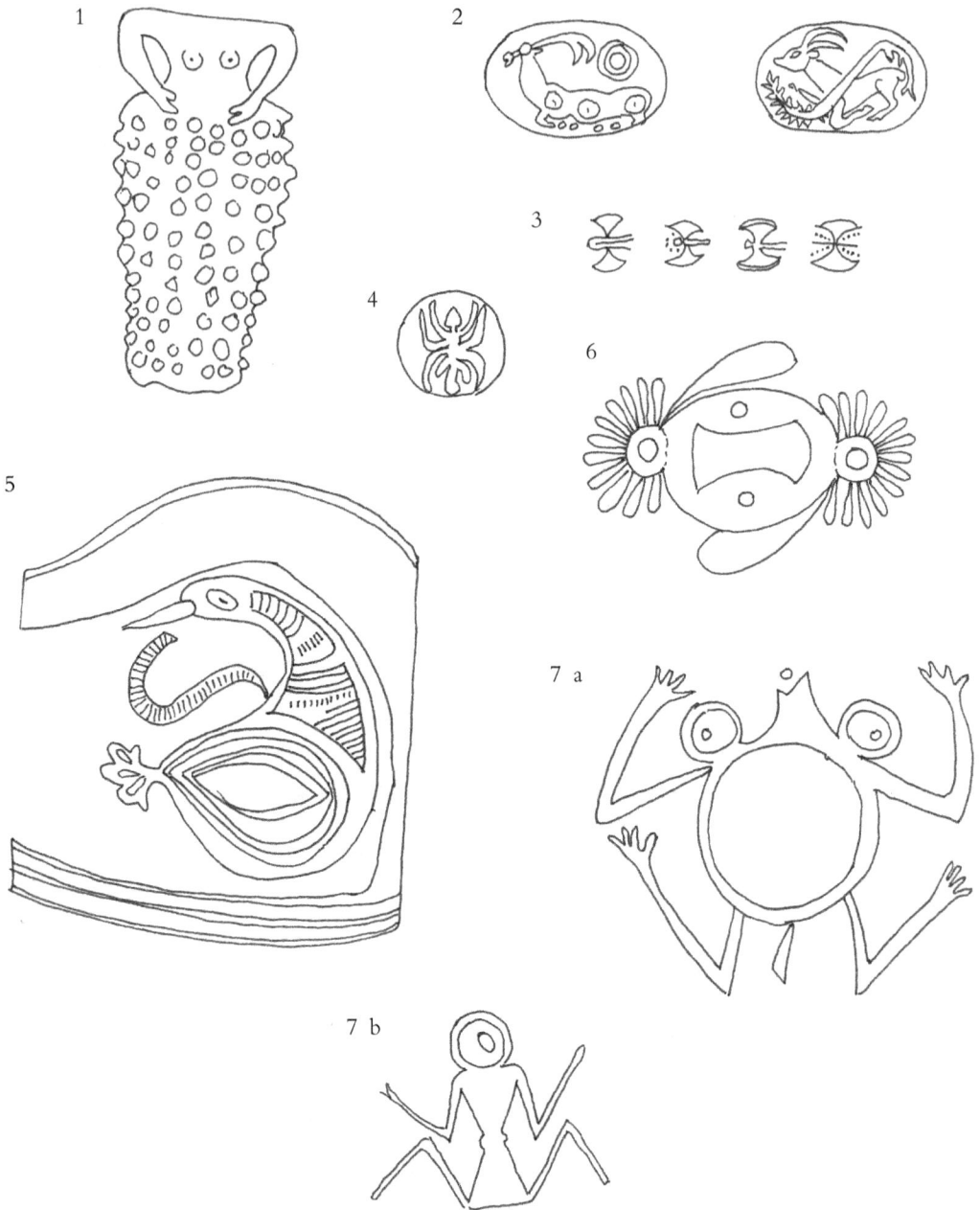

HEDGEHOG GODDESS AND OTHER ANIMAL IMAGERY

1. *Minoan hedgehog goddess*
2. and 4. *Stamp seals with animal designs, a spider motif*
3. *Butterfly designs*

5. *Bird motif* painted on ceramic, 3,400 BP
6. *Butterfly design* on vase
7. *Two frog motifs*, 4,000 BP
   (Source: Gimbutas, Marija, 1989)

All line drawings © Judy Foster, 2013

were organised. They were the chief centres of religious life since they featured very many sacred rooms and shrines and displayed much religious symbolism. Large rooms and courts provided a backdrop for ritual games and ceremonies.

Jacquetta Hawkes describes the palace of Minos at Knossos (one of several, due to earthquakes and fires destroying palaces over a period of time) as covering 20,000 square metres, with three storeys, and one wing with five storeys. It contained living rooms for numerous people, workshops, administrative offices, and huge storerooms with lead-lined pits for storing liquids such as olive oil, wine, various grains and other goods. Workshops for highly valued craftspeople, such as the (female) potters and gem-cutters, were provided within the palace-temple and indicate their importance. Woodworkers and weavers of textiles were shown similar attention at Çatal Hüyük.

The palace-temple featured a large rectangular north-south central court. This meant that the building was oriented towards the four points of the compass which was probably a ritualised position. It is interesting that at Çatal Hüyük too, the walls of the shrines were always facing certain directions; the north wall was the death/regeneration wall, the west wall was the wall of birth, and so on, while the Irish mounds were oriented to the seasonal equinox. Even the houses of the city surrounding the palace-temple were oriented similarly.

The west side of the central court was the sacred area, with a throne, lustral basin, sacred columns, double axes and the sacred cattle horns perhaps associated with a female deity. Decorated bovine heads were thought to be important symbols of the male–female procreation aspect of the female deity as they were at Çatal Hüyük. Arthur Evans (1936) pointed to many Anatolian influences at Knossos, and James Mellaart (1967) confirms the influences of Knossos were clearly seen in the earlier artefacts at Çatal Hüyük. Dorothy Cameron (1997) notes that a further similarity is the so-called throne in the Throne Room at Knossos, which is similar to the throne at Çatal Hüyük.[50]

The main court at Minos was overlooked by windows and balconies, while the stairs which went up several storeys were of stone, supported by huge, tapered, painted timber columns. The roofs featured terracotta sacred horns reminiscent of those used in the shrines at Çatal Hüyük. Running water was laid on, and drainage for rainwater and sewerage was provided throughout. The rooms reserved for the head priestess featured frescoes, a bathroom, running water, and a 'flushing' lavatory with the familiar wooden seat.

Entry to the palace-temple was by a northern gate and the most sacred of the rooms was on the right side of the front entrance. The throne room held one throne, each side of which were two brilliantly painted symbolic couchant griffins; thus the throned figure of the priestess would appear to divide the two confronting griffins. One room in the palace-temple included runnels and cavities probably for ritual libations.

Minoan religion, art and pottery

The religion of Crete was centred around a female deity or spirit of nature which seemed to have been familiar to all Neolithic people. The manner of building what may have been shrines, their layout, furnishings, and the symbols relating to rituals known at Çatal Hüyük, were repeated in the palace-temple of Minos. Jacquetta Hawkes (1968) explains that the symbols and rites of a multi-form protective female deity were integrated into people's lives.

Most images of female deities were more stylised than other representations of people. Images from the neighbouring islands of the Cyclades, found in Crete, represented a possible female deity with a wider range of attributes whom Jacquetta Hawkes describes as "the abundant mother [...] tall, slender, small-breasted, and with an abstract simplicity."[51] Lucy Goodison and Christine Morris (1998)[52] describe her as stylised in shape, her arms folded, her legs tapered, with a flat and enigmatic tilted face. Cycladic figurines have often been found in graves, sometimes underneath other objects; occasionally there would be two or more, or as many as 14; they were sometimes fragmented, perhaps for ritual reasons. These figurines could have represented deities, votaries or priestesses, protective beings, or companion spirits.[53] Marija Gimbutas emphasises that because these figurines were found in graves in Old Europe, they were part of the rituals associated with death, and symbolised the person's change from death to regeneration.

Two other well-known female figurines depict a snake deity robed in the typical dress of the palace-temple women: one of these has snakes around her breasts and along her arms, while the other holds a snake in her hand. The snake was thought to be the guardian of the palace-temple, where it kept rats and mice away from the grain stored in huge urns or pithoi. Carol Christ (1995) says the coiled snake and the snake biting its tail indicate wholeness. The shedding of a snake's skin symbolises rebirth and immortality. Because snakes operate above and below the ground, they link the underworld with the upper world. Dorothy Cameron (1997) equates the snake symbol with the umbilical cord metaphor of birth and rebirth. (The snake has always been a symbol of fertility and regeneration in societies present long before the coming of the warrior cultures.)

Lucy Goodison and Christine Morris describe the above-mentioned prominent snake deity figurines as being found together with other precious artefacts within two stone-lined cists in the earliest palace at Knossos, in a room opening onto a central court used for rituals. One of the three original figurines was found in pieces, the only remaining imagery decorating it being a snake wound around an arm, and part of a skirt and apron. The bared breasts of such images are thought to represent the deity's nurturing role, an interpretation supported by accompanying images on faience relief plaques featuring goats and cows feeding their young. They note that the deity idea was also supported by images of the marine environment such as flying fish, rock art, and seashells decorated with painted designs. Although they are critical of Marija Gimbutas's analysis, their description owes much to the earlier Gimbutas interpretation.[54]

Cattle horns, and both decorated and undecorated bull heads, were an important feature of shrines in both Çatal Hüyük and Crete, according to Jacquetta Hawkes (1968). The bull (or cow) was considered a sacred symbol of a female deity and sometimes thought to represent her female–male procreation aspect. Marija Gimbutas (1989) sees a relationship in the fact that women and bison each have a nine-month pregnancy. Bovine horns were a symbol of becoming: they were connected to new life as symbolised by bees or butterflies emerging from the sacred skull. Jacquetta Hawkes describes one depiction of the ritual bull-leaping game at Knossos where a man is depicted supporting his body with his hands on the bull's back and facing backwards, about to somersault over. A woman waits to catch him, while another stands on tiptoe near the animal's head with its left horn under her left armpit.

Two typical Cretan ritual objects, a circular pedestal-table and a bowl, each feature dancing women wearing bell-skirts perhaps taking part in ritual actions, as recorded by Lucy Goodison and Christine Morris. The central figure featured on the tabletop raises her hands,

NEOLITHIC MINOAN CRETE: KNOSSOS

1. The *snake goddess*, 8,000–7,500 BP
2. *Bird goddess*, early Minoan, c. 7,000 BP
   (Source 1–2: Gimbutas, Marija, 1989)

3. and 4. Two famous Minoan faience *snake goddesses*, 3,600 BP
   (Source: Baring, Anne and Jules Cashford, 1991)

All line drawings © Judy Foster, 2013

in which she holds flowers. Other dancers wearing bird masks bend towards her. The image of the central figure inside the bowl has no legs, while accompanying figures 'float' on each side of her. She could represent a priestess or deity.[55]

Anne Baring and Jules Cashford (1991)[56] record the ancient symbol of the double axe, featured among the wall symbols at Knossos, as also being found as far afield as the Palaeolithic cave of Niaux in south-western France, to the Neolithic culture of Tell Halaf in Iraq. It does not represent a war weapon, but a ritual implement used to mark the altars and shrines of the goddess, or to cut down sacred trees, or sacrifice the bull in Crete. Men are never depicted holding double axes in Cretan imagery, and double axes were also not associated with later Aryan symbolism of the god of thunder and war.

The people in Crete who had lived (and buried their dead) in the caves before they built their houses considered caves as being very important. Carol Christ suggests that in 'goddess' symbolism the cave always represented the connection between women's wombs and the womb of the earth, wherein all life comes out of the dark and in the darkness life is transformed, reborn. Jacquetta Hawkes notes that they were certainly thought to be the birthplace of the female deity and thus especially associated with women and childbirth. Marija Gimbutas explains that burial rites in Crete were communal burials in circular or beehive-shaped tombs called 'tholoi', and somewhat similar to those of Neolithic Brittany, Ireland and England. Sometimes two or three tombs were placed together, always near settlements. Also of interest is the position of the entrances to the tombs, most of which faced the east, suggesting possible 'sunrise' symbolism relating to women's worship of the sun as part of earth's natural cycles.

Minoan crafts and trade

Trade with neighbouring countries, such as Egypt and the Levant, was extensive and included items such as olive oil, honey, fish, fruit and herbs which were exported around the Mediterranean. According to Anne Baring and Jules Cashford, other exports included such objects as decorated ceramics, textiles, tools and vases; but in a sense, some artistic aspects of Minoan culture were also exported, since their influence may be seen in nearby countries. An example is the very fine and highly distinctive pottery made by Minoan women as another item of trade. Late Minoan pottery, such as wine cups and bowls decorated with red, white and yellow designs on a background of iridescent black paint, influenced pottery design in surrounding countries. Finely crafted cups of gold and silver were also produced in Crete.

Artisans and craftspeople made implements and jewellery from copper and gold, and were skilled in the cutting and polishing of beautifully designed vases, jugs and other vessels, from finely coloured and patterned stone. Jacquetta Hawkes says such skills would have been brought from Çatal Hüyük where they had earlier been used. Jewellery included crystal beads, gold chains and armlets, sprays of fine gold leaves and flower-headed hairpins, and gold stars which could be sewn onto women's skirts. There were also stamp-seals made of stone and ivory.

Stamp-seals were a common item at Çatal Hüyük where they were made from clay. It is therefore no surprise to find them in use in Crete. The seal-makers of Crete incised pictures and designs on the flat surface, and sometimes carved the handles in animal and bird shapes. The pictures included: ships; fish and fishermen; wildlife, such as ibex and boar; a potter; a man under a tree playing draughts; monkeys; sheep; and doves. The images of people, animals and birds are not always accurate or three dimensional, but they are vibrantly alive, and the very natural tranquil poses of many of the female figurines suggest they were based on real people.

Wall paintings were often frescoes which were made by applying paint to wet plaster. But there were no portraits of royalty, nor any great hunting or battle scenes. The emphasis was on nature which was featured in order to create an atmosphere of "all-pervading-moving-springing-life"[57] in most of Minoan art. This was in contrast to the Sumerians and Babylonians for whom nature had to be always subservient to the male gods, according to Jacquetta Hawkes (1968). While the Egyptians depicted nature, it was always as a backdrop to human and divine life. From late Minoan Crete a form of written text, known as the Linear B tablets, informs us that numerous female and, to a lesser extent, male deities were present.

End of the Neolithic Period

The beginning of the Warrior Age (4,500 BP)

The Indo-Europeans had begun expanding from Mesopotamia to Central Europe from the steppes between the Carpathians and the Caucasus to the north of the Black Sea by 4,500 BP. They were pastoralists, nomadic tribes who invaded other peoples' land without regard for the gentle peaceful agricultural life and religious rituals, according to Anne Baring and Jules Cashford (1991). All the life-giving symbolism of the earth-centred female deity was turned around forever by their arrival.

No one knows why the city of Çatal Hüyük was abandoned. There is no physical evidence of violent disruption. Perhaps the people moved to the city on the mound across the river (which is of later date) because of some imminent natural disaster, such as volcanic action in nearby mountains, or a fatal human or plant disease.[58]

But everything in the Irish Neolithic changed about 4,500 BP with the first appearance of the Bronze Age Indo-European 'Beaker' people who came to Ireland from Britain. Just as the change at Çatal Hüyük occurred abruptly, so it did also in Ireland. According to George Eogan "the end of that culture is as enigmatic as its beginning."[59] The Beaker people were so named because of their distinctive inverted, bell-shaped, flat-bottomed, highly decorative and regionally specific pottery. They were part of a vibrant farming culture with larger settlements and huge circular enclosures (fortifications), and have been credited with the first use of metallurgy (although, as Marija Gimbutas and James Mellaart[60] have found, metallurgy was already present in Neolithic Europe). The Beaker lifestyle included pastoral activities which were typical Indo-European practices.

Ritual practices included different kinds of burial sites, notably the barrow tombs which were placed on hilltops and held males of high status together with many grave goods including the first Irish metal objects, flat axes, and metal blades. Barrow tombs were small circular mounds, usually made of earth, with a ditch or an external bank surrounding them. George Eogan reports secular sites as including embanked and ritual enclosures, and stone circles, together with the first appearance of metal war weapons, daggers, halberds (dagger-like blades), and spearheads. Michael O'Kelly (1989) notes that the Beaker people were not necessarily Celts. They built large fortified mounds and were a warlike people. While the

Celts were of Indo-European descent, it is currently thought that they may have emerged as a specific group by about 5,500 BP in Europe, but did not appear as a distinct people in Ireland until about 2,400 BP.

Jacquetta Hawkes (1968) describes the situation on Crete between 3,400 and 3,300 BP: the palace-temple of Minos was burnt down and was never rebuilt – this marked the beginning of the end for the Minoan civilisation. Anne Baring and Jules Cashford record that the Mycenaeans, who were Indo-Europeans (Aryans) from Greece, did not invade Crete but established relations with the Minoans about 3,450 BP, introducing a king, hierarchy and warlike activities. Later invaders were the Dorians who were far more destructive, bringing the Minoan civilisation to an end.

Threads

The most important aspect of the civilised society of Çatal Hüyük is its sophisticated antiquity. While the position of women within earlier societies is not always clear, the experience of Australian Indigenous women for over 80,000 years, and the Neolithic women of Çatal Hüyük, suggest it is likely that they enjoyed a position and respect not experienced by their Bronze Age sisters.

There was certainly a female principle present at Çatal Hüyük, whether represented by a deity, spirit or ancestral being. This can be deduced by the preponderance of female images and symbols painted on the walls, the many symbolic female figurines found and, at the Mellaart site, the manner of burial, and even the layout of the houses. Women's visibility can be inferred by the remarkable discovery of such transient artefacts as fine pottery, wooden vessels and fine woven fabrics. It is not surprising that there should be some differences in the discoveries by James Mellaart and Ian Hodder because there are now new ways of collecting evidence, including greater emphasis on context and scientific proof and very much less time on interpretation of non-material evidence. Also the part of the city excavated by James Mellaart was not the same as the area Ian Hodder continues to examine.

It is remarkable that so much evidence of a civilised society has survived at Çatal Hüyük, obviously due to the dry climate, but also because the city was apparently suddenly abandoned, leaving everything in situ. It seemed to be a much more sophisticated culture than Neolithic Ireland, but is this only because life was easier for the Anatolians? The people of Çatal Hüyük certainly had more opportunity for wide contact with other cultures, whereas Ireland was wet and cold and cut off from neighbours by the sea.

When one considers the similarities between Knowth/Newgrange and Çatal Hüyük, although 2,000 years separate them, there are notable implications. They are examples of the way in which environmental differences and distance could affect two apparently similar societies. Both had sophisticated architectural and engineering skills, were highly artistic and technically proficient, and were agrarian societies in which women were visible, making pottery, weaving, cultivating crops and keeping some domestic animals. Both were religious, with female nature/earth-centred deities, spirits or ancestral beings, and a strong ritual life. Each society was obviously peaceful and communal, and both centres supported comparatively large populations for their time. Furthermore, they exploited the natural materials available to them for building well-constructed homes and places of worship despite very different environments.

People everywhere have been hampered by the limitations of their environment and the tools and materials available to them. Thus, although there were no stones available for building around Çatal Hüyük, the hot dry climate allowed the use of versatile mudbricks for the construction of houses, and these could be easily made to any size. But for the Irish the options were much more limited; the wet and cold Irish climate restricted building materials to wood or stone. (This would have also made it difficult to use mortar or plaster.)

While much evidence of Anatolian (Turkish) civilised societies survived because of the hot dry climate, the situation was very different in Ireland. Neither bone nor the normally durable pottery pieces have lasted in many parts of Ireland because of the long-term destructive nature of the wet, acid soils. In addition, because wood was the most appropriate material for making most utilitarian and art objects, they were the first to vanish, thus creating an unbalanced art scenario. It is also possible that art objects were destroyed by successive incoming warrior cultures with their radically different ideologies, deities, and rituals.

It is that evidence which has not survived in Neolithic Ireland, which is remarkable. From at least the beginning of the Neolithic era people in general had a very high standard of wood and textile crafts. For example, a few thousand years earlier, at Çatal Hüyük, weavers had produced and dyed fine fabrics for garments, as well as heavier woven wool mats (kilims) with geometric designs; while woodcarvers had created graceful wooden dishes, beakers, forks, spoons and eggcups as fine as the best pottery of the Neolithic world. There is no record of such refined objects at Knowth and Newgrange, yet there is no reason why the Irish would not have had similar skills as long as they had suitable materials. The competent artistic and creative people who engraved and carved the stone of Knowth and Newgrange would not have stopped with the building and art of the temple mounds; other equally impressive and beautiful objects would have been created and perhaps some remain to be discovered in the future.

The story of Minoan Crete is important because it was a civilised society in which Neolithic ideas survived to be practised alongside Bronze Age warrior cultures without being influenced by their ideologies. However, the Hawkes interpretation of a prominent female deity, and the symbolism as interpreted by Marija Gimbutas and Dorothy Cameron, continue to be compelling evidence for a goddess religion. The important consideration for us is that the female principle was paramount, and women were highly visible in Minoan Crete. The end of Minoan Crete marks the end of women's important status and, in the main, the end of the peaceful Neolithic period in the Northern Hemisphere.

James Mellaart comments that we do not give the highly skilled Upper Palaeolithic and Neolithic people credit for their civilised lifestyles and achievements, nor are we prepared to concede they may have been far more sophisticated than the Indo-European warriors who began to destroy their cultures 6,000 years ago. It needs to be stated that not only was a female principle notable in each Neolithic culture, but also women's high visibility and contribution to such a period of innovative achievement ought to be openly acknowledged.

PART TWO

The Indo-Europeans: 'Civilisation' and History Begin

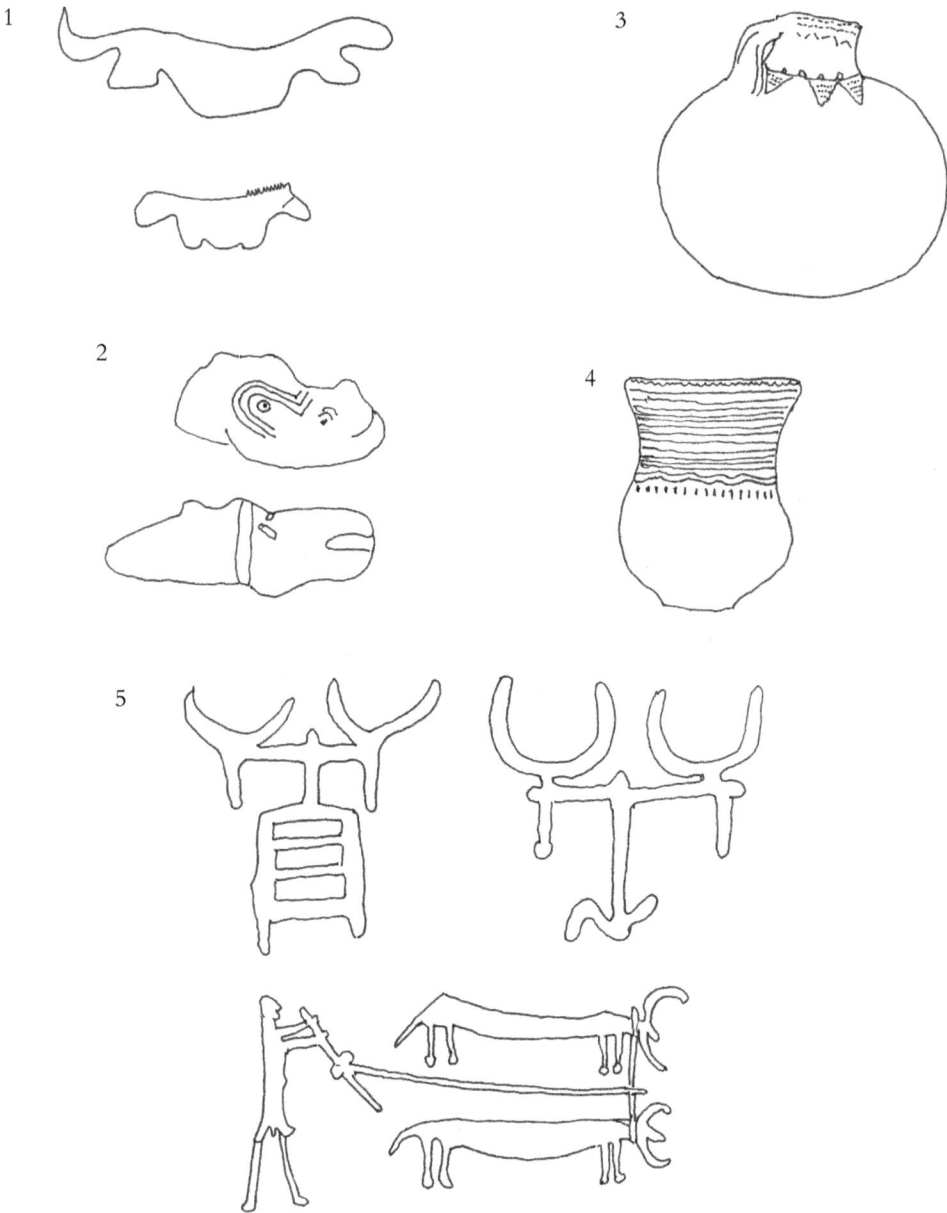

PROTO-INDO-EUROPEAN SCULPTURES, POTTERY, AND ROCK ENGRAVINGS

1. *Two Proto-Indo-European horse sculptures,* 7,000 BP
2. *Horse-head sculptures,* Kurgan
3. *Vase from Lower Dneiper region,* 6,500 BP
4. *Old European Bell Beaker vase,* 5,500 BP

5. *Two rock wall engravings of yoked oxen,* North Pontiac, 5,500 BP
(Source: Gimbutas, Marija, 1991)

All line drawings © Judy Foster, 2013

114

CHAPTER 8

THE FIRST INDO-EUROPEANS: THE BEGINNING OF 'CIVILISATION' AND WRITTEN HISTORY

Marija Gimbutas (1991)[1] summarises life in Old Europe after 12,000 BP as being gentle and peaceful and lived according to the cycles of the seasons. Hunter-gatherers further developed their semi-settled lifestyles: they hunted an increasing variety of animal life; added to and refined their tool kits; harvested and prepared wild grain for food; made fishing nets and sleeping mats; carved antler, bone, stone and ivory body ornaments and figurines; engraved ritual and everyday images upon rock walls; and accompanied the burial of their dead with ritual.

At about the same time in southern Russia, north of the Black and Caspian Seas on the forest-steppes of the Middle Volga Basin, where the country was heavily forested, dark, wild and mountainous, there were hunters who lived very differently, according to Marija Gimbutas. There were few varieties of edible plants available in the narrow valleys beside the rivers and streams, and the only animals suitable to hunt were a few wild cattle and the more numerous wild horses which in Old Europe had become extinct. The people moved around constantly as they hunted the herds, so there is little record of their nomadic lifestyle at this time. The hunters' tool kits which have survived included simple weapons used for killing animals; there is no record of the harvesting and preparation of wild grain as there was in Europe and Africa. Other researchers are less specific, but according to the still highly relevant Gimbutas scenario, by 9,000 BP these people, identified by Marija Gimbutas as the Early Yamna, were breeding stock and practising small-scale farming, and were the first to begin to domesticate the horse, since the earliest archaeological evidence for the practice is in this region. Key evidence for the non-aggression of these Neolithic peoples was the absence of weapons except implements for hunting found in grave sites until the emergence of the Proto-Indo-Europeans in Europe about 6,500 BP.

The lifestyle and mobility of the Proto-Indo-Europeans depended on the domesticated horse, possession of herds of large animals and a pastoral economy. They ran large herds of horses on the pastures, with some kept near the camps to provide milk, meat and hides. Horses were also regarded as sacred animals as the remains of sacrificed horses have been found placed over human graves along with miniature horse figurines carved from flat bone. Discovery of bridle parts made of antler dated to 7,000 BP suggested to Marija Gimbutas that these hunters, who were later to become known as the Indo-Europeans, had begun to ride the horses which they had tamed.

Since Marija Gimbutas wrote about this, David Anthony and Dorcas Brown (2007)[2] have provided further evidence that wild horses were indeed hunted for food and hides from 7,200 BP, but men only began to ride them from around 6,500 BP. They have studied 6,000-year-old bridle bits and horses' teeth, and estimate that more than 300 hours of riding has caused the often considerable wear they display. Further evidence for the ritual value of horses has appeared in the form of horse-head maces found in graves.[3] Marija Gimbutas (1991) observes that horseback raiders could well have brought about the end of the Old European cultures, as evidence shows that tribal raiding beyond the Danube valley began from 6,000–5,500 BP.[4]

She also mentions miniature clay models of wheels found in Old European settlements from about 7,500 BP which show that they also trained cattle to pull wagons, so it is not surprising to find wheeled vehicles in use in southern Russia from this time. Cattle were very important, and were considered the main draught animal because of their strength, while horses provided speed. The increasingly mobile lifestyle on horseback also allowed long-distance travel to steal cattle and horses. Horse owners became wealthy through accumulation of large herds, trading and eventually warfare, gradually moving further afield, conquering and settling in new regions as they went. Two-wheeled horse-drawn chariots which may have been used during war appear in the south-eastern Ural steppes about 4,100 BP according to David Anthony and Dorcas Brown.[5]

Marija Gimbutas did not speculate as to why and how the Proto-Indo-Europeans became warlike but we suggest two possibilities:

- The new freedom gained by horse-riding at a time when people had to walk everywhere led to the development of individual ownership of horses by a few men. Herding and taming a horse allowed personal freedom; owning one horse led to the desire for more, perhaps for trade or exchange. The more horses one man could tame and train, the more power-over and ability he had to trade more goods. Larger herds of horses also led to the need for more pastures, so the individual horseman, along with other horse riders, began to look wider afield. As a group, at first the tribal horsemen invaded or took over neighbouring lands, and eventually were able to rapidly move further forward and outward because of the strength, speed and flexibility of the horse. Individual ownership of horses, unheard of in other prehistoric societies of the time, was also the beginning of the ownership of women.

- The development of male violence and warlike practices.
  It would seem that all indigenous communal societies held that even in the rituals of conflict resolution it was considered unthinkable that any protagonist be deliberately killed. In order for the idea of killing others to arise, it is possible that quarrelling and violence between one or two hotheaded individuals eventually led to killing for gain. Self-gain and individual ownership led to possession of more horses, land, buildings, and eventually to ownership of people (slaves) especially women.

We should mention that up until European invasion of Australia, when some brave men attempted to defend their country, the Indigenous people had observed the rules of peace and communal ownership, and ritual conflict resolution in which the deliberate taking of life was avoided whenever possible.

The Early (Proto-) Indo-European homelands

Marija Gimbutas had researched and reported specific information about the origins and homelands of the Indo-Europeans in the late 1980s, and it is worth noting that her information is still relevant today, although now it has become more specific as more details have become known. In recent years different hypotheses have been presented by other researchers who argue that the Proto-Indo-European people may have come from anywhere within a certain area of southern Russia close to the Black Sea. However, the evidence David Anthony and others have found is that from between 7,000 and 4,000 BP there were many distinct cultures and growing population problems for the peoples in the steppe-desert regions of Russia.

From 7,200 BP onwards there were large herds of horses and hunter horse-riders spread over an enormous area of southern Russia, in the area between the Lower Dnieper River on the west and north of Kazhakhstan, also east of the River Don and between the Middle Volga, the Caucasus and Ural Mountains. A recent map by David Anthony and Dorcas Brown indicates that around 6,200 BP, the Proto-Indo-Europeans occupied lands from north-west of the Black Sea around to the west, from the Dneiper River region as far as the Danube River area.[6] These were the Proto-Indo-Europeans whose language evolved out of those spoken by earlier hunter-fisher groups, who lived along the southern river valleys.

Other evidence is provided by Elizabeth Barber (1999)[7] who has found that because of the presence (or absence) of a certain kind of weaving method, the Proto-Indo-Europeans must have lived east of the Dnieper River (north of the Black Sea) because one important weaving tool used in central Europe on the warp-weighted loom 7,500 years ago was not known in this region. The further east towards the Dnieper River one goes, the less evidence there is for this style of loom. The Indo-Europeans in the extreme south and east had different looms and those who lived west of the Dnieper borrowed words from other languages to describe activities to do with the warp-weighted looms which had originally come from central Europe.

Geneticist Luigi Cavalli-Sforza (2000) has found the Kurgan nomads could have been descendants of Middle East or Anatolian pre-Proto-Indo-European agriculturalists who came to the steppes through Macedonia and Romania about 10,000 to 9,000 BP.[8] His work confirms the accuracy of Marija Gimbutas's dates and position of the Proto-Indo-European homelands, evidence which has been further supported by David Anthony's more recent excavations on the Kurgan steppes.

He also records the Proto-Indo-European genetic expansion outside Europe as spreading widely: east to Iran and India, and to Arabia and northern Africa, where new desert conditions caused the people to rapidly die out by about 5,000 BP. He argues that more modern (Indo-European) peoples eventually replaced them in what is now known as the Sahara Desert. Indo-European farmers also expanded into Europe, mixing their genes with the local hunter-gatherers. There were many migrations of people from the Kurgan region, towards southern Asia around 5,000–4,000 BP en route to Iran, Pakistan and India, eventually causing the end of the Indus civilisation around 3,500 BP.

Marija Gimbutas describes the societies in this very large region as highly mobile, utilising remarkably similar decorative items, tools, and weapons, while living in camps often thousands of kilometres from each other. Cultures included the Yamna, the Maikop or Mikhailovka, and the Late Yamna. These warlike patriarchal and hierarchical original Proto-Indo-Europeans, described by Marija Gimbutas as 'Kurgans'[9] (semi-nomadic pastoralists), were identified by their circular funeral mounds. The Kurgans were the first people in the world to be armed with offensive weapons including long dagger-knives, spears, halberds, and bows and arrows.

According to Marija Gimbutas, increasing use of radiocarbon dating means that it is possible to trace the several 'waves' of 'steppe pastoralists' or Kurgans across Europe. These early outward movements occurred over three periods:

- the Early Yamna mounted warriors moved outwards from the Volga Steppe between 6,400 and 6,300 BP[10]
- the outward movement made by the Maikop warriors from the North Pontiac area to between the Lower Dniester River and the Caucasus Mountains occurred about 5,500 BP[11]
- movement initiated by the Late Yamna warriors from the Volga Steppe took place about 5,000 BP.[12] (Elizabeth Barber records slightly later dates.)

Marija Gimbutas (1991) also considers that dramatic changes took place between 4,000 and 3,700 BP when the people became more unified, adopting better ways of living including the development of houses, settlements and ritual practices, and the use of more efficient pottery and weapons. There were three major developments: the domestication of cattle and sheep; the introduction of horse-back riding and heavy-wheeled vehicles;[13] and the spread of cattle and sheep herds east of the Ural Mountains after 4,000 BP; together with the development of metallurgy and mining, horse-drawn chariots, and Indo-Iranian rituals which were widely adopted in the new region.[14]

She argues that it was the Yamna horsemen of 5,500–4,500 BP who, when moving to invade new territories, utilised oxen to haul ponderous solid-wheeled wagons and carts which were capable of transporting their families and enough supplies to live for long periods in distant lands. They eventually became so mobile that their settlements gradually disappeared from their homelands. They were the first to mine steppe copper ores, and make tanged daggers, pins, flat axes, and metal staffs and clubs, using arsenical bronze metal, and also used iron for daggers and pins, developments which did not reach China until 3,500 BP.

As Marlene Derlet has explained earlier (p. 30), study of Indo-European language families has provided a good deal of information in recent years about the Proto-Indo-Europeans. For example, the breeding of cattle and animal domestication and herding was extremely important as shown by the use of words specifically for horses, cattle, pigs and goats. That the people lived among mountains is indicated by the many words for mountains and hills; and there were words for certain trees and plant life found in the European and Middle Eastern countryside. Linguistic evidence suggests they also knew about the sea and were familiar with ships and watercraft.

In 2005, two other proposals were presented as to why the emergence of violent patriarchal forces occurred: James DeMeo's geographical explanation; and Heide Göettner-Abendroth's theory which considers men's character traits and defects as the reason for patriarchy.

James DeMeo (2009)[15] has studied global patterns of social violence, linked these with prehistoric periods of climate change and argues that this affected family life, sexuality, child-rearing methods and women's status. He confirms the presence of peaceful egalitarian societies lasting until between 6,000 and 4,000 BP, when they changed into male-dominant cultures as a result of severe and repeated drought conditions which turned wet and fertile lands into arid plains. The most abrupt changes took place in northern Africa, the Near East, and central Asia between 6,000 and 5,300 BP, resulting in "famine, starvation, and mass migrations among subsistence-level cultures", which in turn disrupted child–adult and male–female bonds, and increased "patrist attitudes, behaviours and social institutions."[16]

It is interesting that James DeMeo's map of the diffusion of violence closely resembles Marija Gimbutas's and others' point of origin for the Proto-Indo-Europeans and their outward movements into other regions. The biggest problem with his argument is that the experiences of Australian Indigenous people do not support such evidence. They adapted early to frequent changing climates on the Australian continent, and for over 80,000 to 100,000 years, adapted their lifestyles as the climate changed, yet they maintained their peaceful egalitarian way of life very successfully until interrupted by the European invasion 200 years ago. They continue to maintain it where they can today. In fact, Indigenous academic Eve Fesl says that the people had comfortable lifestyles in good health, and had no need to move beyond their own country except to attend seasonal festivals (such as that of the emergence of the Bogong moth, for the harvesting of Bunya pine nuts, or seasonal eel trapping).[17]

The story in the Americas is somewhat similar, although contact with the Chinese at 4,000 BP did have minor influences within the whole of the Americas. The major changes came with the Spanish invasion 500 years ago. They too, had to adjust to changing climates and desertification for over 13,000 years of living their peaceful matrilineal, matriarchal lifestyles.

Heide Göettner-Abendroth (2009)[18] argues against the Gimbutas scenario, citing biological paternity, technical innovation, cattle herding, division of labour, and men's character defects[19] as cause for the rise of patriarchy. She concludes that although the theory of Marija Gimbutas was well documented, she "could not convincingly explain how this [Indo-European] nomadic culture actually developed, and how it became patriarchally organised."[20] However linguists, geneticists, and other archaeologists support Marija Gimbutas's thoroughly researched theory.

Heide Göettner-Abendroth puts forward six points explaining the origins of patriarchy and the recognition of paternity:

- Droughts in central and western Asia 6,000–7,000 years ago forced entire societies to move in order to survive; this happened very slowly, and probably led to the breaking-down of matriarchal agricultural practices.
- The men reverted to hunter-gathering in order to survive, leaving the female clans to manage to support themselves through agriculture, a move which eventually

demoted women, but increased men's importance. Undisciplined groups of men migrated to the west or south, taming and riding horses. However, this did not yet lead to patriarchy.[21]

- Continued drought forced people of southern Russia to move onto lands near the Black Sea, eastern Europe and northern India, lands which were already occupied by many people.

- So the newcomers had two choices: either to turn back to the steppe, thereby risking hunger and death, or to proceed on into already occupied lands, for the first time using armed force. Thus the reason behind the Indo-European invention of invading and war-making was "a need to survive."[22]

After 5,000 BP:

- Conquering the new regions required power over the indigenous inhabitants by the invading strangers which resulted in the invention of rulers (upper classes) and the ruled (lower classes). Heide Göettner-Abendroth says: "At this point patriarchy begins" as does male domination, along with "patriarchal consciousness."[23]

- Warrior-kings dominated and ruled, "[m]atriarchal clans were destroyed" (re-placed by patriarchal clans) and women became valued only for their birth-giving abilities: this was the beginning of the inventing of paternity issues and "patriarchal genealogy, so powerful in patriarchal societies."[24]

However, we suggest that this explanation still does not account for the fact that Australian Indigenous people, who came to Australia 50,000–100,000 years ago, also experienced extreme weather and catastrophic geological events over time, yet developed ways to survive by living co-operatively, and using sets of rites and obligations within a social structure where both patriliny (patriarchy) and matriliny (matriarchy) were successfully combined. Conflicts were communally resolved without the use of extreme violence or wholesale killing and there were no powerful rulers. It should also be mentioned that Australian Indigenous people developed methods of birth control very early, and never allowed population build-up on their lands, so that there was never a need to take over other people's land. Their spiritual relationship with their own land, and their careful concern to be good neighbours with surrounding groups, also contributed to peaceful relations.

Recent new evidence suggests that outside influences brought the dingo with them at some time between 4,000 and 18,000 BP, but otherwise it seems this way of life persisted more or less unchanged until the arrival of the Indo-European (English) invaders just over 200 years ago.[25]

Interesting information has also been provided by indigenous matrilineal societies still extant today in many parts of the world, who shared their cultures at the 2nd World Congress on Matriarchal Studies held in San Marcos, Texas, in 2005. The first (groundbreaking) World Congress on Matriarchal Studies (2003) was held in Luxembourg and "brought together for the first time international scholars who had previously been working on this issue in relative isolation from each other."[26]

Early Indo-European society

Linguistic evidence shows that the Proto-Indo-Europeans were patrilineal and patriarchal and ruled by a warrior chief or king, according to James Mallory (1989).[27] Marija Gimbutas (1991) records Indo-European languages and kinship terminology as providing ample

1

2
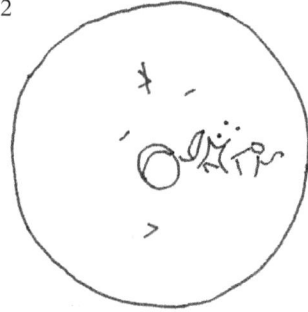

3
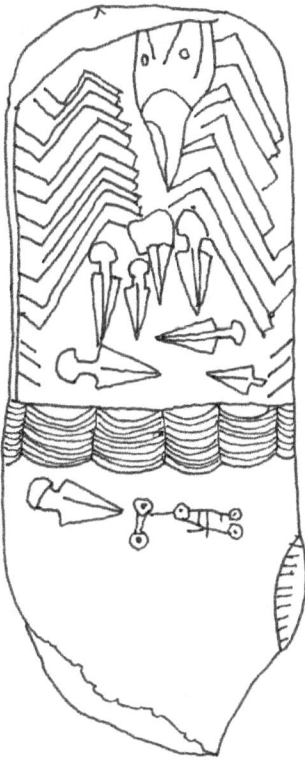

4

5

EARLIEST WARRIOR EQUIPMENT

1. *Clay model cart*, Budapest, 5,000 BP
2. *Engraved amber disc*, 5,000 BP
3. *Carved stone warrior god*, Italy, 5,000 BP
4. *Breast plate*, Bohemia, 5,500 BP
5. *Etched boat on pot*, Yugoslavia, 7,500 BP
   (Source: Gimbutas, Marija, 1991)
   All line drawings © Judy Foster, 2013

evidence of Indo-European patriliny, patrilocality and patripotency. Tribes included small mobile patrilocal families whose men had to marry outside their own group. Women's status depended on their association with male relatives, as they had no rights of their own. As the ideology of the Indo-Europeans took hold of the Old European cultures, Neolithic women lost their influence and were regarded as private property, and from that time forward women were regarded as male possessions. As C. Knight (1991)[28] explains, in women-centred societies blood relationships are basic and indestructible wherein all are equal and all human life is respected. In patriarchal societies the link between husband and wife, "between the ruler and ruled",[29] is more important than blood ties: male authority, female obedience, as well as hierarchy, predominate. These views were to transform the status of women everywhere over the following centuries and they became 'private property' in the new trading and raiding societies.

Early Indo-European religion

Central to the Indo-European culture was the 'god of the shining sky'. As Jacquetta Hawkes (1968)[30] has noted, because the forests were so dark, the warriors were very aware of the bright sun above, and the powers of nature which always seemed to come from over the mountain ranges; they therefore looked to gods who ruled the skies. Marija Gimbutas explains how the ideas of 'father-sky' and 'mother-earth' have their origins very early in history, as the Proto-Indo-Europeans recognised the god of the shining sky who took over the role of the Old European 'goddess of birth and regeneration'. The 'god of thunder' is late Indo-European, evolving with the emergence of class societies among the tribes. Language evidence tells us that this god could be found high in the sky or on mountain tops, on high rocks or on the top of the tallest trees. The 'sun god' was also important as a merciless force in desert conditions, and people living in these areas made sacrifices pleading for a milder sun and more moist conditions for growing food. But those living in colder northern Europe wanted more sunshine, and held important solar festivals in honour of the sun god every year in spring and summer. The fecundity of the thunder god was thought to be transferred by the touch of an axe to awaken nature. Opposite the thunder god of the skies was the 'god of the underworld kingdom of death', deep beneath the earth.

The new Indo-European societies no longer revered the earth-mother as the source of new life, but considered that male warrior gods created and ended life.[31] The roles of the self-generating goddesses were gradually reduced to those of ordinary brides, wives, and daughters, who were now viewed as erotic sexual love objects in the new patriarchal, patrilinear cultures. Marija Gimbutas notes a few exceptions, such as Irish 'Brigit' and Baltic 'Laima' ('Birth and Life Giver', 'The Fate', or 'Three Fates') who retained their powers.

The Old European goddesses were disempowered and their temples disappeared along with their sacred signs and vessels and most of their images, a movement beginning in east-central Europe and soon spreading all over central Europe and beyond. The Aegean Islands, Crete, and the west Mediterranean continued worship of a female deity for a time and on Crete it lasted until well into the Bronze Age before going underground. According to Marija Gimbutas there became a gradual mix of two different symbolic systems: the matristic and the androcentric. Because the Indo-European ruling class were androcentric, it became the norm to recognise it as the 'official' belief system of Old Europe. These new

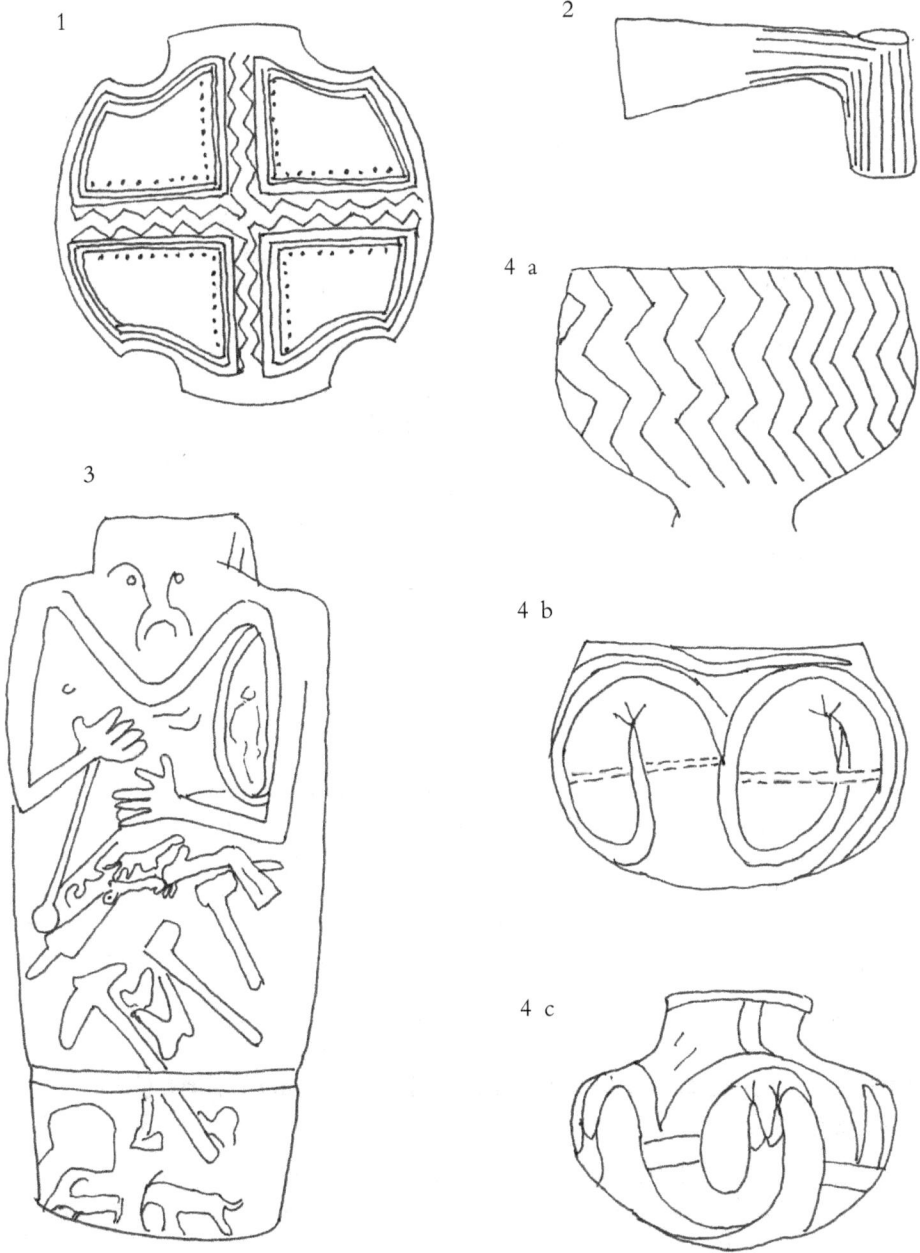

INDO-EUROPEAN WEAPONS AND POTTERY

1. *Royal burial shield*, Kurgan, 6,000 BP
2. *Silver axe*
3. *Thunder god*, Maikop, 6,900 BP
4. *Three Indo-European bowls with zigzag and snake designs*, Germany, 7,000–6,500 BP
(Source: Gimbutas, Marija, 1991)

All line drawings © Judy Foster, 2013

systems, although they may have since experienced some minor changes, remain with us to this day, and are so much part of the warrior culture and society that we find it hard to believe they were ever different.

Early Indo-European ritual burials

The numerous remains in burials of the Proto-Indo-Europeans shows they had predominantly more massive and robust features than the graceful finely-boned Balkan Neolithic people, and were also taller than the populations with whom they integrated, according to James Mallory (1989). Burial customs reveal that this warrior-hunter society was the earliest example of a hierarchical culture. One particular burial was that of an upper-class child who was accompanied by elaborate grave goods including a dagger (which was apparently an unusual inclusion in a child's grave), along with bones of sacrificed horses and cattle. There were no sacrificial graves anywhere in the world before this time.

The first known offensive weapons were daggers up to 56 centimetres long with flint or quartzite blades inset each side of the bone shafts. They were usually buried with the warriors who used them and such graves sometimes included personal possessions such as metal spiral rings. Marija Gimbutas records largely unchanged burial traditions which were similar over a huge area in later periods. Graves now included pottery, egg-shaped with out-turned rims, along with weaponry and tools. As the warrior hunters moved into Old Europe, they brought back goods such as the copper and gold objects made by the Neolithic agriculturalists which they had buried with them. For the first time ritual suttee, the sacrifice of a wife or mistress, appeared alongside the sacrificed horse in elite male graves.

The earliest Indo-European graves found in Old Europe date from 6,500 BP, and were almost exclusively male burials. Their tombs were cairns or earth-covered, used only for elite warriors and included their favourite weaponry, spear, bow and arrow, and flint dagger or long knife. Single grave sites in Neolithic Ireland are thought by Michael O'Kelly (1989)[32] to have been private burials containing the remains of a wealthy or important (male) person. They marked the arrival of the first few Indo-European warriors who had lived alongside the passage tomb people but kept their own distinct culture. As Marija Gimbutas points out, the appearance of single-male burials under small round mounds in eastern Ireland and central England directly contrasts with the local practice of communal burials.

Early Indo-European invasions and the beginning of the Warrior Age

People appear to have lived predominantly peaceful lives throughout the Palaeolithic and Neolithic eras worldwide since there is almost no evidence to the contrary. That is not to say that the societies were trouble-free, but any discord would likely have been quickly settled through methods of conflict resolution, as in the case with Australian Indigenous cultures. For example, there is evidence of one or two isolated instances of violence against people in Africa in the Palaeolithic era, according to David Phillipson (1995)[33] who cites evidence of one rare occurrence of a number of violent deaths which was found in a cemetery at Qadan in the Nile Valley dating to the period between 18,000 and 11,000 BP. He suggests this may have been the result of over-population of the area caused by social or political pressures, or competition for resources. At 13,000 BP, in Italy at one site, an arrow-like flint flake was embedded in the pelvis of an adult female; at a second site, an arrow was found in the vertebra of a child buried at Balzi Rossi. Paul Bahn (1998)[34] records these two European examples as the only known instances of inter-human violence during this period.[35]

Evidence today suggests that Indo-Europeans spread extensively around the world, causing abrupt changes as they invaded or infiltrated Europe, Asia and Africa. As the southern Russian warrior cultures expanded into Old Europe, the refined skills of the Neolithic agriculturists disappeared and were replaced by the more crude Indo-European technology. Marija Gimbutas lists the changes, including: the cessation of temple building; the creation of finely-crafted vases, sacrificial containers, temple models, altars, and sculptures; and use of the sacred script. General evidence of violence, such as the presence of war weapons, and the remains of people murdered with spears or axes, first appears 6,500 years ago. All settlements were now fortified against enemies, a practice which had been unknown in the peaceful Neolithic societies.

The disappearance of the Sesklo and Vinča cultures in Eastern Europe after 6,300 BP was the result of the earliest invasions by the Proto-Indo-Europeans. The chiefs used mounted and armed warriors to fight land owners, and gradually moved out of their homelands to invade lands belonging to their gentle unarmed Neolithic farming neighbours in Europe, eventually spreading further afield to China in the east, south to India and beyond. Some invasions occurred somewhat later, for example, at 4,500 BP in Ireland, and 3,450 BP in Crete. We note that invasions/infiltration in India, China and East Asia did not occur until after 4,000 BP, and as recently as 2,500 BP in countries such as Thailand, Indonesia and the Pacific region.

Africa, across the Mediterranean Sea from Anatolia, is a later example which illustrates the changes Indo-European invaders brought about. Frank Willett (1995)[36] describes northern African life from about 8,200 BP when agriculturists kept cattle, goats and sheep, made pottery, polished stone axes, grindstones, engraved images on stones, and painted cave walls with pastoral scenes. He notes a change which abruptly took place sometime after 3,200 BP when after the arrival of mounted warriors, the practice of engraving ceased in this part of Africa, and the content of the paintings changed. He states that "these paintings seem to reflect Cretan influence not only in the style of the drawings (such as the flying gallop of the horses) but the weapons too are Cretan."[37] Here he is clearly describing the invasion of the Sahara via the Chariot Road coming from Tripoli to Gao on the Niger River by Cretan horsemen after the end of the Minoan period in Crete. Frank Willett emphasises that African paintings before 3,200 BP contained peaceful content, while later less skilful paintings depicted subjects such as battle scenes. David Phillipson argues that after 3,200 BP villages surrounded by defensive stone walls began to be located on high ground away from the banks of lakes and rivers.

Tangible evidence for Indo-Europeans in China 4,000 years ago

Elizabeth Barber (1999) reports intriguing new examples of perhaps the earliest evidence of movements of Indo-Europeans from Europe into Western China which, although first discovered in 1900 CE, was not properly examined until the 1980s by Victor Mair who found the mummified bodies displayed in a museum in Urumqi, a city in Uigur region. The 4,000-year-old mummies were of a number of people of Caucasian origins who had

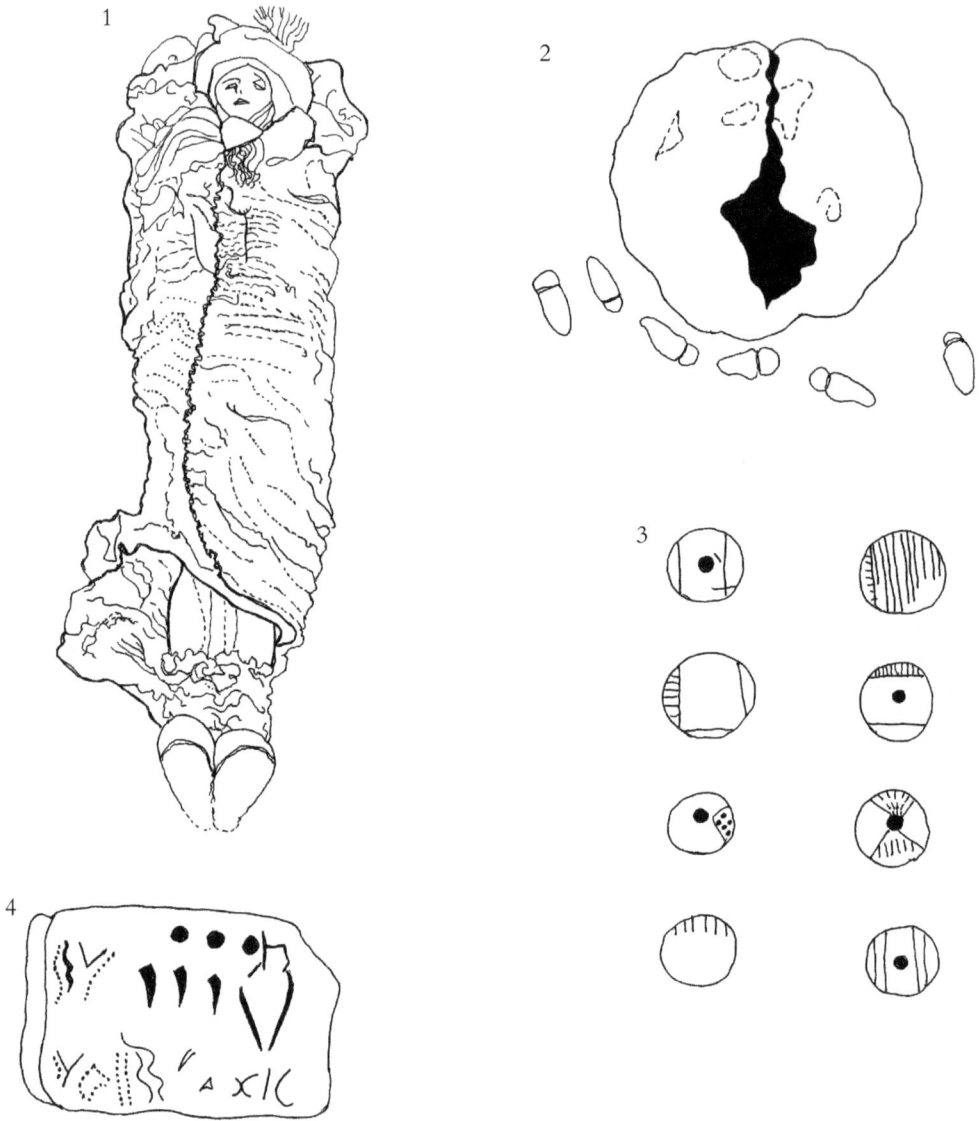

A LOULAN BURIAL, TOKENS

1. A 4,000-year-old *female mummy* similar to those described by Elizabeth Barber (1999) at Urumchi, north-west China (Source: Wade, Nicholas, 17 March 2010)
2. The *clay tokens* which archaeologists often ignored, discovered by Denise Schmandt-Besserat (1996). This example is a 6,000-year-old clay 'envelope' from Iraq in which 6 incised clay tokens were kept. (See also Fig. 3)

3. *Early clay discs*, some perforated, from Iraq, 6,000 BP
4. According to Denise Schmandt-Besserat, this incised tablet from Iran features an account of 33 jars of oil (?) and is about 5,300 years old. She argues that tokens like these led to the first writing.

(Source 2–4: Schmandt-Besserat, Denise, 1996)

All line drawings © Judy Foster, 2013

been discovered buried in hollowed-out tree trunks or curved wooden coffins, graves marked by groups of tall burial poles set in the Taklamakan desert, the salty sands having perfectly preserved their remains, their clothes and any items buried with them. The people were tall, with blond, red or dark hair, with some men wearing beards. DNA tests suggested they were of Indo-European origin, possibly Tokharian-speakers.

These people, who were known as the Loulan, Cherchen and the Hami, had apparently belonged to the Bronze Age since some metal objects were found with them, and had probably migrated in three waves from the west. Elizabeth Barber explains that the first wave of Loulan people 'pioneered' what was to become known as the Silk Road from Europe to China 1,000 years later. The Cherchen people led the second wave; and the Hami people formed the third wave. The Hami were the ancestors of the present Uigur people who are of Caucasian descent. Inscriptions written in the ancient Indo-European-based Tokharian language which was spoken by the Hami are to be found in early Chinese written records, but the Tokharian people were gradually assimilated into the surrounding tribes and by the 10th century CE had disappeared.

Loulan was situated in about the middle of the Tarim Basin, Hami in the north, and Cherchan further south. The Tarim Basin itself is in western China, north of Tibet and India, directly east of the Black Sea and the homelands of the Proto-Indo-Europeans. So it is easy to see how these people would have moved east towards China, passing en route through or around the Tarim Basin.

Besides the Caucasian appearance of the mummies, there are two other reasons for assuming these people came from the west. The mummies from Loulan had among their grave goods items such as a winnowing tray, and a basket, inside which were a few grains of wheat. The staple food of northern China was millet, while in Mesopotamia wheat and barley were grown. Elizabeth Barber thus concludes that because of the Loulan woman's basket with wheat grains, her winnowing tray, her woollen garments and her Caucasian features, her origins must have been from within an early central Asian culture.

The second source of evidence was the width and style of fabric worn by the mummies and studied by Elizabeth Barber. Egyptian weavers used portable horizontal looms which would have produced similar woven fabrics, so these people must have come from the west. This proves the migration took place later than 6,000 BP in the Near East which is when sheep developed woolly coats. They were most likely to have been semi-nomadic herders of sheep, but must have stayed in one place long enough to grow an annual crop of wheat. Arrows in the grave suggest they also hunted game such as wild boar, antelope, hares, ducks, geese and swans which all lived in the vicinity of the rivers they would have followed.

The most remarkable aspect of the finds was the beautifully crafted clothes worn by the people found preserved in the sand. Their simple wraps, moccasins and woollen puttees were skilfully made with plainly coloured simple weaves. Elizabeth Barber describes the women's costumes as including under-girdles (or skirts?) with hanging strands which may have indicated their motherhood status, and the men wore fringed waist sashes covering and emphasising the genital area. The Hami and Cherchen clothes were more elaborate with sleeved shirts, sheepskin boots, coats and trousers featuring zigzag, spiral, and striped designs in brilliant colour combinations. The Cherchens also wore hats. At Hami, twill plaids and tartans similar to Celtic fabrics were found. Elizabeth Barber explains how closely these fabrics resembled similar plaid twills found in Upper Austria where they had been preserved in the Halstatt Bronze Age salt mines. She deduces that these tartan fabrics had been woven by ancestors of the Celts, an Indo-European group linguistically related to the ancient Tokharians, thus demonstrating a relationship between the central Asian mummies and the Proto-Celts of Europe.

Burials were single or in families. Loulan men's graves were deep, and featured wooden posts which formed circles around their separate grave sites. In one grave, three women who were buried with a man showed no signs of violent deaths, and therefore were not the victims of suttee. It is thought they were more likely to have died as a result of an epidemic or some other catastrophe. Elizabeth Barber mentions that later graves, 3,000 years old, included a "saddle with bone buckles, a bridle with an iron bit, [and] a horse's leg stuffed with reeds"[38] indicating horse-riding. Some of the women wore tall, pointed hats similar to witches' hats. Small bundles of a stimulant, the ephedra plant, were also found in the graves suggesting they may have been placed there as part of the burial ritual. This could also indicate that they were shamans or wise women skilled in medicine.

The grave of a three-month-old baby included a carved wooden spindle decorated with spirals. According to Elizabeth Barber, the body was also accompanied by "a small cow's horn cup and what may be the world's earliest preserved nursing bottle, fashioned, nipple and all, from the udder of a sheep."[39] When filled with milk and tied at the end, it formed a baby's bottle complete with teat.

In this chapter we have noted some of the different theories put forward as to the reasons for the complex movements made by many different people around the old world over a long period of time, and how this related to the radical social changes which eventuated. The scenario Marija Gimbutas proposed as to the changes from peaceful communal prehistoric cultures to violent patriarchal class-based societies has much supporting evidence from linguists and other specialists. However, we need to keep an open mind and be aware that new evidence is appearing all the time which may change the story, the ending of which we may never know.

CHAPTER 9

THE FIRST CHANGES TO WOMEN'S STATUS

The new male-dominant culture with its subordination of women was the result of a number of emerging activities stemming from the domestication and taming of the horse. Men became more powerful as they kept ever-larger herds, leading to the need for more land, which in turn allowed greater production, and a larger surplus. More surplus goods led to individual ownership of goods and services, a class system and more male power. The most powerful men controlled those with less power, and all women.

Women's status: Equality or oppression?

Women's inferior status under patriarchy has always been constructed as biologically and 'naturally' based, but both Marija Gimbutas (1991)[1] and Leila Ahmed (1992)[2] argue that archaeological evidence shows women were well respected before the rise of urban societies, but lost their status as archaic states arose. The decline in women's status is also revealed by evidence gathered from mythology and oral traditions in early written history. Elizabeth Barber (1994)[3] uses the design of prehistoric weaving looms and equipment, as well as the variety of textiles which have survived over the millennia to further support this theory.

As we have already seen, there is little doubt that the presence of a single powerful goddess (or multiple goddesses), together with the high status of women, is strongly suggested through the mythological strata which can be traced back to the early Bronze Age and further into the distant past, and there is significant evidence that myths, as we now know them, most often began with the first historical dynasties. Hilda Davidson (1998)[4] gives examples of myths which indicate the equality of female and male gods in the Neolithic period. Women usually needed to be near their home base because of childbearing and rearing responsibilities and caring for the old; for practical reasons they took on work which could be performed near the centre of the home, work which did not endanger small children, and could be resumed after any interruption. Through mythology Hilda Davidson traces evidence of women's skills and knowledge including care of domesticated animals, grain growing and harvesting, spinning, weaving, and embroidery, as well as domestic and communal work.

Elizabeth Barber remarks on the status of Palaeolithic women, specifically in reference to the string apron of the female deity of Lespugne, that her clothing is symbolic rather than utilitarian, suggesting the importance of women's work. Women worked together close to their homes while men could be more mobile. The ornately woven and decorated textiles indicate that women had plenty of time in which to experiment, design and make their increasingly complex and beautiful fabrics during the Neolithic period, a situation which was later to change radically in the Bronze Age. From then on women had to labour long hours as slaves at such tedious occupations as field work and weaving production owned by powerful male individuals. Elizabeth Barber gives the example of Minoan women who were free to create beautiful textiles in Crete, a peaceful place with ample resources to live in comfort. Women looked after their gardens and weaving, while men hunted, fished and traded in distant lands. So it was not surprising that the women had time and energy to make beautiful fabrics. This implies that Neolithic women and men enjoyed equality despite differences in their roles.

Archaeologist Nicholas Platon (1990),[5] while working in Crete, found that the standard of living seemed to have been high for everyone in Knossos as he did not find any houses of poor standard. This suggests that there was equality in Knossos society at that time. Furthermore, worship of the creative and peaceful female deity meant people enjoyed harmony, respected laws and hated tyranny. Personal ambition was unknown; artists did not claim authorship of their work; male exploits were not recorded.

Leila Ahmed observes that there were other centres in the Middle East, such as Mesopotamia, Elam, Egypt, as well as Crete, Greece and Phoenicia, which also provided literary proof of an important goddess or goddesses, and where all women enjoyed elevated status until around 4,000 BP. James Mellaart (1989)[6] explains that in the case of Anatolia, although the goddess religion became demoted with the arrival of 'higher' religions (those of the in-coming Indo-Europeans) it never fully disappeared but lived on in the minds of peasants and others lacking wealth and political influence (including women, of course) who were ignored and thus able to continue following the rules of the goddess. James Mellaart goes on to state that these were the people who kept the goddess narratives/symbolism alive and strong, some aspects of which are still recognised in Anatolia today, and featured on Anatolian kilims which women still weave, although the original meanings of the imagery have not survived.

Agriculture and women's status

Women's status is generally assumed to have begun to deteriorate with the invention and development of agriculture by men. However, Margaret Ehrenberg (1989)[7] argues that agriculture was more likely to have been developed by women since foraging had been their occupation in hunter-gatherer societies.[8]

Mircea Eliade (1991)[9] suggests that inherited skills of women passed down to daughters, enhanced women's social and economic position, giving them a new power, although he does not say when this might have occurred. Because women were responsible for plant domestication they had status as natural owners of the cultivated fields leading to such practices as, for example, matrilocation, wherein husbands live in wives' houses. Yet women had experienced equal status already throughout the Palaeolithic period. Furthermore, with the expansion of communities into new settlements, women, since they were the repositories of specialised knowledge, would have decided where these settlements might be placed, such as being close to a water supply in positions with favourable soil for crop growing.

According to Margaret Ehrenberg, early Neolithic farming or crop cultivation, involving the use of simple technology including hoes and digging sticks, was defined as 'horticulture'. Margaret Ehrenberg describes the later use of ploughs, for tilling the soil in preparation for crop growing, as 'agriculture'. Late in the Neolithic period, with the use of ploughs pulled by domesticated animals, men shifted the emphasis from horticulture to mechanised agriculture, thus taking over the control of farming from women. This is the commonly held view promoted by conservative archaeologists. However, Marija Gimbutas (1991)[10] stresses that although men may have become more involved in mechanised agriculture, women remained in control of such practices as planting times, until after the Indo-European invasions.

Farming and urbanisation

Marija Gimbutas explains how settlements now grew into towns, and there were more of them. More villages formed with the increasing utilisation of the land, and social organisation became more refined. As time went on, agricultural and animal-raising technologies gradually improved. More specialised crops included wheat, linseed, and barley, and there was indirect evidence of ploughing. Regional traditions with diverse symbolic images developed from the original Neolithic culture and a new specialisation in copper metallurgy and other crafts took place. There was much evidence of strong religious beliefs, but no sign of the emergence of a new hierarchy and associated violent practices as would have been the case had men taken full control of farming.

The growth of animal domestication led to the 'Neolithisation' of the western coastal Mediterranean region. Sheep, goats, and pigs were among the main domestic animals. In southern France, around 10,000 BP, the people gradually began to specialise in the cultivation of pulse crops and greens. There were many reasons why these developments came about, such as improved climatic conditions, more settled fishing and shell-gathering communities and the natural environment.

Marija Gimbutas argues that the effects of ever-increasing urbanisation which came about after invasion/contact by the Indo-Europeans resulted in the gradual loss of women's knowledge of sustainable practices and their management of natural resources, and as a consequence, their status.

The beginning of the decline in women's status

Margaret Ehrenberg is convinced that when agriculture and settled urban life became the norm this led to the possession of surplus goods, which people began to store and/or exchange. But there is nothing in the archaeological record to show that the surplus was anything but communal at this time.

However, one of the biggest changes which characterises the distinction between the Neolithic and the Bronze Ages was the loss of equality for women. Leila Ahmed (1992) identifies the chief reason for this loss as the necessity for more (farming) labour power. Women were 'stolen' to provide labour power in early patriarchal societies, and tribes also abducted women because of their sexual and reproductive capacity which became the first 'property'.[11]

In the Neolithic period food and valuables had been communally owned and would have been recorded, stored, managed and distributed by women from a central point such as a temple or other communal building. This practice continued in the early part of the Indo-European period when household management and administration was women's work. Women had always been keepers of records and Tikva Frymer-Kensky (1992)[12] argues that they were therefore most likely to have been the inventors of writing, as they made and used inscribed clay tokens when recording aspects of goods and services or livestock numbers.

Denise Schmandt-Besserat (1996)[13] is convinced that the use of tokens was invented by patriarchal male farmers and merchants, but this attribution overlooks women's long involvement with horticulture and early agriculture. As Tikva Frymer-Kensky comments, women had always been the 'wise ones', leaders in the 'cultural arts', such as weaving, making garments, teaching young children, and the cultivation of plants useful for medicinal and other purposes, all of which required technologically sophisticated knowledge.

Tikva Frymer-Kensky explains that during the early part of the first thousand years of recorded history, the Sumerians and the Akkadians, two distinct peoples who spoke different languages but wrote their histories in Sumerian, intermingled with each other. The writings of this period give us an idea of women's status early in the Indo-European period. She mentions the gifted and politically astute Enheduanna, the High Priestess of Ur, and daughter of the Sumerian king, Sargon of Akkad. Enheduanna was considered to be "the Shakespeare of ancient Sumerian literature in that her beautiful compositions [poems and hymns] were studied, copied and recited for more than half a millennium after her death."[14]

Roberta Binkley (1998) describes Enheduanna as "the world's oldest known author whose works were written in cuneiform approximately 4,300 years ago."[15] Her three most important works are:

- *The Exaltation of Inanna* (her major work)
- *In-nin-sa-gur-ra* ('A Hymn to the Goddess Inanna by the en-Priestess Enheduanna')
- *The Temple Hymns.*

Enheduanna writes:

> 139. That which I recited to you at (mid)night
> 140. May the singer repeat it at noon! to you[16]

Gerda Lerner (1986) refers to Enheduanna as 'protohistoric', living as a high priestess during the second of three stages leading to the final demise of the Neolithic period and immediately before the beginning of the patriarchal period, a process which took 2,000 years. She mentions three stages of changes in Sumer (Mesopotamia):

- the emergence of temple-towns 5,000 BP: first changes to women's status occurred
- (first kings) = growth of city-states (4,000–3,000 BP); Enheduanna was prominent during this time, when lower-class women's status was gradually eroding away
- (military/kings) = the development of national states from 3,000 BP onwards. Women were now fully subordinate with low status.[17]

Roberta Binkley stresses that creative women such as Enheduanna speak personally, with authority and power.

Enheduanna and the other early Sumerian writers put gods and goddesses into the Sumerian context where the main deity of the city could be male or female. At this

EARLY WARRIOR GODDESSES

1. *Early patriarchal goddess Ishtar*, Mesopotamia, 3,800 BP
2. *Inanna-Ishtar, goddess of war* (detail)
3. *Artemis of Greece* (detail)
4. *Athena, warrior goddess*
5. *Goddess of the double axe*, 3,500 BP
All were painted on pots, bowls, etc.
(Source: Baring, Anne and Jules Cashford, 1991)
All line drawings © Judy Foster, 2013

time upper-class Sumerian women were equal to men socially and economically, but later, Akkadian Semitic influences were to gradually 'downgrade' the status of goddesses "in relation to gods and of women in relation to men."[18]

Goddesses defined the role of women within the thought and practice of society; they behaved as all women were expected to behave, and reflected the way society thought all women ought to be. According to Tikva Frymer-Kensky, goddesses not only reinforced society's expectations and gave women a sense of esteem within these roles, but also inhibited any changes, leading to the dichotomy of 'good' (wife) and 'bad' (prostitute) which continues to this day.

She observes that gradually over the first thousand years of recorded history the role of the goddesses – and women – was diminished, along with the status of women, with the balance of power between male and female shifting increasingly toward men. The biggest change to the goddess's power was the loss of her control over the reproductive aspects of humans, animals and agriculture, all of which became attributed to a male god. This marked the beginning of the loss of power of the female principle which continued during the following Sumerian/Mesopotamian periods and beyond.[19]

Leila Ahmed adds that the changes in women's status brought about by the patriarchal warrior newcomers led to an increase in male control and the diminishing of male respect for women's wisdom and nurturing qualities. These ideas heavily influenced Western and Middle-Eastern societies of the time, and even today are alive and well.

The new 'invisibility' of women

Before the advent of patriarchy, generally all societies were matrifocal or matrilineal. Cheikh Diop (1974) provides an example of what he describes as prehistoric traditional matriarchal (matrilineal) African societies, prior to Indo-European invasion and interference:

1. Women have political rights since heredity is matrilineal.
2. The man pays the marriage dowry to the woman/family and the woman is not purchased as a slave.
3. Women can instigate divorce as soon as almost immediately after the marriage if necessary.
4. Women are assigned the least onerous tasks.
5. Women control all aspects of food, therefore they have economic rights.[20]

Some aspects of the great changes which contributed to the invisibility of women are identified by Leila Ahmed (1992) and Gerda Lerner (1986)[21] who argue that separating women into categories of 'respectable' and 'disreputable' was fundamental to the new patriarchal system. A new hierarchy meant people were identified by their 'high' or 'low' *class*. Furthermore, women's class position was dependent upon firstly, their relationship to the men who 'protected' them, and secondly, their sexual relationship to men, rather than their occupation or work.

According to evolutionary biologist Elizabet Sahtouris (1999b),[22] historical records tell us that weapons and wealth gave some men great power, allowing them a world view which rested on the certainty of their own superiority. This resulted in the creation of a new authoritarian and violent male god, who justified the domination and ownership of women to be guarded and sold or exchanged like other goods.

She describes two general changes made by the Indo-Europeans: firstly, they changed the world view, social structure and rules of the existing societies they invaded/infiltrated; and secondly, these new societies engaged in fighting each other, making warriors their heroes, imposing their cultural beliefs upon the conquered, and enslaving them. They defined the role of the goddess as secondary, wife or daughter, to their major god. Sometimes the goddess was completely removed through the construction of new stories in which the god was emphasised and the goddess became a mere troublesome mortal woman, for example, Pandora and Lilith. They also decreed that gods and people were separate from nature, ruled over by one god who was external to nature.

Leila Ahmed and Gerda Lerner summarise the steps during the transition from matrilineal and matrilocal Neolithic societies to patriarchal societies, some of which commenced within Proto-Indo-European cultures before their invasions of Europe and beyond.[23] These run as follows:

1. Men appropriated the sexual and reproductive capacity of women before they introduced the notion of private property and class society. This, Gerda Lerner argues, is the foundation of private property and was the critical step in the change to patriarchy.

2. The clan, and later, the state, became interested in maintaining the patriarchal family.

3. Men began to dominate all members of society by making slaves of conquered women and those men they considered inferior. These first three steps took place during the transition from the Neolithic to the Bronze Age.[24]

Later more gradual changes meant that:

4. State laws were made to enforce women's subordination. Women became economically dependent on the male head of the family; class privileges were awarded to those dependent women of the upper classes who conformed; women were divided into 'respectable' and 'not respectable' categories.

5. Male class and power depended on whether they owned or were employed in the means of production; this meant that the more one owned the more power one gained. This also applied to the amount of land a man owned and controlled. Patriarchal societies became expansionist, and colonisation and warfare to gain extra lands became integral to the prevailing culture. Women's class position and access to material resources depended on their sexual ties. Men owned women's sexuality; and their virginity, because it ensured certainty of paternity, became a valuable trade item for their male owners, and heads of the family.

6. Even though women lost much independence they still fulfilled roles as mediators, (priestesses, seers, diviners and healers).

7. The change to patriarchal societies and royal dynasties marked the breaking down of the peaceful, powerful female deity into numerous goddesses with limited powers. A dominant male 'god of war' then ruled supreme.

8. The emerging Judaic and Islamic monotheistic religions (based on earlier Mesopotamian law) changed the creativity and procreativity of the goddesses and replaced them with a powerful creator/procreator god/king/lord.[25]

9. Women were confined to the private sphere as mere mothers.

Leila Ahmed (1992) speaks of the Arab experience around 5,350 BP where the Egyptian civilisation was remarkably egalitarian with absolute equality in men's and women's laws until the Greek conquest. As the dominant Greek and Roman values and laws spread, Egyptian women gradually lost most of their rights.

The writings of such (Christian) 'church fathers' as Augustine, Origen and Tertullian, for example, were highly influential, reflecting "the concept of the female as inferior, secondary, defined by her biology and useless to men",[26] thus becoming the cause of temptation, corruption and evil. Gerda Lerner confirms that Aristotle's philosophy strongly reinforced the idea of women's subordination.

Leila Ahmed reveals that a polytheist religion arose in Arabia in which there were three important goddesses: al-Lāt, Manāt, and al-ʿUzzā, and various marriage customs. Islam inherited and reaffirmed a male god and the patriarchal family and the subordination of women from Christianity. Leila Ahmed comments that according to Islam, the prophet Muhammad followed in the Judeo-Christian tradition. Many biblical stories, such as those of the creation and fall were incorporated into the Koran. Thus Islamic civilisation rewrote its story, describing past history as 'The Age of Ignorance'. It hid all knowledge of previous civilisations, especially the fact that women in some cultures had enjoyed a higher status before the coming of Islam. Not until Western researchers examined the past to discover the roots of Western 'civilisation' in the Middle East was the history of Islam discovered, and a different way of life revealed to Islamic women.[27]

The role of Indo-European myth and folklore in the diminishment of women

Marlene Derlet gives an overview of other long lasting effects of the new Indo-European warrior ideologies which emerged in a changing focus in the myths and folklore away from the female to the male. Gods now became more powerful than the numerous goddesses with considerably diminished power who had replaced the great goddess of the Palaeolithic and Neolithic periods. Since the gods (and some goddesses) were warriors, revenge and battles were now featured in myth and folklore literature.

Although women still featured in some rituals and myth, their position changed too. Their roles gradually diminished and were mostly associated with agricultural and home-based rituals. However, men were the heroes and therefore the major focus.

This new emphasis is perhaps best explained with a look at the meanings of legends and folklore and the way women's powers were diminished and women came to be viewed in a less favourable light in the Warrior Age.

Customs and rituals: Fear of women

Many customs and rituals, especially in regard to human and vegetal fertility, have survived from prehistoric times, and in some parts of the world are still practised. Jane Harrison (1913/1978)[28] records some examples of those relating to the earliest historic goddesses of Sumeria and Egypt, where the prehistoric goddesses' roles were gradually eroded to be replaced by the activities of male gods during the spring/summer vegetation rituals. Anne Baring and Jules Cashford (1991) tell us that one of the earliest images of Inanna, the

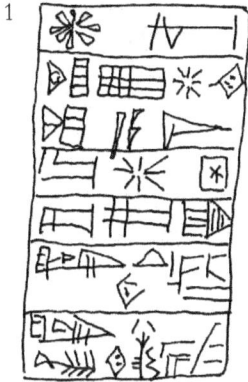

MORE INDO-EUROPEAN IMAGERY

1. *Sumerian script*, 4,100 BP
2. *The Sacred Marriage*, Herakleion, 3,700 BP
3. *Journey from the Underworld*, Sumerian, 5,300 BP (Ship-of-the-dead image?)
4. *Isis, an Egyptian goddess*, c. 5,000 BP
5. *Europa and the Bull*, Archaic Greek, 2,600 BP
   (Source: Baring, Anne and Jules Cashford, 1991)
   All line drawings © Judy Foster, 2013

137

Sumerian 'goddess of spring', "queen of the sky, earth and underworld"[29] depicts her wearing lunar horns on her head, a reference to the importance of the phases of the moon in these rituals.

Enheduanna, the Sumerian high priestess mentioned earlier in this chapter who was devoted to Inanna/Ishtar, must have understood these goddesses in both roles – in their earlier 'spring/new life' role, and their later 'regenerative/death' role as she wrote her poems part-way through this transformative period. In her major work *The Exaltation of Inanna*, Enheduanna is connected with Inanna, a goddess of life and love, whom she considered equal to the Sumerian god An. She also depicts Inanna, as a goddess of battle who keeps humanity in check, thus uniting Inanna with the 'warlike' Akkadian goddess Ishtar.[30] Having later been exiled from Uruk, Enheduanna implores the 'moon god' Nanna, to help her, and exalts Inanna "to equal status with the supreme god of pantheon, An."[31]

Anne Baring and Jules Cashford maintain that the prehistoric goddess Ishtar began as a 'goddess of love, life and joy' in early history, but later changed into a 'warrior goddess', so powerful as to "overturn mountains … bringing fear to the heart and destruction to those named as enemies."[32] At the same time, as a priestess and as a woman, Inanna "had to watch the destruction of people, temple and sacred rites"[33] (perhaps a reference to the gradual erosion of women's status at the time).

It was interesting (but perhaps not unexpected) to find that Enheduanna's poem was only translated as recently as 1968 so she would not have been found in earlier literature. Roberta Binkley comments that her works "foreshadow her own history and the history of women in religion, literacy, and western civilisation for the next 4,800 years."[34] As Enheduanna wrote:

> 70. They approach the light of day, about me, / the light is obscured
> 71. The shadows approach the light of day, / it is covered with a (sand) storm.[35]

Jane Harrison (1913/1978) provides an early historic version of the 'spring' myths where Ishtar's young lover, Adonis (or Tammuz), 'the true son' and 'god of spring', dies and passes into the earth "to the place of dust and death."[36] Inanna's role is not mentioned in this version. Jane Harrison explains that yearly rites celebrated the death of Adonis (the dying vegetation) but not the spring growth or harvesting of crops (his resurrection).[37] Ishtar follows him, causing life above and under the earth to cease: "no flower blossomed and no child of animal or man was born."[38]

Another example she gives is that of the Egyptian god Osiris whose effigy was ritually 'planted' into the spring crops (barley, spelt, and flax) and when the crops began to show (his 'body sprouted'), it was dug out of the earth (resurrected).[39] No goddess is mentioned in this story. Jane Harrison (1924/1963) explains that the annual rituals of 'death' and 'resurrection' of food crops "are essentially periodic",[40] emphasising the circular patterns of time; "plants die down in the heat of summer, trees shed their leaves in autumn, all Nature sleeps or dies in winter, [and] awakes in spring."[41]

Marija Gimbutas (1999) mentions Athena, an early historic goddess whose name is not Indo-European, who appears in Mycenaean Crete, and is also known as 'Lady (Mistress) Atana'.[42] She is depicted as the 'stiff white (marble or alabaster) tomb goddess', with her "large life-regenerative pubic triangle"[43] symbolising life and regeneration.

There are two early historic Cretan 'pregnant vegetation goddesses': Ariadne, who married Dionysus; and Demeter, 'goddess of grain and the care of plants' (who went to Greece). Demeter was married to Iasion, an heroic hunter, also known as Triptolemos, who is mentioned in Hesiod's *Theogony*, according to Anne Baring and Jules Cashford.[44] Ariadne 'died annually' along with Dionysus, "in order to bring new fertility in the spring."[45] Demeter symbolised "revived and growing vegetation", and her daughter, Persephone, "the spirit of the grain, [which] dies and is born again." Harvested seeds, stored underground, were 'fertilised' through "contact with the dead."[46]

According to Marija Gimbutas, the Mycenaeans (early Greeks) "glorified war and male warriors held prominence in society."[47] She stresses that they represent the transition from Old European 'gynocentric cultures' and the in-coming male-dominant classical Greek culture. About 3,200 BP, new people from central Europe arrived and overwhelmed Greece and the Aegean Islands, introducing a Dark Age "from which, much later, the classical Greek civilisation arose."[48] All art and artefacts and the Linear B script vanished, although archaic Greek language persisted, as did the same Greek gods and goddesses. Marija Gimbutas emphasises that the most radical change was the diminished role of women, who could no longer take part in all social, political or intellectual activities, and the goddesses "now served male deities"[49] just as Enheduanna had forecast.

A more recent aspect recorded by Marlene Derlet is the reconstruction and the fear of women, and their consequent assigned unimportance, a theme which Clarissa Pinkola Estes takes up in *Women Who Run with the Wolves* (1992).[50] She argues that it is not hard to understand in the Warrior Age "why old forests and old women are viewed as not very important resources. It is not a mystery." Wolves, coyotes, bears and 'wildish women' all "share related instinctual archetypes, and as such, both are erroneously reputed to be ingracious, wholly and innately dangerous, and ravenous."[51]

Women and wolves have many characteristics in common. Clarissa Pinkola Estes lists the following:

- keen sensing
- playful spirit
- heightened capacity for devotion
- deeply intuitive
- relational by nature
- inquiring
- possessed of great endurance of strength
- intensely concerned with their young, their mate and their pack
- have experience in adapting to constantly changing circumstances
- fiercely stalwart and very brave.

And both have been:

- hounded and harassed
- imputed to be devouring and devious, as well as overly aggressive
- less valued [than] their detractors
- targets of those who would clean up the wilds.[52]

Clarissa Pinkola Estes goes on to say that the predation on wolves and women by those who misunderstand them is strikingly similar.

Another example of a wolf myth is Diane di Prima's 'oral epic' poem-cycle entitled *Loba* (the female form of *lobo*, the Spanish word for 'wolf'). According to Gloria Orenstein (1990),[53] Diane di Prima takes a new look at history, literature and myth in this ever-changing poem, which is continually being added to. She is writing it for all the women who remain "oppressed by patriarchal myths."[54] The goddess in the poem is symbolised as 'Wolf Woman', and combines the myths of Artemis, known as the 'Huntress Maid', originally 'Lady of the Wild Things', who is also associated with the bright moon (moonlight), and as "death-dealer ... reflecting the darker underworld side of the Earth Mother";[55] and Hecate, "goddess of the dark phase of the moon, and the underworld, and of dogs"– symbol of death and rebirth.[56]

Gloria Orenstein states that in the Navajo myth, the Native American 'Wolf Woman', who was Wolf Chief's wife, tired of being subordinate, challenges the men into action when she decides not to be mother, wife or servant any longer. Thus Wolf Woman symbolises contemporary women who decide to take control of their lives.[57] Gloria Orenstein relates that she is also Artemis, "the Lady of Wild Things, the Lady of the Beasts", identified with Hecate and with witchcraft. "All wild things were sacred to her."[58]

The 'dark moon goddess' Hecate is only one symbol of the 'goddess of the dark side', which the wolf and others represent in the *Loba* poem. When the 'Wolf Goddess' is confronted by the poet, she is found to have survived as the nurturing protectress, rather than the ferocious hunter. Gloria Orenstein reveals that the dominant theme in the cycle, "the metaphor of the Hunt ... pleads for a return to our human-animal nature ... the sacred animal nature of the Goddess as Lady of the Beasts ..."[59] She points out the main lessons of the cycle:

- Women become connected to "a mythic matrilineage" through women writers, who awake them to their great possibilities.
- Women are enabled to identify with the various depictions of female deities, "heroines and creators of cultures."
- Women re-discover the source of their strength and power within and begin to appreciate the female deities so degraded and demonised by history.
- Through 're-membering' the images of the goddesses and female figurines contemporary women are also transformed.
- Women artists allow other women to be re-energised and strengthened by the re-discovery of their past prehistory.
- Women need to be critical of their past, and recognise the root causes of their loss of status so they are not repeated in the future.[60]

It is notable that for Marija Gimbutas (1999) the Lithuanian goddesses, gods, and spirits were still very much part of her early life, and their nature-based images and rituals remained active "even in the early part of the twentieth century."[61]

The Indo-Europeans and changes to the meanings of symbols

With the ideological changes brought about by the Indo-Europeans Marija Gimbutas (1991) records other radical changes to the systems of visual symbols in the 'new' territories. Yet despite these new powerful influences the female visual symbolism of Old Europe never died out completely, but went underground. Some of the early traditions especially birth, death and earth fertility rituals, have continued until recent times with very little change in some places, while in others they were assimilated into Indo-European ideology. For example, Athena, the Old European 'bird goddess', was now shown wearing a helmet and carrying a shield. In the Bronze Age, the 'owl goddess' carried a sword or dagger in some areas including Sardinia, Corsica, Liguria, southern France and Spain.[62]

The bull (or cow?), an Old European symbol of the source of life and of regeneration so much associated with the female deity, in Indo-Europe became symbolic of the 'thunder god', strength and maleness. The horse which was not known to the Old Europeans since it had earlier become extinct in that region, was for the Indo-Europeans a sacred animal, a symbol of the 'sky god', the 'moon god', the 'god of death and underworld', and the 'dawn goddess'. Gods were often depicted riding horses, or with horses pulling their chariots.[63]

The Old European serpent symbolised benevolence and life energy, while the poisonous snake was symbolic of the 'goddess of death and regeneration'. For the Indo-Europeans, the snake was a symbol of evil and the finality of death, of the 'god of death and the underworld', and adversary of the 'thunder god'. For Christians, snakes are evil and represent 'the devil'; today many people have a hate/fear relationship with them. Yet Indigenous Australian people respect the snake as both life-giving and vengeful, for example, the well-known Rainbow Snake.

Also symbolic of the Indo-European gods were solar motifs, daggers, halberds and other weapons of war. After the invasions of the Indo-Europeans into Neolithic Old Europe symbols of the Neolithic goddess disappeared or their meanings were reversed.[64]

With the arrival of the Indo-Europeans some of the meanings of the main symbolic colours of the Old Europeans were radically changed. Examples of the transition to new meanings include:

- *White* was the colour of bones, and symbolised death without regeneration for the Old Europeans. In today's world this has completely changed to a (Western) understanding that white/light is 'good' (positive), while dark/black is 'bad' (negative). Other colours associated with death were yellow, gold, amber, marble and alabaster. The Indo-European meaning linked these colours with eternal life and the 'god of the shining sky'. White remains the colour of death in some cultures, for example, China and parts of Indigenous Australia.

- The colour *black* became associated with death, a radical change of meaning which today we would argue is a 'natural' response to dark places, yet it was not so in the deep past. While prehistoric people viewed the fertile dark of the regenerative cave as the womb of the Old European goddess, for the warrior societies the cave became symbolic of the finality of death and the evil powers of the underworld, the world of the dead – cold, damp and final – ruled by the Indo-European sovereign male god. For indigenous peoples, death is not feared as final but understood as a passage into another life.

- The *Yellow* Sun. In Old Europe the sun symbolised regeneration. But in Indo-Europe the sun was the all important life-giving symbol of the 'god of the shining sky', who was a 'year god'. He represented the birth of the sun; the young sun of spring; the triumphant sun of summer; and the old sun of autumn. The important new aspect of the sun (light) was that it was 'up there' in that special place away from 'corrupt' earth. In Christian belief 'up there' is the wonderful place of the afterlife which is open to those who fulfil the right conditions.[65]

141

It seems impossible for us today to realise that there could be any other way to react to the symbols described above. We might find it difficult to understand that the people living prior to the Bronze Age warriors were not afraid to descend into the deep dark of sacred caves for rituals of one sort or another. For prehistoric people, the dark cave was a place to get close to one's beginning, so they could spend time creating beautiful paintings and engravings deep underground without concern. The earlier meanings of such powerful symbols merits closer consideration.

CHAPTER 10

INDO-EUROPEAN PHILOSOPHIES: THEIR DEVELOPMENT AND EFFECTS

The philosophies which differentiate prehistoric world views from historic Indo-European (Western) ideologies can help us to comprehend how historical Western peoples have been able to justify their colonisation of territories belonging to 'the other'.[1] The change in focus to a patriarchal emphasis which took place with the entry of the warrior societies into Europe marked the beginning of radically new philosophies where women and nature could be owned and used as men wished, which is why attitudes towards the natural world are an important part of the debate. If attitudes to nature can change, then the position of women can also change. Plato, who is said to be the 'father' of Western philosophy, based his thinking about women and nature on some of the fundamental principles which originated with the pastoralist Proto-Indo-Europeans.

The Pre-Platonic world

Many peoples throughout human history and prehistory have perceived interfunctioning worlds, that is, without clear separation between the material and the immaterial, the physical and the metaphysical. As a result, certain animals, birds, reptiles, sea creatures, the heavens, and even natural features of the earth, such as rocks, hills, and rivers, can be infused with vital force or 'spirit'. Many contemporary ecological activists also understand the world this way. Humans, like all other life forms, are part of the whole living world, and it is arrogant to think otherwise. An understanding of prehistoric philosophies may be revealed by investigating two Indigenous philosophic traditions which, according to their informants, have remained more or less unchanged over the millennia.

Indigenous Australian philosophies

According to Val Plumwood (1993), the 60,000-year-old Indigenous Australian philosophies of nature are remarkably elegant. In these traditions, people understand death as "returning to the earth"[2] within the country from which they came. For the Gagadju people of Kakadu, Indigenous elder Bill Neidjie (1989) explains that continuity rests on their own particular land where their ancestors lived in the past, and from where their descendants will arise. This gives them their human identity; and responsibilities for, and connection with, their land, for the past and for the future: "[T]he land for us never change around, never change."[3]

143

For the Kaititj people of central Australia their land (Country) is not individually owned but is the source of both spiritual and emotional well-being and identity, according to Diane Bell (1983/2002).[4] Both women and men are bound to their land by rituals of reciprocity.

Patricia Baines (1988)[5] explains that for the Nyungar people of the Perth region in Western Australia the land and its life forms are personalised: "Old trees are parents and seedlings are children." Birds and animals, especially those who act differently or look unusual could be deceased ancestors. The land most often is understood as "the body of one's mother." To damage the earth in any way (mining, road making, building fences etc.) is "to cut into one's mother."[6] From a Nyungar perspective, the essential relationship of generation and regeneration is regarded as being shared by all living things, with which the people identify as if they are members of one's family. Thus Nyungar people view the endangering or destruction of any aspects of nature as "murdering ... personalised forms". Living entities such as trees which sheltered past people now represent these old people. The tree becomes an icon, and is the sign of "immanent ancestral presences" because in the past it had shared old people's lives. Certain parts of the landscape are integral to particular rituals and stories.[7]

Diane Bell (1998a)[8] speaks of Ngarrindjeri elder, Doreen Kartinyeri, who explains the reason for her close connection to her land which meant that her people could

> talk to the ancestors, but this relied upon the proper rituals having been observed. In a spiritual and physical sense the land contains the power of the ancestors. To disturb burial sites causes a rupture in the Ngarrindjeri world and it has consequences for the living.[9]

Sarah Milera, when discussing Indigenous Law which forms the basis of Ngarrindjeri philosophy, says as a descendant of that important law, she is unable to talk about certain things except to those with a right to hear, and she has responsibility for their accuracy in the retelling. Val Plumwood (1993) argues that by trying to understand such Indigenous philosophies we may all hope to find a better world view.

In the Americas, the First People fulfilled all the preconditions to create the best conditions for wildlife, for the creation of open plains, and the growing of large trees and forests. Starhawk (2002) reveals:

> Their interaction with the land was so elegantly attuned that European invaders missed it entirely, believing they had found a wilderness untouched by human intervention (and open to exploitation) when what they had actually found was more in the nature of an exquisitely cared-for wild garden.[10]

(The first European invaders thought the same of the Australian landscape when they first saw it.)[11] Starhawk comments that in reality there was no 'untouched' wilderness anywhere except perhaps on very high mountains or on glaciers. It was the Europeans whose preconceived Western superiority and racist ideas led to the creation of the fantasy of the 'virgin' wilderness. The first people everywhere successfully supported their clans in such a way as to preserve their lands, wildlife and vegetation for the future. This way of thinking and acting left behind very little evidence of their long occupation, something that cannot be claimed today.[12]

The earliest Indo-European philosophies

The world views before patriarchy were concerned with nature as the immanent goddess and did not divide nature into "living and non-living parts";[13] for prehistoric people 'non-living' meant something dead which had originally been alive. These ideas lasted until replaced by the Indo-European god who was 'external' to nature, according to Elizabet Sahtouris (1999a)[14] who describes the gradual changes in thinking about women and the human relationship to nature in the 600 years leading up to the emergence of organised religions such as Christianity.

These early scientific thinkers were described as physicists or philosophers. They thought that if they could understand natural order (a *dynamic* natural process) it would reveal to them a better way to order personal and social aspects of human life. Elizabet Sahtouris mentions such thinkers as: Lao-tse and Confucius (China); Vedic Hindus and Gautama Buddha (India); Zoroaster (Persia); and Thales, Anaximander, and Heraclitus (Milesian Greece – Turkey); all of whom understood nature

> as striving to create its own balance and order through an endless dance of opposing forces (dualisms?) such as male and female, light and dark, hot and cold, inward and outward, storm and calm, creation and destruction. In this dance, opposites clashed or simply got out of balance so that things grew, say, too cold or too stormy or otherwise disorderly. Yet somehow new forms and patterns created themselves to bring about new balance and harmony.[15]

They agreed that nature always strives for order and balance rather than chaos, and recognised humans as part of nature. They came to realise that chaos meant a lack of pattern; lawlessness or disorder. Order (the opposite of chaos), was named *kosmos*, the Greek word for 'world' and 'the pattern of things', "orderly rhythms, balance and harmony in the pattern of stars and planets, the cycles of seasons, the beautiful form of plants and animals."[16] These could be interfered with by chaos but then renewed and restored to their former order; for example, old leaves became mulch, restoring soil in which new plants could grow; earlier forms could become new forms in nature's cycle.

Anaximander's teacher, Thales (c. 624–546 BCE) was an early scientist in the Western tradition who observed nature and recognised a pattern of evolution, seeing it as interconnected with everything else and constantly moving towards balance and harmony. According to Elizabet Sahtouris (Western) scientists today are beginning to understand nature in this way. The pre-Socratic Eleatic Greek philosophers from Elea in southern Italy and from Sicily understood a cosmos which was perfectly mathematical in its balance and harmony, and remaining forever unchanged. They held that nature only appeared to be imperfect because people could not see its hidden perfection. Unlike the dynamic philosophies of prehistory, their worldview was static. They considered the Earth as central, with stars and planets revolving around it. There was no kind of evolutionary change, but "a perfect repetition of the same cycles" in the sky and among Earth's creatures. Elizabet Sahtouris notes that some Hindu traditions today understand time and events as cyclic. For those early scientists "everything had been just as it was now from the very beginning of the cosmos."[17] This idea of an unchanging universe was later to re-emerge in Christian thinking.[18]

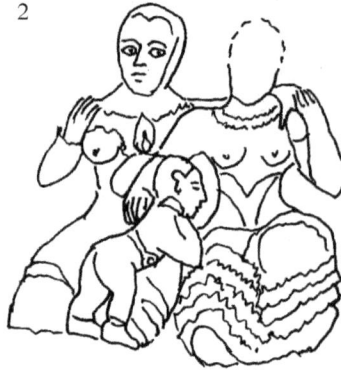

EARLY INDO-EUROPEAN GODDESSES

1. *The goddess Astarte* (detail)
2. *Ivory goddess sculpture*, Mycenae, 3,100 BP
3. *Persephone with dove*, Italy (detail), 2,400 BP
4. *Aphrodite*, sculpture, Graeco-Roman, 2,350 BP

5. *Goddess with the double axe* (detail), Knossos, 4,000 BP
All were painted on pots, bowls, etc.
(Source: Baring, Anne and Jules Cashford, 1991)
All line drawings © Judy Foster, 2013

Plato's philosophy

The Eleatic search for perfection greatly influenced the Greek aristocratic philosopher Plato (c. 428–348 BCE) and was the foundation for his philosophy. Western thinkers and writers continue to admire his work: "[E]ven after 23 centuries Plato's work remains the starting point for the study of logic, metaphysics and moral and political philosophy" states the cover blurb on R.M. Hare's *Plato* (1982).

In *Feminism and the Mastery of Nature* (1993) Val Plumwood describes 2,500-year-old Western philosophy as white, elite, and male-dominant, and although Western philosophers claim to speak for the rest of society, they take their authority for granted; they do not question their relationship to the rest of the world, nor are they at all self-critical.[19]

Plato's ideas were based on the philosophy developed by the warrior society, that of the Proto-Indo-Europeans, which introduced changes to the status of women and war practices. As Leila Ahmed (1992)[20] observes, these changes included those which increased male control over women, and those which diminished women's humanity. Although women had probably earlier invented writing, it was not long before Indo-European men appropriated the skill thereby excluding women from its use.[21] Patriarchal philosophies gained traction through the spread of writing, as writing was then held by many powerful men as their secret or sacred knowledge. Women, the lower castes and classes, and foreigners, were mostly excluded but they kept alive their oral traditions through storytelling, song, dance and folk traditions. But it was Plato who took up these earlier ideas and refined and extended them to form a mode of thought and practice which has continued to underlie Western thinking ever since.

According to Elizabet Sahtouris,[22] Plato's teacher, Socrates (whose own teacher was Diotima,[23] a priestess) was less interested in how the natural world worked than in the workings of the human mind and ways to improve its performance in ordinary people. Plato took Socrates' ideas further and concluded that there must have been perfect ideas behind our imperfect world. He claimed our senses limited us from seeing a perfect world, an unchanging world which must have been created by a god apart from it. Elizabet Sahtouris states that the earlier philosophy of a living, creative nature with all its imperfections was replaced by "the perfect and rather mechanical creation of a single though yet unknown god."[24]

Val Plumwood (1993) gives us an insight into aspects of Plato's philosophy in which his treatment of women, slaves, minority groups and Indigenous people parallels his treatment of nature. For Plato, women and slaves fall into the same category as non-human creatures and the earth. Nature is seen as political: the Western construct of reason places elite human males as masters, and nature, like women, as subordinate, not equal. Just as Nature is non-human, so are people who are sexually, racially and ethnically different – nearer to animals than humans, without full rationality or culture. Nature is the passive environment, an invisible background, while in the foreground white Western male experts or entrepreneurs provide reason and culture. Nature was considered 'terra nullius', an empty purposeless and meaningless resource, part of a naturally subordinate lower realm, along with marginalised groups such as women and slaves.

Platonic philosophy is centred on a hierarchic dualism of reason over nature. Val Plumwood observes that for Plato everything has a higher side and a lower side: the higher side relates to the 'realm of reason', while the lower side relates to nature and the physical world. For example, love between men falls into the higher category, while male heterosexual love, and the creation of children, belongs in the lower category. Plato's world is divided into spheres: the higher world is that of the changeless, immaterial, and incorruptible; and the biological world is the lower changeable, sensual world of living and dying.[25]

According to Judith Genova (1994) Plato incorporated an earlier version of dualism into his thinking, that of Pythagoras, whose table of opposites included:

limited	/	unlimited
odd	/	even
one	/	multitude
right	/	left
male	/	female
resting	/	moving
straight	/	twisted
light	/	darkness
good	/	bad
square	/	oblong.[26]

The male/female dualisms were never regarded as equally important by Plato, and nor was equality ever an aim of individuals, states, or the cosmos.

Val Plumwood lists the most important elements which lie behind the 'dualistic structure' of Western thinking and the ensuing practices of colonisation, a number of which first emerged in Platonic thought:

culture	/	nature
reason	/	nature
male	/	female
mind	/	body (nature)
master	/	slave
reason	/	matter (physicality)
rationality	/	animality
reason	/	emotion
mind, spirit	/	nature
freedom	/	necessity
universal	/	particular
human	/	nature (non-human)
civilised	/	primitive
production	/	reproduction
public	/	private
subject	/	object
self	/	other.[27]

The notion of dualism involves concepts which are given oppositional identities by dominant forces. Val Plumwood argues that dualisms assume and reinforce difference; concepts are seen as either superior, or inferior and alien, and are closely connected with "domination and accumulation."[28]

In the 1600s CE a major development in Platonic-based thought emerged with Descartes (1596–1650 CE) who focused upon "mind/body (physicality); subject/object; human/nature and human/animal."[29] Later philosophers Hegel and Rousseau concentrated on "public/private; male/female; universal/particular and reason/nature."[30]

Plato and women

Val Plumwood identifies several assumptions lying behind Plato's dualisms in Western thinking:

- women are linked with the physical and nature
- both women and nature are inferior
- the concept of dualistic contrasts, which involves 'women/nature' is in opposition to 'reason/humanity'.[31]

All dualisms act for men's domination over women and nature since the separation between the rational and the inferior non-rational can be used to support the presumed inferiority of women, slaves, other racial groups, and other (barbaric) cultures, also manual (non-intellectual) workers who are seen as 'less rational', therefore inferior and closer to nature and animality.

Plato disliked women as sexual beings, and made constant derogatory comments about them in his literature. Val Plumwood explains that women were seen as beings without reason and belonging to a chaotic lower order of nature, lacking form and discipline. It was considered to be even worse when men adopted behaviours usually associated with women. While Plato depicted 'elite' women as equal to men, at the same time he consistently made disparaging statements about them. These 'elite' women included high-class courtesans for whom sex was central to their status. Although he considered such women inferior, he did admit that they were useful when waging war. However, unless they were as strong and athletic as men, they could not achieve citizenship.

According to John Cottingham (1996)[32] Plato's distrust and dislike of women is perhaps most clearly demonstrated in his 'metaphor of the cave' where he argued that knowing and truth are like the sun, belonging to a higher place; the sun, the light, knowledge and the soul lie within in the male realm. Women have no place in such a realm since they have irrational opinions rather than any capacity for real knowledge.[33] Plato most wished to be free of the corrupt 'world of appearances', represented by the (female) dark or 'twilight' of the cave (the dark of the uterus), and move onto the higher plane of reason, into the sunlight, the wonderful unchanging eternal (male) world of reality. The dark of the cave 'world of appearance' is in contrast with the 'blinding light' of reason, the 'world of reality'.[34]

Plato and the warrior hero

The earliest colonising warriors were the marauding Proto-Indo-European horsemen who invaded Neolithic settlements and farmlands. Val Plumwood (1993) describes Plato's identification of the 'warrior' as not entirely new but based upon the earliest patriarchal ideas. He used 'reason' to justify the devaluation of human life and the glorification of death so that war, a central organising principle in Plato's thought, could be waged in order to keep the masters' lifestyles comfortable. He considered war to be closely associated with reason which allows disconnection from humanity and thereby justifies killing without any emotional interference – 'for a higher good'. Thus it is a noble thing for the warrior-hero to be prepared to fight to the death. By doing so he believes he gains status and honour. But for those men who 'survive defeat' their only 'reward' is dishonour and relegation to the lower orders as slaves. By risking death the warrior demonstrates his control over and disregard for the body, self-preservation and life.[35]

Plato and animals (nature)

Although Plato admired war and war heroes, he was very scathing about the value of animals. Plato considered that 'land animals' descended from ignorant inferior men who were not thinkers and who did not use 'reason' or believe in 'spirit': "Animals, like women, are created after and as adjuncts to men."[36] Val Plumwood quotes him from *Timaeus* as stating that because of these deficiencies

> their forelimbs and heads were drawn by natural affinity to the earth, and their forelimbs supported on it, while their skulls were elongated into various shapes as a result of the crushing of their circles through lack of use.

The reason why some animals

> have four legs and others many was that the stupider they were the more supports god gave them, to tie them more closely to the earth.

The most stupid of the land animals

> whose whole bodies lay stretched upon the earth, the god turned into reptiles, giving them no feet, for they had no further need of them.

Water creatures were the most stupid of all since

> they live in the depths as a punishment for the depths of their stupidity. These are the principles on which living creatures change and have always changed into each other, the transformation depending on the loss or gain of understanding or folly.[37]

Plato and Earth: The natural world

This view of creatures explains Plato's view of women and nature as subordinate. The dualisms mind/body and human/nature lie behind the *radical exclusion* of nature in most of nature's senses and contrasts. In no way can (male) humans be linked to (female) nature because men and nature are so different. As Plato identified elite male human character as 'divine' (only elite men had souls), nature along with women is assigned a negative lower position. In almost every sense nature and women lie outside the realm of reason, goodness and value.

In *Phaedo* Plato regarded the earth as 'spoilt and corroded'; there was another higher world "pure and incorruptible, pure and fair ... the place of the true heaven and the true light and the true earth", while the visible world of nature, its conditions and status as negatively associated with the feminine

> is an earthly prison ... a dump, a place where refuse and sediment from the higher world above accumulate ... Biological change, the decay of organisms and their change into other organisms ... as disease and foulness.[38]

Some philosophies influenced by Plato

It is no secret that Platonic rationalist thought was a major influence upon early thinkers such as Aristotle (384–322 BCE), Augustine (354–430 CE), and Thomas Aquinas (1226–1274 CE). These men were prominent among those responsible for further formation and refinement of the intellectual and philosophical basis, not only of Christian doctrine, but also all later Western intellectual and philosophical traditions. Interestingly, Denise Schmandt-Besserat (1992/1996)[39] asserts that the first early cuneiform writing appeared at 6,500–6,000 BP in Sumeria, and the earliest records of practices such as making war and taking slaves go back to the third stage of the early recorded history of humanity (that of the first Sumerian and Greek rulers) just over 4,900 years ago. It is not surprising therefore that Plato and his student Aristotle took these practices for granted, assuming that war and slavery were inevitable. But even in their time there were still vestiges of the earlier peaceful cultures telling a different story. Not until after the appearance of the Indo-Europeans did the early zealous rulers destroy all but the last traces of these cultures in Europe; even then not all aspects were destroyed because folk (women's) traditions preserved them. Archaeological evidence today shows peaceful early cultures, so we no longer have the excuse that making war and the taking of slaves are inevitable.

Jonathon Barnes (1982)[40] observes that Aristotle studied under Plato. Although he may have disagreed with some of Plato's ideas, Aristotle agreed with Plato in principle. Aristotle held similar views concerning women and nature as lower forms of life where men were hierarchically placed above other living things. Women and slaves could have no freedom; only men were considered citizens, but even many of those were meant to be slaves. In every aspect women and slaves were property of the master. This view continues to influence colonialist societies today.

John Ralston Saul (1995/1997)[41] considers Augustine to have been greatly influenced by Plato and his philosophy. He identified three basic qualities: memory, reason and will. John Cottingham adds that it was Augustine who proposed, among other aspects of thought, the influential notion of 'original sin', which related to "the fallen nature of man" caused by women, and "the need for salvation by divine grace."[42] For Augustine, like Plato, the world of nature/body (which included women and slaves) was of a lower "perishable inferior realm", of use only as an instrument "to gain salvation ... in heaven", and where women were naturally subordinate to men, according to Val Plumwood.[43] Genevieve Lloyd (1990) explains that women, like 'irrational' animals, were apparently meant to be under the control of 'rational' men who were the only humans made in God's image.[44]

Thomas Aquinas was greatly influenced by Aristotle and is best known for his 'five ways' or proofs of the existence of God. He drew on Plato and his concept of the separated soul which lives on after death. John Cottingham (1996) states that Thomas Aquinas's views of intellect and will prepared the way for Descartes' "radical mind/body dualism"[45] ideas which were to be developed subsequently. Thomas Aquinas argued that men were made in the image of God, but women, it seems, were made in the image of men. He also claimed that woman was naturally subordinate to man because in reproduction she is passive, while men's 'seed' is the active factor in creating new life.[46]

John Cottingham describes French philosopher Rene Descartes (1596–1650 CE), as being among the key people who dispensed with ideas grounded in Aristotle's traditional 'scholastic' philosophy. He took a fresh approach to the sciences, basing it on distinctly mathematical ideas. According to Charlotte Witt (1996),[47] Rene Descartes was both as explicitly and covertly misogynist as Plato and Aristotle; but he was often more subtle, deliberately not expressing his theories in gendered terms, and giving the impression that he was personally committed to equality of the sexes. For some feminists, both his mind/body dualism theory and the way he abstracted his presentation of reason, implied gender bias by assuming that women are essentially "identified with emotions and the body."[48]

Val Plumwood (1993) reveals that for Descartes and his followers, the Cartesians, nature (women and the natural world) was a machine in which principles of physics, geometry and pure mathematics were able to explain everything concerning all natural phenomena. Descartes regarded nature (and women?) as easily moulded – a machine to be controlled. To understand the workings of mechanistic nature was seen as a means of power over it. Further knowledge of bodily mechanisms allowed the possibility of control over death itself. It is notable that these attitudes concerning nature parallel patriarchal philosophical attitudes towards women who, since Plato, had been bracketed with nature as 'less than human'.

Cartesian thought and the later humanist movements are focused on and emphasise unified dualisms of human/nature and mind/body as mindless mechanisms. Humanists recognised a common human nature, but inferior humans were still associated with inferior nature, especially in colonialism, according to Val Plumwood. Reason now had a new role, where the elite men were not only the 'possessors' of women but also of 'non-mindful' nature, which was lacking mind or thought. Nature was only as valuable or significant as humans wanted to think it was, and because humans saw nature in this way they could treat it any way they chose. Thus humans were free to dispose of or otherwise damage irreplaceable beautiful living things as they pleased. This view of nature coincided with the advent of capitalism which regards nature as a market commodity and a free resource.

Vandana Shiva (1989) explains the Indian philosophy of nature: unlike Cartesian thought where nature and the environment are considered separate from humans, in Indian thought people and nature (Purusha-Prakriti) are "a duality in unity."[49] All of creation shows signs of a principle unifying unity and diversity in nature known as Prakriti which organises everyday life. There is continuity between humanity and nature, and nature is seen as actively creative, productive, and diverse in every way, connected and inter-related, and all of life is sacred.

Philosophies of today: Scientific and economic rationalism, globalisation and corporatisation

Scientific Rationalism, referred to by Michael Dames (1992/1996),[50] is the dominant world ideology today. Now everything can be manipulated and improved scientifically by such innovations as genetic engineering; and every environmental problem can be fixed by science.

Corporatisation in the 19th century was regarded as an alternative to democracy, even though it promoted the rights of the group over the rights of the individual. This idea had its roots in Plato's contempt for the individual, and the superiority of the (male) elite. Corporatisation is all about *power-over* or domination as Starhawk (2002) explains. Domination allows a small powerful group to limit or control the resources of others. But it is not only small groups who can dominate; multi-national corporations and other agencies also wield power over individuals, organisations and nations which is enforced by police or military violence. However, Starhawk emphasises that power can also come *from within* – our creativity can allow us to dare to dream and to do. Power from within is 'unlimited' and is what we call 'spirit'.[51]

Scientific and Economic Rationalism as John Ralston Saul (1995/1997) observes, are based on and continue Platonic philosophy into the present day. We only have to read Plato's *The Republic* to find the basis of the corporate model which is so much part of business life today. We see it in the way the corporate elite use the law to inspire fear, as well as to administer their form of justice.

Scientific and economic rationalism, women and nature

Scientific Rationalism combines Platonic and Cartesian philosophies but without any concept of deities or metaphysics, according to eco-feminist Susan Griffin (1989).[52] She argues that humans are no longer the centre of the universe, the biosphere, the earth. In order to survive we believe we must 'take control of our environment'. We see ourselves and life as meaningless and we transfer this idea to nature. To illustrate this idea Susan Griffin uses the metaphor of the (female) mountain which is 'transformed' to destruction by mindless (male) 'progress' where

> believing a mountain to have no inner reason, no sacredness unto itself, the modern technologist takes coal out of the soil simply by cutting away half of the face of the mountain. Suddenly the whole of the mountain begins to erode.[53]

The erosion releases chemicals into the streams, upsetting the natural balance and killing trees, plants, fish and animals, and thereby causing the death of those people who depend on them for food. (A devastating example in recent times is the Ok Tedi mine in Papua New Guinea). Then the previously beautiful countryside becomes ruined, beyond repair. The modern technologist has transformed the mountain, just as society "transforms those who have become symbols of nature (women and Indigenous people) into objects of degradation"[54] claims Susan Griffin. She likens this necessity to control and transform nature (the mountain) to the "false sense of triumph" felt by the early explorer finally reaching his goal, then feeling a twinge of regret as he cannot avoid seeing in the image of the destroyed mountain the "devastation [of] his own inner life ..."[55]

Eco-feminist Judith Plant (1989)[56] argues that modern science now aims to use methods of genetic engineering to control procreation; this is the final solution to the 'problem' of (female) nature. She echoes the earlier arguments of radical feminists active in the fight against reproductive technologies.[57]

Female-focused philosophies

Val Plumwood (1993) notes that there are some hopeful responses to the Cartesian mechanistic world view in more recent times:

- A recognition of a 'New Age Goddess' or immanent deity who lifts and enlivens the whole of nature away from the purely material world. This deity is thought by many Western women to be the re-emergence of the Palaeolithic/Neolithic 'goddess'.[58] The notion is based on the similarity between the various forms of female symbolic imagery throughout the diverse societies of Europe.

- There are new scientific theories, for example, quantum theory which, unlike other scientific concepts, recognises a continuous relationship between humans and nature.[59]
- There is also a growing recognition that certain spiritual concepts are not as opposed to scientific knowledge as had been previously thought. Some scientific theories are now recognised to be 'universal truths', at once metaphysical and physical (for example, the continual 'birth', 'growth' and 'death' of stars). Sidney Liebes, Elizabet Sahtouris and Brian Swimme (1998)[60] claim that evolution is circular in the sense that organisms and species not only evolve and become extinct, but amazingly fuse together to make another entity. Everything, even human thinking, is in a constant state of evolution.
- Val Plumwood notes that the theory of pantheism has been understood as worship of (female) nature as a deity; an inclusive worship "that admits or tolerates all gods."[61] Today this understanding has widened to include the belief that nature's forces and natural substances are as one with a (male) metaphysical being. Panentheism, a philosophy in which a deity is understood as being present within everything created, attempts to counter the effects of dualisms by promoting an immanent god, or female earth-centred deities, as underlying nature.
- In process philosophy the human mind and nature are closely connected, and everything in nature and the universe is in a constant process of change, development, and finishing or decaying. Those who understand nature as a living, pulsating entity, with everything in it having a diverse purpose and reason for living, see themselves as part of this activity, not alienated from it. This allows us to be intentionally open to exchanges with the natural world which we have not set in motion ourselves but which can open us up to tremendous new possibilities. Val Plumwood observes that women especially resonate to this way of thought.

Threads

Val Plumwood comments that "the master's logic of colonisation is the dominant logic of our time."[62] She identifies three stages in the development of philosophic thought from the time of Plato onwards:

Stage One. Plato and early rationalists establish the notion of the master identity versus the lower orders (women, slaves, nature); colonisation of culture and human self is established. (These ideas are based on 6,000-year-old Indo-European notions.)

Stage Two. According to Descartes and later rationalists, all non-human nature has no mind, but is there to be annexed and moulded at will. This view underlies attitudes towards women in many instances.

Stage Three. Nature as an instrument is appropriated as a resource, a tool to be searched out and exploited for its usefulness, as are women in many cultures, for example, when corporations take their business offshore to take advantage of women's cheap labour. This leads to the way men continue to 'divide' women and deny them a fair living.

These three stages include the dualising process wherein "reason progressively divides, devalues, and denies the colonised other which is nature."[63]

There is a fourth stage which Val Plumwood identifies as 'devouring the other'. (Her example is Indonesia's relationship with East Timor). Here the colonised could decide between being eliminated, or assimilated into the coloniser culture. This is an example of 'reason' devouring the other, now unable to resist or answer back "because it no longer has a voice and language of its own."[64]

In *Wild Politics* Susan Hawthorne points out Ariel Sallah's description of 'corporate colonisation' in its most basic form:

Man is 1 (one)   woman is 0
point   hole
coloniser   colonised[65]

During her long career Marija Gimbutas discovered over 30,000 prehistoric female figurines, as well as other artefacts, in Old Europe, many over 32,000 years old; she also examined others which were very much older and found elsewhere in the Northern Hemisphere. But could more female figurines also be found in the prehistoric Hidden Worlds (Africa, India, China and East Asia) or in the New Worlds of Australia, the Americas or the Pacific Islands? And when did the Indo-Europeans first reach these regions; what were the changes which took place?

As will be shown, the signs were there, recorded in indigenous mythologies; they marked changes to the cultures in question, particularly those which affected the status of women. For example, the early Austronesian-speaking Lapita people from Taiwan lived peaceful lives in the Pacific, but later migrating Austronesian-speakers from China brought violence to the Pacific. By the 19th century colonialist era, all of the islands of the Pacific were inhabited by violent cultures. Our recorded human 'history' begins with dynastic cultures ruled by kings, queens or presidents: we choose to forget the hidden prehistories of communal consensual social organisations.

PART THREE

THE HIDDEN AND NEW WORLDS: PREHISTORIES, THE FEMALE PRINCIPLE AND INDO-EUROPEAN INFLUENCES

THE GREAT HORNED GODDESS

The great horned goddess: Aouamrhet/Oya
(wall painting), Tassili, North Africa, 10,000 BP
(Source: Lhote, Henri, 1959)

All line drawings © Judy Foster, 2013

THE HIDDEN AND NEW WORLDS

In order to reveal prehistoric women in the Hidden and New Worlds, we begin in Africa, from where, as archaeological evidence suggests, the first humans emerged. We then follow their possible early prehistoric routes through India, to China, Korea, Japan, then to Thailand, Indonesia, and Australia, to Oceania, and the Americas. The currently agreed timelines relating to these arrivals are of considerable interest but can change at any time as new archaeological and other evidence is constantly emerging.

The European terms 'Bronze Age' and 'Iron Age' are of little help in describing social development in Asia, the Americas, or the Southern Hemisphere, since metals were often used alongside other Neolithic practices in the countries under discussion, and were not utilised at all in the Americas (although these terms have been used in this text for comparative reasons). Gina Barnes (1993)* explains that each Asian country uses its own method of dividing prehistory into archaeological periods and developmental stages, and this can be particularly confusing when examining Chinese, Korean and Japanese prehistory.**

---

*   Barnes, Gina (1993) *China, Korea and Japan.*

**   Northern time periods are based on certain phases of technological progress: Palaeolithic (Old Stone Age); Neolithic (New Stone Age); the Bronze or Iron Age; so are not necessarily appropriate to describe cultural developments in the Southern Hemisphere, India or East Asian countries, because these periods often overlap each other or fall within different time frames. The Upper Palaeolithic period of India in the north-west dates from 45,000 BP but in other areas it can occur several thousand years later, while the Bronze Age in Thailand was a continuation of the Neolithic period, where bronze metal was used in decorative items rather than for war weapons.

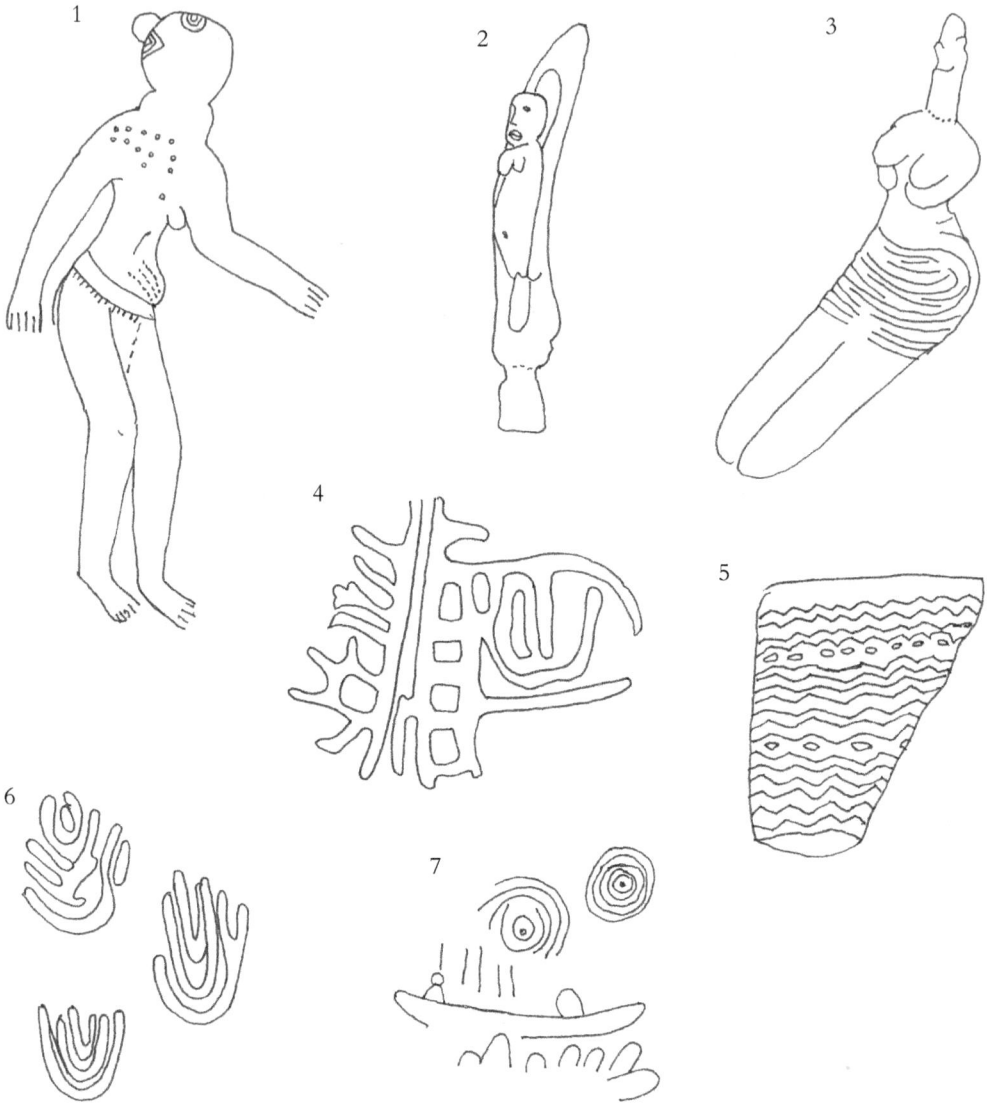

AFRICA: NEOLITHIC IMAGES

1. *The White Lady of Tassili, rock wall painting,* 7,000 BP (Source: Willett, Frank, 1995)
2. *Early historic figurine, wood sculpture*
3. *Neolithic clay figurine,* Sudan, c. 4,000 BP (Source: Dashu, Max, 2008)
4. *Early rock wall engraving* (Source 2–4: Phillipson, David, 1985)
5. *Pottery fragment with repeated meander design* (Source: Department of Arts of Africa, Oceania, and the Americas, October 2004)
6. *Hand prints in African cave,* prehistoric decorated hands prints, painting on rock wall by Khoi herders, Eland Bay, Western Cape, South Africa (Source: Department of Arts of Africa, Oceania, and the Americas, 2001)
7. *Uganda canoe design with spirals (Ship of the Dead?)* (Source 6–7: Chakravarty, Kalyan and Robert Bednarik, 1997)

All line drawings © Judy Foster, 2013

CHAPTER 11

HIDDEN WORLDS: AFRICA

African communities (2,000,000–6,000 BP)

William Petrie (1853–1942)[1] made the earliest excavations in Africa in the Nile Valley at Nagada and Ballas in the early 1900s. He found no war weapons in nearly 1,200 graves and was convinced that the early cultures were 'peaceful' and possibly 'united' everywhere in prehistoric Egypt and Sudan. Other excavations at Al-Badari took place in 1928 and revealed cultures of the 7,500-year-old Badarian people who preceded the ancient Egyptians by at least 2,000 years. Only since the end of the 19th century has the rest of Africa been archaeologically explored, enabling the first overviews of middle and southern African prehistory to be produced as recently as the 1980s. David Phillipson (1985)[2] explains that communities of the African Palaeolithic and Neolithic periods from 2 million years until 6,000 years ago were found to be non-aggressive, and notes evidence of only one or two instances of violent death involving no more than a few individuals.

In northern Africa's[3] Western Desert region until 70,000 BP the climate was generally moist, according to Fred Wendorf and Romauld Schild (1998).[4] The early northern African people were peaceful and nomadic, living in temporary shelters and following water sources in response to the prevailing climatic conditions which fluctuated between wet moist conditions and dry periods of varying lengths. They hunted large animals, such as buffalo, camel, giraffe, antelope and gazelle, and gathered a wide variety of plant foods.

From 12,500 BP until 5,900 BP the climate was hyper-arid and the large animals disappeared. The nomadic hunters had to dig wells for water and were restricted to catching small game, hares, jackals, small rodents and birds, while the gatherers collected seeds, fruits and roots. A 1998 report by Fred Wendorf and Romauld Schild explains that a typical settlement was discovered near the Egyptian and Sudanese border at Nabta Playa (dated after 11,000 BP). It had been occupied over a long period as the people had dug wells for use as a reliable year-round water source. Evidence there shows that cattle had been domesticated from 11,000 BP by small family groups living in semi-permanent seasonal camps. Cattle were an important and reliable food source, providing milk products and blood, and were regarded as sacred animals, not to be butchered for meat.

There was no evidence of permanent dwellings until 8,900 BP. After this time settlements with large oval stone huts, smaller circular huts and numerous bell-shaped storage pits appeared. Many deep wells were built and sheep and goats were now herded alongside

161

A Timeline for Prehistoric Africa

Period (BP)	Place/People	Evidence
Lower Palaeolithic	African Continent	
7,000,000–5,000,000	Ethiopia	• Earliest ape/human
3,000,000	Africa	• *H. habilis*
2,500,000	Ethiopia	• *H. habilis*
		• Earliest stone tools
		• Jaw of *Homo* (Hadar)
2,000,000		• *H. erectus*
1,800,000	Southern Africa	• Makapansgat hominid head
1,500,000		• Collection of red ochre pebbles, quartz crystals
800,000	Hunter-gatherers	• First use of fire
600,000		• Red ochre crayons (ritual)
200,000		• Archaic (early) *H. Sapiens*
100,000		• Modern *H. sapiens*; incised lines in Blombos Cave
Upper Palaeolithic		
30,000	The San people	• Rock art, ochres, ritual
29,000		• 40,000 paintings in 500 shelters
28,000		• Painted gravestones
28,000	Namibia	• Earliest portable paintings
		• Foundation for what later became the Egyptian 'civilisation'
19,000	Nile area	• Hunter-gatherers
18,000	Northern Africa	
15,000		• Harvesting, grinding of wild grains
11,000	Nile Valley	• Semi-settled communities
Neolithic		
10,000	Sahara	• Earliest pottery
9,000	Zambia	• Settlements, pottery
		• Wooden bows, arrows, other tools; leather bags and clothing, shell and stone beads, pendants
8,000	Nile	• Settlements with mud daub houses, bone harpoons
		• Ivory statuettes, triangular heads (females)
7,500	Tassili	• Stone monoliths (male and female)
	Senegal	• Bone female figurines
	Al-Badari	• Badarian culture (Egypt) peaceful; ivory female figurine
6,500	Egypt	• Pastoral period; clumsy stiff animal paintings suggest possible contact with Indo-Europeans?
5,500	Egypt	• Beginning of Egyptian 'civilisation'
	Coincides with early wave of Indo-European invasions	• Earliest monumental tomb
5,000	Nubia	• Stone vessels, copper tools, palettes, amulets; domestic sheep, goats, cattle, houses
4,200	North Africa	• Famous pyramids appear from this time
		• Indo-European horsemen invade southern Africa
3,000	Tripoli – Gao (Coast to Niger River)	• Chariot Road built, opening up northern Africa to invaders

the cattle. Some decorated pottery was made, perhaps used for rituals as pot sherds were not commonly present. In the late Neolithic, pottery was made more frequently and burnished, with impressed or incised decorations. Huts had central hearths and stone wall bases, and in some instances holes indicated that posts may have supported brush or woven grass matting walls and roofs.

At El Nabta, the researchers found the remains of a large, oval-shaped regional ceremonial centre with a north-south orientation dated to between 7,500 and 7,400 BP. It was built from "nine large sandstone blocks 100 metres apart" and "beyond the north end of the alignment there was a 'calendar circle' of smaller sandstone slabs." A number of "sandstone tumuli containing the remains of cattle"[5] suggested the sacrificing of cattle in ritual, but no human remains were found. This stone ceremonial centre, with its evidence of cattle 'sacrifices', may have been the precursor of another larger, more complicated, oval-shaped ceremonial Ness of Brodgar stone temple complex discovered in 2002, and excavated in 2008 and 2011 in the Orkney Islands (north of Britain) dated to 5,200 BP. The remains of shin bones of 600 cattle left behind at the end of a 'feast' (or ritual sacrificial ceremony?) held shortly before the site was abandoned was probably due to the influx of new people with very different cultural practices (the in-coming Indo-Europeans?).

The Ness of Brodgar site[6] holds 100 oval-shaped (Marija Gimbutas would say 'womb-shaped') buildings, the most recent a 25-metre-long oval building set within a 5-metre-wide monumental stone walled enclosure. Each building is thought to have featured thick stone walls and the earliest Neolithic stone slate-tiled roofs, according to site director Nick Card. Archaeologist Mark Edmonds suggests that the original Ness of Brodgar people took their cultural practices south to Scotland and England. Perhaps it is possible that the people who occupied Malta (revealed by Cristina Biaggi in 1994) and built monumental temples, although smaller in scale, may also have come from the Ness of Brodgar. She dated the monumental temple sites in Malta to 4,000–2,500 BP; the Orkneys to 4,500–1,800; and the Shetland Islands to 4,000–2,500 BP; so this is a distinct possibility since the Ness of Brodgar is 800 years older.

From 19,000 BP the foundations for what was to become the Egyptian civilisation were being laid, according to Cheikh Diop (1974).[7] During this time, climatic conditions caused people to move north, from the Sahara to the Upper Nile, while there was also some movement south into Equatorial Africa as climatic conditions improved. In the Upper Nile region people prepared for seasonal flooding, developed irrigation using geometry to redefine and restore flood-damaged farm boundaries, and built dams. They also developed the earliest form of hoe suitable for ploughing in the Nile Valley.

Neolithic Black African societies were gentle, idealistic, peaceful, women-centred and agricultural, and enjoyed a spirit of justice and light-heartedness, attributes which were very necessary for successful daily coexistence. Cheikh Diop explains that northern Africa, like various parts of Europe, was invaded by the aggressive Eurasian steppe nomads (Indo-Europeans). He states that despite the fact that Black Africans had been the creators of early African civilised societies such as that of Egypt, they were regarded by the incoming white Western colonisers as mere animals, although it was admitted that some were artists.

African American scholar and mythologist Clyde Ford (1999)[8] regrets the fact that so little of African prehistory is generally known because Africa was for so long considered 'primitive'. He explains that as early humans expanded their territories throughout the world, they took their world views with them, including a fundamental belief in female deities, spirits or ancestral beings. He considers the Chariot Road (built by Indo-Europeans around 3,000 BP, which ran from near Tripoli on the Mediterranean Sea to Gao on the Niger River) as being the means by which horse-drawn chariots, as part of highly mobile destructive marauding bands, were used to invade and destroy the African inland peoples, forcing the African earth/nature goddess underground. While many previous generations of writers have considered Africa 'primitive', scholars such as Martin Bernal (1987)[9] have challenged this and instead shown evidence for the development of classical Greek culture from both African and Asiatic roots. Ivan van Sertima (1988)[10] also argued for the importance of women in African antiquity.[11]

The African Nile experience

In Blombos Cave, flat ochre surfaces of rocks incised with linear parallel markings have been found suggesting ritual activity 100,000 years ago, and are among the very early African rock art images. To date the earliest modern human remains of a young Black African man dated to between 37,000 and 32,000 BP, have been found at Luxor in 1980, together with a flint tool. How the early artists lived has not yet been recorded but their lifestyles could have been similar to that of later cultures. David Phillipson (1985) describes typical northern African Palaeolithic lifestyles about 18,000 BP as a time when people gathered, fished, and hunted wild cattle and other large animals. Major cultural developments followed a vaguely parallel course in different parts of Africa. In fertile places, such as the Nile Valley, the population gradually increased, causing competition for space within the small central area, and resulting in some groups having to move to the drier periphery.

From as early as 18,000 until 11,000 BP, in some Nile Valley communities, such as Al-Badari in Upper Egypt and Nubia, the women developed crop cultivation by weeding and watering patches of wild grasses, and clearing more ground to allow for the grassed areas to expand. They were harvesting wild grains, as evidenced by the many grindstones found in settlements. Microliths were apparently used for cutting wild barley and other grasses. David Phillipson maintains that these practices would have led to the earliest development of crops which were quite different from wild grain.

The people buried their dead in cemeteries; in one rare instance it appeared that a considerable number of people died violently, perhaps as a result of territorial defence, but David Phillipson considers that this was a very unusual occurrence in the Palaeolithic period. The movement of people to the Nile Valley as conditions elsewhere became drier was partly responsible for an increase in population.

About 10,000 BP, people of Afro-Mediterranean stock settled along the Mediterranean coast and moved down through eastern Africa parallel to the coastline. These people were later forced by drought to migrate to the Nile area. A semi-settled hunter-gatherer lifestyle continued along with the growing of grain and the keeping of some domestic animals. By 9,000 BP, pottery, worked copper, and fine ceramics and sculpture appeared in Sudan. The Tassili people of the Sahara had domesticated sheep, goats, and cattle. Many cave paintings recording changing climate and featuring animal migrations, as well as human activities, appear over this period. Not until about 5,000 BP did the Sahara become drier and as it is today. James Demeo (2009) explains that, before 6,000–5,000 BP, Saharasia had been "a semiforested grassland savannah"[12] where many different animals grazed, and waterways supported fish, shellfish and other aquatic species. Today this region is very dry with little vegetation. James Demeo argues that this was the result of "a major ecological transition from relatively wet to arid desert conditions"[13] due to climatic instability (and not to human population expansion).

Settlements included a base camp with small seasonal outer settlements. This allowed women to make Africa's earliest pottery, which they gradually refined over time. The Early Khartoum pottery was decorated with parallel meander (wavy) lines and later, jabbed 'dots' in patterns around the pots. There were also signs of sun-dried daub which indicates possible buildings.

In Nigeria, dugout canoes were apparently in common use, according to Peter Breunig of Frankfurt University. One example made of African mahogany, with finely crafted bow and stern, found buried in sand, has proved to be the world's oldest known dugout. He states that it represents the result of a long tradition of canoe building and use of watercraft in Africa.[14]

There is much rock art in the northern Sahara region and in southern Africa, but it can only be dated by testing any deposits which might cover the art. At Tassili in the Sahara, rock art presents a picture of a green Sahara and an evolutionary record of a region which has since become sandy desert.[15] The earliest dated Tassili rock art is 10,000 years old, and features dynamic graceful, flowing images of animals now extinct in the region, while their agile hunters carry clubs, throwing-sticks, axes and bows but no spears.

Food production in northern Africa was not widespread until about 8,000 BP, some time later than plant cultivation and animal domestication in the Near East. Climatic problems may well have influenced this later start. There was also some experimentation with the domestication of wild or semi-wild animals at this time.

Also by 8,000 BP the Saharan people were making their own style of pottery. Their tools became more specialised, some with 'crescent' edges used for sharpening spear and harpoon shafts, and bone harpoon heads. Stone rings weighed down the fishing nets, and women used them as loom weights. Mummification of the dead began at this time, according to Myra Wysinger.[16]

By 7,500 BP the peaceful Badarian people of Neolithic Egypt who preceded the much emphasised 'ancient' Egyptian 'civilisation', became efficient farmers, hunters and miners, and successful traders, exchanging goods over considerable distances. They grew barley, wheat, and flax, wove fine linen cloth, and made beautiful pottery and carved objects. In 1928, archaeologists Guy Brunton and Gertrude Caton-Thompson recorded 1,200 graves in 600 tombs. They found no buildings, but as these would have been made of mud daub they could not have survived regular flooding events in the Nile Valley.[17]

Burials took place in the desert, well away from living areas, and bodies were oriented southward, facing west and curled in a foetal position. Grave goods included clay bins for storing grain, and pots with pottery ladles for serving food. Bread was among the foods provided for the next life. People were buried with their clothing, jewellery and cosmetics, craft tools, vases and bowls, ivory spoons, cooking pots, baskets, and religious items such as ivory female figurines. Other precious objects including glass, crystal, and copper appeared in some graves. Polished stone palettes on which to grind green malachite ore (an ingredient used in eyeshadow to enhance the eyes) were also found, while oil from the castor plant was provided to cosmetically oil the body, or to burn in lamps. Other objects included beads, bone needles, copper pins, clay model boats, combs, mirrors, bracelets, ivory finger rings, nose and ear studs, arrowheads, and amulets of animal heads such as gazelles or hippopotami.

Evidence of trade with neighbours included items such as basalt vases from the Delta region, elephant ivory from the south, shells from the Red Sea, turquoise from Sinai, copper from the north, black pottery with white designs from the west, porphyry slabs from the Red Sea mountains, and (imported) steatite beads. Significantly, there were no offensive weapons in any graves, nor any signs of violent deaths.

Specialised fishing equipment, such as bone harpoon heads barbed along one edge, found along the Nile at 7,000 BP led David Phillipson to conclude that in this period both fishing and hunting activities increased. Permanent homes were made of mud daub. It was around 6,500 BP when pottery began to feature many incised wavy lines or dotted design motifs. Harpoons used for fishing may also have been used occasionally for weapons, as evidenced by the rare discovery of a harpoon head found buried in a skeleton in Nigeria. Fishing, grain gathering and hunting along rivers led to a much more settled lifestyle not present elsewhere.

By 6,000 BP, in the Khartoum area, pottery was burnished, and new styles emerged which were not unlike predynastic Egyptian ware. Designs on the pots featured various grains, a clue to popular crops of the time. Ammonite beads were traded. There were large herds of goats, cattle and sheep, and farming practices.

In Nubia around 5,800 BP, manufactured goods such as stone vessels, copper tools, palettes, and amulets were exchanged for wool and animal skins from Egypt. The Nubians fished and hunted, kept sheep, goats, and cattle, cultivated wheat and barley, and used linen cloth which may have been imported. Some people lived in rectangular houses with up to six rooms. This lifestyle is very similar to that of Anatolia's Çatal Hüyük a few thousand years earlier. Around 5,100 BP the first signs of the dynastic period in Egypt appeared, and there were also signs of hierarchy as demonstrated by the different standards of dwellings used by the elite and the workers, indicating the presence of Indo-European pastoralists or their ideologies and practices.

Southern Africa

David Phillipson (1985) describes the early lifestyles of southern African people as being similar to those of the north. At the Klasies River Mouth region on the extreme south coast, from 120,000 until about 1,000 BP there were tools used for hunting land- and sea-creatures, and the gathering of shellfish rather than fishing.

At 50,000 BP the first southern African people, the Xhoisan (San) hunter-gatherers, lived in the region from Zimbabwe to Cape Town, including the Kalahari Desert. They created many engravings and wall paintings, used bows and arrows and decorated digging sticks.

There is evidence of hunter-gatherers between 9,000 and 4,500 BP living in dry caves and at a few waterlogged sites, such as those at Gwisho hot springs in Southern Zambia, which includes remains of organic materials such as wooden bows, arrows, digging sticks, pegs, wedges and bark trays. There is also evidence of hides which had been skilfully stitched together to make clothing, and leather bags. Valuable items were wrapped in leaves and beds were made using soft grasses. Camps were seasonal, with people moving according to the availability of a wide range of vegetable foods. Burials were within the settlements, and included grave goods, such as jewellery consisting of beads and pendants of bone and shell, and other personal items which suggest a belief in an afterlife. Antelope horns or warthog tusks were sometimes included and David Phillipson suggests that these may have been trophies. There were many painted gravestones, some of which could be 28,000 years old.

Art, religion and ritual

Ochres and other 'colouring' materials were commonly found in settlements around Africa from 30,000 BP, according to Clyde Ford (1999). The San of southern Africa have some of the oldest African art traditions known today; their oral traditions were passed down through their rock art, engravings and paintings, reflecting past and present myths and rituals.

Elands are symbolic animals for the San, and are sacrificed as part of initiation rituals for both young women and men. The San use death to describe shamanistic trance (a 'voyage' into inner space) as, in their words, shamans "die when they cross over into the spirit world."[18] The connection between an eland's death and the shaman's trance is suggested in San rock art imagery. Engravings or sculptures of human-like figures with very long bodies/ legs symbolise trance-related elongated figures.

Cheikh Diop mentions ivory statuettes (possibly female) with triangular heads dated to 7,500 BP which he suggests are similar to those found later in Crete. Stone monoliths found in Senegal were symbolic of the female and male, and were made by early Black Africans to represent the symbolic union of sky and earth (by depicting the two sexual organs). Rain was symbolic of the fertility of the 'earth mother' (goddess), and the 'sky father' (god) in Africa (as it was in some parts of Indigenous Australia).

A fine example of female figurines of this period in Africa is a slender ivory female deity from Al-Badari 7,500 years old which is carved from the lower canine tooth of a hippopotamus. She has facial features and a bare head, well-proportioned breasts, arms on hips, and is wearing an incised cross-hatched pubic covering as she stands confidently on well-shaped legs and feet. Numerous other sculpted ivory objects including figurines are mentioned but not described.

Max Dashu gives another example of a 6,000-year-old ceramic female deity of Neolithic Sudan who is seated and features arms and hands under breasts, with broad hips and long legs tapering to narrow 'feet'. The figurine appears to be wearing a 'skirt' draped in folds over her hips and thighs (or the incised lines could represent ritual scars). She has a long neck and incised oblique 'eyes'. Max Dashu (2004b) suggests that "the hands-to-breasts motif remains a central sign of African sculpture in the maternal statues of the Yoruba, Bamilake, BaLuba and other cultures."[19] There are similar images from Old Europe around this time among the female deities recorded by Marija Gimbutas; and others from Mehrgarh in India, although these female deities also display elaborate hairstyles.

Of interest are a further series of photographs of the northern African predynastic Kemetic (Egyptian)[20] priestesses (or goddesses?) with their female attendants standing in boats on the Nile. This imagery, dated to 6,200–5,600 BP, appears on ceramic pottery, in rock art and on the haft of a flint dagger.[21] The boats are long, large and slender, with high curved prows and sterns, and are powered by numerous oarsmen (suggested by the rows of oar-like parallel lines along the lower edge of the boats). The painted boat shapes often follow the bottom line of the pot.

The number of priestesses differs (one, two or three figures) and they are always depicted larger in size than other figures. The priestesses have their arms raised in supplication, with fingers closed and wrists bent to form a shape similar to that of cattle horns of the time. Large or small fans, palm trees, flamingos, deer and other animals may be included, as well as other abstract symbols such as parallel rows of zigzags (water symbols) and dots. The symbolism of the late Mehrgarh/early Harappan Indus Valley priestess/goddess in the 'cow boat' with attendants (described in the following chapter) held similar meanings for people of the time.

A second group of female figurines[22] of similar date, also with arms raised in supplication or praise, are made from ceramic or stone, and sometimes painted with skin colour to the waist, with yellow or white skirts. They feature vulture-like heads and faces, and are long and slender with well-proportioned figures, legs held together, and standing on tiptoe. (Marija Gimbutas would identify them as 'bird goddesses'.) Similar female figurines (although not with raised arms) have been found at Mehrgarh (see next chapter).

In southern Africa some rock art sites have paintings with many layers of images, the earliest perhaps belonging to the Palaeolithic period. As in the north, these beautiful naturalistic and peaceful images feature wild animals and sometimes human hunters. Frank Willett (1995)[23] notes portable art consisting of small stone slabs featuring stylised animals which could be over 27,000 years old.

He explains that from 6,000 BP onwards the art became less skilful, with stiffly posed cattle predominating, their horns always frontally facing even when their bodies might be in profile. This is the period in which sheep, goats and cattle were first kept in herds, indicating a possible first contact with Indo-European ideas. It ended with the arrival of Indo-European horsemen about 3,200 BP when later paintings appear clumsy and include detailed depictions of ceremonies, raids and battles indicating the time of change from peaceful cultures to warrior societies. David Phillipson notes that villages with defensive walls were beginning to appear. Sculpture would have been important during these early periods but, due to the limitations of dating methods, it is difficult to determine whether the stone images which remain today might belong to earlier times. According to Frank Willett, sculpture has traditionally been made from wood and other materials which deteriorate over time, so that the imagery we see today mostly belongs within the Warrior Age.

With the exception of the early Egyptian Black African civilisation with its large monuments and strong, rich and vibrant cultural history, there seem to be no large settlements or towns remaining today. That omission could well be corrected with further archaeological discoveries, as has occurred recently in India and China.

The African 'goddess'

According to Clyde Ford, the female principle, the goddess in African mythology, is an inseparable part of African culture and society, expressed through feelings and actions, beliefs and behaviours, affecting artistic creations and myths, world views, and actions towards others. She became hidden in African myths as her role was changed or edited out by the early Western (missionary) recorders, but Clyde Ford has found that she remains very much central to African prehistory and mythology. She has always been present in three basic symbols: the tree, the earth, and the stone. These images often represent her in creation stories, which have been preserved in traditional oral histories by African mothers, and passed

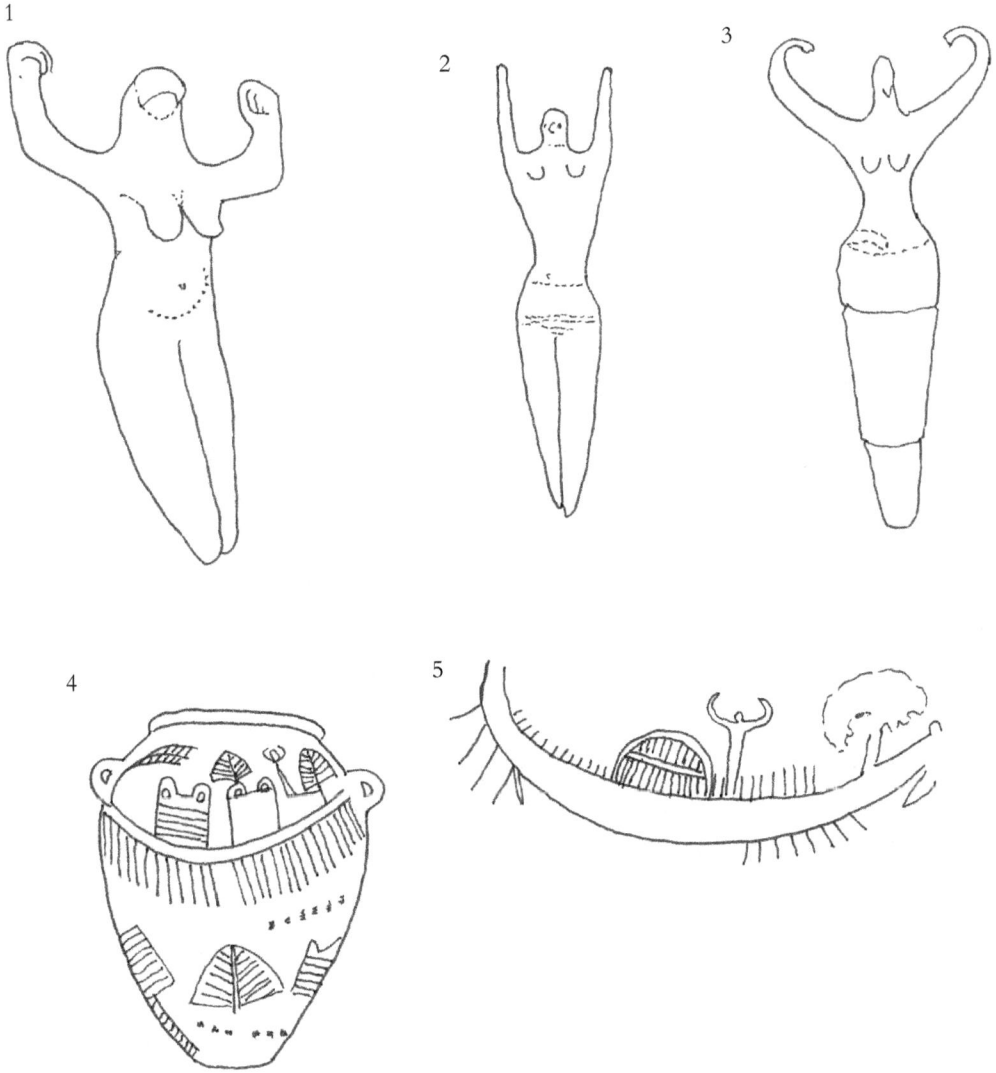

NEOLITHIC EGYPTIAN FIGURINES

1–3. *Three Kemetic female figurines in the 'supplication/praise' position* (6,200–5,600 BP), Egypt

4. *Design on a pot featuring the Kemetic priestess/goddess in a boat, reminiscent of the Indian Lady of the Spiked Throne (in next chapter)*, Egypt

5. *Petroglyph of the Kemetic priestess/goddess in a boat*, Egypt
(Source: Dashu, Max, 2005a)
All line drawings © Judy Foster, 2013

on to their children. The more recent scarcity of imagery representing the female principle can therefore be explained by a belief in her presence within these symbols. Sacred rocks and stones represent the goddess or ancestral being throughout Africa just as they do in India, and in Indigenous Australia where ancestral beings are often represented in (sacred) natural features of the land, sky and water.

Runoko Rashidi (1988) explains that the predynastic African goddess had "an all-encompassing influence and was universally acknowledged as the greatest and ultimate seat of power."[24] He identifies Neith (Tanit) as "one of the earliest of the northern African goddesses [who] can be traced back to at least 6,000 BP."[25] Neith appears as the 'Great Mother' and is represented as a white vulture, at once nurturing and destructive. Neith, as the wild cow and milch cow, was "guardian of the Nile Delta … both the donor of life and protector of the dead",[26] 'goddess of love and sensuality', linked with dance, music and song. She was associated with Hathor, who was a fertility goddess represented as the predynastic sacred cow. (The sacred cow symbolism perhaps originated here and then was transferred to other cultures, such as India.) It seems the attributes of the African goddess listed above held similar meanings to those of the Old European goddesses and those elsewhere – a truly worldwide goddess.

For Rosalind Jeffries (1988) the African goddess was rainmaker, and "Primal Mother Creator … [H]er powers of fertility in the universe … could be magnified to affect vegetation, animal husbandry and the atmosphere."[27] These symbolic aspects can be seen all over Africa, and particularly in the 10,000-year-old cave paintings at Tassili (seven examples of which appear in *Black Women in Antiquity*, 1988).[28] The first of these spectacular paintings depicts the 'horned goddess' (c. 10,000–8,000 BP) who features tattooed arms, breasts, body and lower legs, wears an apron skirt, and large horned headdress (cow horns, used to carry medicinal herbs, symbolised healing, death and the afterlife).[29] Other paintings feature women dancing, and one portrays the goddess transforming herself into a cow. Rosalind Jeffries explains that it was generally believed that the goddess "utilised the temperament and power of various animals to help people"[30] in times of trouble.

Camille Yarborough (1988)[31] records another example of 5,000-year-old Tassili rock art in which a woman breastfeeds her baby. The pattern and number of braids in her hairstyle is symbolic, designed to inform other women of her status, clan and village.

Other symbolic images of the deity include the snake (vitality of life), while the serpent, death, and the goddess are all related because the serpent sheds its skin just as the womb sheds its inner lining. The 'serpent eating its tail' motif represents the eternal cycles of life, death and regeneration. The deity is associated with the sun, moon and stars (a worldwide theme), and male and female horns are linked with (sacred) cattle in Africa (as they are in India, Anatolia, and Crete). Palaeolithic hunters and the goddess image are engraved on rock near Algiers. She has always been connected with the abundance of animals.

Clyde Ford tells us that the Sahel bards forecast that the African deity awaits her rediscovery, and this time she will be so deeply absorbed within that she will never be forgotten. An African goddess that fulfils that promise is the Yoruba goddess, Oya from West Africa.[32] She is a weather goddess and "manifests herself in various forms: the river Niger, tornadoes, strong winds generally, fire, lightning and buffalo."[33] Judith Gleason connects Oya with the Tassili wall paintings at Aouanrhet in Algeria which depict a horned woman with outstretched arms that resemble buffalo horns, as well as horn-like breasts.[34]

170

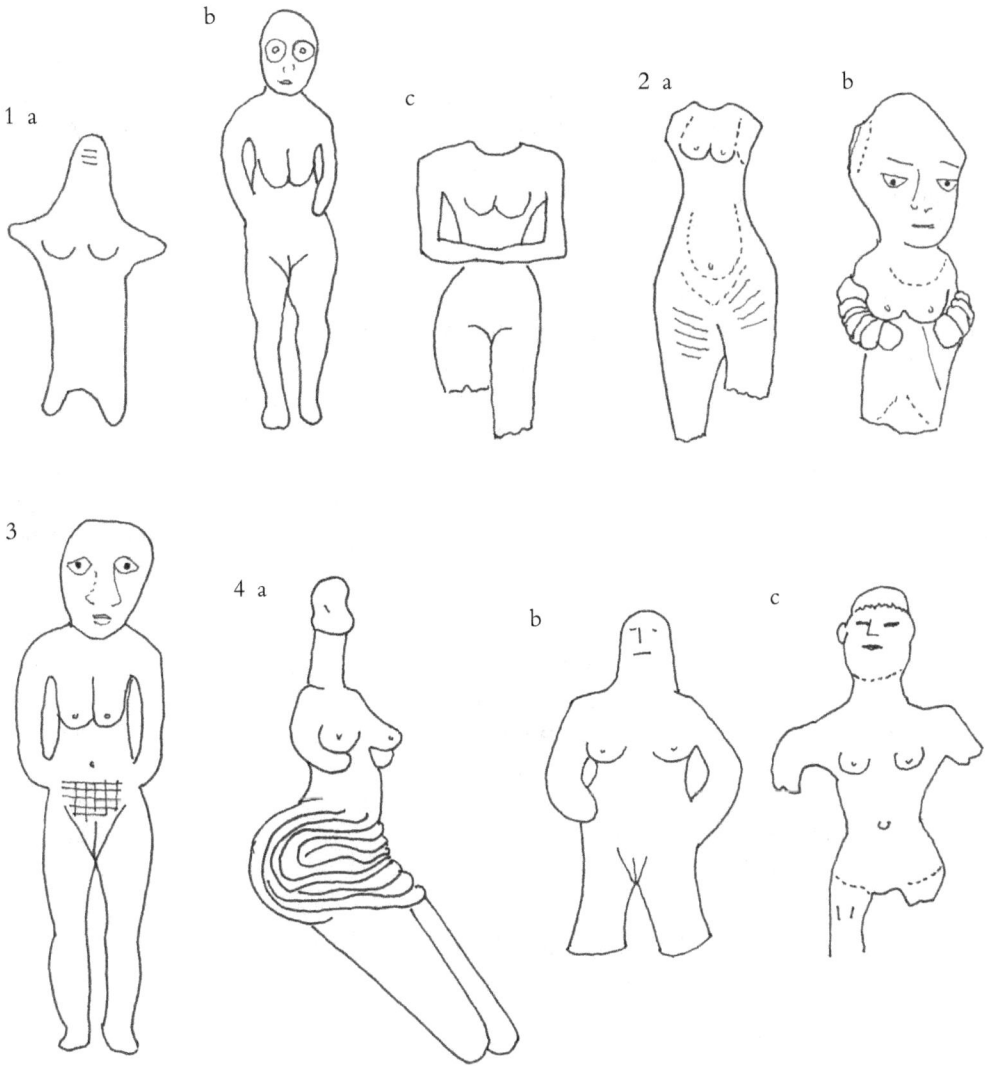

AFRICA: GODDESS FIGURINES

1. *Three figurines* from the Badarian culture, 7,000 BP (Source: Wysinger, Myra, n.d.)
2. Prehistoric *female deities* from Sudan and Nigeria (Source: Dashu, Max, 2008, poster)
3. *Ivory figurine* from the Badarian culture, 6,500 BP (Source: Wysinger, Myra, n.d.)
4. *Three female figurines*: from Sudan 6,000 BP; Kenya and Chad, n.d. (Source: Dashu, Max, 2008, poster)

All line drawings © Judy Foster, 2013

African matriarchal societies

Examples of matriarchal/matrilineal societies with roots in prehistory were presented at the First and Second World Congresses on Matriarchal Studies (2003 and 2005)[35] and demonstrate the importance of women in the past. Papers were presented by northern African Kabile (Berber) Makilam, and by southern African Akan (Asante) Wilhelmina Donkoh, each of whom spoke of some fundamental traditions of their cultures. Both examples include a number of similarities to Indigenous Australian societies.

Matriarchal societies: Northern Africa

In 'The central position of women among Berber People of northern Africa: The four seasons life cycle of a Kabyle woman'[36] Makilam describes the Kabyles, an ethnic sedentary sub-group of the Berber people who, together with the nomadic Tuareg people, are the oldest known (modern human) people of northern Africa. Traditionally the Kabyles are matrilineal, with women central to the clan, and the mother of the clan is regarded as the 'central pillar' of her house, symbolised by the central supporting pillar of the building. She is responsible for the passing down of knowledge, oral traditions, values, conventions and customs to her children and her children's children. The teachings, knowledge and words of all female elders are considered sacred.

Houses and land are owned by the community, and each village is independent from all others, and governed by the elders. Members of the clan are related through bloodlines to the mother. Endogamy allows for marriages between clan members of the community, with harmonious, mutually supported social relationships based on blood-ties and affiliation to the community land.

Mothers choose the wives for their sons; the mothers make these arrangements together after the birth of a son. Young people are married early – when they reach puberty – to ensure that any children are legitimate. Girls who become pregnant before marriage have

THE GREAT HORNED GODDESS

The great horned goddess: Aouamrhet/Oya
(wall painting), Tassili, North Africa, 10,000 BP
(Source: Lhote, Henri, 1959)
All line drawings © Judy Foster, 2013

to leave the community with the child's father until the baby is born; they are eventually accepted back into the clan after purification rituals, although the child always bears a stigma. Men's responsibility is to name their children (establishing legitimacy?).

There is belief in an afterlife, and ancestral veneration is part of daily life expressed in all social activities. Agricultural practices follow the seasonal cycles, observing circular time. Every step of every activity is accompanied by ritual according to the season, including the production of cloth and garments, the preparation of food, and the sowing of grain; each step is consistent with one of the four seasons of the year (gestation, birth, marriage, old age/ death). In this way nature and the earth are respected and cared for by everyone.

Makilam gives an important and lovely example of the symbolism of ritual activity by African women in the creation of pottery. Each step of pottery-making follows the season, and there is symbolism in each act of forming a clay pot:

- first, *a ball* of clay is formed = woman (who is the centre of the pot)
- second, *a coil* of clay is rolled and formed around the ball = man (who forms the sides of the pot) = symbolism of the circle/spiral = both together symbolise *the whole*, new life.

Similarly in weaving:

- the threads of the *warp* = woman
- and the *weft* threads which cross over and are interwoven into the warp, the weft = man
- both together form *the whole* = the cloth = living creation = *birth of new life*.

Makilam also speaks of the symbolism of the imagery women hand-paint onto pottery and on house walls, which is a secret symbolic language meant only for women; its meaning is passed down from mother to daughter with each stage of her initiation connected with special knowledge relating to the stages of a woman's life. (This symbolism is also present in South-East Asian women's traditional weaving.)

The traditions Makilam describes are those which have been preserved by women through centuries of waves of colonisation in Algeria, Tunisia, and Morocco, and are now in danger of extinction. She does not mention male traditions, although some can be inferred.

Matriarchal societies: Southern Africa

In 'Female leadership among the Asante',[37] historian Wilhelmina J. Donkoh describes the matrilineal Akan-speaking people of Ghana, where origins are derived from one female ancestor, the descent is through the female line, and ownership of property and inheritance are based on blood affiliation to the matriliny. Social, economic and political responsibilities are sex-specific. The Asante are a matrifocal society whose oral traditions and knowledge are recorded in folk tales, names, drum language, pottery, and the creation of sacred sites for ritual use.

Asante spiritual beliefs include three levels of existence forming a circular life pattern: future unborn life in the spiritual realm; the present physical existence; and death and regeneration in the spiritual realm. There are many female and male spiritual beings or deities, symbolised by rocks, mountains, rivers, and lakes. The supreme being is male: Onyame; the most sacred female earth deity is Asaase Yah (Mother Earth). These two spiritual beings symbolise balance through harmony.

In this clan system there is a common ancestress, and matrilocality is the preferred living arrangement. No child is considered illegitimate; every child is valued. In the kinship system each child is made legitimate through being named by the father. If he does not, the mother's lineage has the right to name the child.

In the Asante kinship system there can be no marriage between the mother's children and her sister's children; the mother's brother's children can marry the father's sister's children, who are cross cousins. (These rules are similar to those in kinship systems of Australian Indigenous societies.) Married women never leave the lineage or ancestral home, but the group may have more than one house. Sometimes a woman may live in her husband's family's house.

Women are considered very important because of their childbearing capacity, and socially both female and male are equally respected. Men's role is to provide meats, game and fish, while women provide vegetables and fruit. A man has the right to build a house on his mother's land, and he has rights and responsibilities within his mother's home. A father gives his children spiritual protection, and may assist in raising them, but will pass his goods on to his siblings.

Conflict was traditionally dealt with by council in which all adult clan members, together with male and female traditional leaders, met to discuss domestic matters, and any decisions were made by consensus. Today, colonisation has meant that the people have been dispossessed of their traditional law and order system which is now more complex and hierarchic, and there have been changes to leadership roles brought about by contact with modernity and politics.

Max Dashu (2005c) speaks of the Bantu cultures in central and southern Africa which are matrilineal, with land inherited by daughters; women's ritual activity also bestows power. She argues that many cultures "are not only matrilineal but also matrilocal with powerful female offices and a history of important foundational women."[38] The Goba clan, for example, are matrilineal, where sisters and their children are central; the men marry out, with one brother remaining with his mother's kin, and representing them in matters outside the family. His sisters, who choose him, can stop anyone unsuitable from taking control. The female elder "has important responsibilities to the ancestors."[39] The women evoke and commune with the spirits in dance "to clear harmful influences from the village while the young men drum."[40] There are women's councils, and men's councils, each of which take part in important decision-making, and in settling disputes. Senior women and men take part in some rituals, and a group of female elders always take part in all other council activities.[41]

Threads

It is interesting to note the number of similarities between African traditional life and the traditions of Australian Indigenous people:

- peaceful communal societies; everything is held in common; no individual ownership
- conflict is avoided and disputes are settled through ritual
- decisions are made in consultation with the elders by group consensus
- respect for elders, whose traditional knowledge is highly valued
- elaborate kinship rules for relationships and marriage which ensure harmony
- every child is valued

- equality found through sex roles adapted for context
- high respect for the land and nature, and a strong sense of the spiritual in everyone and everything.

Despite women's efforts to preserve their roles, responsibilities, and rituals, African traditional societies underwent tremendous change under the pressure of colonisation, beginning at least by 4,500 BP with the arrival of Indo-European ideas and practices, and they have continued to change with more recent waves of colonisers. It has been due to the strength of the people in passing down oral traditions that so much information has survived until today.

Colonisation and dispossession

The traditional women of Nigeria and Kenya

The work of traditional village women around the world is often hidden and not taken into account, yet it has been the major source of food for their families for generations, according to Susan Hawthorne (2002).[42] She provides two examples where the colonisation of women's traditional food cultivation has had problematic effects: for the growing of the staple crop, cassava, in Nigeria, and njahe beans in Kenya, but there are many other similar examples around the world.

Cassava has symbolic meaning for Nigerian women: it has supernatural power and is sacred; while the njahe bean has special uses for Kenyan women and their reproductive functions because of its high protein content. According to Nigerian woman, Flora Nwapa, it is below a man's dignity to grow cassava, although he is very happy to eat it "but when he becomes affluent, he is ashamed of eating it."[43]

Women plant cassava roots between the rows of maize or other crops (a process known as 'intercropping') which are grown by the men for cash and export. Traditionally cassava is easy to grow and harvest, versatile in cooking, and healthy to eat. It is also important for conservation and improvement of the land and environment. Vandana Shiva (1993)[44] comments that intercropping has been basic to African farming techniques and demonstrates the most sustainable approach to farming.

Colonisers want to restrict these cultural practices by replacing the use of cassava-root cuttings with specially developed cassava seeds, to 'improve' the yield, and they require the plants to be grown separately from the men's crops. This makes it harder for the women to grow the plants, and those who rely on cassava as the staple of their diet can be deprived of a cheap, sustainable, environmentally friendly food source.

For the Kenyan women there are similar problems: njahe beans are a trade commodity and at the same time are a special food for women who eat them at certain times: while pregnant, after childbirth, and after menopause. The beans are small and black with white caps, and are symbolic for the Kikuyu people. They are high in protein and nutritionally superior to, and complementary with, millet and maize.

Colonisers want njahe beans to be replaced with other exotic crops because they do not like their taste or colour, or do not like the plants intermixed with other more economically valuable crops. They believe the best results are achieved by separate group plantings, although in the longer term this is not sustainable. Poorer women and their families are then deprived of a cheap nutritious and available food source, and lose their traditional cultural practices and symbolic meanings. As Susan Hawthorne explains, "women and small farmers are disempowered, genetic diversity is reduced ... [and] farmers are increasingly vulnerable to agricultural disasters through exposure to a wide variety of crop diseases"[45] and famine.

The Tonga from the Zambezi River Valley

Sekai Nzenza-Shand (1997)[46] describes the plight of the Tonga people of the Zambezi River valley, on the northern border of Zimbabwe, as another example of dispossession as a result of colonisation. The Tonga people's traditional hunter-gatherer, semi-nomadic lifestyle had remained largely undisturbed over the millennia because they lived in a deeply forested region abounding in wild game, fruits, nuts and seeds. They lived along the banks on each side of the mighty river, in which several varieties of fish were plentiful. Their settlements contained clusters of temporary houses, small and low-roofed, and thatched with grass, a style suited to seasonal occupation.

According to Sekai Nzenza-Shand's informant, traditional Tonga society was matriarchal (matrilineal), wherein women inherited land and possessions. Upon the death of the chief, the title was passed on to his sister's son. The man moved in with his wife's family upon marriage, and each time he married a new wife, he would live with her family for a time, afterwards dividing his time between all his wives within their families. Such a system would have been advantageous for both parties since wives and mothers would have been assured of a support network even if they were widowed or divorced.

This changed in 1953 when the British-owned Northern Rhodesia (Zambia), Nyasaland (Malawi), and Southern Rhodesia (Zimbabwe), were divided into two separate countries to form a federation. The river became a border between North and South Rhodesia, and so the Tonga had to buy passports if they needed to cross the river, the banks of which were guarded by armed men who did not hesitate to shoot. When the construction of the Kariba Dam was completed, the Tonga traditional lands were flooded by the lake (the dam covered land 200 kilometres long, and up to 40 kilometres wide). The Tonga people were moved away from the river to the Zambezi Escarpment, which was dry and mainly infertile wild scrub country, where they were told to build their houses and cultivate the land for their food, something they had never done before. Many of the men were employed to build the dam, and there were numerous accidents during which men died. There were plenty of wild animals in Omay (their new country), but hunting required the purchase of permits, and the Tonga were simply too poor to do so. They received little or no government help. With growing tourism on the shores of Lake Kariba, the needs of the Tonga were ignored, according to Sekai Nzenza-Shand, and although independence was achieved in the 1980s, few changes have resulted.

The people continue to live in traditional houses rather than permanent residences because it is all they can afford. HIV/AIDS and other illnesses cause many deaths but there are few clinics, and shortages of health carers and medicines.

Sekai Nzenza-Shand was told that the Tonga people were always very healthy when they lived their traditional way in the Zambezi valley. However, because of the different plant ecology and growing conditions in the new region, they did not know which plants were useful as medicines, or as food for people and animals. She states that tourism has been of no benefit to them, and the government ignores them. Theirs is a life of poverty: where once they had been self-sufficient, now they are "the forgotten people."[47]

The African semi-settled hunter-gatherer lifestyle lasted much longer than it did north of the Mediterranean (most likely because of difficult environmental factors which prevented the heavy farming practices of Europe and East Asia), and in some instances it is still practiced today. Environmental problems have ensured that the nomadic and semi-nomadic lifestyles have remained in parts of Africa.

The fact that the prehistoric African goddess was visible in so many forms indicates a prominent female principle which lasted well into the historic period, and she can still be seen today in the wonderful cave paintings. The imagery of the sacred cow and the cattle horns appear in different motifs and circumstances, not only throughout Africa but also in numerous other cultures, and all of these are traditional women's symbols. The 7,500-year-old ritual sacrificing of cattle in Africa is also significant in different ways in the relationship between humans and their highly valued animals (for example, in the Nile Basin, Mehrgarh, Çatal Hüyük, Crete, or Ness of Brodgar in the Orkney Islands).

CHAPTER 12

HIDDEN WORLDS: THE INDIAN SUBCONTINENT

The prehistory of India[1]

The subcontinent of India is separated from the rest of Asia by mountains which extend from the north-west corner of Baluchistan right across to the south-east border with Myanmar (Burma). Borders are also shared with Iran, Afghanistan, Russia, Tibet, and China. While Pakistan, Kashmir, Nepal, Bhutan and Bangladesh are all part of the subcontinent of India, it is only since European colonisation that political borders separating these countries have been drawn. The earliest 'civilisations' (Mehrgarh, Harappa and Mohenjo-daro) on the Indian subcontinent were in the north-west, associated with the Indus River valley. Tools dated to 2 million BP and used by *Homo erectus* are spread all over India, although little skeletal evidence has been found as yet. The Indo-Europeans seemed to have seeped into India from Iran between 5,000 and 4,500 BP. The name 'India' is derived from the Greek word *Indos* and the Sanskrit word *sindhu*, meaning 'the Indus River'. Sanskrit, Greek and Latin are related Indo-European languages. Dilip Chakrabarti (1999) states that an earlier name for India was Bharatavarsha "the land where the progenies of the mythical king Bharata live."[2] (However, the association of the idea of a king suggests that this name is also of Indo-European origin.)

India is important in the story of Asia and the Hidden and New Worlds because it is situated on a likely route taken by *H. erectus* and *Homo sapiens sapiens* (modern humans) on their journey eastwards through Myanmar (Burma) to Java in Indonesia, and to China which lies on India's eastern border. It was from India that skills including iron-mongering, cotton-growing and certain textile-weaving methods were brought to South-East Asia together with other Indo-European ideas and practices. India is also important in the search for the prominent female principle in prehistory because, as Dilip Chakrabarti explains, the 'mother earth goddess' has always been powerful in the Indian psyche.

In the late 1800s Western colonialists considered that India could only develop culturally when exposed to 'outside forces' and this mindset caused India's long and culturally rich prehistory to be ignored. Dilip Chakrabarti explains that any earlier records were compiled by British colonialists and were focused on the racially 'superior' Aryans, who had invaded India about 5,500 BP and established the well-known Indus 'civilisation'. Sir Mortimer Wheeler's archaeological survey (1944–1948) was responsible for the emphasis

A TIMELINE FOR PREHISTORIC INDIA

PERIOD (BP)	PLACE/PEOPLE	EVIDENCE
Lower Palaeolithic **2,000,000** **900,000** **800,000**	Throughout India Narmada River Valley, central India Bhimbetka in Madhya Pradesh	• Stone tools used by *H. erectus*; no skeletal evidence • Part of Archaic *H. sapiens* skull • Engraved cupules and meander line in cave. Red ochre (ritual) quartz crystals, stone disc
Upper Palaeolithic **(c. 26,000–11,000)** **c. 11,000** End of Palaeolithic	North-west to north-central India Baghor I Ganga River Valley	• More diverse tools, crescent shaped sickles (harvesting), hafted wood- or bone-handled tools; seasonal camps • Triangular coloured stone on rubble-built platform (worship of female principle) • Scarcity of evidence before 12,000 BP
Mesolithic **(c. 12,000–5,000)** **12,000** **9,000** **8,000** **8,000–5,000**	Baghor, north-west India Baghor II, north-central India Uttar Pradesh Bhimbetka	• First semi-settled communities; stone floors; ritual burials; hammer stones; shallow querns; grinding stones • Circular stone pieces; shelters with wooden posts; fragile pottery pieces; woven mats (?); rice cultivation • Early village, ritual burials, grave goods; bone necklace, pendant; plastered floors; stone platforms • Rock art: hunters, large animals, women and food; linear images in red ochre Later: earliest images of 'mother goddesses'; no weapons, no battles
Neolithic **(c. 9,000–5,000)** **9,000** **7,500** **7,000** **6,500** **c. 6,500–4,600** **6,000–4,500**	North of Indus River: Mehrgarh Mehrgarh Kerala, Tamil Nadu Mehrgarh Late Mehrgarh; Early Harappa Dravidians Beginning of Indo-European Period Indo-Aryans	• City of Mehrgarh (equates with Çatal Hüyük in Anatolia): mudbrick houses; courtyards; cemeteries; stone vessels; necklaces etc. in semi-precious stones; many human figurines • Terracotta bead stamp: small copper ingot, 2 beads (earliest metallurgy?); earliest wheat and cotton growing; wheel and handmade pottery; extensive trade with the west • Cave paintings; figurines; pottery; wattle and daub huts • Bow drills (engraving, dentistry); terracotta crucibles (copper smelting); a variety of wheel-made pottery; no war weapons reported; first terracotta cattle (religious ritual?); diverse grave goods; female figurines • Pre-Indo-European period • These cultures are widely considered to be the beginning of India's history and are warrior cultures.

PERIOD (BP)	PLACE/PEOPLE	EVIDENCE
5.400–4,800	Tamil Nadu	• Rock art, copper and bronze objects
c. 5,500–5,000	Mohenjo-daro, Classic Harappa Indus script, Hinduism Baluchistan	• Many copper and iron war weapons; iron-mongering was exported to China about 5,000–4,500 BP • Evidence of pastoralism; fortified villages; clay toy horse and cart with wheels • Sacrificial platform, drain with skull; 'Zhob'-style female figurines denote Indo-European influence; many cattle figurines
4,000	Quetta	• Large pottery kiln (market economy?); early signs of Indo-European influences
3,500–1,000	Rest of India	• Villages, farming, paintings in caves and on rock walls, tools, querns, etc.

on Mohenjo-daro as one of two typical major cities of the Indus civilisation, the other being Harappa. Dilip Chakrabarti has found these accounts to be erroneous in a number of ways. Early Harappa developed alongside the earlier city of Mehrgarh about 6,000 BP, with similar villages whose inhabitants cultivated a wide variety of crops. As Mehrgarh gradually disappeared Harappa grew and by 5,000 BP had become a centre within a large area of farms and irrigated fields.

Since Sir Mortimer Wheeler's excavations there had been few archaeological surveys of prehistory carried out by Indian researchers until the 1970s. They have faced considerable difficulties created by the bureaucratic and authoritarian control of governments and provincial bodies over sites, which have often been left unprotected and greatly damaged by increasing population pressures.[3]

Palaeolithic India (2,000,000–12,000 BP)

According to Dilip Chakrabarti, it is unfortunate that very little attention is given to cultural, social and ritual life when most archaeologists excavate and record early sites; they concentrate only on tools and bones while ignoring stone formations and other signs of habitation dated before 12,000 BP.

The earliest tools found throughout India, such as hand axes, flakes and choppers, were possibly used by *H. erectus* since they are 2 million years old and are similar to those found in Africa, Europe and Asia. Dilip Chakrabarti (2006)[4] argues that the only skeletal evidence of early people in India indicates that they were archaic *H. sapiens* rather than *H. erectus*, although such evidence is still under review. Part of Namarda Man's skull was discovered in 1982 and its age is thought to be between 900,000 and 730,000 years old. A human collarbone has been found more recently but its age is as yet undetermined, while a fossilised skull of a baby found at Odai in southern India is 166,000 years old.

At Bhimbetka in Madhya Pradesh, central India, there are rock engravings of cupules (cupmarks) and a meander line in a cave dating to around 800,000 BP which may have been associated with women's rituals, just as they are today in parts of India. Artefacts include a stone disc, six small quartz crystals, and a piece of red ochre, all of which suggest the presence of early ritual life. According to Kalyan Chakravarty and Robert Bednarik (1997) there are many other sites in central India such as in "the extreme north, north-west and the Deccan as well as the extreme south [which] seem to have a dominant tradition of rock engraving"[5] including cupmarks on a pillar in Uttar Pradesh, central India.

Dilip Chakrabarti (2006) describes more recent Palaeolithic tool kits as including scrapers, perforators, chisels, scoops, shouldered points, barbs and spatulae. He notes one example of fragments of an (imported) engraved ostrich-shell decorated with cross-hatching between two parallel lines, and a bone harpoon from Bhimbetka dated to between 25,000 and 19,000 BP (perhaps indicating early use of cord?). Upper Palaeolithic tools became more diverse over time and are common in the current Indian landscape, although very few of these deposits have been fully excavated as yet. During this time tools also became more complex, with new crescent-shaped sickles for harvesting grain crops and other geometrically shaped tools which could have been arrowheads and drill points. Sickles and saws had hafted wood or bone handles.

By 12,000 BP flat grinding-stone slabs with grinding stones and split pebbles appeared which would have been used in food preparation. Typically, people lived near water sources in the summer and moved further afield in the wet season so that women could make use of a wide range of edible plants, fruits, berries, pods, mushrooms, leafy vegetables, and one or more seed species. Men hunted a variety of animals including cattle, elephant, buffalo, deer, wild cats, sheep, and goats.

Houses were temporary shelters formed of reeds, tree branches or leaves, sometimes with stone blocks arranged around the base; people also lived in caves or rock shelters. Sometimes shelters were supported by wooden posts, as indicated by postholes. One example had posts placed in pairs which Dilip Chakrabarti suggests indicated a thatched superstructure similar to those used by nomads today in India. They had floors made from stone slabs.

At one site there was a rubble-built platform on which was placed a triangular piece of natural stone. This platform arrangement dates to between 11,000 and 10,000 BP and marks the end of the Upper Palaeolithic period in northern India. Dilip Chakrabarti considers this arrangement to be the earliest tangible indication of recognition of the female principle/deity in India. Similar stone and platform arrangements continue to be constructed in Indian country villages and people still regard the triangular stone as representing the female principle or *Shakti*, symbolic of one or another *Mai* (mother). According to Marija Gimbutas (1989),[6] the triangle in Old Europe symbolises the 'goddess of birth, death and regeneration', as do the three spirals on the entrance wall within Newgrange which are arranged point down (two spirals above, one below). The triangle pointing up is a male symbol (as in the Trinity triangle).[7]

Mesolithic (Early Neolithic) India (12,000–5,000 BP)

Because of its comparative isolation and often difficult environments, India (unlike many other countries) had a long and distinct Mesolithic period which falls between the Upper Palaeolithic and the Neolithic periods. Dilip Chakrabarti (2006) maintains that during this time people became more settled, as food production and animal domestication developed. The Mesolithic period in India fell between 12,000 and 7,000 BP, and the metal-bearing

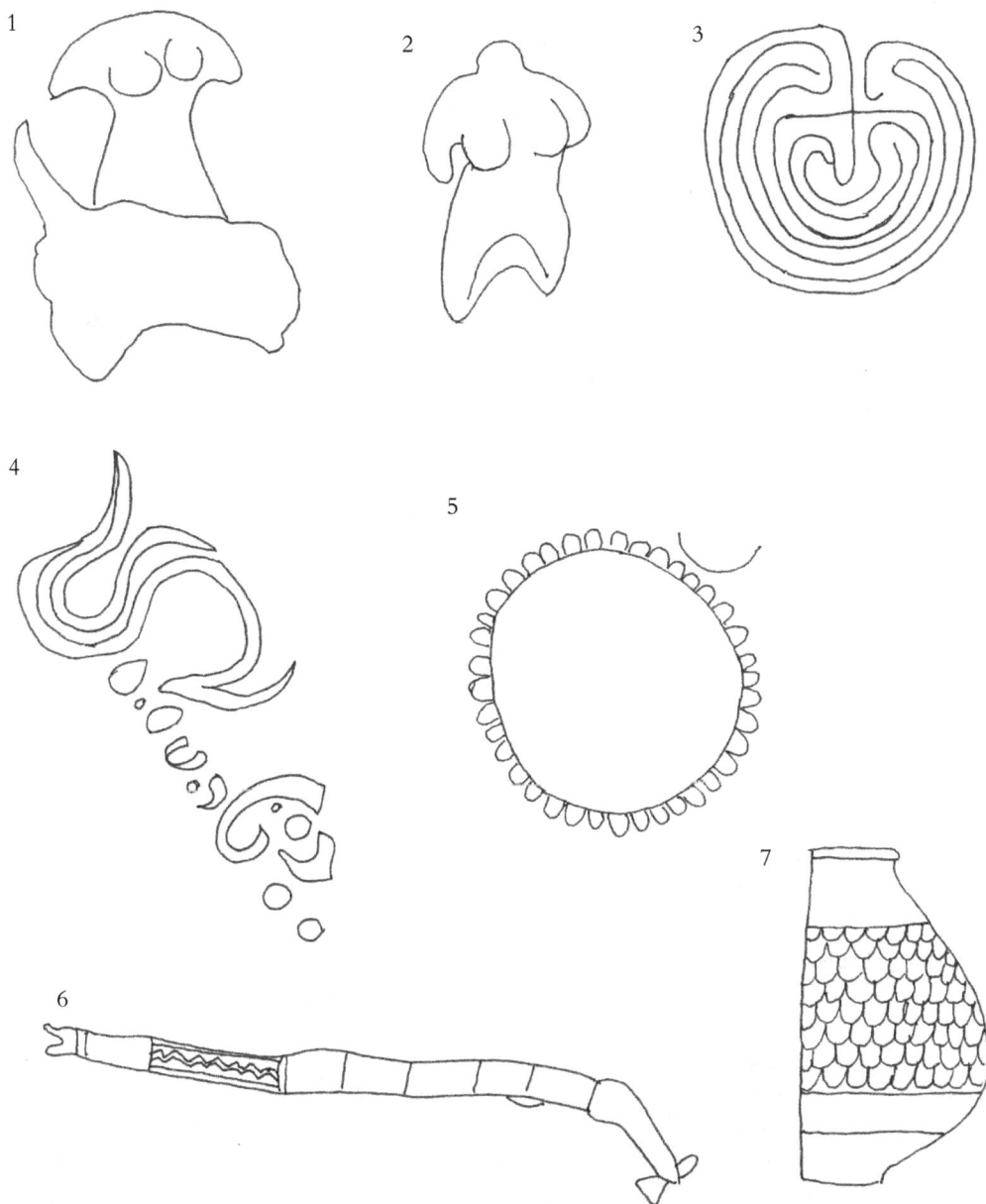

FIGURINES AND ROCK ART

1. and 2. *Two female figurines* (note similarity to figurines from Europe and China) (Source: Chakrabarti, Dilip, 1999)
3. *A circular design motif on rock wall*
4. and 5. *Rock art paintings*
6. *Wall painting of a snake*
7. *A repeated design on pottery* (Source 3–7: Chakravarty, Kalyan and Robert Bednarik, 1997)

All line drawings © Judy Foster, 2013

Mesolithic between 6,000 and 5,000 BP. It is notable that copper and bronze metal beads, stamp seals and other small objects were made in India during the Neolithic period sometime before the European Bronze Age, indicating a sophisticated culture.

Dilip Chakrabarti gives four examples of Indian life during this time demonstrating the growth towards a Neolithic civilisation which was present long before the Indus 'civilisation':

- Baghor I, north-west India

  Between 12,000 and 9,000 BP small huts had floors made of slabs of quarried schist, and were sometimes circular in shape and delineated by stone blocks; in one instance a burial site featured a carefully placed fully extended skeleton with an arm draped over the body, lying on a stone block. Quartz and chert tools, together with a few small pieces of pottery, lay among the dwellings but these may have been left by later people. Short tubular and barrel-shaped beads of banded agate, carnelian and garnet, and tiny bone beads were also found. Hammer stones, pieces of red ochre, broken shallow querns and grinding stones were evidence of food preparation using seeds and plants, and there were many animal bones.

- Baghor II, north-central India

  This is another early site, dated to 9,000 BP, where children apparently played with a few small, chipped, circular pieces of stone, although these could also have been weights or measures of some sort as Denise Schmandt-Besserat (1996) has argued. Wooden posts were used to support shelters, and other pieces of stone were perhaps used as sleeping or storage platforms, head rests or hearths. At another similar settlement fragile handmade pottery pieces, anvils, hammer stones, querns, mullers and ring-stones were found. Burnt clay lumps with reed marks suggest the use of woven reed mats. There were also possible storage bins made from bamboo and clay, found together with charred rice, indicating a settled village and early agriculture.

- Uttar Pradesh

  Dated to about 8,000 BP, ritual burial practices were this early village's most notable feature. Although dwellings were similar to earlier ones, further signs of early ritual burials included graves in which bodies were carefully laid upon loose 'cushion-like' soil with heads towards the setting sun, and right (male) or left (female) hand across the abdomen. Grave goods included shells and microliths. One male had a microlith arrow in his body, which suggests he may have been a victim of an accident or conflict resolution. Grave goods at another site include a bone necklace and pendant, while microliths were made of chert, chalcedony, quartz crystal, agate and imported carnelian. These tools could have been trade items. At a further site, Dilip Chakrabarti records plastered hearths and floors, the hearths probably used for roasting game. Prepared foods would have been served from stone platforms near the hearths. At this site there were some collective graves, but in all cases bodies had been treated with respect as demonstrated by the way they had been carefully placed with heads either towards the west or east, indicating ritual burials.

- Southern India

  Dilip Chakrabarti (2006) records that the only direct evidence of Mesolithic people in southern India is 7,000-year-old painted wall art in a rock shelter in southern Kerala near the west coast. There is more Neolithic evidence in Tamil Nadu, including pottery, small human figurines, animals and birds, as well as rectangular wattle-and-daub huts, hearths, querns and many stone tools. The pottery featured channel-spouts, and dishes-on-stands. In a later period there is late Neolithic rock art and some copper and bronze objects, and evidence of cattle from 5,400 to 4,800 BP.

Mesolithic rock art

Rock art painted with red ochre is thought by Dilip Chakrabarti to date to this period and is found on walls and ceilings of the numerous caves and rock shelters in central India. They feature hunter-gatherer life, with elegant and graceful linear images of hunters and animals in movement, women preparing food, and imagery which could represent plant foods or animal traps. Men carry bows and arrows, spears and hatchets. He found no scenes of human violence in this period, although later paintings in the same area, which include horse-riding and elephant-riding warriors with metal weapons, and royal processions, indicate that these activities belong to the Warrior Age.

While early paintings mainly featured large animals, in the next stage of the Mesolithic men are depicted using hunting weapons and large broom-shaped traps, and women are also represented hunting the animals, some of which are decorated with geometric and abstract designs within body outlines, in a wider range of colours. At a later stage of the hunter-gatherer/village period are the earliest representations of 'mother goddesses' which have been so prominent in Indian prehistory.

Indian rock art has continued into the historic period and it is not always easy to recognise earlier art. Dilip Chakrabarti states that the meanings are not known to present day Indians. (This is not the case in Australia where the Indigenous people still identify with the earliest traditional oral and art evidence of their beginnings.) The best-known rock art is at Bhimbetka near Bhopal and is painted in red and white ochre, while more colourful painted images are usually more recent.[8]

The Indian Neolithic Period (9,000–5,000 BP)

The earliest evidence of the Neolithic in the Indus River Valley lasted for 2,000 to 3,000 years, and may have spread from Anatolia through Iran. By 6,000 BP agriculture had spread throughout India. The Indus River area was the area most suited to agriculture, the growing of wheat and barley, and the domestication of cattle, sheep and goats. Women produced painted pottery.

The Mehrgarh civilisation

The most important Neolithic site in India is the recently rediscovered city of Mehrgarh situated near the Bolan Pass in Baluchistan, which is in north-west subcontinental India near the Iranian border. The city evidently covered an area of 250 hectares along the banks of the Bolon River. Mudbrick houses occupied the site, with each layer of houses built over a previous level as at Çatal Hüyük. Recent excavation levels reveal that this city was occupied

India: Mehrgarh Figurines

1. *Group of clay bird goddesses* from Mehrgarh (8,000 BP)
2. *Two clay bird goddesses*, 8,000 BP
   (Source 1–2: Mahmood, Mahmood, 2009)
3. A *female figurine from Mehrgarh*, 5,000 years old, National Museum of Pakistan, Karachi

4. *A figurine from Mehrgarh*, c. 3,000 BP
   (Source 3–4: Wikimedia Commons, 2013)
5. *Romanian figurine* (note the similarity to an Old European snake goddess), front and side views, Romania, 7,800 BP
   (Source: Gimbutas, Marija, 1991)

All line drawings © Judy Foster, 2013

well into the historic Indus civilisation. Archaeologist J.F. Jarrige began to excavate Mehrgarh in 1974 and archaeological work lasted until the end of the 1980s. There are a number of reports providing details of the prehistory of Mehrgarh, including those of Gregory Possehl (1982),[9] and Dilip Chakrabarti's *Oxford Companion to Indian Archaeology* (2006). These reports record the five earliest levels of Mehrgarh occupation which fall within the Neolithic period.

Level one (11,000–9,000 BP)

This date equates Mehrgarh with Çatal Hüyük in Anatolia. There is evidence here of the earliest domestication of barley, cattle, sheep and goats. Around 9,000 BP rice cultivation is apparent, watered by an early form of irrigation.

Houses with a number of rooms, including storerooms, were made of mudbricks with floors covered in reeds. They were interspersed with open spaces, possibly courtyards used for domestic functions, rituals and burials. Some houses featured interconnecting rooms and doors with lintels. One large broken pot, decorated with external ridged lines and an interior design of a snake, was found along with several complete goblets and other beautiful painted vessels. The reports make no mention of the city layout at this point.

Tools included microliths, harvesting tools, a few stone vessels, and some unbaked clay figurines but no pottery. Burials contained grave goods including goats, baskets of food, and lumps of red ochre. Shell, dentate shells, calcite beaded necklaces, mother-of-pearl and shell pendants, steatite beaded belts, anklets of calcite beads, bone rings and, sometimes, turquoise and lapis lazuli beads which could have been traded from Afghanistan, were also found in graves. Some burials were contained within specially constructed low brick walls, and occasionally bodies were compacted to make room for later burials. Nothing is known as yet about the sex or status of the dead. Terracotta human figurines (probably representing the female principle) are significant at this time, with one well-executed example with a tubular body, pinched nose, and legs joined, suggesting a new form of imagery emerging. These figurines depicted women with long hair and garments decorated with raised designs of flowers reaching to the ground, their arms positioned to draw attention to exposed breasts.

Level two (9,000–7,500 BP)

A small copper ingot and two beads were found, as well as a terracotta bead incised with a design which could have been used to make patterns on wet clay. Wheel-made pottery made its appearance alongside earlier handmade pottery. Cotton was apparently grown under irrigation, and trade was very important to the economy. Red ware pottery featuring pipal leaves was common, while the first use of fired grey pottery items was evident. Distinctive female figurines from this period displayed carefully modelled complex hairstyles, round heavy breasts and joined legs.

Gregory Possehl's 1982[10] account reports that there was also evidence of an early form of dentistry with artificial drilling on the teeth of some individuals. It is thought that the method of drilling using flint drill bits was similar to the technique used for making holes in beads. There is no further evidence of dentistry after 6,500 BP. According to the original report in *Nature*, A. Coppa et al "describe eleven drilled molar crowns from nine adults discovered in a Neolithic graveyard in Pakistan that dates from 7,500 to 9000 years ago … [providing] evidence for a long tradition of a type of proto-dentistry in an early farming culture."[11] (This period equates to level one at Harappa).

187

Level three (7,500–5,500 BP)

There was an indication of possible changes to social organisation, for example, a large complex of storerooms suggested a surplus of crops. There was more craft specialisation including bow drills, suggesting shell engraving; and terracotta crucibles with traces of copper indicated copper smelting which was most likely used in jewellery, as no war weapons were reported. Wheel-made pottery featured a variety of regional designs. A few terracotta humped cattle were found, and were perhaps of religious significance as they had been at Çatal Hüyük. Terracotta female figurines retained the tubular body but one type of image now featured broad hips, and cloth draped around the waist, while a second style had a similar-shaped head with pinched nose, pendulous breasts, broad hips and legs joined together. (See illustration on p. 186.)

Level four (5,500 BP)

Although houses were similar to those in the past, rooms were now interconnected through doorways with wooden lintels which could be quite low in height as they were earlier in Çatal Hüyük. There was one room which may have had a special purpose, according to Dilip Chakrabarti. It contained grinding stones, pestles, a storage jar, a large broken basin with ridges and snake decorations inside, fine undamaged goblets, beautifully painted vessels, blades, bones, and various kinds of pottery. He also noted a new form of tubular-shaped terracotta female figurine, still with joined legs, featuring large coils of hair on each side of the head, incised eyes, and strands of necklaces around neck, large breasts and hips.

Level five (5,300–4,500 BP)

Brick walls were no longer associated with burials. Dilip Chakrabarti describes how the heads of bodies were carefully placed on brick 'pillows', laid east-west, and sometimes turned to face the south. There was only one collective burial. The first sign of the importance of women was demonstrated by the inclusion of two painted wheel-made pots as grave goods. Another grave contained a circular, compartmented stamp-seal of copper/bronze placed near the woman's head. Jewellery was often included in graves; necklaces and head ornaments, and sometimes pendants of semi-precious stones worn with or without the necklaces, were placed on what were presumably female graves. People's teeth were in good order because of a naturally high incidence of fluoride in the local water. Mahmood Mahmood[12] refers to the importance of the female figurines over this period as representing the earliest form of the 'matriarchal' goddess Indria (Early Harappa period).

Mehrgarh level five evidence gradually disappears at about the same time as the beginning of the mature stage (classic period) of the Harappan civilisation (4,800–3,900 BP) and it is also around this time that Indo-European influences began to appear in the Indus Valley.[13]

Although the pre-Indus civilisation is dated to between 5,500 and 5,000 BP, the brief glimpse of Mehrgarh that is available at this time is not extensive enough to discern the signs of change into a hierarchic society. In fact at level five (4,000 BP) there is not much change, but at level six (3,500 BP) the first signs of Indo-European influences are immediately apparent. For example, a large pottery kiln suggests pottery production for a market economy. Pottery had always been a specialised craft/skill practiced exclusively by women in the past but now it appears that they may have had to work for others. According

188

INDIA: HARAPPA FEMALE FIGURINES

1. *Two terracotta female figurines* from Early Harappa/Late Mehrgarh
2. *Female figurine* with painted features (Source 1–2: Clark, Sharri R., 2001)
3. *Female figurine*, Late Harappa/Early Mohenjo-daro period

4. *Female figurine with infant* from Early Mohenjo-daro period
5. The famous *Dancing Girl*, Late Mohenjo-daro/Early Historic period
6. Early *example of the Indus script* (Source 3–6: Kenoyer, J.M., 2008–2010)

All line drawings © Judy Foster, 2013

to Dilip Chakrabarti, at Quetta around 4,000 BP the signs are more obvious; there was a room with a sacrificial platform, a drain with half a human skull in it, and 'Zhob' style mother goddess figurines. Male figurines now appeared alongside the female figurines.

At another site in Baluchistan the signs are even clearer, with evidence of pastoralism in the mountains at 5,500 BP. The first appearance of fortified villages and a clay toy horse and cart with wheels, an Indo-European invention, occurs at 5,000 BP. Thus, although the latter part of the village era is considered Neolithic by Dilip Chakrabarti, all the signs point to the beginning of the Indian Warrior Age with its hierarchy, materialism, violence and loss of status for women. The other result of the warrior takeover in India was the development of the caste system with all its inequities for both women and men.

Max Dashu has drawn our attention to a remarkable recent discovery of a ceramic 'boat' entitled 'The Lady of the Spiked Throne', which has been dated to the Late Mehrgarh/ Early Harappa period. Massimo Vidale (2011)[14] refers to the sculpture as 'a cow boat' made in red-orange ware style, similar to those of Mehrgarh and early Harappa. It is shaped in the form of a horned bovid, with an elongated 'body', the far end covered with a ceramic canopy: the four legs are folded beside the 'body', front legs facing backwards, back legs bent forwards. Cobras writhe along each leg, their hooded heads resting on the bovid's shoulders and flanks. The bovine head, with curved horns, proudly bows forward, and features black linear "vegetal, zoomorphic and geometric patterns."[15] There is a hump behind the bovine head, upon which is painted a sun symbol and there are other symbolic designs on the neck and body, including winding spiraling aquatic plants with triangular-shaped leaves, and a meander water design. Black painted lines meander up the horns, while the eyes of the 'cow' are formed with black line almond-shaped concentric circular pupils and arched brows, and the muzzle is incised with double black outlined almond-shaped nostrils. From the front, the body appears as a triangular shape, topped with the horned head gazing benignly towards us, and more aquatic plant designs cover the shoulders and chest.

The prominent female figurine, a 'queen' (the goddess) is seated under the canopy, upon her 'spiked' throne, her arms above the backs of two small horned 'bulls' (bovids). She wears a high headdress, while lozenge-shaped almond eyes and large beaked nose are the only facial features; her wide square shoulders and finely-shaped upright figure are framed by her throne, which features five triangular-shaped spikes across the back, with another spike each side. (Could these shapes represent the star rays of the Seven Sisters of the Pleiades?)

Two male attendants stand against the curve of the canopy (one on each side of the goddess), with two more by the inner hollow of the bovid head. There are eight figurines sitting "on low square stools … separated by a central isle" and "arranged in alternating female and male couples, females coming first and being slightly larger than males."[16] (The style of these figurines is similar to those of the Late Mehrgarh/Early Harappa period 4,800–4,600 BP.) This artefact is significant because it is of a form not found before at the Indus sites of Mehrgarh, Harappa and Nausharo.[17]

In his brief description of India's prehistory, Dilip Chakrabarti makes no mention of clear evidence of women's and men's roles but there are some notable points which suggest women's prominence:

- The Palaeolithic period featured hunter-gatherer societies where women and men would have shared complementary roles.

1

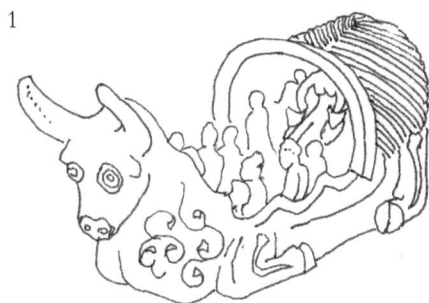

2

3

THE LADY OF THE SPIKED THRONE

1. *The Lady of the Spiked Throne* ('cow-boat')
   ceramic sculpture, red/orange clay with black
   painted details, India, 4,800–4,600 BP
2. *The 'cow boat'* (detail)
3. *The queen/priestess/goddess on her throne* (detail)
   (Source: Vidale, Massimo, 2011)

All line drawings © Judy Foster, 2013

- According to Dilip Chakrabarti, traditional Indians regard the earth as "Dharitri, a mother which never dies";[18] and the 'goddess' is still represented by certain rocks and other natural features, as she has been in Africa.
- Respect for the dead was demonstrated by the care taken with the placement of bodies, and the presence of grave goods demonstrates ritual practices and an awareness of the metaphysical. The content of graves does not suggest hierarchy or violent deaths (with one exception which could have been accidental).
- Indo-European influences and practices seem to have infiltrated into India even before the Aryan invasions/incursions of the early historic cities of Harappa and Mohenjo-daro. Although the power of the female principle was weakened by the new male dominance, it has never been fully removed from view.

Origins of modern India

Wendy Doniger (2009)[19] posits that the first modern humans had come to India by sea in watercraft, blown there by the monsoon winds from eastern Africa 50,000 years ago, rather than by land via Iran as others suggest. She also argues that the Dravidians were descended from the Proto-Indo-Europeans (who were the first to domesticate the horse). She argues that prehistoric horses did not flourish in India because of climatic conditions, and the only evidence of prehistoric horses has been found in India's north-west.

191

Trade was possible from 6,300–4,600 BP between southern Turkmenistan, central Asia, northern Iraq and India, with caravans carrying pottery, seals, figurines, and ornaments, and this allowed the exchange of languages and cultures on the Indian subcontinent. The Indo-Aryans were the first to bring horses back to India as part of the extensive northern trade network and came to the Indus Valley about 5,000–4,500 BP. The Indo-Aryans also established India's caste system.

The original inhabitants of the Indus valley and Mehrgarh were indigenous tribes whose languages related to Austroasiatic Munda languages. Wendy Doniger comments that a number of different languages were spoken and many words derived from these original languages are to be found in Hindu languages today. Munda-speaking people remain in India today.

The earliest elements of Hinduism, India's oldest religion (with the exception of those of the indigenous Indian tribal peoples), were present sometime before and during the early Harappa period, and may reach back into the early Mehrgarh civilisation, as there were many different peoples/cultures reaching these regions around this time.

From 5,300–4,600 BP Early Harappa included a citadel surrounded by high walls, within it some buildings at first identified as palaces, but later described as possible granaries (since no evidence of kings or armies has been found). More recent suggestions for the high walls are as protection against flooding.[20]

The earliest examples of the Indo-Aryan Indus script date from about 5,000 BP.[21] The discovery of steatite seals, with imagery including animals, people and inscriptions (for example geometric motifs and other markings) in Harappa, are considered to be part of the as yet undeciphered Indus script.[22] (These early seals appear to be similar to the earlier incised tokens found in Iran and Iraq by Denise Schmandt-Besserat, which she identifies as a forerunner to the first writing; this is quite possible because of early contact between these countries and the Indian subcontinent.)

According to Luigi Cavalli-Sforza (1994) Indians are genetically three times closer to West Europeans than to East Asians. As well, a 2009 study of genetic sources "suggests that modern Indians descend from two prehistoric genetically divergent populations",[23] one of which is referred to as the 'Ancestral North Indians' (40,000 BP), and the other as the 'Ancestral South Indians' (60,000 BP).[24]

There are four major language families in India, each encompassing numerous languages:
- *Indo-Aryan* in the northern part of India
- *Dravidian* in the southern part
- in the middle regions, a number of tribal languages, including
  Munda, an Austroasiatic language family
- *Tibeto-Burman languages* in the north-eastern hills of India.

The Dravidians, while being in southern India, are also present in central India, Sri Lanka, Bangladesh, Pakistan, Afghanistan and Iran. Dravidian subgroups are Tamil, Telugu, Kannada and Malayam. Most Indian people today are a mix of Dravidian and Aryan, hence the importance of the record of Dravidian origins. Dravidian languages link with northern Africa, Europe, and western Asia.

Origins of the Indian goddess/goddesses

Many small sculptures, especially those of female figurines, have been found in archaeological digs on the subcontinent of India, particularly in Upper Palaeolithic and Neolithic/ Chalcolithic (late Neolithic) periods, although unfortunately few have been fully recorded. Some of those found in prehistoric Mehrgarh (10,000–5,000 BP) and Early Harappa have been photographed and provide a glimpse of the way in which women were viewed in these periods.[25] These images could well be the forerunners to the goddesses of the Hindu and other cultures on the Indian subcontinent. Marija Gimbutas has recorded thousands of images of female deities in Europe and surrounds, so it is plausible that there would also be numerous goddess images on the Indian subcontinent around the same time.

The earliest Indian goddess figurines we can describe (and illustrate) are the figurines from Mehrgarh dated from 7,000 BP, and others from about 6,000–5,000 BP. The early images of women, children and animals are simply formed in red clay with small modelled or pinched details.

Later images of the female deity/deities demonstrate a refinement of form in fine white clay, with large rounded and detailed hairstyles and breasts, but with arms merely indicated, wide hips, legs joined together and shaped, narrowing to a point. (Images similar to these, and approximately the same age, were recorded by Marija Gimbutas in Europe, and were also found in Africa.)

In the first two levels at Harappa (late Mehrgarh period) goddess figurines were also present, and examples photographed by Sharri R. Clark (2001)[26] of Harvard University, include several early examples of women, children and animals and, later, figures of men and more animals. Again there are the small simple pinched clay modelled female figurines with details added. The first red clay female figurine depicts hair and face, simply modelled arms held away from the body, hands joined, with breasts added, and wears a wide belled skirt. She has been painted with black hair, a collar or necklace around her neck, and a net design on her skirt. A second female figurine has a wide headdress, modelled necklace, and breasts, and is armless, with short skirt and legs joined together.

The goddess figurines became more detailed during the Classic Harappan period, with jewellery, headdresses, and dress decorations becoming more complex. However, they do not have the refinement and finish of the 5,000-year-old Mehrgarh figurines, which is a strong indication of less-skilled crafts people belonging to the incoming Indo-European period. Although female figurines at Mohenjo-daro appear within the very early historic period, they are similar in style to Harappan goddesses. Although the early figurines do not resemble contemporary images of the Hindu goddesses, their meanings have remained unchanged.

After the beginning of the Indo-European period, goddess imagery was less common, and the focus had moved to male figurines. The Hindu religion, with roots in prehistory, has inherited a goddess or many goddesses from the late prehistoric and the earliest historic cultures in India. Therefore the Hindu goddesses are possibly the closest in meaning to the long-lasting European goddess or goddesses of prehistory uncovered by Marija Gimbutas.

The *Dictionary of World Mythology*[27] summarises the complexities of the Hindu goddess Devi who, it is said, may have originated from the earliest mother goddess of the Indus civilisation from Mehrgarh. Other names for her are Mahadevi, 'great goddess'; also

Parvati, 'the mountaineer'; and Kali or Durga, 'the fierce goddess' (the Old European 'goddess of death and regeneration'?). As the female manifestation of the supreme lord, she is also called *Prakriti* as she balances out the male aspect of the divine addressed as *Purusha*."[28]

- Lakshmi: represents wealth, maternal fulfilment
- Parvati: power, love, spiritual fulfilment
- Sarasvati: learning, arts/cultural fulfilment
- Kali: holds both creative and destructive power of time.

Durga is the 'supreme goddess' for many Hindus and "represents the empowering and protective nature of motherhood."[29] (Her contemporary image has eight arms each holding a symbolic item.) Durga is the 'invincible, eternal goddess' who "becomes manifest over and over again to protect the world."[30]

As the goddess Maya and Prakriti, she relates to the cosmos and the earth, and she is also *Shakti*, the "feminine energy ... the motive force behind all action and existence in the phenomenal cosmos in Hinduism."[31] All of the various Hindu female entities form the many aspects of the same female deity. (These meanings are perfectly in accord with the Gimbutas Old European scenario.)

Religion, nature, and women's status

The peoples prior to colonisation were imbued with the female principle. Vandana Shiva (1989/2010)[32] explains that 'Terra Mater' the 'great earth mother', who creates and protects, has inspired ecology movements in the West. In prehistoric India, nature embodied the female principle which produced life and provided sustenance.

In early historic India *Shakti* was a primordial dynamic energy which pervades and sustains nature. Vandana Shiva explains that

> Nature, both animate and inanimate, is thus an expression of *Shakti*, the feminine and creative principle of the cosmos; in conjunction with the masculine principle (*Purusha*), Prakriti creates the world.[33]

Nature as Prakriti is both active and diverse; she is present and identified within stones, trees, water, fruit and/or animals. Humans are not divided from nature, nor are women and men divided, because the female principle creates life in all its forms. There is no difference between the masculine and feminine, between person and nature, Purusha and Prakriti; although distinct, they are as "one being."[34]

Vandana Shiva identifies the first Indo-European-based colonisation of India from Iran around 5,000 BP as beginning the destruction of the female principle generally, while the female principle in men changed from creative activities to destructiveness and domination. Thereafter 'passive non-violence' in women and violence and aggression in men became accepted as biological norms. (These are socially constructed concepts and not necessarily associated with gender.)

Max Dashu (2010) speaks of 'cultural stratification' where "older layers are retained and appropriated, even hidden by indigenous or common people, and appropriated, modified, transformed or superseded by newly dominant groups."[35] This is a fair description of the time when indigenous or other original peoples in the Hidden and New Worlds came into contact with Indo-Europeans and their ideologies/practices. She gives an example in India, noted by Frederique Apfel Marglin and Purna Chandra Mishra who point out the manner in which

> an aboriginal goddess known as Mangalaa is incorporated into a brahmanized superstory, while oppressed-caste groups maintain their own tradition of the goddess as a forest and a river being who is venerated in the form of a pot. People from outcaste groups are not permitted to enter the temple but their rites nevertheless remain a central part of the festivals originated by their ancestors.[36]

It seems that the goddess of the indigenous tribes, such as the Munda, Warli or Maithili, is still recognised in the central parts of India today, although she may be integrated with one or more Hindu goddesses. Numerous other creation stories include a goddess who, while she is still the creator of all things, gradually becomes subordinate to one of her creations.

Traditional Indian life today

The traditional Munda: India's Indigenous people

The Munda and Mahatos people, originally from Bihar and northern Rajshahi, have retained their indigenous cultures and lifestyle.[37] Munda language groups live in parts of northern and central India, and there are about 4 million people today. They are known as hard workers who are agriculturalists where possible, and fishers or urban workers elsewhere, some with small businesses.

They now observe some Hindu rituals and deities (although not the caste system); theirs was, and remains, a 'nature' religion, with their main god being Sing-bonga, 'the sun'. There are many spirits (good and bad) of trees, hills, forests, the village and ancestral beings; (female?) deities associated with snakes, monkeys, and other wild animals; and deities representing different aspects of human and natural life, celebrating the seasonal changes, and the harvesting of crops.

The Munda and Mahatos people live simply, are peaceful, and rarely quarrel with neighbours. There is a *montri,* a minister who, with village representatives, settles arguments and any conflict problems. There are male priests, while shamans may be male or female, although the family group is patriarchal. Some clan groups are wood carvers, others paint ritual wall art, but there is no indication of whether female artists are involved.[38]

South Indian Dravidians: The people of Kerala

Kerala is a peaceful province in south-west India, and the population is predominantly Hindu, Christian and Muslim. The original Negritto tribes and Dravidians did not appear to have a formal religion, but worshipped the spirits of trees, animals, and snakes; and the sun, moon, forest guardians, and hill gods. It was a nature religion, perhaps similar to that of the Munda people, with goddesses such as Mari Amman (cured chicken pox/small pox) or Karrupan Swami (protector of travellers), or some goddess spiritualities.

The Aryans brought organised religion to Kerala: including Hinduism, Vedic rites, gods and goddesses, but these were integrated into the original Keralan society's spiritual belief system. For example, the original Kerale god Ayyapan became integrated with Hindu gods, such as Shiva or Krishna, as son of Shiva and Vishnu's feminine form, Mohin. The

Melayali Hindus recognise the goddess Bhagavathy. The societies of Kerala remain firmly matrilineal, although the Hindu caste system is still important. Women tell the myths and legends of Kerala to the children to teach them traditional moral values, and about their origins.

Kerala women's traditional art of female body painting remains prominent. This is mylanchi (henna) tattooing, or staining fingertips, nails and palms of hands with a paste made from the mylanchi plant. Over time, design motifs which are based on flower and plant imagery have become richer in contrast and patterns. Complex traditional face and body paintings are worn by the female dancers for weddings or other celebrations.

Kerala women also create wall paintings based on traditional motifs/stories from Neolithic cave art; examples include the Pandiyan art of Tamil Nadu, and the Warli art with northern influences from Maharashtra. Wall paintings are part of Kerala lifestyle. Another art of the Malayali women is *chedikkalam* which is drawing on floors in many and various innovative styles and designs.[39]

Traditional matriarchal societies

Two women from India spoke of their knowledge and experience of their traditional matriarchal/matrilineal cultures during the World Congresses on Matriarchal Studies held in 2003 and 2005. Patricia Mukkim was from a Khasi clan, in Meghalaya in north-east India, and Savithri Shanker de Tourreil, was from a Nayar culture in Kerala, south-west India.

In 'Khasi matrilineal society: Challenges in the twenty-first century'[40] Patricia Mukkim explains that the indigenous Khasi people live in the hills of north-east India and believe they are descended from seven celestial families who lived on earth long before humans. Could they have been connected with the Seven Sisters of the Pleiades? Indigenous Australian Munya Andrews (2004), for whom the Seven Sisters of the Pleiades has traditional meanings, has investigated the meanings of the Pleiades in a number of countries including India. She explains that in one Hindu myth of the seven sisters, the stars of the Pleiades are known as the 'Krittika', who had once been married to the seven Rishis (Sages). She notes that according to Gertrude and James Jobes (1964) "[t]he association of the seven Krittika as wives of the seven Sages might explain the custom of many newly married couples in India worshipping and praying to the Pleiades before entering their matrimonial homes."[41] Munya Andrews suggests that such a ritual originates in the home country from which the Aryans had come. The Pleiades in India also relate to the moon and lunar cycle. She mentions another Indian celebration, Diwali (Feast of the Lanterns), held to honour the goddess Lakshmi. This is a five-day festival held in late October to mid-November, the Pleiades month which is named Kartik, after the son of the Pleiades.

According to Patricia Mukkim[42] some anthropologists have suggested that the Khasi may have originally come from South-East Asia, while linguists favour Myanmar or Cambodia. They preserved their traditions, rules and values in their oral history until 1842 when missionaries came to 'Christianise' them, and radically changed many aspects of their culture. Despite such interference some of the most important traditions have been preserved.

In this matrilineal society descent is through the female line. There is a clear distinction between relatives from the mother's line, and relatives from the father's clan (kinship group). Most clans relate to their great-great-grandmother's lineage. The grandmother is the matriarch, and her daughters and their children all live in the ancestral house, the original home. Members of the same clan cannot marry each other.[43]

Matrilineal solidarity is reinforced by religious rituals connected with the ancestral home, which is where the families from the mother's descent always gather with families from the father's descent, and engage in rituals connected with significant occasions, such as marriages or funerals. This ensures that the young people from each clan descent can get to know one another, so that they do not inadvertently become romantically involved. The eldest maternal uncle acts as 'priest' "who offers sacrifices to the household deity as an act of appeasement for wrongs committed against her by any members of the family."[44] (In Old European houses Marija Gimbutas found evidence of many household female deities whom she thought may have occupied a similar role.)

The youngest daughter becomes custodian, inheriting the ancestral home and considerable responsibilities, including the management of the land and other property (which is held in common) belonging to the family members. She sees to the distribution of some land to each married daughter for their new family unit, and some property (managed by maternal uncle/uncles) for the sons for their use. Senior male members are appointed by the family to represent them in clan council, and the clan council elects representatives to local government councils. If the youngest daughter has no daughters, her sons will be given any self-acquired property of the parents, and the next eldest sister's youngest daughter will receive the ancestral home. Originally the Khasi had no inheritance law because everything was held in common. Today, when there is no property, the youngest daughter is required to look after the parents and unmarried siblings and may have to support them with her own resources.

Patricia Mukhim points out several advantages of matriliny which may have changed since contact with colonisers' patriarchal ideology:

- the clan was perpetuated through the mother's bloodline
- no need for a dowry system
- women did not have to marry
- women could choose a partner, marriages were not arranged
- there were no specific rules against co-habiting with a partner.

There are more problems than advantages in present day Khasi society with the weakening of matrilineal traditional practices, such as individual ownership of land, and the rise of a marked sexual division of labour. Men and boys are not involved in the domestic arena. Women are no longer valued or celebrated as in the past.

Savithri Shanker de Tourreil's account of Nayar matriliny is somewhat similar to the above, although the Nayar have been exposed to contact with patriarchal societies for a longer period. In 'The Nayars of Kerala and Matriliny Revisited' she describes the Nayar people from Kerala, situated on the south-west coast of the Indian peninsula, who have been matrilineal "for a very long time."[45] Contact with China (4,500 BP?) and ancient Greece and Rome has had some effect on Nayar lifestyles, and more changes have occurred with British and other colonisers. She has collected information about traditional Nayar societies of 100 years ago (as close to the original traditions as is possible today).

Savithri Shanker de Tourreil's great uncle was the eldest man and head of the matrilineal family unit. He only managed the family property and assets, which belonged to all family members. If there happened to be no adult male to fill this role, the nearest adult female would be the head, but this was not common. The uncle would lead the daughter's puberty ceremony; boys did not experience such a ritual. The female was central to matriliny, "with a civil and legal status independent of men."[46] Members in the matrilineal family unit were related through a common ancestress, and the lineage could only continue through the female line. Young women from another branch of the family had to take the position if there were no females in a generation. Female births were greatly celebrated (part of the mother-daughter-granddaughter tradition), as baby girls were potential ancestresses. She observes that originally "sisters, female cousins and nieces on the mother's side were seen as the real heiresses by brothers, male cousins and uncles."[47] This ensured that these men considered it their duty to look after these relatives. Thus these women had closer ties to their brothers than to their sexual partners, and vice versa. Women who were married or had partners continued to live in the matrilineal home, with their children raised by a maternal uncle. Given these circumstances divorce was relatively simple to procure.

More recent developments have meant that sons are now more valued and daughters regarded as burdens. The extended family structures have broken apart, property is controlled by the men, and women have to work much harder. Other traditions have been lost, such as respect for nature and caring for the land.

Colonisation and 'development'

Those who hold the view of mother earth as a creative sacred power have had the most to lose under colonisation. Although Vandana Shiva (1989/2010)[48] generally discusses the Indian experience under British colonisation, she recognises the similarities between India's experiences and those of other 'Third World' countries.[49]

Vandana Shiva explains that forests have always been central in the Indian experience, as is Aranyani, the 'goddess of the forest'. The forest, which is diverse, harmonious and self-sustaining, represents a model of community which is the basis for the organisation of Indian societies and civilisation. Forests are fundamental to the survival of all religions and cultures of the southern Asian region because of their ecological value and interconnection. Rather than being thought of as dark dangerous places, Vandana Shiva states that traditionally they were considered as intimate and harmonious communal habitats for all creatures.

For indigenous forest scientists, trees had diverse forms and functions. They supplied most vegetable foods, such as seeds, grains, fruits, roots, rhizomes, leaves, and medicines, as well as their value as wood for tools, artefacts and homes. Since food gathering and fodder collection have always been women's responsibility, women as foragers were critical for the management and renewal of forest diversity. When the British colonisers took control, they were only interested in the commercial value of timber; indigenous knowledge became irrelevant, and was replaced by a narrow, male-oriented 'science of forestry'. Colonisers' interests generated poverty by replacing women's forest-based subsistence economy. The affected women have fought back but their contributions towards saving the forests are all but invisible. Forests, clear-felled for agricultural land use, now grow such things as 'useful' cash crops to be sold in other locations, while the local forest women's families struggle to survive.

Giti Thadani (2004)[50] speaks of another sad effect of British colonisation in India which has affected the seven islands which used to form part of the archipelago on which the city of Mumbai now stands. These seven islands were sacred, "governed by the trinity of Goddesses Mahakali, Mahasarasvati, Mahalakshmi."[51] The linguistically and visually limited English were uninterested in local names or places and did not hesitate to change them;

hence the beautiful seven islands were redeveloped to become connected to each other: "water ... transformed into land. A causeway was constructed."[52] They became "an industrial dream", "one landmass" and Mumbai (named for the local goddess Mumba) became destined to be "the Gateway to India."[53] The sacred stories of the three goddesses have disappeared along with their islands.

Gradually the enlarged city became industrialised – with cotton and silk weaving mills – and the population increased to work in the mills. According to Giti Thadani, the population has continued to increase but the wealthy mill owners and their friends and visitors still enjoy beachside living, marinas and promenades, "while the natives had the 'black' city. The sea disappears into a stinking open lavatory ... the more land is reclaimed, the more human density ..."[54] This is just one example of the grim changes colonisation has brought about which Giti Thadani pondered over on her journey through India. She documents the destruction of goddess imagery and ritual places. The result, she says, is the hiding of Indian women's prehistory and the rich goddess mythology. The female figurines of Harappa and Mohenjo-daro gradually disappeared and were replaced by increasingly developed male images of priests and kings. This process continues for the world's women today.

Colonisation, the Arts and 'development' today

A careful look at the visual imagery in India's prehistoric period reveals signs and symbols of the goddess, and they are often still present in the tribal arts today, perhaps disguised in the forms of familiar images such as birds, animals or plants, even in so-called decorative patterns. The oral histories, art and artefacts (still surviving) of India's indigenous and traditional people provide the only information available which tell the story of prehistoric women's experiences in India, and teach us about their rich cultural heritage.

Jyotindra Jain (1995)[55] explains the effects of 'development' upon the traditional arts of India since colonisation, where the content, production and quality of painting, sculpture, relief-work and pottery, and everyday items such as lamps, *hukkas* and nutcrackers have been greatly affected by commercial interests.

For example, there has been mass production and marketing of traditional tribal arts, such as Madhubani wall and floor paintings made by women and used in women's rituals, and Gujarati embroideries including wall-hangings, door panels, and mirror-studded skirts and blouses (girls' dowry items). This has resulted in their status being lowered from art to handcraft, emphasising a new cultural division between art and folk art. The handloom textile industry has been replaced by textile mills in this new mass production environment, and as a consequence, quality has been lost.

Traditional tribal and folk art was once communal, created by a group for celebrations and ritual; this had allowed each individual to be inspired by another group member, resulting in some surprising elements and a sense of mystery to their creations. But the imposition of aesthetic and cultural criteria to promote trade does not allow the application of inherited artistic vision or creative experimentation and is considered authoritarian, unethical and unfair according to Jyotindra Jain. Many of these arts have been the province of women, who are doubly penalised by market controls which pay low wages and cause many fine skills and inherited content of the arts to be lost. It has also ensured that Indian women remain subservient to men and largely invisible.

199

1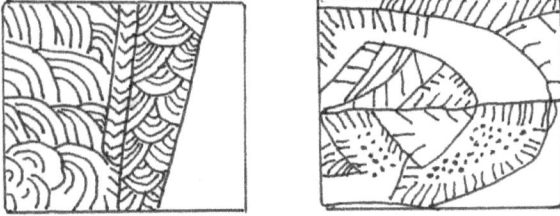

2

3

4

INDIA: TRADITIONAL WOMEN'S ART

1. *Two examples of Gond Art*
   (Source: Tara Books, 2009–2010)
2. *'Scene of Childbirth'* by Manjula Thakur,
   Maithili wall art
   (Source: Thakur, Manjula, 2010)

3. Prehistoric *Indian cave art,* unidentified site
   (Source: Chakrabarti, Dilip, 1999)
4. Detail *of dancing figures* from a Warli woman's
   wall painting, white paint on earth-coloured
   wall (Source: Indianetzone, n.d.)

All line drawings © Judy Foster, 2013

Nonetheless, in the early 2000s an independent publisher appeared which is feminist and collectively owned. It designs, prepares and makes handmade books, with art work individually screen-printed, and text letterpress printed, on special handmade paper composed of cotton cloth waste mixed with either tree bark, rice husks or grass. Tara Books[56] is a women's village industry which has produced "more than 160,000 handmade books ... so far"[57] according to their catalogue. They believe that they could be "the only publishing press that produces so many books by hand in the world" as "more than a dozen skilled craftspeople from local villages make the books."[58]

The artists who design, paint or draw the illustrations (each an individual work of art) include Gond tribal artists of central India who create intricate symbolic patterns "which fill the surface [with] images in amazing profusion."[59] Similar symbolic motifs have been painted on mud walls and floors (and originally on cave walls) by women – and sometimes men – to celebrate events, or tell traditional stories which have been imparting knowledge to the family viewers for millennia. The catalogue writers say that Gond artists today draw on inherited conventions and create distinctive symbolic patterns unique to each artist. The example featured in the catalogue is *Signature*, a picture book for adults, featuring the work of a number of Gond artists, one image of which is that of a coiled snake motif forming a complex spiral pattern in which the snake awaits discovery.

Other artists include the Meena tribal women in Rajasthan, who repeat on paper the painted imagery they depict on the mud walls and floors in their homes using the traditional art form known as Mandana, "to mark festivals and changing seasons."[60] An example is *Nurturing Walls – Animal Art* by Meena Women, in which a photograph (also taken by a tribal artist) provides glimpses of a traditional painting revealing tantalising images of a large plant with birds, and the female artist on a ladder in the act of painting another motif in white paint on a house wall. The wall art of the Meena women is part of "a rich and quietly thriving tradition ... largely unknown outside the walls of Meena villages"[61] and the art tradition continues to be passed down from mothers to daughters.

The Warli women from Maharashtra, in western India, paint on house walls in a style of "a series of brilliantly drawn pictograms."[62] Warli traditional wall art dates back into the Neolithic period, at least 4,500 BP. The people are agriculturalists, and their thatched-roof mud huts are built surrounding a circular courtyard. Their wall art celebrates the harvest, births, weddings and daily events, recording customs and beliefs. The paint used is white on earth-coloured walls, and the imagery features: figures of people in action; traditional geometric patterns, including spirals, circles, concentric circles, rectangles, and loops; animals, birds and plants, all "in lively rhythmic movement",[63] a style based on prehistoric cave art.

In the example from *Do!,* a children's picture book, there are numerous vibrant symbolic figures of plants, animals and people in an informal narrative design on a plain background. Because the style of the art is not unlike early rock art of the region it raises the question: Could Warli women have painted at least some of the early cave art?

The tribal wall painters published by Tara Books are not the only wall artists. There are other peoples who specialise in wall art, including the Maithili women of north-east India, near Bihar; and the Karnataka women of Malnad. The art of the Maithili and Madhubani women is the expression of inherited wisdom used as a focus for village rituals. The paintings, which have very old origins, enhance the walls of homes in the villages of Bihar, celebrating seasonal festivals, and weddings. The motifs used have symbolic meanings, for example: a ring of lotus flowers and bamboo trees – fertility and children; the moon – a source of heavenly nectar, long life; or the sun – fertility. The servants of the goddess Durga appear in corners of the room, while other images based on Vedas, Puranas, and scripture may be used, indicating Indo-Aryan influences integrated into traditional imagery and stories. Other motifs include those of the universe (sun, moon, stars) and plants, trees, birds, fish, turtles, and other animals. Durga is the only goddess mentioned, but perhaps the Bihari prehistoric goddess has become integrated with her as has happened elsewhere.

Wendy Doniger (2009) provides another view, stating that the women of Mithila traditionally use coloured rice powder to paint ritual designs on the floors and courtyards of their homes for celebrations, during which the family's bare feet 'carry' the sacred message of the imagery into the house. Sometimes such ritual art is painted on very fragile paper so that, through its destruction, it impresses its images upon the minds of those who walk over it. Because the art agents of tourist corporations can indirectly 'force' the often very poor artists to make their designs permanent on quality art paper or canvas for sale, this process of exploitation of indigenous or traditional art can result in the removal of the ritual power of the art from the women and their families.[64]

The Karnataka women's paintings on walls are known as *chittaras*, and the design arrangements of lines and patterns symbolise and celebrate aspects of nature, or the spiritual, social or agricultural lives of the people. The women make their own colours from natural sources – tree barks, rocks, minerals, and plants. The designs are common to all the community, but the colours differ from one family or clan to another. The women also make: *butti*, cane baskets coated with red mud; *madake*, clay pots; *torans*, door hangings of dried paddy; and *irike*, circular rings of dried grass.

These examples of women's and men's tribal arts from their varied cultures provide a contemporary record of art works which come from very old traditions that are still very much alive. If these works of art can still be found throughout India today, then women's (and men's) traditions also remain alive, and are perhaps enjoying a resurgence. In the case of women, this suggests an increasing reclamation of their original status before the historical period, and their importance within the social organisation.

CHAPTER 13

HIDDEN WORLDS: CHINA, KOREA, JAPAN

China

China's prehistory

Homo erectus seems to have moved from China to Java around 2 million BP, as there are traces of both *Homo habilis* and *H. erectus* in China at this time. Another school of thought argues that the first humans could have evolved independently in China and Java.[1] Archaic *Homo sapiens* were certainly present in China around 200,000 BP and in Java around 100,000 BP. A report in 2000 explains that *H. erectus* in China did not have the same tools as did African *H. erectus* which suggests that *H. sapiens* in East Asia may have descended from East Asian *H. erectus*.[2]

Gina Barnes (1993)[3] notes that fluctuating sea levels, due to increasingly severe warm and cold phases, meant that at different times there were land bridges between the mainland and islands in East Asia which also allowed movement of people to places as far away as Japan. She records that pottery was not always associated with agriculture as it was during the various eras of western Northern Hemisphere prehistory. Hunter-gatherers in Indonesia and Iron Age Thailand had been exposed to Chinese influences, and Indian influences in East Asia are also apparent. David Anthony (2007)[4] records that from the Bronze Age the people of Xinjiang in China had close connections with the western steppes, as shown in their physical type, fabrics, wheeled-vehicle technology, and burial rituals. There was two-way traffic across the steppes, the 'bridge' to the east crossing the centre, allowing exchange of cultures and ideas.

From around 4,000 BP the Han Chinese warriors brought Indo-European Eurasian pastoralist ideas and practices from southern China to South-East Asia, Mesoamerica and the Pacific Islands.

China's Neolithic period

Until at least the year 2000, the commonly held view of the beginning of pottery making in China was consistent with that given by the Heilbrunn Timeline of Art History[5] which stated that China's Neolithic period originated 12,000 years ago and ended 8,000 years later with the introduction of metallurgy, and the beginning of individual settled farming

A Timeline for Prehistoric China*

Period (BP)	Epoch/People	Stage	Evidence
1,800,000		*H. erectus* *H. habilis*	• Different stone tools from those used by African *H. erectus* raises questions of origins as to the descent of modern humans from China's *H. erectus*
700,000	Palaeolithic		
200,000		*H. sapiens*	
20,000–18,000			• First pottery sherds
12,000–10,500			• Beginning of settled farming communities; first rice growing
	Early Neolithic	Nanzhuangtou culture	
7,800–7,400		Dadiwan pottery culture	• Earliest city – first pottery, millet crops
7,500–6,000	Neolithic Period	Yangshao matrilineal culture, Banpo village	• Beautiful jade tools and other artefacts – female deities, matrilineal society
7,000		Dawenkou culture	• Rice growing in southern China
6,100–4,600		Hongshan culture	• Coastal region
5,500–4,900	Late Neolithic		• Matrilineal culture village with goddess
		Liangzhu culture	• Temple, clay female deities, jade goddess figurines pottery, large central clan meeting house
5,000			
to 4,000	Bronze Age	Longshan culture	• Metallurgy; first violence; hierarchic societies
3,000	Beginning of Historical Period	Shang Dynasty	• Dynasties begin
2,551–2,479		Confucius	• Sets the way of life values which are still used today
2,100	Iron Age Han Chinese		• Movement into Thailand and South-East Asia

*Note: A comparative timeline that includes Japan and Korea appears in chapter 14.

communities and animal domestication. This was particularly evident along the two major river systems: the central and northern regions of the Yellow River; and the southern and eastern regions of the Yangtze River. The two regions each developed their own distinctive traditions, with differences in architecture, ritual burials and artefacts, including pottery styles.

Although Gina Barnes in 2010[6] had noted the first pottery making appearing in China as dated to as early as 16, 000 BP, further important new evidence reported in 2012 takes the date of the beginning of pottery making in China back to as early as 20,000 BP. A number of thick, coarse sherds of pottery, some pieces with impressed decoration, were found by Xiaohong Wu of Peking University in north-west China's Jiangxi Province, in Xianrendong Cave which lies one hundred kilometres south of the Yangtze River.[7] The cave had been occupied from the Upper Palaeolithic (25,000–15,000 BP) and through three Neolithic phases. The first period was the Palaeolithic-Neolithic Transition from 19,780 to 10,870 BP (Early Neolithic) with evidence of the first pottery, fishing, hunting deer, and gathering of wild rice and other plant foods. Grinding slab stones were also found.

The 20,000-year-old pottery was made using either of two methods: 'sheet laminating', or 'coil and paddle'. The red clay pots had a round base with thick, roughly finished walls and featured impressed cord or basket markings. The pots may have been used in cooking, or for storage beside a fire, as some pieces have scorch-marked areas. Stone tools consisted of chipped flakes, scrapers, burins, drills, and in some cases the stone was polished; while bone tools included fishing spear-points, arrowheads, shell knives, and also bone harpoons and needles (evidence of string or thread use?).

Gideon Shelach (2012)[8] of the Hebrew University in Jerusalem, describes the use of new technology which included small flake tools and grinding slab stones (early querns?) allowing the collection of a wider range of plant and animal foods which could be ground-up and cooked in pots. These inventions were perhaps in response to climate-change or food scarcity. He also states that although the early use of pottery occurred long before the beginning of agriculture and use of grinding stones, unusually, in this instance, pottery was not made again until the Early Neolithic period. (We are reminded that evidence including grinding stones used by Australian Indigenous people to grind wild plant roots and grass seeds dated to 30,000 BP, were found by Judith Field et al at Cuddie Springs, New South Wales. The ground seeds were mixed with water into 'cakes' and cooked in camp fire ashes.)[9]

Xiaohong Wu records that in the second Early Neolithic (12,430–9,700 BP) period in Xianrendong Cave, the first rice growing took place, with two varieties of rice being cultivated. Different types of clay were now used for pottery, which had become more refined and decorated with geometric designs. Many more polished stone tools were used, along with a small number of stone adzes and perforated stone discs.

In the following Neolithic period (9,600–8,825 BP), Chinese archaeologists regarded Neolithic societies as communal, with the late Neolithic marking the transition from women-centred to warrior societies.[10] Gina Barnes (1993) records that in Korea (the Jeulmun culture), and Japan (the Jomon culture), while pottery was well developed, the abundance of seafood and edible plants meant that agriculture was unnecessary. From 9,000 BP the abundant food supply provided women with time to spend developing more advanced, refined pottery techniques as shown in the complex and very fine examples of the period. Gina Barnes describes many different vessel shapes, such as pottery with handles,

1

2

4

3

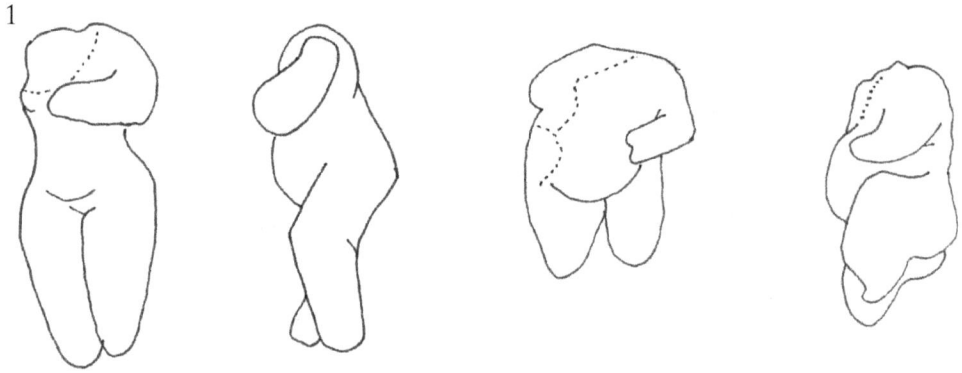

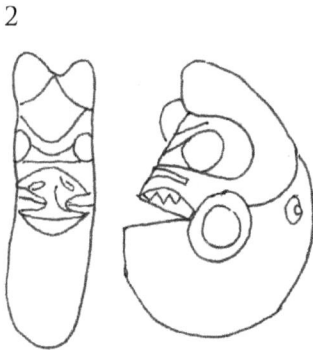

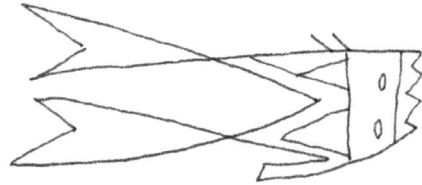

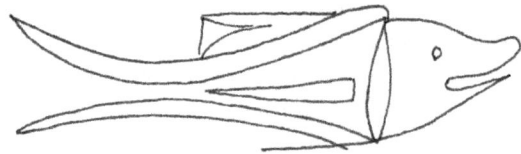

CHINA: HONGSHAN FIGURINES

1. *Two figurines,* Hongshan culture, 6,500 BP, front and side views of each
2. *A polished pendant of a Hongshan pig-dragon,* 6,000 BP
3. *Sculpted stone head of a woman* (goddess) of similar date (6,000 BP)
   (Source 1–3: Nelson, Sarah M., 1994)
4. *Two fish designs on a pot,* Banpo
   (Source: Treistman, Judith M., 1972)
   All line drawings © Judy Foster, 2013

tripods, quadrupods, perforated vessels and angled vessel supports. Decorations included eight-pointed stars, five-petal 'flower' designs on red or blue bowls, with other designs including square and circular spirals, hand stencils, and lines arranged in swirling patterns.

Edmond Capon (1977)[11] observes that some jugs featured animal or bird shapes with handles of twisted pottery 'rope'. These decorated vessels were in considerable contrast to the simple textured deep, wide-mouth pots made by other forager cultures of the same period. The most sophisticated pottery was the technically superior wheel-turned black pottery. Bone and stone tools of the time were also varied and functionally specific, implying a complex civilisation. Plant, animal and human motifs appeared on ceramic and bone artefacts, and small animal figurines were made.

He divides Neolithic China into three broad cultural regions: in the central northern plain of the Yellow River, the Yangshao culture; in the east, the Lung-shan culture; and in the far west, the Pan-shan culture. Pottery from the Lanchou region is known as the Pan-shan type, and consists of red pottery urns and bowls, painted with broad and energetic spiral designs, suggesting a sophisticated and developed material culture. Yangshao pottery was the most notable because it originated in this region; this pottery features semi-abstract fishes and human faces. Tool kits included bone needles, harpoons and arrowheads.

Jade from the east was widely used by the Chinese artists and artisans for tools and other artefacts because of its beauty, strength and toughness, and its ability to be formed into interesting shapes, according to the Heilbrunn Timeline of Art History. It not only appeared aesthetically pleasing when used for jewellery, ornaments, bowls, dishes and utensils, but could also be used for those tasks where highly durable implements were needed. It required the careful application of harsh abrasives over a long period to create a design on objects, as they could not be easily incised or carved; these techniques were mastered very early by the Chinese makers. Ritual objects, such as fine bowls or dishes found in burials, rarely show any signs of wear or deterioration, testifying to the durability of jade.[12]

Gina Barnes (1993) records Chinese Neolithic houses as usually being made of wattle and daub, and featuring mortise and tenon joints in their wooden frames (such joints are still used today); some buildings had a number of rooms, and usually included grain-storage pits. Some villages were surrounded by ditches to keep animals out, while others were built on stilts over marshy ground. There was often a large communal building, while houses and ritual burials were arranged in groups, perhaps in kinship or clan groupings.

The first cultivation of plants, animal domestication and pottery-making occurred in China's Neolithic period, with the Nanzhuangtou culture in the Middle Yellow River region.[13] According to Li Liu, "the earliest pottery, grinding slabs and rollers, possibly domesticated pigs and dogs, and domestic features (hearths and ash pits)"[14] occurred at 10,500–9,700 BP. On the Central Plains the small settlements remained static, although steppe grasses gradually gave way to broadleaf forests over this period.

The Dadiwan cultural site in north-west China, dated to 8,500 BP and lasting until 5,000 BP, is described by Li Liu as being a city of 240 houses and other buildings, including a remarkable palace-like structure, although only a very small part has been excavated to date. There are 98 cooking stove ruins, storage pits and cellars, 71 mausoleums, 35 kilns and 12 irrigation canals and ditches, as well as pottery, stone and jade artefacts, bone, horn, teeth and mussel artefacts, and 17,000 faunal remains. The earliest dry millet crops, the oldest decorated

1

2

3

4

5

6

7

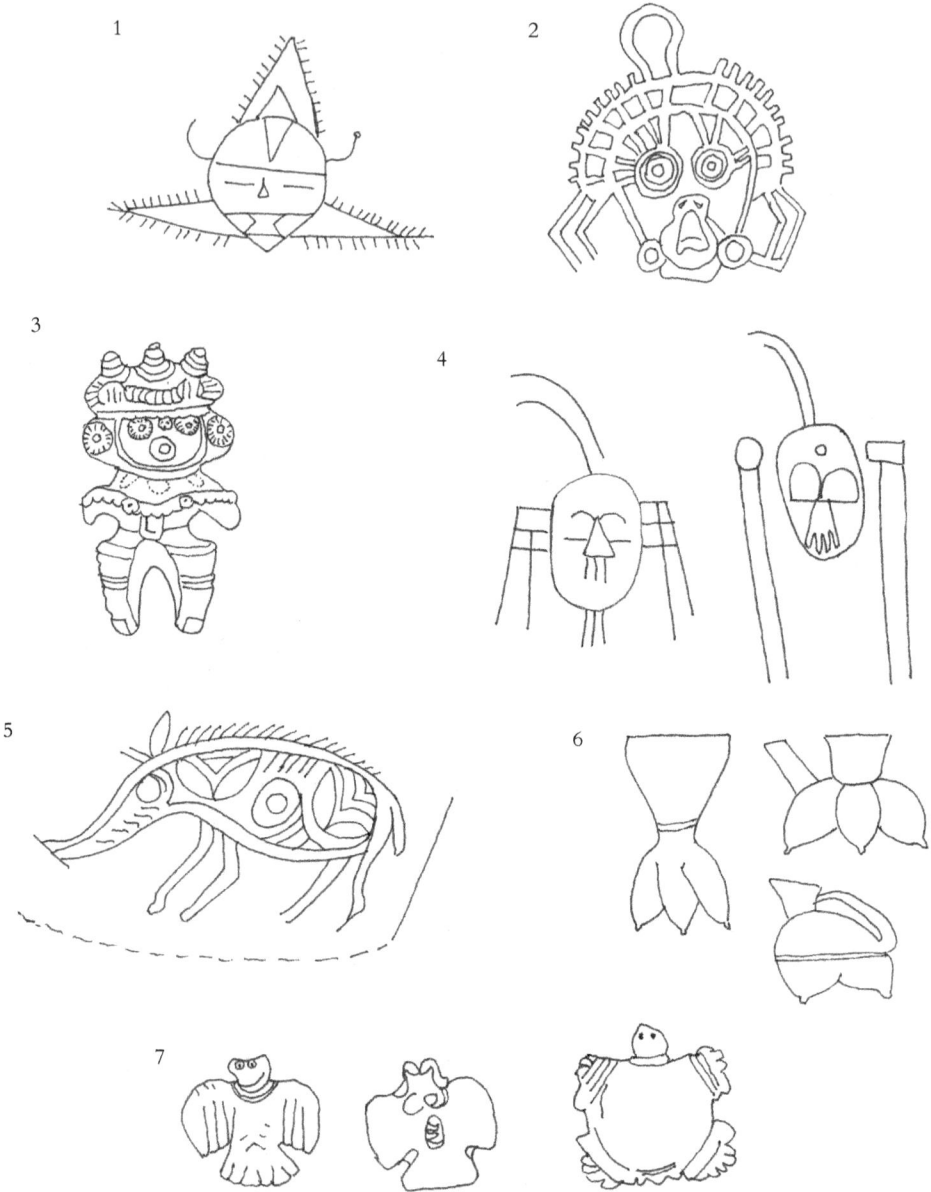

SYMBOLIC IMAGES FROM CHINA

1. *Neolithic Yangshao face design motif on pottery*
   (Source: Capon, Edmund, 1977)
2. *Prehistoric rock wall engraving,* 'mask'
   petroglyph, Helankon, Ningxia Hui
   Province, China
   (Source: Chakravarty, Kalyan and Robert
   Bednarik, 1997)

3. *A Neolithic dogu female pottery figurine*
4. *Two faces incised on rock wall,* Yangshao culture
5. *Yangshao pig design on pot*
6. *Breast-shaped Neolithic pots,* Dawenkou culture
7. *Three carved jade creatures,* Neolithic
   Hongshao/Liangzhu cultures
   (Source 3–7: Barnes, Gina, 1993)

All line drawings © Judy Foster, 2013

purplish-coloured pottery featuring pictographs dated to 9,000 BP which are considered to be the earliest examples of Chinese characters, and the earliest floor paintings, all appear here in an excavated palace-like building.[15]

The clan meeting place, or palace, was a 420-square-metre multi-room composite construction,[16] consisting of a main room, two side rooms, front room, and a back room (with large mid-floor pit fireplace). The main room was divided into nine sections by eight wooden pillars (only their bases remain), and the floor was very flat and smooth, and as hard as concrete.[17]

Li Liu describes the early Yangshao culture (7,500–6,000 BP) as including "both semi-subterranean and ground-level houses"[18] in small or medium round shapes, with some others square or rectangular, sometimes placed around a central plaza, near a large communal building. Tools included axes, whetstones, pottery files, scrapers, awls, and small pottery kilns. By the middle Yangshao period (6,000–5,500 BP) larger settlements were present, as was a more complex social organisation. Ground-up cinnabar powder was used for painting pottery, house floors, and for ritual use in tombs.

The matrilineal Yangshao culture, situated in the middle and lower Yellow River Valley in China's north-west, is noted for the prehistoric village of Banpo, which consists of 45 houses, 200 storage pits, and 6 kilns, 174 adult graves, and 76 children's graves.[19] According to Edmond Capon, Banpo village provides insights into the Chinese Neolithic way of life. Like many Neolithic villages it was built on raised ground close to a river, and was quite large with around 300 residents. The village was circular, and divided into living areas, and manufacturing zones for items such as pottery, and a graveyard. The houses of Banpo were large (up to 15 metres in diameter) and rested upon circular or rectangular low earth walls. Floors were above ground level, wooden pillars supported thatched roofs reinforced with clay, and the interiors were furnished with clay ovens, cupboards and benches, while outside there were large grain storage bins.

Distinctive pottery made at this time included mammary-shaped water bottles at Yangshao and rounded pots mounted on three hollow tripod breast-shaped legs, further indication of a Dawkenkou matrilineal culture on the coast. Dawkenkou women were buried with their spades, sickles, needles and spindle whorls. Gina Barnes (1993) argues that these artefacts indicate that women were likely to have been in charge of plant cultivation.

According to Eva Sternfeld (1995)[20] Chinese researchers agree that Yangshao culture was matrilineal and this is demonstrated by the gravesites. Men and women were buried separately: men with four offerings; most women with six offerings, with one young (priestess?) girl's grave holding 79 objects; suggesting that females had higher status. The large buildings found featured common rooms and clan meeting rooms with women's living areas, and were surrounded by small circular huts. The beautifully decorated pottery was women's creation for everyday and ritual use. The men hunted and fished, while women worked the fields, and their pottery often displayed symbolic motifs/designs of fishers and fish.

Banpo tool kits included items of chipped stone, polished axes and arrowheads. Edmond Capon gives one example of Banpo pottery which featured a stylised human face painted in black on red pottery, and also included possible female pubic symbols (three lines fanning out from a central point forming a 'V' shape) placed around the pot's rim. Other items included such tools as bone needles and harpoons, and curved stone sickles for harvesting the staple millet crops. Domestic animals included dogs, pigs, goats and cattle, while rice growing, both here and throughout much of China, was well in place after 6,000 BP.

In the north-east of China, the matrilineal Hongshan culture of 5,500 BP featured the important 'goddess temple' at Niuheliang. It is significant that sites in two different parts of northern China appear to have been women-centred as this may indicate that matrilineal cultures were generally present in prehistoric times.

Jeffrey Hays (2008a)[21] records the village as including "houses with murals, massive stone architecture, clay female figurines of various sizes, a stepped platform ... and graves with ritual jade pieces and hundreds of pottery tubes of unknown purpose."[22] He also notes the pig-dragon pendants, which archaeologists suggest may be 'fertility symbols'.[23]

Sarah Nelson (1994) maintains that Hongshan is unique in China because of the 'goddess temple'. It features: larger than life-size statues of women; 'body' fragments, and part of an incense burner; outdoor platforms (perhaps altars?); and numerous symbolic jade figurines of female deities and fauna, turtles, and birds. She describes the temple as being 25 metres long, and varying from 2 to 9 metres in width.

> [It] has three lobes at one end and an asymmetrical extension at the other. The few centimetres of flooring that remain contain raised and painted designs in geometric patterns. Fragments of statues made of unbaked clay were found in the temple, including a life-sized female face with green jade eyes.[24]

Unfortunately her article does not include a detailed description of any of the other accompanying illustrations of female figurines, and makes no reference to the jade 'bat goddess'[25] who was present at this time. She notes that small female figurines and larger fragments of other figures (but no large statues) had been found at another related site at Dongshanzui.

Li Liu's reports of prehistoric excavations reveal no evidence of violence, although she suggests there may have been forms of hierarchy in some instances which could also mean the presence of powerful female deities. According to Gina Barnes there were no indications of violent deaths, although female graves often included more grave goods than male graves which suggest women were respected and enjoyed high status as in the Yangshao culture. Historian Brian Griffith (2012)[26] agrees that Neolithic settlements have revealed female figurines but few, if any, war weapons or signs of hierarchy, and were similar to those "described by Marija Gimbutas, Merlin Stone or Riane Eisler."[27]

The Bronze Age in China

The Bronze Age in China seems to have occurred somewhere around 4,800 BP, with the first appearance of dynasties. The first indication of the Indo-European presence was the east coast pottery-laden male burials in mainland China in the Late Neolithic period between 5,000–4,000 BP, according to William Watson (1961).[28] Although wild horses, and perhaps sheep, were now present in mainland China, it is not known when they were first domesticated.

Throughout China's Neolithic period women had been preparing and weaving hemp (plant fibre) for cloth, but it was not until 4,000 BP that they began cultivating silkworms for making silk cloth which provided better insulation and absorbed dyes well. The availability of a range of colours facilitated the development of clothing codes indicating

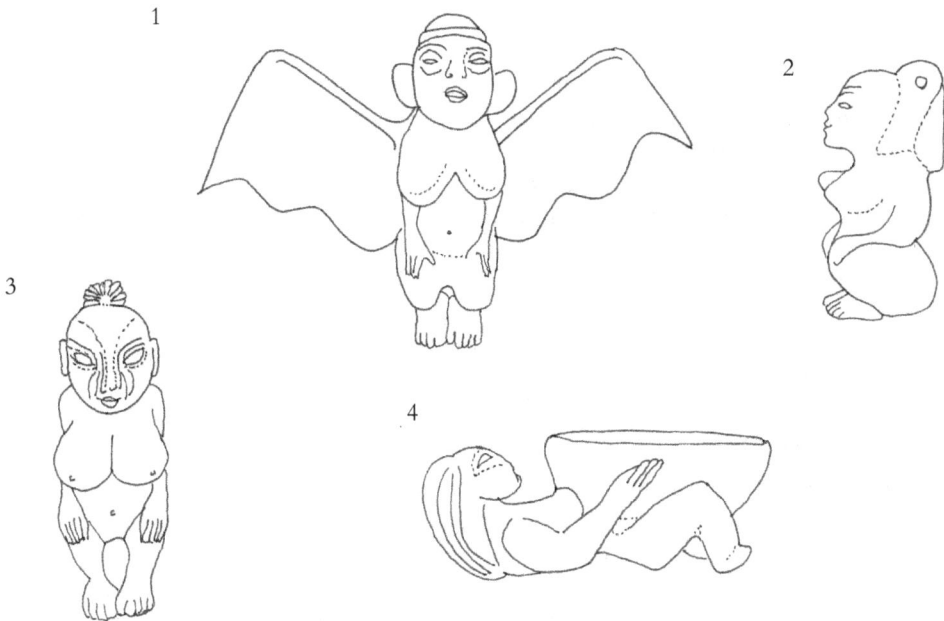

MORE HONGSHAN FEMALE FIGURINES

1. The Hongshan matrilineal culture: *Jade Nugua (Nuwa) bat* (5,000–3,000 BP), a female creator deity (Source: Fabisch, Gunter, 2010)
2. *Neolithic yellow-ochre agate female figurine* (Source: DashiVillage.com, 2008)
3. *Jade Neolithic mother goddess Nugua (Nuwa),* who has many aspects
4. *Pregnant female deity* holding a cup, Neolithic (Source 3–4: Fabisch, Gunter, 2010)

All line drawings © Judy Foster, 2013

specific social meanings, for example, white for mourning, and red for celebration. Elizabeth Barber (1994)[29] considers that the availability of comfortable and colourful silk cloth was one of the reasons why nomadic pastoralist Eurasians (Indo-Europeans) moved into China.

Judith Treistman (1972)[30] argues that pastoralism, which had prevailed on the vast Eurasian steppes, then spread into northern China. Nomadic pastoralists first appeared in northern China about 5,500 BP then moved throughout the countryside changing peaceful agricultural communities into large centralised commodity-driven hierarchic settlements. Elizabeth Barber's description of the 4,000-year-old human remains found in the Tarim Basin which lies on the route to China also shows the contact with, and influence of Indo-Europeans. Gina Barnes records class distinction, a social elite, specialised crafts and public architecture as now being common along with the insidious addition of violence, especially in the Central Plain region. This was most likely the beginning of the East Asian Warrior Age.

Certainly the end of the late Neolithic and the beginning of the Bronze Age were marked by such innovations as walled enclosures, and human sacrifice including a sudden proliferation of headless and footless corpses which, in one instance, were found 'stuffed' inside a well along with numerous projectile points. Other changes included the building of larger dwellings, and the placement of sacrificed humans and horses, bronze vessels, and war weapons, in some burials. William Watson describes an example where there were large numbers of burials containing men sacrificed in rituals concerned with the "erection or function" of the buildings. He speaks of men "buried outside the gates, some holding bronze vessels, others facing outwards with halberds in their hands"[31] and other victims placed at intervals around the perimeter. Burials also included dogs, and there were chariots complete with their charioteers buried in the central court. Outside the city, enormous cruciform pits thought to be royal tombs, held human victims similarly sacrificed. These drastic changes flowed south through Thailand to the rest of South-East Asia with the southern thrust of the aggressive Iron Age Han Chinese around 2,100 BP.

Archaeological, linguistic and other evidence suggests that 4,500 years ago Yunnan Chinese came to South-East Asia bringing patriarchal ideas, practices, and the dog. Sea traders from Indonesia introduced the dingo to north-west Australia which was subsequently partly domesticated by Australian Indigenous people.

The Chinese goddess

The Neolithic Hongshan 'great goddess' Nu Wa (or Nuwa, Nu Gua, Nugua) is estimated to be around 8,000 years old but may be much older. According to N.S. Gill she is "a Chinese creator goddess who made humans (as opposed to creator gods who made the universe ...)."[32] She is known as "the Repairer of the Universe, Transformer of the Myriad Creatures, a wind goddess, a female shaman and a raindancer." The historical Nugua sometimes appears with human torso and serpent's tail and is associated with "water, earth and caves."[33]

Brian Griffith (2012)[34] records that Chinese creation stories "picture the world as a family [and] portray the cosmic mother and father as roughly equal." Goddesses "symbolise the original equality of men and women in primitive clans ... [as] not a matriarchy but a partnership" and are focused upon in this book "partly because Western religions came to exclude them."[35] He has traced the goddess through the earliest written documents, and describes Nu Wa as giving birth "to all creatures in ten days ... [O]n the seventh day she gave birth to human beings."[36] Nu Wa saved the world from disaster caused by the 'gods of water and fire' by "patching the sky with stones of five colours", and used the "the severed legs of a giant turtle" to prop up "the four corners of heaven."[37] In another story, Nu Wa's status and powers were greatly reduced with the coming of patriarchy, when she became "the goddess of matchmaking."[38]

According to Brian Griffith, among her other attributes, Xi Wang Mu, the "Queen Mother of the West" was "a deity for women who determined their own lives and vocations"[39] and the version of her story which he records is basically similar to that of Max Dashu's account which follows.

Xi Wangmu, the Shamanic 'great goddess' of China

The 7,000-year-old Xi Wangmu (Hsi Wang Mu) was an important Neolithic goddess in China. Max Dashu (2010)[40] describes the great grandmother, female ancestor, 'Spirit Mother of the West' as being found in a garden hidden in the clouds in the western Kunlun Mountains where heaven and earth meet. An enormous tree, "a cosmic axis that connects heaven and earth, a ladder travelled by spirits and shamans"[41] is to be found in the garden. Time, space, and stars are under Xi Wangmu's control and she can create and destroy, control life and death, disease, healing and new growth. (These are the same attributes Marija Gimbutas found in the Old European goddess.) She wears a headdress symbolic of a loom, and holds a weaving tool, each representing her role as "cosmic weaver who creates and maintains the universe."[42] She often sits on a dragon (yin) and tiger (yang) throne, as depicted on a Banpo burial stone in Henan.

The Kunlun Mountains (also called 'Jade Mountains') had great symbolic meanings. They were known as the 'heavenly' mountains, mysterious and outside time, pain, or death; a place of everything wonderful. Dancing jade maidens accompany images of Xi Wangmu in some instances. In some of her portraits Xi Wangmu is associated with the Sheng crown headdress. An important festival for women, during which they displayed the results of their weaving skills, was celebrated "on the seventh day of the seventh month at the seventh hour", representing the time when Xi Wangmu "descended among humans."[43] This symbolised the mid-point of the year and the balance of cosmic energies.

This goddess is sometimes associated with certain animals, sometimes appearing with tiger's teeth and leopard's tail, with 'wild hair' under her headdress. She is said to call loudly, to 'roar', to make long sounds such as shamans make, "to rouse winds and call spirits."[44] In the Indus valley around 4,400 BP she was depicted on stamp seals as a 'tiger-woman'. She is known as 'Snake Shaman' in some depictions.

Max Dashu (2009) remarks that from the Han Dynastic period onwards the image and symbolism of the goddess changed to become aristocratic and hierarchic, and was subsequently replaced by kings and lords, although she has never disappeared entirely from view. She appears still as "the Weaving Maid who oversees women's fabric arts, silk cultivation, and needlework."[45]

There were a number of other Chinese goddesses including: Bixia Yuanjin, 'Princess of the Clouds', who looks after dawn, childbirth, and destiny; Feng Pho-Pho, 'goddess of the winds', riding a tiger; Gaomei, originally 'First Mother', changed by patriarchy into a male deity; Ma-Ku, Ma-Gu, 'goddess of spring, health and healing'; Tien Hou, 'ocean goddess' who protects sailors; Xi-Hou, 'Lady of Ten Suns', who 'gives birth to the sun' each day; and Yaoji, represented and worshipped as a sacred rock.

Nüshu: Women's secret script

It is not known when or where *nüshu,* women's secret script, originated but it is known to have been used for over a thousand years, and could even have been present in the late Neolithic period. According to Gina Barnes (1993), marks and signs incised on Mainland China's Neolithic pottery suggest they form the earliest stage of writing in East Asia, as they are descriptive motifs appearing in columns similar to modern Chinese characters. Could these markings be the forerunners of *nüshu* script?

According to Cathy Silber (1995), *nüshu* "is a writing system used solely by women ... in one small part of south-western Hunan."[46] *Nüshu* characters were slim, elongated, graceful and elegant, balanced as they were by shorter curves and dots, when compared with the squat, square standard Chinese characters. This secret language of women came into use because Chinese Confucian cultures were very patriarchal, and women were excluded from education.

Before the time of Confucius (2,551–2,479 BP) women were relatively free, according to Bret Hinsch (1995).[47] Gina Barnes explains that Confucius "taught moderation and harmony in all things in an era of incredible violence and change"[48] and affirmed that governments and men needed to be authoritarian and hierarchical. Bret Hinsch confirms that among other things, Confucius dictated women's position in relation to men as being subordinate. For example, women were generally thought of as 'polluting' when menstruating, and their subordination was considered part of the 'natural order' of things. The division of labour based on sex was also supported by the teachings of Neo-Confucianism. (These views advanced by Confucius seem very similar to early Indo-European ideologies. Indeed some of his ideas/views also resemble those of the early Christian Church 'fathers', including Thomas Aquinas and Augustine.)

Because women were not taught how to read or write standard Chinese characters, they developed their own written secret language which men could not understand, and this allowed women to express themselves without fear or misunderstanding, a freedom not previously available to them. They could keep diaries of everyday problems and joys, and express themselves creatively in poetry or story, which they could share with other women. It was used by mothers to pass down secret women's knowledge and teachings to their daughters and granddaughters. Although they could not change men's attitudes or "the dominant textual tradition"[49] they could encourage and support each other without interference.

Sadly women could no longer use *nüshu* after the 1949 revolution, and rather than risking the possibility of women's secret literature falling into the wrong hands, much of it was either buried with its writers or otherwise destroyed, with only a few examples still surviving to the present. There are a few women today who can still read and write *nüshu*, and it is now being taught to some young women (and three young men) at Tsinghua University in Beijing, and by Hu Mei Yue in a village in Jiangyong county.[50]

Matrilineal traditions in China

In *Societies of Peace: Matriarchies past, present and future*, two Mosuo women from Yunnan and Sichuan provinces in south-west China speak of their matrilineal societies: Lamu Gatusa,[51] who comes from the Lake Lugu area; and Hengde Danshilacuo (He Mei),[52] from Sichuan. Lamu Gatusa states that 60% of Mosuo people "still live in matriarchal societies today."[53]

According to Lamu Gatusa in 'Matriarchal marriage patterns of the Mosuo people of China', the Mosuo people had little contact with the outside world until recent times, despite living on an important caravan trade route, the Tea Horse Road, which was the route between China and Tibet. Although they traded for some items they were largely self-reliant and self-managed, with their own distinct language and oral traditions.

Eva Sternfeld (1995) describes life for the Mosuo who belong to the Naxi minority in the Yongning region, where people live on an isolated plateau surrounded by 1,200-metre-high mountains near the Jinsha River, off the Yangtze River. Here the people farm, raise animals, fish and hunt. In this region there are more women than men.

There is an important goddess who is represented by a sandstone ridge bearing her name, Ganmu (Woman Mountain). In 1952 the communist People's Liberation Army tried to convert the now 'liberated' Mosuo to a patriarchal society: "The Region was declared a commune and the villages transformed into brigades, decisively weakening the power of the matriarchal families as economic units"[54] according to Eva Sternfeld. They built roads and brought in trucks to the originally inaccessible region, to 'modernise' it. Electric power plants were constructed and electricity supplied to the houses, schools were provided, and new marriage rules introduced, but the patriarchal practices were never fully successful and traditional ways of living and matriarchal traditions have been reclaimed.

Lamu Gatusa relates a number of traditional rules:

- All in the family descended from the mother support each other. There are no disruptions between brothers, wives, uncles or nephews.
- Love marriages are "not affected by political, economic or religious factors."[55] There is one exception: there may be no marriages between members of the same clan, or between those who are too closely related.
- All Mosuo clan members are cared for: young, old, weak, or disabled.
- There is equality between the sexes; and although girls are preferred, boys are welcomed.
- Some Mosuo have 'visiting' marriages. A young pregnant girl shares her mother's bedroom to 'protect' the unborn baby.
- The family property always remains intact so as to support all members, and is not inherited outside the family.
- A flexible division of labour allows every member to work at tasks according to their special skills.
- A balance kept between work and other aspects of living ensures a peaceful family life.
- Although Mosuo culture is women-centred, men's roles are also important, thus creating an equality between women and men, and this shows in family, property and marriage patterns.[56]

She states that "in matriarchal families, difficulties among the members can be easily negotiated because they all come from the same mother and are more considerate of each other."[57]

In her discussion of 'Mosuo Family Structure', Hengde Danshilacuo (He Mei) confirms that most people continue to live in the maternal family home, and never marry their lovers. She explains that Mosuo cultures have very different structures to other Chinese societies. In various Mosuo areas marriage systems differ, leading to diverse family structures. Other systems she discusses concern "the 'visiting' (matriarchal) and monogamous (patriarchal) patterns [which] coexist in a complex family structure."[58] She comments that the more common patriarchal and monogamous family structure also exists in China today.

China's traditional minority cultures

There are two other traditional cultures which, although they have been patriarchal throughout the historical period, have prehistoric links and traditions. Until relatively recently, the people lived as they had done for millennia, but with increased contact with the outside world, changes to their lifestyles are happening.

Huangnan Prefecture is a small and isolated area in high altitude mountainous land in the south-east corner of Qinghai, which is accessible by road. Pamela Tan (1995)[59] describes the Qinghai Region as once being part of Eastern Tibet, and the people include farmers and nomads who have continued their traditional lifestyles. It is interesting that the province includes the Kunlun Mountains, and a national park contains the headwaters of the Yellow, Yangtze and Mekong Rivers. (Was the important Neolithic goddess Xi Wangmu [Hsi Wang Mu] 'Spirit Mother of the West' ever recognised in this region?) In recent times the population is comprised of: Han Chinese (54%); Tibetans (23%); and Hui (16%); with small groups of other peoples including Sala, Tu and Mongul peoples (although in 1995 Pamela Tan recorded that 66% of the people were Tibetan).[60]

Not only are the cultures diverse, but also the landscape, flora and fauna. Pamela Tan observes that "the spoken dialects differ considerably; even the physical features of the people are as different as are many customs, attitudes and lifestyles."[61] Most people are agriculturalists in this region of high altitudes, long distances and bad roads.

In Qinghai, the farms are small, with traditional pise-walled houses and high-walled courtyards (an outer one for stock, and an inner one for family) enclosed by a large wooden gate to keep out the bitterly cold winter winds. Some houses feature finely carved wooden rafters and have trees and flowers growing in their courtyards. The mixed groups of people live peacefully together in the villages, growing wheat and/or corn for the following year. Collecting water can be problematic if the previous season has been dry; women and children – and the men if available – collect water every day. The men plough the fields, sow grain and spread manure over the fields, and women weed the crops, all by hand. If the crops fail, the men have to leave to find employment elsewhere for a period of time to supplement their income. The women have to manage as best they can when this happens.[62]

Extended families tend to live in the village, or in nearby villages. The Han Chinese have arranged marriages, while the Tibetans have 'love' marriages. Women are highly regarded, perhaps suggesting an equality in relations between women and men. Women spin and weave the wool from their sheep, and mohair from the goats, for clothes and carpets, and embroider items for domestic use and for exchange; the men take some items away with them to be sold. Women also grow Chinese spice pepper trees (for cooking) and rhubarb (for medicines), and raise chickens, pigs, goats, sheep and cattle.

Korea

In prehistory, China, Korea and Japan were one geographical landscape known as 'East Asia'. Cold phases during the Glacial Maximum periods – at 70,000, 50,000 and 37,000 BP – meant low sea levels, when people could easily move between previously sea-covered regions. Towards the end of the last Ice Age, the coastal regions of Korea and the Japanese Islands, although they were not covered in ice, were greatly affected by the rise and fall of sea levels (by up to 120 metres higher or lower). Gina Barnes (1993) states that this event either exposed or drowned much coastal land until after 18,000 BP, when the climate gradually became warmer. The land became covered by the seas from 10,000 BP, and then again between 6,000 and 4,000 BP, during which time Korean and Japanese people increasingly exploited sea resources. Although this was the agricultural period in China, in Korea and Japan it was the 'New Stone Age', the era of polished stone tools and ceramics, but no agriculture.[63]

There was no interest in archaeology in Korea until the Japanese occupation from 1910 to 1945 according to Gina Barnes (1993). The earliest presence of humans has been tentatively dated to 50,000 BP. Palaeolithic people could move freely over Korea and Japan during cold phases. Between 18,000 and 9,000 BP, like their counterparts in mainland China, the Jeulmun people of Korea who came from the Alti region of southern Siberia,[64] and the Jomon people of Japan also made pottery, were sedentary and did not practice agriculture.

Toolkits included arrowheads, and artefacts included pierced bones, pebbles, and animal teeth (perhaps used in necklaces); and incised pebbles, dated between 20,000 and 10,000 BP. Gina Barnes records rock art, including pecked linear images of reindeer and grey deer in Korea.[65]

The earliest substantial Korean house is dated to 21,000 BP; its five-square-metre floor is outlined by rocks, and includes a burnt patch which was probably a hearth. Post holes indicate that a roof of some kind was present. There are suggestions of groups living in settlements, with huts organised into clan groups, while burials were in communal graves. Women and men wore animal skins in winter and woven fibre (tapa cloth) garments in summer, and women's clothing was often ornamented with shell and pebble jewellery. There were many regional variations involving technologies, social organisation and material culture during the long-running Jeulmun and Jomon periods.

The first settled Neolithic Korean communities made Yungimun pottery 10,000 years ago, and by 9,000 BP the Jeulmun or 'comb-pattern' pottery appeared, together with polished stone tools. Gina Barnes comments that in Korea, the Jeulmun Neolithic period (8,000–2,700 BP) was characterised by hunter-gatherers who fished and collected plant foods, including fruit and nuts, but not until near the end of the Neolithic period (about 2,700 BP) was millet, and later, rice, cultivated.

All pottery in East Asia from the very beginning featured textured surface decoration, including stamped, punched, grooved, pinched, and geometric incised designs. The textured patterns included multiple linear arc-shaped arrangements, cord marks, vertical repeat zigzags, shell impressions, and applique markings. Pots in the north of Korea featured flat bases, and in the south, conical bases, and were very different to the Jomon pottery shapes. Gina Barnes notes the only appearance of 'crude' clay figurines in Korea, and also artefacts which may have been masks, consisting of large shells with 'eye' and 'mouth' holes, perhaps used in rituals.

By 5,000 BP the pottery was decorated with painted designs. Jeulmun pottery was very similar to that produced in Mongolia and parts of Manchuria. Pit houses were apparently now more permanent; as the name suggests, they were equipped with pits (some with stairs) in which groups of large storage pots were kept. Generally pots of the time were "wide-mouthed, pointed-bottomed pots with bands of simple incised geometric designs"[66] some with perforated rims to secure lids. Gina Barnes argues that inland Jeulmun settlements were not affluent due to the seasonality of resources, and their tools and ornaments were limited, unlike Middle Jomon cultures of the same period.

There is no mention of whether the clan social structure was patrilineal or matrilineal, although Brian Griffith (2012) reports that, just as in China and Japan, there were traces of earlier women-centred cultures in Korea after the beginning of the historical period, in which nurturing, kindness, harmony and selfless giving were encouraged, with the same values expected of both women and men.[67] He states that "Min Jiayin (1995)[68] claims the general pattern [in East Asia] is that women were buried with more symbols of honour and status, while men were buried with more tools of production."[69] However, there are Korean goddesses: Aryong Jong, 'the goddess of rainfall'; Mulhalmoni (Healing Waters) who is the special matron of female shamans, and may be called upon especially to heal eye ailments; and Yondung Halmoni, a 'wind goddess', who is offered rice cakes in shamanic rituals.[70]

The Early Historic Mumun pottery culture[71] ran from 3,500 to 2,300 BP and during this time the first agriculture appeared, including intensive dry farming and paddy-field crops of many kinds. The Middle Mumun pottery period from 2,800 to 2,550 BP brought the first

1 hierarchic cultures; and the first elaborate elite burials and violent activities began in the Late Mumun period from 2,550 to 2,300 BP with the beginning of Korea's Bronze Age. Gina Barnes mentions bronze weapons (the Manchurian type) appearing about 2,300 BP, and iron about 2,400 BP, indicating contact with Indo-European (Eurasian) influences from China. There were huge mounded tombs constructed during this latter period. Populations were sedentary due to rich resources. Early written texts did not appear until after 2,300 BP.

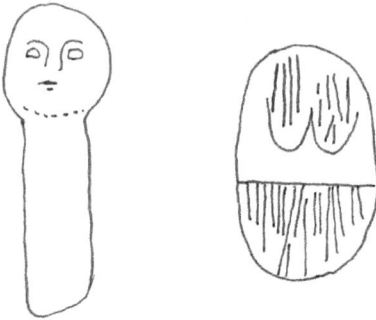

EARLY SYMBOLIC KOREAN
IMAGES

1. *Cylindrical stone with human head* (perhaps a pestle?) 20,000–10,000 BP; and an incised pebble with female image
(Source: Barnes, Gina, 1993)
All line drawings © Judy Foster, 2013

Japan

Evidence shows that the Palaeolithic period in Japan lasted from 50,000 BP until 18,000 BP and the people were hunters, fishers and gatherers who used micro-blade stone tools. Little else is known about them. Jomon pottery originated with the ancestors of the present-day Ainu 'aboriginal' people of Japan about 18,000 BP.[72] They have a legend which says they have lived there for 100,000 years (for almost as long as the Indigenous people say they have been in Australia).[73] DNA tests indicate that the Ainu may originally come from Tibet, the Andaman Islands, Mongolia, or even Taiwan.[74] (There have been suggestions that 10,000-year-old skeletal evidence of early Ainu people resembles that of indigenous New Guinean and Australian people.)[75]

The indigenous Ainu people lived in the northern and central islands and their culture and language was different to that of the Jomon people. They were mainly hunter/fisher people with an animist religion. Their houses were built from cogon grasses, bamboo grass, or bark, and were placed alongside rivers and the coastline. Typical houses had reed-thatched roofs, and were seven metres by five long with three windows, a central fireplace, and a storage area at the western entrance. People usually sat on woven reed or flag mats. The largest house in a settlement was used as a communal meeting place.[76] Ainu clothes were made from feathered bird-skin, tree bark (barkcloth), and hides of bear, deer, fox, seal and dog; men's hats were made from wood fibre with partially shaved wood bundles, and women's hats consisted of an embroidered headband.

In terms of societal structures, there were various forms of marriage: that of a child "promised by arrangement", marriage "based on mutual consent of both sexes",[77] or sometimes a daughter was given a room of her own to receive her followers, one of whom the parents would choose for her to marry. Men and women were considered to be adult at 15 to 16 years of age; girls received their first tattoos at 12 to 13 years of age, and the remainder by adulthood, when they were to marry.

Conflict resolution was mediated by a number of clan elders who decided suitable punishment. Ainu people also hunted in groups within their own territory; sometimes several village units hunted within joint territories. They were peaceful people until the arrival 3,500 years ago of the Yayo people.

The Ainu have: the 'sun goddess' Chup-Kamu (who was originally the moon goddess); Fuji, an ancient 'fire goddess' as represented by Mount Fuji; Kamui-fuchi, 'Lady Hearth', the Ainu Supreme Ancestress, a deified tribal mother, or spirit of 'female productivity and the home'; and Onne-chip-kamui, 'Grandmother Tree'.

The Jomon people were similar in appearance to modern Ainu people, descendants of an ancient Palaeo-Asiatic lineage which may also have included the Jeulmun people of Korea. This date is in accord with Luigi Cavalli-Sforza's genetic evidence in 2000 concerning the likeness of northern Chinese to Manchurians, Koreans and Japanese.[78]

The Jomon hunter-gatherer cultures lasted from 18,000 until 2,300 BP. Jomon pottery is the earliest known pottery, and pot sherds have been found which are marked with band appliqué and 'fingernail' impressions. According to the Heilbrunn Timeline of Art History, during Japan's Neolithic period the Jomon people were semi-sedentary hunter-gatherers and fishers, living in pit houses arranged around central open spaces. Women made coiled clay pots, the clay often mixed with other adhesive materials, such as mica, lead, fibres, or crushed shells, finely shaped and finished, and low fired.[79]

This long stage falls into several periods:

- The *Incipient Jomon* period (18,000–10,000 BP) marks the transition between the Palaeolithic and Neolithic periods, and the pottery made during this time is thought to be the world's oldest. Their low-fired pots were deep, with pointed bottoms and simple cord markings around the rims. Applique and fingernail impressions were used in decoration, although otherwise pottery was not well finished. Pots were used for cooking vegetable and meat, as well as storage. Tools included polished-edged axes, stone drills, arrowheads, and arrow shaft smoothers similar to eastern Siberian tools.[80]

- The *Initial Jomon* (10,000–7,000 BP) appeared during the time when Shikoku and Kyushu Islands separated from the main island of Honshu because of rising seas. Warmer seas meant richer sea and land resources supporting more people, and artefacts from that time include stone tools, grinding stones, knives, and axes.

- During the *Early Jomon* (7,000–4,500 BP) abundant seafoods were widely used, and pit houses were square-shaped, organised into small villages. Trade between the islands included many handcrafts, cord-decorated clay pots for cooking and storage. Shells or carved sticks were rolled over the surface of some pots, and others had decoration made from the edge of shells forming a rippled-patterned design. Woven baskets, bone needles (for sewing garments?), bone fish hooks and more abundant stone tools were used during this period.

- During the *Middle Jomon* period (4,500–3,500 BP) the people moved permanently up into the mountains, lived in larger villages, and began to cultivate small crops. The many stone figurines, and some phallic imagery, found in the shell-mound graves suggest increased ritual practices. Pottery now sometimes included decorative elements made "by carving or sculpting the clay", although "the clay fabric was coarse"[81] with patchy finish.

EARLY DOGU FIGURINES

1. *An early stone figurine,* Incipient Jomon period
2. *Painted dogu 'cat' figurine,* Middle Jomon
3. *Dogu figurine with snake 'crown',* Middle Jomon
4. *Clay figurine,* Late Jomon (Source: Early Women Masters East and West, n.d.)
5. *Some broken dogu figurines in situ*
6. *A prehistoric pot with interesting rim design* (Source 1, 2, 3, 5, 6: Heritage of Japan, n.d.)

All line drawings © Judy Foster, 2013

- The *Final Jomon* period (3,500–2,300 BP) was marked by population decline due to less food being available, and as a consequence, villages became smaller. There was now more ritual activity and increased artefacts including stone rods, stone phalli, and figurines, and a return to simple cord-marking and incised designs on pottery.

The (patriarchal) Yayoi culture now appeared, along with the growing of domesticated rice in dry riverbeds or in swamps. The Yayoi people merged with the Final Jomon culture between 2,300 and 2,000 BP (marking the beginning of the historical period) and became the ancestors of the modern Ainu people.[82]

Japanese matriarchy

In 'Amaterasu-o-mi-kami, Japanese Sun Goddess: The matristic roots of Japan'[83] Susan Gail Carter states that this Japanese goddess has been revered for a long period and is still recognised today. The Jomon period began at 18,500 BP and the first fired clay female figurines and other ritual clay artefacts also appeared along with the first evidence of matriarchal cultures about this time (see below). Susan Carter notes seven attributes of Japanese matriarchy:

- women as preserving social values, familial identity, teachers of traditions, bearers of children
- egalitarian, with complementarity between the sexes, no hierarchies
- respect for nature and all living things
- conflict resolution through formal intervention and mediation
- female veneration
- worship of female deities, symbolic of all life
- the sacred and the secular are inseparable.

These attributes appear to be common to most prehistoric societies.

The earliest Jomon figurines are stones incised with symbolic markings, including 'breasts', found in Japan's late Palaeolithic; in one instance a figurine is accompanied by a bowl. Figurines range in size from 3 to 30 centimetres, usually standing, a few crouching, and overwhelmingly depict female forms. Over 10,000 figurines have been found all over the country, according to Susan Carter. These deities may have generous figures, with large breasts and hips, and feature symbolic colours such as red, and triangles, pubic triangles, spirals, running spirals, and zigzags. They are thought to have been used in rituals.

The earliest of the very few female clay figurines which date to the Initial Jomon period feature clean curved lines and a semi-abstract shape, and are thought to represent 'the earth mother'. In the Middle and Final Jomon periods there were many more figurines, usually of pregnant women. For prehistoric central Asian and Eurasian peoples, female deities (*dogu*) represented the 'earth mother' of creation and childbirth or 'Great Mother of Earth and Nature'; and in the Late Jomon, they represented agriculture, fertility and rice cultivation. Northern Middle Jomon *dogu* figurines were slab-shaped, while later ones were heart-shaped, triangular, horned owl-shaped, cat-faced or with slit goggle eyes. Others featured large buttocks and breasts, some crowned with a coiled snake ('snake goddess').[84]

Susan Carter cites other evidence which includes stone circles, some of which may have been sundials, and some perhaps used as calendars in relation to the movements of the sun. Female figurines have been found in these formations, as well as possible burial pits.

1 a   b

2   3   4

JAPAN: DOGU FEMALE FIGURINES

1a. and b. *Two Jomon figurines*, 3,000 BP
(Source: Department of Asian Art, October 2002)

2. *A Jomon Dogu female figurine*
(Source: Nielson, Paula I., 2010)

3. *Dogu ceramic figurine*
(Source: Barnes, Gina, 2010)

4. *Dogu figurine*
(Source: British Museum, 2009)

All line drawings © Judy Foster, 2013

The great goddess of Japan, Amaterasu-o-mi-kami, has been the symbol of the sun, birth, regeneration and new growth over a very long period. Although with patriarchy she has become absorbed into the nature-embedded Shinto religion, according to Susan Carter, she continues to 'shine' brightly as a role model for Japanese people. According to the 'Far East Realm' she was the "highest expression of the Spirit of Nature."[85]

Other goddesses include Ama no Uzume, 'goddess of persuasion'; Inari, a Shinto goddess represented as a female fox, who looks after love and prosperity; Izanami, 'goddess of the legends'; Tatsu-ta-hime, 'Lady Wind', who looks after the harvest; Uta no Mitanna, Japanese 'rice goddess', whose messengers are the foxes; Wakahirume, 'goddess of weaving'; Yaya-zakurai, 'cherry-tree goddess'; and Yuki-Onne, 'The Snow Maiden', spirit of a quiet and painless death.[86]

Brian Griffith (2012) observes that the East Asian prehistoric goddesses were not forgotten with the coming of written history, but lived on in the lives of village people, who have continued to pass down their values and meanings to the following generations.[87]

CHAPTER 14

HIDDEN WORLDS: THAILAND AND INDONESIA

Thailand

Thailand's prehistory

Archaeological excavations are now being carried out more frequently in countries such as Vietnam, Thailand and Indonesia. In Thailand collaborative digs have been undertaken between Thai and Western archaeologists, such as Rachanie Thosaret and Charles Higham[1] since 1956. They contend that Thailand's prehistory is important because it was the gateway through which people passed as they expanded into South-East Asia at least 1 million years ago.

The most recent evidence of *Homo erectus* to be found in northern Thailand is that of 'Lampang Man' and stone tools dated to about 1 million BP. According to Charles Higham and Rachanie Thosaret (1998) most researchers agree that people arrived by at least 1 million BP. Bones of *H. erectus* found on the banks of the Solo River in Java have been dated to 1.8 million BP, and traces of *Homo habilis*, an earlier hominid, have been found in China and Vietnam dated to the same age, according to Robert Bednarik (1996).[2] He notes that 700,000-year-old tools were found at two places in Thailand. It is thought that *H. erectus* may have come from Africa to China, Vietnam and Thailand, or through India and Burma, to Thailand.

Somewhat later, hunter-gatherers left behind remains of their fires, dated to about 38,000 BP in areas above sea level; unearthed tools included chert scrapers, knives and choppers, with a few being made of stone and one of deer antler. It is surmised that bamboo was used to make traps, spears and arrows although, as in other tropical countries, no wooden artefacts have survived. However, it is fair to assume that the freely available timber would have been extensively used both for utilitarian and ritual purposes.

Evidence of hunter-gatherer groups, dated from 11,000 to 7,500 BP, has been found in north-west Thailand in Spirit Cave, which is situated on a hillside overlooking the Salween River.[3] The people were Hoabinhian hunter-gatherers from North Vietnam as demonstrated by their stone tools.

A Timeline of Prehistoric Influences in East and South-East Asia

Period (BP)	China	Korea	Japan	Thailand	Indonesia
c. 1,800,000	H. erectus Different stone tools from African H. erectus			H. erectus	H. erectus in Java (2,000,000)
700,000	Palaeolithic H. sapiens	500,000 H. erectus			H. erectus in Java, the world's first sailors
100,000					H. floresiensis
		Late Palaeolithic hunter-gatherers	Ancestors of the Ainu lived from 50,000–18,000 Pottery-making hunter-gatherers	38,000–27,000 Hunter-gatherers	29,000–17,000 Hunter-gatherers
18,000	Pottery			Wild cereals	
16,000			Pottery Beginning of Jomon culture		13,000 H. floresiensis disappears
13,000		Pottery		13,000–7,500 Pottery sherds Neolithic?	
12,000	Rice growing (c. 12,000–9,000)				
10,000	Dadiwan pottery culture	Hunter-gatherers	Female figurines		8,000 Sulawesi Toalian period
7,800–7,400				10,000–3,000 Pottery, houses on stilts, ritual burials	
7,000–5,000	Yangshao Matri culture	Neolithic	These were the original Ainu people		
7,000	Neolithic Period (rice growing in southern China) No violence	Jeulmun period Pottery making hunter-gatherers (no rice or millet yet); semi-settled	Early Jomon Period	No violence	No knowledge of cultures during this time
6,000	Weaving				
6,100–4,600	Dawenkou culture Hongsan jade culture				Pottery
5,000–4,900		Comb-pattern pottery			
5,000	Liangzhu culture	Jeulmun period	Middle Jomon No rice or millet yet		
4,000	Indo-Europeans reach China	Clan settlements, small scale cultivation of wild plants: millet, rice		Agriculturalists Silk bundle in grave	Neolithic agricultural activities, animal domestication, rice growing, woven textiles
	Longshan culture Late Neolithic hierarchic societies, first violence		Late Jomon	No violence Bronze Age non-violent	
			Modern Ainu		Lapita pottery
3,000	Shang Period hierarchies		Final Jomon Violence		
2,800	Zhou hierarchies	End of Jeulmun Early hierarchy Early Munman pottery Early Bronze Age Mid-Munman pottery Hierarchies Warfare	End of Jomon Hierarchies	Iron Age (c. 2,500) Weapons in graves signify violence	Bronze and iron Dong Son culture from China (first violence) wars, headhunting
2,200				Hierarchic social organisations, dynasties, etc.	Buddhism
2,100				Han Chinese in Thailand	Hinduism, metallurgy
1,600 CE					European invasion, Christianity

226

Thai hunter-gatherer civilisations (European Neolithic Period)

Ralph Coffman (2002)[4] describes the communal Chinese Neolithic peoples of Yunnan who lived along the Yangtze, Mekong and Salween Rivers about 8,500–7,800 BP, as being semi-sedentary, and living in houses built on stilts so that they could be close to food sources including wild rice and fish. These were the people who migrated to South-East Asia. Essential to this mode of living was the building of wooden weirs used to trap fish as flooding rivers receded. The use of bamboo, stone, or wood for fish traps, a method of construction which had originated deep in the past, has also long been used in Australia and the Pacific.

In Thailand's Neolithic period (around 11,000 BP) settlements were permanent and the use and cultivation of wild cereals commenced; later, farming developed with the domestication of cattle and pigs, and a variety of crops, including betel, beans, peas, nuts, pepper and cucumber. Charles Higham and Rachanie Thosaret (1998) report that between 13,000–7,500 BP pottery sherds, stone adzes and slate knives appeared. In other parts of the world the remains of pottery usually indicate the past presence of agriculturalists rather than hunter-gatherers, but this is not so in Thailand.

Like the Jomon people of Japan, Thai hunter-gatherers were able to live in settlements with a well-established cultural life. Women were able to make beautifully constructed pottery because they had abundant food readily available. Their diet included a variety of plants, fruit and seeds, as well as small animals and fish. Between 10,000–3,000 BP Thai clay pottery was burnished black in colour and featured cord-marks and incised designs. Fish hooks made of bone, pottery anvils (for forming pots), and burnishing stones have been found at one site on an ancient shoreline now situated inland.

Remains of ancient post holes indicate that some of the houses were built on stilts over the sea while others were on nearby land. As Brian Griffith (2012) observes,

> typical houses of early [Neolithic] coastal villages were similar around the Pacific Rim from Japan to Melanesia. They were generally built on wooden stilts, with walls of woven reeds and large overhanging roofs of thatch or palm fronds.[5]

Charles Higham and Rachanie Thosaret record that in the coastal settlements, men fished and hunted, and women made pottery vessels. There was exchange of goods with inland people from whom the men obtained stone suitable for making adzes. Their fertile environment meant that they did not have to cultivate plants or domesticate animals. Burials were ritualised, with bodies placed in a seated position, and accompanied by numerous pottery vessels and grave offerings. Similar burials have been found in central and northern Vietnam.

These Thai people were similar in appearance to modern Thais. Despite a good diet, their life expectancy was around 30 years (occasionally up to 50 years). Archaeological evidence shows that there was a high mortality rate for infants, and many people suffered from anaemia-related diseases. Charles Higham and Rachanie Thosaret suggest that this was due to the annual cool dry winters and warm wet summers.[6] They describe Thailand's environment as diverse with uplands, long coastlines and many rivers.[7]

At another 4,500-year-old settlement, remnants of cloth made from beaten bark (tapa) or naturally occurring asbestos sheets, demonstrated that these fibres were used to wrap bodies for burial. Burials were laid out in a chequer-board design. Grave goods included bone harpoons; pottery featuring intricate decoration; many shell beads, some in

1

2

3

4 a

b

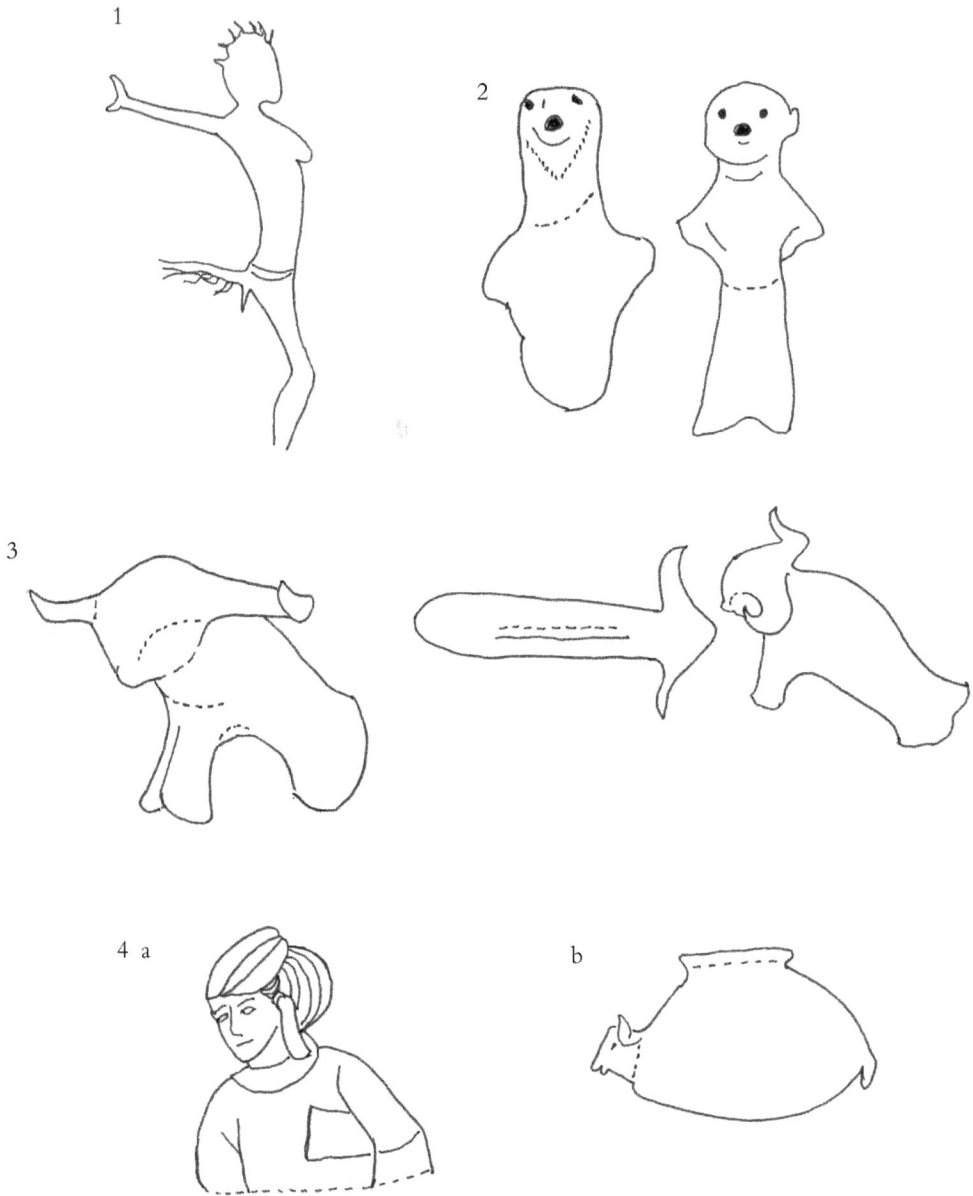

THAILAND: PREHISTORIC FEMALE FIGURINES

1. Southern central Thailand: *Prehistoric female figure* in a cave painting
2. *Two Bronze Age clay figurines*, probably female, found in central Thailand
3. *Neolithic clay cattle figurines* (possibly pestles) suggest female symbolism, central Thailand

4a. Detail of a very *fine female figurine* engraved on a Bronze Age bowl
b. A beautifully formed Neolithic pot in the shape of a cow, western Thailand
(Source: Higham, Charles and Rachanie Thosaret, 1998)

All line drawings © Judy Foster, 2013

barrel and funnel forms; cowrie shells; bangles; and clay pottery anvils. In later periods at this site, men were buried with turtle shells, and women's burials included clay anvils indicating their pottery skills.

There was some form of hierarchy in these increasingly larger settlements as demonstrated by the rich goods in some graves; for example, one woman was buried with thousands of dazzling shell beads; others, with elegant and beautifully decorated pottery, or expertly made and polished stone adzes, and their bodies wrapped in expensive woven cloth. Alternatively, this may indicate that women enjoyed respect and status, as was the case in the northern European societies.

The Thai Neolithic Period

In Thailand there is no evidence for a transition from hunter-gatherer societies to farming societies, yet the earliest agriculture in Thailand appears to have occurred about 4,300 BP. There is also no physical evidence for rice cultivation originating in Thailand. It seems that the first farmers in Thailand may have come directly from southern China, since rice was first cultivated in the Yangtze Valley. The earliest evidence of rice farming in southern China is rice-husking implements dated to 8,500–7,800 BP. Dogs, descended from China's wolves, are thought to have been brought in by the first rice farmers.

In South-East Asian countries women's importance was signified not only by the making of fine pottery but also by their creation of woven cloth via cultivation, collection and spinning of the fibres through to weaving and dyeing of the cloth. According to Elizabeth Barber (1994)[8] the cloth itself was not just the result of labour but was also a symbol of creation and fertility. Special cloth with specific motifs related to its purpose was prepared by women for use at initiation, marriage, childbirth and burial. These cloths offered protection for the well-being of the wearer.

Charles Higham and Rachanie Thosaret (1998) describe grave goods from this time as including incised and impressed designs of arcs and snakes on pottery vessels, adzes, shell disc beads, tubular stone beads, worked shell, bone harpoons, anthropomorphic pots, and even a carved sandstone phallus. Bodies of both sexes were oriented north-east to south-west, often in groups. Some later graves were superimposed over earlier ones without disturbing them. No Neolithic burials contained bronze implements or defensive weapons.

There is no evidence of social disharmony in early Thailand, and the subsequent Lapita[9] people of the Pacific were also peaceful, so it would seem that any conflict was caused by the interference of incoming Indo-European warriors, or their ideas and practices which would only occur much later, after the Bronze Age.

The Bronze Age in Thailand

Bronze Age communities were usually no larger than 250 people. They grew rice, made pottery and mined copper in the dry season. In their graves there were bronze socketed axes, bronze socketed spearheads and arrowheads. The Thai Bronze Age (which lasted from 3,500 to 3,000 BP) is interesting because just as in Bronze Age Crete, Thai people were making beautifully executed bronze objects but no weapons of war. Charles Higham and Rachanie Thosaret did not find any evidence to indicate aggression or conflict. Even in the following early Thai Iron Age (after 2,500 BP), while bronze (and copper) was used to make increasingly complex artefacts such as bowls, bracelets, finger rings and bells, of the many bronzes found, none of these related to war or conflict, but were perhaps used in rituals or for display. Other settlements containing bronze objects similar to these dated to the Bronze Age are found from as far north as Hong Kong and southern China, and throughout Vietnam and Thailand. Even objects of Chinese jade have occasionally been found in Thai burials, indicating long held trade routes from China to the south.

Social organisation

In Bronze Age social organisation, there were minor differences in wealth between some families, perhaps suggesting the presence of a senior descendant of the 'founding ancestor', particular skills in communicating with the spirit world, or the creation of 'desirable objects.' In independent communities such as these, all decisions were reached by consensus, with no consultation with outside influences. This scenario is typical of Old European Palaeolithic and Neolithic civilisations, as well as of non-hierarchic social organisations, such as prehistoric indigenous societies. Women in these societies would have enjoyed respect and status.

Charles Higham and Rachanie Thosaret say of the people of Ban Chiang in the north of Thailand that again "there is no evidence for conflict or strife"[10] during the Bronze Age, even though a number of people with broken bones were found. They believe this was due to hard living conditions, as people at this time did not live longer than 40–50 years. Although bronze arrows were found among grave goods, they stress that there were no war weapons present. Remaining traces of Bronze Age Thai villages and settlements also did not indicate any defensive formations or evidence of hierarchy. (Hierarchy is assumed by the presence of some graves being more elaborate than others, some with more grave goods.) Graves held either men or women, indicating peaceful innovative communal societies in which religious leaders or clan elders of either sex were especially honoured by the group.

The Thai Iron Age

By 3,000 BP the Iron Age had brought with it "exotic goods and ideas" from China and India, resulting in "the emergence of a social elite."[11] Later, around 2,500 BP, iron artefacts including weapons appeared.

The warlike southern Chinese Yin and Han dynasties (earlier influenced by nomadic Eurasian [Indo-European] ideas and practices) introduced aggressive weaponry about 2,100 BP. Charles Higham and Rachanie Thosaret record that from around this time some graves held war weapons, such as swords, knives and spearheads, indicating that the change from a peaceful Neolithic period to a warrior Iron Age had occurred in Thailand.

We know that Indo-Europeans had reached China by at least 4,000 BP as indicated by the 4,000-year-old Caucasian mummies found in Loulan. They were certainly already present in India, as they had likely ended the 4,500-year-old Mohenjo-daro civilisation of the Indus valley. It is also likely that the warrior ideology of armed aggression brought by the Yin and Han warriors brought about many shifts, including changes to women's status, and the rise of competitive social groups who increasingly wished to outrank others in power and status.

For Charles Higham and Rachanie Thosaret 'civilisation' is based on hierarchic social structure, the rise of social classes, and the consequent power struggle leading to violence. In 2,100 BP the Han Chinese began so-called civilisation in Thailand by introducing the Pali

Indo-European languages, and later, increased Indian trade brought with it Sanskrit along with the Buddhist religion. Yet communal social organisations vanished with the advent of these new 'civilisations', and women's status changed to one of subservience.

Matriarchal/matrilineal societies in Thailand?

The 'Far-East Realm'[12] mentions one Thai goddess named Tap-Tun, a relatively unknown deity whose Bangkok temple is filled with the *palad khik* or 'representative phallus' used in phallic worship. Was she a goddess whose purposes were originally intended for women, but with her meaning and status changed by patriarchy? Or is she a patriarchal fertility goddess for men?

Arts of Thailand

According to William Warren and Luca Invernizzi Tettoni (1994)[13] there are many traditional arts and crafts which have been preserved and are still practised in present-day Thailand, particularly in villages in remote regions. Early Thailand was predominantly rural with agricultural occupations utilising handmade agricultural tools, many constructed from bamboo. Deities or ancestral beings resided in all living things, and were shown respect by ritual practices. Dynasties appeared about the same time as the Dong Son culture in Indonesia (2,800 BP) and Buddhism did not appear until the 3rd century CE.

Early houses were small and made with bamboo walls and thatched roofs, and were equipped with utensils made from woven bamboo, baked clay pottery, rattan, coconuts and various leaves. Emphasis was placed on practicality rather than decorative design, while wood was not used for tools until somewhat later. Earthenware pots were made in large sizes for storing water, and cooking pots were round in shape and often sat on pottery trays. Many large and small storage containers were made from tightly woven bamboo which was sealed with lacquer. Stronger large bamboo baskets were used in the fields and elsewhere for carrying heavy loads.

Women wove hemp cloth and tapa (barkcloth) for clothes, on simple looms often kept under the houses. Cloth was coloured using natural vegetable dyes and decorated with limited designs using clay rollers. Girls learned the required skills from their mothers, and were expected to weave two superior lengths of cloth by the marriageable age of 15–16 years: one length for their wedding, and one for their prospective husband. Cotton cloth was utilised for everyday clothing, and silk for special occasions. Weaving patterns were traditional, with limited design motifs repeated in particular order according to the family or clan design. Today, these designs have some similar features throughout South-East Asia, although a wider range of colours and symbolic imagery allows them a greater variety between cultures, and they are often more complex and very beautiful. It is interesting that in more recent times, a 4,000-year-old bundle of silk thread was found in a grave in north-east Thailand, suggesting woven silk may have been worn by prehistoric people long before contact with the Han Chinese arrival 2,800 years ago.

1

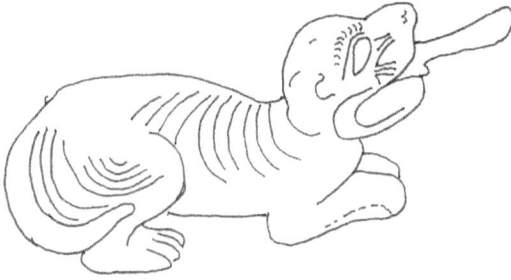

2

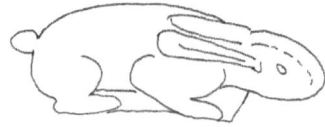

4

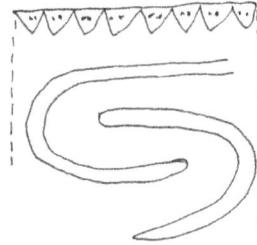

3

5

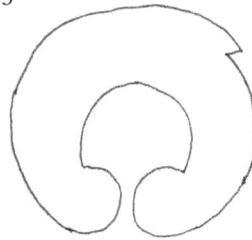

6

7

TRADITIONAL ARTS OF THAILAND

1. *Traditional carved wood animal*
2. *Carved wood rabbit*
3. *Two carved wood water bird bowls*
   (Source 1–3: Warren, William and Luca
   Invernizzi-Tettoni, 1994)

4. *An incised Lapita design on pottery*, 3,000 BP
5. *A stone bracelet*
6. *A Lapita pottery design motif*
7. *A decorated bowl*
   (Source 4–7: Higham, Charles and Rachanie
   Thosaret, 1998)

All line drawings © Judy Foster, 2013

Indonesia

Indonesia's prehistory

Irwin Hersey (1991)[14] records that there was an early Ice Age land bridge between Thailand, Malaysia and Indonesia which allowed *H. erectus* and the later hunter-gatherers access to most of South-East Asia. Indonesia is made up of 13,667 islands and many of the smaller islands remain uninhabited.

Indonesia's Palaeolithic Period

According to skeletal evidence, *H. erectus* was certainly present on the island of Java 2 million years ago, and it is significant that tools were found on this island which is separated from the next nearest island by a significant distance and a deep permanent sea passage.

Robert Bednarik (1995)[15] argues that the kinds of fauna present on Flores Island suggest that it has been separated from Java since the beginning of the Ice Age. Flores was also settled by *H. erectus*, as stone artefacts have been found together with (now extinct) primitive elephant bones used by *H. erectus* 700,000 years ago. He contends that Javanese *H. erectus* must have developed a form of language together with the ability to design, sail, and navigate some kind of watercraft, perhaps similar to the rafts or canoes used by present-day people in the area. These would have been necessary to take people across the stretch of sea separating Flores from the other islands of the Indonesian chain. Such evidence points to the development of complex skills, including the 700,000-year-old invention and building of boats, together with their navigation, which demonstrate the ever increasing sophistication of early humans in South-East Asia.

Flores Island lies between Bali and Timor, and could have been used at any time after 700,000 BP by early humans as a stepping-stone on the southern route to Australia. Stone tool evidence, including red ochre stones, flaked tools, and stone balls, shows that hunters-gatherers could have lived on any of the accessible islands from 29,000 to 17,000 BP. There are cave paintings of hand stencils which are 29,000 years old; also stone arrowheads; and tools for cutting bamboo and grass, used in making mats, according to *Indonesian Heritage* (1996)[16] researchers. They mention the Toalian period of 8,000 BP in Sulawesi, evidence for which includes new versions of stone tools, including arrowheads with serrated edges similar to those in the Americas; and caves with paintings where the Toalians lived.

A new human species named *Homo floresiensis* (dated to 18,000 BP) was discovered by Peter Brown and Mike Morwood (2004)[17] on Flores in a cave which has been inhabited since 95,000 BP. This early human co-existed alongside modern humans, but stone tools suggest a very much earlier emergence. Adult skeletons show that these people grew to no more than 1 metre tall, perhaps due to isolation and inbreeding as they were originally the same size as modern humans. (By contrast, so-called pygmies[18] – the shortest *Homo sapiens* – are about 1.3 metres tall). *H. floresiensis* are thought to have died out by 13,000 BP, although there is speculation that some might still exist hidden in remote deep cave systems. Their finely crafted tools show they may first have emerged as early as 700,000 BP and were probably mariners, since Flores has always been inaccessible by land from the rest of Indonesia.

Indonesia's Neolithic Period

Indonesian Heritage (1996) researchers[19] identify the Indonesian Neolithic period as occurring around 4,500 BP. This period heralded the beginning of agricultural practices and domestication of animals. The oldest pottery in Indonesia yet known dates to around 5,500 BP, while rice was first cultivated just over 4,000 years ago. (The earliest pottery making in China dates to 18,000 BP and the skills were imported to Japan by sea at that time. It was made much later in South-East Asia, perhaps because of the distance from China or because South-East Asians used other kinds of vessels, such as bamboo sections, seashells or coconut shells.)

It is conjectured that Neolithic Indonesians lived in individual communities of up to 250 people with a settled village lifestyle. Centralised authority occurred in the latter stages of the Bronze Age with the emergence of a social elite. Later still in the Neolithic, imported bronze was made into ceremonial axes and other refined objects (with the exception of war weapons).

Indonesian Neolithic pottery was usually made using carved wooden paddles and featured a smooth red finish often decorated with wrapped-around cord designs. Art motifs included spirals and circles. This Lapita-style pottery, dating to 3,500 BP, was incised, carved, and stamped, and it indicates that the Lapita ancestors of Polynesian and other Pacific communities very likely came from Indonesia.

Patrick Kirch's archaeological report describing the earliest (3,500-year-old) pottery in the Pacific region reveals evidence of a similar style of pottery on most of the islands in Melanesia and Polynesia, which also suggests an Indonesian origin. According to Patrick Kirsch (1997) the richly designed motifs on the pots indicate "elaborate and sophisticated design systems ... all sharing the same formal 'grammar' and obviously produced within a common semiotic tradition",[20] and are strong evidence for communal cultures. He excavated on Massau Island, which is located at the northern point of the Austronesian-speaking Bismark Islands. The early Massau pottery was low-fired earthenware (baked in open fires rather than in kilns) made using paddle and anvil tools but no wheel, a method still used today in Fiji and elsewhere in the Pacific. Most symbolic designs were featured on bowls, and bowls with pedestals; other bowls were plain, and all were burnished, and sometimes painted with red slip. Large globular jars, perhaps used for storage, were plain. No pottery was ever placed directly on a fire for cooking or serving at this time.

The early pottery features many geometric motifs similar to those found on woven fabrics in South-East Asia. As Patrick Kirch explains, the women who produced Lapita pottery "worked within a framework of explicit rules for the creation and application of motifs."[21] Motifs were restricted in range, combination and placement, suggesting the designs had traditional meanings passed down through each generation, with "special words for certain design elements and motifs part of a code."[22] North African Kabile woman, Makilam, earlier explained the symbolism involved in making and decorating a pot (chapter 11). Every step of every activity has a certain meaning, and the imagery on pottery and other objects form a secret language understood only by women.

The designs could be applied using special tools, dentate-stamps, or by incising or carving. Basic elements include the arc, circle, egg-shape, eye-shape, straight line, parallel lines, 'V'-shape, zigzag, cross-hatching, triangle, diamond, rectangle, 'U'-shape, square, and pointed or square arch. Early decorated pottery was not made for trade purposes, but intended for

INDONESIA: FEMALE FIGURINES

1. Two views of a *prehistoric female figurine* from central Sulawesi, Indonesia, no date (Source: Miksic, John, ed., 1996)
2. Late Prehistoric *carved wood female figurine* from the Molucca Islands (Source: Hersey, Irwin, 1991)
3. *Three Old European 'ship-of-the-dead' symbols*, 6,000 BP (Source: Gimbutas, Marija, 1989)
4. An Indonesian example of the *'ship-of-the-dead' symbolism* which is still in use in weaving; ship-of-the-dead symbolism relates to the transition from death to regeneration (Source: Hamilton, Roy W., ed., 1994)
5. Late Prehistoric *wooden female figurine* from Irian Jaya (Indonesian New Guinea) (Source: Hersey, Irwin, 1991)

All line drawings © Judy Foster, 2013

ritual or home use. They sometimes included anthropomorphic designs or stylised human faces among other repeat designs. Some design elements and forms are still used today on pottery and woven cloth.

C.L. Chen (1968)[23] stated that the Taiwanese Austronesian speakers personified their ritual pots, giving them sexual characteristics symbolising the "ancestors of certain families [who] were born from the pots." There were "male and female pots exchanged upon marriage and kept in a special place in the ancestral dwelling houses."[24] Patrick Kirch regards this information as support for the existence of strong connections between pottery designs within East Asia. B. Chiang (1992) informed Patrick Kirch that when people moved house, they were careful with the pottery, and "they organised themselves into social groups based on the house", and considered "worship or ritual recognition of ancestors very important."[25]

Patrick Kirch has found only one small Lapita figurine on Massau Island, featuring a large head, small body, short legs and no sex characteristics, carved from porpoise bone. In the Pacific region female symbolism came in other forms, such as land features, motifs in woven textiles or on pottery.

Roy Hamilton (1994)[26] records that Austronesian-speaking Indonesian people were most likely descended from seafaring agriculturalists from Taiwan who arrived about 4,500 BP, bringing women's skills of weaving and the making of barkcloth (tapa) with them. Cotton growing and complex dyeing procedures perfected in India did not reach Indonesia until around 1,000 years ago, although Elizabeth Barber (1994)[27] believes that weaving was well established in China at 6,000 BP and by 4,000 BP in Thailand. Woven textiles remain integrated in social and religious life to this day, and are central to Indonesian society for economic, cultural and artistic reasons.

Bronze Age Indonesia

Around 2,500 BP the first use of both bronze and iron metals appeared. Currently it is not yet possible to describe the Indonesian prehistoric sequence because the sparse evidence is so widely distributed throughout Indonesia's 13,667 islands. Only recently have Indonesian archaeologists begun to excavate for remains of societies present before 2,500 BP.[28]

Wanda Warming and Michael Gaworski (1981)[29] explain that the highly influential Dong Son culture from northern Vietnam (which was influenced by earlier Indo-European contact in China) appeared in Indonesia about 2,800 BP, and brought about great changes to the peaceful Neolithic societies.

Earlier arrivals were peaceful non-hierarchic people, although they were culturally different from the preceding peaceful hunter-gatherer people. The Dong Son people introduced hierarchic social structures, including drastic changes to the status of women despite their sole ownership of the important weaving skills. Warp ikat weaving techniques, the introduction of the horse, emerging warriors and war practices such as headhunting, were other innovations. Dong Son influences live on in the more inaccessible regions of Indonesia today (although headhunting no longer occurs).

Indian influences were established in Indonesia by 2,100 BP as evidenced by the appearance of the Hindu religion and metallurgy, particularly the use of iron. Later in the Neolithic imported bronze was made into ceremonial axes and other refined objects. Hindu, Buddhist and Islamic influences eroded the status of women who came to be considered subservient to men.

European colonialists invaded in the 1600s CE reinforcing earlier Indo-European influences, especially the reduced status of women, and introducing Christianity. With their coming many older traditions died out.

The symbolic arts

In South-East Asia and the Pacific, traditionally the dead have been buried at sea in boats, according to Wanda Warming and Michael Gaworski. According to Ralph Coffman (2002),[30] 'death ship' imagery (as seen on the Dong Son drums) originated in south-west China's Mekong/Red Rivers area, and was adopted by the Han Chinese who came to Indonesia about 2,800 BP. This was also the time when the first war weapons appeared.

Irwin Hersey (1991) describes these ships as symbolised by the inclusion of dedicated 'ship plazas' in Flores and Tanimbar village squares supporting "the age-old belief that the souls of the dead go to the land of souls by ship."[31] For instance, Sikka, a village on Flores Island, has a greatly treasured three-dimensional early bronze sculpture of a ship which represents "the ship of the Dead."[32] 'Ship of the dead' motifs found on traditional ritual woven ikat textiles today originated from motifs found on the early Dong Son metal drums brought from Vietnam and China.

Other Indonesian textile motifs within the Dong Son sphere of influence (but which are probably much older) depicted on warp ikat ritual cloth include: the snake (rebirth and long life), lizards, birds, frontally-viewed human figures, monkeys, fish, insects and seahorses. The horse motif was introduced by the Dong Son people, as there were no horses in South-East Asia before this time.

In her gallery catalogue, curator Robyn Maxwell (2010)[33] describes the arts and crafts of Indonesia for the last 2,000 years which demonstrates that women's traditional weaving has been prominent over a long period of time, and is still present today among minority groups living in remote mountain regions. Prehistoric techniques and designs continue to be used, and they retain their spiritual beliefs and special relationship with the deities and/or ancestral beings of the natural world. All South-East Asian people shared similar beliefs in the past.

She states that "memories of those ancient travels appear everywhere in the art of South-East Asia from prehistoric cave paintings to 19th century textiles."[34] The ship motif is common in many shapes and repeat designs. The 'body' of the boat is a female symbol, while the prow is a male phallic symbol, and the spiral and hook motif represent the prow and stern. Boats on textiles symbolise "the journey over water through life"; and the life cycle of "birth, puberty, betrothal, and marriage";[35] and funerals. An early form of cloth, found in the mountain regions of Sulawesi in Indonesia and in the Philippines, is abaca (woven wild banana leaves), but tapa (beaten bark) has been used elsewhere, indicated by evidence including mallets (for beating bark pulp), clay whorls and spindle weights (for preparing thread), and perforated clay discs (for spinning thread). Vegetable fibres were twisted into thread and string; and later, silk was used. All of these fabrics are still created by women and worn by everyone in remote areas.

Robyn Maxwell explains that fabric designs are unique to particular groups; for example: the Pasisir people from Lampung, Sumatra, use ship designs; the Sa'dan Toraja people from Sulawesi use people and cattle designs; the Paminggir people from Lampung, use semi-abstract birds and zigzags; the Minangkabau people from Solok, West Sumatra, use

EARLY INDONESIAN ART

1. *Traditional indigenous Dayak figurine* (early historic)
2. *Timor figurine*, probably Early Historic
3. *Early Historic Flores figurine* from a shrine
4. *Three pottery design motifs:* a. *repeat faces;* b. *design with spirals;* c. *fruit and leaf motif* (Source: Kirch, Patrick Vinton, 1997)
5. *Traditional Dayak 'ship-of-the-dead' painting on pot* (Source 1–3, 5: Hersey, Irwin, 1991)

All line drawings © Judy Foster, 2013

repeat star designs; and the Minangkabau people from Syunung, West Sumatra, use more formal complex woven repeat patterns (possibly because they have now been in contact with Islam). Today much of the cultural diversity of the different islands is being lost as exposure to tourism increases.

Traditional matrilineal/matriarchal societies?

While he provides no information about the earlier indigenous inhabitants, Roy Hamilton (1994) does reveal that the villages "were composed of a number of clans or lineages, but the most important social units were named [ancestral] 'houses' that make up the clans."[36] He states that there were many patrilineal clans, but also some matrilineal clans and villages/ regions. These clan lineages could be considered to be remarkably similar to currently known matrilineal social organisations, such as the Minangkabau.

A modern Indonesian matrilineal women-centred society: The Minangkabau

The social organisation of the South-East Asian Minangkabau people of central Sumatra in Indonesia could well be representative of early societies in the Pacific region which still regard themselves as matrilineal, although the Pacific women in most cases have gradually lost their centrality in society to some degree through the influence of colonisation. Peggy Sanday (2002)[37] describes the foundation of Minangkabau society, *adat*, as establishing the rules for all social and cultural law/expression for the Minangkabau people, and it is used across Indonesia to describe local customs.[38] (The Minangkabau are present in other parts of Indonesia and Malaysia.) Of the 300 ethnic groups in Indonesia the Minangkabau are the fourth largest, and the most stable of the world's matrilineal societies.

Minangkabau matriarchy/matriliny

Peggy Sanday defines matriarchy in its original sense as referring to the centrality of women's activities rather than to a female-dominant society. The matrilineal system means that Minangkabau people are permanently linked to their ancestral land which is held 'in perpetuity' for succeeding generations. Land is passed down through the maternal line to daughters; if there is no daughter, the line ends. The husband goes to live at the wife's house on their wedding day. A husband will be asked to leave if he does not behave as he should. Fathers have close bonds with their children and help discipline, guide and nurture them. A chief male leader, the *penghulu*, can help manage the land but cannot pass it on to his children.

Peggy Sanday speaks of *adat matriarchaat* (Minangkabau matriarchy) as the original indigenous code underlying Minangkabau culture which operates together with the more recent Islamic religion and the laws of the state, forming a "three-stranded rope",[39] the fourth strand of which is magical knowledge. *Adat* has its origins in the prehistoric animistic period, when indigenous cultures derived their code of conduct from nature's fertility and growth. The good (benign) aspects of nature were incorporated into social and cultural rules, while nature's bad (destructive) aspects were discarded. Imitating nature's actions teaches people what will support life and what would destroy it. The good aspect of nature is its provision of the tools to obtain food and shelter; just as plants grow and develop, so people must also be nurtured. Thus *adat* is designed to protect and nurture the weak while renouncing brute strength.[40]

There is a Minangkabau concept of evil in nature "where the strongest will conquer the weak, the tallest will defeat the shortest, the largest will hold down the smallest."[41] This is the harsh side of nature, where *adat* has no influence. The curses of ancestors, and black and white magic, acting independently of human action, punish any people who do not observe the rules governing matriliny, particularly when the rights to use or dispose of ancestral land are abused.

Women's *adat*, known as *adat ibu*, points to the right way to guide and protect individual people as it integrates them into social relationship patterns; while men's *adat limbago* applies the rules and passes them on to the next generation, thereby upholding *adat's* legitimacy. *Adat* shows people a way of life and a world view concerning proper relationships. Through the life cycle ceremonies which women organise and stage, *adat* social relations are promoted. Women aim to uphold *adat* law and ensure children grow up the right way within an acceptable lifestyle. It is considered that if women do not uphold *adat* or pass this knowledge on to their children, the meaning of *adat* will be lost and so will they.

Men contribute to *adat* by discussion and making speeches which preserve *adat* law, applying it when settling disputes. They share with their sisters the care of ancestral land. There are 22 rules in *adat*, passed on to sons and nephews by fathers. *Adat* law is never written down but exists in oral traditions passed on to each new generation. Some traditional speeches used by men in their ceremonies contain these rules, often within proverbs and metaphors. Although the men know the ritual speeches, the women organise the appropriate context and time in which the men speak.

The core of *adat* philosophy is "good deeds and kind heartedness, democracy and thoughtfulness"[42] and as Peggy Sanday explains, it is directed towards human morals and feelings. No force is applied in decision-making, there can be no rivalry, and much time is allowed for thought before action. It is considered normal for some people to disagree since consensus can only be achieved by discussion and a search for the truth. The *penghulu* or male leader in the village who holds the hereditary matrilineal title, along with other important men in council, settles disputes and upholds *adat* law. Anyone who does not support the truth, "who is rude or uses force, is shunned or expelled from the community."[43]

The Western concept of power and dominance/subordination as understood today is considered by Benedict Anderson (1972)[44] to have emerged after the end of the European Middle Ages when societies became secularised, and came to be expressed through the colonisation of perceived 'primitive' countries.[45] Conquest, expansion, and the acquisition of wealth were the keys to power. No longer were the aspects of life associated with women, such as "the family, life cycle rituals, religion and magical lore"[46] relevant or desirable. Force was now the overwhelming power in civil society, while "the power associated with the regeneration of life"[47] became obsolete. Minangkabau societies are based on this second concept, the power of nature, although they manage somehow to integrate the power of the state with *adat*, and have thus avoided the Western practice of power through male domination/female subordination. *Adat* somehow manages to preserve female/male equality through systems which do not allow physical domination in any form. Wealth is always shared.

Visual symbols in Minangkabau society

Peggy Sanday defines Minangkabau matriarchy "in terms of cultural symbols and practices associating the maternal with the origin and centre of the growth processes necessary for social and individual life."[48] This definition reflects the true meaning of the word matriarchy. The central female symbol, Bundo Kanduang (Our Own Mother) recognised as the (first) common ancestress, was the Queen Mother of the Minangkabau people, and established *adat* at the very beginning. All women are descended from her, and continue the ceremonies and rituals of *adat*. There are many other important symbols:

- The butterfly symbol of the first ancestress symbolises the 'common good' and is also associated with the oldest pillar (the first to be erected) and centrally placed in the traditional house.
- The symbol of women's 'fertility, well-being and maternal nurture' is the sheaf of seven rice seedlings known as 'Sonan Sari'. It also is the symbol for a bountiful harvest.
- *Adat* matrilineal longhouses and *adat* council houses have roofs shaped like buffalo horns, which have been long recognised as female symbolism. (For example, Marija Gimbutas and Dorothy Cameron identify the early symbolism of the 'U'-shape of buffalo horns with female reproductive organs as seen at Çatal Hüyük, in India and Crete). The 'U'-shape can also be seen in designs on Minangkabau men's and women's ceremonial dress. In some regions it is used to form the shape of women's headdresses, and is symbolic of Minangkabau ethnic identity.
- Standing stones, menhirs, thought to be originally put into place by the first people to mark clan land or grave sites, are engraved with arrangements of spirals. They are likely to be prehistoric because any early bodies in human burials were oriented towards an important mountain, for example, Mount Sago. (In the Islamic period bodies are always oriented towards Mecca.) It is considered important that *adat* longhouses are oriented towards Mount Merapi while the menhirs face Mount Sago, thus they could be linked to the ancestors and the afterlife.
- A strong male symbol is the coiled fern frond which represents the way "a man should wrap himself around his family, custom and affairs of the village."[49]

Peggy Sanday's account of the Minangkabau demonstrates women's equal status in this society, and it is remarkable and a tribute to their strength, determination and wisdom that they have preserved values which are opposite to those of the dominating West. The integration of Islam with *adat* did not happen easily but was the result of much negotiation between Islamic and *adat* leaders who were resolved to end the tensions and conflicts which had divided them. The Matrilineal principle, nature, and the maternal have become interconnected with Islam in Minangkabau society. There are very few reported instances of rape or wife abuse because respect and harmony cannot be dislodged as prime social values. Women's *adat* ceremonies are still part of daily life, although men's *adat* has lost ground because of changes to systems of regional government. Peggy Sanday argues that despite these and other colonialist pressures, the matrilineal system will continue for some time to come, because of the Minangkabau ability to accommodate difference through *adat*. Although there are differences and similarities in this society as in all societies around the world, once again it suggests similar social principles to those of the female-centred Old European cultures and symbolic system.

One other Indonesian matrilineal group, the Sikka Natar on Flores Island, is described by E.D. Lewis for whom textiles are "the principal medium of cultural expression [and] are the product of women who possess and control a large corpus of specialized knowledge."[50] Each (ancestral) house has its own exclusive number of "bands [*hura*] in the structure of cloths worn by the women of the house"[51] representing the clan.

The *hura* are associated with men and passed down through groups of men, although they are woven by the lineally related women who use their own inherited traditional motifs in the design. Girls are taught about the motifs which pass from grandmothers to mothers, to daughters, and to mother's sisters. While the girl is single, she uses her matrilineal clan motifs within the *hura* belonging to her father's house. When she marries, she uses her clan motifs in her husband's *hura* design, so all know her clan relationship.

E.D. Lewis states that in the past the encoded information within the design motifs and the design structure of the cloth symbolised events, mythical people, and creatures of Sikkenese traditional stories, the meanings of which have almost entirely been lost. It seems likely that this society has only matrilineal aspects and few, if any, other features of true matriarchy, but it is included in this exploration of matriarchal/matrilineal societies because of the strong likelihood that societies such as this existed before the intervention of Indo-European ideologies/practices.

As previously mentioned, the concept of *adat* is a complex system of laws, customs and rituals governing almost every part of life, which evolved in prehistoric times, and was affected by Dong Son influences. Peggy Sanday (2009)[52] emphasises that matriarchal values, such as those of the Minangkabau, demonstrate a system of social interaction where each person in a social group has equal power. Through her study she hoped to show how matriarchal values are related to a philosophy of cooperation. The way the Minangkabau understand it, matriarchy is not about being ruled by women but about female-influenced social principles and values through which both sexes work together to promote human well-being. Growth in nature is the primordial foundation and principle for the construction of a Minangkabau social model.

She goes on to say that the Minangkabau are concerned as to whether they can retain the *adat* social ideology and build democracy in the face of increasing danger posed by the influences of Western capitalism and anti-Western Islamism on their culture. They wish to keep matrilineal *adat* which is considered sacred, and never to be changed. Peggy Sanday argues that "the mutually supportive role played by *adat matriarchaat* and Islam stands out as a major theme ... Backed by religion, *adat* is better able to withstand the global capitalist formations sweeping Indonesia."[53]

The Minangkabau women are organising ceremonies to make clear to the young men their cultural inheritance, and their responsibilities, so that they do not turn to indiscriminate violence as has happened in so many other countries. According to Peggy Sanday this demonstrates how matriarchal values can influence what happens. Although she has not mentioned other societies in Indonesia with similar values, it would seem likely that they were there in the past, as previously seen in China, Korea, and Japan.

CHAPTER 15

NEW WORLDS: AUSTRALIA

Women have never been invisible in precontact[1] Indigenous Australia. Women have left traces in Australia's landscape in rock art, and in stories and ceremonies, some of which continue to this day. Deborah Bird Rose (1994)[2] discusses her experience of one particular female creation being, the Black-headed Python, who sometimes appeared as a woman and sometimes as a python. She created the physical land features of a certain area in northern Australia, scattering seeds of plants, and even leaving behind some of her children who became ancestors of the present people of the area. "Although she kept travelling she also stayed, becoming a certain rock at a certain place. The rock is the living and conscious body of the Python ancestral being today."[3] One side of this sacred site belongs to the women, the other to the men. Neither can enter the other's area.[4] There is agreement that

> Python Woman created the country, the plants, the people, the language and the Law ... Further along the track she was accosted by some men who took some of her Law. That Law, an extremely important men's ceremony, is now controlled by men.[5]

However, women still control the rest of her Law, including the major rituals which once belonged exclusively to women but are now shared by both sexes.

In 2008, Emily Kame Kngwarreye, one of Australia's pre-eminent Indigenous artists, explained the past and present meaning of 'country' for Indigenous people:

> I was born on this Country — right here. This is my Country. When I'm been a little girl we walked around in this bush. I been grown up here, Alkhalkere Country — my Country. I've never been moved from this Country.[6]

The artist's life and painting were about "one story, her story, her Dreaming, embodied in her Country, Alkhalkere." It was where

> the essence of her being resided ... [H]er Dreaming ... was the source of the creative power, of her knowledge ... [I]t infused her life and her belief system, governed her kinship relations and connection with other people ..."[7]

This understanding of belonging to a particular part of the land was, and still is, critical to the well-being of the long-lasting Indigenous Australian cultures.

Aboriginal and Torres Strait Islander peoples (Indigenous Australians) have been present for a very long period. Estimates range from 40,000 years to around 140,000 years. For example, Mike Morwood suspects "that people have been living in Australia for much

A TIMELINE FOR INDIGENOUS AUSTRALIA

PERIOD (BP)	PEOPLE	PLACE	EVIDENCE
1,800,000	*H. erectus*	Java	• Bones, stone tools
900,000–800,000	*H. erectus*	Indonesia	• Stone tools
700,000	*H. erectus*	Flores Is.	• First seafarers cross to Flores by watercraft
140,000	Archaic *H. sapiens*	Lake George (New South Wales) & Great Barrier Reef (Queensland)	• Core samples suggest regular use of 'firestick' farming; suggests first purposeful management of the environment
120,000	Modern humans (*H. sapiens sapiens*)	Java/Australia	• People first came to Australia by land from Java via Papua New Guinea?
100,000	Semi-nomadic hunter-gatherers		
80,000–9,000		Papua New Guinea and Australia (incl. Tasmania)	• Were joined together by land bridge until separated by rising seas 9,000 BP
60,000		Northern Australia	• Ground red and yellow ochre 'crayons' were used for ritual rock painting
50,000–48,000	Semi-nomadic hunter-gatherers	Lake Mungo (New South Wales)	• Ritual burial of 'Mungo Woman' suggests her importance as a woman of the clan • Later burials of men and women of either 'gracile' (light) build or 'robust' (heavy) build suggest people had different origins
48,00–42,000		Olary (South Australia)	• Rock engravings
42,000–40,000		Koonalda (South Australia)	• Deep cave on Nullarbor Plain features ritual finger markings and incised lines
		Tasmania (Hobart)	• Stone tools dated to 40,000 BP recently discovered revealing Ice Age occupation
30,000		Western Australia	• Pilbara and the Canning Stock route feature the Cleland Hills 'faces'
		Cuddie Springs (New South Wales)	• Earliest known seed-grinding implements found so far (30,000 BP)
		Lake Mungo (New South Wales)	• Large collection of human footprints – men, women and children – running or walking, preserved in newly exposed dry clay
23,000–19,000	Semi-nomadic hunter-gatherers		

PERIOD (BP)	PEOPLE	PLACE	EVIDENCE
18,000–8,000		(Burrup) Murrunjuga Peninsula (Western Australia)	• Large collection of rock engravings and stone arrangements (now threatened by building of a large industrial complex)
17,000	Semi-nomadic hunter-gatherers	Kimberley region	• Gwion Gwion paintings
10,000		Papua New Guinea Australia	• The first horticultural practices • The Jinmium cupules
8,000	Semi-nomadic hunter-gatherers	Lake Condah (western Victoria), Gippsland (eastern Victoria); also along streams and coastline around Australia	• Circular, semi-permanent brush huts built over stone foundations. Also stone-walled huts thatched with peat slabs. Extensive systems of water channels connected to ponds used for trapping eels. Coastal rock channels trapped fish.
5,000–4,000	Semi-nomadic hunter-gatherers	Contact with Indonesians and/or others	• First dingoes brought to (or arrived by land in) Australia any time between 18,000 and 4,000 BP
(CE)			
1600–1700	Semi-nomadic hunter-gatherers	Australia	• Contact with Dutch, Portuguese and French shipwrecked sailors was not always friendly; new artefacts
1770 onwards	Semi-nomadic lifestyle begins to disintegrate	Australia	• Captain Cook 'discovers' Australia and European invasion of Australia ensues
1800s		Australia	• Infectious diseases, massacres decimate clans; remnants herded into mission stations; dislocation, dispossession of peoples
1869–1970s		Australia	• Mission stations; reserves; Stolen Generations. Alia Hoyt[8] reports: 100,000 children taken, adopted by white families
1967		Australia	• Referendum removes discriminatory clauses against Indigenous people which resulted in Aboriginal people being counted in the census. Referendum also gave the Federal government concurrent rights to make laws regarding Indigenous people.
2009		Australia	• Prime Minister apologises to Indigenous people for past wrongs

longer than the 60,000 years we originally thought" as "early human occupation dates for East Timor [are] for over 100,000 years",[9] and he suggests that further careful investigations and dating of Kimberley rock art sites will provide proof of this.

It is important to recognise that Indigenous Australians and non-Indigenous people often comprehend the world differently. Indigenous world views include cyclic notions of time (and this is also true of pre-Enlightenment societies in Europe). They also include notions of linear time as represented in storytelling, again comparable to other societies. Indigenous traditional creation stories (the Dreaming/the Law), handed down from generation to generation, could be as old as 100,000 years or more, while the period of written history is less than 6,000 years.

Australian Indigenous cultures have living traditions extending over a very long time; all Australian rock art is their cultural heritage, telling of their origins. Indigenous people have understood the idea of evolution; their Dreaming ancestral beings indicated that humans and animals were sometimes interchangeable. Indigenous stories show that they understood themselves as part of an interdependent and interfunctional world, not a hierarchical pyramid. This and much more has been preserved in oral traditions which have been dismissed as 'myth' (fiction) by non-Indigenous people prior to being 'authenticated' by 'literate' scientists.

Josephine Flood (1995)[10] states that around Australia there are differing Indigenous creation stories which explain the origins of the people, and of their land and its features. Some oral traditions tell of the Ancestral Beings rising out of the earth, or coming from the sky or the sea. Others tell of the coming of the Creation Beings from across the ocean. Many northern Australian creation stories tell of "the Great Earth Mother, symbol of fertility and creator of life."[11] Another example is given by Wandjuuk Marika of the Riratjingu people:

> The giant Rainbow Serpent emerged from beneath the earth, and as she moved, winding from side to side, she forced her way through the soil and rocks, making the great rivers flow in her path, and carving through mountains, she made the gorges of northern Australia.[12]

As is shown in the timeline, the presence of red and yellow ochre crayons dated to 60,000 BP suggests the earliest rock art. Accurately dating rock art is still proving to be difficult, and currently accepted dates relating to early occupation are likely to change in light of new discoveries and research.

Australia's first people

The evidence about how people first came to Australia, New Guinea and the Pacific is uncertain and some of it is circumstantial. It's clear that the prehistory is very long and has been greatly influenced by environmental factors. There are a number of competing hypotheses.

According to Josephine Flood (1995) there is uncertainty about the origins of the first Australians (and whether they developed independently from *Homo erectus* in Australia, as modern humans may have done in Asia). There has also been controversy as to when they might have come to Australia.

Robert Bednarik (2006)[13] refers to evidence which suggests that *H. erectus* could have drifted across the Lombok Strait, a 30-kilometre stretch of deep, fast-running water between Bali and Lombok in Indonesia, around 900,000 BP using (bamboo) rafts. The feasibility of people rafting this strait is supported by the evidence of elephants swimming this stretch of water around 700,000 BP. The butchered bones of elephants dated to that period have been found, together with stone tools, on Flores Island.

It has also been argued that core samples taken by Gurdip Singh[14] in Lake George in the early 1990s suggest that humans regularly used fire in Australia, perhaps to aid in the hunt, from about 140,000 BP until after the Western invasion. Future firm evidence in the form of art, artefacts or skeletal material could change this theory.[15]

Generally accepted theory suggests that the appearance of archaic *Homo sapiens* in Java around 100,000 BP was the catalyst for the first people to cross the waters to Australia, perhaps because they could see the distant smoke from big bushfires rising to as high as 5,000 metres, well above sea level. The sea gap between Australia and Asia at the time was probably less than 90 kilometres wide. There has almost always been a wide sea barrier between Timor and Australia except during four periods of low sea level when the gap narrowed to between 90 and 100 kilometres.

Seas were low between about 160,000 and 140,000 BP and again between about 70,000 and 55,000 BP. During these periods the 'greater Australian continent' included Papua New Guinea, Tasmania, the Gulf of Carpentaria and the North West Shelf. People could walk from Burma to Indonesia, from Papua New Guinea to Australia, or through Sulawesi to Papua New Guinea and on to Arnhem Land. These were the most likely times for human migration between Indonesia, Papua New Guinea and Australia.[16]

The watercraft those early people used are not known, and few of the recorded types would have been durable enough to survive the distance. Only one kind of raft, used until recently by 'tide-rider' people on Australia's north-west coast, could have made the distance, if made from bamboo (available in Java) instead of mangrove (the Australian medium). The people coming from Java had bamboo resources, but once having arrived in Australia, would most likely have been there to stay since mangrove wood was not suitable for a return journey. Curiosity, overpopulation, and a desire to move on to better land and resources could have most likely triggered the desire to leave South-East Asia.

Because of their fertile land and suitable climate, Papua New Guineans have been practising a form of agriculture, the cultivation of gardens for growing crops (horticulture), for at least as long as the peoples of the Old World (over 10,000 years). The land bridge which joined Australia to Papua New Guinea from around 80,000 BP until about 9,000 BP meant that Australian Indigenous people could also have practised agriculture had environmental factors been more favourable. According to Tim Flannery (1994),[17] the apparent 'primitiveness' of Australian Indigenous people is a falsehood.[18] Humans developed ways of life in Australia as sophisticated as the environment allowed; the agricultural revolution took place as early, or even perhaps earlier, than in Europe. One form of land management in Australia (the use of a system of broad-acre land clearing by fire) was utilised up until the European invasion, which is why so many of the first Europeans commented on the 'park-like' tidiness of Australia's countryside.[19] Mosaic burning was a practice of using low intensity fires to clear the understorey. It was carried out before the dry fuel built up. They therefore avoided the high-intensity fires that have occurred regularly since colonisation. Some native Australian plants (for example *Banksia*) depend on fire to facilitate seed germination.

Another agricultural practice was 'small-scale curation', where competing species were removed, small streams diverted to allow the watering of desired plants, and other useful plants were transplanted (most likely by women). But in general it would not have been practical to cultivate much of the land due to unpredictable weather conditions, poor soils and the shortage of water. Most recent evidence indicates that the northern part of Australia was the first to be settled, but people were obviously able to follow river systems down through central Australia to the Willandra Lakes region about 70,000 BP when the lakes were full, game was plentiful and the land was lush.

Lake Mungo: Early ritual life

The view of early Australian human prehistory as provided at Lake Mungo in New South Wales is one of world significance. Josephine Flood (1995) explains that:

- it provides evidence for the dispersal of modern humans anywhere in the world, together with their successful adaptation to semi-arid living conditions
- there is evidence of fishing which suggests that these humans had net-weaving skills
- their transport and use of coloured ochres in Australia suggests the presence of a very early aesthetic sense
- it is not only evidence of a sophisticated cultural and ritual life, but also suggests the importance of the role women played within Indigenous groups – as demonstrated by the ritual burial of the young Mungo woman
- it is evidence of Indigenous cultural continuity from the time of their first arrival in Australia until early contact times.[20]

The earliest proven use of red ochre as part of ritual was found in 1968 at Lake Mungo by archaeologist Jim Bowler in a burial site dated to at least 48,000 BP.[21] The first skeleton to be found was that of a slender young woman of small stature. Her body had apparently been cremated, her bones broken up, collected and placed in a small hole near the cremation site. The bones and surrounding sand was stained pink in colour, indicating that ochre powder had been scattered over the remains as part of ritual.

Two skeletons of men, found nearby, each had two teeth missing from their lower front jaws, a practice which continues today (although it now involves removal of teeth from the front top jaw instead of the lower jaw). It is possible that tooth avulsion has an ancient history, but it is equally possible that in some cases teeth are missing for entirely different reasons.

Indigenous Australians have probably come from several different places at different times during pre-history.[22] Mungo Woman, for example, has a body type described by archaeologists as 'gracile', a generally lighter build. Others such as the more recent remains of a man found near Lake Mungo which could be as old as 60,000 years, has a body type described as 'robust'. Josephine Flood states that both groups of humans were present in Australia at the same time.

The Lake Mungo region also includes a more recent discovery of a very large collection of human footprints, made by running and walking family groups and single hunters, which are between 19,000 and 23,000 years old. They are preserved in hard, dried clay near the Willandra lakes, and Indigenous owners of the area say it used to be a meeting place for the Ngiyampaa clan since the Dreamtime. The skeletons of two 17,000-year-old

AUSTRALIA: ROCK, BODY AND SAND ART FORMS

1. and 2. *Cave paintings of dancing women* (ancestral beings?)

3. *Owl figurine, wall painting,* Northern Territory (Source 1–2: Chaloupa, George, 1993)

4. *Circle design,* Central Desert (Source: Layton, Robert, 1992)

5. *Sand drawings,* 'Yawulyu' women's art

6. *Three women's ceremonial body designs*

7. *Basic design elements used in sand drawings* (Source 5–7: Munn, Nancy, 1973)

8. *Two 'X-ray' paintings of a turtle*

9. *Footprints of desert animals* (Source 8–9: Layton, Robert, 1992)

All line drawings © Judy Foster, 2013

males were found nearby. During this long period the area around the lakes would have been wooded and lush and the lakes filled with fish, mussels, crayfish, and occupied by various water birds.[23]

In March 2010 new evidence emerged of the earliest Ice Age Indigenous people living along a river near Hobart in Tasmania. It consists of numerous stone tools which have been dated to 40,000 BP.[24]

Cultural traditions: Australian Indigenous art, religion, and early rock art

The best information, apart from Australian Indigenous myths which indicate the wealth of knowledge acquired over the millennia about the sophistication of the Australian prehistoric way of life, is to be found in the many rock engravings and paintings found around the country. In Australian Indigenous cultures, knowledge was valued much more highly than any material aspects of life and nowhere is this more apparent than in visual imagery. It is more than likely that women were among the producers of visual imagery, just as they have traditions of weaving and other forms of art connected to storytelling and knowledge transmission. But women's art and ritual production is less likely to survive in the archaeological record as women generally worked with perishable materials, whereas men often worked with stone.

Josephine Flood (1995) proposes the possibility of body and wall painting proving the presence of humans in Australia at least about 60,000 BP. Until 1999, a rock shelter known as Malakunanja II, situated in what is now known as Kakadu National Park, was thought to be one of the first places where the earliest settlers in Australia set up camp. Old and faded paintings appear on the shelter's overhang, and many tools were found in the deepest floor layer of sand. These included core-scrapers, flakes, and many other artefacts of unknown use, together with a grindstone and dolerite (volcanic rock used in the grinding of tools), haematite (which was a source of a red pigment), and red and yellow ochre 'crayons'. These artefacts have been dated to between 61,000 and 52,000 BP. Ochres and pigment such as haematite were used for rock painting and for ritual body decoration. The presence of ochre at such sites indicates that these early people painted pictures perhaps even before they created petroglyphs (rock engravings).[25]

These early paintings utilised many different forms and techniques. George Chaloupa (1993)[26] describes the symbolic images as not only depicting humans, animals and fish, but also as recording the development of tools, ritual dress of both women and men, and people's religious and celebratory actions. The earliest motifs were probably hand or grass prints, or were prints of objects including ochre-filled bundles of grass which had been covered with pigment and thrown or pressed against the rock walls, sometimes forming designs. Different weathering of the pigment suggests that hand prints have been an important part of ritual since 'the beginning'. Pigment blown over the hand or other objects leaves a silhouette – this stencil method is also very old. These images reflect the local social and cultural economies when cereal grasses were a staple food of the local people.[27]

Naturalistic motifs of now extinct animals, such as the giant kangaroo, as well as painted human figures, are present in some early shelters. Many of these tantalising images are very faint and often they have been over-painted by more recent images. But some include enough detail to allow identification of specific animals and also demonstrate the early use of the 'X-ray' style.[28]

The overlapping worlds of human beings and animal beings are reminiscent of similar rock art in European caves. It is possible that the regenerative power of women and of female animals was considered important.

There are many different styles of Indigenous art to be found throughout Australia. In the north there is the X-ray style and the Gwion Gwion (Bradshaw) figures, and some imagery which is more figurative. Various styles include the geometric central Australian imagery, and other motifs in southern Australia, both geometric and figurative, with as many individual differences as there were languages across the land. The variation in styles could be an indication of waves of immigrants over thousands of years.

Early symbols

Engraved motifs

Petroglyphs (engravings) are found all over Australia but those at Olary in South Australia are considered to be very old.[29] There are 50 petroglyph sites in this region alone. Josephine Flood (1995) has little doubt that these rock art symbolic images are very old since people had been in the Mungo area for at least 60,000 years.[30] These motifs have become known as examples of the Panaramitee style, which is generally found in Australia's inland desert country and consists of a very large number of small images, usually no bigger than 10 centimetres, engraved onto rock faces either in outline or in solid form.[31] These motifs are simple or complex circular shapes, and tracks which include animal, bird and human footprints. The circle images include pecked pitted dots, linear crescent shapes, radiating lines, or 'mazes'. There are a few naturalistic images of lizards, human figures, faces or vulvas. For Josephine Flood and others, these images often show similarity with motifs of similar age at sites such as Olary, the Pilbara, or Cleland Hills.

Engraved cupules (cupmarks)

Groups of engraved cup-like marks are widely distributed throughout Australia, and also found worldwide. The Kimberley cupule site is an example of the collections of similar symbols/depictions which are present in numerous sites across northern Australia. These cupule sites are perhaps the earliest identifiable Kimberley form of deliberately incised shapes that are familiar to us, and might suggest the beginnings of ritual practice.

There are two varieties of cupules identified by Graham Walsh (1994): the 'pecked pits', which are usually found on walls and near-vertical panels; and the larger 'prebraded cups', formed by pecking then abrasion, to create smoothly finished depressions.[32] These are usually found on horizontal surfaces or on large portable slabs. The prebraded cups have usually been explained as hollows caused by the grinding of ochre or food.

In late September 1996, archaeologists announced in *The Australian*[33] that rock engravings (cupules) and stone artefacts found at Jinmium in the Northern Territory had been dated using the thermoluminescence technique, and were originally thought to be around 117,000 to 176,000 years old. Paul Tacon described the thousands of rock engravings as semi-circular in form, systematically pecked, and approximately the size of a 20 cent coin.

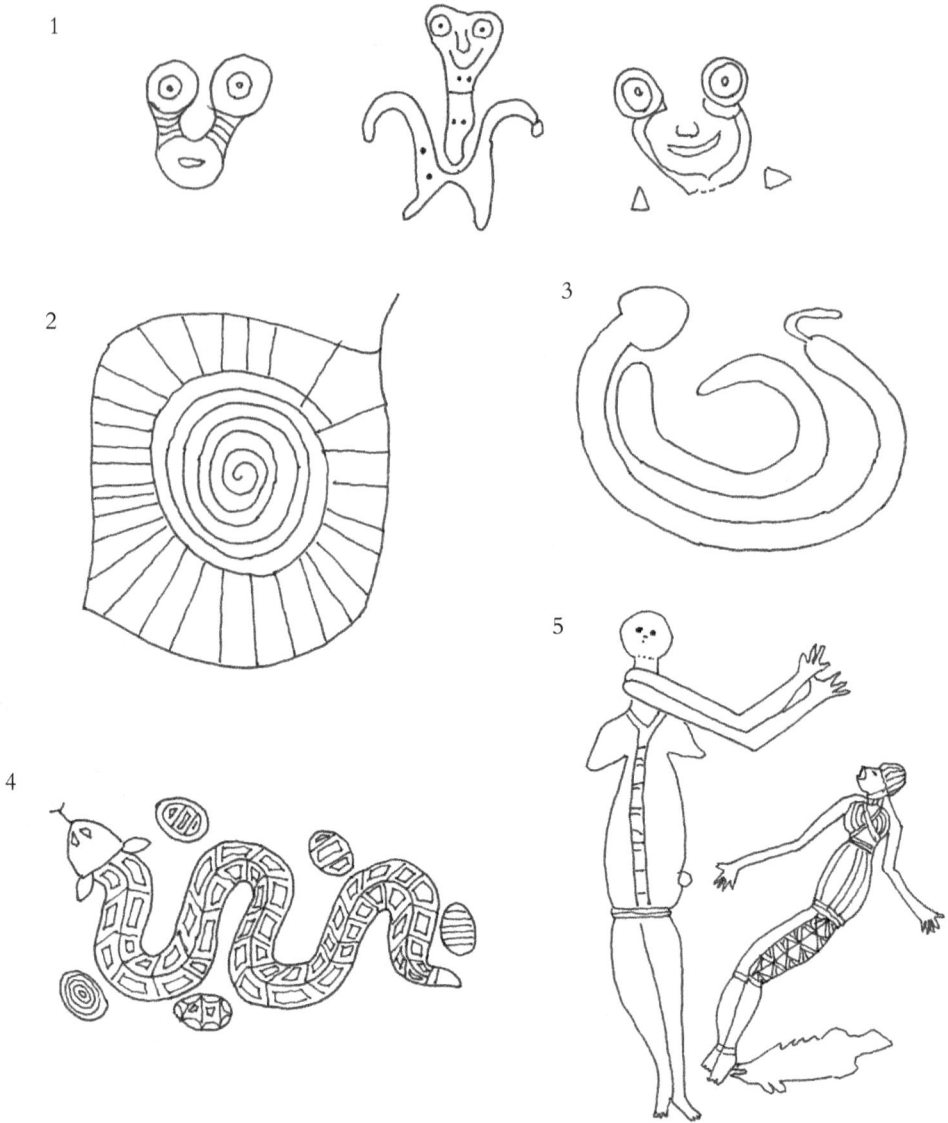

1

2

3

5

4

AUSTRALIA: VARIOUS SYMBOLIC IMAGES

1. *Rock engravings*, Cleland Hills, western Central Australia
(Source: Flood, Josephine, 1990)

2. *Pintupi pencil drawing*, artist unknown (c. 1976?) This *circle motif* precedes the double circle so well known in Central Desert art.

3. Detail of *'Snake Family Dreaming'*, Pintupi
(Source 2–3: Bardon, Geoffrey and James Bardon, 2004)

4. *Fitzroy Crossing Women's painting* on paper, *'The Rainbow Serpent'*, c. 1997 (personal collection)

5. *Wall painting of a female ancestral being and woman* in the 'X-ray' style (date unknown), Northern Territory
(Source: Chaloupa, George, 1993)

All line drawings © Judy Foster, 2013

Evidence of rock art using ochre dated to 60,000 BP was also found. Subsequent tests in 1998 found these early dates to be incorrect. It should be noted that cupule sites in other parts of the world are known to be much older than the adjusted date of 10,000 BP for the Jinmium cupules. Thus, while there is no firm date as yet, the speculation continues.

The Jinmium cupules: Women's symbols?

It is notable that the current Indigenous custodians of the Jinmium cupule site are women. Women in India and North America have traditionally made similar cup marks in association with birth rituals. Indian women still make dots as part of a ritual, according to G. Kumar (1996)[34] who says that in rural India it is common for women to place lines of dots of *roli* or *sindur* in the temples of their deities, with the desire to be given the deities' blessings.

In North America, Robert Heizer and Martin Baumhoff (1962)[35] describe earlier cupule sites which were still used in historic times by both men and women. There were 'rain rocks' used in ceremonies to make or prevent rain. Other Native American clans used pitted rocks known as 'baby rocks', pecked by women wishing to conceive children. Such ancient practices have persisted until recent times.

The Indigenous women of Jinmium do not comment on the making or meaning of the Jinmium cupules perhaps because they may be men's rituals, and women have their own rituals about which they will not speak. Indigenous women, unlike the men, have been very successful at keeping secret their sacred places, stories, and rituals, so it is still often falsely assumed that Indigenous women have no secret-sacred life of their own.

The Rainbow Snake

The Rainbow Snake is well known throughout northern Australia and Josephine Flood (1997) describes it as an "ancestral creative snake (male or female)" which may feature "supernatural attributes such as horns or antlers or front legs."[36] It inhabits rivers and waterholes, and traces of it can be seen in the land marking the 'Dreaming tracks.' Paintings and engravings of Rainbow Snakes are also found in many other parts of Australia, at sites such as Mootwingee, north of Broken Hill, although their stories and meanings may no longer be known to present day people.

Traditional body and ground painting

Women and men across Australia carry out a range of ritual practices. They include painting of bodies as well as of sacred objects. Women in central Australia paint their breasts using the arch, dots and lines. In desert areas women and men make ground 'paintings', and in the 'Top End'[37] tall sculptural forms are made. It is impossible to generalise about the meanings, except to say that sacred images in Australia, as elsewhere in the world, are layered with meaning. Knowledge acquisition is incremental and women and men learn different parts of sacred knowledge. There is 'women's business' and 'men's business'. This can be a life-long process, with the deepest meanings known only by a very few older, fully initiated women and men.

While figurative art is usually found in rock paintings, Josephine Flood observes that geometric images may be engraved on sacred objects, painted on the human body or incorporated into ground paintings. In contemporary dot paintings only a few different motifs are used but they are arranged in various ways to produce thousands of visual stories. They often represent maps of country, or tell of ancestral movements across the land. She explains that contemporary central Australian Indigenous people who still paint and engrave tracks of animals, birds and humans have described these as depicting "the earth's view of the creatures who walk on its surface."[38]

Early (finger) engravings: Koonalda Cave

Rock engravings in Koonalda Cave (South Australia) could be around 42,000 years old and are evidence of the great antiquity of Australian Indigenous cultures, according to Josephine Flood (1995). Koonalda Cave features wall engravings which generally consist of large groups of vertical and horizontal lines with some grid or lattice arrangements. It had previously been thought that the images were incidental markings formed as the result of the collection (by hand) of the fine powder on the walls; or marks produced in the course of sharpening bone points. However, Josephine Flood challenges this view.[39] She is convinced that there are also a few definite symbolic motifs present, such as two sets of 20-centimetre concentric circles, and an unusual herringbone design. This design, consisting of 37 short diagonal finger markings, has below it a second row of 74 incised diagonal lines. Josephine Flood argues that it would seem to be no accident that the number of incised lines is twice the number of finger markings, making it a significant symbolic design. She concludes that these designs were probably produced during some form of ritual since, in hunter-gatherer societies, most art is part of religious ritual, and this is certainly true of traditional Indigenous societies in more recent times. There are comparable markings of similar age in the Snowy River Cave at Buchan in Victoria.

Dynamic figures of Arnhem Land

The dynamic figures in Arnhem Land (Northern Territory) which are possibly younger than the above artwork, mainly feature human figures in action, shown in profile. Ornaments, such as animal-fur bracelets worn by the figures, are quite detailed. Subject matter includes hunting with boomerangs, two men fighting and other ritual activities, throwing spears, copulation, and dancing. There are often narratives involving people and animals. According to George Chaloupa (1993), the images are most often male animal-headed beings (anthropomorphs or zoomorphs), animal tracks, and geometric motifs. Men wear headdresses or elaborate hairstyles, pubic and buttock coverings, and hold objects such as spears and boomerangs, while women carry dillybags and digging sticks, firesticks or spears.

Josephine Flood (1997)[40] was told by contemporary informants that the age of the women depicted in the paintings is indicated by their stylised hair (or occasionally lengths of twisted hair). Older women might also be represented with short hair due to cutting after the death of kin. Age is readily identified by the size of the women's breasts (girls have small breasts, young women have medium breasts, and old women have large breasts).

Another important feature of these paintings are the 'battle' scenes. These show men dodging flying spears and boomerangs, or with upraised spears as they chase each other in one-to-one combat. But no dead men are featured, indicating that the conflicts consisted of small skirmishes where few, if any, men were killed or badly injured.

The Gwion Gwion figures of northern Australia

The stylistic features of this important group of symbolic images could indicate contact with visitors (such as in the example of the early hunter-gatherer images in the Bhimbetka caves, as described in chapter 12). The Gwion Gwion figures (or 'Bradshaw paintings' as they were known until recently) of the Kimberley region of Western Australia are thought to be of considerable antiquity, possibly somewhere between 10,000 and 17,000 years old, but could be much older. People today say that the paintings carry information about the foods, tools, customs and ritual dress worn by Indigenous people until relatively recently. There are similarities in style between the Gwion Gwion of the Kimberleys and the Mimi figures of Arnhem Land, suggesting possible lines of communication between these regions.

The paintings depict silhouetted figures in red or dark ochre paint which has little or no residual surface material left but has formed stains which have bonded into the surface of the rock. They are sinuous figures, usually depicted in movement whether dancing or ritually enacting some kind of narrative. The figures are wearing distinctive varied elaborate headdresses sometimes ornamented with tassels, tasselled 'skirts' or waist sashes, ankle tassels or bands, and wrist bands. They display no distinguishing sexual characteristics and therefore could represent men or women. Their elongated, highly stylised, sometimes almost abstract appearance is quite different from any other Australian Indigenous art in technique and style except for those which George Chaloupa calls the 'dynamic figures of the Arnhem Land plateau' which are thought to belong to a similar period. The Gwion Gwion figures are comparable in artistry to the more famous European cave paintings of similar age.

The Cleland Hills 'faces'

The Cleland Hills 'faces', situated 320 kilometres west of Alice Springs (Northern Territory), feature triangular and heart-shaped faces similar to the mask-like tiki faces found in southern China, South-East Asia, Papua New Guinea, New Zealand and the Pacific Islands. Some of the Australian faces feature large circular 'eyes', sometimes with a pitted dot in the centre. They may have a 'U'-shaped or vertical line 'nose', and no mouth, with pointed chin; or a large 'U'-shaped smiling mouth above a square or rounded chin. One face is attached to a stylised body with outstretched 'arms' or 'wings', and with legs wide apart, a similar form to those found in South-East Asia, indicating considerable antiquity. Others may or may not have bodies but are associated with other imagery. Josephine Flood (1977) observes that the most noticeable feature of the faces are the eyes which are circular, sometimes filled in, sometimes dots, dot-in-circle, or concentric circles, sometimes including 'rays' of short lines. She considers that some of the images could symbolise owl or emu faces, but what is most unusual is that they display emotions of happiness or sadness. These rock art images could indicate contact with visitors from nearby countries, and their location well away from the northern coast makes them all the more remarkable.

Other faces appear in the Pilbara and along the Canning Stock Route (both in Western Australia), and in north-west New South Wales, the Mount Isa region of Queensland, and the Victoria River district in Northern Territory. The early petroglyphs at Mount Cameron West in Tasmania are deeply pecked and abraded so as to seem almost sculptural. Indigenous people of today say they do not know the meanings of these ancient images, which could be at least 30,000 years old, as their stories have vanished over time.

In the 1840s American whalers camping on the Murujuga (Burrup) Peninsula (Western Australia) first saw the extensive petroglyph sites located there. Other shipwrecked sailors over the period before White settlement had also reported them. In 1968, Robert Bednarik (2006) began recording some of the 600,000 petroglyphs, 1 million motifs, and five

ENDANGERED BURRUP PENINSULA ART

1. The above images are examples of *the endangered rock art engravings* on Burrup Peninsula in Western Australia, which could be many thousands of years old.
2. More prehistoric rock art engravings from Burrup Peninsula
(Source: Bednarik, Robert, 2001).

3. *Traditional engraved mother-of-pearl shell ornament (featuring a female figure?)* traded from Broome, northern Western Australia to Wiluna, southern coast of Western Australia. These ornaments could be secular, or have secret meanings, worn hung from the neck or waist, by both women and men.
(Source: Ackerman, Kim, 1994).

All line drawings © Judy Foster, 2013

different styles of stone arrangements within the eight-square-kilometre area. Unfortunately, between 1963 and 2004 around 900 of the 3,000 plus sites were destroyed by industrial developments with further developments planned including a large natural gas plant.[41]

The imagery includes faces which are similar to the Cleland Hills faces, plus numerous animals and birds in many different styles, and various abstract motifs. There are standing stones, together with rock arrangements, reminiscent of the Irish standing stones. There are few remaining descendants of the original peoples of the area who know the meanings and the stories of the rock art, as the violent occupation by white pastoralists resulted in a number of large massacres of Indigenous people dating from 1868. Rock art specialists and some traditional owners continue to fight for the preservation of the sites.

The similarities and variations in art styles across Australia are likely to be the result of exchange between people. The variations demonstrate both continuity and change in the traditional images. Contemporary art of the regions includes both figurative secular images, and the more secret/sacred geometric art.

Indigenous symbolic images used by both women and men have a range of meanings, both public and secret. According to Josephine Flood (1995), the public interpretations include:

- the circle: a waterhole, campfire, cave, tree, or hill
- a straight line: a straight path, spear, kangaroo's tail, backbone, a person lying down
- the 'U'-shape: a seated person
- the 'S'-shape: snake, smoke, string, tail, lightning, or flowing water
- groups of small dots: rain, ants or eggs
- the double arc: ribs, clouds, or a boomerang
- arrow-like shapes: footprints.

The variety of geometric elements such as circles, lines, tracks, or crescents in different combinations can form the story of a myth "in a plan or bird's eye view."[42] Circles might represent a certain site, while connecting lines form "the paths taken from one place to another."[43] The concentric circle "usually relates to the presence of an Ancestral Being."[44] In this system the number of classes of meaning can be increased without increasing the number of motifs in the repertoire.[45] All of them constitute a symbolic vocabulary, some of which may have had shared meanings, while others were restricted to particular groups. Symbols are multivocal and can be read in different ways at different times. The use of symbols allows for surface public readings (for example, for children and people from outside the society) and deep or restricted readings, according to age and extent of knowledge.

Early Indigenous life in Australia

At the time of European invasion there were approximately 250 language groups which varied in size and range of their territory according to ecological niche. The Yolŋu people of Arnhem Land say that they

> … owe their languages to the Djan'kawu sisters, Yolŋu ancestral beings who also gave form to the land. When the sisters travelled across the land from east to west, they drove their digging sticks into the land at different places. Every time they put their digging sticks into the land, water came out.

The water represents Yolŋu knowledge, languages, songs and law. Each time the Djan'kawu sisters spoke, they changed their languages as they crossed from one territory to another. This is how the different languages came about.[46]

Some groups were able to live semi-sedentary lives in the well-watered coastal regions. In the sparser desert regions people congregated in times of plenty but spent most of the year in small family groups. Groups were closely affiliated with certain tracts of land by virtue of place of birth, burial of close relatives and descent from ancestors associated with places and region. Permission was needed to visit or hunt on the country of another group. Marriages were arranged between groups and thus access to resources was extended.[47]

Modes of subsistence in Australia reflect the various environmental challenges encountered by early people. In areas such as Gippsland and Lake Condah in western Victoria people had a semi-settled lifestyle.[48] Since the early 1800s, explorers, settlers and archaeologists had provided a number of different interpretations of settlements such as Lake Condah and other areas around Australia. Until recently these reports have been largely disregarded because it had been assumed that Indigenous people had always been hunter-gatherers incapable of living any other way.

However, Josephine Flood (1995) records the possibility of eel 'farming' at Lake Condah where there is evidence of arrangements of stones which she considered may have been used as foundations for semi-permanent brush huts; it was the presence of these stone arrangements which led Heather Builth (2000, 2002)[49] to investigate further. Her revelatory new evidence, reported in *The Age* (13 March 2003),[50] showed that the precontact Gunditjmara people had lived in villages of circular stone huts, probably thatched with readily accessible peat slabs supported by wooden 'beams', in the vicinity of Lake Condah 8,000 years ago. This style of building was well known in other parts of the world, such as India and Africa, during the same period. For example, there were "the remains of 103 dwellings and storage structures that occurred in clusters, some of which had shared walls … and an opening at the east or northeast"[51] for protection against cold winter winds. Heather Builth identifies six different 'plan forms' of the stone structures:

1. different sized circles, some with pits which may have been hearths
2. "up to five intersecting or interlocking circle segments" which form a cellular type
3. "oval exterior wall with an internal cross partition – a bi-cellular form"
4. "single circular wall" with attached "small circular chamber … near the entrance"
5. "spiral wall enclosing a circular space … known to the living Gunditjmara as a 'number 6' shape" (perhaps for wind protection)
6. "a normal circular wall with a smaller diameter circular wall attached at the entrance."[52]

Her investigation also revealed extensive systems of water channels connecting a number of artificial ponds in which eels, collected from the ocean as hatchlings, were grown for harvest as a staple food and for trade. The eels were preserved by smoking them in large hollow trees in the area. The water channels extended 30 kilometres and featured stone walls with provision for large woven eel traps at intervals. This was a highly sophisticated system, the equivalent of any others to be found elsewhere in the world at the time.[53] Traditional subsistence practices were significantly curtailed by farming practices, water management, natural resource management and other systems imposed by the colonising people. As Heather Builth points out, when the fertile land of Victoria was invaded by the first European settlers, the impact on Indigenous people and their ways of life was significant.[54]

Similar well-organised villages associated with 'farming' (the conservation and controlled collection of plants or fish) were reported by government officials, explorers, and first settlers, in various parts of Australia – they were more common than has been generally known. For example, George Grey (1841)[55] recorded "abundant populations in clusters of well-built, clay-plastered and turf-roofed huts" alongside 'warran grounds' (yam) which he said supported "at least a hundred and fifty natives."[56] Similar cultivated areas of plant foods were reported in a number of other places in south-western Australia.

Other villages with huts made from various materials (and waterproofed) had been reported at Boulia on the Georgina River (circular, with stone walls and domed waterproof roofs); in the Western Desert (numerous timber-framed huts, with domed roofs cladded with spinifex grass, called 'wiltja'); and the Kimberley (huts "with circular stone walls and roofs of various materials").[57]

Arrival of the dingo

The ways in which Australian Indigenous people lived in the past are of great importance because the living cultural tradition is very long. It is both an asset and a challenge. Ritual and cultural traditions are never static; Australian Indigenous people have adapted and absorbed new happenings and experiences without disturbing the original conceptual world views. This has been their great success: to accommodate change within an oral culture without violating basic conceptions of an interrelated world.

It has generally been considered that contact with Macassan traders from Indonesia contributed to cultural change and adaptation and possibly the introduction of the dingo about 3,500 years ago. However, recent new evidence by geneticist Alan Wilton,[58] a researcher from the University of Sydney, suggests that "[c]learly the land route is much more feasible for dogs than the sea route."[59] He was one of a team of researchers "who took mitochondrial DNA samples from more than 900 domestic dogs across Asia, South-East Asia, Indonesia, New Guinea, the Philippines, and Taiwan",[60] Polynesia and Australia. They argue that most likely the dingo and the New Guinea singing dogs came overland from southern China any time between 18,000 and 5,000 BP. The dingo, though a relative newcomer, was comprehensively incorporated into stories across the Australian mainland. Such incorporation shows the ways in which cultural change and continuity were manifested.

Indigenous Australian trade: An extensive activity

Extensive trade routes radiated across Australia, and it was not unusual for valued items, or important news and knowledge, to be transported great distances for exchange. Among the items traded were shell, ochre, pituri, possum skins, whale oil, granite, flint quartz and other igneous rocks useful for tools. Kim Ackerman (1994)[61] highlights the trade in white or bright red ochre from the Flinders Ranges in the southern region of South Australia, which was highly desirable for ritual purposes, such as body or wall paintings. Good quality coloured ochres were found only in certain regions, and small quantities could be easily carried for long distances to be exchanged for pearl shell pendants from the Broome area on the north-west coast of Western Australia.

Kim Ackerman states that oval and egg-shaped pendants made of baler and pearl shell were extensively traded from two areas in Australia, with the largest network from the north-west coast, and another lesser network from Cape York. The Western Australian network reached south to what is now Geraldton, and east across to the Yalata/Port Augusta area in South Australia; and pearl shell from the Broome region was found thousands of kilometres away along the Great Australian Bight. Shells were sent north-east to the Boulia area in Queensland, and to around Carnarvon in New South Wales.

The pendants could be worn by men, women or children, and either suspended from the neck on hair string, or worn around the waist, hung from a hair belt. In Kim Ackerman's study of pearl shells in the Kimberleys, he notes that they were incised with a variety of zigzag or maze designs, and sometimes left plain. Some shells were used in secret-sacred rituals, and others in public ceremonies, such as those for more rain. Kim Akerman links pearl shells to the Rainbow Serpent story:

> [I]ts flashing [is] the lightning that precedes the summer storms ... symbol of life in its own right ... water, rain, lightning: factors in the seasonal re-awakening of the land after long dry periods ...[62]

The Australian Indigenous kinship system

Australian Indigenous kinship systems ensure that each individual is located within a complex of relationships which define who are family, who are potential marriage partners, who are neighbours, and who are potential trade partners, as well as those who are beyond one's kinship reckoning. Within the Aboriginal cosmologies every person, every creature and every physical feature of land and water are regarded as interconnected.

Dislocation, disease and disruption have affected peoples around Australia. In spite of this, patterns of kinship and marriage persist and deeply embedded notions of relatedness to people, country, and story endure. Other small kin-based societies around the world have been similarly disrupted by colonisation.

The 'Arandic system' of classificatory kinship means that one's father's brothers will be called 'father', one's mother's sisters will be called 'mother', and the children of one's mother's sisters will be considered brothers and sisters, while the children of one's mother's brothers will be regarded as cousins.[63]

There are different names given for each of four categories, of which two are matrilines and two are patrilines. To make it even more inclusive (and complex) there are categories of matrimoieties and patrimoieties.[64] As Diane Bell (1983/2002) explains, the most important aspect of the Australian Indigenous social systems is

> the relations of people to land [which] is a web of circulating relationships wherein reciprocity is indeed achieved. It is not a system of isolated patriclans each maintaining and jealously guarding a discretely owned territory.[65]

In central Australia, the subsection system (also known as the 'skin' system) is generated by the cross-cutting classifications of patrimoieties, matrimoieties and generational moieties such that everyone is born into a subsection and has a 'skin'. The skin is a shorthand way of knowing how one is related. Part of the fascination with desert systems of classification is that small children can operate them whereas outsiders require computers to decode them!

As Diane Bell (1983/2002) states, the European 'kinship' systems trace relationships through a limited number of ancestors and distinguish blood relations from in-laws. She explains that these distinctions are drawn in central Australian systems, but

> within each category further distinctions are drawn. For example, four lines of descent, one from each of the grandparents (that is, father's father, father's mother, mother's mother and mother's father) are distinguished terminologically. In English, I need to speak of maternal or paternal grandparents to make this distinction. In the Arandic system, each of the lines has a particular set of rights and responsibilities in respect of land, marriage arrangements, and ceremonial organization, and different rules of behaviour apply to each. For instance, one may engage in obscene joking with one's mother's mother and her brother but not with one's father's mother.[66]

The importance of kin can be found in the stories people tell one another. Peggy Rockman Napaljarri begins a story with the following kinship structure laid out:

> At a place called Wawalja, there lived a Jungarrayi man with many women. Many women lived with him at that place. He had wives of all the wrong skins, all sorts, Napangardi, Napaljarri, Nangala, Nungarrayi, Napanangka, Nampijinpa. He was married to all of them. That Jungarrayi took the wrong women as wives.[67]

The story continues and tells of the social strife that results when kinship rules are not followed.

Traditional social practices

Many present day Aboriginal and Torres Strait Islander people, particularly urban people who had so much of the earlier traditions and practices taken from them, are reaching back to rediscover their culture, and seeking the traditions which still exist. In doing so, they are creating new traditions based in part on what is remembered of the old ways. The impact of colonisation has been pervasive but cultural stories continue, and connection to country continues.

Following the passage of the 1967 Referendum[68] and legislation at the Federal level, new spaces opened up for enquiry (for example, The Stolen Generation).[69] Other consequences of the 1967 Referendum included the possibility of making land claims and Native Title Claims, while the Heritage Act allowed for the protection of important cultural sites. People are now speaking out, and this in turn has created a space for cultural resurgence including creating art within a cultural frame of connections to country, family and story.[70]

Australian Indigenous women's traditional role

Anthropologist Diane Bell lived with Aboriginal women in central Australia in the 1970s and reported on the beliefs and practices of women that had continuity with the past. Previously, the dominant picture of ceremonial activity in Aboriginal society had been focused on men and their beliefs.

Hunter-gatherer societies are as varied as other social systems; in some, women have a high status. Diane Bell argues for both the continuity and change throughout the living tradition of 60,000 years of Aboriginal Law.[71] She gives examples of central Australian societies today where women are autonomous and substantially independent of men in both economic and ritual areas. She records the older women saying that "[w]hite fellas always ask the men, but, we know too."[72] The men stress that the women should also be consulted because they are unable to 'speak for' them. But because researchers are usually men, much more is known of men's perspective of the gendered landscape. Diane Bell (1998a)[73] explains that there are degrees of exclusion of the opposite sex depending on what activity is happening at a site. There are things which should not be seen, and some which should not be heard. Both men and women have great respect for one another's stories and places.

In fact many social and cultural practices are divided equally into 'women's business' and 'men's business' and conducted separately. For example, once boys attain the age of six or seven they join with the men, while the girls remain with the women. However, there are some tasks where everyone joins in. Other tasks involve women acting co-operatively with the men, or acting independently of them.

It is women's responsibility and practice to place emphasis on their nurturing role where they care for land through their land-based ceremonies; conflict and social harmony are achieved through health and healing rituals, while emotions are managed by 'love rituals'. Women's business is about the sacred business of being a woman, and includes all aspects of women's lives – birth; knowledge of medicinal plants, of the seasons and collection of food; preparation of girls for womanhood, modes of behaviour, demeanour and speech.

In south-eastern Australia, before European invasion there were birth-associated rituals and exchanges (such as the baby's umbilical cord being exchanged between certain relatives, in the case of the Ngarrindjeri) or ceremonies involving firestick marriage rituals (when families of the couple symbolised the new union with a new hearth). In a number of Aboriginal societies, including the Ngarrindjeri, men and women are named as they progress on their ritual journey from childhood to adulthood.

In the south-east, women's puberty rites begin with their first menstruation and continue through cicatrisation (the practice of cutting the skin to form ritual scars) until the next significant rite of passage, that of giving birth. There are special practices and rites associated with birth giving, when the women are separated from the general camp and cared for by older women. The period of isolation required at menstruation and birth giving are special times when much sacred information is passed on to the girls and young women. (It should be noted that men have their times of seclusion also.) Women's reproductive rites were in the hands of women.

Birth was an important time and the passage through birthing gave women access to knowledge not available to women who were not yet mothers. Women were critical to survival, and the status of mother had both physical and spiritual connotations. Colonisation saw a marked shift in how birth was treated and consequently women lost power. Colonisation targeted women's ceremonies and birth was the moment when women would be taken to hospital, thereby breaking the cultural and ritual paths. In missions, schools and domestic service where many women found themselves, they were expected to be obedient. This changed the relations between women, men, country and their long history.

There are two contexts for the beliefs and practices of religion, public and private, noted by Deborah Bird Rose (1994).[74] Sex, age and locality define these restrictions. Certain people in each locality have rights to certain knowledge of that locality, according to the country they come from and their relationship to the people in it. The fact that a stranger is female or male does not mean that she or he has rights to particular knowledge.

- *Certain adults have the right to certain knowledge and not to other knowledge.*
  The old men and old women allow these rules to be relaxed so they can discuss certain aspects of that knowledge. Otherwise these restrictive rules, if broken, are punishable by death, carried out by specially appointed men (and women?) or by the Dreaming beings.
- *Men's and women's spiritual systems are interrelated: matter and spirit are interrelated.*
  Deborah Bird Rose notes that this includes the Dreamings, land, plants, animals, living and dead bodies, also including the bodies of trees, stones and ground. Continuity is everything. Life is continually created by the actions of responsible moral agents including not only humans, but also the earth and all living creatures. There are many aspects of the above description which could be recognised in the picture of female prehistoric life provided by Marija Gimbutas.

Interrelated women's and men's business

There is women's space and men's space in this physical landscape. The land does not grant the rights of women over men, nor does it grant women the right to operate in opposition to men, although it recognises a competitive element of desire. But it is women who are the givers of life, bringing it "forth from within the earth ... giving birth ... the powerful transformation from ... being to becoming."[75] Shedding blood in this context, be it women's blood, or arm blood, or red ochre, is important for both women and men. For Indigenous people the world is as it is, with its power to destroy as well as its power to regenerate and to create. This is the world of the Dreaming and of the people.

So it seems certain that women have never been invisible in precontact Indigenous Australia.

CHAPTER 16

NEW WORLDS: OCEANIA

The prehistory of Oceania, a huge and varied expanse of islands, reflects that diversity in terms of language and cultural differences, dates and material evidence of settlements. Remarkably there are traces of matrilineal cultures still present in a number of the islands, including Papua New Guinea, Hawai'i and New Zealand, and traditional people of this region have spoken of this in recent times. Only Papua New Guinea, the Bismark Islands and the Solomon Islands have been settled for a similar length of time as Australia by modern humans; consequently Non-Austronesian languages are prominent throughout these islands. They were settled very early by peaceful cultures, most likely from one source. People did not arrive at any of the other Pacific islands until after 4,000 BP, and appeared in New Zealand even more recently (1,000 BP). Between 4,000 and 3,000 BP several waves of people arrived from either Taiwan or southern China, each bringing their own different cultural influences.

Although they have cultural and social similarities, the Pacific cultures are diverse, each with their own different kinship rules, social organisation, political structures and religions. They have been (until recently) classified into three groups: Melanesians, Micronesians, and Polynesians; but these categories do not take into account their varied histories and origins. However, Patrick Kirch (1997)[1] explains that new studies of linguistic grouping suggest the presence of two fundamental groups rather than the above three:

- The *Non-Austronesian speakers* are from prehistoric South-East Asia (dated to at least 70,000 BP) and include the language speakers of inland Papua New Guinea, Palau, the Marianas in western Micronesia, a few small places in the Solomon Islands, the Bismark Archipelago and Australia.
- The *Austronesians* (known as the Lapita people, originally from Taiwan, dated to 4,000–3,600 BP) are Micronesian, Melanesian and Polynesian language speakers. Their homelands include South-East Asia, part of the north and east coasts of Papua New Guinea, and the Pacific Islands.

(There was a second migration via South-East Asia by Chinese Han Austronesians around 2,500 BP.)

Near Oceania

Near Oceania, which includes part of Papua New Guinea, the Bismarks and the Solomons, was settled over 70,000 years ago by hunter-gatherers who most likely came from Thailand and Indonesia at around the same time that Australia was first settled. These first

A Timeline for Prehistoric Oceania

Period (BP)	Place/People	Evidence
1,800,800	Java, Indonesia (Flores)	• *H. erectus*
700,000	Flores (Indonesia)	• Earliest evidence of oceangoing sea craft used by *H. erectus* • Cutting tools from New Britain Island indicate overseas trade
140,000 1770 (CE)	Lake George (New South Wales) also Great Barrier Reef (Queensland) Australia	• Core samples suggest humans regularly used fire, perhaps as a hunting aid
100,000	Java	• Archaic *H. sapiens* may have crossed the sea to Australia on bamboo water craft
100,000–70,000	**Near Oceania:** Consisting of Australia and Papua New Guinea	• Were first settled by modern humans? Non-Austronesian language speaking hunter-gatherers from South-East Asia
18,000–13,000	*H. floresiensis*	• Remains found in cave on Flores suggest *H. floresiensis* coexisted with modern humans
10,000–8,000	Australia and Papua New Guinea	• Separate because of rising seas • Stone figurines of animals, birds, mortars, pestles, PNG highlands
6,000–4,000	New Guinea	• Pottery
4,000	**Remote Oceania:** Consisting of all other Pacific islands	• People are Austronesian speakers: the Micronesian, Melanesian and Polynesians who were originally from Taiwan
3,600	Remote Oceania	• Settled by Indo-European language speakers: the Lapita people
	Massau Island	• Talepakemalai stilt-house village
Up to 2,100	Pacific Rim	• Peaceful cultures in the Pacific
1,600		• Polynesians settled Hawai'i
1,100		• Polynesians settled Easter Island
1,100–800	New Zealand	• The Polynesian people arrive

Non-Austronesian people were descendants of earlier peaceful hunter-gatherers from the supercontinent of Sahul.[2] (Remote Oceania which includes the rest of the Pacific Islands was not occupied until the Lapita people arrived around 3,600 BP).

Sahul consisted of New Guinea, Australia and Tasmania, and was formed during several periods in the past by falling sea levels. There are two routes from Asia to Sahul proposed by Patrick Kirch: the first was via Sulawesi to western Papua New Guinea; the second followed islands east of Java (Bali via Flores to Timor, and directly onto Sahul; or via Leti to Sahul near the Aru Islands).[3] These early inhabitants of Near Oceania must have possessed ocean-going sea craft in order to sail from one island to the next. Remains of *H. erectus* and obsidian cutting tools from New Britain dated to 700,000 BP were discovered on Flores Island which could not have been reached by a land bridge as the sea passage separating it from the main island has always been too deep.

Papua New Guinea

At around the same time that Australia and Papua New Guinea became separated from each other, Thailand and Indonesia, which were originally part of the Asian mainland, became separated from it by rising sea levels 9,000 years ago. So it seems that Australian Indigenous people and inland Papua New Guineans originally came from the same place in South-East Asia, however, they developed very different lifestyles due to the dissimilar climatic conditions. According to Tim Flannery (1994),[4] Papua New Guinea was very different environmentally to Australia, with deep fertile soils, reliable rain, and numerous plants suitable for food through gathering and cultivation.

Most researchers report successive and constant arrivals of immigrants and visitors from the north to the Pacific Islands and Australia after 3,800 BP. Charles Higham and Rachanie Thosaret (1998)[5] mention two Indo-European languages, Pali and Sanskrit,[6] present in Thailand which is en route to Oceania, thus other influences are also likely to have migrated along with these cultures. It would seem that everyone led predominantly peaceful lives which only changed when Eurasian/Indo-European influences flowed down from China as they did in South-East Asia after 4,000 BP. (Incidentally, it is worth noting that Australia, Papua New Guinea and Pacific societies have myths which tell of the women originally 'owning' the creation secrets[7] which were later taken over by the men at one point in the past.) According to Tim Flannery, the planting of root crops, such as taro and bananas, with their simple propagation needs (cutting up tubers and replanting), has been practised for over 10,000 years in Papua New Guinea. There is evidence of the early use of irrigation from about 9,000 BP to regulate the flow of water over the cultivated land. In order to grow plants such as taro, the soil needed to be both watered and drained. Agriculture may have become increasingly important over time in Papua New Guinea as the elusive animal species became more scarce and difficult to hunt in the dense forests.

The wet and humid climate has ensured that few prehistoric artefacts have survived. Also the terrain is such that archaeological exploration has been limited. While contact with the Spanish and Dutch 500 years ago would have introduced some social changes, when the British arrived in 1905 even more traditional indigenous knowledge was lost, according to G.S. Hope, J. Golson and J. Allen (2006).[8] They explain that traditionally, one or two clans lived in small villages scattered throughout the heavily forested land and linked by narrow pathways, which allowed social contact and exchange of goods with other clans. The men cleared land for garden cultivation, and built the houses and fences, while women prepared food, planted the gardens, raised pigs, and cared for the family. Tim Flannery explains that when explorer Mick Leahy saw them in 1931, he described Papua New Guinean villages as neat and organised, with each house having a fenced-in garden featuring square beds of sweet potatoes, beans, cucumbers and sugar cane, and here and there "a clump or two of feathery bamboo, a few banana trees and a grove of casuarinas, and invariably flowers and ornamental shrubs."[9]

G.S. Hope et al. record that both women and men looked after the children. Extended families lived next to the parents, and everyone gathered frequently for communal meals, ceremonies and work. Marriages were arranged, and land passed down from parents to children. Young children of both sexes were allowed to play freely until girls reached five or six years old, at which time they began to help with light domestic work; while boys of seven or eight were expected to accompany the men. Separate initiation rituals took place when both boys and girls were older. Household decisions were made by consensus and clan decisions by customary law.

All of these aspects are still present today. David Simmons (1979)[10] explains that generally people of the region believe the world includes both humans and spirits. Indeed spirits of recently dead important ancestors are part of everyday life. Birth, initiation, marriage and death rituals are always marked by offerings to the ancestral spirits and non-human spirits. The people also believe that spirits can be kindly or cruel, depending on the way they are treated in ritual or during other daily activities. Australian Indigenous women had their own strong ritual and cultural life apart from the men, and it is reasonable to conclude that this would also have been the case for Papua New Guinean women.[11]

Prehistoric arts of Papua/West Papua and related Pacific islands

Prehistoric tools found in the Highlands include stone pestles and mortars, grinding stones, and figurines, which today are considered objects of power. The Heilbrunn Timeline of Art History[12] has photographs of these early stone sculptures found in different parts of Papua New Guinea, especially in the Highlands. (Although they are not as yet securely dated they could be around 8,000 years old) Some of the pestles have human or bird heads or bird figures on their tops, while mortars may feature geometric motifs or anthropomorphic or avian imagery on rims and/or sides. The figurines depict humans, phalluses, birds and animals. Many of these tools would have been used by women in food preparation, although some may have been ceremonial, or used by men in ritual. The Heilbrunn examples include a pestle with a zoomorphic top, a pestle in the form of a semi-abstract bird, and two figurines, which are well designed, and simple in form. The accompanying article identifies them as bird sculptures, but their similarity to female deities in early European societies suggests they are more likely to be female figurines. It is possible the symbolic meanings of these figurines and birds could be similar to those studied by Marija Gimbutas.

Chris Boylan and Greta North[13] provide some information about the prehistory of Papua New Guinea which they say is in the process of being unveiled by new excavations. There are very old wall paintings in caves which are still used for rituals, and the images are similar to motifs commonly used today, although the local people say that their meanings have changed. Chris Boylan and Greta North give one example, 'the segmented coloured circle' which appears on modern shields, and is featured in the old paintings. There have been no prehistoric wooden artefacts discovered so far.

Figurative sculptures and anthropomorphic headdresses (also used in the past for rituals) are made from ephemeral materials. Many early examples of these were burnt or otherwise destroyed with the arrival of the first Europeans 500 years ago. Today these take the form of headdresses worn solely by men, and kept in the (men's) spirit house. Body art, including painted motifs, masks, costumes and figures made from plant and animal matter, together with traditional symbolic motifs from the past, are widely used today. Some examples include: the circle, symbol of the sun, or the human navel; and opposing triangles, which may symbolise butterfly wings, the spider, teeth, waterfalls, or humans. Imagery can be representational or abstract with particular combinations of elements or colours.

Pottery

It can difficult to find evidence of prehistoric women's material arts and culture which, even today, seem to be considered unimportant by many researchers.[14] In a study of the traditional pottery of New Guinea by Patricia May and Margaret Tuckson (2000)[15] they record that there was much pottery made from 6,000 to 4,000 BP on the New Guinea mainland, while the 3,300-year-old Lapita-style pottery (described by Patrick Kirch later in this chapter) was rare, and was more commonly found in the numerous Pacific islands. Patricia May and Margaret Tuckson travelled extensively through the Papua New Guinea countryside over ten years and found many different pottery styles still made by women's paddle-and-anvil technique, or men's coil technique. The earliest pottery had been made by women in some regions, and by (Austronesian) men in other regions although the majority of pottery was women's creation. Pottery decorated with bird and animal heads (and sometimes human genitalia) were made by men but their meanings are unknown today.

There was no pottery in the Highlands or in Western Papua, New Britain or New Ireland, (although some was traded in these areas); instead earth-ovens or sections of bamboo were used for cooking food, and gourds and bamboo segments are still used to carry or store water even today. Women of coastal regions and small islands have always made their pottery using the wooden paddle-and-anvil technique to create "light and thin-walled ... round-based and full-bellied" pots, "typically female in form", with some exceptions which were "spherical or sections of spheres"[16] with distinct shoulders; all examples were very finely finished and beautiful in appearance.

In the Central Province, the mountain people are non-Austronesian, with some Austronesians living along the coastal areas. Women have clan designs which are used in their tattoos (on arms, chest and thighs) and also on their pots and barkcloth. Symbolic clan design motifs include the frigate bird, lizard tail, clouds in line, frog's hind leg and foot.

In the Milne Bay Province (south-east Papua) women continue to be prolific potters, although the men collect the clay and distribute the finished pots for trade or exchange. Early pots displayed a wide range of applied and incised design motifs, probably representing aspects of traditional stories and made as part of women's rituals, as was barkcloth (see following pages). The women gathered to make the pots in special 'club' houses. Early small pots were used to contain food for the dead in burials, with larger pots used for bones and skulls.

In the Northern Province, in the north-east of the mainland, women make their pots using the coil method (a method elsewhere used by men) but also use paddle-and-anvil to finish forming the pot. Here the pots feature a wide circular mouth and bowl, gradually shaping to a narrow point at the base, with little (if any) decoration. Pottery making is gradually disappearing in this area. Traditionally these items were very important in 'bride transactions', with pots and ornaments being considered a form of wealth. Patricia May and Margaret Tuckson describe the process: "After the initiation of boys and girls, the initiate's maternal uncle receives from the initiate's father a pig; from his mother, a gift which frequently includes a pot."[17] Pots are often broken up upon the death of the owner "as

1

2

3

4

5

6

7

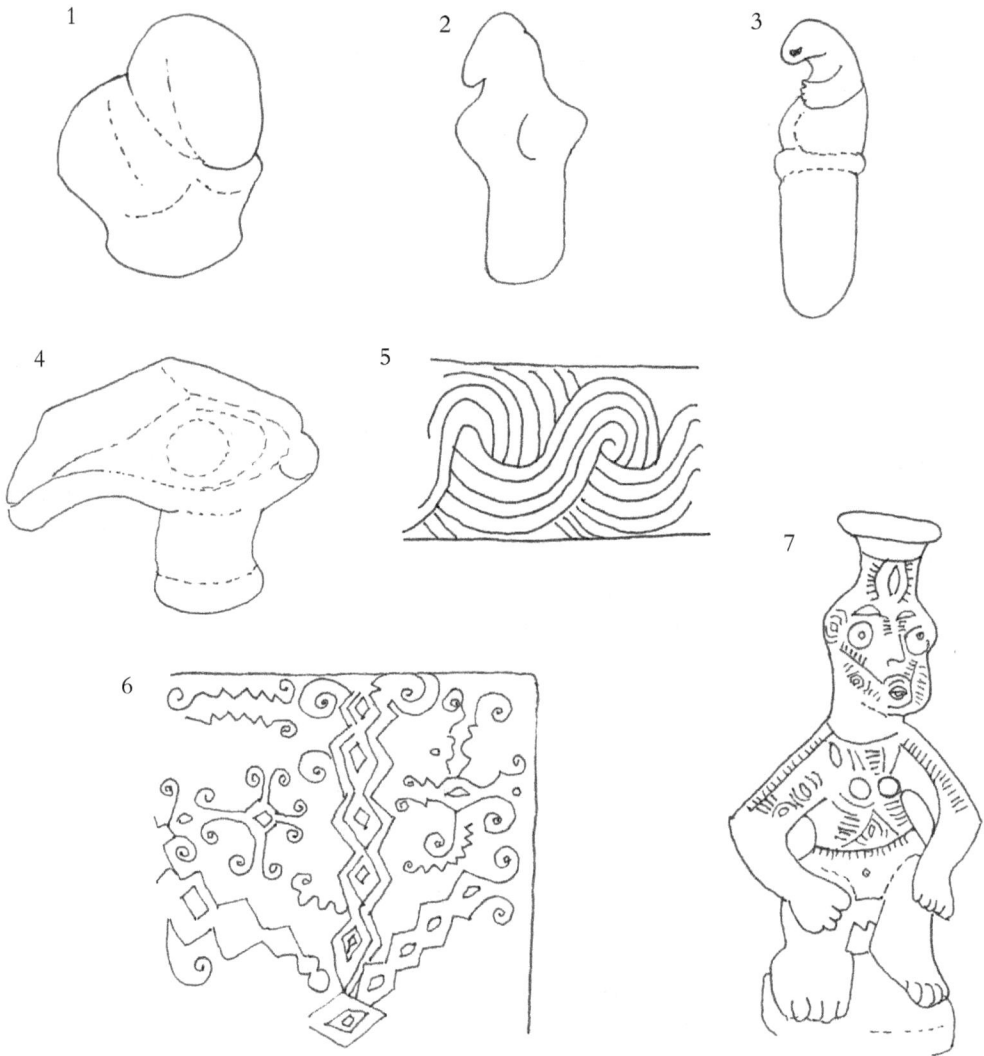

OCEANIA: PAPUA NEW GUINEA ART

1–4. The earliest known Oceanic art: *Four prehistoric stone pestles* from Papua New Guinea. Sculptures 1. and 2. are labelled 'bird sculptures', but could also easily be female figurines (the Gimbutas bird goddess?); 3. Could represent a mammal head with torso; 4. A bird's head (Source: Department of Arts of Africa, Oceania, and the Americas, October 2004)

5. A *women's traditional 'M' design* on a pot rim from Central Province, northern coast of Papua New Guinea (Source: May, Patricia and Margaret Tuckson, 2000)

6. An example of an *Ömie traditional barkcloth* (nioge) *design* (detail) (Source: Balai, Sana and Judith Ryan et al., 2009)

7. An early *carved wood Yaul mythological female figurine* from the Sepik River Province, Papua New Guinea, no date (Source: May, Patricia and Margaret Tuckson, 2000)

All line drawings © Judy Foster, 2013

a display of grief." A widow wears "a hood of barkcloth or netted string and around her neck, mementoes of her dead husband, including sometimes a piece of the pot in which she cooked his food."[18] Early pots featured zigzag patterned rims or incised abstract or plant forms, or spirals around the necks of pots, the meanings of which are no longer known. An Austronesian clan group in the area traded pots inland, exchanging them for feathers, reptile skins and barkcloth, with obsidian, shells and canoes traded by coastal people.

In Morobe Province (north of the Northern Province) men make the pottery, while young married women (not yet having produced a child) collect the clay at certain specific times. The women must wear traditional dress, not smoke, only use their own language, and not be witnessed digging the clay, according to the necessary ritual. One unusual clay item the men make is a drum, using a hollow clay tube, mounted on a hollow bowl-shaped base, and topped with a similar baseless wide hollow clay bowl, over which they stretch a lizard or snake skin.

There are few pottery-making clans in the Highlands as clay is not readily available. These are non-Austronesian people who are mainly agricultural. The few pots which are made by either women or men are distinctive tall oval-shaped vessels with high necks and rounded bottoms, sometimes decorated with painted designs. In one area, men make ocarinas in the shape of a pig's head with eyeholes and open mouth.

In the Sepik River region close to West Papua's border and along the north-west coast, men make all of the decorated ceremonial clay pots and other items, carve wood, hunt and plant certain foods used in ritual. The women make the plain utilitarian pots, look after the children and the gardens, prepare food, and carry water and firewood.

Aibom pottery from the central Sepik region is made by men, has figurative imagery on some pot rims, and painted motifs on ceremonial pottery. In this region women also know how to make the pots. Patricia May and Margaret Tuckson record versions of a myth of the principal female deity, an animal and bush spirit named Kolimangge

> who [in one myth] created pottery for the tribe and taught the women to pot. The little stick used by potters to press designs into the relief decorations is [her] pencil and the water in the coconut shell which keeps the clay from sticking is her 'ink'. She subsequently transformed herself into earth and clay and is thus [named] *kolimangge*.[19]

Another version of the myth tells how the clay, fuel and the sago sealing solution all came to her when she called them. On her command the fuel prepared itself for firing, the pots settled themselves on the fuel and later took themselves to market and stood in a row. After marrying a man called Korumblaban she lost her command over the raw materials and pots and since then all the women potters must carry their own clay, build their own fires and take their own pots to market.[20] (Does this indicate that perhaps they originally made the pots, a traditional practice taken from them by the men with the introduction of Indo-European customs as mentioned earlier?) A further mythological female deity's body is credited with the creation of two of the most useful plants in the region, the red coconut palm, and the black palm.

The authors note that the Aibom pottery is analogous to Neolithic Jomon pottery, both in form and decoration (with perhaps similar meanings?) and also to Minoan and South-East Asian Neolithic pottery. (This is quite likely since the second-wave Austronesians came from southern China). No identifiable female ritual imagery on women's pots has been recorded, and very few if any images of female figurines apparently exist today. But it could well be that any visual references to female deities are portrayed in semi-abstract design motifs, the meanings of which were/are only known to the women concerned, which is the case in many parts of Indigenous Australia.

Barkcloth (tapa) making

Barkcloth (or 'tapa' as it is known in some of the islands) was widely made by women throughout Papua New Guinea and the Pacific Islands, and this tradition continues today. The main producers of barkcloth are: Samoa (*siapo*), Tonga (*ngatu*), Hawai'i (*kapa*), Fiji (*masi*), Tahiti (*ahu*), Santa Cruz (*lepau*), New Zealand and Cook Islands (*arite*), Bougainville (*nuung*), Papua New Guinea (*nioge*) and West Papua Lake Sentini region (*maro*). There are some differences between techniques of construction and colours of the design motifs in each region or clan. Traditionally, women made barkcloth, although there are two exceptions, Samoa and Fiji, where both women and men make the cloth.

One region in Papua New Guinea which has been able to continue making barkcloth the traditional way is described by Sana Balai, Drusilla Modjeska, and Judith Ryan (2009)[21] in the exhibition catalogue *Wisdom of the Mountain: Art of the Ömie* in which a number of beautiful *nioge* are presented. Sana Balai explains that the Ömie individual must earn the right through initiation to create the *nioge*, with its accompanying rituals including customs, stories, songs, and dances. She says this matrilineal culture is diverse, complex, highly organised, but also flexible enough to accommodate changing traditions.

The tree barks used for *nioge* are from the paperbark mulberry and varieties of fig trees, and are ceremonially removed from the trees by the women. The prepared bark is placed on a special wooden anvil and repeatedly beaten using wooden mallets to produce a fine creamy cloth. This process may be accompanied by the beat of the *kundu* drum, and by songs, stories and dance. The colours of the 'paint' used to create the designs are traditional and obtained from plants and ash. For example, black is made from the burnt leaves of a small bamboo; red, and a range of brown paint, from scraped tree bark and burnt ferns, and the like; and yellow, from a certain green guava-like fruit which when cut, becomes yellow.

The Ömie live high up on the steep slopes of Mount Lamington in eastern Papua and have been somewhat isolated as, in order to go elsewhere, they have to cross the lands of the clans living on the plains below, who are powerful, with different culture and language. This isolation has helped the Ömie to retain their traditional culture and society, despite the effects of ongoing colonisation. They have many uses for *nioge*: for wrapping up babies, for blankets on cold nights, for women's and men's garments and cloaks, and for ceremonial wall hangings.

There are creation stories of the first *nioge*-making reproduced in the design motifs on the cloth. Much knowledge used in the *nioge* rituals is not available to uninitiated women, but they learn new design meanings with each stage of initiation.

Perhaps the most used visual symbol on the *nioge* is the 'climbing vine with thorns and tendrils'. This motif features the odunaige, a sinuous climbing vine with sharp hooks and searching tendrils which "when painted double with the two stems drawn parallel and the hooks curling outwards"[22] suggests the male and female dancers peeling away to left and right during the dance. This design was originally also tattooed onto newly initiated women's faces. It is a highly versatile and interesting motif and there were many variations of it within the *Wisdom of the Mountain* exhibition catalogue.

Another symbolic motif associated with men is the concentric circle, representing the strength and purpose of the Ömie people, while other images much used in this instance are the 'V', 'M', and diamond-shaped motifs in repeat designs (just as had occurred in Old European designs recorded by Marija Gimbutas). Imagery also includes lizard bones, snake skin, cassowary eggs, certain tree barks, caterpillar markings, spider webs, frogs and snails, all of which are likely to have both everyday and secret meanings, as in Australian Indigenous cultures.

Judith Ryan speaks of the *nioge* as being "central to the Ömie creation story and Ömie identity, and every woman involved in creating *nioge* is recreating the original story."[23] The Ömie people, although they had only occasional contact with the outside world until 2004, had been greatly affected by the Second World War, and the 1951 volcanic eruption of Mount Lamington with both events killing many people and making life hard for survivors. Earlier loss of culture was also caused by missionaries and other Western influences, for example, the loss of traditional ritual tattooing of symbolic design motifs on the body and on *nioge* as part of initiation, which was an important aspect of ritual ceremonies and a diverse iconographic medium used by the Ömie. Judith Ryan mentions other symbolic motifs used on *nioge*, including cross-hatching, the double butterfly, pig's tusk, and weaving textures.

The *bilum*

One traditional item that is still made throughout Papua is the *bilum*, a 'string' bag used for functional or ceremonial reasons, which may be crafted from knotted or woven string made from reeds or other suitable plant material. It may be carried by both women (with short handles, on their heads)[24] and men (with a long looped shoulder handle). Grass or reed fibre may be coloured black, or shades of rust red through to light to dark brown, and woven into traditional geometric patterns according to each clan. Men hang them from their shoulders down the back to carry tools for the hunt, while women's shorter *bilum*s hold babies, or gathered foods and so forth. There is a lovely traditional story associated with the *bilum*s of the Papua New Guinea Ömie people where 'the old woman' climbs up the mountain and puts the sun into her *bilum* at sunset, and takes it out in the morning.[25] Today, women crochet *bilum*s in bright colours and patterns, often as a tourist item. Other woven items include head, arm and waistbands, as well as baskets and mats.[26]

Remote Oceania

The Lapita People: Ancestors of the Pacific Islands and New Zealand

Evidence left by the early Lapita peoples includes the many rock art sites found throughout the Islands. David Roe (1992)[27] states that some of the engravings in the Solomon Islands have been found inside caves, and on boulders near streams, and those in taro fields which perhaps were used as boundary markers. Images include 'canoe' designs, anthropomorphic figures, cupules, concentric circles, 'wheels', meanders and other geometric motifs. Rock art recorded in New Britain, Vanuatu, and New Caledonia is also believed to have been made by the Lapita people since the motifs relate to those found on Lapita pottery. Patrick Kirch

(1997)[28] mentions rock art on New Ireland which has been dated to 30,000 BP and is likely to have been created by earlier peaceful hunter-gatherers. He records the first Austronesians from peaceful Taiwan as travelling in sea-going canoes to the Bismark Archipelago about 4,000 years ago.

About 3,500 BP descendants of the Lapita people, the Polynesians, settled Vanuatu, New Caledonia, Fiji, Tonga, and Samoa. Later (around 1,600 BP) Polynesians settled Hawai'i. Tim Flannery (1994) theorises that they went to Easter Island around 1,100 BP. New Zealand was the last place they settled and this did not occur until somewhere between 1,100 and 800 years ago. The term 'Lapita' is used to identify a certain kind of pottery originally found on the west coast of New Caledonia at a beach named Lapita, according to Patrick Kirch, who states that it is now used to identify Oceanic ancestors, and artefacts belonging to their cultures.[29]

Tim Flannery describes the lifestyle of the Lapita people as seafaring; they settled on small islands and built their houses raised on poles over shallow water. Patrick Kirch discovered the oldest Lapita site known as Talepakemalai, dated to 3,600 BP, on a coral island in the Massau Island group. It was a stilt-house village built over tidal flats. Some wooden posts were preserved, along with seeds and nuts of plant foods, as well as beautifully decorated Lapita pottery, shell beads and bracelets, fish hooks, numerous obsidian flakes and other artefacts.

Their long canoes had large sails, were stabilised with outriggers, and able to carry heavy loads over long distances. Lapita settlements were permanent, usually placed on what Roger Green[30] names 'beach terraces' facing reef passages; or situated on small offshore islands. The people gathered shellfish and caught fish; they also kept pigs and fowls, and grew plant crops.

Patrick Kirch suggests that one of the reasons why the later Lapita people and their descendants moved to settle in new locations in Oceania was because of their (patriarchal) type of social organisation where eldest sons inherited the ancestral home and land. Younger family members would therefore look for new lands with plentiful resources where they could raise their own families. This knowledge has been passed down through oral traditions, and in the past was a major incentive for these voyages of discovery.

Navigation in the Pacific

Munya Andrews (2004)[31] explains the navigation methods used by the Polynesians in the Pacific. They observed a number of natural signs to find their way including: the position of the sun, moon, and stars; wind direction; the swells and currents of the ocean; the colour and temperature of the water; the presence of birds, their numbers, and direction of flight; the movement of clouds; and even phosphorescence, to develop the sophisticated navigation system used by all prehistoric and early historic Austronesians and non-Austronesians.

This method was used successfully by the Phoenicians and Vikings who had no instruments when navigating, according to Munya Andrews, so it is plausible that early humans used similar methods 700,000 years ago. She identifies the stars and explains how the relative position of certain islands to latitude and longitude were all critical for successful navigation purposes in the Pacific, and had to be learnt over a long period by intending navigators. This would have included knowing the traditional art, songs, stories and teachings passed down from generation to generation. She explains how certain stars, such as the

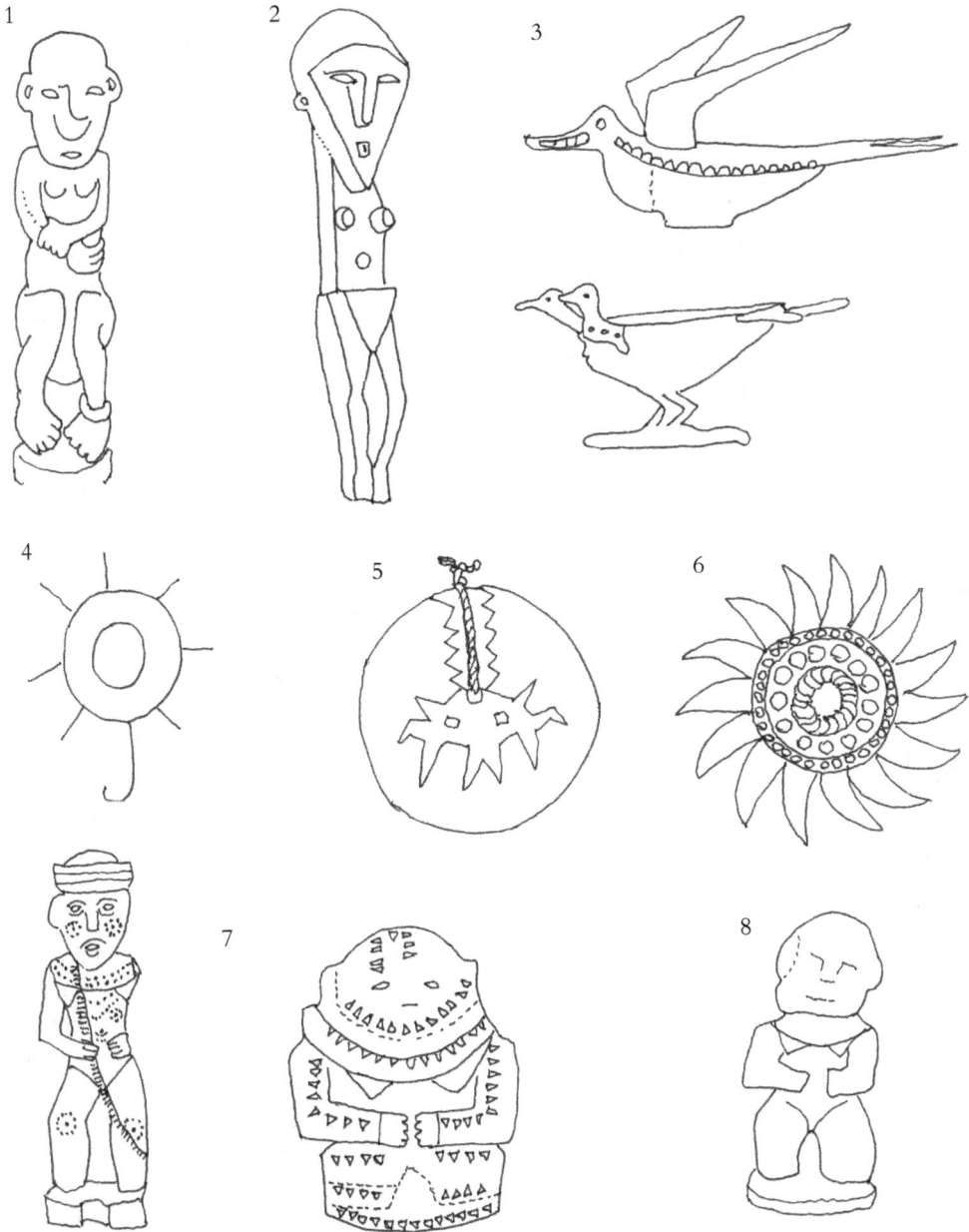

SOLOMON ISLANDS AND PAPUA NEW GUINEA: FEMALE IMAGERY

1. *Carved wooden house post representing female figure,* Solomon Islands
2. *Traditional carved figurine,* Papua New Guinea
3. *Two frigatebird bowls*
4. *A women's tattoo design*

5. *A frigatebird ornament,* turtle/pearl shell
6. *An ornament made of porpoise teeth and beads*
7. *Two ritual wooden female figurines*
8. *A figurine made from lava*
   (Source: Archey, Gilbert, 1965/1967)

All line drawings © Judy Foster, 2013

Southern Cross constellation, appear in very different positions in the sky depending on where one is positioned in Australia and the Pacific, and are not seen at all in the Northern Hemisphere.

Lapita pottery in the Pacific Islands

Pottery (which was in many cases women's creation), with its increasingly innovative designs of shape and decoration, has always been an indication of the complexity of a civilisation. In the Pacific region there are many interesting varieties of pottery styles and techniques, sometimes made by men using the slab-and-coil method, more often by women using the paddle-and-anvil method. (It is likely that the early Lapita pottery, which was more finely made and decorated, was made by women). The finest, best decorated, early Lapita pottery was used for serving foods, while the plainer pottery was used for storage vessels. The later Lapita coarse pottery was made and decorated by men for ritual purposes.[32]

Evidence of the arrival of the Lapita people consists of a highly distinctive earthenware pottery which women low-fired on open fires (there is no evidence of early pottery kilns). After hand-forming using slab and coil techniques, women made vessels using a paddle and anvil, as is still the tradition in Fiji. To finish, the vessel was burnished or covered with a layer of red slip which appeared red-brown or brown in colour after firing.

Patrick Kirch describes Lapita-style pottery as featuring repeated combinations of sets of 'dentate' or 'toothed' stamp designs pressed into the clay prior to firing. These designs were very evenly and carefully applied on a band around the upper parts or on the rims of the pots, usually on the exterior, but also sometimes along the inside rim. Sometimes the patterns formed motifs. The tools used for making the incised or pressed patterns have not been found so they are likely to have been made of wood or bamboo. Some pots had pedestal feet; others were flat-bottomed, or had flaring rims, while plain pots were often large and globular, with narrow necks and flaring rims. Earlier pots were more decorative than later ones. Plain pottery was for serving or storage of food and water, while decorated pottery would have been used in ritual.

Repeat designs were restricted to certain forms, and there were special words for design elements which were part of an inherited artistic code. Each set of design elements would have had particular meanings which could be 'read' by those who used the pottery. Some imagery (which is still seen today) included geometric shapes, such as triangles, zigzags, cross hatching, parallel wavy lines or meanders, and half circles. Often elements were repeated in such a way as to form anthropomorphic face designs, featuring eyes, nose, arms, digits, and even a 'headdress'. (As we have already seen, these motifs are present in many other prehistoric regions and are remarkably similar to the patterns decoded by Marija Gimbutas.)

Later, paddle-and-anvil techniques were still mainly used by women, whose fine, beautifully crafted pottery (used for storage vessels) was a valuable trade item. But the heavier, less accomplished decorated pottery was made by men for ritual purposes. Decoration hid the clumsy forms and thick walls of these pots. David Simmons compares the Lapita geometric patterns with tapa designs, and also Samoan body art (tattoos), designs on Tongan clubs, and carved designs on Austral Island ceremonial paddles. One pottery sherd from the Solomons featured a face mask similar to those found in areas of Melanesia, and often used in Polynesian sculpture.

Agnes Sullivan (1985)[33] explains that Lapita women also made woven baskets, nets, rope and cord, as the raw materials were readily available in nearby forests. Other Lapita items included earth ovens, stone adzes for woodworking and carving, and small chisels for tattooing. Patrick Kirch describes tool kits as including shell adzes, flake tools, shell scrapers and peelers, anvils, polishers, sling-stones, shell beads, bracelets, rings, discs, needles, awls, shell fish hooks, and net sinkers (or loom weights?). There are no aggressive weapons among these artefacts, perhaps because there was no need to attack others or defend their own property. Trade was frequent with other Lapita communities; trade items usually included obsidian, chert, pottery and oven stones used for cooking.

Agnes Sullivan says changes to Lapita cultures which occurred around 2,500 BP included new triangular-shaped motifs on axes, while pottery lacking decoration became heavier, with thicker walls, and was eventually no longer made. The style of pottery also changed over the earlier Polynesian stages – from classic dentate-stamped Early Eastern Lapita to a Late Eastern Lapita phase (when decoration greatly declined and certain pots were no longer made) and later to a terminal Polynesian Plain Ware. By 2,000 BP pottery had ceased to be made or used, and changes had also taken place in regard to tool kits, settlement and subsistence patterns. Polynesian culture and technology around 300 CE certainly represented a divergence from the Lapita tradition, and it seems quite possible that this occurred because of newcomers to the area. However, Patrick Kirch stresses the continuity between the Lapita societies and the societies which followed, as the Polynesians are directly descended from at least one group of Lapita people.[34]

Although the Lapita peoples brought decorated pottery with them, Christine Price (1980)[35] reports that its making ceased after their disappearance around 2,500 BP. Gilbert Archey[36] in 1965 referred to the Lapita people as 'Neolithic proto-Polynesians' who seemed not to have possessed metal arts, but did initially bring looms and pottery to Samoa and the Marquesas. He theorises that pottery and the weaving loom most likely disappeared from the islands through lack of resources, such as the availability of suitable clay for pottery, or perhaps because the people preferred to make quick and simple coconut containers and tapa cloth from the readily available materials. Wooden artefacts would have been used but have not survived because of the humid climate.

One wonders whether these early people disappeared with the arrival of later more aggressive and hierarchic Austronesian newcomers. Only in Fiji or parts of New Guinea and the New Hebrides is there a pottery tradition extending into the present. Far more widely known is the practice of making wooden vessels, such as kava bowls and food containers.

The 'myth' of early fierce warrior cultures in the Pacific is contradicted by its prehistory. Most commentaries allude to warfare as being always present among the Islanders, and the people themselves believe this to be the case, but recent discoveries show this was not the practice among the first Lapita peoples from whom the Polynesians are descended. Tim Flannery agrees that intermarriage and cohabitation, rather than violent conflict, was the norm among the Lapita peoples, as there is no evidence of any massacres or fortified villages. The complexity of Lapita pottery, the rock art, and other artefacts, and the remains of early Lapita lifestyles, indicate a peaceful culture in the Pacific in accord with other civilisations of the Pacific Rim until at least 2,100 BP.

Torres Strait and Aotearoa/New Zealand: Female Imagery

1a. and b. *Frigatebird-shaped ear ornaments for a bride,* Torres Strait
2. *Ritual female sculpture*
   (Source: Chick, John and Sue, eds, 1978)

New Zealand
3. *Carved wooden panels featuring traditional spiral design motifs*
4. *Other basic spiral design motifs*
   (Source: Barrow, Terence, 1984)

All line drawings © Judy Foster, 2013

Matriliny/matriarchy in the Pacific

Zohl dé Ishtar (1994) has recorded the Pacific women speaking of their traditions before European colonisation, with her first informant being Margarita Sarapao[37] of the Northern Marianas, who explains that traditional life meant that the women of the Pacific enjoyed equal status, "made decisions for the land", and "had a say"[38] in who the (male) chief should be. Chailang Palacios[39] explains that theirs was a matrilineal society. "The chiefs are the old people, very powerful because they have experienced so much."[40] She adds that behind the chiefs are the women. Their power is subtle: they are in charge of the house, of decision-making; they have the last word.

Concerning traditional cultures and religion, Chailang Palacios explains that before the Spanish came to the Northern Marianas in 1521, nature, the land and the sea were valued, respected, contemplated and appreciated, and were the heart of indigenous ritual and cultural life.

Bougainville is an island close to Papua New Guinea's south-east coast. Theresa Minitong[41] explains that in 1990 Bougainville was still matrilineal, with the land and the wealth controlled by women. Before colonisation, everyone acted as a community, as 'equal partners'. Following colonisation women's status was eroded as the men forgot their traditional position and decided that they were more important.

Lijon Eknilang[42] states that the people of the Marshall Islands are traditionally matrilineal, and the women are responsible for the land which is inherited from the mother. They consult with the community, and make the final decisions. The clan mother (oldest woman), together with the women, decides what major tasks need to be done, and the men carry them out. However, the men represent the women at meetings, just as in Maori society.

The land inherited through the mother (owned and shared by everyone) provides clan identity, power, social organisation and political status; women enjoy equal status with men, but each sex has different responsibilities. The clan land can never be sold or given away. Food is shared to ensure that all are fed. Everyone helps prepare the food for the community and all eat together. The traditional law system includes, for example, rules of behaviour concerning men's access to women when they are menstruating or pregnant, just as under Australian Indigenous Law where women can go to women's camps which no man may enter.

Gabriela Ngirmang[43] of Belau adds that the family house also belongs to the ancestors who are buried "right here in this graveyard."[44] The land belongs to the clan, in Gabriela Ngirmang's case, "going back seven mothers." The clan inherits the title which belongs to the land and which establishes their identity and their position in Koror. She adds that "the land ... is our identity. Without it we are lost."[45]

Also from Belau, Isabel Sumang[46] comments that the women can't do without the men who fill many roles and provide a balance. Men's jobs are as important as women's jobs. Women make decisions for women, and men make decisions for men. Before colonisation "even in the Council of Chiefs they have a system – they have different roles, each clan has a role."[47] Women are brought up to be strong and to know their role – they assume their matrilineal power. "Titles are handed down through women."[48] This is because a woman always knows that her baby belongs to her, but a man may not necessarily know whether he is the father of a child. The family bloodline is certain in the woman's child so the title is passed from mother to daughter. Manami Suzuki (1987) remarks that "female values still operate in Belau. But modern masculine culture and technology have been invading Belau ... [and] the modern society and traditional society confront each other."[49]

For the Hawai'ians also, their ancestry is connected to their land, while the natural forces, such as the moon, the stars, rain, native plants and animals, and ocean life, are the deities. According to Ku'umea'aloha Gomez[50] they love their land. Native American Dine (Navajo) woman, Lenora Hill,[51] adds that her people are taught that their spiritual way of life preserves the universe, which is continually being healed "by their offerings and prayers to the earth."[52]

Pacific women's arts and status

Penelope Schoeffel (1995)[53] provides an overview of Pacific women's arts and crafts with their links to women's status. Although the production of women's traditional crafts has been undermined by importation of cloth and craft commercialisation, arts and crafts continue to be important for ceremonial, economic and cultural reasons.

Women have traditionally used feathers, seeds, shells, vegetable matter and dyes to decorate some of their crafted objects. Animal fur and feathers are used for warmth, insulation, and aesthetic effect in the cold highlands of New Zealand and Papua New Guinea. Specialised and therapeutic items, including cosmetics (scented coconut oil, turmeric and ochre), and medicinal herbs (such as infusions of plant matter) continue to be made by women in many Oceanic societies. Prestige goods including clothing and ornaments have always been ceremonially exchanged for use in rituals, such as marriages, funerals, and the installation of chiefs.

Shell discs, into which women laboriously drilled holes, are today considered a form of 'wealth'. Small shells were originally used in the creation of symbolic design motifs on cloth or other artefacts; today they are strung on cords and have become the principal prestige goods of many Solomon Island societies. Other 'hard' prestige goods made by men include carved ornaments, such as tortoise shell or pearl-shell discs featuring intricate filigree designs.

In most Melanesian and some Micronesian societies, women's role in food production was, and still is, central to their economies (and their status). Women produce staple foods, tend livestock, and sometimes fish. In other Micronesian and all Polynesian societies, women's main role continues to involve the creation of handcrafted goods for domestic use and exchange. They are repositories and dispensers of knowledge about resources. Men's role includes hunting, fishing, clearing and preparing land for cultivation, and growing certain crops linked to men's rituals.

Papua New Guinean women exclusively craft fine hemp cord used for net construction; while Polynesians utilise coconut fibre for nets and cordage used in house and boat building. But men always use 'hard' materials for decorative ritual objects, drums, weapons, canoes, fish hooks, food bowls, headrests and hanging hooks. There are exceptions, such as some Micronesian men traditionally plait objects for ritual use, including cane baskets, because of the strength needed to weave the cane. In the past, in Yap and Palau, men even used special looms to weave 'currency cloth'. Men in some parts of Papua New Guinea make craft objects while women fish and process the staple food, sago. But everyone knows how to make coconut baskets as needed.

Since colonisation, the overall cultural value, producer prestige, quality and diversity of traditional arts and crafts has been eroded by commodification. This especially applies to women's prestige goods throughout the Pacific. While most goods have ceremonial and cash value, the emphasis is now on quantity rather than quality, and this has had considerable effect on women's work in particular. While men's status has remained high, because of their seemingly more prominent woodcarving, less value has been assigned to women's arts and crafts, leading to lowering of the status both of women and their work. However, this trend is not necessarily present everywhere in the region and traditional forms of exchange of certain goods has meant that women's crafts continue to be necessary in many Pacific societies, even though there is an overall decline in quality, even in ceremonial goods.

Tonga

According to Phyllis Herda (1995),[54] in Tonga traditional decorated barkcloth (tapa) made from beating the bark pulp of the paperbark mulberry tree, is still considered an important prestigious, ceremonial and economic creation of women. Women's labour (*koloa*) is "wealth, riches or what one values."[55] Men's labour is considered work (*ngaue*). *Koloa* establishes women's status, and influences the rank of the women who make it. Sex and age establish rank: female outranks male, older outranks younger. Women still produce *koloa*, despite changes to the traditional lifestyle through colonisation, and it is still central to social and economic exchange, and has formal economic value. Fine woven mats are also *koloa*; they can be long lasting, and one fine, beautifully woven mat can be more valuable than a large bundle of barkcloth. They can be handed down through generations.

The Philippines

In the Philippines, as Alice Guillermo (1995)[56] explains, weaving has always been women's work with both cultural and economic value. Weavers are "the [traditional] active agents"[57] of clothing, protection and healing in the community through the art and inspired craft of weaving. Woven textiles are "narratives of social and environmental exchange, protecting and unifying the body and spirit of a community." They reflect "the female point of view of cosmological relationships and cultural interactions by creating alternative narratives to those of war and military might."[58] They document everyday life, and challenge the Western colonising notion of 'high art' and 'low' craft.

Norma Respicio (2003)[59] tells us that the implements, materials (yarn, and so forth), and natural dyes define the landscape and demonstrate the people's resourcefulness. Yarns consist of natural fibres such as cotton, bast fibres such as abaca and ramie, pineapple leaf fibres, and silk; and colours are derived from plants, seeds, roots, bark and fruits. Each of these materials has its own spirits or soul, and these become as one new spirit in the new fabric. Female spirits are connected with certain designs and can reside in the fabric, so preparation of the yarn, weaving and dyeing must be perfect in every way.

Imagery includes human figures and the boat (ship) of the dead, as occurs in Indonesia on cloths used in death rituals; the 'wind god' is symbolised by dazzling optical illusionary whirlwind and whirlpool motifs which act to protect men and women from the anger of the wind god. Bird motifs, symbolic crocodiles and/or big lizards, snakes, crabs, frogs, turtles, spider and scorpions all become woven 'vehicles' of the spirits. There are numerous flora and fauna images. Symbols which indicate early contact with East Asia (and the Indo-Europeans) include the horse rider motif, geometric designs with *dong son* curvilinear designs.

Ikat weaving in the Philippines dates to the Philippine Iron Age (2,200 BP). Before this date barkcloth was used, as it was also in Thailand. As in other Oceanic islands, weaving was 'soft' work assigned to women, while 'hard' woodcarving was men's business. Women used geometric designs because of constraints of the woven image; men's designs were curvilinear and floral; the limitations/techniques inherent in weaving and in woodcarving determining the emerging forms of design motifs. Men's woodcarving was considered of a higher status than women's weaving and perhaps this is related to the length of time such materials might last or to Indo-European contact, thus it seems Philippine men enjoy a higher status than women.

Yet the women can pass on their world views and values more easily in woven fabrics than men can with woodcarving. Philippine women in traditional times were always the central powerful mediator between community, spirits and the forces of nature. As weavers women were also priestesses and female spirit healers. Philippine imagery includes natural forms, birds, animals, plants, the heavens, water, sea creatures and so forth. Today, not much domestic cloth is woven as it is mostly commercially produced for low prices, by women who are exploited by colonialist powers. Originally indigenous women were proud of their power as weavers, but today weaving has become the background for their struggle for recognition, self-determination and freedom from exploitation.

Polynesian New Zealand

Maori women

Although Maori culture is relatively young, it has its roots in late Austronesian and Polynesian cultures of the past. One Maori artist, Robyn Kahukiwa,[60] through the search for her own identity, became determined to correct the biased assumptions made by Western researchers about what they see as Maori male dominance. For example, such researchers assume that because men are the public 'face' of Maori societies (apparently making all decisions and creating all the highly publicised art of the sacred carvings), that Maori women are therefore subordinate and have no culture of their own. This biased view unfortunately has had an effect on traditional Maori societies where it has become one factor contributing towards destabilisation of the balance of complementarity between Maori men and women.

That women have an important role to play in all aspects of life is made clear by the myths. Robyn Kahukiwa observes that "although the males are usually the protagonists, the females, by their actions, hold the plot together and provide the knowledge and *aroha* [love] necessary to enable the heroes to perform their deeds and fulfil their tasks." She emphasises that "these *wahine* all have great strength and it is fitting they be accorded the awe and respect which is theirs."[61] All Maori men have strong women alongside them, and nowhere is this seen more clearly than when men make formal public speeches in meetings where decisions are made which affect everyone in the tribe. In this situation women have the power to prompt the speaker, helping him to remember all that must be said; or if he speaks incorrectly or foolishly, they prevent him from further speech by singing a traditional song.

Through a brief look at one Maori cultural practice we may gain some further insights into Pacific Island women's culture. Although it is not recognised as an art form by (usually male) anthropologists, the weaving traditionally created exclusively by highly skilled Maori women is aesthetically beautiful, and in every way an art form. Weaving traditionally involved the use of carved decorated wooden pegs between which the weaving was suspended. These pegs and other items, such as the wooden *waka huia* feather boxes, may have been carved in the past by the women who used them. Contemporary Maori weaving has meanings which go far beyond the function of the item.[62]

In her art, Robyn Kahukiwa is attempting to search out the 'shadowy' Maori women in mythology as part of the process of reclaiming her own Maori identity. In one series of paintings, she appropriates images of carved sacred figures which belong to an exclusively Maori male aspect of culture, in order that the past can be used to correct today's injustices. She believes that not only the Maori as a people, but also Maori women in particular, need empowerment and unity to become a force for good. Robyn Kahukiwa says her work is about "the mana of the people; about strength, energy, dynamism and continuance."[63] She wants Maori mythology to be no longer confined to the domain of children but to regain some of the great meaning for adults, as was the case in the past. She says this might be achieved if people just took the time to read or listen to the myths.[64]

Trying to discover Pacific women's roles and status is problematic; women's cultures, rituals and symbols are there, although little has been known about them until very recently. Pacific women are only now speaking out about themselves and their cultures and it is through their words that one can gain a true perspective. Western colonialism has been responsible for upsetting the harmonious balance between the sexes, and for bias against women which has rendered them invisible in the New World.

Colonisation in the Pacific Region

Zohl dé Ishtar (1994) has recorded the experiences of Pacific Island women speaking about what colonisation has meant for their people since first contact with Europeans. Colonisers such as Britain, Spain and France and, in more recent times, America and Japan, have brought great changes to indigenous life in the Islands. Changes to cultural and religious practices, the loss of language, and the reduced status of women were among the first effects of colonisation. Zohl dé Ishtar gives an example: before colonisation, menstruating and pregnant women were protected from unwanted male attention by laws governing modes of behaviour; after colonisation these laws were gradually broken down, at first by the missionaries, and later were 'distorted' by the imposition of the colonisers' own moral standards. Consequently, women's knowledge of contraception has been disrupted and "[m]odern forms of contraception, for example, have not adequately replaced age old systems."[65]

Later changes included people being removed from homelands to provide space for tourist complexes, military bases, mines and plantations. More recent changes have included political, social and economic programs relating to the nuclear industry wherein unwanted waste can be disposed of in the 'empty' Pacific. For example, nuclear bomb testing at Murorora Atoll and Fangataufa Island by the French in 1966 had terrible effects, including increased levels of cancer; children born with deformities; and ocean poisoning resulting in further deformities, disease and chronic illness. Chailang Palacios[66] considers that these tests were carried out in the Pacific because it is inhabited by Black people and that if only White people lived there, testing would not take place.

Zohl dé Ishtar explains that the result of colonisation, as described by the above women, has been the institutionalised oppression of women, and as this shift moves further into the local populations, there is an increase "in the more 'private' male pursuits of wife bashing, rape, incest, pornography and other crimes."[67] Sue Culling,[68] a Maori, comments that what has been lost is land, language and culture, resulting in

> a warped development and worst of all, the colonisation of people's minds so that they no longer trust their own traditions and history but look to Europe for answers. And Europe has nothing to offer but death.[69]

In the case of Fiji, Indians were brought to the islands between 1879 and 1916 as cheap labour for the British colonisers. The British applied the idea of 'divide-and-rule', keeping the Indians isolated in the cane fields, and the Fijians in the villages, to prevent them from uniting and protesting against their oppression. However, the relations between the two groups have not necessarily been antagonistic. For example, Fijian market women have on occasion protected Indian women by hiding them under their stalls or behind piles of vegetables when youths were rioting. Rusula Buretini[70] states that Fijian women are always strong "but colonisation has placed them second to men."[71] However, now the women are making changes and are working towards regaining equal status.

Zohl dé Ishtar summarises the colonisation experience of the Pacific which she considers echoes that of Old Europe where

> the people [were] subdued through massacres and bloodshed; the land stolen and violated; women raped and devalued; the spiritual belief of the Earth as a dynamic force denigrated; a foreign culture imposed; the language, oral traditions and cultural practices banned; and many men seduced by the promises of male domination.[72]

It is difficult to compare the symbolic life of cultures in South-East Asia and the Pacific region with those of the female-centred Old European societies beyond observing the similarity of ritual symbols (although not necessarily their meanings). It would seem that women were as important in the Southern Hemisphere as in the North until Indo-European ideas and practices were introduced. Since then the female principle has been subverted and the women of this part of the world have become dominated and made invisible by the legacy of the Proto-Indo-Europeans from southern Russia, just as they had in the Northern Hemisphere.

CHAPTER 17

NEW WORLDS: THE AMERICAS

The earliest civilisations in the Americas were present long before the well-known 2,000-year-old Mayan and Toltec civilisations, while the Aztecs and the Incas were not on the scene until shortly before European invasion in 1492. The communities and civilisations of North and South America are as diverse as their environment which ranges from sub-arctic to tropical and hot desert.

The First People of the Americas

North America was one of the last land masses to be settled by modern humans. No traces of *Homo habilis* or *Homo erectus* have been found anywhere on the American continents,[1] although signs of their occupation could well have been lost when covered by the rising seas during the melting of the ice around 12,000 BP. Tom Dillehay (2008)[2] tells us that the earliest evidence of human occupation so far has been found along the west coast of South America dating to between 15,000 and 13,000 BP. (A more recent date is 14,600 BP for the earliest occupation at Monte Verde in southern Chile, according to Tom Dillehay,[3] while an earlier controversial date of 15,500 BP for stone tool evidence in the Buttermilk Creek area has recently been argued by Michael R. Waters et al.[4]) Cold, dry ice-covered land, water shortages and great distances meant that the only place humans could cross was over the Bering Strait after 50,000 BP. During this period the sea level was lower than it is today, exposing a grassy, swampy land which originally joined Alaska with Siberia. Known as 'Beringia', this country could support large animals suitable for humans to hunt until it later vanished under the waves. The first and second migrations were groups of Palaeo-Indian nomadic big-game hunters from Siberia who lived in small peaceful communities. They would have entered via Beringia until the seas rose again, removing all evidence of their occupation.

Only in the past 20 years or so has the prehistory of the Americas begun to be more thoroughly studied using modern technologies, so many of the dates in the following timeline could change in the future as new evidence appears. Brian Fagan (1991b)[5] presents one interesting piece of evidence which suggests that the first migration of people may have come from two different sites in Siberia: the (non-Asian) people from Mal'ta (originally from the Ukraine) with a 'unifacial edge-trimmed' stone tool tradition; and (Asian) people from Dyukhtai (with Mongolian origins) who used 'bifacial tradition' stone tools.

A Timeline and Prehistory of the Americas

BP	NORTH AMERICA	EVIDENCE	MESO-AMERICA	SOUTH AMERICA	EVIDENCE
22,000	First people (open to revision)				• Stone tools; date unreliable
15,000	Yukon, Alaska	• Siberia: Dyukhtai tradition (Asian) stone tools			
14,600–13,000				**First people:** hunter-gatherers, fishers (non-Asian) west coast	• Stone tools, unifacial edge-trimmed tradition came via Bering Strait from Siberia to southern Chile
12,500				Patagonia	• Wood, stone artefacts
11,500	**First people** (Asian)	• Bifacial tradition stone tools • Highly mobile small bands exploit varied environments • Small game hunter-gatherers, fishers		Second migration Clovis culture	• Fine stone arrows/spear points, bifacial tradition • Figurative paintings • Waisted polished stone axe
11,000–10,000				Chile	• Fishing nets, huts, seeds, tools, cord, baskets
10,000–9,000	Clovis culture	• Mammoth hunters where megafauna available		Proto Archaic culture	• Settlements along shorelines • Wooden tools • Plant cultivation, basketry, clothes, maps • Large coastal settlements, fishing nets (Chile), circular stone foundations for huts • Use of controlled burning
9,000–5,000				Atacama Desert	• Mummification of the dead
8,000	Palaeo-Indians	• Diversified activities in response to local conditions • Temporary shelters, bones, more stone tools	Palaeo-Indians Mexico	Palaeo-Indians Peru Ecuador	• Andes – mummification, plant cultivation • Maize growing, non-Asian bones in cave
7,000		• Sandstone querns, roasting pits used over many years • Controlled burning to promote new growth • Large corrals to catch bison		Patagonia	• Men's clothes – breech cloths; women's clothes – grass skirts • Clay figurines, wall paintings, engravings • Ceramic cultures, pottery
6,600–6,000		• Mortars and pestles, basketry, obsidian trade networks • Circular stone foundations for tepees or lodges • Peaceful co-operative groups		Ecuador Valdivia	• Carved, decorated gourds for storage • Larger settlements. Small circular huts surround central area. • Distinctive pottery • Female figurines of generous proportions

BP	NORTH AMERICA	EVIDENCE	MESO-AMERICA	SOUTH AMERICA	EVIDENCE
5,000	Archaic cultures	• Wood and stone artisans, pottery • Some settled, some mobile groups	Archaic hunter-gatherers	Peru, Caral Uruguay	• Peaceful pyramid city • Irrigation-grown cotton and woven goods • Mound building begins. Burial mounds?
4,500	Bison hunters			Amazonia	• Tutishcainyo, Saladoid, Barrancoid traditions • Complex pottery vessels, clay griddles, pottery figurines, female and male
4,000	East Woodland people		Contact with Chinese visitors		
4,000	Most parts of North America	• Settlements, some are male dominant, most are peaceful • A time of abrupt changes, advanced woodwork and craft skills • New art traditions, hierarchic large populations 'advanced' social and political organisation (time of patriarchal ideologies/ practices?)	Olmecs settlements trade kaolin figurines, ceramics, monumental stone carvings Violent end	Brazil El Paraseo	• Mound building, some large, some used for burials have bone and shell jewellery and utility items • Beginning of patriarchal period? Extensive changes to social organisation, cultural and ritual practices. These changes occurred earlier in the north. (Could be the result of contact with Han Chinese landing in Mexico around 4,000 BP as recorded by Alice B. Kehoe?[6])
3,000	Adena mound builders		San Jose Magote farming villages	Sechen Alto	
1,500	Anasazi	• Grave goods			
(CE) 100	Adena (end) Followed by: Anasazi Hopewell Hohokam Mimbres		Teotihuacan, Monte Alban, Olmecs and Preclassic Maya	Twanaku, Chavin Da, Huautar, Nayca, Moche, Huari, Nayca (end) and Moche (end)	
600	Hopewell (end)		Monte Alban (end), Preclassic Maya, Classic Maya	Huari (also called Wari)	• The most documented period in Mesoamerica/North America is also the most violent. Former women-centred peaceful clans had to fight for survival. Most in North and South did not want war.

287

BP	NORTH AMERICA	EVIDENCE	MESO-AMERICA	SOUTH AMERICA	EVIDENCE
900	Mississippian		Teotihuacan (end) Classic Maya	Huari (end)	
1200	Mississippian (end)		Toltecs Chichen Itza Aztecs	Tiwanaku (end); Chimú (end) Incas	
1492	Christopher Columbus arrives				
1500		• Colonising patriarchal practices replaced former ways of peace	Aztecs (end)	Incas (end)	• Colonising patriarchal practices replaced former ways of peace

Around 13,000 BP the first people from Mal'ta who came to South America were expert hunters, foragers and fishers. They appear to have travelled south along the coastline, bypassing mainland North America to settle on the west coast of South America. Around 11,500 BP the second migration occurred, this time to North America, by people from Dyukhtai who were highly mobile Palaeo-Indian mammoth hunters equipped with efficient lightweight spears.

Both groups were very adaptable, with the ability to successfully respond to the many varied environments which they encountered. While stone tools were readily preserved, other tools were extremely perishable and only found in exceptional circumstances. Hence, the following timeline has limited detail but enough to provide a brief overview.

North America

In the Arctic, the first humans from Mal'ta in Siberia had settled only along the shores of Alaska. Later, small groups of musk-ox hunters from Dyukhtai went to the east following the shores of the Arctic Ocean into an area of numerous islands known as the Canadian archipelago.

Kalyan Chakravarty and Robert Bednarik (1997)[7] record evidence which includes cupules and grooves found in North America along the west coast from Alaska to Mexico, which are possibly the country's oldest art dated to 13,000 BP. Researchers say this is possible because the first settlers could have travelled to South America via the Aleutian Islands, passing from island to island by water craft.[8]

Around 11,500 BP, the second group, who used the bifacial tradition, became the first North Americans, entering the continent via the inland. Their tradition is known as the Clovis culture – so called because of the shape of their distinctive tools, beautifully made arrowheads, named after the town of Clovis in New Mexico near where they were first found. According to Brian Fagan (1991b),[9] the hunters killed quite large animals with these spears. Clovis arrowheads from both North and South America were similar to those used in Eastern Europe and the Ukraine.[10] Clovis hunter-gatherers tracked and hunted the herds of mammoth and bison, using every part of the animals – hides, tusks, bones and pelts – for

NORTH AMERICA: DESIGNS AND SCULPTURAL FORMS

1. An interesting *engraved wall design motif* similar to the earlier example from China (Source: Heizer, Robert, and Martin Baumhoff, 1962)
2. Various *circle, spiral and meander motifs in Native American rock paintings or engravings* (Source: Petroglyphs.US., 2010)
3. *Incised medicine bags on rock wall* (Source: Petroglyphs.US., 2010a)

4a. and b. *Two 'keeper-of-animals' spirits incised on rock*
5. *Early Woodland pottery figure, 3,000–2,500 BP*
6. *Shaman's rattler frog*, pipestone
7. *Carved female figure tilling the snake-earth*
8. *Early Woodland engraved pottery bowl* (Source 5–8: Illinois State Museum, 2000)

All line drawings © Judy Foster, 2013

the household, for weapons, for shelter and clothing. Their fat was melted down to burn in lamps. All Native Americans, Indigenous Mesoamericans and South Americans are apparently descended from these Ice Age hunters from Mal'ta and Dyukhtai.

Robert Bednarik (1995)[11] mentions artefacts, such as very faded 10,000-year-old figurative paintings which have been found in South America, as well as a piece of a pigment ball which may have been worn as an ornament, dated to 13,000 BP. Pieces of pottery dated to 9,000 BP, and a fine-waisted and polished olive-grey granodiorite axe, have also been found.

Christian Feest (1992)[12] notes that early humans had to be adaptable because of slowly occurring environmental changes taking place in different parts of the continent. As the Ice Age came to an end, the changing climate caused the extinction of some large game, such as mammoths, mastodons, fossil bison and wild horses, leaving only the smaller animals. This occurred at the same time as other large animals disappeared in Europe, Eurasia and Australia. Horses were not present again in the Americas until the Europeans arrived in 1492.

The descendants of the Clovis hunters, the Palaeo-Indians and later Archaic societies, had varied lifestyles. Plains hunters continued to hunt bison while those in desert areas harvested seasonal plants and hunted small game. Others living near water sources, marshes, lakes, rivers or along the sea coast became more sedentary and developed more complex cultures because of the rich food resources. Brian Fagan describes the eastern Woodlands people, for example, as hunting deer and other game and taking advantage of the availability of wood for building, food resources, and household needs. Hunter-gatherers understood their local environment, and worked together for the good of the whole clan, their aim being to live sustainably for the long term.

According to Andrew H. Whiteford and S.Z. Herbert (2002)[13] the earliest Native North American arts, such as basketry, pottery and textiles, appear around 9,000 BP. Basketry included plaited, twined and coiled methods. Deep baskets coated with resin were used for carrying water; and tightly woven baskets were used for cooking. The earliest pottery occurred in the south-east at 9,000 BP, and later in the central and eastern regions. It was created via the 'coil and paddle' technique, still traditionally used today.[14] Textiles at this time included "rush mats and fibre sandals"[15] made by both women and men. Other techniques included fabric weaving (in the south-west), finger weaving, and spinning of wild animal hair over the thigh. Back-strap looms and vertical looms appeared somewhat later.

At one cave site on the American central plains, Brian Fagan records artefacts which reveal something about Native American culture of this region between 9,500 and 6,000 BP. These include stones incised with patterns of nets, 'V'-shapes, parallel lines, and notches, and anthropomorphic figurines made from 'Y'-shaped twigs, rush leaves, and string. Various woven objects, such as both coiled and twined baskets, winnowing baskets, and nets for snares, were used. Men's tool kits featured spear throwers, stone-tipped and wooden spears, stone-tipped knives and scrapers, while women's tools included awls, needles, and grinding stones and mortars. Foods eaten included ground seeds, and nuts. They wore clothing, such as fur and leather cloaks and sandals, all of which were created by women.

Brian Fagan suggests that the communal status of the hunter-gatherer Palaeo-Indian cultures was vital to their well-being (as it was to Australian Indigenous people). The precontact North American population consisted of 500 clans with 200 languages, similar to the numbers of Indigenous clans in Australia.

At 5,500 BP, north-west coast people lived a complex and settled lifestyle in permanent large villages. They worked stone and wood with great expertise, producing split, cut and bent timber for various uses, and were capable of splitting 30-metre-long trees for house planks, or constructing boxes from steamed and scored planks, sculpting wooden oil bowls and stools, and making an ingenious variety of tool handles. Boxes were decorated with incised and painted designs comprised of local animals, such as bears, beavers, birds, seals, whales and wolves, and in the forms of supernatural beings and mythical ancestors.

The land mass of North America contained many different and often challenging environments and, as a result, Native American clans were often unable to live in large sedentary groups as people did in South America, because of food availability. By 4,500 BP some Native Americans of the plains had become expert bison hunters who built artificial corrals, often situated in low-lying streams and hidden from the bison they were stampeding until the last minute. Christian Feest notes that over time lifestyles gradually became more settled which allowed the making of pottery, and the carrying out of elaborate burial rituals. The East Woodland people, for example, began to cultivate staple food plants about 4,000 years ago, then eventually as their populations further expanded, large-scale crops, such as maize and beans, were grown to supplement the hunter-gatherer diet.

Around 3,000 BP some clans began to bury their dead in funeral mounds. These burial grounds were placed on natural ridges above rivers, which were traditionally associated with mythical and human ancestors. Brian Fagan (1991a)[16] records that the Adena people of the Ohio area (and the related Hopewell people of the Illinois area) had elaborate burial practices, and those for high-status people were quite spectacular, consisting of enormous earthworks. Sophisticated grave goods indicated similar cultural, social and political organisation. Local plants were cultivated, alongside hunting, fishing and gathering practices. It was around this time (4,000 BP) that contact with East Asia occurred in Mesoamerica (Mexico and Central America).

With the fading out of East Asian male-dominant ideologies of the Hopewell cultures after 400 CE, new societies evolved (or arrived) in the Mississippi River Valley. Burial mound traditions were increasingly influenced by Mesoamerican ideas and practices involving new and unusual materials, foods and ritual imagery. Corn was now widely grown, ceremonies became more elaborate, and the arts flourished.

Native American social organisations became more sophisticated, small towns appeared, tribal confederations were formed, and centralised chiefdoms became increasingly common where environmental conditions allowed. The title 'chief' did not necessarily carry the Western meaning in Native American societies but referred to the spokesperson for the clan who may have been female or male. Christian Feest also assumes the presence of military practices, but as Native American Paula Gunn Allen (1986)[17] explains, although after 3,000 BP a few Native American clans did become warlike, most remained peaceful and women-centred. Where individual male initiates did fight each other, these duels were not competitive in the same sense as in Western clan warfare, but were a part of each man's ritual of initiation, and strictly controlled by the councils (much like Australian Indigenous fighting rules).

By 2,000 BP, certain Native American societies became class-based, with the chief as the head, and some elite office holders, while shamans and commoners had the least power. These societies began to quarrel over land and food supplies and this eventually led to warfare.

First Peoples of North America

Paula Gunn Allen notes that, according to Native American historian, anthropologist and author D'Arcy McNickle

> at least 70 per cent of the tribes were pacifist, and the tribes that lived in peacefulness as a way of life were always women-centered, always gynocentric, always agricultural, always sedentary … and always the children of egalitarian, peace-minded, ritual, and dream/vision-centered female gods.[18]

Paula Gunn Allen's informants speak for a number of tribes including the Cherokee, Iroquois, Pueblo, Navajo, Hopi, Abanaki, Crow, Pomo and Kiowa, and South American Bari and Mapuche tribes, but there were many others.

When history books assume that Native American states and political systems were similar to the hierarchic patriarchal Western systems they could not be more mistaken. Powers of law and decision-making were held by councils composed of 'men's councils' and 'matrons' councils'. The 'matrons' (senior women) were the ceremonial centre of the system and therefore the decision-makers in matters of policy. Native Americans framed power as "supernatural and paranormal, a matter of spirit involvement and destiny."[19] Moreover, women's power could only be directed and controlled by other women of equal power – usually older women. Young women were trained by older women to use their power carefully so as not to harm anyone. Women who showed unusual attributes could become medicine women.

European colonisation so affected the Native American societies that they could no longer be the cooperative, autonomous, and peaceful people they were in the past. Their social systems had in the main been balanced by complementary institutions and organised relationships and these were so radically changed by the new patriarchal influences that they became dysfunctional. The male-dominant secular-based colonisers almost completely destroyed the social and political status of Native American men, whose previous status had depended upon their ritual and political relationship to clan women (whose own status had a spiritual base). Even the Plains men, who have long been thought of as the most patriarchal, received their power through women's influence.

Traditional Native American life as we know it today is based on contact with the Spanish invaders who brought widespread violence, and the horse, to the Americas in 1492. Christian Feest argues that these basic changes led to a new kind of nomadic and competitive way of life in North America, where the sedentary farming tribes lost advantage to the small bands of roving raiders.

Native American oral traditions

As is the case for Australian Indigenous people, for Native Americans stories are truths, and mythic stories are an important and unique dimension of human expression. They describe ideal or actual human capacities with a special sense of reality, re-creating and renewing Native Americans' relationship to the universe. The most informative commentators concerning precontact indigenous cultures today are the people themselves. According to Paula Gunn Allen Native American societies were kept from total destruction by their strong oral traditions which continue to contribute to their survival. Oral traditions which preserve clan identity, spiritual traditions, and connection to the land and its creatures, provide the basis for Native American resistance to cultural takeover and assimilation by non-indigenous America.

So much of the oral traditions and knowledge, only known to certain initiated people, has been lost. It is not only women's position, but also Native American oral traditions and cultural practices which have been undermined and almost destroyed by Western cultures. Native American women were responsible for the preservation and use of oral traditions but these teachings have rarely been properly appreciated or examined in context by Euro-Americans. The destruction of the context of their oral traditions runs parallel to the loss of status previously held by women.

In the Native American world everything is regarded as interconnected, everything relates to everything else. Many Native American societies recognise an important deity, 'the Great All-Spirit', who is female. Female-centred power fostered people to live in peace and harmony with the spirits and one another. This also meant that selected clan members (women or men) had rights to certain knowledge and rituals, but there were some rituals and knowledge which everyone could share. These women-centred clans were spiritually based. In Mohawk clans, for example, women were the decision makers. In the Council Longhouse, the 'clan mothers' (women past menopause) would sit on one side, while the chiefs (women or men) were on the other; the clan mothers made decisions and the men spoke on their behalf. Native American men respected women, and men's and women's work was highly valued. Paula Gunn Allen states that, in fact, the mother or matron was the highest position which could be achieved.[20]

Paula Gunn Allen states that within the Native American world view the spiritual centre was female, known by "many names and many emblems."[21] She explains that the Great Spirit is everywhere and is owed everything: life, thought, balance, harmony and ordered relationships. It is offensive and demeaning to women to refer to the Great Spirit as a 'fertility goddess' since she fulfils a far greater role in the lives of Native Americans. She is known as 'Thought Woman', although she fills other roles in Keres theology. Thought Woman is both mother and father to all living things, and wishes her people to live in peace, so the Keres people are traditionally non-violent and non-hostile. Everyone was equal in Keres society, and it was the women who saw to fair and equal distribution of goods and services among men, women and children.

Paula Gunn Allen explains the relationship of Keres people to the land: "We are the land, and the land is mother to us all."[22] There are two principles: the male principle which is transitory, that is, "it dies and is reconstituted"; and the female principle which is permanent, "immanent and present in the earth (minerals, crystals, stones, wood) and in water."[23] He is transient, she is permanent.

There are several important aspects of the Keres world view. Firstly, a Keres person has a dynamic, creative and responsive place in creation which allocates equivalent or even greater privileges to all things, including animals, vegetables, minerals – and humans. Secondly, for Keres people, space is talked about as circular, and time too is cyclic.[24] Paula Gunn Allen explains that Native Americans tend "to view space as spherical and time as cyclical, whereas the non-Indian tends to view space as linear and time as sequential."[25] This circularity means that all things have a necessary and significant function.

1

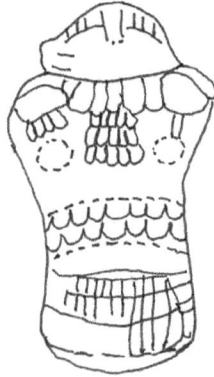
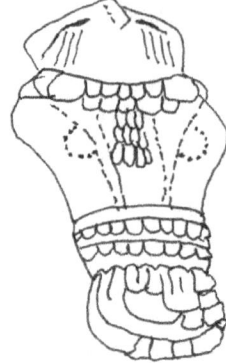

2 a   b   c

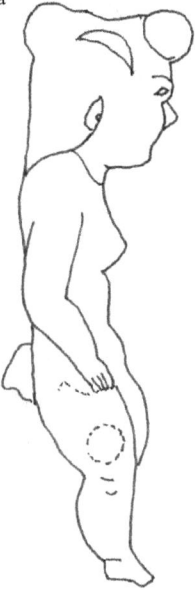
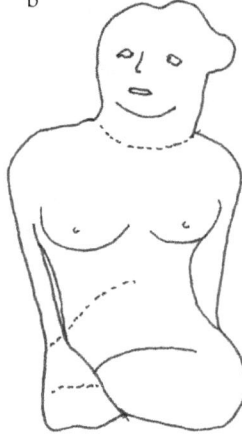
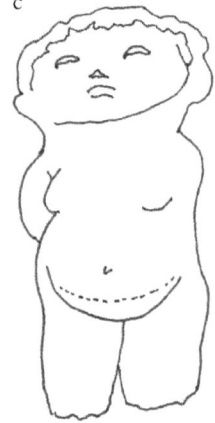

NORTH AMERICA: FEMALE FIGURINES

1. *Three unfired clay figurines* from Utah, the
   Fremont culture
   (Source: Wikipedia contributors, 2012)
2a. *Illinois figurine*, date unknown
  b. *Louisiana figurine*, 3,500 BP
  c. *Georgia figurine*, date unknown
   (Source: Dashu, Max, 2008, poster)

(According to Max Dashu there is very little
information about these female figurines,
although the Louisiana figurine was found in an
important archaeological site at Poverty Point.)
All line drawings © Judy Foster, 2013

Conflict resolution

Paula Gunn Allen speaks of the role of hand-to-hand combat as a means of resolving conflict in Native American societies. The Keres, for example, so hated war that in very early times any antagonism between people or groups was dealt with through ritual institutions, just as is the case in Australian Indigenous societies. There were rituals to purify those who had taken part in warfare, especially if someone had been killed. This was to make sure that sickness would not infect the people, the land or its creatures, and droughts would not occur. It was important for people to belong; if they were removed from their community for severe violations of laws they had to be ritually reinstated to be recognised again as clan members.

Although fighting was controlled and ritualised as a male shamanistic practice in Native American societies, its purpose was less about power over others than it was about endowing each Native American warrior with certain spiritual powers. It did not matter whether the warriors won or lost; they still gained sacred power.

A Native American man's near encounters with death in war were an important part of his initiation, leading to direct participation in his transformation. Because of women's menstruation and birth giving, they had ready access to transformative power. Women's rituals were concerned with continuity. They received increased sacred power as they reached each of the four female life phases (first initiation at puberty; marriage; childbirth; menopause).

The role of the shamans

According to Paula Gunn Allen (1986) shamans could be men or women, performing similar roles and dispensing certain knowledge to all suitable others, with some knowledge being kept to themselves or taught to apprentices, and some shared with other shamans. We have already seen how important they were as spiritual councillors among the leaders in the councils.[26] In Brian Fagan's account, it is assumed that the role of the shaman was always performed by a male who always operated under drug-induced trances, and taught 'fictional' creation 'legends' rather than myths with their truths. The implication is that this no longer takes place in more recent post contact societies. He also states that the descendants of these male shamans were to become the "mighty Lords and priest Kings"[27] of the later Aztec and Inca kingdoms, which no doubt was true, but he does not point out that these later Mesoamerican cultures only occupied a small niche within the whole of the Americas.

Brian Fagan assumes that precontact male shamans also played a pivotal role in the growing of plants, establishing the right time for planting and harvesting, and for their associated fertility and initiation ceremonies. However, in most other areas this role was usually filled by female shamans because of women's traditional horticultural and agricultural knowledge.

'Invisible' Indigenous women of the Americas: Colonisation and appropriation

Paula Gunn Allen's account of contemporary Native American cultural values is especially important in providing a balanced, informed view of the invisible lives of America's indigenous peoples, in particular the women who are rarely consulted by (usually) male researchers. According to Alice Kehoe (1998)[28] little has changed since the reporting of the typical 19th-century typical view of all women (including Africans, Native Americans, and radical labour leaders) as unable to reason. There are still many assumptions made concerning the 'primitive' nature of prehistoric American cultures even today, especially those present before the much publicised Incas and Aztecs (neither of these 'civilisations' occurred until after the first century CE).

A few male and most female researchers today are more aware of the indigenous knowledge base which would provide a more accurate picture of prehistoric and contemporary indigenous life in the Americas. A number of women have been prepared to consult directly with the people who know the stories. But women who wish to work with Native American nations generally remain outside the archaeological mainstream. As Alice Kehoe explains, "it took the Native American Grave Protection and Repatriation Act, 1990, to persuade many male Euro-American archaeologists to recognise whose history they work in."[29] Because some female archaeologists have been sensitive to Native American cultures, a cohort of male archaeologists consider them to be emotional, weak, and too concerned with personal relationships, and regard their work as subjective rather than 'pure' objective science. Because they insist on truthful accounts gained through living with the clans, female archaeologists help to prevent the usual portrayal of Native Americans as a 'primitive' and vanishing group "doomed by its cultural retardation to conquest and domination."[30]

Starhawk (1998)[31] speaks of the similar experiences of cultural and identity appropriation of the Native American communities as for Australian Indigenous people. Native Americans have become increasingly angry when Euro-Americans take rituals, chants, myths, and sacred objects out of their context, diluting their meanings, making financial gain or dishonestly claiming unearned authority and expertise over them. Euro-Americans often wrongly assume that the traditions of Native Americans are "sadly but safely dead"[32] and so can be freely adapted for other purposes. By raising the cultural appropriation issue Native Americans can proclaim that their culture is still very much alive.

Since colonisation, Native American identity has been manipulated: the colonisers' priority was to remove women's powers to ensure that all memory of the precontact gynocratic Native American cultural identity was obliterated (although they could never destroy it completely since woman-centred societies still exist today). According to Paula Gunn Allen there are still those Euro-Americans who categorise Native Americans as either 'the noble savage' or 'the hostile savage'. The first stereotype portrays a 'doomed victim' of the evolution of humans from primitive to 'civilised', and accordingly the Native American is a victim who has to 'assimilate or perish'. The second stereotype underlies the deeply embedded fiction in the American unconscious that 'Indians' were always bloodthirsty, fierce and cruel, freely slaughtering 'innocent' colonists and pioneers; this thinking influences the social oppression of "the other."[33] According to Jared Diamond (1991),[34] yet another stereotype is the idea of "fierce mounted warriors"[35] of the Great Plains who 'terrorised' their neighbours, which really only took hold during the period from 1660 to 1770, and even then was in response to European colonisation rather than Native American tribal expansion. Native Americans, like Australian Indigenous people, traditionally stayed on their own lands. These same Euro-Americans today see modern Native Americans as 'worthless', 'lazy', 'alcoholics,' not willing to progress and prosper to achieve the 'American dream'.[36] As long as such attitudes exist there can be little opportunity for change.

Matrilineal/matriarchal societies in North America

As a member of the Bear Clan of the Ohio Seneca Iroquois, Barbara Alice Mann (2009)[37] argues that traditionally the political, economic, spiritual and social roles of clan mothers were accepted by all eastern Nations (and still are by traditional people). The Mound Builders, "an ancient North American culture",[38] emerged around 5,000 BP. Their priests ruled "through terror and brutality ... [specialising] in spiritual terrorism, waged wars, controlled all commodities, and gang-raped young women."[39] Then a law ensuring peace between all was agreed upon in the 9th century CE by voters belonging to the Seneca, Cayuga, Onondaga, Oneida, and Mohawk Nations following the settlement of a long-running war with the violent, patriarchal and aggressive priests of the Mound Builders, who had claimed power 2,500 years before.

Eventually, in the 9th century some of the people left the Mound Builders, led by a clan mother, and moved to the Quebec area, then later, to the eastern New York area. Another clan mother led the future Attiwendaronk[40] people to Ontario, and this group formed an agricultural 'government' based on the sharing of power between women and men.

According to Barbara Alice Mann, the rules which were decided by consensus included three principles. These three foundational principles were: The will of the people was sacred, "high ethics", and "public health and public welfare." In addition to this:
- "women were the *sole* [local] councillors"
- "women were the *sole* keepers of peace and war"
- "the *sole* keepers of Mother Earth"
- "the *sole* keepers of lineages and names."[41]

The clan mother was "wise, quick, intelligent and forceful."[42] Collaboration between women and men was based on a cyclic concept "that Two make One, One cannot exist alone, to have One, there has to be Two first."[43] All existing things are at once 'independent yet interdependent', for instance, "male and female, farm and forest, day and night, youth and old age."[44] They are not dualities as in Western thought, but one half of the other. Each person "has two spirits within, a sky spirit for her father, and an earth spirit for her mother."[45]

Like Paula Gunn Allen, Barbara Alice Mann agrees that Native American wars were not the same as Western wars, but were more like martial arts, with ritualised contests between male protagonists of equal size, weight and skill level. It was similar for women who had their own "martial arts competitions."[46] If participants were killed or badly injured it was considered a disaster. Wise grandmothers 'governed' the cultures and settled disputes by facilitating discussion and negotiation between the opposing clan grandmothers. Another law included the right of women and children to peace, safety and security. Everything was shared, and this was made certain by the women, who controlled and distributed goods and services for all.

The symbolic arts of the Native North Americans

Janet Berlo and Ruth B. Phillips (1998) record that for Native Americans "all artistic creation involves the utilisation of materials in which power may reside, including wood, stones, grasses, and pigments."[47] This applies equally to a woman "making a basket out of grass fibre or a man carving wood from a living tree ... [I]t is impossible to draw a line between what is sacred and what is secular."[48] They argue that in the Native American world view, women's and men's activities are complementary to each other as two parts of a whole. However, men usually carve wood or stone, while women create using clay, fibre and basketry.

Just as in some Australian Indigenous societies, in Native American societies today (as it was in the past) the act of preparing leather for clothing and the weaving of baskets is intimately linked with the telling of women's stories and the passing down of sacred knowledge to the next generation. The making of baskets symbolises the circle which reinforces the solidarity of the clan. According to Paula Gunn Allen (1986), basket making was a special act for Native American women. Women only became basket makers when they reached the proper age, and then it was taught by a spirit teacher. The most sacred Pomo baskets made under these conditions held psychic and spiritual power, were created under the direction of the maker's spirit guide, and could only be given as a gift by the maker/owner, and never bought or sold by the new owner. David Guss (1998),[49] commenting on South American baskets, notes that their true symbolic meanings can only be considered within their cultural context, as they provide an expression of Native American spiritual concept of the universe.

Franz Boas (1928/1955)[50] refers to basket and pottery making in the Americas as women's arts (although in certain circumstances men might also make them), and woodwork as a men's art, in early societies. Depending on the materials available, Native Americans made most utensils, carriers and storage containers out of wood or basketry. Examples include boxes, buckets, kettles, cradles and dishes. Pottery was a later innovation because it was too heavy to be carried by people who were constantly on the move.[51] When the clans became sedentary, women began to make pottery using rolled coils of clay in a similar fashion to using fibre in the making of baskets. (Although Franz Boas, like other researchers of the time, described basketry and pottery as 'women's arts', when describing the method of making a basket or pot, he always referred to the maker as male when giving examples of the rhythmic complexity of their creation.)

Symbolic geometric shapes and colours were used in the creation of Native American sand paintings. According to Franz Boas, in the case of the Cheyenne, certain colours relating to the deities were: *green*, symbolising growth and development; *yellow*, maturity and perfection; and *red*, life and good fortune. These colours may not have carried the same meanings for every tribe, and nor would the geometric shapes. Also the meanings of geometric shapes would not necessarily be the same in every design. For example, a triangle might represent a woman's pubic covering in one instance, or a flying bat in another. Other symbols used in many combinations include such motifs as stars, spirals, meanders, circles, squares and zigzags, and these were used as border designs on garments, basketry, and pottery, sand paintings, in rock art, on men's tools and other objects. All motifs had meaning, and were often part of a narrative. Imagery could also include geometric and figurative representations of living creatures, anthropomorphic and zoomorphic motifs, and sculptures, and masks.

Leatherwork was of a superb standard. Women spent much time curing and preparing soft leather for garments worn by all the clan. Garments could be decorated with coloured motifs, have seeds, shells or beads attached, or have coloured stitching, fringing or other decoration applied, according to the purpose for which they might be used, or as a mark of the status of the wearer. Strong leather boxes decorated with imagery were also made for storage. Women's sacred objects, such as Pomo baskets, were specially woven and were usually decorated with whatever beautiful objects were available.

Rock art included similar motifs. Robert Heizer and Martin Baumhoff (1962)[52] describe the petroglyphs they studied as being pictographic narratives. For the ordinary viewer, they would seem to represent a symbolic language, as they can include repetitive images which could be linear images of humans in a variety of actions, as well as animals and other objects. These images should be understood as the ritual aspect of hunting. Only the people who used them could know the meanings of abstract imagery. Perhaps, like Australian Indigenous petroglyphs and rock paintings, they were used as prompts for telling stories of the hunt, or creation stories.

Mesoamerica

The Olmec culture

The Olmec culture which emerged in Mesoamerica around 3,500 BP, appeared at a time when small villages gradually developing into large settlements which were built on the first gravel platforms of the region. Trade with other centres brought in materials, such as basalt, greenstone and obsidian. By 3,250 BP unusual kaolin figurines, ceramics and monumental stone carvings first appeared.

Brian Fagan (1991a) describes one city belonging to the emerging Olmec culture which came to a violent end just as had so many cities and societies. San Lorenzo was a city built on an artificial platform rising 50 metres above the river basin. A rectangular courtyard, a group of mounds, and small pyramids had been constructed on the summit of the platform. This was most likely a centre for ceremonies, marked as it was by eight Asian-influenced huge stone heads and several throne-like stone monuments, many of them brought from basalt quarries 80 kilometres away. By 2,700 BP these monuments had been damaged, possibly during a violent takeover of the site. Mesoamerica, with its warlike hierarchic 'civilisations', was the region most influenced by Eurasian/Indo-European ideas and practices; in all other regions of the Americas the societies were more peaceful. This evidence supports Joseph Needham's and Alice Kehoe's[53] convictions that migrants from Asia arrived in the region around 4,000–3,000 BP.

Matrilineal/matriarchal societies in Mesoamerica

Dona Enriqueta Contreres (2005)[54] explains that her people, the Zatopecs ('People of the Clouds'), live 2,700 metres above sea level in pine forests near Oaxaca City in Mexico. They have preserved, and continue to maintain, their spiritual life, the practice of their traditional medicines, and their communal lifestyle. They have maintained their mother tongue in the face of widespread use of the colonial Spanish language. The sacred law contains four principles: everything has life; Mother Nature is revered; ancestors are revered; and they recognise a special relationship between people and nature. There is equality between communities and between women and men.

All people deserve and value respect. This attitude is passed on to the children, leading to mutual respect between family and the community. Presumably this means that disputes are settled through discussion and mutual agreement as in many other indigenous societies, and aggression punished through ritual means. She states that everyone "works together ... on any project that is taken on for the benefit of the community."[55] Women and men have the same rights; and the village elders assign certain duties to women.

Dona Enriqueta Contreres suggests that, for a peaceful world future, it is the women who must initiate change and restore respect for nature. She asserts that we are "mentally, physically and spiritually ... all one ... [and] we must take back [our] authority."[56]

South America

Tom Dillehay (2008)[57] mentions some controversy as to whether the first people to come to South America arrived on the west coast in 17,000 BP, 15,000 BP or 11,000 BP, while Rodrigo Navarrete (2008)[58] argues for first arrivals to the northern coastline of Venezuela where evidence of stone tools, apparently 20,000 years old, have been found. However, a date of 13,000 BP seems to have general acceptance by most researchers in *The Handbook of South American Archaeology* (2008).[59] According to Tom Dillehay, the climate of South America 20,000 years ago was much colder than today, and sea levels were approximately one metre lower, so more fertile coastal land was exposed, and this would have allowed people to easily move down the coastlines. It would also have ensured that most of the evidence left by those first people did not survive.

The first (non-Asian) South American people to settle on the western coast in Columbia were small-game hunters, foragers and fishers who prospered in the coastal environment. Tom Dillehay states that particular plants were grown for food, and fire was used to clear land for more plant growth. By 10,000 BP crops were grown in some areas. He notes two kinds of tools: the earlier type were edge-trimmed and found along Peruvian coastlines; while later, after another migration, the bifacial projectile points of the mammoth hunters were found in southern Chile. Here there were no large animals because of the dry climate and environment, so people also lived along the coast and by rivers and lakes. Fishing grounds were rich and extensive, and hunters sought seals, walrus, whales, fish and shellfish. In fact, hunting and fishing were predominant all the way along the coastlines of both North and South America over a very long period.

Tom Dillehay considers that the earliest human activity in Patagonia, the most southern region, occurred at 12,500 BP, and evidence consists of wood and stone artefacts found in caves. Also in caves are wall engravings, finger markings, and incised lines dated to between 10,000 and 7,000 BP. Wall paintings include hand negatives and images of guanacos (similar to alpacas or lamas). Some paintings in the Cueva de las Manos cave have a possible date of 9,320 BP.

From 10,000–6,600 BP people of the Las Vegas culture (a major archaeological site on the coast of Ecuador)[60] grew maize on the slopes of the Andes, and made carved decorated gourd utensils for storage. By 6,600–6,000 BP in Ecuador, the climate along the Andes was tropical from sea to summit as far south as the Peruvian border. Rich marine resources also meant that hunter-gatherer societies in regions such as Peru (11,000 years ago) were able to settle in one place very early, and become highly complex cultures even though the nearby inland was desert. The Proto-Archaic people here lived in villages as early as 10,000 BP. One example of an early village had simple huts encircling what could have been a central 'plaza'. Because they were sea hunters they utilised reed rafts for fishing and hunting seals and other marine animals.

In northern Chile, between 11,000 and 10,000 BP, people were living in settlements and using fibre fishing nets to take advantage of the rich sea, river and lake resources, and were also hunting small animals inland. In central and southern Chile, and at Las Vegas there are remains of several huts, and collections of many plant seed varieties (used for food, clothing, and so forth), plus wood for tools and other equipment, and reeds for baskets, mats, cord, and clothing. The earliest agriculture occurred around this time. Tom Dillehay sums up the situation: "Early foragers were knowledgeable and flexible, shared social values and goals, had ethics and principles of belief and practiced ritual and ceremony."[61] Brian Fagan (1991a) argues that the practice of mummification of the dead by both Peruvians and northern Chileans first occurred in the Atacama Desert region between 9,000 and 5,000 BP as a result of their belief that ancestors continued to be active in people's lives. It seems this practice took place in South America long before it was known in 'ancient' Egypt. Not everyone was mummified, but those who were included men, women and children, with some receiving more elaborate treatment than others.

Tom Dillehay reports that there were few grave goods before 4,000–3,500 BP, and these included cactus needles and fish hooks, cotton handlines, stone sinkers, bone and shell hooks, and many harpoons. In other graves they found bone necklaces, marine shells, small leather bags, coloured pigments and reed 'paintbrushes', also red-painted woven reed headbands, and the occasional dried clay figurine. Bodies were often wrapped in coloured twined-reed mats; women wore grass skirts, and men wore breechcloths.

In one instance in a Peruvian village (just as at Çatal Hüyük in Anatolia), families buried their dead under the floor of their houses, with the first burial at the western side of the building, and others inside the four outer walls. The first grave held an adult male, perhaps the head of the house, but grave goods indicated an egalitarian society. Burial goods included animal skin burial mats wrapped around the bodies, also bone and shell beads. By 4,000 BP nearby powerful agricultural states had taken over the coastal village region and the village was abandoned. That they lived an egalitarian lifestyle which had to be abandoned following the 'take over' by powerful neighbours is yet another clue as to possible contact with Eurasians/Indo-Europeans.

The development of agriculture in the Americas seems to have taken place after 10,000 BP. The earliest evidence of plant growing found in a cave in the central Andes shows that the inhabitants hunted deer and rabbits, and utilised various plants for food, bedding, clothing, containers, shelter, and weapons. Many plants, such as fruits and tubers, beans, lima beans, and chilli peppers, were probably brought over the Andes and grown in cultivated patches along the rivers.

One of Brian Fagan's few references to women's roles acknowledges the important activities of the first Mexican farmers of 8,000 BP, who cleared land and planted bean crops in small plots, while the men hunted deer and other game. Even when the families had to move, the women returned to water, weed and harvest their crops which were the mainstay of their diet.

The staple food of the Americas, maize, was developed from a native grass called teosinte somewhere between 15,000 and 8,000 BP. Maize was a labour-intensive crop, so could only be grown around settled communities. It lacked protein, and therefore had to be grown in association with protein crops, such as beans and squash, and required specific growing conditions which were not available in the lands above the North American south-

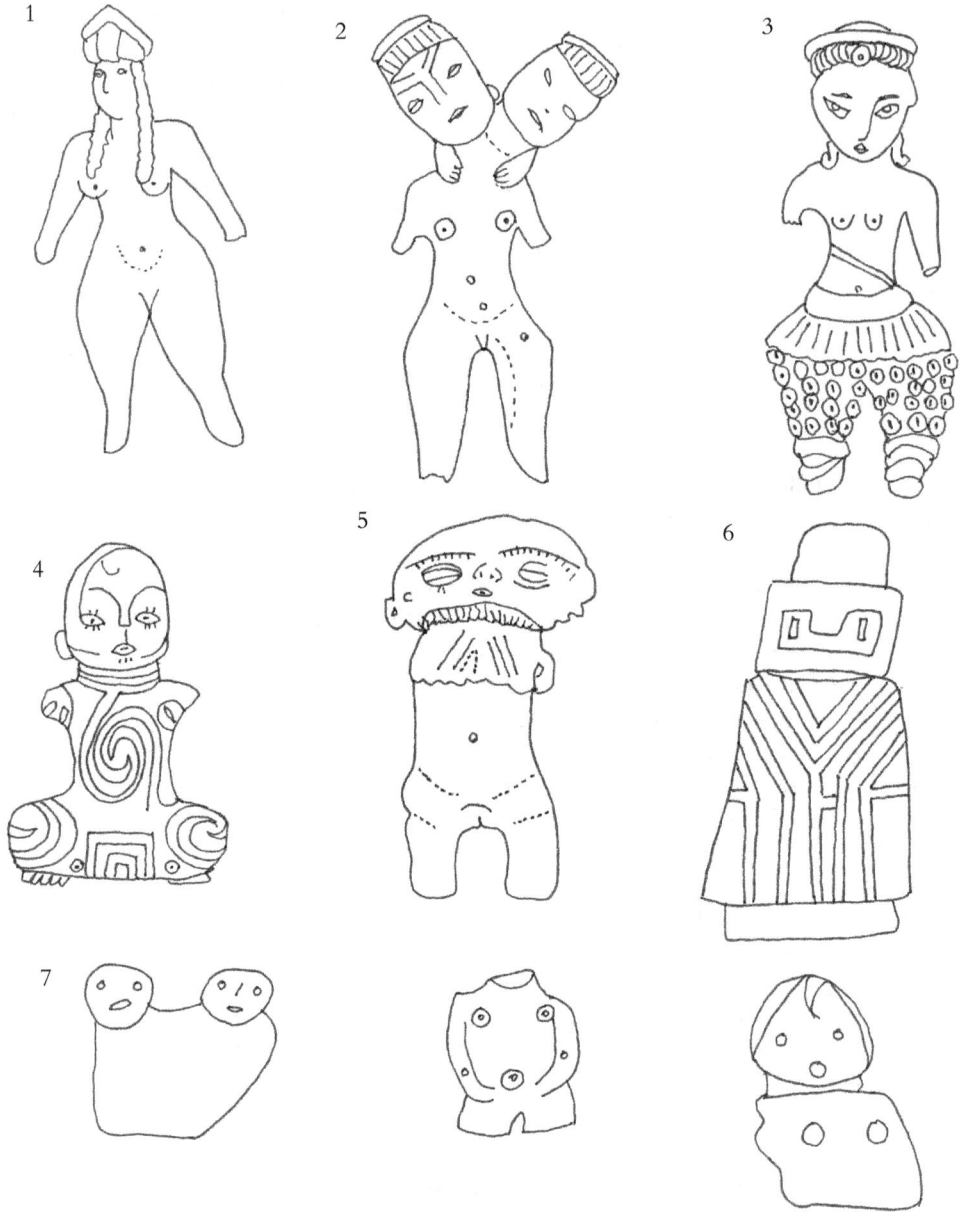

FIGURINES OF MEXICO AND SOUTH AMERICA

1. *Tlapacoya ceramic figurine,* central Mexico, 3,500–3,300 BP (Source: Wikimedia Commons: Snite Museum of Art, 2012)
2. *Double-headed figurine,* Late Prehistoric
3. *Late Prehistoric figurine,* Mexico (Source 2–3: Arte Historia, 2011, no longer available)
4. *A ritual female figurine*
5. *Female figurine,* Venezuela
6. *A Valdivia owl figurine*
7. *Three small unbaked clay female figurines and animal head* (Source 4–7: Silverman, Helaine and William H. Isbell, eds, 2008)

All line drawings © Judy Foster, 2013

west. It was a common crop throughout Mesoamerica by 4,500 BP, as there is evidence of maize cultivation in the Andean highlands. Along the coast of Peru, Proto-Archaic people grew maize in irrigated fields around 5,000 BP.

According to J. Scott Raymond (2008),[62] the Valdivia region of Ecuador was noted for the growth in size of its settlements, which featured circular huts arranged around a central courtyard, some of them quite large, perhaps used for rituals or extended families. Around 6,000–5,500 BP, the people of Valdivia created the first known representational images in the Americas. They made finely crafted pottery vessels in large numbers, featuring distinctive symbolic designs, the bowls being the most highly decorated with incised geometric motifs, and finished with burnished red slip. There were many figurines, with the earliest made of stone, and later ones of clay; many were broken, and found in 'rubbish heaps' which J. Scott Raymond suggests "were part of common household rituals and not curated items"[63] (indicating they could not be considered sacred?). He describes the well-rounded female figurines as "frequently exhibiting female genitalia and breasts."[64] Marija Gimbutas (1991)[65] would have interpreted such items as being sacrificial offerings in women's home rituals which she stressed were just as important as others held in temples.

The Heilbrunn Timeline of Art History[66] describes the small, stone, carved figurines as featuring well-formed faces, and both female and male sexual characteristics. The earliest ceramic figurines were similar, usually female, and with more varied elaborate headdresses, and some with ample curves. They appeared in different contexts, in burials, in houses and in rubbish piles, but mainly in association with women's activities such as food preparation, and close to the home hearth, so would most likely have had a similar function to those of Old Europe which, according to Marija Gimbutas, represent the goddess. One example even has two heads and four breasts on two upper torsos joined at the waist, standing with legs apart, but with no delineated pubic region. All of the figurines have their arms held close to the body.

The earliest ceramics in Amazonia appeared at 8,000 BP and J. Scott Raymond states that by 4,500 BP important Amazonian cultures had emerged, including the Tutishcainyo, Saladoid, and Barrancoid traditions, each with their own distinctive complex pottery vessels, and female and male figurines. The Saladoid pottery tradition, for example, had a wide range of vessels, and clay griddles.

In Brazil and Uruguay the first mounds were built about 5,000 BP, some quite large and impressively high (many appeared to be rebuilt or added to over the following centuries). There were sometimes traces of buildings left on the summits in which people may have lived, or which may have been used in rituals and ceremonies. Some mounds were also used for ritual burials. Most mound building lasted until between 3,000 and 2,000 BP.

Asian influences and the famous 'great' South American civilisations

It is interesting that mound building in North America did not begin until 3,000 BP. This raises some important questions, for example: Why did some of the South Americans build mounds so much sooner than the North Americans? Was this because South America was first settled some time before North America, or does this indicate increasing exchange or trade of goods and cultural practices between different regions? Joseph Needham (1971)[67] and Alice Kehoe (1998) certainly considered both a possibility. In fact, Joseph Needham was certain that contact with pre-Columbian America by early Chinese sailors took place

1

2

3a

b

SOUTH AMERICA: VALDIVIA FIGURINES

1. *Three Valdivia figurines* from Equador, 6,000–5,000 BP, made from carved stone (Source: Dashu, Max, 2010, and Department of Arts of Africa, Oceania, and the Americas, October 2004)
2. The unique *double-headed Valdivian figurine* is similar to Old European figurines recorded by Marija Gimbutas (Source: Department of Arts of Africa, Oceania, and the Americas, October 2004)

3a. *A mother and daughter figurine,* Vinča culture, Romania, 7,000–6,750 BP (Source: Gimbutas, Marija, 1989)
 b. The *'Gumelnita Lovers'* figurine, southern Romania, 7,000–6,750 BP (Source: Gimbutas, Marija, 1999/2001)

All line drawings © Judy Foster, 2013

between 4,000 and 3,500 BP, a theory unpopular with many mainstream archaeologists despite their knowledge of a widespread use of suitable watercraft capable of long distance travel, including all varieties of boats and rafts with sails. He and his Asian colleague, Lu Gwei-Djen, spent many years tracing and following contacts and influences throughout Eurasia and were able to demonstrate how cultural aspects and diverse knowledge could have been derived from many distant places, especially East and South-East Asia, despite the great difficulties posed by differing languages.

There may have been contact with East Asia and other Northern Hemisphere countries in early times, at least by 3,500 BP. For example, some burial practices may well have been brought from Europe by Indo-European newcomers. This is quite possible since we now know (through Elizabeth Barber's 1999[68] study of the mummies of Urumchi in northern China) that Caucasians were present in China at least by 4,000 BP, and it is now generally accepted that people came from China by boat, or continued to follow the route across to the Bering Strait taken by the first people to arrive in the Americas. Symbolic art appearing after 2,000 BP shows decidedly Asian influences in Olmec sculptures and other Mesoamerican art and artefacts.

Other similarities between Mesoamerica and eastern Asia include aspects of calendar astrology, a notion suggesting "that the movements of stars correlate closely with human events",[69] an idea which Alice Kehoe (1998) describes as "unnatural" and "fantastic." Other technology found in Mexico which suggests contact with Eurasia includes clay figurines of animals fixed to axles with wheels, assumed by mainstream researchers to have been used as toys, since such an invention as carts pulled by animals was considered too sophisticated to attribute to the 'barbaric Mexican Indians'. It's important to remember that carts pulled by animals first appeared in southern Russia nearly 7,000 years ago, well within the prehistoric Mesoamerican time frame.

Another similarity provided by Alice Kehoe is the use of corbelled arches rather than true arches in South-East Asian temples, a practice which was adopted by the Mayan Late Classic architects. She adds that corbelled arches are apparently more earthquake-proof than true arches which is why they were preferred in Mexican temples. It is notable that they are features of the 5,000-year-old Irish passage tombs of Newgrange and Knowth.

We add a further similarity, where complex woven fabric designs and use of coloured dyes reflect a distinct Asian influence, for example, ikat weaving featuring geometric designs, which originated in China and has been much used in South-East Asia. The recent discovery of the 4,900-year-old pyramid city of Caral in the Supe Valley of northern Peru (see next section) proves the existence of cotton growing and the creation of textiles in this region. Presumably earlier visitors from Asia would have brought cotton seeds with them since it seems cotton originated in India and was exported to East Asia after 6,000 BP.

According to Sharisse and Geoffrey McCafferty (1996),[70] spinning and weaving were very important women's work in pre-Columbian and Mexican societies and communicated status, rank, ethnic affiliation and sex. They also defined and reified female identity. Spinning and weaving designs could symbolise sexuality, childbirth and female life cycles as well as female initiation. Complex ikat weaving on backstrap looms features in traditional *rebozos* (long shawls with many uses) which have been worn by women in Mesoamerica and Peru almost continually at least since first contact with China, the Philippines and South-East Asia 2,500 to 3,000 years ago.[71]

The sacred city of Caral

The recent 'great' civilisations of the Mayans (300 CE), the Toltecs, the Incas and the Aztecs (1200 CE) could never have existed without the ever increasing fertile maize fields, and the ready supply of water which could support very large sedentary groups of people. In North America the water supplies were intermittent and unreliable and the difficult environment meant that maize could only survive in the most southern parts. Brian Fagan (1991a) argues that these factors prevented the establishment of large civilisations in North America. In South America the 4,600-year-old pyramid city of Caral, first investigated by Peruvian archaeologist Ruth Shady Solis in 1997,[72] has caused researchers to rethink the origins of civilisation in the Americas.

Dated to at least 5,000 BP, Caral is set in the Supe Valley Desert, 25 kilometres from the coast and north of Lima. Ruth Solis describes the city as an interesting early example of urban planning featuring several pyramids of varying sizes, plazas, and buildings spread over 65 hectares. The accurate date for the city was obtained from woven reed bags holding stones placed at the base of the inner walls of the largest pyramid which covered a large area almost as big as four football fields. At around 25 metres tall, it features a 15-metre-wide staircase leading down to a circular plaza, with three terraced levels, at the top of which is a platform with a fireplace and ruined atrium. Remains of coloured plaster walls and squared brickwork were also found. Ruth Solis considers that there could have been a form of hierarchy after 3,600 BP, since the best houses (for governing council members, just as in other Native American cultures of the time) were on the top of the pyramids, while craftspeople lived at ground level. Some houses were built of stone, others of wattle and daub. Social organisation is thought to have been based on social equality but with some distinctions underlying kinship and age groups.

The workers apparently lived in the poorest huts on the outskirts of the city. However, these structures may have been used only during the building of the pyramids or at certain ceremonial times, since the cotton farmers would have lived on site at their fields, and the fishers in villages along the coast. Caral was a peaceful city, not unlike other Neolithic cities of the time, since no defensive walls or war weapons of any kind were found. The one grave found so far held a baby who had died of natural causes, and had been lovingly prepared for the afterlife.

Caral was a trade centre built in close proximity to the rainforests of the Andes from which the inhabitants obtained food, wood and other necessities. Evidence of their diet includes: fruit seeds, cocoa beans (and medicinal plants) from the forests; squash, sweet potatoes and beans from irrigated fields; and snail shells, and the bones of birds and fish (such as sardines and anchovies) from the coast. But the biggest crop was cotton – seeds, fibres and textiles – irrigated from the river by a series of criss-cross trenches and canals throughout the valley. Woven fishing nets and other woven goods would have been traded with the coastal people, who exchanged them for fish and shellfish.

Ruth Solis has found no pottery and postulates that storage vessels would have been made from readily available hollowed-out squash and wood. Food was baked in the ashes. Other artefacts include a number of flutes made of pelican and condor bones, and cornets of deer and llama bones which suggest music was an important part of rituals. One engraving on a rock face features a spiral and a linear figure with a square-shaped head. Other imagery appears in a number of geoglyphs pecked onto the smooth rock surface of the earth. The

MESOAMERICA AND SOUTH AMERICA: FEMALE FIGURINES

1a. *Clay figurine*, Puebla, Mexico, 3,000 BP
 b. *Female figurine* from southern Peru,
   2,500 BP
 c. Max Dashu records this *Argentinian figurine*
   as "hollow, with painted body designs."
   (Source: Dashu, Max, 2008, poster)
2a. *Brazilian figurine* from an important cultural
   centre at the mouth of the Amazon River
 b. An *El Salvadorian figurine*, date unknown

 c. A *clay figurine* from Chile, n.d.
   (Source: All the above were recorded by Max
   Dashu and appear in her poster 'Female Icons,
   Ancestral Mothers', 2008)
3. South America: A *prehistoric geoglyph* near
   Caral, Peru, as seen from the air, date
   unknown
   (Source: Turnbull, David, 14 November 2011)
       All line drawings © Judy Foster, 2013

most spectacular example, dated to 4,500 BP, is a huge human profile incorporating ear-length hair, eye, nostril, and wide open mouth, which is best viewed from the air. Other smaller geoglyphs feature squares, parallel lines and crossed lines. Their meanings are not known.

The peaceful Caral civilisation began to wind down around 3,600 BP and the buildings and pyramids were covered with sand to protect them. There was no sign of a violent takeover of Caral. A report in *National Geographic* (July, 2001) by Hillary Mayell[73] suggests that climatic changes due to El Niño may have caused the people to move elsewhere because of prolonged drought or excessive flooding. According to Tom Dillehay, other nearby settlements discovered more recently had also been abandoned for similar reasons.

Ruth Solis continues to excavate in the Caral region, as there are many questions still to be answered. Caral has only just begun to reveal its secrets, so it is still too early to draw many conclusions. However, it seems likely that the rich textile traditions of Peru today may well have developed from, or at least been greatly influenced by, the textiles of Caral.

Although pyramids and mounds were relatively common throughout the Americas, for example, the well-known Teotihuacan's Pyramid of the Sun, the temple at Monte Alban, the Andean pyramids, and the Pyramid of the Sun in the Moche Valley, they were not necessarily the result of contact with the Northern Hemisphere. This has now proved to be the case since the Caral pyramids, and some South American pyramids, are at least as old as most (if not all) of those in Egypt, Mesopotamia, and South-East Asia, suggesting to Brian Fagan (1991a) the universality of human imagination and engineering skills.

Prehistoric and traditional life in South America

The presence of the Neolithic-style pyramid city of Caral goes a long way toward showing the peaceful nature of the Americas before 4,000 BP when life changed radically with the rise of Mesoamerican and South American warrior cultures, such as the Olmecs, Aztecs and the Incas. As Native North American, Paula Gunn Allen (1986)[74] stresses, most prehistoric South Americans were peaceful women-centred societies. Only those in Columbia (part of Mesoamerica) were violent and patriarchal (no doubt due to the 4,000-year-old contact with China).

Where is the prominent female deity/deities in the above descriptions of American cultures in prehistory? Many clay female figurines have been reported, but contemporary informants do not mention them, or their role in traditional cultures. Max Dashu explains that for the matrilineal Kogi people of the Santa Marta Mountains in Columbia, a "primordial Mother Essence from whom everything originates"[75] is central to their spiritual belief. "She is the unborn and eternal source. She is the Mother of Songs."[76] For the Wayuu culture, Juya (Rain) is their father, and Mma (Earth) is their mother, and "the trees, mountains and animals are [their] relatives ... [while] the earth [is] a fountain of sustenance ... the creator of life."[77] According to Max Dashu, for the Canelos Quichhua in Ecuador, Ningui, "the soil of their fields", is the Garden Mother. "She is also Mother of clay and ceramics, and the very spirit of culture."[78] She mentions the many terracotta female figurines found along the Amazon, symbolic of land/water; fish, frogs and other aquatic creatures; the sun, moon and stars. The Tupi of Brazil make "jade amulets often in the form of frogs",[79] and also fish, tortoises and other related forms.

Max Dashu also found that in certain specific traditions spread across South America, men "seized the sacred ceremonies, instruments, and masks"[80] from the women, just as had occurred in Australia and the Pacific region. (Australian Indigenous women say this was the time when the men first stole the women's secrets, perhaps with the introduction of the dingo 4,000 years ago.)[81] The theft of women's ceremonies and artefacts marks the entrance of patriarchal forms in many places around the world.

A matrilineal culture

An account is given by Carolyn Heath (2009) who was given permission by the Shipibo people of the Upper Amazon to "make their voice heard in the West, to give voice to invisibility."[82] They come from a lowland forest region in Peru which has always been relatively inaccessible to the outside world, so they have been able to maintain their traditional matriarchal and matrilineal egalitarian lifestyle until recent times (even though they had been affected by the Spanish invasion). Today, capitalism threatens them by 'consumption' of their rainforests, thus their need to record their culture is pressured.

The Shipibo women's culture is strong; they remain "assertive, independent, vigorous, self-confident, and perceptive ... socially extraverted and creatively intuitive",[83] says Carolyn Heath who spent 12 years with the people experiencing their culture. Furthermore, women and men experience equality, only being differentiated by their activities rather than their sex. Everyday life is harmonious, while public and family life remain one entity.

They live in matrilocal family compounds, central to which is the matrilineal clan mother and her daughters. All of the women are blood relatives, and married daughters set up their own houses next to the clan mother's house. Men in the compound are unrelated, as husbands move in with their wives and live there until the birth of the first child. Unmarried daughters continue to live with the clan mother. The land is communally owned.

All decisions are made by the clan mothers, and girls are favoured because they "attract more sons-in-law to the family."[84] Divorce is easily obtained: if sons-in-law are lazy or otherwise lacking, they can be sent back to their families. Women control the cooking pot and eat separately from the men to whom they dole out food. Economically women are autonomous, and are highly proficient in producing textiles and pottery, skills which they learn from an early age.

Designs containing symbolic imagery representing the structures of authority and politics, rules of behaviour, regulations and levels of hierarchy are incorporated by the women (in the form of a symbolic 'language') into their textiles and pottery designs; or integrated into women's songs and men's oratory. The intricately formed geometric designs record the Shipibo cosmological belief system, and their vision of the universe is sometimes featured on pottery, woven into the cloth, or painted upon it. Wild tree cotton is available for fabrics and thread, as are large deposits of clay and minerals suitable for pottery making; these resources have been used for at least 4,000 years and probably much longer. Today, women trace symbolic designs onto men's wooden tools and weapons for them to carve and engrave, but in earlier times they also traced designs onto house walls and so forth.

Men recognise the 'skyworld', symbolic of the spirit; for women, it is the 'inner world' in opposition to the material world; each approach complements the other. Women's interpretation of never-static, ever-dynamic spiritual designs comes from their inner world; they are inspired by everything in nature and life; such designs, through repetition, "create order out of chaos."[85] They never explain to outsiders the complex spiritual and other meanings shown in the designs (just as Australian Indigenous people never reveal all the meanings expressed in their paintings or other art works, beyond the most obvious).

Instead of producing woven or ceramic symbolic articles, men are the orators in a strong oral tradition, and are the re-interpreters of traditional myths, while women have sacred songs relating to them. As Janet Catherine Berlo (1996) comments: "Men speak, women make cloth ... cloth makes manifest deeply held cultural values that may otherwise be imperceptible. In fact, it may be women's very crucial job to translate these ephemeral values into material objects."[86] It has been generally assumed that Shipibo men are dominant because men's oratory is public and apparent; but (supposedly subordinate) Shipibo women, while less conspicuous, are the 'active agents of culture' through items usually taken for granted, such as their pottery and cloth.

WEAVING THE THREADS

Stitch by stitch,
Circle by circle,
Weaving is like the creation of life,
All things are connected.

Ellen Trevorrow[1]

The weaving (the wavy lines) are for weaving, not just women's weaving, but they show that everything is connected: land, water, *ngatji*, spirit world, everything. The winding trails that lead towards the island represent where paths cross into other people's territory. They are like guidelines for people and stories.

Audrey Lindsay[2] (describing one of her paintings)

When one considers the similarities and differences in the lives of prehistoric women one can see how each of these arrangements of threads forms a unity – the spiral, the symbolic circle – is there as it is in basketry. Strands of threads – similarities and differences, complex patterns and shapes, colours and textures – all these make the whole.

When we began our journey to investigate the lives of the invisible women of prehistory, we did not really know where the search might take us. Our aim was to attempt to find out what women's roles were in prehistory, 'to re-write' women's story into the prehistoric archaeological record.

Marija Gimbutas set the stage for our search by defining the idea of the goddess, the female deity, who represents the female principle. She opened up the world of prehistory in Old Europe, where prehistory began and where and why it ended. Marija Gimbutas identified the early suppression of knowledge of women's prehistory, beginning with our understanding of the word 'matriarchy' – we've always been told that it means the opposite of 'patriarchy'. But Marija Gimbutas provided another meaning, along with that other misunderstood word, 'civilisation'. When we see these words, their biased patriarchal meanings influence our thinking and obstruct the truth about prehistory. The remarkable picture of women's lives in Old Europe helped us understand what we needed to look for as a starting point in our search, especially in the previously unknown regions of the world which we have named the 'Hidden Worlds' (Africa, India, China, South-East Asia), and the 'New Worlds' (Australia, Oceania and the Americas). It is difficult for many to imagine a world where people have not always cold-bloodedly killed one other to gain power and prestige, and some argue that Marija Gimbutas presented an impossibly perfect peaceful world. Prehistoric societies did indeed have to deal with deaths caused by anger, greed and other human passions, but developed social mechanisms which helped defuse or avoid these situations. Since all life was respected, there was never wholesale killing as has been experienced in much of the world for the past 6,000 years.

One important discovery was the sophistication of the so-called primitive prehistoric societies of East Asia and the New Worlds, who were found to have cultures that were complex, successful and peaceful, what in other contexts is called 'cultured'. We found numerous signs of the female principle which included natural visual symbols and the presence of a strong and highly developed traditional textile legacy, as well as matrilineal (women-centered) cultures of the type described by Peggy Sanday, most of which became heavily influenced or almost disappeared because of colonising influences beginning 5,500 years ago.

Strand 1: Myth; intangible evidence

Marija Gimbutas's body of work on visual symbolism demonstrates the importance of myth in the search for the invisible women of prehistory. When linked with enigmatic visual imagery, myth can open up external meanings of symbols, particularly when explained by the people who have inherited them. For example, Indigenous Australian Munya Andrews, a Bardi and Nyul Nyul woman from north-west Western Australia, in her examination of just one symbol, that of the star formation known as Seven Sisters of the Pleiades, has described some of the remarkably similar myths relating to this symbol found all around the world. Of special interest are the differences, although not necessarily the truths, underlying the Pleiades story found between the 600 linguistic groups in Indigenous Australia.

Informed analysis helps reveal meanings of imagery for which original meanings have been lost. Many people find it hard to tune in to prehistoric symbols because non-indigenous – and especially urban[3] people – have become so far removed from the natural world. Meanings of symbolic imagery cannot be measured or scientifically proven, but researchers such as Marija Gimbutas, Dorothy Cameron and Michael Dames have shown that there are other ways to decipher them. And how much is missed if we ignore them as the processual archaeologists and rock art scientists of today are inclined to do. The basic symbols are just that – repeated over time and space, they will always have a contemporary meaning.

Strand 2: Bias

Early in our journey it was necessary to identify some of the different forms of bias against women used by those who have recorded prehistory (usually men). To find the women – and the female principle – has meant careful reading of the evidence provided by a number of archaeologists and related specialists. Unfortunately, archaeological evidence and archaeological reports are now limited to the scientific aspects of any artefacts and their environment, with symbolic imagery and other aspects recorded, but otherwise ignored, and the processual archaeologists usually record only one side of the story.

One persistent form of bias held by contemporary researchers is the firm belief that "brutality and violence are at least as old as humanity",[4] and that prehistoric people were so ignorant they were not capable of caring for those who were incapacitated in any way. Yet the *evidence* suggests otherwise: that prehistoric people did indeed care for one another, and care for those with disabilities. Evidence also supports the view that prehistoric *women* cultivated medicinal plants for their treatment of illnesses. What *is* lacking is any substantial evidence of the supposed widespread violent activities; it does not appear in engravings, paintings or graves until after the emergence of Proto-Indo-Europeans around 6,000 years ago.

Another example of prehistoric intelligence is the great range of engraved rock art imagery found around the world, and the hauntingly beautiful art of the Upper Palaeolithic caves, which remind us of the great skill and talent of those early prehistoric artists. How could anyone today continue to refer to such proficient creative peoples as 'ignorant' and 'savages' when they could engrave, paint and draw with such dynamism and skill?

Strand 3: Cord, string and weaving

There are now many more reports than in the past by an increasing number of female researchers who have been able to examine – and publish – aspects of archaeological evidence previously ignored by male researchers. In this way we have found (to our amazement) that many early innovations in prehistory had been created by hunter-gatherer women in both the 'Old Worlds' of Europe and surrounds, as well as in the Hidden and New Worlds!

One sequel to Marija Gimbutas's achievements has been the raising of our awareness concerning prehistoric innovations and the realisation that many of these were actually women's creations designed for practical purposes in everyday living. Prehistoric women's activities have rarely (if ever) been mentioned, yet through necessity and over time they would most likely have invented: the use of cord or thread[5] (for spinning, weaving, cloth thread, mats and baskets, fishing etc.); pottery (cooking, storage, and portage); forms of accounting and writing (incised baked clay counters); medicines and healing; agriculture; and methods for the conservation of nature.[6]

The earliest clothing worn around the world (before the Upper Palaeolithic) would most likely have been that of animal skin sewn together using animal sinews or fibres from plants to make warm garments. In Australia, Indigenous woman Maree Clark,[7] artist and curator, provides another early example, that of the possum-skin cloaks reported present in Victoria at least 5,000 years ago (and probably very much earlier):

> Every Aboriginal person in south-eastern Australia would have had a cloak because of our climate … You'd get one as a little baby and as you grew, the cloak grew with you, and it would have traditional markings of your clan, your family, and who you were … [8]

The possum-skin cloaks made by the women featured traditional designs carved into the skins, and were worn in ritual ceremonies and when a person was buried.

Animal skins were also widely used by both women and men in the Americas for tepees, clothing and many other purposes from 15,500 BP in North America and 14,600 BP in South America. According to Heather Pringle (2013) the pre-Clovis people "dressed in warm, tailored hide garments stitched together with sinew and bone needles",[9] lived in hide tents when moving overland, and travelled down the west coast in boats covered with hides stitched together.

In Indonesia, cord or string must have been available by 700,000 BP (stone tools and butchered elephant bones were present), as it would have been used in the construction of the first watercraft. In the somewhat later (around 120,000 BP) Australian hunter-gatherer lifestyle it would have been hard to move seasonally[10] from place to place without a means of bundling and carrying such objects as tools and other equipment, or babies and small children (there were no pack animals in Australia). Over time, more ways of using these materials were likely to have been developed by women, including baskets, string bags and baby carriers, and so forth, and the woven grass matting used for walls, floor coverings and roofs of houses. These developments could be found in early societies around the Old World, as well as in the Hidden and New Worlds.

Weaving was likely to have been undertaken all over Australia, wherever the women could find suitable materials available, over a very long period. Ngarrindjeri weaving was certainly present when the first settlers arrived in South Australia. In 1833, the explorer Charles Stuart[11] commented on the circular mats used by the local Indigenous women, while in the 1840s the artist George French Angas made drawings of the mats.[12] As Tom and Ellen Trevorrow comment:

> We teach our Ngarrindjeri basket-weaving techniques. We tell of our stories relating to the land, waters, trees, plants, birds and animals – people call them our Dreaming stories. They are our way of life, our survival teaching stories.[13]

Strand 4: Matriliny

The most compelling evidence of the female principle and matrilineal cultures we have found is the presence of numerous small female 'goddess' figurines of unbaked clay, ceramic, stone or wood, which archaeologists have very often found in archaeological digs in most parts of the world, but which they still consider too 'unimportant' to record in any detail because they represent females. The meanings of some of these earliest female sculptures found in Old Europe were interpreted by Marija Gimbutas through their shape and 'decoration' which included certain repeat motifs ('M', 'V', 'III', and so forth) forming a language of meaning, and information about their context. Female figurines have also been found almost everywhere in the Hidden and New Worlds – and if they are now absent in some of these regions it is probably because ephemeral materials such as wood, were used in their creation.

As is clear from the artefacts and material evidence referred to in this book, there were female deities/spirits/ancestral beings (or their associated symbolism in patterns of motifs such as those on pottery) dating well back in prehistory throughout the world. The evidence therefore is not restricted to some small region or specific period but appears on *every* continent across a vast expanse of time. They were there in Africa, India, China and Japan. In South-East Asia, Papua New Guinea and the Americas, numerous examples were found. Female symbols, such as engravings of vulvas or physical aspects of country, have been found across Australia, and in the northern areas, there are cave paintings of female ancestral beings.

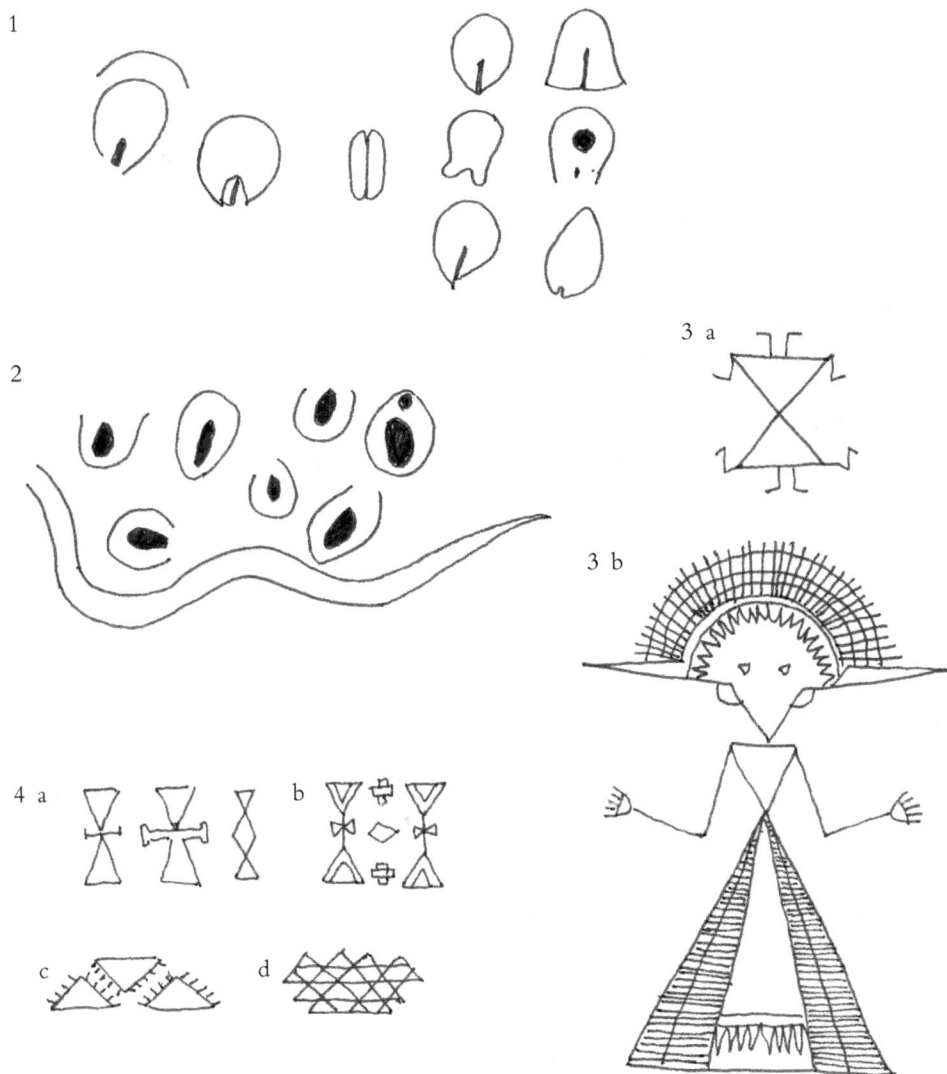

VULVAS AND DOUBLE TRIANGLE FIGURINES

1. *Vulva or sprouting seeds symbols* from Old Europe dated between 12,000–7,000 BP (Source: Gimbutas, Marija, 1989)
2. An example of *engraved vulva symbols* from Australia, at least 10,000 BP; a large collection of the symbols cover one rock wall in Carnarvon Gorge, New South Wales, Australia (Source: Photo by Foster, Judy, 1997)
3a. *A double triangle goddess* from Old Europe dated to 8,000–7,000 BP (Source: Gimbutas, Marija, 1991)

3b. *A double triangle figurine* from a contemporary Indonesian woven image
4. Franz Boas recorded these *double triangle motifs* in 1927 in North America:
   a. An *Arapaho* symbol
   b. A *Sioux* symbol
   c. A *Pomo* symbol
   d. *Native American* symbols
   (Source: Boas, Franz, 1928/1955)
   All line drawings © Judy Foster, 2013

Remarkably, the intangible evidence of matrilineal cultures is also still present in the traditional lives, stories and practices preserved by indigenous people around the world. There is an academic tension between those who write from within their inherited tradition and those who come from outside as scientists, academics or journalists. Perhaps it is time to listen to the insiders. Matrilineal societies existed extensively before patriarchy emerged and are still present today despite the pressures of colonisation. Prehistoric communities were women-centered – women were respected, and shared equal status and responsibilities with men. Social interactions in prehistory were, in the main, peaceful, with conflicts being settled by ritual means rather than by violence. Having once been peaceful, human communities can become peaceful again. Just as patriarchy began with the emergence of *history*, so it can end with the beginning of a '*new era*'.

Strand 5: Agriculture

It should not be assumed that if prehistoric people did not practise some form of agriculture that they must have been 'ignorant savages' who were incapable of such an activity. There are those who still hold this bias, and there are also those who consider the beginning of agriculture (possibly a women's invention since they were gatherers) as something of a landmark in human development; yet when we look at where and when the practice first appeared, it was not in Old Europe, but in Africa after 18,000 BP, the Near East around 12,000 BP, and Papua New Guinea around 11,000 BP. What is more, early semi-agriculture (or 'pre-agriculture') had been practised long before agriculture by hunter-gatherer women who had developed methods of conservation and caring for wild grains, grasses, fruits, and other food plants (depending on what was available), collecting only what was needed.

In Australian inland regions, it has been found that wild millet grain (and related grass seeds) had been collected and ground for food since 30,000 BP. Ngarrendjeri elder, Ellen Trevorrow, explains how she collects rushes suited for basket-making:

> I pick and move around and just thin out the good places ... But I move around in a circle. I pick and move and let the other lot grow; they grow very quick. I never pick them out completely. Later, I can return when the young ones have come up again. You can see where I've been.[14]

Further examples of semi-agriculture are provided by Josephine Flood (1995). She mentions that in early Australia, on the grassy plains and in the Darling River region, the explorer Sir Thomas Mitchell[15] (in 1835) recorded the long green native millet grass being cut by women using stone knives, and stacked in one large heap so that when it dried out, the grains would fall in one place ready for them to collect. According to Josephine Flood "stone knives were also used for reaping in the early days of cereal-growing in the Middle East, so this is important evidence of semi-agricultural practices in inland Australia."[16] Agriculture could not be developed in Australia because of infrequent and erratic rainfall and poor soils. In places such as Papua New Guinea and some of the Pacific islands which were also not suited to agriculture, horticulture – the cultivation of gardens – was developed, at least by 11,000 to 10,000 BP; in South America, by 8,000 BP, and in North America, by 6,000 BP.

Rhys Jones (1980) notes that in tropical Australia (and elsewhere), while the women were digging yams they "left the top of the tuber still attached to the tendril in the ground so [it] would grow again."[17] They also threw away seeds, nuts, and tubers around the camps so they would grow again.[18]

Another semi-agricultural practice, perhaps as old as 140,000 years and not taken seriously until very recently in Australia, was 'fire-stick farming'. It involved the carefully controlled clearing of land using 'cool fires' which were lit during suitable weather (before the bush became too dry) to clear away any buildup of dead branches and so forth, thus preventing the destructive wild fires we experience today. The ashes left behind promoted new growth of grass and bush foods, attracting animals for easy hunting, and providing space for human and animal movement. Such fires were regular and of low intensity.[19] Tom Dillehay (2008)[20] also mentions firestick farming in parts of South America between 14,000 and 9,000 BP.

Strand 6: Housing

There is also bias with regard to the forms of prehistoric housing around the world. It is assumed that the more complex the design and form of houses, the more developed the country or region must be. This was the case in the Old European region. It was certainly thought by the English first settlers that because Australian Indigenous huts or shelters were usually simple and impermanent that Indigenous people had little attachment to their housing, and were too ignorant to construct more permanent dwellings.

In fact, there were many factors involved when building Australian shelters, including the climatic and social circumstances, the availability of materials, the length of occupation, and the numbers to be sheltered, which also affected the layout of the settlement. Shelters were of simple construction, with space carefully planned, and the people regularly followed the same pattern of rotation between each camp according to the seasons.[21] Paul Memmott and Carroll Go-Sam (2001)[22] explain that there were also cultural symbols connected with ancestral beings encoded in the building of dwellings which had to be taken into consideration. Elsie Roughsey explains the difficulties when building the huts the traditional way:

> When the huts were built it was very hard work to be done. We people went so many miles out bush to get all our barks, spent all day just collecting barks … We all came home with great loads of barks on our heads and on our sides, hung down from the shoulder by a string or belt. That's how we carried extra load more, was that way. The men had much heavier loads on their heads … We had no other way to carry all the load.[23]

Paul Memmott and Carroll Go-Sam describe one style of house still erected in Arnhem Land, built on stilts and with curved stringy-bark sheets forming a dome roof over one or two rooms, one platform (made of bare branches) placed above the other, used for sleeping spaces reached by climbing poles. A fire underneath helped discourage the swarms of mosquitoes. A "complex religious symbolism [was] associated with these houses" drawn from "the mythological activities of the Wagilak sisters, ancestral heroines who built the first vaulted dwelling in the region."[24]

Strand 7: Women's symbolic languages

Women's secret languages were everywhere too. Indigenous and traditional cultures of a number of regions in the Hidden Worlds (Africa, India, and China) mention that women traditionally communicated through the content and/or arrangement of imagery on pottery, in woven mats, baskets and so forth, or in motifs within the designs on fabrics woven on looms. Both the rituals involved in the making of objects, and the imagery displayed upon them, conveyed certain information to other women, and such knowledge was passed down from grandmothers to mothers to daughters. We have seen how special marks on tokens and seals formed a symbolic language used by Middle Eastern women to record amounts and contents on storage pots and jars during the Neolithic period; since they were responsible for this task, it is possible that only they understood the meanings of at least some of the incised motifs on these tokens and seals. In South-East Asia, designs on woven fabric were/are the source of women's secret and public language.

In the New Worlds, including Australia, women communicated in many ways: through symbolic imagery in sand drawings, through ritual activities, in body painting, and basket making. Six thousand years ago, women communicated in Papua New Guinea through the shapes and imagery on their pottery, as well as on barkcloth; in North America, through the shapes and designs of basketry and pottery; and in South America, through barkcloth, pottery and female figurines.

Strand 8: Writing

Another significant surprise (which most male recorders never mention) is the invention of writing by women in the Middle East, beginning with those first clay tokens 10,000 years ago. The first early historic cuneiform writer was the Sumerian female poet, Enheduanna, whose hymns and poems were famous.

And although it possibly falls within the earliest historic period, *nüshu*, a secret writing created by women in one part of China, has existed until very recently. *Nüshu*, which was used only by women, was partly based on some of the Chinese characters which women were never taught and only men were educated to use. This allowed women freedom to communicate with other women in a way previously denied to them, in a culture in which women existed but were never heard.

Strand 9: Effects of colonisation

Indo-European colonisation had drastic effects on Hidden and New World peoples, *especially the women*. Some have managed to preserve earlier traditions despite colonisation, but it is an on-going process. Women in the past had been responsible for their families, for the care and welfare of the forests, the plains, mountains and rivers and lakes, as well as the coastal regions, conserving these food, medicinal, and building resources for future generations. To use an expression of the Australian Indigenous people, 'they cared for country'. Women in particular have lost control of nearly all these responsibilities under colonisation, resulting in loss of identity and of status. A state of poverty and subservience/servitude has often been the outcome.

A 2004 United Nations report summarises the situation for indigenous women which includes problems such as poverty, lack of health care and education, as well as armed conflicts, pollution, large-scale mining and logging, invasions of illegal miners, unsympathetic governments, loss of their lands, and human trafficking ... less pay, lowest jobs, subject to discrimination, humiliation, and sexual abuse.[25]

Yet, as Susan Hawthorne explains in *Wild Politics*, traditional women

still have access to the knowledge which can help sustain the planet through the twenty-first century and beyond. Obviously there are men too with this knowledge, but perhaps it is time to listen to the women.[26]

One aspect of the emerging resurgence of Indigenous Australians has been given voice by Hetti Perkins in her recent brilliant documentary series and accompanying book *art + soul: a journey into the world of Aboriginal art* (2010).[27] She explains that the artists speak of their lives before 'contact', and record their stories and knowledge in powerful art works for "the coming generations" so that "living memory of our country before contact will [not] be lost."[28] Hetti Perkins says:

In many ways *art + soul* marks this moment and celebrates the phenomenal endurance of our culture ... the world's oldest continuous cultural tradition and one of its most dynamic art movements.[29]

Indigenous woman, Nganyintja, reminds us: "In all these different places all over Australia, lots of Aboriginal people have always lived since the beginning."[30]

Our experience when researching women in prehistory was not unlike discovering an old, large unfinished, carefully folded hand-woven cloth, the patterns once varied and vivid in colour and texture, hidden low in a deep, dark place six thousand years ago. The fabric was full of holes and faded so much in places that the patterns of threads could barely be discerned; so fragile that without great care, it could not yet be safely unfolded to reveal the whole design. But there were traces/signs of patterns within patterns and a unity underlying the multiple arrangements of life threads of those prehistoric women. They could be still glimpsed here and there by lifting just one small corner of this prehistoric fabric. Clearly the fiercely patriarchal forces of the short historic period have insidiously unravelled or lost most of those essential threads of the lineages of our ancestral mothers. But hopefully women today and in the future will be able to retrace those threads deep into the past and reconnect them so that more of our prehistoric heritage is made known to everyone. Women can once again reveal the female deity, goddess – the female principle – and reconstruct that peaceful and dynamic existence. Then when the intricately interwoven patterned design is fully unfolded, the brilliantly coloured images will reveal a new harmonious whole – a world of equality – and of peace.

Acknowledgements

Judy Foster

With a background in art and design, I have always been interested in symbolic imagery. I'd also been exposed to the wonders and mystery of Australian Indigenous art; and to women's inequality, and found there was much to learn. As a mature-age student at Monash University I focused on the visual arts, sociology, and Australian Indigenous studies, while concentrating on the position of women within these disciplines.

It was frustrating to find that at the beginning of every art history book consulted during the course of study there was reference to widespread early societies which had been violently disrupted or destroyed by incoming historic peoples. There was little or no information provided about these early people yet they were obviously cultured, as demonstrated by such evidence as the very old and wonderful painted symbols and engraved rock images of northern Australia, and the famous animal paintings in the French and Spanish caves. The question which emerged from this experience had two aspects:

When did symbols first appear, and why? Who were the people who used them, and why did they disappear?

Why was there such an emphasis on women (as seen in symbols and artefacts) in these early times, and when and why did this change? Was it similar in the Hidden Worlds of Africa, India and China/East Asia, and the New Worlds of Australia, the Pacific, and the Americas?

The search for answers to these questions after I graduated from university was a revelatory experience. Over ten years or more of investigation into prehistory, inspired by Marija Gimbutas and her ground-breaking discoveries, our distant female ancestors and the prehistoric worlds of Old Europe and the Hidden and New Worlds were gradually revealed. To discover women's roles, and their contributions, beyond those of childbearing and nurturing, required insight and careful reading between the lines. We had to look even harder to find out how and when these changes took place. As can be seen in the timelines, there were a number of surprises!

I am aware that these ideas and theories can probably never be proved beyond doubt, but there do seem to be strong reasons for believing that Marija Gimbutas and those following her are on the right track as to the realities of women's position in prehistory. Although I did see some extracts of his text, I was never able to find a copy of James Mellaart's The Goddess from Anatolia to see the illustrations (but several are viewable on the web). His meticulous and thoughtful examination of the Çatal Hüyük civilisation is complementary to the work of Marija Gimbutas.

Although Marlene Derlet was still teaching at Monash University's Centre for Indigenous Studies when we began researching, her role in the preparation of this book went far beyond her written contributions to the chapters on language origins, Indigenous oral literature and mythology, and the customs and rituals which perpetuate fear of women. Numerous discussions, her critiques, and patient editing were invaluable, and kept the project ongoing over the 12 years it took to complete it. Thank you, Marlene.

I would also like to thank Susan Hawthorne for taking the time to read and comment on the early manuscript in 2003 which helped me to develop the ideas, and especially her second reading over the 2008 Christmas period, after which her further encouragement, recommendations of new books, and the pile of other useful books, spurred us to complete the task. Thanks too, for her careful final editing – the book looks great.

Special thanks to Maree Hawken, for her meticulous editing over the period of the project, and patience when inserting updates – and forever having to add new references to the bibliography!

Thanks to the Spinifex Press team, the Palmer Higgs team, and the designer Deb Snibson, who all did a great job, and to McPhersons Printing.

Also many thanks to my husband, Graham, for organising all the timelines and converting the illustrations into JPEG, as well as getting me out of holes when my computer played up. Thanks to our daughters, Sarah, Carolyn and Edwina, for their ongoing encouragement.

As a mark of respect for the work of the many women whose publications we consulted, and in order to differentiate our format from that of the exclusive male mainstream, we chose to include women's first names wherever possible throughout our text.

Judy Foster
Blackburn, Victoria, Australia

Marlene Derlet

The interest in the type of society we live in, the culture and behaviour it values, and the status women hold in it, goes back a long way for me – back to my childhood. I belong to a generation where war and victory were celebrated, where the heroes were the men of battle, and history did not include women. I learnt very early that being a girl meant restriction in behaviour and aspirations, and as a woman I would always hold a lower status than a man.

I realise now that the seed for questioning the type of society I live in was planted in those days long ago. I used to ask myself such questions as: Why do countries have to go to war with each other? Why are there hardly any heroines in the history books? Why are women assigned to a lesser status? Why the general unimportance of women? And most importantly, where did these attitudes and perceptions originate? Was there ever a society that had no wars and where women and the feminine were celebrated and given importance?

The search for answers to these questions was difficult and long. I found some answers through my studies in anthropology, sociology, linguistics and Germanic studies, and through my involvement in feminism and women's groups. But the best answers to my search for a different society came through my work at university as a researcher in Australian Indigenous issues and as a tutor of Australian Indigenous studies, where I developed (amongst other courses) a course in the study of Australian Aboriginal women. Here I found a society where people lived generally in peaceful co-existence with other groups and where, until colonisation, there existed a strict separation between men and women. (In some parts of Australia this is still so today). However, what is very hard for non-Indigenous people to comprehend is that this separation does not mean inequality and unimportance. Each sex was (and still is) valued in its own right. I also found in my field of work that, until very recently, there was an entrenched prejudice by scholars and researchers against prehistoric and Indigenous societies, and against any society that did not measure up to the so called civilised (Western) model.

When I was asked to contribute to this book, I was instantly enthusiastic because I saw it as a way to finally get answers to my questions. My research also awoke again my interest in language and literature, especially folk literature. I always felt sad and disturbed by the way women are portrayed in folklore. They are presented as somebody to be feared: she is the temptress who brings destruction to men; the evil witch to be avoided at all costs. Why? Was it always like this?

To look back into history, it is necessary to understand its transmission – the recording of history and who owns it; who judges (or judged) what is in history and what is omitted; what are the problems inherited in oral transmission of history, folk literature or, as in the Indigenous case, the Creation stories – the Dreaming. Since the invention of the writing system, the accuracy and credibility of oral transmission of folk literature has been questioned. So much value has been put on written records that the content of oral folk literature as a guide to history has been unacceptable to most historians, and any truth and accuracy it may contain is usually dismissed. There is (and always has been) a purpose behind this denial and denigration of other societies' culture and folklore – that of domination and power.

Did I get the answers I was looking for? Yes, the archaeological, anthropological and linguistic evidence shows that before the Indo-European invasion there existed societies which were peaceful; where war and victory, with their male heroes, were not part of the culture; instead, the feminine was celebrated and women had equal status. Language did not contain words for destructive weapons; women were not witches, but healers, educators, and the like, who were celebrating birth, life, death and regeneration.

The exercise of compiling material for this book has also been a rewarding journey into the discovery of the origin of humankind and of language, and has helped me to better understand and appreciate folk literature. However, the journey has induced a sadness in me because of the way generation after generation has devalued the importance of women and made women invisible in history; and because this state of affairs did not begin to change until recently.

I want to thank Judy Foster for her hard work, her patience and endurance to keep our project going.

Marlene Derlet
Basel, Switzerland (formerly East St. Kilda, Victoria, Australia)

NOTES

CHAPTER 1 The Theory of Marija Gimbutas

1 'Old Europe' is a term used by Marija Gimbutas (1999) to describe a region which covers Hungary, south/central Yugoslavia, Bulgaria, Roumania, eastern Austria, southern Czechoslovakia, southern Poland, east to Ukraine and Kiev, southern Italy, Malta, Greece, Crete, Cycladic, Ionian, Aegean Islands, and western Turkey.

2 Marler, Joan (ed.) (1997) *From the Realm of the Ancestors*, p. 9.
According to Joan Marler (1997), between 1968 and 1980 Marija Gimbutas directed four major excavations in south-east Europe: at Silagroi, Greek Macedonia (7,000–4,000 BP); Starcevo and Vinca at Anza, Macedonia (8,300–7,000); Sesklo at Achilleion, Thessaly, Greece; and Scaloria cave sanctuary near Manfredonia, south-east Italy (7,600–7,300 BP). Her earlier excavations were in the Baltic area, although she thoroughly examined Neolithic artefacts found throughout eastern Europe, as well as those in museums and collections in the Northern Hemisphere.

3 Gimbutas, Marija (1989) *The Language of the Goddess*, p. xv.

4 In Western texts, the period from 10,000 years until 2,000 years ago was, until recently, known as BC, 'Before Christ'; now replaced by the more neutral BCE, 'Before the Common Era', which links up with the discovery of radiocarbon dating in the late 1940s. The period after 2,000 years was known as AD, Anno Domini or 'In the Year of Our Lord' (Renfrew and Bahn, 1991, p. 102). This sets the fixed point of the beginning of what is now known as 'the Common Era' (CE). The years of prehistory (the period before 6,500 years ago) are described as 'Before the Present' (BP). BCE, CE and BP are used in this book.

5 That many consider the ideas of Marija Gimbutas to be still relevant is demonstrated in the 1996 volume of all her papers published by the *Journal of Indo-European Studies*, and also Joan Marler's *In the Realm of the Ancestors: An Anthology in Honor of Marija Gimbutas* (1997), in which some 60 contributors voice their belief in, and support for, the Gimbutas scenario. Marija Gimbutas provided a picture of Neolithic and Proto-Indo-European life as no one else has yet done. In 2009, a series of papers by indigenous women from Africa, India, China and the Pacific region, *Societies of Peace: Matriarchies Past, Present and Future* was published, and showed striking similarities between these prehistoric cultures and those Marija Gimbutas researched.

6 Starhawk (1997) 'Marija Gimbutas' work and the question of the sacred' in Marler, Joan (ed.) *From the Realm of the Ancestors*.

7 Starhawk, and film-maker Donna Read of Belili Productions, produced a documentary in memory of Marija Gimbutas entitled *Sign Out of Times*, released in 2003.

8 Barlow, Maureen (1998–1999) 'In Memory of Marija Gimbutas'.

9 Dames, Michael (1997) 'The Gimbutas gift' in Marler, Joan (ed.) *From the Realm of the Ancestors*.

10 Spretnak, Charlene (1997) 'Beyond the backlash', p. 400.

11 Christ, Carol (1997a) 'A different world', p. 408.

12 O'Murchu, Diarmuid (2000) *Religion in Exile*.

13 Sahtouris, Elizabet (2000) *Earthdance*.

14 In Steven Pinker's new book, *The Better Angels of Our Nature: The decline of violence in history and its causes,* he has revived the old argument that chimpanzees and humans are innately violent. According to reviewer Frank Carrigan, Steven Pinker argues that both psychology and history reveal "the interdependence of a fixed human nature with changing historical circumstances", pointing out that "civil society is nothing but a thin crust covering a volcanic set of primeval impulses." Steven Pinker

argues that humans were not "completely enslaved" by biology despite having to compete "for physical resources", which "ensured that humans were wired for violence from the outset." Evidence, however, suggests this is not the case.

We have found in our research that archaeologists almost always admit they find no signs of violence either in prehistoric graves or in excavations, while art historians often comment that prehistoric rock art paintings and engravings do not record anything other than hunting, gathering, dance, or everyday activities. It is also notable that any signs of violence towards other people appear at or after the beginning of the historical period.

According to Frank Carrigan, Steven Pinker, a psychologist and professor at Harvard University, is "one of the top 10 global public intellectuals", so what does it say about the level of intellectual engagement that this book ignores the considerable evidence which reveals a remarkably peaceful human prehistory. (Based on a two-page book review: Carrigan, Frank, 18–19 February 2012, *The Weekend Australian Review*, pp. 18–19.)

15 Rosenfeld, Diane (2009) 'Sexual coercion, patriarchal violence and law'.

16 Marler, Joan in Harris, Paula (1997) 'Old Souls: Joan Marler's Realm of the Ancestors', p. 1.

17 Dexter, Miriam Robbins in Gimbutas, Marija (2001) *The Living Goddesses*, p. xvii.

18 Gimbutas, Marija (2001) *The Living Goddesses*, p. 3.

19 Processual archaeology was a reaction against earlier archaeology in which cultural dimensions were explored based on the evidence of a people's material culture. Processual archaeologists claim to take a 'scientific' approach, but they ignore the material culture, the symbols and the prehistorical connections between societies. This has resulted in a significant loss of contextual studies which allow for a greater understanding of the societies being examined.

20 See Renfrew, Colin (1974) *The Explanation of Culture Change*, pp. 78–830.

21 Mandt, Gro (1997) 'The Women of Vingen', p. 163.

22 Marler, Joan (2004) 'A letter to the editor', *Scientific American*, p. 21.

23 Fagan, Brian M. (1991a) *Kingdoms of Gold, Kingdoms of Jade*.

24 Hodder, Ian in Marler, Joan (2004) 'A letter to the editor', *Scientific American*, p. 21.

25 ibid.

26 ibid.

27 Liberal feminists reify individual choice and independence and tend toward taking a libertarian view of social relations thereby ignoring systems of oppression; radical feminists consider that the well-being of the individual arises from the well-being of the group. An analysis of systematic oppression and how it functions is central to radical feminism. Because of the group-based or collective analysis, radical feminist approaches have more in common with the less individualistic philosophies and social structures that prevailed throughout our long human *pre*history.

28 Goodison, Lucy and Christine Morris (1998) *Ancient Goddesses*.

29 On the other hand, the liberal feminist processual archaeologists mentioned above, featured in *Ancient Goddesses* (Lucy Goodison and Christine Morris, 1998), are often reluctant to interpret the imagery in any way, thus omitting what would be considered an important aspect of the prehistoric picture. Is this not another form of bias?

30 Conkey, Margaret and Ruth Tringham (1996) 'Cultivating thinking / challenging authority', p. 225.

31 Starhawk argues that the power women had in prehistory was 'power-within', rather than 'power-over'.

32 Marler, Joan (2003) 'The myth of universal patriarchy'.

33 Sanday, Peggy Reeves (2002) in Marler, Joan (2003) 'The myth of universal patriarchy', p. 4.

34 Brown, David J. and Rebecca McClen Novik (Interviewers) (1992) 'Learning the language of the goddess'.

CHAPTER 2 Identifying Bias in Research

1   Note on use of gender and sex:
    In archaeology we cannot know anything about gender, since it has to be based on findings. We can
    know the sex of an individual, but not whether they behaved according to what we know as the cultural
    forms of 'feminine' and 'masculine'. This is particularly so given the argument of this book, namely
    that women and men – that is, the sexes – acted in culturally different ways than those prescribed by
    patriarchal societies. Therefore, unless we are discussing cultural gender norms, in this book we use the
    word 'sex' to give greater clarity to our meaning.
2   Daly, Mary (1973/1986) *Beyond God the Father.*
3   Twohig, Elizabeth Shee and Margaret Ronayne (eds) (1993) *Past Perceptions.*
4   Lerner, Gerda (1986) *The Creation of Patriarchy.*
5   Gero, Joan (1996) 'Archaeological practice and gendered encounters with field data'.
6   Robin Morgan's *Anatomy of Freedom* (1982) includes an excellent discussion of objectivity.
7   Christ, Carol (1980) *Diving Deep and Surfacing*, p. x.
8   Dames, Michael (1997) 'The Gimbutas gift'.
9   Ehrenberg, Margaret (1989) *Women in Prehistory.*
10 McGaw, Judith (1996) 'Recovering Technology'.
11 Mellaart, James (1970) *Excavations at Hacilar.*
12 Kehoe, Alice Beck (1998) *The Land of Prehistory*, p. ix.
13 Renfrew, Colin and Paul Bahn (1991) *Archaeology.*
14 More recently, in the 2008 *Handbook of South American Archaeology* (Silverman, Helaine and William H.
    Isbell eds), little has changed. For example, prehistoric non-material evidence, such as the many female
    figurines and imagery on early pottery, are barely mentioned, although those which appear in the early
    historic period are shown in some detail.
15 Sahtouris, Elizabet (2000) *Earthdance*, p. 115.
16 Lorblanchet, M. (1977) 'From naturalism to abstraction in European prehistoric art', p. 50.
17 For example, scholars such as Franz Boas (1955) attempted to trace styles of shapes and decoration of
    objects from the Native American present back to the past in order to discover origins for the designs.
    He worked in the field and built up large inventories of designs on such objects as pots, baskets and
    clothes (all of which were made by women), to get some idea of 'primitive' (male) Native American
    cultural traits.
18 This involved limited work with experts in other related fields to discover a more complete picture of
    a particular ancient community. Research would reveal what materials people (men) had used to build
    their shelters, what kind of food they ate, what sort of animals they killed in the hunt, even the details of
    their physical environment.
19 Eisler, Riane (1990) *The Chalice and the Blade.*
20 Bednarik, Robert (1995) 'Concept-mediated markings in the Lower Palaeolithic', pp. 605–634.
21 There are also two views of the movements of the earliest humans: the conservative one which doubts
    the 'humanity' of those early hominids, and holds that modern humans came out of Africa at the
    beginning of the Upper Palaeolithic. The second, more progressive view, argues that modern humans
    evolved from *Homo erectus* independently in different parts of the world around about the same time; and
    that *H. erectus* humans ought to be credited with possessing far more intelligence than they have been.
22 Sanday, Peggy Reeves (1998) 'Matriarchy as a Sociocultural Form', p. 2.
23 Marler, Joan (2003) 'The myth of patriarchy', p. 4.
24 Bachofen, J.J. (1967) *Myth, Religion and Mother Right.*
25 Peggy Reeves Sanday (1998) describes the origins of the term: Louis Henry Morgan (*Ancient Society,*
    1877), Jane Harrison (*Prolegomena to the Study of Greek Religion,* 1903), Sir James Fraser (*The Golden
    Bough,* 1911–15), and Robert Briffault (*The Mothers,* 1927) all described early societies as egalitarian and
    matriarchal in the first sense. Carl Gustav Jung (1950) and Erich Neumann (1955) built upon the notion
    of the 'Great Mother Goddess'. James Mellaart's revealing excavations at Çatal Hüyük (1967) and Marija

Gimbutas's ground breaking *Gods and Goddesses of Old Europe* (1974), provided tangible evidence which further developed this theme. Dorothy Cameron (1981) followed with her images of Neolithic goddess symbolism in *Symbols of Birth and of Death in the Neolithic Era*.

26 Allen, Paula Gunn (1986) *The Sacred Hoop*.

27 Dashu, Max (2004a) *Icons of the Matrix*.

28 Dashu, Max (2004b) *Suppressed Histories Archives*, p. 6.

29 *The Australian Concise Oxford Dictionary* (1995), p. 697.

30 mātṛi: Sanskrit; meter: Greek; mater: Latin – all words for mother are the source words for matrix which, in Latin, means womb.

31 Sanday, Peggy Reeves (2002) *Women at the Centre*.

32 The Greek word *barbaros* originally meant a non-Greek speaking person. The word is onomatopoeic, in the sense that it mimics a person whose language sounds like a series of 'barbars', that is, foreign 'gobbledygook'. The politics of language infuses the discipline of archaeology.

33 Flannery, Tim (1994) *The Future Eaters*.

34 Past glaciation broke up the rocky surface over time causing the release of rich nutrients and the build up of deep soils which were continually spread around by the numerous rivers.

35 Semi-permanent circular huts made with stone bases supporting wooden beams upon which peat turf was laid, were present at Lake Condah in southern Victoria around 8,000 BP, according to Heather Builth (Phillips, Graham, 13 March 2003, 'Life was not a walkabout for Victoria's Aborigines'). They were used by Indigenous people in association with eel 'farming'. See chapter on Australia.

36 Gimbutas, Marija (1991) *The Civilization of the Goddess*, p. viii.

37 Gimbutas, Marija (1999/2001) *The Living Goddesses*.

38 Schmandt-Besserat, Denise (1992/1996) *How Writing Came About*.

39 Schmandt-Besserat, Denise (2007) *When Writing Met Art*, p. 50.
    According to Denise Schmandt-Besserat, the earliest markings indicated units and numbers of goods, descriptions of goods, etc. Gradually a formal organisation of information emerged, for example, the signs could be 'read' lineally; the location of motifs above/below was linear; the order of signs was linear, with the direction of lines of signs leading left to right.
    There were six stages of development of the accounting tokens:

    - plain geometric tokens
    - plain clay envelopes holding tokens were used
    - markings (signs) were impressed into the wet clay of the envelopes
    - impressed tablets recording numbers and identity of goods were developed
    - pictographic motifs were impressed or incised on the tablets indicating numerical information
    - the cuneiform script, the first pre-writing in the Near East appeared around 5,100 BP during the early historic period.

40 She does not mention the earlier Vinča script as recorded by Marija Gimbutas perhaps because it has not yet been deciphered, or perhaps she feels the origins of the Vinča script bear no relation to the art and writing in the Near East. She argues that not until after 5,500 BP did art become narrative, and writing move beyond accounting to become a comprehensive medium of communication.

41 Rudgley, Richard (1998) *Lost Civilizations of the Stone Age*.

42 According to Richard Rudgley (1998), civilisation today is clearly not superior to that in the times before history. For example, we consider prehistoric people as superstitious and believing in 'magic', yet superstitions such as not walking under ladders, or touching wood, together with the magic of occultism and astrology, are very much part of Western life today. Body mutilation is also much in vogue – pierced body parts, breast implants, and circumcisions are as much used today as initiation scarring, tattoos, sub-incision, and ear-piercing were in the past.

43 Bednarik, Robert (1997a) 'Origins of navigation and language'.

CHAPTER 3 Intangible Evidence

1   Bohm, David and Mark Edwards (1991) *Changing Consciousness.*
2   Marshack, Alexander (1977) 'The meander as a system'.
3   Leakey, Richard and Roger Lewin (1992) *Origins Reconsidered.*
4   Bednarik, Robert (1997b) 'Makepansgat hominid head'.
5   Bednarik, Robert (1994b) 'The Pleistocene art of Asia'.
6   Jespersen, Otto (1922) *Language: Its nature, development and origin* cited in Danesi, Marcel Vico (1993) *Metaphor and the Origin of Language*, pp. 6–7.
7   Depending on their field of expertise and interest, linguists might concentrate on the reconstruction of a proto-language and how the diversity of languages came about, or how language and concept making are connected, and the question of humans possessing an innate language faculty or capability, and the existence of a universal grammar.
8   Aitchison, Jean (1996) *The Seeds of Speech.*
9   More recent information, such as evidence of the 700,000-year-old seafaring ability mentioned previously, suggests much earlier origins for language.
10 Ruhlen, Merritt (1994) *The Origin of Language.*
11 For comparative source material on goddesses across the Indo-European language spectrum see: Dexter, Miriam Robbins (1990) *Whence the Goddess: A Source Book.* Pergamon Press: Athene Series, New York.
12 Ruhlen, Merritt (1994) *The Origin of Language*, pp. 30–31.
13 Pinker, Steven (1994) *The Language Instinct.*
14 Going further back, it has been established that the languages of the Angles and Saxons evolved from Proto-Germanic, a language spoken by a tribe occupying northern Europe in the first millennium BCE. It belongs to the western branch of the tribe and together with German, Yiddish, Dutch, Afrikaans, Swedish, Danish, Norwegian and Icelandic, it originated from the northern branch which settled in Scandinavia. For an example of an Indo-European language tree see: InterSol Inc. (1996–2010) 'The Proto-Indo-European Language Tree' (Diagram); and Wikimedia Commons (18 October 2008) 'Partial tree of Indo-European languages' (Diagram).
15 Pinker, Steven (1994) *The Language Instinct.* See map p. 241.
16 For instance, it was discovered by the famous fairy tale collector and linguist, Jacob Grimm (of the Grimm brothers), that the 'p' and 't' sounds in Proto-Indo-European changed to 'f' and 'th' in Germanic. For example: Sanskrit *piter* → Latin *pater* → English 'father' (Pinker, Steven 1994, p. 252).
17 Pinker, Steven (1994) *The Language Instinct*, p. 253.
18 On the basis of some similarities found between most languages (although this may be very speculative) the above mentioned linguists assign all of these languages to a common ancestor proto-proto-language they named 'Nostraic'. This theory is based on the hypothetical Nostraic root *marja* which then is compared, for instance, with the Proto-Indo-European *mor* for 'mulberry', the Proto-Uralic *marja* for 'berry', and the Proto-Kartvelian (Georgian) *mar-caw* for 'strawberry'. In the same way a resemblance has been found between the Indo-European word *melk* for 'breast' and *mlg* for 'to suckle' in Arabic.
19 Campbell, Joseph (1959/1969) *The Masks of God*, p. xvii.
20 ibid., p. 22.
21 Stone, Merlin (1991) *Ancient Mirrors of Womanhood.*
22 It is interesting to note that the literal meaning of the word 'heathen' is 'from the heath' (countryside), while the word 'pagan' (Latin *paganus*) means 'country person' or 'other than Christian, Jew or Mohammedan' (ibid., p. 7).
23 Dames, Michael (1992/1996) *Mythic Ireland*, p. 14.
24 ibid., p 10.
25 Barber, Elizabeth Wayland (1994) *Women's Work.*
26 Lauter, Estella (1984) 'Steps towards a feminist archetypal theory of myth-making'.
27 In a similar vein, see Orenstein, Gloria Feman (1990) *The Reflowering of the Goddess.*
28 Barber, Elizabeth with Paul T. Barber (2004) *When They Severed Earth From Sky*, p. 246.

29 Clunies-Ross, Margaret (1983) 'Modes of formal performance in societies without writing', p. 1.

30 ibid., p. 16.

31 The consequences of a people adopting the writing system (literacy) have been far reaching. It is not only the forms of communication which are affected but also thinking processes, social organisation and technological developments (ibid., p. 16).

Comparing written with non-written text, Margaret Clunies-Ross argues that, although the written text has a fixed form, it may acquire some minor variations. However, there are non-literate societies or groups who are adamant that the nature of the oral form they use is unchanging. This is especially so with Australian Indigenous societies who insist that the content and form of their oral performances were created in the Dreamtime when the world was created (this topic is discussed later in this book, including in chapter 15). However, "there are various mechanisms … whereby innovation is introduced into the repertoire." There is a general recognition that "every performance is in a sense a new creation … created from within the possible manifestation of a particular form" variance depending on particular circumstances, the individual performer and the expectation of the society (ibid., p. 21).

32 According to Isidore Okpewho in *African Oral Literature* (1992), in the past some scholars seemed to have difficulties in applying the term 'literature' to any oral performance or transmission of culture, history, etc. because of its association with folklore. The term literature, in its restricted sense, is usually assigned to written texts which are creative and imaginative (such as stories, plays, and poems). In the more common sense, literature may refer to any type and volume of written or printed text. In general, the term 'oral literature' is today used for "literature delivered by word of mouth" (p. 3). (For similar reasons the term 'pre-literate' infers that prehistoric people and indigenous people are too primitive to have any form of story telling – or oral literature.)

Two East African scholars define oral literature as spoken, recited or sung compositions in performance which display accurate observation, vivid imagination and ingenious expression (Nandwa and Bukenya in Okpewho, Isidore 1992, pp. 4–5).

33 ibid.

34 ibid., p. 7.

35 Terms such as 'folk literature', 'traditional literature' or 'folklore' are often linked to images of uneducated or 'primitive' societies, an association that goes right back to the evolutionist theory of the earlier stages of humankind. According to the evolutionists, any text, be it oral or written, is the survival of an earlier one, and by transmission over time and generations, lost qualities which had appeal to the original owners, and thereby had weakened considerably. Therefore, to this scholar, the genre of fairy tale presupposes a 'civilised' society, according to Alexander Krappe.

36 Goodall, Heather (1992) 'The whole truth and nothing but … '.

37 Michaels, Eric (1987) *For a Cultural Future.*

38 Bell, Diane (1998a) *Ngarrindjeri Wurruwarrin.*

39 Goodall, Heather (1992) 'The whole truth and nothing but … ', p. 110.

40 ibid., p. 111.

41 Flood, Josephine and Bruno David (1994) 'Traditional systems of encoding meaning in Wardaman rock art'.

42 Myth and The Dreaming: The term 'The Dreaming' is constantly present in any reference to Australian Indigenous people and their way of living and thinking, and it is undoubtedly best defined by them. Indigenous Professor Marcia Langton sees the Dreaming "as a world view … the Aboriginal reality and not the dream" (in Coombs, H.C. et al 1983, p. 34) while according to poet Kevin Gilbert

> [t]he Dreaming, the Dreamtime, not only refers to an historic era in the long distant past but is a living continuation of spiritual life and instruction that continues today (ibid., p. 35).

For non-Indigenous anthropologist John Stanner it is 'The Everlasting Present', and is

> [a] philosophy in mythology attained as the social product of an indefinitely ancient past, and [the Aboriginal] proceeds to live it out 'in life', in part through a ritual and an expressive art, and in part through non-sacred social customs (ibid., p. 34).

According to non-Indigenous Deborah Bird Rose, Dreaming refers to

> the creative beings who make possible the continued coming into being of the world; and they are living powers in the world ... [T]he earth is referred to by some people as 'Mother'; she brings forth life. Some of this life is male and some is female. Males and females, whether pythons, or kangaroos, or human beings, travelled the earth creating among other things, a gendered landscape (1994, 'Flesh and blood and deep colonising', p. 328).

43 The very creation of such skilfully manufactured objects must have had meaning or they would never have been made. Their creation would have involved the collection and selection of raw materials, and tools such as drills and sharpeners, grinding stones, and string or thongs; the ability to make string and tie knots would also be necessary.

44 Ungurmarr-Baumann, Miriam Rose (1998) '*Ngangkurungkurr* (Deep Water Sounds)', p. 3.

45 Atkinson, Judy (2002) *Trauma Trails, Recreating Song Lines*, p. 18.

46 Bell, Diane (1998a) *Ngarrindjeri Wurruwarrin*, p. 223.

47 Munn, Nancy (1973) *Walbiri Iconography*.
Nancy Munn was apparently one of the few female researchers of the time to come to Australia to study the symbolic images used by the Desert people at Yuendumu in 1956–1957. Her mentors were well-known male anthropologists, such as Mervyn Meggit and W.E.H. Stanner. She recorded a great deal of imagery concerning both women and men in some detail but, like her mentors, considered that men's imagery was always the most important and the only sacred imagery. Any women's imagery was apparently considered secular. At first she was not allowed to see men's secret rituals, nor preparation for these or for secular ceremonies. (This is not surprising given what we now know from Diane Bell's experience: as an uninitiated female visitor with little understanding of Indigenous protocol, she probably was not given sacred meanings of men's 'business' either). The only female imagery she was shown was women's body painting (but not its sacred aspects). She did not learn anything about women's own secret ritual objects and ceremonies.

48 Napanangka, Tjama in dé Ishtar, Zohl (1994) *Daughters of the Pacific*, p. 144.

49 Nancy Munn gives an interesting overview of *yawulyu* from the public aspect including both men's and women's roles relating to it, although her version largely misses the depth of meaning revealed by Zohl dé Ishtar. Since her informants were mainly men, it could not have been otherwise.

50 dé Ishtar, Zohl (2005) *Holding Yawulyu*, p. 43.

51 ibid., p. 26.

52 Bell, Diane (1983/2002) *Daughters of the Dreaming*.

53 Gunn-Allen, Paula (1986) *The Sacred Hoop*.

54 ibid., p. 107.

CHAPTER 4 Tangible Evidence

1 Bednarik, Robert (1997a) 'Origins of navigation and language'.

2 Gimbutas, Marija (1989) *The Language of the Goddess*.

3 Early images of lunar symbolism include circles surrounded by rays, circles, and half circles, and apparently represented the cyclic mode of nature, linking it with the waxing and waning of the moon, where all in nature is born, grows, and dies in cyclic pattern, where "all is bound together by the same lunar rhythm" (Eliade, Mircea, 1976, 'Symbols – patterns, transitions and paradises', p. 349).

4 Campbell, Joseph (1959/1969) *The Masks of God* (Vol. 1), p. 4.

5 Leroi-Gourhan, Andre (1968) *The Art of Prehistoric Man in Europe*, p. 287.

6 Marshack, Alexander (1977) 'The meander as a system'.

7 Janson, H.W. (1986) *History of Art*, p. 9.

8 Bednarik, Robert (1994c) 'Art origins'.

9 Bahn, Paul (1998) *Prehistoric Art*.

10 Bednarik, Robert (1995) 'Concept-mediated marking in the Lower Paleolithic'.

11 Lewis-Williams, J.D. and T.A. Dowson (1988) 'The signs of all times'.

12 Bahn, Paul (1998) *Prehistoric Art*.

13 Furthermore, because hallucinations derive from the human nervous system, all people who enter certain altered states of consciousness, no matter what their cultural background, are liable to perceive these non-real mental images. Other causes of hallucinations and the like include psychoactive drugs, fatigue, sensory deprivation, intense concentration, auditory driving, migraine, schizophrenia, hyperventilation, and rhythmic movement (Lewis-Williams, J.D. and T.A. Dowson, 1988, 'The signs of all times', p. 202).

14 Feliks, John (1998) 'The impact of fossils on the development of visual representation'.

15 Feliks, John (2006) 'Musings on the Palaeolithic fan motif', p. 1.
See replies to John Feliks's, 'The impact of fossils on the development of visual representation', by John Bradshaw, Laurence Straus; and response by John Feliks (1998) in *Rock Art Research* 15 (2), pp. 109–134.

16 Feliks, John (2006) 'Musings on the Palaeolithic fan motif'.

17 Chakravarty, Kalyan and Robert Bednarik (1997) *Indian Rock Art and Its Global Context*, p. 129.

18 Gimbutas, Marija (1989) *The Language of the Goddess*, p. 322.

19 ibid., p. 56.

20 Gimbutas, Marija (1991) *The Civilization of the Goddess*, p. 400.

21 Bell, Diane (1998a) *Ngarrindjeri Wurruwarrin*.

22 The pattern appears circular when completed. The weaving begins at the centre and works outwards. A number of different shapes may be produced. The circle produced through weaving is a metaphor for connectivity, family and community.

23 Bell, Diane (1998a) *Ngarrindjeri Wurruwarrin*, p. 69.

24 ibid., p. 69.

25 ibid., p. 88.

26 ibid., p. 542.

27 Liebes, Sidney, Elizabet Sahtouris and Brian Swimme (1998) *A Walk Through Time*, p. 127.

28 Andrews, Munya (2004) *The Seven Sisters of the Pleiades*.

29 ibid., p. 3.
Munya Andrews was told how, in the Dreamtime, the Seven Sisters came down from the sky to land on a high hill. Underneath was a cave, from which the Sisters came and went, and it was a home for them on earth. They would skilfully hunt and gather food for their stay. One day an old man saw them returning to the cave and followed them so he could get himself a wife. He hid behind a bush and grabbed the youngest sister, while the other Sisters escaped back to the cave, climbed through a secret passage to the hilltop and flew back into the sky carrying their digging sticks. The youngest sister called for them to help her but they had already gone. She vigorously fought the old man until she was able to escape, and followed her sisters into the cave. She kept calling them even as the old man followed her back up to the sky. Her star is harder to find as she is always in the distance trying to catch up with her sisters. "According to our elders", says Munya Andrews, "you can still see that old man in the night skies as they point to the evening and morning star [(Venus)]. There he goes, they say, still chasing the Seven Sisters" (p. 3). This is the children's version of the story, as the versions of stories for older children and adults become more complex, and there are secret sacred versions which may only be told to certain women and men who are entitled to hear them. Around Australia there are slightly different stories, with different names for the Sisters. More than seven stars have been noted by the people of Northern and Central Australia, made possible by the exceptionally clear night skies.
Munya Andrews has researched the meanings of the Pleiades in other parts of the world, noting how many similarities there are in the various versions of countries such as Greece, Europe, the Americas, and India. (See *The Seven Sisters of the Pleiades*, 2004.)

30 ibid., p. 31.

31 ibid., p. 30.

32 ibid., p. 51.

33 An example of the meander symbol as it appears on a 300,000-year-old ox bone found at Pech de l'Azé includes: a broken central double arc which continues with further parallel arcing; one double arc

with lines running from wide to narrow spacing; one set of lines in the image of a 'U'; and one which includes multiple stroking, such as those lines formed by running one's spread fingers across a surface (Marshack, Alexander, 1977, 'The meander as a system', p. 291).

34   However, there were many other symbols, not mentioned here, first appearing in the Neolithic period which are illustrated in Marija Gimbutas's extensive collection in her *Language of the Goddess* (1989) for those who are interested.

35   Richard Rudgley (1998) *Lost Civilizations of the Stone Age*, p. 73.

36   Gimbutas, Marija (1989) *The Language of the Goddess*, p. 56.

37   dé Ishtar, Zohl (2005) *Holding Yawulyu*, p. 32.

38   Gimbutas, Marija (1989) *The Language of the Goddess*, p. 213.

CHAPTER 5   Northern Hemisphere

1   Bednarik, Robert (November, 2001) 'An Acheulian figurine from Morocco', pp. 115–116.

2   Rudgley, Richard (1998) *Lost Civilizations of the Stone Age*.

3   Bahn, Paul (ed.) (1992) *Collins Dictionary of Archaeology*.

4   Whitaker, Alex (n.d.) 'Chauvet-Pont-d'Arc Cave'.

5   Clottes, Jean (2003) *Chauvet Cave: The Art of Earliest Times*, p. 3.

6   Grand, P.M. (1967) *Prehistoric Art: Paleolithic painting and sculpture*.

7   Janson, H.W. (1986) *History of Art*.

8   Bahn, Paul (1998) *Prehistoric Art: Cambridge illustrated history*, p. 196.

9   Conard, Nicholas J. (14 May 2009) 'A female figurine from the basal Aurignacian of Hohle Fels Cave in southwestern Germany', pp. 248–252.
     See also: Conard, Nicholas J. 'From Cave painting to the Internet', <http://www.nature.com.nature/videoarchive/prehistoricpinup/>.

10   Smith, Deborah (14 May, 2009) 'Busty "Venus" is first human in art', p. 11.

11   The misuse of words like 'pornographic' and 'erotic' to describe ancient figures is not at all useful in understanding the imagery. As argued in this book, these figures are powerful emblems and represent women in respectful and sometime awe-filled ways. By contrast, pornography refers to demeaning and degrading portrayals of women for (in the main) the male gaze. Likewise, referring to these as erotic is a misrepresentation of the metaphysical purpose of these figures.

12   Pericot-Garcia, Luis, John Galloway and Andreas Lommel (1967) *Prehistory and Primitive Art*.

13   Clark, Graham (1961) 'The first half-million years'.

14   Marshack, Alexander (1991) *The Roots of Civilization*.

15   Feminist archaeologists Margaret Conkey and Ruth Tringham point out that the term 'goddess' is not recognised by most archaeologists because "[they] seem to have difficulty in dealing with the symbolic or spiritual" (in Wright, Rita, 1996, *Gender and Archaeology*, p. 231).

16   Dashu, Max (2010) 'The Meanings of Goddess' (Part 2), p. 4.

17   Dashu, Max (2010) 'The Meanings of Goddess' (Part 1).

18   ibid., p. 4.

19   Lerner, Gerda (1986) *The Creation of Patriarchy*.

20   Marshack, Alexander (1977) 'The meander as a system'.

21   Barber, Elizabeth Wayland (1994) *Women's Work*.

22   Kvavadze, Eliso, Ofer Bar-Yosef et al (11 September 2009) '30,000-year-old wild flax fibers'.

23   Eliso Kvavadze and Ofer Bar-Yosef, and five other archaeologists, announced the discovery in *Science* (11 September, 2009).

24   Olga Soffer of the University of Illinois in *British Archaeology Magazine* 52 (April 2000).
     See update in Soffer, Olga, J.M. Adovasio and D.C. Hyland (2000) 'The "Venus" figurines', pp. 511–537.

25   When she tried wearing a similar skirt for a time, Elizabeth Barber found that the swing of the skirts gave her a feeling of power.

26   Davidson, Hilda Ellis (1998) *Roles of the Northern Goddess*.

[27] Cameron, Dorothy (1981) *Symbols of Birth and Death in the Neolithic Era.*

[28] Marshack, Alexander (1991) *The Roots of Civilization.*

[29] Schmandt-Besserat, Denise (1992/1996) *How Writing Came About.*

[30] Tikva Frymer-Kensky (1993) had first noticed women using clay tokens to "assist them in keeping an account when storing household supplies in the late prehistoric and early historic Sumerian societies" (pp. 34–35).

[31] Gimbutas, Marija (1989) *The Language of the Goddess.*

[32] Baring, Anne and Jules Cashford (1991) *The Myth of the Goddess.*

[33] Gimbutas, Marija (1999) *The Living Goddesses*, p. 5.

[34] The symbolism of making (the pot), baking and sharing of bread is discussed by Beth Hensperger (1997) in Marler, Joan (ed.) *From the Realm of the Ancestors.*

[35] At Cuddie Springs in northern New South Wales a large number of grinding stones were found in 1997 which suggest "a broad-spectrum plant-processing economy much earlier than previously known" (Fullagar, R. and J. Field, 1997, 'Pleistocene seed-grinding implements …', p. 300). New evidence in 2001 substantiated the dates in the first excavation. See: Field, Judith, R. Fullagar and Gary Lord (2001) 'A large area archaeological excavation at Cuddie Springs', pp. 252–702.

[36] Dames, Michael (2009) 'Footsteps of the goddess in Britain and Ireland'.

[37] Gimbutas, Marija (1989) *The Language of the Goddess.*

[38] Harrod, James (1997) 'The Upper Paleolithic "Double Goddess"', p. 494.

[39] Dames, Michael (1976) *The Silbury Treasure.*

[40] Biaggi, Cristina (1994) *Habitations of the Great Goddess*, p. xxiv.

[41] ibid., p. xxvi.

[42] One or two examples of what seem to be all-over pitted stone blocks at tomb entrances are reminiscent of the small (ritual?) cupules which it is thought women who wanted babies may have made on rock walls or pillars in India, and North America. (Are the Jinmiun cupules, near Kununurra, Australia [an Indigenous women's site] or those accompanying vulva symbols on a rock wall in Carnarvon Gorge, Queensland, further examples of similar women's rituals?)

[43] New evidence found at Stonehenge reveals it is part of a very large complex, with a second older 'henge' made of timber found near the stone monument. Both buildings were originally beside a long avenue leading to a river. More discoveries are likely in the future. Further information may be found at the Ancient Wisdom website <www.ancient-wisdom.co.uk/englandstonehenge.htm>.

[44] Perhaps it is this symbolism which Plato found so abhorrent, as it focused too much on the importance of female aspects. He would have viewed death as final, as do all Indo-European cultures today, and the cave or grave as a menacing underworld, places to be avoided and feared. (See later chapter in Part 2.)

[45] Chakrabarti, Dilip (1999) *India, An Archaeological History*, p. 82.

[46] If these symbols are placed together vertically with points touching, they form the prehistoric hourglass or double-triangle regenerative symbol, and the borrowing of a so-called pagan symbolism.
For those who wish to further investigate the Neolithic goddess see Miriam Robbins Dexter (1990) *Whence the Goddess.*

CHAPTER 6   Hunter-Gathering, the First Horticulture and Agriculture

[1] Robert Bednarik (1996) revealed that there are now signs that *H. habilis* had been present in Asia as well as in Africa, suggesting that humans may have evolved simultaneously in more than one part of the world.

[2] Bednarik, Robert (1996) 'The Origins of *H. habilis* in Africa and Asia'.

[3] Sloan, Christopher (November 2006) 'The origin of childhood', pp. 48–159.

[4] Morwood, Mike, Thomas Sutikna and Richard Roberts (April 2005) 'World of the Little People'.

[5] ibid.

[6] Fischman, Josh (April 2005) 'Family Ties', pp. 16–27.

7 In March 2012, Deborah Smith (*The Age*) and *National Geographic Daily News* published news of evidence of a prehistoric group of previously unknown humans which was discovered in Red Deer Cave in Yunnan, China, dated to between 14,500 and 11,500 BP (Smith, Deborah, 15 March 2012 'Scientists stumped by prehistoric human …', pp. 1, 6; Owen, James, 14 March 2012 'Cave Fossil Find'.)

8 O'Kelly, Michael (1989) *Early Ireland*.

9 Bednarik, Robert (1996) 'The Origins of *H. habilis* in Africa and Asia'.

10 However, the notion concerning the descent of all humans from one woman, 'African Eve', through the examination of genetic chromosome sequences (DNA) in order to find a common ancestor for all present-day humans is not a viable proposition because DNA evidence is not always reliable (Bednarik, Robert, 1994e, 'African Eve DNA').

11 Ehrenberg, Margaret (1989) *Women in Prehistory*.

12 Bell, Diane (1983/2002) *Daughters of the Dreaming*, pp. 54–55.

13 Bell, Diane (1998a) *Ngarrindjeri Wurruwarrin*.

14 Barber, Elizabeth Wayland (1994) *Women's Work*.

15 Soffer, Olga (2000) 'Woven clothing dates back 27,000 years', pp. 2–3.

16 Bednarik, Robert (1997a) 'Origins of navigation and language'.

17 Sahtouris, Elizabet (1999b) 'Living systems in evolution'.

18 ibid., p. 1.

19 Gimbutas, Marija (1991) *The Civilization of the Goddess*.

20 Conkey, Margaret and Ruth Tringham (1996) 'Cultivating thinking / Challenging authority'.

21 Eisler, Riane (1990) *The Chalice and the Blade*.

22 Sahtouris, Elizabet (2000) *Earthdance*.

23 Gimbutas, Marija (1991) *The Civilization of the Goddess*.

24 ibid.

25 ibid., pp. 21–22.

26 Mellaart, James (1975) *The Neolithic of the Near East*.

27 More recent descriptions of the Natufians differ little from this information. Today the information about art and artefacts is no longer researched in accordance with post-processual archaeological methods.

28 Hauptmann, Harald (1988) 'Nevali Cori: Architekur', pp. 99–110.
   See also report 'Nevali Cori' at <http://en.wikipedia.org/wiki/Neval%C4%B1%C3%87ori> (accessed July, 2011).

29 Moore, Andrew, Gordon Hillman and Anthony Legge (2000) *Villages on the Euphrates*. Also a report 'Tell Abu Hureyra' at <http://archaeology.about com/od/althroughadterms/qt/Abu-Hureyra.htm>.

30 Moore, Andrew, Gordon Hillman and Anthony Legge (2000) 'Tell Abu Hureyra', p. 2.

31 Mann, Charles C. (2011) 'The birth of religion' [Klaus Schmidt], pp. 34–59.
   Scham, Sandra (November/December 2008) 'The World's First Temple' [Klaus Schmidt].

32 Scham, Sandra (November/December 2008) 'The world's first temple' [Klaus Schmidt], p. 1.

33 Banning, Ted (6 October 2011) 'Archaeologist argues world's oldest temples were not temples at all'.

34 ibid.

35 Banning, Ted (2011) 'So fair a house', p. 621.

36 Shou, Benjamin (2010) 'Jerf el Ahmar' at <http://wki.sjs.org/wiki/index.php/Jerf_el_Ahmar>.
   The Jerf el Ahmar site is possibly the first complex farming town in Syria, built by sedentary hunter/ farmers, according to Benjamin Shou (2010). The main circular stone-walled (ritual?) building is erected partly below ground level, and is divided into eight irregularly shaped small rooms around a central 'court'. Other houses nearby are rectangular with four rooms. (A photograph can be found at <http://wki.sjs.org/wiki/index.php/Jerf_el_Ahmar>.)

37 Akkermans, Peter (2011) in 'Comments' to Banning, Ted (2011) 'So fair a house', pp. 641–660.

38 Banning, Ted (2011) 'So fair a house', p. 621.

39 Harrigan, Peter (2008) 'Art rocks in Saudi Arabia'.

[40] Bednarik, Robert in Harrigan, Peter (2008) 'Art rocks in Saudi Arabia', p. 2.
See also the original report: Bednarik, Robert and Majeed Khan (2005) 'Scientific studies of Saudi Arabian rock art', pp. 49–81.

[41] A series of excellent photographs of some sites by Lars Bjurstrom accompany the 2008 article 'Art rocks in Saudi Arabia' in *Saudi Aramco World* 59 (7), <http://www.saudiaramcoworld.com/issue/200807/art. rocks.in.saudi.arabia-compilation.htm> (accessed January 2012).
More photographs are included in 'Introduction to Saudi Arabian rock art and petroglyphs' in *Sandladder* 234, December 2010, pp. 30–37, <http://ancient-cultures.info/attachments/File/RR_article_petroglyph> (accessed January, 2012).

CHAPTER 7   Three Prehistoric Civilisations

[1] The timing and length of the Neolithic period varies in different parts of the world, and in most places in the Northern Hemisphere (with the exception of Crete) it had ended by 4,500 BP.

[2] Bednarik, Robert (1994d) 'Miscellanea'.

[3] In *The Goddess and the Bull* (1995), journalist Michael Balter (the Hodder 'official' biographer), tells the (biased) story of the eventual banning of James Mellaart from the Çatal Hüyük site after an ancient treasure trove disappeared without a trace from another village site. The Turkish government prevented James Mellaart from continuing the dig because he had previously published the find in 1959, and because they "assumed [the treasure] had been smuggled out of the country" (p. 44) although there was never any evidence of this having occurred. Suspicions still lingered and James Mellaart could no longer visit Turkey. The dig has been continued by his colleague, Ian Hodder, the post-processual archaeologist who had apparently reinvented the way archaeology is practised with the new benefits of science (but without regard to most other aspects). James Mellaart is now considered 'of the old school' because of his 'historical' approach to archaeology, and consequently his considerable contribution to the world of archaeology is today largely ignored.

[4] Mellaart, James (1967) *Çatal Hüyük*.

[5] James Mellaart was later greatly criticised for making too many 'unscientific' assumptions about his discoveries at Çatal Hüyük, with the processual archaeologists considering that he had 'a vivid imagination'. Yet if one examines his 1967 report, the photographs alone of his discoveries are compelling evidence, even without the text.

[6] Unfortunately the Berkeley University team led by Mirjana Stevanovic and Ruth Tringham will very likely ignore important goddess aspects if they intend to record using current narrow scientific methods (Hodder, Ian, December 1998, *Catalhoyuk Newsletter* 5).

[7] Hodder, Ian (2006) *The Leopard's Tale*.

[8] This practice still takes place today. The plastering assisted the durability of the houses, which generally lasted up to 100–120 years. Some houses had as many as 60 layers of plaster, by which time they would become so unstable as to need to be pulled down and rebuilt over the flattened walls of the previous house (Mellaart, James, 1975, pp. 50–56).

[9] Gimbutas, Marija (1991) *The Civilization of the Goddess*.

[10] Ian Hodder compares Çatal Hüyük culture with that of Tikopia, which is one of the most remote of the southern Solomon Islands. Tikopia is five square kilometres in size, and 350 metres above sea level. The people are not Melanesians (as are those of the rest of the long-settled Solomon Islands and Papua New Guinea), but Polynesians who still observe Polynesian patrilineal and matrilateral traditions. Considering that Polynesian cultures are only 3,000 years old, it is hardly a fair comparison with the 7,000–9,000-year-old Çatal Hüyük!

[11] A press release in 2008 noted there were experts from eight countries working with the Turkish archaeologists in a new seasonal dig. New finds included wall paintings, stamp seals and several small figurines, probably female. Two burnt houses have also been found in one area, and large ovens in another, but few details of these have been provided (Hodder, Ian, December 2001, *Catalhoyuk Newsletter* 8).

12 *The Goddess from Anatolia*:

- Volume 1 – contained photographs from the site
- Volume 2 – James Mellaart wrote about the content and interpretations of the unpublished wall paintings at Çatal Hüyük
- Volume 3 – Udo Hirsch wrote on early economies and culture of Anatolia, its mythology and kilim weaving methods
- Volume 4 – Belkis Balpinar wrote on the history of Anatolian kilims and designs, also the Turco-Islamic period and Anatolian kilim design groups.

Rug dealers and textile experts Marla Mallett (1990 and 1993) and Peter Davies (2000) were strongly critical of James wMellaart's careful reconstructions of the Neolithic kilim designs found on the walls of Çatal Hüyük and published in *The Goddess from Anatolia* (1989). Their claims were not true then and are not true today, but these attacks persist, as do those critiques focused on the work of Marija Gimbutas.

13 Brown, David J. and Rebecca McClen Novik (3 October 1992) 'Learning the language of the Goddess', p. 5.

14 Barber, Elizabeth (1994) *Women's Work, The First Twenty Thousand Years*.

15 Gimbutas, Marija (1989) *The Language of the Goddess*.

16 This was a very early agricultural society so these were early domesticated wild cattle which usually had horns when featured in rock art, etc. Elizabeth Barber says woolly sheep were selectively bred from 6,000 BP, so presumably wild cattle were also selectively bred to minimize horns. Because the 'bull's head' is associated with women's reproductive organs, and cows are the most productive, via their milk and its by-products, it is quite likely that the symbolism of many bovine head motifs were actually intended to represent early domesticated cows' heads. Hornless cows probably did not occur until the historic period. It possibly also displays a Western or European ignorance of the cattle that probably inhabited these areas. For example, buffalo have huge horns whether they are cows or bulls.

17 Gimbutas, Marija (1989) *The Language of the Goddess*, p. 225.

18 Cameron, Dorothy (1981) *Symbols of Birth and Death in the Neolithic Era*.

19 Tony Judd (May 2007) in 'Presumed cattle petroglyphs in the Eastern Desert of Egypt: Precursors of classical Egyptian art?' examined the depictions and frequency of prehistoric long-horned cattle petroglyphs in Eastern Desert rock art. Tony Judd uses the term 'bovid' or 'cattle' (seldom 'bull') as he says the cattle could also represent Neolithic aurochs (long-horned bovids) or buffalo. Although he only examined the 5,300-year-old petroglyphs of the Eastern Desert of Egypt he found that there were thousands of these prehistoric and early historic images recorded throughout western Egypt (and presumably the rest of northern Africa, wherever the climate allowed). Most of the images had 'exaggerated' long horns; only a few had the short horns of Asian cattle (introduced in the Egyptian predynastic period for cross-breeding purposes). Some of the images could be identified as bulls, others as cows, but all had "differently curved long horns" (p. 69) the ends of which were curved inwards or outwards.

According to Robert Bednarik, Saudi Arabia does not have many recorded sites as yet, but he says there are thousands more prehistoric art sites in the region waiting to be re-discovered and recorded. The online sources listed below do include images of long-horn cattle, both male and female, so the scenario on the Arabian Peninsula could be similar to northern Africa (Bednarik, Robert and Majeed Khan, 2005, 'Scientific studies of Saudi Arabian rock art', pp. 49–81).

Bjurstrom, Lars (photographer) (2008) 'Art rocks in Saudi Arabia' in *Saudi Aramco World* 59 (7), <http://www.saudiaramcoworld.com/issue/200807/art.rocks.in.saudi.arabia-.compilation.htm> (accessed January 2012).

Photographs are included in: Thomas (pseud.) (December 2010) 'Introduction to Saudi Arabian rock art and petroglyphs' in *Sandladder* 234, pp. 30–37, <http://ancient-cultures.info/attachments/File/RR_article_petroglyph> (accessed January, 2012).

20 Mellaart, James, Udo Hirsch and Belkis Balpinar (1989) *The Goddess from Anatolia*, p. 23.

21 Gimbutas, Marija (1989) *The Language of the Goddess*, pp. 225–226.

22 In Mellaart, James, Udo Hirsch and Belkis Balpinar (1989) *The Goddess from Anatolia*.

23 Barber, Elizabeth (1994) *Women's Work*.

24 ibid., pp. 80–81.

25 Rudgley, Richard (1998) *Lost Civilizations of the Stone Age*.

26 Schmandt-Besserat, Denise (1992/1996) *How Writing Came About*.

27 O'Kelly, Michael (1989) *Early Ireland*.

28 Knowth was still being excavated and restored in 1998, and new finds of engraved orthostats occurred regularly. Restoration was completed and the whole surrounding area opened up to the public in 2003. It seems even more spectacular than Newgrange, as it is larger in size, with "18 satellite passage tombs around it, each one a major monument in its own right" (p. 3) according to Jeffrey May (October 2003) in 'George Eogan: Knowth Excavations', an article in *Current Anthropology*. The Knowth Passage Tomb area covers 12 phases of occupation, the earliest being the central Passage Tomb, and following this came the Late Neolithic Grooved Ware Phase. The mound continued to be used by the first Indo-European Beaker people, and was further used on and off until the 12th century CE, when Irish monks built a grange over the 'roof' (see photographs). This article as well as some excellent aerial photographs may be viewed on <http://www.knowth.com/current- archaeology.html>.

29 Dowth passage tomb features two western passages, shorter in length and with lower roofs than those at Newgrange or Knowth. Engraved symbolism is also less accomplished and more sparse. There are curb stones surrounding the base of the mound, only some of which feature engravings. The northern passage is 3–4 metres long, and formed with large orthostats, and lintelled roof, as is another passage running off the right-hand arm of the cruciform chamber, within which lies a large stone basin. The southern passage has one recess off the circular chamber into which the roof stones had collapsed, and were removed at some time in the past. The more recent roof was made using cement.

Cristina Biaggi remarked on the astounding similarity of the stone-lined passages at Knowth, Newgrange and Dowth to those she recorded in Malta. Photographs are provided in her book (*Habitations of the Great Goddess*, 1994) and in the websites mentioned below, which also have links to comparative photographs of the Maltese passage tombs.

Dowth passage mound, Ireland: <http://www.ancient-wisdom.co.uk/irelanddowth.htm> (accessed April 2012).

Murphy, Anthony (n.d.) 'Dowth megalithic passage tomb' *Mythical Ireland*, <http://www.knowth.com/dowth.htm> (accessed April 2012).

30 Gimbutas, Marija (1999/2001) *The Living Goddesses*.

31 Dames, Michael (1976) *The Silbury Treasure*.

32 Brennan, Martin (1994) *The Stones of Time*.

33 Gimbutas, Marija (1991) *The Civilization of the Goddess*.

34 Eogan, George (1986) *Knowth and the Passage Tombs of Ireland*.

35 Paul Bahn (1992) describes a corbelled vault as formed by rows of stones, each of which overlays the previous one, until they meet in the centre. They support a capstone and are an early form of the domed roof.

36 Twohig, Elizabeth Shee and Margaret Ronayne (eds) (1993) *Past Perceptions*.

37 Knowth has two passages, the eastern one which runs east-west and ends in a central cruciform; and a second passage which runs west-east. Specific internal use of light and shadow marks each equinox and accompanying spiral engravings in certain positions confirm this (Brennan, Martin, 1994, *The Stones of Time*, pp. 102–3).

38 Brennan, Martin (1994) *The Stones of Time*, p. 127.

39 It is also worth noting that, as with other Neolithic communities around the world, there is no evidence of ritual human sacrifice, warlike practices, war weapons, fortifications, or battle scenes in Ireland until the arrival of the Indo-European Beaker people ended the peaceful Neolithic existence about 4,500 BP.

40 In 1993, processual archaeologist Elizabeth Shee Twohig argued that while she considers there is no 'goddess' symbolism associated with the Irish mounds, there are some suggestions of a female religion ('cult'). (We argue that the use of the word 'cult' disparages early so-called primitive religions.) Elizabeth Shee Twohig agrees the mounds were used as "burial places and for ceremonies associated with

ancestors" (although not like places of sacred ritual symbolic of the goddess, as Marija Gimbutas and Michael Dames suggest) and she notes that they are very similar to the passage tombs in Brittany from where the Irish builders may have come ('Prehistory: A present perception', pp. 1–5).

41 Gimbutas, Marija (1991) *The Civilization of the Goddess*, p. 305.

42 O'Sullivan, Muris (1993) *Megalithic Art in Ireland*, p. 10.

43 Evans, Arthur (1936) *The Palace of Minos at Knossos*.

44 ibid., p. 108.

45 In Baring, Anne and Jules Cashford (1991) *The Myth of the Goddess*, p. 121.

46 Cameron, Dorothy (1997) 'The Minoan Horns of Consecration'.

47 Hawkes, Jacquetta (1968) *Dawn of the Gods*.

48 ibid., p. 30.

49 Christ, Carol (1995) *Odyssey with the Goddess*.

50 Arthur Evans gave hierarchic names to the furniture, art works and objects in the so-called palace in Crete, whereas Marija Gimbutas identified it as a large and important communal building with religious and other purposes.

51 Hawkes, Jacquetta (1968) *Dawn of the Gods*, p. 27.

52 Goodison, Lucy and Christine Morris (1998) *Ancient Goddesses*.

53 According to Lucy Goodison and Christine Morris, the mixing of bones and objects together in tombs does not suggest hierarchy but rather "social values and organisation different from contemporary Western culture" with a focus on "the natural world, sun, plants and animals" (1998, *Ancient Goddesses*, pp. 117–120). They feel that the jumbled bones in the graves at places such as Mesara, in Crete, suggest a possibility of ancestor worship and a non-hierarchic society.

54 For processual archaeologists Lucy Goodison and Christine Morris not all such apparent female figurines should be considered divine. They argue that although there were many more female than male, unsexed, or animal figurines, we cannot assume from such evidence that female figurines were divine. They note that John Evans recently excavated Neolithic Knossos and found only one female figurine "in a possible religious context" (1998, *Ancient Goddesses*, p. 113); most were found in the remains of homes. But we know from Çatal Hüyük and other Neolithic towns in Old Europe described by Marija Gimbutas that homes were also places in which there were shrines dedicated to the goddess.

55 Lucy Goodison and Christine Morris argue that there is little or no evidence for the 'great goddess' in Minoan Crete. They argue that, although there is a predominantly female emphasis, as shown in the greater proportion of female to male (or non-sex) figurines among artefacts, this could suggest polytheism, or other ritual or secular use.

56 Baring, Anne and Jules Cashford (1991) *The Myth of the Goddess*.

57 Hawkes, Jacquetta (1968) *Dawn of the Gods*, p. 100.

58 Perhaps Ian Hodder's team may eventually find further evidence, as he will be excavating until 2017.

59 Eogan, George (1986) *Knowth and the Passage Tombs of Ireland*, p. 220.

60 Marija Gimbutas (1989, *The Language of the Goddess*, p. 67) reports metallurgy items made by 7,200 BP, and James Mellaart (1967, *Çatal Hüyük*) says metallurgy was present by 7,000 BP. Metal items included copper and lead "beads, tubes and possibly small tools" (p. 22).

CHAPTER 8 The First Indo-Europeans

1 Gimbutas, Marija (1991) *The Civilization of the Goddess*.

2 Anthony, David and Dorcas Brown (2007) *The Horse, the Wheel and Language*.

3 Anthony, David and Dorcas Brown (n.d.) 'Harnessing horsepower'.
  See also Anthony, David and Dorcas Brown (2007) *The Horse, the Wheel and Language*.

4 Gimbutas, Marija (1991) *The Civilization of the Goddess*, p. 394.

5 Anthony, David and Dorcas Brown 'Harnessing horsepower'.

6 ibid.

7 Barber, Elizabeth (1999) *The Mummies of Urumchi*.

8   Cavalli-Sforza, Luigi (2000) *Genes, People and Languages*, p. 120.
    6,000 years ago Indo-European speakers spread rapidly through Europe, the Middle and Near East, India, central Asia, and western China, and Indo-European languages today remain widely spoken. The vast steppes of East Europe and Asia allowed easy dispersal of nomadic cattle-breeding tribes (Eurasian steppe pastoralists), although these migrations are not necessarily the same as the movements proposed by Marija Gimbutas.

9   Marija Gimbutas (1991) says that the Kurgans can be described as a 6,000-year-old patrilineal society "under the leadership of a warrior chief. Females possessed an inferior status elevated only by association with their male relations" (p. 395) "to become 'private property' in the new trading and raiding societies" (p. 394).

10 To view a map of Early Yamna movement visit: <http://en.wikipedia.org/wiki/Kurgan_hypothesis>.

11 To view a map of Maikop movement visit: <http://en.wikipedia.org/wiki/Maykop_culture>.

12 To view a map of Late Yamna movement visit: <http://en.wikipedia.org/wiki/Yamna_culture>.

13 Marija Gimbutas (1991) gives an example of a miniature clay ox-drawn cart from 5,000 BP found in a grave along with the sacrificed oxen (p. 374).

14 Gimbutas, Marija (1991) *The Civilization of the Goddess*, pp. 393–4.

15 DeMeo, James (2009) 'Saharasia'.

16 DeMeo, James (2009) 'Saharasia', pp. 410, 412.

17 Fesl, Eve (c. 1991) Lecture at the Monash Indigenous Centre.

18 Göettner-Abendroth, Heide (2009) 'Notes on the rise and expansion of patriarchy'.

19 In today's world men are regarded as 'naturally aggressive' but this is not necessarily true.

20 Göettner-Abendroth, Heide (2009) 'Notes on the rise and expansion of patriarchy', p. 427.

21 ibid., p. 430.

22 ibid., p. 430.

23 ibid., p. 431.

24 ibid., p. 431.

25 For further information see 'Arrival of the dingo' in Chapter 15.

26 Göettner-Abendroth, Heide (2009) 'Notes on the rise and expansion of patriarchy', p. 3.

27 Mallory, James P. (1989) *In Search of the Indo-Europeans*.

28 Knight, C. in Gimbutas, Marija (1991) *The Civilization of the Goddess*.

29 ibid., p. 222.

30 Hawkes, Jacquetta (1968) *Dawn of the Gods*.

31 Jane Ellen Harrison talks about this aspect in *Ancient Art and Ritual* (1913/1978).

32 O'Kelly, Michael (1989) *Early Ireland*.

33 Phillipson, David (1985) *African Archaeology*.

34 Bahn, Paul (1998) *Prehistoric Art*.

35 British researcher Nick Thorpe (2000) mentions several instances in Europe where the remains of numbers of 'massacred' men, women and children have been found dating back into the Mesolithic period. In one instance the skulls were covered with red ochre indicating ritual burial. He argues that these apparently violent deaths indicate the origins of war beginning in the hunter-gatherer period. However we cannot be sure all these people died at the same time; and such evidence of ritual burial took place in other peaceful Mesolithic/Neolithic instances such as at Çatal Hüyük where heads of the dead were removed from the bodies and buried separately. The other instances Nick Thorpe mentions involved the use of weapons used for killing animals for food, and in conflict resolution in Australia. (For instance, such weapons were also used to punish very serious breaking of the Law which sometimes resulted in the death of the transgressor). Two further examples given are the "aggressive Yanomams of the Amazon" and Papua New Guineans as violent Mesolithic cultures but we already know that Chinese influences between 4,000 and 2,000 BP imported Indo-European practices and ideas to these formerly peaceful cultures (Thorpe, Nick, 2000, 'Origins of war', p. 1).

36 Willett, Frank (1995) *African Art*.

37 ibid., p. 53.

38 Barber, Elizabeth (1999) *The Mummies of Urumchi*, p. 50.
39 ibid., p. 52.

CHAPTER 9 The First Changes to Women's Status

1   Gimbutas, Marija (1991) *The Civilization of the Goddess*, p. xi.
2   Ahmed, Leila (1992) *Women and Gender in Islam*.
3   Barber, Elizabeth (1994) *Women's Work*.
4   Davidson, Hilda Ellis (1998) *Roles of the Northern Goddess*.
5   In Eisler, Riane (1990) *The Chalice and the Blade*, pp. 32–36.
6   Mellaart, James, Udo Hirsch and Belkis Balpinar (1989) *The Goddess from Anatolia*.
7   Ehrenberg, Margaret (1989) *Women in Prehistory*.
8   We are reminded that seeds which were accidentally spilt during their preparation for food grew around camps and eventually led to their deliberate cultivation. Thus women most likely were the first to discover ways and times to plant crops. They also developed ways to use plants medicinally, and for weaving and dyeing (Ehrenberg, Margaret, 1989, *Women in Prehistory*, pp. 77–78). It is also likely that women invented and made the first pottery, since they were the ones who needed containers for storage and carrying.

    Margaret Ehrenberg observes that interpretations of archaeological evidence can convey opposing meanings. She gives the example of Minoan art, where women are depicted wearing different dress and taking part in a range of activities, which raises interesting questions as to sex roles in Minoan culture. She argues that depictions of women in prehistoric art do not necessarily reveal women's status in that culture, and uses depictions of women today, together with their reduced status, to demonstrate this point (for example, the prominence given to religious statues of Mary in churches does not reflect the reality of women's position either in Christianity or in everyday society). This argument really is not relevant because today's societies are so much more complex, and so separated from nature and earlier cultures, that they cannot really be compared with prehistoric cultures. However, it *is* fair that caution should be applied when interpreting the earlier status of women.
9   In Baring, Anne and Jules Cashford (1991) *The Myth of the Goddess*, p. 50.
10 Gimbutas, Marija (1991) *The Civilization of the Goddess*.
11 Ahmed, Leila (1992) *Women and Gender in Islam*, p. 12.
12 Frymer-Kensky, Tikva (1993) *In the Wake of the Goddesses*.
13 Schmandt-Besserat, Denise (1992/1996) *How Writing Came About*.
14 Frymer-Kensky, Tikva (1993) *In the Wake of the Goddesses*, p. 12.
15 Binkley, Roberta (1998) 'Biography of Enheduanna Priestess of Inanna', p. 1.
16 In Binkley, Roberta (1998) 'Biography of Enheduanna Priestess of Inanna', p. 4.
17 Lerner, Gerda (1986) *The Creation of Patriarchy*, p. 60.
18 Kramer, Samuel Noah in Baring, Anne and Jules Cashford (1991) *The Myth of the Goddess*, p. 182.
    Gerda Lerner (1986) records that women then gradually became relegated to the private sphere, preoccupied with the household economy activities, child rearing and the spinning and weaving of cloth (*The Creation of Patriarchy*). Lower-class women were artisans or domestic industry workers, while slaves provided labour.
19 It is also notable that most of the earliest historical depictions (paintings and sculptures) of the goddesses of this time show them holding, or associated with, war weapons or other warrior symbols.
20 Diop, Cheikh Anta (1974) *The African Origin of Civilization*, pp. 143–144.
21 Lerner, Gerda (1986) *The Creation of Patriarchy*.
22 Sahtouris, Elizabet (1999b) 'Living systems in evolution'.
23 See Gerda Lerner's three stages of the first changes to women's status in Sumer (Mesopotamia) (1986, *The Creation of Patriarchy*, p. 60) mentioned above.
24 Ahmed, Leila (1992) *Women and Gender in Islam*, p. 15.
25 Lerner, Gerda (1986) *The Creation of Patriarchy*, p. 16.

341

[26] Ahmed, Leila (1992) *Women and Gender in Islam*, p. 36.

[27] Leila Ahmed (1992) notes Gerda Lerner's *Creation of Patriarchy* (1986) as a suitable resource (p. 37).

[28] Harrison, Jane Ellen (1913/1978) *Ancient Art and Ritual*.

[29] Baring, Anne and Jules Cashford (1991) *The Myth of the Goddess*, p. 176.

[30] Clarissa Estes (1992) argues that fairy tales, myths and stories provide women with understanding and reassurance and are instructional. They lead women "into their own knowing" (*Women Who Run with the Wolves*, p. 13).

[31] In Baring, Anne and Jules Cashford (1991) *The Myth of the Goddess*, p. 3.

[32] ibid., p. 169.

[33] Binkley, Roberta (1998) 'Biography of Enheduanna Priestess of Inanna', p. 4.

[34] ibid., p. 5.

[35] ibid., p. 4.

[36] Harrison, Jane Ellen (1913/1978) *Ancient Art and Ritual*, p. 6.

[37] ibid., p. 7.

[38] ibid., p. 5.

[39] ibid., p. 5.

[40] Harrison, Jane Ellen (1924/1963) *Mythology*, p. 25.

[41] ibid., p. 26.

[42] Gimbutas, Marija (1999/2001) *The Living Goddesses*, p. 144.

[43] ibid., p. 144.

[44] Baring, Anne and Jules Cashford (1991) *The Myth of the Goddess*, p. 366.

[45] ibid., p. 145.

[46] ibid., p. 145.

[47] Gimbutas, Marija (1999/2001) *The Living Goddesses*, p. 152.

[48] ibid., p. 153.

[49] ibid., p. 153.

[50] Estes, Clarissa Pinkola (1992) *Women Who Run with the Wolves*.

[51] ibid., p. 4.

[52] ibid., p. 4.

[53] Orenstein, Gloria Feman (1990) *The Reflowering of the Goddess*.

[54] ibid., p. 134.

[55] Harrison, Jane Ellen (1924/1963) *Mythology*, p. 87.

[56] Baring, Anne and Jules Cashford (1991) *The Myth of the Goddess*, p. 72.

[57] Orenstein, Gloria Feman (1990) *The Reflowering of the Goddess*, p. 135.

[58] ibid., p. 136.

[59] ibid., p. 136.

[60] ibid., p. 137.

[61] Dexter, Miriam Robbins in Gimbutas, Marija (1999/2001) *The Living Goddesses*, p. 213.

[62] Gimbutas, Marija (1991) *The Civilization of the Goddess*, pp. 318–400.

[63] In the Indian Vedas, these horses and cows are all female, as comes through in the Vedic poem to Uṣas, an ancient dawn goddess (Susan Hawthorne, 1982, pers. comm.).

[64] Anne Baring and Jules Cashford (1991) explain that Artemis represents the new moon, while Hecate symbolises the dark moon. In other words Hecate is Artemis's dark side. They say "it seems as though the original goddess of the moon contained both the light and dark aspects in one whole" (*The Myth of the Goddess*, p. 328), a situation which changed in the early historic period.

[65] Gimbutas, Marija (1991) *The Civilization of the Goddess*, pp. 398–400.

CHAPTER 10 Indo-European Philosophies

1   Although little is known of the kinds of philosophies operating before written history, much of the archaeological, ethnographic and symbolic evidence, especially that of archaeomythologists such as Marija Gimbutas, shows that the societies were peaceful with an emphasis on the earth and the female principle. Women in these societies had status and respect as they did within Australian Indigenous societies (the oldest living cultures) and in Native American societies. Neolithic philosophies would most likely have reflected this scenario.

2   Plumwood, Val (1993) *Feminism and the Mastery of Nature*, p. 89.

3   Neidjie, Bill (1989) *Story about Feeling*, p. 19.

4   Bell, Diane (1983/2002) *Daughters of the Dreaming*.

5   Baines, Patricia (1988) 'A litany for land'.

6   ibid., p. 228.

7   Bell, Diane (1998a) *Ngarrindjeri Wurruwarrin*, p. 307.

8   ibid.

9   ibid., p. 306.

10   Starhawk (2002) *Webs of Power*, p. 162.

11   Gammage, Bill (2011) *The Biggest Estate on Earth*.
     Bill Gammage's research shows that Aboriginal people managed the land in a systematic and scientific fashion.

12   An extensive discussion of differing conceptions of land is made by Hawthorne, Susan (2002) *Wild Politics*, pp. 163–205).

13   Starhawk (2002) *Webs of Power*, p. 1.

14   Sahtouris, Elizabet (1999a) 'WorldViews from the Pleistocene to Plato'.

15   ibid., p. 4.

16   ibid., p. 4.

17   ibid., p. 5.

18   ibid., p. 8.
     For more comprehensive information see Elizabet Sahtouris (1999a) 'Views from the Pleistocene to Plato' in her *Earthdance: Living Systems in Evolution*, <http://www.ratical.org/LifeWeb/Erthdnce/chapter13.htm>, or her hard copy book of the same title, published in 2000 by iUniversity Press, San Francisco.

19   Val Plumwood links the critiques feminists have made about the domination of people on the basis of sex, race and class, with the domination of nature where human identity lies 'outside' nature, while humanity and nature are dualisms which oppose each other. It is this opposition which explains how damaging Western philosophies underlie the current worldwide environmental crisis with its disastrous effects for so-called Third World women (1993, *Feminism and the Mastery of Nature*). (Her description of the concept of mastery [master/slave dualism] is especially relevant to our discussion of the colonisation concept later in this chapter.)

20   Ahmed, Leila (1992) *Women and Gender in Islam*.

21   Denise Schmandt-Besserat (1992/1996, 2007) demonstrates how women were the first to develop the signs from which a system of writing was to emerge, while the famous Sumerian high priestess, Enheduanna, was the first known author of poems and hymns to be written in cuneiform writing (see Chapter 9). In India, Sarasvati is the 'goddess of writing', and Vac is the 'goddess of speech'.

22   Sahtouris, Elizabet (1999a) 'WorldViews from the Pleistocene to Plato', p. 9.

23   Upholders of the conventional philosophical tradition argue that Diotima is a fiction, but see Susan Hawthorne's essay in which she argues the case for Diotima as an historical thinker: Hawthorne, Susan (1994) 'Diotima speaks through the body' in Bar On, Bat-Ami (ed.) *Engendering Origins*.

24   Sahtouris, Elizabet (1999a) 'WorldViews from the Pleistocene to Plato', p. 9.
     Michael Dames explains that Plato's ideas eventually "became institutionalized in academia"; this has meant that researchers in disciplines such as prehistory are limited to methodologies and presuppositions "quite at odds with the ancient societies they attempt to analyse – a discovery which generally goes

343

unnoticed, with predictably tragi-comic results." He gives *Anthropomorphic Figurines* (1968) as an example, in which Peter Ucko concluded that Palaeolithic and Neolithic figurines were dolls rather than goddesses which he considered had "never existed or if they did, they were, like folklore, fit only for infants." Consequently Peter Ucko proved "that the art of synthesis is invisible to a reductionist" (in Dames, Michael, 1997, 'The Gimbutas gift', p. 47).

[25] Plumwood, Val (1993) *Feminism and the Mastery of Nature*, p. 89.

[26] Genova, Judith (1994) 'Feminist dialectics', pp. 42–43.

[27] Plumwood, Val (1993) *Feminism and the Mastery of Nature*, p. 43.
Today the dualism 'chaos v. order' is no longer relevant since it is now realised that even chaotic events such as explosions have their own order even if apparently random in form. The rules of physics underlie every natural event no matter how chaotic it might seem, even to the explosive origins of the universe.

[28] Plumwood, Val (1993) *Feminism and the Mastery of Nature*, p. 42.
Over the ages, different sets of dualisms have been emphasised by different philosophies. Plato emphasised reason/body, reason/emotion, and universal/particular (Plumwood, Val, 1993, p. 43). Another Greek philosopher, Aristotle (384–322 BCE), who succeeded Plato, was concerned with dualisms of domination and hierarchy; human/nature; male/female; master/slave; and reason/body and its emotions; the superiority of the rational and the inferiority of the non-rational (p. 46).

[29] ibid., p. 45.

[30] ibid., p. 45.

[31] ibid., p. 33.

[32] Cottingham, John (ed.) (1996) *Western Philosophy*.

[33] In the 'metaphor of the cave' Plato said: "Behold! human figures living in an underground cave, which has a mouth open towards the light ... here they have been from their childhood, and have their legs and necks chained so they cannot move and can only see before them" (Plato in Cottingham, John, ed. 1996, *Western Philosophy*, p. 67). The metaphor (or allegory) of the cave describes men who desire to be free of women and the 'lower orders'. Men turn their eyes away from the 'dark prison' of ignorance to see the 'light' of Reason. "Yet of all the organs of sense, the [male?] eye is the most like the sun [light]". But for Plato women and nature remain in the dark: "[T]he eyes, when a person directs them towards objects on which the light of day is no longer shining ... see dimly, and are nearly blind; they seem to have no clearness of vision in them" (p. 65).
Plato was referring to men when he said: "[T]he soul is like the eye: when resting upon that which truth and being shine, the soul perceives and understands, and is radiant with intelligence". A woman apparently looks "toward the twilight of becoming and perishing then she has opinion only, and goes blinking about and is first one opinion and then of another, and seems to have no intelligence" (p. 65). In other words, women took account of context, but men wanted universal rules to apply to every situation.

[34] Moving out of the cave and ignoring nature "is the 'great task' of separation [the domination of nature], the Oedipal journey of the establishment of masculinity [toward] the vision of Logos, to true selfhood, [and] to the attainment of human cultural identity defined by rejection and separation from the lower order, which includes the mother, primal matter, the earth, and all that is conceived as belonging to it" (Plumwood, Val, 1993, p. 76).

[35] Plumwood, Val (1993) *Feminism and the Mastery of Nature*, p. 76.

[36] ibid., p. 95.

[37] ibid., p. 95.
Thus for Plato, women and natural forms have no value. Furthermore, Plato regarded the Gaia story, where the worship of the ancient earth goddess Gaia suggests an 'organic' world view wherein the earth is celebrated and respected, as a false but useful idea because "it will encourage citizens to fight for the state." It is a kind of militarism, rather than a suggested environmentalism (Plumwood, Val, 1993, p. 73). Plato would never have accepted what we now realize: that humans, both men *and* women, cannot live without the creatures of the environment; that without nature (or women) there can be no life.

[38] ibid., p. 96.

[39] Schmandt-Besserat, Denise (1992/1996) *How Writing Came About*.

[40] Barnes, Jonathon (1982) *Aristotle*.

[41] Saul, John Ralston (1995/1997) *The Unconscious Civilization*.

[42] Cottingham, John (ed.) (1996) *Western Philosophy*, p. 592.

[43] Plumwood, Val (1993) *Feminism and the Mastery of Nature*, p. 109.

[44] As Augustine puts it in *Augustine's Confessions XIII*, woman has

> a nature equal in mental capacity of rational intelligence, but made subject, by virtue of the sex of her body, to the male sex in the same way that the appetite for action is made subject, in order to conceive by the rational mind the skill of acting rightly (Augustine in Lloyd, Genevieve, 1990, 'Augustine and Aquinas', p. 91).

[45] Cottingham, John (ed.) (1996) *Western Philosophy*, p. 138.

[46] Thomas Aquinas writes:

> [Woman] plays a passive role but the male seed is the active one: [it] tends to the production of a perfect likeness in the masculine sex; while the production of woman comes from defect in the active force or from some material indisposition, or even from some external influence; such as that of a south wind which is moist as the Philosopher observes (Aquinas in Lloyd, Genevieve, 1990, 'Augustine and Aquinas', p. 97).

It is worth noting that these two philosophies are neither accurate nor relevant but unfortunately still seem to influence male thinking.

[47] Witt, Charlotte (2 October 1996) 'How feminism is re-writing the philosophical canon'.

[48] ibid., pp. 5–6.

[49] Shiva, Vandana (1989/2010) *Staying Alive*, p. 40.

[50] Dames, Michael (1992/1996) *Mythic Ireland*.

[51] By speaking out, individuals can use their power to "inspire or illuminate" the thinking of others. "Power-over seems invincible, but ultimately it rests upon the compliance of those it controls." If enough people don't comply or "recognise the legitimacy of the system ... ultimately the system cannot stand" (Starhawk, 2002, *Webs of Power*, p. 6).

[52] Susan Griffin explains dualisms and Scientific Rationalism as occurring when nature (and the female) is separated from powerful (male) human institutional and philosophical concerns which are considered as superior. Power moves from the patriarchal church to the state "and the authority for knowledge from priest to scientist – and yet still retain in a new guise and a new language, the essence of the old point of view." This has happened with what is known as 'the scientific revolution' where "many assumptions, methods and even questions we take to be scientific, actually partake of the same paradigm that in an earlier age we described as Christian" (1989, 'Split culture', p. 8). She explains that science does not necessarily contradict the older patriarchal Western religious ideas of a corrupt earth, the existence of heaven and the 'evils' of sensuality. (Male) church authority is merely replaced by (male) scientific dogma, that of the 'truth' of objective experimental data and the authority of 'scientific experts'. In this way our alienation from a deceiving world and from our senses is supported by science (p. 9).

[53] Griffin, Susan (1989) 'Split culture', p. 12.

[54] ibid., p.12.

[55] ibid., p 12.

[56] Plant, Judith (1989) (ed.) *Healing the Wounds*, p. 16.

[57] For example see:
Arditti, Rita, Renate Duelli Klein and Shelley Minden (eds) (1984) *Test-Tube Women: What future for motherhood?* Pandora, London.
Corea, Gena (1985) *The Mother Machine: Reproductive technologies from artificial insemination to artificial wombs*. Harper and Row, New York.

[58] Here she is presumably referring to the Old European 'goddess' who is today considered to be re-emerging in Western women's thought.

59 According to physicist Peter Derlet, quantum theory is basically a 20th-century theory of measurement in which the 'observer' plays a subtle yet intimate part in the outcome of an experiment. Peter Derlet says that

> in this sense, quantum mechanics can be seen as more holistic than that of traditional classical physics. However, to this day, it remains unclear precisely as to how the quantum nature of the universe transcribes to large complex systems, such as human consciousness and the world it sees and conceives (pers. comm., 9 June 2002).

For further discussion see Morgan, Robin (1982) *The Anatomy of Freedom*.

60 Liebes, Sidney, Elizabet Sahtouris and Brian Swimme (1998) *A Walk through Time from Stardust to Us*.

61 Plumwood, Val (1993) *Feminism and the Mastery of Nature*, p. 128.

62 ibid., p. 192.

63 ibid., p. 192.

64 ibid., p. 193.

65 Hawthorne, Susan (2002) *Wild Politics*, p. 183.

CHAPTER 11 Hidden Worlds: Africa

1 See Petrie, William (1939) *The Making of Egypt*.
See also the following website which has several articles concerning the Badarian culture, based on the reports of William Petrie (1920, 1939), and Guy Brunton and Gertrude Caton-Thompson (1928): Wysinger, Myra (n.d.) 'Pre-history Africa & the Badarian Culture', <http://wysinger.homestead.com/badarians.html>.

2 Phillipson, David (1985) *African Archaeology*.

3 Today 'North Africa', 'Northern Africa', and 'South Africa' refer to specific countries or groups of countries, but for the purposes of this chapter 'northern Africa' and 'southern Africa' are used more generally to refer to the geographic division of the African continent into two regions.

4 Wendorf, Fred and Roumald Schild (1998) 'Nabta Playa and its role in Northeastern African prehistory'.

5 ibid., p. 108.

6 Owen, James (27 January 2012) 'Stonehenge precursor found'.
Virtual photographic images of part of the complex can be seen at <http://www.dailymail.co.uk/sciencetech/article-2081254/Stone-Age-temple-Orkney-signi> (accessed July 2012).
See also Meg Daley Olmert's relevant lecture discussing the relationship between certain animals and humans which goes back until at least their appearance in 32,000-year-old cave paintings and (even older) engravings at <http://www.youtube.com/watch?v=xgWL7RcwVdg> (28 July 2012, 'The human-animal bond: Made for each other').

7 Diop, Cheikh Anta (1974) *The African Origin of Civilization*.

8 Ford, Clyde (1999) *The Hero with an African Face*.

9 Bernal, Martin (1987) *Black Athena: The Afroasiatic roots of classical civilisation Vol. 1*.
Bernal, Martin (1991) *Black Athena: The Afroasiatic roots of classical civilization Vol. 2*.
Bernal, Martin (2006) *Black Athena: The Afroasiatic roots of classical civilization Vol. 3*.

10 van Sertima, Ivan (1988) *Black Women in Antiquity*.

11 Such iconoclastic theories generate aggressive responses, in a way that is very similar to the attacks on Marija Gimbutas.

12 DeMeo, James (2009) 'Saharasia', p. 415.

13 ibid., p. 415.

14 Breunig, Peter in Wysinger, Myra (n.d.) 'Pre-history, Africa & the Badarian Culture'.

15 The *AURA Newsletter* reports that unfortunately this priceless rock art is now being vandalised and stolen for sale elsewhere (Becker, Nancy and Leonard Becker 2003, 'Tassili-n-Ajjer rock art in peril', p. 19).

16 Wysinger, Myra (n.d.) 'Pre-history Africa & the Badarian Culture'.

17 Bard, Kathryn A. (ed.) (1999) *Encyclopaedia of the Archaeology of Ancient Egypt* in Wysinger, Myra (n.d.) 'Pre-history, Africa & the Badarian Culture'.

18 Ford, Clyde (1999) *The Hero with an African Face*, pp. 104–111.
19 Dashu, Max (2004b) *Icons of the Matrix: The Matrikas* (Part 2), pp. 23–24.
20 Aksamet, Joanna (1989) 'The gold handle of a flint dagger from Gebelein (Upper Egypt)', pp. 325–332.
21 Dashu, Max (2005a) 'Predynastic Kemetic priestesses' (photographs).
22 Dashu, Max (2005b) 'Women in North African rock art' (photographs).
23 Willett, Frank (1995) *African Art*.
24 Rashidi, Runoko (1988) 'African goddesses', p. 73.
25 ibid., p. 73.
26 ibid., p. 78.
27 Jeffries, Rosalind (1988) 'The image of woman in African cave art', p. 98.
28 Van Sertima, Ivan (1988) *Black Women in Antiquity*.
29 The word 'cornucopia', meaning 'plentiful' is derived from the Latin word for horn, hoof or beak.
30 Jeffries, Rosalind (1988) 'The image of woman in African cave art', p. 110.
31 Yarborough, Camille (1988) 'Female style and beauty in Ancient Egypt', pp. 89–92.
32 Oya is not only important in Nigeria, but also in the Caribbean and Brazil. Slaves transported from West Africa to the Americas took her traditions with them.
33 Gleason, Judith (1987) *Oya*, p. 1.
34 ibid., p. 225.
35 Selected papers from the Congresses appear in Göettner-Abendroth, Heide (ed.) (2009) *Societies of Peace*.
36 Makilam (2009) in Göettner-Abendroth, Heide (ed.) *Societies of Peace*.
37 Donkoh, Wilhelmina J. (2009) in Göettner-Abendroth, Heide (ed.) *Societies of Peace*.
38 Dashu, Max (2005c) 'Daughters of Kasamba'.
    See also: Dashu, Max (2005a) 'Predynastic Kemetic priestesses' (photographs); (2005b) 'Women in North African rock art' (photographs).
39 Dashu, Max (2005c) 'Daughters of Kasamba'.
40 ibid.
41 ibid.
42 Hawthorne, Susan (2002) *Wild Politics*.
43 ibid., p. 209.
44 Shiva, Vandana (1993) *Monocultures of the Mind*, pp. 50, 56, 58.
45 Hawthorne, Susan (2002) *Wild Politics*, p. 216.
46 Nzenza-Shand, Sekai (1997) *Songs to an African Sunset*.
47 ibid., p. 218.

CHAPTER 12 Hidden Worlds: The Indian Subcontinent

1 For ease of reference, in this chapter 'India' refers to the subcontinent.
2 Chakrabarti, Dilip (1999) *India, An Archaeological History*, p. 20.
3 Not only the female sacred sites and imagery were lost to population increases, but also any/all prehistoric remains which were looted, sold or built-over. See Gita Thadani's experiences/comments later in this chapter.
4 Chakrabarti, Dilip (2006) *Oxford Companion to Indian Archaeology*.
5 Chakravarty, Kalyan and Robert Bednarik (1997) *Indian Rock Art and Its Global Context*, p. 34.
6 Gimbutas, Marija (1989) *The Language of the Goddess*.
7 For an overview (in photographs) of the symbols mentioned in many cultures around the world see: Max8899 (26 July 2012) 'Prehistoric Lajja Gauri and the 'M' and 'V' sign' (Lajja Gauri is an Indian 'fertility' goddess).
8 Dilip Chakrabarti is concerned that prehistoric art and artefacts have not been reported, or even respected, by historic India. China and South-East Asia also have this common problem as a result of colonisation. Any paintings/rock art/artefacts found now are usually reported, although they are never as

old as petroglyphs. Robert Bednarik and Kalyan Chakravarty's book records some of these. Population pressures, incoming religious and political influences, and climatic conditions could account for some being destroyed.

[9] In Possehl, Gregory (2006) 'Mehrgarh: Period I, Period II, Period III'.

[10] ibid.

[11] Coppa, A. et al (April 2006) 'Early Neolithic tradition of dentistry'.

[12] Mahmood, Mahmood (n.d.) 'The lost civilization'.

[13] See Kenoyer, J.M. (n.d.) 'Images of Asia: Harappa archaeological research project' or Clark, Sharri (2001) 'Embodying Indus Life'. The story is told in these photographs and dates of the images.

[14] For illustrations and photographs of the 'Lady of the Spiked Throne' see Vidale, Massimo (2011) <http://a.harappa.com/sites/harappa.drupalgardens.com/files/Spiked-Throne.pdf>.

[15] Vidale, Massimo (2011) *Lady of the Spiked Throne*, p. 11.

[16] ibid., p. 15.

[17] Although the artefact has been described as depicting a queen with her entourage seated on a throne within a bull-shaped boat (for example, J.M. Kenoyer has described the bull's horns as representing "the power, strength, and virility of the animal; by analogy whoever wore a headdress with the horns would possess similar attributes") all the symbolism of shapes, visual imagery and design elements are reminiscent of those relating to the Old European goddess as described by Marija Gimbutas (Kenoyer, J.M. in Vidale, Massimo, 2011, p. 16).

[18] Chakrabarti, Dilip (1999) *India, An Archaeological History*, p. 19.

[19] Doniger, Wendy (2009) *The Hindus.*

[20] Mehrgarh may have been deserted for this very reason if the flood events of 2010 in the Indus region are any indication. Archaeologists have often recorded deep layers of silt in excavations of the area.

[21] Kenoyer, J.M. (n.d.) 'Images of Asia: Harappa archaeological research project'.

[22] The Indus script is considered to be a sign of a literate society by many, and considered unique because of the brevity of the inscriptions. Three researchers, Steve Farmer, Richard Sproat and Michael Witzel (n.d.) in their paper 'The collapse of the Indus script thesis: The myth of a literate Harappan civilisation', argue that the Indus system did not encode language but was instead similar to a variety of non-linguistic sign systems used extensively in the Near East and other societies. Denise Schmandt-Besserat has argued that inscribed token images were used by women for 10,000 years to identify and record amounts of goods for storage and distribution in Iran and Iraq. Others consider it an early written language; all part of an interesting debate not yet proved. In any case, the Indus script appeared in the early Indo-European period and does not belong within the time frame of this book.

[23] Cavalli-Sforza, Luigi L. (2000) *Genes, People and Languages*, pp. 101–162.

[24] In another study "Dravidians were connected with other Indian populations and peoples of Malaysia, Singapore and China" (Wikipedia contributors, 2010, 'The Dravidian peoples').
For a reference about the debates on the origins of Vedic culture – and this is an ongoing debate – see Bryant, Edwin (2001) *The Quest for the origins of Vedic Culture: The Indo-Aryan migration debate.*

[25] Images of some of the female figurines found at Mehrgarh may be found under the title 'Mehrgarh' as well as 'Indus Valley Civilization' in Google Images. There are also at least two excellent slide shows online which show the gradual disappearance of female imagery, and its replacement by male imagery. See Clark, Sharri R. (2001) 'Embodying Indus life'; and Kenoyer, J.M. (n.d.) 'Images of Asia: Mohenjo-daro, Pakistan, and Harappa archaeological research project' 1996–2008, <http://www.imagesofasia.com/images-of-asia-php> (accessed January 2011).

[26] Clark, Sharri R. (2001) 'Embodying Indus life'.

[27] 'Devi' (n.d.) *A Dictionary of World Mythology*.

[28] ibid.

[29] ibid.

[30] ibid.

[31] ibid.

[32] Shiva, Vandana (1989/2010) *Staying Alive.*

33 ibid., p. 38.

34 ibid., p. 52.

35 Dashu, Max (2010) 'The Meanings of Goddess' Part 3, p. 10.

36 Marglin, Frederique Apfel and Purna Chandra Mishra 'Death and regeneration: Brahmin and non-Brahmin narratives', in Dashu, Max (2010) 'The Meanings of Goddess' Part 3, p. 10.

37 Parkin, Robert (n.d.) 'Munda – Religion and expressive culture'.

38 ibid.

39 Kerala Travel Tours (n.d.) 'Religion in Kerala'.

40 Mukkim, Patricia (2009) 'Khasi matrilineal society'.

41 Jobes, Gertrude & James (1964) cited in Mukkim, Patricia (2009) 'Khasi matrilineal society', p. 193.

42 Mukkim, Patricia (2009) 'Khasi matrilineal society', p. 193.

43 Patricia Mukkim (2009) explains that Khasi matriliny distinguishes between relatives 'from the mother's line' and those from 'the father's clan', which itself is a kinship group. Clans can "trace their roots to their great-great-grandmothers." Patrilineal descent "connects the man with his kinsmen who are related to him through males only." Matrilineal descent "assigns an individual to a group consisting exclusively of relatives through the females only" ('Khasi matrilineal society', p. 194).

44 ibid., p. 194.

45 Shanker de Tourreil, Savithri (2009) 'The Nayars of Kerala and matriliny revisited', p. 205.

46 ibid., p. 208.

47 ibid., p. 208.

48 Shiva, Vandana (1989/2010) *Staying Alive*.

49 For example, forests in South-East Asia, Central America, Amazonia and India are rapidly being cleared to the extent that the forests, soils, waters and air are being gravely degraded. In the years since Vandana Shiva wrote about this topic, there have been huge fires in Indonesia which have burnt for weeks, long droughts in Africa, and floods and landslides in India and South America, which have killed many people. We have been warned that with global warming sea levels will gradually rise, covering whole Pacific islands and inundating land and cities along coastlines around the world.

50 Thadani, Giti (2004) *Moebius Trip*.

51 ibid., p. 151.

52 ibid., p. 152.

53 ibid., p. 152.

54 ibid., p. 153.

55 Jain, Jyotindra (1995) 'Art and artisans' in Kaino, Lorna (ed.) *The Necessity of Craft*, pp. 24–34.

56 Tara Books, <http://www.tarabooks.com>.

57 Tara Books (2009–2010) 'Catalogue', p. 11.

58 ibid., p. 11.

59 ibid., p. 11.

60 ibid., p. 14.

61 ibid., p. 14.

62 ibid., p. 25.

63 ibid., p. 25.

64 Unfortunately the ritual art of Indigenous Australian people is just as much at risk of exploitation as that of indigenous people everywhere else. The Central Desert Indigenous people also make ritual designs on the earth for ceremonies. The designs may be very elaborate, formed of coloured earths and ephemeral materials such as native flowers, etc. The story telling of the myth, and the ritual dance accompanying it, gradually destroys the design as part of the ceremony. So the ritual wall and floor art of the Indian women is part of a larger, very old tradition indeed, as old as 100,000 years or more.

CHAPTER 13 Hidden Worlds: China, Korea, Japan

1   Bednarik, Robert (1996) 'The origins of *H. habilis* in Africa and Asia', p. 93.
2   Theobald, Ulrich (2000) 'Prehistoric cultures of China: Paleolithic China'.
3   Barnes, Gina (1993) *China, Korea and Japan*.
4   Anthony, David and Dorcas Brown (2007) *The Horse, the Wheel and Language*.
5   Department of Asian Art (October 2004) 'Neolithic Period in China' in Heilbrunn Timeline of Art History.
6   Barnes, Gina (2010) 'Prehistoric ceramic figurines in Japan'.
7   Wu, Xiaohong et al. (June 2012) 'Early pottery at 20,000 years ago in Xianrendong Cave, China'.
8   Shelach, Gideon (28 June 2012) 'The earliest known pottery'.
9   Field, Judith, R. Fullagar and Gary Lord (2001) 'A large area archaeological excavation at Cuddie Springs'.
    It is possible that Australian Indigenous people may also have used a basic unbaked clay arrangement of 'pebbles' on which to cook their ground-seed cakes, as the remains of ancient hearths marked by patches of burnt clay rubble still remain on claypans at Lake Mungo and in the Mallee country close by the Murray River.
10 Gina Barnes uses the term 'Neolithic' in East Asia to refer to the Agricultural period, as in the case of China, or in the sense of 'New Stone' era as in Korea and Japan.
11 Capon, Edmund (1977) *Art and Archaeology in China*.
12 Department of Asian Art (October 2004) 'Neolithic Period in China' in Heilbrunn Timeline of Art History.
13 Liu, Li (2004) *The Chinese Neolithic*, p. 24.
14 ibid., p. 24.
15 ibid., pp. 86–87.
16 Lin, Chen (8 November 2002) 'Dadiwan relics break archaeology records', p. 1.
17 Ministry of Culture P.R. China (2003) 'Dadiwan site' in Liu, Li (2004) *The Chinese Neolithic*.
18 Liu, Li (2004) *The Chinese Neolithic*, p. 79.
19 Hays, Jeffrey (2008a) 'China's earliest cultures 7,000–2,500 BP'.
20 Sternfeld, Eva (1995) 'A Stone Age matriarchy', in Gertsclacher, Anna and Margit Miosga (eds) *China for Women*.
21 Hays, Jeffrey (2008a) 'China's earliest cultures 7,000–2,500 BP'.
22 ibid.
23 Hays, Jeffrey (2008b) 'Yangshao, jade, the Yellow River and China's early cultures'.
24 Nelson, Sarah M. (December 1994) 'The development of complexity in prehistoric northern China'.
25 Gill, N.S. (n.d.) 'Nugua' (Bat goddess).
    A photograph of this goddess may be found at: Hongshan Culture Jade Nuwa-Bat Entity, <www.exoticjades.com>.
26 Griffith, Brian (2012) *A Galaxy of Immortal Women*.
    Brian Griffith quotes Min Jianyin concerning partnership cultures in Neolithic China and both books are of interest for those who want further information. See: Jiayin, Min (1995) 'Introduction' and 'Conclusion' in Jiayin, Min (ed.) *The Chalice and the Blade in Chinese Culture*.
    See also Griffith, Brian (23 June 2011) 'The goddess realms of prehistoric China'.
27 Griffith, Brian (2012) *A Galaxy of Immortal Women*, p. 81.
28 Watson, William (1961) 'China: The civilization of a single people'.
29 Barber, Elizabeth Wayland (1994) *Women's Work*.
30 Treistman, Judith M. (1972) *The Prehistory of China*.
31 Watson, William (1961) 'China: The civilization of a single people', in Piggot, Stuart (ed.) *The Dawn of Civilisation*, p. 269.
32 Gill, N.S. (2012) 'Ancient/classical history: Nugua', <http://ancienthistory.about.com/od/godsand goddesses/g/061010/Nugua.htm> (accessed July 2012).
33 Gill, N.S. (2012) 'Ancient/classical history: Nugua'.

34   Griffith, Brian (2012) *A Galaxy of Immortal Women.*

35   ibid., p. 29.

36   ibid., p. 27.

37   ibid., p. 29.

38   Gill, N.S. (2012) 'Ancient/classical history: Nugua'.

39   Griffith, Brian (2012) *A Galaxy of Immortal Women*, p. 35.

40   Dashu, Max (2010) 'The Meanings of Goddess'.

41   Dashu, Max (2009) 'Xi Wangmu, the Shamanic great goddess of China', p. 1.

42   ibid., p. 2.

43   ibid., p. 2.

44   ibid., p. 2.

45   ibid., p. 9.

46   Silber, Cathy (1995) 'Women's writing from Hunan', in Gertsclacher, Anna and Margit Miosga (eds) *China for Women*, pp. 13–19.
     There are websites with more information including an example of *nüshu* script compared with a Chinese translation. See '*Nüshu* – Women's script', <http://www.crystalinks.com/nushu.html> (accessed April 2010).

47   Hinsch, Bret (1995) 'Views of the feminine in early Neo-Confucian thought' in Gertsclacher, Anna and Margit Miosga (eds) *China for Women*, pp. 21–32.

48   Barnes, Gina (1993) *China, Korea and Japan*, p. 22.

49   ibid., p.13.

50   Lo, Lawrence (n.d.) 'Nüshu'.

51   Gatusa, Lamu (2009) 'Matriarchal marriage patterns of the Mosuo people of China' in Göettner-Abendroth, Heide (ed.) *Societies of Peace.*

52   Danshilacuo, Hengde (He Mei) (2009) 'Mosuo family structure' in Göettner-Abendroth, Heide (ed.) *Societies of Peace.*

53   Gatusa, Lamu (2009) 'Matriarchal marriage patterns of the Mosuo people of China' in Göettner-Abendroth, Heide (ed.) *Societies of Peace*, p. 240.

54   Sternfeld, Eva (1995) 'A Stone Age matriarchy: The Yangshao culture' in Gertsclacher, Anna and Margit Miosga (eds) *China for Women*, p. 139.

55   Gatusa, Lamu (2009) 'Matriarchal marriage patterns of the Mosuo people of China' in Göettner-Abendroth, Heide (ed.) *Societies of Peace*, p. 240.

56   ibid., p. 241.

57   ibid., p. 243.

58   Danshilacuo, Hengde (He Mei) (2009) 'Mosuo family structure' in Göettner-Abendroth, Heide (ed.) *Societies of Peace*, p. 249.

59   Tan, Pamela (1995) 'Women farmers in Qinghai Province' in Gertsclacher, Anna and Margit Miosga (eds) *China for Women.*

60   ibid., pp. 317–329.

61   ibid., p. 317.

62   For more information see: United Nations Sustainable Development Department (1998) 'Asia's women in agriculture, environment and rural production: China'.

63   Barnes, Gina (1993) *China, Korea and Japan*, p. 17.

64   New World Encyclopedia contributors (6 November 2008) 'Prehistoric Korea'.

65   For information (and pictures) about these and more recent rock art discoveries, see Van der Suijs, Marinus (2008) 'Korea's prehistoric past'.

66   Griffith, Brian (2012) *A Galaxy of Immortal Women*, p. 78.

67   ibid., p. 127.

68   Jiayin, Min (1995) 'Introduction' and 'Conclusion' in Jiayin, Min (ed.) *The Chalice and the Blade in Chinese Culture.*

69   Griffith, Brian (2012) *A Galaxy of Immortal Women*, p. 93.

70 'Far-East Realm: Here the old Asian goddess shall dwell again', <http://inanna.virtualave.net/fareast. html> (accessed July 2012).

71 New World Encyclopedia contributors (6 November 2008) 'Prehistoric Korea'.

72 Nielson, Paula I. (2010) 'Origins of the Ainu people of northern Japan'.

73 Olson, Steve (2003) *Mapping Human History*, p. 133.

74 Nielson, Paula I. (2010) 'Origins of the Ainu people of northern Japan'.

75 Olson, Steve (2003) *Mapping Human History*, p. 133.

76 Ainu Museum (Japan) (n.d.) 'The Ainu people'.

77 ibid.

78 Cavalli-Sforza, Luigi L. (2000) *Genes, People, and Languages*.

79 Department of Asian Art (October 2002) 'Jomon Culture (ca. 10,500–ca. 300 B.C.)' in Heilbrunn Timeline of Art History.

    According to Marilyn Stokstad (Heilbrunn Timeline of Art History website) the Jomon Period was peaceful, with pottery made by women throughout East Asia. Excellent photographs of middle Jomon pottery can be seen at this site: <http://www.earlywomenmasters.net/masters/jomon/index.html> (accessed August 2012).

80 Niigata Prefectural Museum of Prehistory (n.d.) 'The Jomon Period in Japan'.

81 ibid.

82 Kawagoe, Aileen (n.d.) 'Jomon Dogu'.

83 Carter, Susan Gail (2009) 'Amaterasu-o-mi-kami, Japanese Sun Goddess' in Göettner-Abendroth, Heide (ed.) *Societies of Peace*, pp. 394–404.

84 Kawagoe, Aileen (n.d.) 'Jomon Dogu', p. 2.

85 'Far-East Realm: Here the old Asian goddess shall dwell again', <http://inanna.virtualslave.net/fareast. html>.

86 ibid.

87 Griffith, Brian (2012) *A Galaxy of Immortal Women*, p. 17.

CHAPTER 14 Hidden Worlds: Thailand and Indonesia

1 Higham, Charles and Rachanie Thosaret (1998) *Prehistoric Thailand*.

2 Bednarik, Robert (1996) 'The Origins of *H. habilis* in Africa and Asia', p. 93.

3 Higham, Charles and Rachanie Thosaret (1998) *Prehistoric Thailand*.

4 Coffman, Ralf J. (2002) 'Voyagers of the Pacific'.

5 Griffith, Brian (2012) *A Galaxy of Immortal Women*, p. 86.

6 Brian Griffith (2012) explains that from 12,000 BP, with the ending of the last Ice Age, sea levels slowly rose and flooded low-lying regions in China and South-East Asia. He states that

    melting ice caps meant that the average annual temperatures rose from around 4 degrees Celsius colder than present (during the Ice Age) to near 4 degrees warmer than present before 5,000 BP. This meant more evaporation of the sea, more clouds and more rain (ibid., p. 83).

    By 4,000 BP the climate became cooler and drier, and seas fell back to their present levels.

7 The broad central plain is a rice-growing area and like the rest of Thailand, is subject to a tropical climate with a wet and dry season. Movement across the land from east to west is made easier because of the lower sea level and the narrow width of the Kra Isthmus and people can move from north to south via the major river systems.

8 Barber, Elizabeth Wayland (1994) *Women's Work*.

9 'Lapita' is an early pottery style found in Papua New Guinea and the Pacific Islands, and the people who introduced it are known as the Lapita people.

10 Higham, Charles and Rachanie Thosaret (1998) *Prehistoric Thailand*, p. 110.

11 ibid., p.170.

12 'Far-East Realm: Here the old Asian goddess shall dwell again', <http://inanna.virtualave.net/fareast. html>.

13 Warren, William and Luca Invernizzi Tettoni (1994) *Arts and Crafts of Thailand.*

14 Hersey, Irwin (1991) *Indonesian Primitive Art.*

15 Bednarik, Robert (1995) 'Concept-mediated marking in the Lower Paleolithic'.

16 Miksic, John (1996) 'The hunting and gathering stage in eastern Indonesia' in Miksic, John (ed.) *Indonesian Heritage Volume 1*, pp. 32–33.

17 Morwood, Mike, Thomas Sutikna and Richard Roberts (April 2005) 'World of the Little People', pp. 5–13.

18 The term 'pygmies' as used by anthropologists refers to groups of humans where "adult males grow to less than 59 inches (150 cm) in average height" (*Encyclopaedia Britannica Online*, 2012).

19 In Miksic, John (ed.) (1996) *Indonesian Heritage Volume 1.*

20 Kirch, Patrick Vinton (1997) *The Lapita People*, p. 119.

21 ibid., p. 125.

22 ibid., p. 125.

23 Chen, C.L. in Kirch, Patrick Vinton (1997) *The Lapita People.*

24 ibid., p. 143.

25 Chiang, B. in Kirch, Patrick Vinton (1997) *The Lapita People*, pp. 143–144.

26 Hamilton, Roy W. (ed.) (1994) *Gift of the Cotton Maiden.*

27 Barber, Elizabeth Wayland (1994) *Women's Work.*

28 Miksic, John (1996) 'The hunting and gathering stage in eastern Indonesia' in Miksic, John (ed.) *Indonesian Heritage Volume 1.*

29 Warming, Wanda and Michael Gaworski (1981) *The World of Indonesian Textiles.*

30 Coffman, Ralf J. (2002) 'Voyagers of the Pacific'.

31 Hersey, Irwin (1991) *Indonesian Primitive Art*, p. 13.

32 ibid., p. 13.

33 Maxwell, Robyn (2010) *Life, Death and Magic.*

34 ibid., p. 17.

35 ibid., p. 20.

36 Hamilton, Roy W. (ed.) (1994) *Gift of the Cotton Maiden*, p. 24.

37 Sanday, Peggy Reeves (2002) *Women at the Centre.*

38 In order to gain the trust of the Minangkabau people, it was important for Peggy Sanday to be accepted by one widely respected and honoured important female leader, who became her guide and informant.

39 Sanday, Peggy Reeves (2002) *Women at the Centre*, p. 16.

40 This knowledge was interpreted from an *adat* proverb (with men's assistance) by Peggy Sanday.

41 Sanday, Peggy Reeves (2002) *Women at the Centre*, p. 28.

42 ibid., p. 20.

43 ibid., p. 202.

44 Anderson, Benedict (1972) 'The idea of power in Javanese culture' cited in Sanday, Peggy Reeves (2002) *Women at the Centre*, p. 113.

45 ibid., p. 231.

46 ibid., p. 231.

47 ibid., p. 231.

48 Sanday, Peggy Reeves (2002) *Women at the Centre*, p. 237.

49 ibid., pp. 25–26.

50 Lewis, E.D. (1994) 'Sikka Regency' in Hamilton, Roy W. (ed.) *Gift of the Cotton Maiden*, p. 165.

51 ibid., p. 165.

52 Sanday, Peggy Reeves (2009) 'Matriarchal values and world peace' in Göettner-Abendroth, Heide (ed.) *Societies of Peace.*

53 ibid., p. 325.

CHAPTER 15 New Worlds: Australia

1   The word 'ancient' is somewhat ambiguous as it is often used when referring to a time/date at the end of prehistory and the beginning of the historic period, for example 'Ancient Egypt'. Therefore, referring to Indigenous people as 'ancient' wrongly suggests that they have only been in Australia for 5,000–6,000 years. Similarly, 'prehistoric' in this instance would suggest that they are not modern humans, which is also false. Therefore, I prefer the term 'precontact'.

2   Rose, Deborah Bird (1994) 'Flesh and blood and deep colonising'.

3   ibid., p. 349.

4   Women and men operate in separate ritual spheres, and as elders, they each have some understanding of the other sex's ritual and knowledge.

5   Rose, Deborah Bird (1994) 'Flesh and blood and deep colonising', p. 334.

6   Emily Kame Kngwarreye in Neale, Margo (ed.) (2008) *Emily*, p. 218.

7   Neale, Margo (ed.) (2008) *Emily*, p. 218.

8   Hoyt, Alia (20 October 2008) 'What was Australia's Stolen Generation?'.

9   Mike Morwood in Burdon, Amanda (April–June 2009) 'Written in stone', p. 56.
   (See also Kershaw, Peter A., 1993, 'Palynology, biostratigraphy and human impact', p. 15.)
   This *Australian Geographic* story includes further information and Hugh Brown's beautiful photographs of rock art in the Kimberleys. Other early evidence for human impact in Australia via firestick farming has been provided by Peter Kershaw (Queensland) and Gurdip Singh (Australian Capital Territory); see endnote 28.

10 Flood, Josephine (1995) *Archaeology of the Dreamtime*.

11 ibid., p. 27.

12 ibid., p. 27.
   Robert Bednarik comments that there are examples of early creation 'myths' which refer to previously existing natural features, such as the Ice Age land bridges between Kangaroo Island and the mainland; or the freshwater lake that once occupied what is currently the Gulf of Carpentaria. Scientific evidence now supports these eyewitness accounts (2006, *Australian Apocalypse*).

13 Bednarik, Robert (2006) *Australian Apocalypse*.

14 Singh, G., A.P. Kershaw and R. L. Clark (1981) 'Quaternary vegetation and fire history in Australia' cited in Flood, Josephine (1995) *Archaeology of the Dreamtime*, p. 18.

15 Further core samples from off the Queensland coast taken more recently by Peter Kershaw confirmed the earlier hypothesis (1993, 'Palynology, biostratigraphy and human impact', p. 15). However, in the absence of other evidence to support the claims, the core samples were not regarded as very significant. Yet further core samples, taken in 1996, again raise the issue of human intervention in the landscape by the regular use of fire ('Ancient seabed discovery rewrites human history', September 1996, *Research*). See also endnote 26.

16 Kalyan Chakravarty and Robert Bednarik (1997) argue that the first people to come to Australia were 'accomplished seafarers' who often travelled the oceans, sometimes establishing small colonies as they went (*Indian Rock Art and Its Global Context*).

17 Flannery, Tim (1994) *The Future Eaters*.

18 See the discussion defining 'civilisation' in chapter 2.

19 See Gammage, Bill (2011) *The Biggest Estate on Earth*.

20 Flood, Josephine (1995) *Archaeology of the Dreamtime*, pp. 38–55.

21 In 2003 this date was disputed by the discoverer, Jim Bowler, and reduced to 40,000 BP so that it fits in with conservative theories as to the time of the emergence of modern humans in Africa (Bowler, Jim, 19 February 2003, in 'New age for Mungo Man [and Mungo Woman]').

22 However, according to evolutionary geneticist Toomas Kivisild of Cambridge University, DNA analysis from Indigenous Australians and Melanesians suggests that they had come from the same recent migration from Africa as did Europeans and Asians (in Leung, Chee Chee, 10 May 2007, 'Aborigines' genesis in Africa'). In his paper, 'Revealing the prehistoric settlement of Australia by chromosome and

mtDNA analysis' (22 May 2007) he argues that Indigenous Australians and Papua New Guineans were descended from the same founding population and developed in relative isolation with little outside contact.

See also the online abstract of his paper: Kivisild, Toomas (22 May 2007) 'Revealing the prehistoric settlement of Australia by chromosome and mtDNA analysis', <http://www.pnas.org/content/104/21/8726.abstract> (accessed November 2012).

23   Smith, Deborah (22 December 2005) 'Feet of clay offer glimpse of life 23,000 years ago'.

24   Darby, Andrew (11 March 2010) 'Highway threatens ancient Aboriginal site'.

25   George Chaloupa (1993) has described these earliest paintings as belonging to what he calls the pre-estuarine period which lasted from 60,000 BP until 8,000 BP, and which covers the time when the sea rose after the last Ice Age and 'an estuarine environment' developed along the north-west Arnhem Land plateau. The climate changed from dry to wet, the sea rose and fell, and rose again, separating Australia from New Guinea, although not before association with the New Guineans brought an exchange of cultural and social traits to northern Australia (*Journey in Time*, pp. 91–92).

26   ibid.

27   The thrown imprints are often illegible because they could not easily be controlled. George Chaloupa suggests that some images could have been made using textiles, such as skeins of bush cord or hair string. In other places animal tails have been used. Both the grass prints and the thrown object imprints are usually placed very high on the rock walls, perhaps to better preserve them, as any images painted within general reach would most likely be overpainted many times across the millennia.

28   The 'X-ray' style of northern Australian Indigenous art displays the ritualised symbolic anatomical features within the body shapes of animals, birds, fish or other creatures.

29   At the time of the announcement, anthropologist Rhys Jones questioned the accuracy of the sandstone material tested, but this new time frame does in fact coincide with other projected dates for the first occupation of Australia. A date of 150,000 to 140,000 BP for human occupation in the bed of Lake George near Canberra had earlier been indicated by evidence of the sudden change to vegetation due to the regular use of fire shown in core samples taken by Gurdip Singh in 1981 (see Flood, Josephine 1990, p. 18; White, Mary 1994, p. 149; Walsh, Graham 1994, p. 75). In late 1996 two other scientists announced another core sample dating possible human habitation to 200,000 BP ('Ancient seabed discovery rewrites human history', September 1996, *Research*.)

30   See also Kleinart, Sylvia and Margo Neale (eds) (2001) *The Oxford Companion to Aboriginal Art and Culture*.

31   Josephine Flood (1983) explains that petroglyphs are made using three methods:

   • friction – where an implement is used to scratch, abrade or rub an area on the rock face in order to form a groove or rubbed area

   • percussion – using a hammer and chisel-like implement to form indentations in the rock surface, and

   • twisting and twirling a pointed tool in order to drill small pits in the surface which are made closely together to form lines of varying widths.

The second and third methods produce a 'pecked' effect, and allow more control over the making of the image and are thus more clearly defined than are designs produced by the friction method (*Archaeology of the Dreamtime*, p. 121).

32   Walsh, Graham (1994) *Bradshaws*.

33   Leech, Graeme (23 September 1996) 'Challenge to the origin of Man'; and Leech, Graeme (30 May 1998) 'Between rock art and a hard place', p. 8.

34   Kumar, Giriraj (1996) 'Daraki-Chattan'.

35   Heizer, Robert and Martin Baumhoff (1962) *Prehistoric Art of Nevada and Southern California*.

36   Flood, Josephine (1997) *Rock Art of the Dreamtime*, p. 307.

37   The northernmost section of the Northern Territory.

38   Flood, Josephine (1997) *Rock Art of the Dreamtime*, p. 187.

[39] Flood, Josephine (1995) *Archaeology of the Dreamtime*, pp. 152–154.
She refers to: Wright, R.V.S. (ed.) (1971) *Archaeology of the Gallus Site, Koonalda Cave*. Australian Institute of Aboriginal Studies, Canberra; and Martin, H.A. (1973) 'Palynology and historical ecology of some cave excavations in the Australian Nullarbor', *Australian Journal of Botany* 21, pp. 283–316.

[40] Flood, Josephine (1997) *Rock Art of the Dreamtime*.

[41] Bednarik, Robert (2006a) 'Dampier fact sheets'.

[42] Peterson, Nicolas (1981–1982) *Aboriginal Australia* (Catalogue), p. 46.

[43] ibid., p. 46.

[44] ibid., p. 46.

[45] Archaic petroglyphs with similarities of style (although not necessarily of the Panaramitee style argued by Josephine Flood) are to be found across Australia: from the Pilbara (Western Australia) to N'dhala Gorge (Northern Territory); from central western Queensland to Olary (South Australia); and as far as Mount Cameron West (Tasmania). Petroglyphs featuring ancient face-like symbols which occur at one site along the Canning Stock Route, on the Dampier Archipelago, and in the Cleland Hills, are very weathered and heavily patinated and could also belong to this early period, although they have not been dated as yet.

[46] *Aboriginal Indigenous Languages* (1996), p. 41.

[47] For a map of Australian Indigenous languages visit: <http://www.aiatsis.gov.au/asp/map.html>.

[48] Evidence of a semi-settled Indigenous village lifestyle, noted in a number of regions around precontact Australia, was often reported by the earliest explorers/settlers, and until recently these reports were not followed up. However, in 2000–2001 findings from Heather Builth's unpublished PhD thesis were released and enthusiastically received internationally.
Paul Memmott (2007) has collected and reported many of the early accounts and further information in *Gunyah, Goondie & Wurley: The Aboriginal architecture of Australia* to reveal a very different Indigenous scenario.
An interesting overview of Paul Memmott's book which includes Heather Builth's research, is given by M.H. Monroe, 'Aboriginal shelter' in 'Australia: The land where time began. A biography of the Australian continent', <http://austhrutime.com/aboriginal_shelter.htm> (accessed November 2012).

[49] Builth, Heather cited in Monroe, M.H. (n.d.) 'Aboriginal shelter' in 'Australia: The land where time began'.

[50] Phillips, Graham (13 March 2003) 'Life was not a walkabout for Victoria's Aborigines' [Heather Builth], p. 15.

[51] Monroe, M.H. (n.d.) 'Aboriginal shelter' in 'Australia: The land where time began'.

[52] ibid.

[53] There is limited evidence that such practices also took place at Tooradin further east of Melbourne but there has been no archaeological investigation in this area as yet.

[54] It is worth noting that although the local Gunditjmara people in the 1970s argued that these stone circles "were the remains of ... the village huts", an official 1990 (40-day study) survey commented "that most of the circles were not hut foundations ... [but] were more the product of overly active and untrained imaginations misinterpreting natural formations" (Phillips, Graham, 13 March 2003, 'Secrets of the stones') prompting Heather Builth to investigate them more fully. Her PhD thesis was never published, and she had some local critics such as Annie Clarke, whose critical paper 'Romancing the stones' (Victorian Archaeological Report, 1990) presented "alternative explanations for the circular stone remains" (Phillips, Graham, p. 3). As a result "archaeologists were more reluctant to claim human engineering in the formations of some structures" (Phillips, Graham, p. 3). However, Heather Builth's findings were well received and presented in some Australian journals, as well as internationally. See Phillips, Graham, 13 March 2003, 'Secrets of the stones', <http://www.smh.com.au/articles/2003/03/12/1047431096364.html> (accessed December 2012).

[55] In Hallam, Sylvia J. (1975) 'Fire and hearth'.

[56] ibid., p. 13.

57 Monroe, M.H. (n.d.) 'Aboriginal shelter' in 'Australia: The land where time began'.
More examples may be found in Memmott, Paul (2007) *Gunyah, Goondie & Wurley*.

58 Wilton, Alan (8 April 2010) 'Genome-wide SNP and haplotype analysis reveal a rich history underlying dog domestication' in Nature 464, pp. 898–902. Also at *Nature International Weekly Journal of Science*, <http://www.nature.com/nature/journal/v464/n7290/full/nature08837.html> (November 2012).

59 In Muller, Natalie (13 September 2011) 'Dingoes originated in China 18,000 years ago', p. 2.

60 ibid., p. 2.

61 Ackerman, Kim with John Stanton (1994) *Riji and Jakoli*.

62 ibid., p. 37.

63 Bell, Diane (1983/2002) *Daughters of the Dreaming*, p. 257.

64 For more extensive information there is a comprehensive description of these aspects and others in Diane Bell's *Daughters of the Dreaming* (1983/2002).

65 Bell, Diane (1983/2002) *Daughters of the Dreaming*, p. 269.

66 ibid., p. 256.

67 Rockman Napaljarri, Peggy and Lee Cataldi (trans.) (2011) *Walpiri Dreamings and Histories / Yimikirli*, p. 151.

68 The 1967 Referendum is generally known as the referendum that gave Aboriginal people the vote. In fact, some Aboriginal people had been voting in various jurisdictions across the country for some years. What the 1967 Referendum did was to count Aboriginal people in the census, thereby acknowledging them as a people. It also omitted reference to Aboriginal people which allowed the Federal government to make laws that applied to Aboriginal people. For more information see: <http://en.wikipedia.org/wiki/Australian_referendum_1967_(Aboriginals)>.

69 This refers to the children of Aboriginal and Torres Strait Islander people who were stolen from their families by governments (at federal and state levels) as well as their agents such as churches and missions. The practice occurred over a roughly one-hundred-year period from 1869 until the 1970s. For further information see: <http://en.wikipedia.org/wiki/Stolen_Generations>.

70 Hughes, Paul (1987) 'Aboriginal culture and learning styles'.
Harris, Stephen (1990) *Two-way Aboriginal Schooling*.

71 Culture is not static and while it is possible to draw some conclusions based on archaeology, and some from present-day cultural forms, one also has to accept that the inference could be mistaken, and that change will have happened all the way through the 60,000 or more years.

72 Bell, Diane (1983/2002) *Daughters of the Dreaming*, p. 23.

73 Bell, Diane (1998a) *Ngarrindjeri Wurruwarrin*.

74 Rose, Deborah Bird (1994) 'Flesh and blood and deep colonising'.

75 ibid., p. 335.

CHAPTER 16 New Worlds: Oceania

1 Kirch, Patrick Vinton (1997) *The Lapita People*.

2 Papuans speak 750 languages which have roots in earlier cultures.

3 For a map of the area go to: <http://en.wikipedia.org/wiki/File:Map_of_Sunda_and_Sahul.png>.

4 Flannery, Tim (1994) *The Future Eaters*.

5 Higham, Charles and Rachanie Thosaret (1998) *Prehistoric Thailand*.

6 There is some discussion about which Indo-European languages were the first to reach Thailand and beyond; some researchers contend that Pali and Sanskrit are the most likely options, while others argue in favour of Austroasiatic languages. See pages 70–72 in Higham, Charles and Rachanie Thosaret (1998) *Prehistoric Thailand*.

7 This is mentioned in Teillhet, Jehanne (1983) 'The role of women artists in Polynesia and Melanesia', pp. 47–48.

8 Hope, G.S., J. Golson and J. Allen (2006) 'Paleoecology and prehistory in New Guinea'.

9 Flannery, Tim (1994) *The Future Eaters*, p. 293.

[10] Simmons, David (1979) *Art of the Pacific*.

[11] In 2004 Indonesia divided the region of West Papua (formerly Irian Jaya) into 27 regencies with two cities and 830 villages, the boundaries of which did not necessarily correspond with the different clan cultures originally present. There are Melanesians, Micronesians, and Papuan clans, as well as a growing number of Austronesian Indonesians present today in West Papua.

[12] Kjellgren, Eric and Jennifer Wagelie (2001) 'Prehistoric stone sculpture from New Guinea' in Heilbrunn Timeline of Art History.

[13] Boylan, Chris and Greta North (n.d.) 'Highlands art of New Guinea'.

[14] Although women have varied access to political and economic status in the different Pacific cultures, it is usually the preserve of men to use 'hard' materials such as wood, ivory, stone and bone for carving and engraving art objects with certain explicit or implicit masculine values and ideologies to gain their (external) powers, while women are 'limited' to the use of 'soft' materials, such as clay, gourds, tapa, skins and woven threads, according to Jehanne Teillhet (1983, 'The role of women artists in Polynesia and Melanesia'). She classifies men's 'religio-political' works (such as sculpture) as 'art', but women's 'secular utilitarian' work as 'craft', making the point that all Oceanic cultures distinguish between the art produced by men and that produced by women. Jehanne Teillhet considers that the possible reason for this is that women, as creators of life, have no subliminal need to create anthropomorphic representations. If we are to accept this argument it would seem that Pacific Island women have no ritual life (yet in every other culture women have their own rituals).

[15] May, Patricia and Margaret Tuckson (2000) *The Traditional Pottery of Papua New Guinea*.

[16] ibid., pp. 6–7.

[17] ibid., p. 112.

[18] ibid., p. 113.

[19] ibid., p. 239.

[20] ibid., p. 239.

[21] Balai, Sana and Judith Ryan, with Drusilla Modjeska and Alban Sare (2009) *Wisdom of the Mountain*.

[22] ibid., p. 28.

[23] ibid., p. 34.

[24] See photograph on p. 43 in D'Alleva, Anne (1998) Arts of the Pacific Islands.

[25] Drusilla Modjeska records the myth of the old woman who carries the sun and moon in her *billum* while climbing the mountain. She hangs the sun in the sky "so everyone could see the wondrous light" (Balai, Sana and Judith Ryan, with Drusilla Modjeska and Alban Sare, 2009, *Wisdom of the Mountain*, p. 26). When she finishes her work for the day she climbs back up the mountain and replaces the sun with the moon.

[26] David Simmons (1979) has recorded photographs of some art objects from the Pacific region (in *Art of the Pacific*) which include beautifully woven items, such as a complex three-dimensional crocodile, a face mask, and a magnificent ceremonial woven shield decorated with numerous circular shell beads forming a design, and it is likely that all of these would have been also made by women.

[27] Roe, David (1992) 'Rock art of North-West Guadalcanal'.

[28] Kirch, Patrick Vinton (1997) *The Lapita People*.

[29] In the words of Patrick Kirch (1997):

> A great majority of prehistorians and historical linguists have now come to regard Lapita as the archaeological manifestation of those people who spoke Proto-Oceanic and its immediate daughter languages. Lapita – which spans a time period between about 3,600 and 2,000 years ago, and is distributed in space from the Bismarks to New Caledonia and eastwards to Samoa and Tonga – has come to be recognised as the ancestral cultural stock from which the modern diversity of Oceanic-speaking peoples and cultures ultimately arose (*The Lapita People*, p. xxi).

[30] Green, Roger in Kirch, Patrick Vinton (1997) *The Lapita People*, p. 14.

[31] Andrews, Munya (2004) *The Seven Sisters of the Pleiades*.

[32] Kirch, Patrick Vinton (1997) *The Lapita People*, pp. 120–123.

[33] Sullivan, Agnes (1985) 'Nga Paiaka O Te Maoritanga'.

34 Much of the *art of the Pacific* Islands now present belongs to the time of first contact with Europeans, so it is difficult to picture the art of the earliest cultures except through the remnants of designs on the pottery.

35 Price, Christine (1980) 'Clay for the potter'.

36 Archey, Gilbert (1965/1974) *The Art Forms of Polynesia*.

37 In dé Ishtar, Zohl (1994) *Daughters of the Pacific*, pp. 88–89.

38 ibid., p. 89.

39 ibid., p. 89.

40 ibid., p. 88.

41 ibid., p. 11.

42 ibid., p. 28.

43 ibid., p. 43.

44 ibid., p. 47.

45 ibid., p. 47.

46 ibid.

47 ibid., p. 55.

48 ibid., p. 65.

49 Suzuki, Manami (1987) in dé Ishtar, Zohl (1994) *Daughters of the Pacific*, p. 55.

50 In dé Ishtar, Zohl (1994) *Daughters of the Pacific*, p. 7.

51 ibid.

52 ibid., p. 7.

53 Schoeffel, Penelope (1995) 'Craft, prestige goods and women's roles in the Pacific Islands'.

54 Herda, Phyllis S. (1995) 'The creation of wealth'.

55 ibid., p. 164.

56 Guillermo, Alice (1995) 'Weaving: Women's art and power'.

57 ibid., pp. 35–39.

58 ibid., p. 9.

59 Respicio, Norma (2003) *Our Pattern of Islands*.

60 Kahukiwa, Robyn (1984) *Wahine Toa*.

61 ibid., p. 10.

62 Weaving "is a vehicle that can link the past to the present, and the present to the future. The threads of continuity are the Maori values. These threads can be in many shades. The strongest is the *wairua* (the spiritual aspect)." A weaver draws together "customs, traditions, history, music, oratory, legends, and the needs of *iwi* (tribe), *hapu* (sub-tribe), and *whanau* (family) … [She] creates or weaves not for herself alone, but for the *mana* (prestige) of the people" (*Taonga Maori: A spiritual journey expressed through Maori art*, Exhibition catalogue, 1989, National Museum of New Zealand and the Australian Museum, p. 54).

63 Kahukiwa, Robyn (1984) *Wahine Toa*, p. 10.

64 Robyn Kahukiwa contends that myths explain the way things are. They show the way to act and the results of certain actions. As an example she reveals that "one does not have to search too deeply in Maori mythology to find that incest was taboo in traditional society ... It was also important that people be identified from their birthplace in order to establish tribal connections" (1984, *Wahine Toa*, p. 10). Another important aspect was the preservation of accuracy in the passing down of myths and rituals. For example, if the recitation of a ritual *karakia* was not correct the consequences could mean death or bad luck.

65 dé Ishtar, Zohl (1994) *Daughters of the Pacific*, p. 39.

66 ibid.

67 ibid., p. 216.

68 ibid.

69 ibid., p. 216.

70 ibid.

71 ibid., p. 128.

72 ibid., p. 234.

CHAPTER 17 New Worlds: The Americas

1 Originally North America was part of the northern supercontinent of Laurasia, while South America was a part of the southern supercontinent of Gondwanaland, and eventually drifted towards its present position. Together they are referred to as 'The Americas'.

2 Dillehay, Tom (2008) 'Profiles in Pleistocene history'.

3 Heather Pringle (2013) mentions Tom Dillehay, who also "found traces of early Americans who slept in hide-covered tents and dined on seafood and a wild variety of potato 14,600 years ago" (Pringle, Heather, 'The First Americans', p. 70) in Monte Verde in southern Chile, and suspects other earlier evidence has since been covered by the sea.
See also Dillehay, Tom D. et al. (2008) 'Monte Verde', pp. 784–786.

4 Waters, Michael R. et al. (25 March 2011) 'The Buttermilk Creek complex and the origins of Clovis at the Debra L. Friedkin site, Texas' (in Pringle, Heather, 2013, 'The First Americans'). Also at <http://www.sciencemag.org/content/331/6024/1599.abstract> (accessed January 2013).
Heather Pringle (2013) reports that the new occupation date for North America by the pre-Clovis people has been revised to 15,500 BP due to the discovery of 15 stone tools together with numerous knapping flakes on the level below the Clovis tool finds. The revised date is based on the date of the soils within which the tools were found, and therefore remains controversial and not yet generally accepted (Pringle, Heather, 'The First Americans').
See also Polyak, Victor J. et al. (1 November 2012) 'Climatic backdrop to the terminal Pleistocene extinction of North American mammals', pp. 1,023–1,026.

5 Fagan, Brian M. (1991b) *Ancient North America*.

6 Kehoe, Alice Beck (1998) *The Land of Prehistory*.

7 Chakravarty, Kalyan and Robert Bednarik (1997) *Indian Rock Art and Its Global Context*.

8 Yet evidence, in the form of early stone artefacts and charcoal remains of fires found at Pedra Furada, has not been generally accepted since critics insist the 'artefacts' are stones fractured naturally in rock falls. The charcoal is thought to have come from seasonal fires. The Brazilian archaeologist Niede Guidon (1998), who made the discovery, says in support of her claim, that there was no evidence of fire in the surrounding area. One of Niede Guidon's team experimented with rock falls and found that the accidental fractures and flaked stones were quite different to the artefacts found at the site. Richard Rudgley (1998) claims that the bias against her discovery is because Niede Guidon is both female and a Brazilian, and therefore is considered "a less 'acceptable' kind of archaeologist than if she were a North American man" (*Lost Civilizations of the Stone Age*, pp. 256–259).

9 Fagan, Brian M. (1991b) *Ancient North America*.

10 Dillehay, Tom (2008) 'Profiles in Pleistocene history'.

11 Bednarik, Robert (1995) 'Concept-mediated marking in the Lower Paleolithic'.

12 Feest, Christian F. (1992) *Native Arts of North America*.

13 Whiteford, Andrew Hunter and S.Z. Herbert (2002) *North American Indian Arts*, pp. 23 and 55.

14 According to Andrew Whiteford and S.Z. Herbert the first pottery was made in Mexico by the Cochise people around 9,000 BP (ibid.).

15 Whiteford, Andrew Hunter S.Z. Herbert (2002) *North American Indian Arts*, p. 55.

16 Fagan, Brian M. (1991a) *Kingdoms of Gold, Kingdoms of Jade*.

17 Allen, Paula Gunn (1986) *The Sacred Hoop*.

18 ibid., p. 266.

19 ibid., p. 254.

20 ibid., p. 33.

21 ibid., p. 13.

22 ibid., p. 119.

23 ibid., p. 267.

24 "The circular concept requires all 'points' that make up the sphere of being to have a significant identity and function, while the linear model assumes that some 'points' are more significant than others" (ibid., p. 59).

[25] ibid., p. 59.

[26] We have included the following critique of Brian Fagan's biased account of Native American shamans because his *Kingdoms of Gold, Kingdoms of Jade: The Americas before Columbus* (1991a) has been a recommended university text (at least in Australia at the time of writing) and has been promoted by Paul Bahn's *Collins Dictionary of Archaeology* (1992).

[27] Fagan, Brian M. (1991a) *Kingdoms of Gold, Kingdoms of Jade*, p. 94.

[28] Kehoe, Alice Beck (1998) *The Land of Prehistory*.

[29] ibid., p. 187.

[30] ibid., p. 187.

[31] Starhawk (1989) *The Spiral Dance*, p. 201.

[32] ibid., p. 201.

[33] Allen, Paula Gunn (1986) *The Sacred Hoop*, p. 3.

[34] Diamond, Jared (1991) *The Rise and Fall of the Third Chimpanzee*.

[35] ibid., p. 243.

[36] Allen, Paula Gunn (1986) *The Sacred Hoop*, p. 4.

[37] Mann, Barbara Alice (2009) 'They are the soul of the Councils' in Göettner-Abendroth, Heide (ed.) *Societies of Peace*.

[38] ibid., p. 58.

[39] ibid., p. 4.

[40] This spelling of 'Attiwendaronk' is used by Barbara Alice Mann (2009) however other alternative spellings include 'Attawondaronk'.

[41] Mann, Barbara Alice (2009) 'They are the soul of the Councils', p. 60.

[42] ibid., p. 60.

[43] ibid., p. 61.

[44] ibid., p. 61.

[45] ibid., p. 61.

[46] ibid., p. 63.

[47] Berlo, Janet C. and Ruth B. Phillips (1998) *Native North American Art*, p. 33.

[48] ibid., p. 33.

[49] Guss, David M. (1998) *To Weave and Sing*.

[50] Boas, Franz (1928/1955) *Primitive Art*.

[51] There were no suitable native animals which could be trained to carry goods available to Native Americans until the reintroduction of the horse in the 1490s.

[52] Heizer, Robert and Martin Baumhoff (1962) *Prehistoric Art of Nevada and Southern California*.

[53] Needham, Joseph (1971) 'Science and civilization in China' in Kehoe, Alice Beck (1998) *The Land of Prehistory*.

[54] Contreres, Dona Enriqueta (2009) 'Matriarchal values among the Sierra Juarez Zapotecs of Oaxaca'.

[55] ibid., p. 77.

[56] ibid., p. 78.

[57] Dillehay, Tom (2008) 'Profiles in Pleistocene history' in Silverman, Helaine and William H. Isbell (eds) (2008) *Handbook of South American Archaeology*.

[58] Navarrete, Rodrigo (2008) 'The prehistory of Venezuela', pp. 429–458.

[59] Silverman, Helaine and William H. Isbell (eds) (2008) *Handbook of South American Archaeology*.

[60] See Dillehay, Tom (2008) 'Profiles in Pleistocene history', p. 31.

[61] Dillehay, Tom (2008) 'Profiles in Pleistocene history', p. 31.

[62] Raymond, J. Scott (2008) 'The process of sedentism in north-western South America', pp. 79–120.

[63] ibid., p. 83.

[64] ibid., p. 83.

[65] Gimbutas, Marija (1991) *The Civilization of the Goddess*.

[66] Department of Arts of Africa, Oceania, and the Americas (October 2004) 'Valdivia Figurines' in Heilbrunn Timeline of Art History.

[67] Needham, Joseph (1971) 'Science and civilization in China' (Vol. 4, Part 3, pp. 197–198) in Kehoe, Alice Beck (1998) *The Land of Prehistory*.

[68] Barber, Elizabeth Wayland (1999) *The Mummies of Urumchi*.

[69] Kehoe, Alice Beck (1998) *The Land of Prehistory*, p. 197.

[70] McCafferty, Sharisse and Geoffrey McCafferty (1996) 'Spinning and weaving as female gender identity in Post-Classic Mexico'.

[71] For further information see Davis, Virginia (1996) 'Resist dyeing in Mexico' in Blum, Margot, Janet Berlo and Edward Dwyer (eds) *Textile Traditions of Mesoamerica and the Andes*, pp. 309–336.

[72] Solis, Ruth Shady (n.d.) 'First city in the New World?'.

[73] Mayell, Hillary (July, 2001) 'Fall of ancient Peruvian societies linked with El Niño'.

[74] Allen, Paula Gunn (1986) *The Sacred Hoop*.

[75] Dashu, Max (n.d.) 'Female divinity in South America', p. 1.

[76] ibid., p. 1.

[77] ibid., p. 1.

[78] ibid., p. 4.

[79] ibid., p. 6.

[80] ibid., p. 8.

[81] Indigenous imagery in Australia also was highly focused on the land and its creatures, but there was a strong representation of ancestral beings as anthropomorphic and zoomorphic figures. Many motifs are non-figurative, and these include circles and double circles, spirals, meanders, multiple lines, etc., commonly used symbols which we have noted in the rest of the Southern Hemisphere. There is no obvious sex reference in many of the motifs, especially in the numerous non-figurative symbols, so we cannot discern either a dominant male or female emphasis in Australian Indigenous imagery.

[82] Heath, Carolyn (2009) 'Women and power', p. 92.

[83] ibid., p. 94.

[84] ibid., p. 95.

[85] ibid., p. 99.

[86] Berlo, Janet Catherine (1996) 'Beyond bricolage', p. 440.

CONCLUSION Weaving the Threads

[1] Ngarrindjeri elder Ellen Trevorrow in Ngarrindjeri Tendi et al. (2007) *Ngarrindjeri Nation Sea Country Plan* in Bell, Diane (ed.) for the Ngarrindjeri Nation (2008) *Listen to Ngarrindjeri Women Speaking/Kungun Ngarrindjeri Miminar Yunnan*, p. 51.

[2] Audrey Lindsay, Camp Coorong Museum in Bell, Diane (ed.) for the Ngarrindjeri Nation (2008) *Listen to Ngarrindjeri Women Speaking/Kungun Ngarrindjeri Miminar Yunnan*.

[3] The word 'urban' and its cognate 'urbane' are connected to ideas of civility, refinedness and sophistication. But perhaps our future lies with country people and 'peasants' (which means people from the country) and people who have maintained traditional connections with land, indigenous peoples, farmers and those with long links in particular regions (nomadic peoples and gypsies).

[4] Gorman, James (17 December 2012) 'Ancient bones that tell a story of compassion'.

[5] We include this information because Australian male scientists, archaeologists, anthropologists and other male members of related disciplines rarely (if ever) consult women, or mention their presence anywhere in prehistory, a notable omission. It is also worth noting that, although the earliest solid evidence of string is at 34,000 BP, the first inferred use of string (rope, cord etc.) dates back to at least 700,000 BP, possibly 800,000 BP, along with stone tools and butchered elephant bones, and was used by both women and men.

[6] It is also worth noting that one of the very few male commentators to recognise the presence and inventions of women in prehistory has been the well-known Australian social commentator Phillip

Adams (2010) who, in an article 'The feminists of prehistory', has suggested that "at least one of the Ages of Men was an Age of Woman. The Age of String ... [heralded a 34,000-year-old] technology at least as significant as the smelting of metal ..." (Adams, Phillip, 11–12 December 2010, p. 3).

7   For information about Maree Clark visit <http://museumvictoria.com.au/bunjilaka/about-us/birrarung-gallery/artist-profiles/maree-clark/> (accessed December 2012).
    More information is available at <http://www.vic.gov.au/stories/possum-skin-cloaks/> (accessed December 2012).

8   Maree Clark in Ross, Annabel (21–22 December 2012) 'Traditional culture: "It's almost like an autobiography, this cloak". The skins of the father, uncle, aunt and sew on', p. 24.
    For further information see Gibbons, Helen (May 2010) 'Possum skin cloaks'.

9   Pringle, Heather (2013) 'The First Americans', p. 71.
    See also Waters, Michael et al. (25 March 2011) 'The Buttermilk Creek complex and the origins of Clovis at the Debra L. Freidler site, Texas', pp. 1,599–1,603.

10 There were several more seasons in the Indigenous calendar than the four Indo-European seasons, depending on where one lived.

11 Stuart, Charles (1833) *Two Expeditions into the Interior of Australia*, p. 155.

12 In Bell, Diane (ed.) for the Ngarrindjeri Nation (2008) *Listen to Ngarrindjeri Women Speaking/Kungun Ngarrindjeri Miminar Yunnan*, p. 8.

13 Tom and Ellen Trevorrow in ibid., p. 11.

14 Ellen Trevorrow in Bell, Diane (1998a) *Ngarrindjeri Wurruwarrin*, p. 70.

15 Mitchell, Sir Thomas (1839) *Three Expeditions into the Interior of Eastern Australia* (Vol. 1), pp. 228–229, 290–291.

16 Flood, Josephine (1995) *Archaeology of the Dreamtime*, p. 261.

17 Jones, Rhys (1980) 'Hunters in the Australian coastal savanna' cited in Flood, Josephine (1995) *Archaeology of the Dreamtime*, p. 259.

18 Flood, Josephine (1995) *Archaeology of the Dreamtime*, p. 260.

19 ibid., p. 251.
    See also Sylvia J. Hallam's (1975) *Fire and Hearth: A study of Aboriginal usage and European usurpation in south-western Australia* for an interesting overview of fire-stick farming.

20 Dillehay, Tom (2008) 'Profiles in Pleistocene history', pp. 33, 41.

21 Memmott, Paul and Carroll Go-Sam (2001) 'Living spaces' in Kleinert, Sylvia and Margot Neale (eds) *The Oxford Companion to Aboriginal Art and Culture*, p. 406.
    There were 8 types of shelters used including:
    - In areas where there was a lot of rain "sophisticated styles of strong weather proof shelters were developed ... [which were] tall enough to stand up in ... [and] sited near plentiful resources so that sedentary occupation was possible" (p. 405).
    - In the inland and the hot central desert there were "dome forms covered with a thick layer of spinifex and sometimes mud or clay plastering" (p. 405).
    - In the eastern forests "saplings and canes" were used to make "lightweight, interconnected dome forms ... sometimes covered with carefully thatched grasses or layers of palm leaves to deflect the heavy continuous rain" (p. 405).
    - Paul Memmott and Carroll Go-Sam also mention the "tall conical houses ... clad with earth sods for insulation ... and rock wall cottages" (p. 405). (Presumably here they are referring to the southern Victorian circular stone huts at Lake Condah, and those in Western Australia.)

22 ibid., p. 405.

23 Roughsey, Elsie, Paul Memmott and Robyn Horsman (1984) *An Aboriginal Mother Tells of the Old and the New* in Memmott, Paul and Carroll Go-Sam (2001) 'Living spaces', p. 408.

24 Memmott, Paul and Carroll Go-Sam (2001) 'Living spaces' in Kleinert, Sylvia and Margot Neale (eds) *The Oxford Companion to Aboriginal Art and Culture*, p. 407.
    'Wagilak' is also spelt 'Wagilag'.

[25] United Nations Permanent Forum on Indigenous Issues (10–12 May 2004) 'Indigenous women today', p. 49.

The 2004 United Nations report is concerned with the future for indigenous women and is optimistic since "indigenous voices are being heard more clearly in the United Nations, so too are the voices of indigenous women making themselves heard more distinctly, apart from indigenous peoples, and apart from women in general … [I]ndigenous women are receiving much needed institutional support as they seek to draw attention to the needs of this especially vulnerable group" (p. 59).

[26] Hawthorne, Susan (2002) *Wild Politics*, p. 233.

[27] Perkins, Hetti (2010) *art + soul*.

[28] ibid., p. x.

[29] ibid., p. x.

[30] Ilatjari, Nganyintja (1983) 'Women and land rights' in Gale, Fay (ed.) *We Are Bosses Ourselves*, p. 56.

Bibliography

Aboriginal Australia (1981–1982) (Catalogue) National Gallery of Victoria, Art Gallery of Western Australia, Queensland Art Gallery.

Aboriginal Indigenous Languages (1996) Senior Secondary Assessment Board of South Australia, Adelaide.

Ackerman, Kim with John Stanton (1994) *Riji and Jakoli: Kimberley pearlshell in Aboriginal Australia.* Monograph Series 4, Northern Territory Museum of Arts and Sciences.

Adams, Phillip (11–12 December 2010) 'The feminists of prehistory' *The Weekend Australian Magazine*, Melbourne.

Ahmed, Leila (1992) *Women and Gender in Islam.* Yale University Press, New Haven.

Ainu Museum (Japan) (n.d.) 'The Ainu people', <http://www.ainu-museum.or.jp/en/study/eng01. html> (accessed August 2012).

Aitchison, Jean (1996) *The Seeds of Speech: Language origin and evolution.* Cambridge University Press, Cambridge.

Akkermans, Peter (2011) in 'Comments' to Banning, Ted (2011) 'So fair a house: Gobekli Tepe and the identification of temples in the pre-pottery Neolithic of the Near East', pp. 641–660 <http://www.scribd.com/doc/67961270/Gobekli-Tepe-temples-Ted-Banning-2011> (accessed November, 2011).

—— (n.d.) 'Jerf el Ahmer', <http://wki.sjs.org/wiki/index.php/Jerf_el_Ahmar> (accessed November 2011).

Aksamet, Joanna (1989) 'The gold handle of a flint dagger from Gebelein (Upper Egypt)' in *Late Prehistory of the Nile Basin and the Sahara*, Poznan Archaeological Museum, pp. 325–332.

Alaimo, Stacy (1997) 'Feminism, nature, and discursive ecologies', University of Texas <http://www.altx.com/ebr/ebr4/alaimo.html> (accessed May 2003).

Allen, Paula Gunn (1986) *The Sacred Hoop: Recovering the feminine in American Indian traditions.* Beacon Press, Boston.

'Ancient seabed discovery rewrites human history' (September 1996) *Research* (Monash University Journal) Montage 9.

Anderson, Benedict (1972) 'The idea of power in Javanese culture' in Holt, Clare, Benedict Anderson and James Siegal *Culture and Politics in Indonesia.* Cornell University Press, New York, pp. 1–69.

Andrews, Munya (2004) *The Seven Sisters of the Pleiades: Stories from around the world.* Spinifex Press, North Melbourne.

Anthony, David (1998) 'The horse in mortuary symbolism in the European Steppes, 5,000–4,000 BCE', The Institute for Ancient Equestrian Studies, Hartwich College, Oneonta, NY. <http://users.hartwick.edu/iaes/horseback/horse.html> (accessed April 2003).

—— and Dorcas Brown (2007) *The Horse, the Wheel and Language.* Princeton University Press, Oxford.

—— and Dorcas Brown (n.d.) 'Harnessing horsepower: Horses and humans in antiquity', <http://users.hartwick.edu/anthonyd/harnessing%20horsepower.html> (accessed July 2011).

Apostolakou, Lito (September 2009) 'Ancient Japanese clay figurines', <http://www.Lito-Apostolakou. suite101.com-Museum-Exhibits (accessed September 2010).

Archey, Gilbert (1965/1974) *The Art Forms of Polynesia.* Bulletin of the Auckland Institute and Museum, No. 4. Published by the Authority of the Council.

—— (1967) *South Sea Folk: Handbook of Maori and oceanic ethnography.* Third Edition, Unity Press, UK.

Arditti, Rita, Renate Duelli Klein and Shelley Minden (eds) (1984) *Test-Tube Women: What future for motherhood?* Pandora, London.

Arendt, Hannah (1998) *The Human Condition.* University of Chicago Press, Chicago.

Atkinson, Judy (2002) *Trauma Trails, Recreating Song Lines: The transgenerational effects of trauma in Indigenous Australia.* Spinifex Press, North Melbourne.

Austin, Donald (2010) 'Big Petroglyph Canyon', Rock Art Gallery, Petroglyps.us <http://www.petroglyphs.us/photographs_petroglyphs_big_petroglyph_canyon_california> (accessed July 2011).

Australian Concise Oxford Dictionary (1995) Oxford University Press, South Melbourne.

Bachofen, J.J. (1967) *Myth, Religion and Mother Right: Selected writings of J.J. Bachofen.* trans. Ralph Manheim. Princeton University Press, Princeton. (First published in German in 1848 as *Das Mutterrecht*, 2 vols. Basel: Gesammelte Werke.)

Bahn, Paul (1998) *Prehistoric Art: Cambridge illustrated history.* Cambridge University Press, Cambridge.

—— (ed.) (1992) *Collins Dictionary of Archaeology.* Harper Collins, Glasgow.

Baines, Patricia (1988) 'A litany for land' in Keen, Ian (ed.) *Being Black: Aboriginal cultures in 'settled' Australia.* Aboriginal Studies Press, for the Australian Institute of Aboriginal Studies, Canberra pp. 227–250.

Balai, Sana and Judith Ryan, with Drusilla Modjeska and Alban Sare (2009) *Wisdom of the Mountain: Art of the Ömie.* Exhibition Catalogue, National Gallery of Victoria.

Balter, Michael (2005) *The Goddess and the Bull, Catalhoyuk: An archaeological journey to the dawn of civilization.* Free Press (Simon and Schuster), New York.

Banning, Ted (2011) 'So fair a house: Göbekli Tepe and the identification of temples in the pre-pottery Neolithic of the Near East', in *Current Anthropology* 52 (5), pp. 619–660. Also <http://www.scribd.com/doc/67961270/Gobekli-Tepe-temples-Ted Banning-2011> (accessed November 2011).

—— (6 October 2011) 'Archaeologist argues world's oldest temples were not temples at all' *E!Science News* <http://esciencenews.com/articles/2011/10/o6/archaeologist.argues.worlds.oldest.temple> (accessed October 2011).

Barber, Elizabeth Wayland (1994) *Women's Work: The first 20,000 years.* W.W. Norton and Company, New York and London.

—— (1999) *The Mummies of Urumchi.* Macmillan Publishers, London.

—— with Paul T. Barber (2004) *When They Severed Earth From Sky: How the human mind shapes myth.* Princeton University Press, Princeton and Oxford.

Bard, Kathryn A. (ed.) (1999) *Encyclopaedia of the Archaeology of Ancient Egypt* in Wysinger, Myra (n.d) 'Pre-history Africa and the Badarian Culture', Extract by Gregory Possehl <http://www.wysinger.homestead.com/badarians.html> (accessed 20 April 2010/September 2010).

Bardon, Geoffrey and James Bardon (2004) *Papunya, A Place Made After the Story: The beginning of Western Desert painting.* Miegunyah Press, Melbourne.

Baring, Anne and Jules Cashford (1991) *The Myth of the Goddess: Evolution of an image.* Arkana/Penguin Books, London.

Barlow, Maureen (1998–1999) 'In memory of Marija Gimbutas: Where were the women?' Belili Productions, Canada, <http://www.amazonation.com/Gimbutasll.html> (accessed September 2011).

Barnes, Gina (1993) *China, Korea and Japan: The rise of civilization in East Asia.* Thames and Hudson, London.

—— (2010) 'Prehistoric ceramic figurines in Japan: Exhibitions of primitive art or avatars?' <http://gina-barnes.suite101.com/prehistoric-ceramic-figurines-in-japan-1880362oio-04-27weeklyo.25> (accessed September 2010 – no longer accessible). See: <http://suite101.com/article/prehistoric-ceramic-figurines-in-japan-a188036>.

Barnes, Jonathon (1982) *Aristotle.* Oxford University Press.

Bar On, Bat-Ami (ed.) (1994) *Engendering Origins: Critical feminist readings in Plato and Aristotle.* State University of New York Press, Albany, pp. xi–xviii.

Barrow, Terence (1984) *An Illustrated Guide to Maori Art.* Reed Methuen, New Zealand.

Becker, Nancy and Leonard Becker (2003) 'Tassili-n-Ajjer rock art in peril', *AURA Newsletter* 20 (2) September, Australian Rock Art Research Association (AURA), p. 19.

Bednarik, Robert (February 1990) 'On neuropsychology and shamanism in rock art' [Comment on Lewis-Williams and Dowson] in *Current Anthropology* 31 (1), pp. 77–84.

—— (1994a) 'The earliest known art' *Acta Archaeologica* 65, c/o The Institute of Archaeology, Vandkunsten 5, DK-467, Copenhagen, Denmark, pp. 221–232.

—— (1994b) 'The Pleistocene art of Asia' *Journal of World History* 8 (4), University of Hawai'i Press, pp. 351–375.

—— (1994c) 'Art origins' *Anthropos* 89, Academic Press, Fribourg, Switzerland, pp. 169–180.

—— (1994d) 'Miscellanea' *The Artefact*, Pacific Rim Archaeology 17, The Archaeological and Anthropological Society of Victoria Inc., p. 77.

—— (1994e) 'African Eve DNA' *The Artefact* Pacific Rim Archaeology 17, The Archaeological and Anthropological Society of Victoria Inc., p. 73.

—— (1995) 'Concept-mediated marking in the Lower Paleolithic' *Current Anthropology* 36 (4), University of Chicago Press, pp. 605–634.

—— (1996) 'The Origins of *H. habilis* in Africa and Asia' *The Artefact* Pacific Rim Archaeology 9, The Archaeological and Anthropological Society of Victoria Inc., p. 93.

—— (1997a) 'Origins of navigation and language' *The Artefact* Pacific Rim Archaeology 20, The Archaeological and Anthropological Society of Victoria Inc., pp. 16–56.

—— (1997b) 'Makepansgat hominid head' *The Artefact* Pacific Rim Archaeology 19, The Archaeological and Anthropological Society of Victoria Inc., p. 4.

—— (2000) 'Something Old, Something New ...' *AURA Newsletter* 17 (1) March, Australian Rock Art Research Association (AURA) and International Federation of Rock Art Organisations (FRAO), Archaeological Publications, Melbourne.

—— (2001) 'An Acheulian figurine from Morocco' [The Tan Tan figurine] *Rock Art Research* 18 (2) November, Australian Rock Art Research Association (AURA) and International Federation of Rock Art Organisations (FRAO), Archaeological Publications, Melbourne.

—— (2006) *Australian Apocalypse: The story of Australia's greatest cultural monument.* Occasional AURA publication 14, Australian Rock Art Research Association Inc., Melbourne.

—— (2006a) 'Dampier fact sheets', *AURA Newsletter* 23(2), pp. 5–9. Also at: <http://mc2.vicnet.net.au/home/dampier/web/facts.html>.

—— (2007) 'Antiquity and authorship of the Chauvet rock art' *Rock Art Research* 24 (1) May, Australian Rock Art Research Association (AURA) and International Federation of Rock Art Organisations (FRAO), Archaeological Publications, Melbourne, pp. 21–34.

—— and Majeed Khan (2005) 'Scientific studies of Saudi Arabian rock art' *Rock Art Research* 22 (1), Australian Rock Art Research Association (AURA) and International Federation of Rock Art Organisations (FRAO), Archaeological Publications, Melbourne, pp. 49–81.

Behrendt, Larissa (1993) 'Aboriginal women and the white lies of the feminist movement: Implications for Aboriginal women in the rights discourse' *The Australian Feminist Law Journal* 1, August, pp. 27–44. The Australian Feminist Law Foundation Inc., University of Melbourne.

Bell, Diane (1981) 'Women's Business is hard work: Central Australian Aboriginal women's love rituals' in Charlesworth, Max, Howard Morphy, Diane Bell and Kenneth Maddock (eds) *Religion in Aboriginal Australia.* University of Queensland Press, St. Lucia, pp. 344–369.

—— (1983/2002) *Daughters of the Dreaming.* McPhee Gribble/Allen and Unwin; Spinifex Press, North Melbourne.

—— (1998a) *Ngarrindjeri Wurruwarrin: A world that is, was, and will be.* Spinifex Press, North Melbourne.

—— (1998b) 'Aboriginal Women and the religious experience' in Charlesworth, Max (ed.) *Religious Business: Essays on Australian Aboriginal spirituality.* Cambridge University Press.

—— and Topsy Napurrula Nelson (1989) 'Speaking about rape is everyone's business' *Women's Studies International Forum* 12 (4), pp. 403–414.

—— (ed.) for the Ngarrindjeri Nation (2008) *Listen to Ngarrindjeri Women Speaking/Kungun Ngarrindjeri Miminar Yunnan*. Spinifex Press, North Melbourne.

Berlo, Janet Catherine (1996) 'Beyond bricolage: Women and aesthetic strategies in Latin American textiles', in Blum, Margot, Janet Berlo and Edward Dwyer (eds) *Textile Traditions of Mesoamerica and the Andes*. University of Texas, Austin.

Berlo, Janet C. and Ruth B. Phillips (1998) *Native North American Art* (Oxford History of Art). Oxford University Press.

Bernal, Martin (1987) Black Athena: The Afroasiatic roots of classical civilisation Vol. 1, 'The fabrication of Ancient Greece 1785–1985'. Free Association Books, London.

—— (1991) *Black Athena: The Afroasiatic roots of classical civilization Vol. 2*, 'The archaeological and documentary evidence'. Free Association Books, London.

—— (2006) *Black Athena: The Afroasiatic roots of classical civilization Vol. 3*, 'The linguistic evidence'. Free Association Books, London.

Biaggi, Cristina (1994) *Habitations of the Great Goddess*. Knowledge, Ideas and Trends Inc, Manchester Connecticut.

Binkley, Roberta (1998) 'Biography of Enheduanna Priestess of Inanna', University of Pennsylvania Museum, <http://www.cdde.vt.edu/feminism/Enheduanna.html> (accessed May 2012).

Bjurstrom, Lars (photographer) (2008) 'Art rocks in Saudi Arabia' in *Saudi Aramco World* 59 (7), <http://www.saudiaramcoworld.com/issue/200807/art.rocks.in.saudi.arabia-.compilation.htm> (accessed January 2012).

Blum, Margot, Janet Berlo and Edward Dwyer (eds) (1996) *Textile Traditions of Mesoamerica and the Andes*. University of Texas, Austin.

Boas, Franz (1928/1955) *Primitive Art*. Dover Publications Inc., New York.

Bohm, David and Mark Edwards (1991) *Changing Consciousness: Exploring the hidden source of the social, political, and environmental crises facing our world. A dialogue of words and images*. Harper, San Francisco.

Bone, Pamela (13 June 2002) 'Blokey Australia will have a female PM, says Vanstone' *The Age*, Melbourne, p. 14.

Bowe, Heather (1996) 'Aboriginal languages of Australia', Koorie Studies Lecture, Monash University, Melbourne.

Bowler, Jim (19 February 2003) in 'New age for Mungo Man [and Mungo Woman]' (Media release), University of Adelaide, <http://www.adelaide.edu.au/news/news472.html> (accessed November 2012).

Boylan, Chris and Greta North (n.d.) 'Highlands art of New Guinea', *Tribal Arts Magazine*, <http://www.tribalartsmagazine.com/en/index_auteur_ASC.4.html> (accessed June 2010).

Bradshaw, John (1998) 'Sermons in stones: Fossils and the evolution of representational art' [Comment to John Feliks] *Rock Art Research* 15 (2), Australian Rock Art Research Association (AURA) and International Federation of Rock Art Organisations (FRAO), Archaeological Publications, Melbourne, pp. 125–126.

Brake, Brian, James McNeish and David Summers (eds) (1979) *Art of the Pacific*. Oxford University Press.

Brennan, Martin (1994) *The Stones of Time: Calendars, sundials and stone chambers of ancient Ireland*. Inner Traditions International, Rochester.

British Museum (2009) 'The power of dogu: Ceramic figures from ancient Japan' (photograph) <http://www.britishmuseum.org/images/dogu_tanabatake_325.jpg> (accessed 11 February 2013). Full article: <http://www.britishmuseum.org/whats_on/past_exhibitions/2009/the_power_of_dogu.aspx>.

Brockman, John (n.d.) 'The Three Dimensions of Human History' Edge 3rd Culture: A Talk with Colin Renfrew, <http://www.edge.org/3rd_culture/renfrew/renfrew_pl.htm> (accessed September 2002).

Brown, David J. and Rebecca McClen Novik (3 October 1992) 'Learning the language of the Goddess: Interview with Marija Gimbutas', *Voices from the Edge*, <http://www.levity.com/mavericks/gim-int.html> (accessed April 2003).

Brunton, Guy and Gertrude Caton-Thompson (1928) *The Badarian Civilization and Pre-Dynastic Remains Near Badari*. British School of Archaeology University College.

Bryant, Edwin (2001) *The Quest for the Origins of Vedic Culture: The Indo-Aryan migration debate*. Oxford University Press, Oxford.

Builth Heather (1998) 'Lake Condah revisited: Archaeological constructions of a cultural landscape' (Abstract) *Australian Archaeology* 47 <http://www.library.uq.edu.au/ojs/index.php/aa/article/viewArticle/919> (accessed November 2012).

Bullock, Alan, Oliver Stallybrass and Stephen Trombley (eds) (1988) *The Fontana Dictionary of Modern Thought*. 2nd edition, Fontana, USA.

Burdon, Amanda (April–June 2009) 'Written in stone', *Australian Geographic* 94, Journal of the Australian Geographic Society.

Cameron, Dorothy (1981) Symbols of Birth and Death in the Neolithic Era cited in Gimbutas, Marija (1991) The Civilization of the Goddess. Harper, San Francisco.

—— (1997) 'The Minoan Horns of Consecration' in Marler, Joan (ed.) *From the Realm of the Ancestors: An anthology in honour of Marija Gimbutas*. Knowledge, Ideas and Trends Inc., USA, pp. 508–523.

Campbell, Joseph (1959/1969) *The Masks of God: Primitive mythology* (Vol. 1). Penguin Books, USA.

Capon, Edmund (1977) *Art and Archaeology in China*. Macmillan, Melbourne.

Carrigan, Frank (18–19 February 2012) 'Anger management: Humans were wired from the onset', *The Weekend Australian Review*, Melbourne, pp. 18–19.

Carroll, John (1998) *Ego and Soul: The modern West in search of meaning*. Harper Collins, Sydney.

Carter, Susan Gail (2009) 'Amaterasu-o-mi-kami, Japanese Sun Goddess: The matristic roots of Japan' in Göttner-Abendroth, Heide (ed.) *Societies of Peace: Matriarchies past, present and future*. Inanna Publications and Education, Toronto, pp. 394–406.

Cavalli-Sforza, Luigi L. (1991) 'Genes, peoples and languages' *Scientific American*, November, pp. 72–78.

—— (1996) 'History and geography of the human gene' in *Genes, Peoples and Languages*. Princeton University Press.

—— (1999) 'A panoramic synthesis of my work', International Balzan Foundation, <http://www.balzan.it/english/pb1999/cavalli/paper.htm> (accessed June 2003).

—— (2000) *Genes, Peoples and Languages*. trans. Mark Scielstad, Penguin Books, New York, pp. 101–162; <http://users.cyberone.com.au/myers/gimbutas.htm> (accessed June 2003).

—— (12 February 2003) 'WHO human genetics' <http://www.who.int/nct/hgn/ovrview.htm> (accessed September 2003).

—— (19–22 March, 2003) 'Africa human genome initiative' <http://www.africagenome.co.za/profiles/luigi_cavalli_sforza.html> (accessed June 2003).

—— (15 August 2003) 'The threshold challenge of the new human genetic technologies', Centre for Genetics and Society, Oakland, California <http://www.genetics-and-society.org/overview/threshold.htm> (accessed September 2003).

Chakrabarti, Dilip (1999) *India, An Archaeological History: Palaeolithic beginnings to early historic foundations*. Oxford University Press, New Delhi.

—— (2006) *Oxford Companion to Indian Archaeology: The archaeological foundations of ancient India*. Oxford University Press, New Delhi.

Chakravarty, Kalyan and Robert Bednarik (1997) *Indian Rock Art and Its Global Context*. Narendra Prakash Jain, Bhopal.

Chaloupa, George (1993) *Journey in Time: The world's longest continuing art tradition*. Reed Books, Sydney.

Chandler, Jo (26 April 2010) 'Call to hear the gender agenda', Opinion, *The Age*, Melbourne, <http://www.smh.com.au/opinion/society-and-culture/call-to-hear-the-gender-agenda-20100425-tll1.html>.

Chick, John and Sue (eds) (1978) *Grass Roots Art of the Solomons: Images and islands*. Pacific Publications, Sydney.

Chomsky, Noam (1993) *Language and Thoughts*. Moyer Bell, USA.

—— (1986) *Knowledge of Language: Its nature, origin and use*. Praeger Publishers, New York.

—— (1988) *Language and Problems of Knowledge*. The Managua Lectures: Cambridge, The MIT Press.

Christ, Carol (1980) *Diving Deep and Surfacing: Women writers on spiritual quest*. Beacon Press, Boston.

—— (1995) *Odyssey with the Goddess: A spiritual quest in Crete*. Continuum, London.

—— (1997a) 'A different world: The challenge of the work of Marija Gimbutas to the dominant worldview of Western cultures' in Marler, Joan (ed.) *From the Realm of the Ancestors: An anthology in honour of Marija Gimbutas*. Knowledge, Ideas and Trends Inc., USA, pp. 406–415.

—— (1997b) *Rebirth of the Goddess*. Addison-Wesley, Reading.

Clark, Graham (1961) 'The first half-million years: The hunter-gatherers of the Stone Age' in Piggott, Stuart (ed.) *Dawn of Civilization*. Thames and Hudson, London, pp. 19–40.

Clark, Sharri R. (2001) 'Embodying Indus life: Terra cotta figurines from Harappa', Harvard University, <www.harappa.com/figurines/> 'Figurines from Harappa', 72 slides (accessed January 2011).

Clottes, Jean (2003) *Chauvet Cave: The art of earliest times*, University of Utah Press.

Clunies-Ross, Margaret (1983) 'Modes of formal performance in societies without writing: The case of Aboriginal Australia' in *Aboriginal Studies* 1, pp. 16–25.

Coffman, Ralf J. (2002) 'Voyagers of the Pacific: Rock art and the Austronesian dispersal'
[Part 1] *Rock Art Research* 19 (1), pp. 41–62.
[Part 2] *Rock Art Research* 19 (2), November, pp. 79–97; Comments, p. 104.
Australian Rock Art Research Association (AURA) and International Federation of Rock Art Organisations (FRAO), Archaeological Publications, Melbourne.

Coombs, H.C., M.M. Brandl and W.E. Snowdon (1983) *A Certain Heritage: For and by Aboriginal families in Australia*. CRES Monograph 9, Centre for Resources and Environmental Studies, Australian National University, Canberra.

Collins English Dictionary (1991) 3rd edition, Harper Collins.

Collins, Paul (1995) *God's Earth: Religion as if matter really mattered*. Dove/Harper Collins, Melbourne.

Collon, Dominique (1995) *Ancient Near Eastern Art*. University of California, Los Angeles.

Conard, Nicholas (14 May 2009) 'A female figurine from the basal Aurignacian of Hole Fels Cave in south-western Germany', *Nature* 459, pp. 248–252.

—— (n.d.) 'From cave painting to the Internet: The earliest examples of figurative art circa 38,000–33,000 BCE. A female figurine from the basal Aurignacian of Hole Fels Cave in south-western Germany', <http://www.nature.com.nature/videoarchive/prehistoricpinup/> (accessed October 2010).

Condran, Mary (1997) 'On forgetting our divine origins: The warning of Dervogilla' in Marler, Joan (ed.) *From the Realm of the Ancestors: An anthology in honour of Marija Gimbutas*. Knowledge, Ideas and Trends Inc., USA, pp. 416–432.

Conkey, Margaret and Ruth Tringham (1996) 'Cultivating thinking/Challenging authority' in Wright, Rita (ed.) *Gender and Archaeology*. University of Pennsylvania Press, pp. 204–250.

Contreres, Dona Enriqueta (2009) 'Matriarchal values among the Sierra Juarez Zapotecs of Oaxaca' in Göttner-Abendroth, Heide (ed.) *Societies of Peace: Matriarchies past, present and future*. Inanna Publications and Education, Toronto.

Coppa, A. et al (April 2006) 'Early Neolithic tradition of dentistry: Flint tips were surprisingly effective for drilling tooth enamel in a prehistoric population', *Nature* 440, cited in Posshel, Gregory 'Mehrgarh: Period I, Period II, Period III, craft production in early periods, Period Hordeum vulgare, vulgare' <ahref=http://www.jrank.org.history/pages/6295/Mehrgarh> (accessed January 2010).

Corea, Gena (1985) *The Mother Machine: Reproductive technologies from artificial insemination to artificial wombs*. Harper and Row, New York.

Cottingham, John (ed.) (1996) *Western Philosophy: An anthology*. Blackwell Publishers, USA.

Cowan, J.G. (1992) *The Elements of the Aboriginal Tradition*. Shaftesbury, Dorset.

Crafts and Artisans (n.d.) 'Folk Painting' <http://www.craftandartisan.com> (accessed October 2010.)

—— (n.d.) 'Folk Painting/Hase Chitra of Karnataka' <http://www.craftandartisans.com/folk-painting-hase-chitra-of-karnataka.html> (accessed September 2010).

Crafts in India (n.d.) 'Maithili Painting' An ode to Indian Art, <http://www.craftsinindia.com/products/paint/maithili.html> (accessed September 2010).

Crystalinks (n.d.) 'Nushu – Women's Script', <http://www.crystalinks.com/nushu.html> (accessed October 2010).

Cultural India (n.d.) 'Ancient India – Cultural Timeline and Elements of Indus Valley Civilization', Cultural India <http://www.culturalindia.net/indian-history/ancient-india/indus-valley.html> (accessed September 2010).

D'Alleva, Anne (1998) *Arts of the Pacific Islands*. Yale University Press, New Haven.

Daly, Mary (1973/1986) *Beyond God the Father*. Beacon Press, Boston.

Dames, Michael (1976) *The Silbury Treasure*. Thames and Hudson, London.

—— (1992/1996) *Mythic Ireland*. Thames and Hudson, London.

—— (1997) 'The Gimbutas gift', in Marler, Joan (ed.) *From the Realm of the Ancestors: An anthology in honour of Marija Gimbutas*. Knowledge, Ideas and Trends Inc., USA, pp. 47–49.

—— (2009) 'Footsteps of the goddess in Britain and Ireland' in Göttner-Abendroth, Heide (ed.) *Societies of Peace: Matriarchies past, present and future*. Inanna Publications and Education, Toronto, pp. 313–322.

Danesi, Marcel Vico (1993) *Metaphor and the Origin of Language*. Indiana Press, USA.

Danshilacuo, Hengde (He Mei) (2009) 'Mosuo family structure' in Göttner-Abendroth, Heide (ed.) *Societies of Peace: Matriarchies past, present and future*. Inanna Publications and Education, Toronto, pp. 248–255.

Darby, Andrew (11 March 2010) 'Highway threatens ancient Aboriginal site', *The Age*, Melbourne.

Dashi Village (2008) <http://www.dashicun.com/html_en/view10.htm>.

Dashu, Max (2004a) *Icons of the Matrix* (Part 1) Suppressed Histories Archives, <http://www.suppressedhistories.net/womenpowervd.html> (accessed 2010)

—— (2004b) *Icons of the Matrix: The Matrikas* (Part 2) Suppressed Histories Archives, <http://www.suppressedhistories.net/articles/icons2.html> (accessed 2010).

—— (2005a) 'Predynastic Kemetic priestesses: The testimony of Naquada ceramics and rock art' (photographs) <http://www.suppressedhistories.net/Gallery/kemet/invokers3.html> (accessed July 2012).

—— (2005b) 'Women in North African rock art' (photographs) <http://www.suppressedhistories/Gallery/northafrican/rockart.html> (accessed July 2012).

—— (2005c) 'Daughters of Kasamba: The Goba People of the Zambezi River' (Matrix cultures), Suppressed Histories Archives, <http://www.suppressedhistories.net/matrix/goba.html>.

—— (2008) 'Female Icons: Ancestral Mothers' (Poster) Sacred women, Lifegivers; Suppressed Histories Archives, <http://www.sh.net/catalog/treasures_sha.html> (accessed April 2010).

—— (2009) 'Xi Wangmu, the Shamanic great goddess of China', Suppressed Histories Archives, <http://www.suppressedhistories.net/goddess/xuwangmu.html> (accessed March 2010).

—— (2010) 'The Meanings of Goddess' (Parts 1, 2, 3) <http:// www.goddess-pages.co.uk/index. php?option=com_content&task=view&id=60> or <http://www.suppressedhistories.net/ womenspowerdvd.html> (accessed April 2010).

—— (n.d.) 'Ecuadorian figurines: A taste from the archives', Suppressed Histories Archives, <http:// www.suppressedhistories.net/articles/articles.htm> (accessed March 2010).

—— (n.d.) 'Female divinity in South America', Suppressed Histories Archives <http://suppressed histories.net/goddess/fdivsa.html> (accessed April 2010).

—— (n.d.) 'The matrilineal country of Laos'; 'Daughters of Kasamba: The Goba people of the Zambezi River'; 'Exodus of the Zigula (Somali Bantu)' Suppressed Histories Archives <http://suppressedhistories.net/matrix/motherright.html> (accessed April 2010).

Das, Sushi (16 September 2010) 'Fleeing arranged marriage' *The Age,* Melbourne.

Davidson, Hilda Ellis (1998) *Roles of the Northern Goddess.* Routledge, London.

Davies, Paul (1992) *The Mind of God: Science and the search for ultimate meaning.* Penguin, Australia.

Davies, Peter (2000) *Antique Kilims of Anatolia.* W.W. Norton and Co., New York.

Davis, Virginia (1996) 'Resist dyeing in Mexico: Comments on its history, significance and prevalence' in Blum, Margot, Janet Berlo and Edward Dwyer (eds) *Textile Traditions of Mesoamerica and the Andes.* University of Texas, Austin.

de Beaugrande, Robert (1991) *Linguistic Theory: The discourse of fundamental works.* Longman Inc., London.

dé Ishtar, Zohl (1994) *Daughters of the Pacific.* Spinifex Press, Melbourne.

—— (2005) *Holding Yawulyu: White culture and black women's law.* Spinifex Press, Melbourne.

DeMeo, James (2009) 'Saharasia: The origins of patriarchal authoritarian culture in ancient desertification', in Göttner-Abendroth, Heide (ed.) *Societies of Peace: Matriarchies past, present and future.* Inanna Publications and Education Inc., Toronto, Canada, pp. 407–423.

Denison, Simon (ed.) (April 2000) 'Woven clothing dates back 27,000 years', *British Archaeology* 52 (2) <http://www.britarch.ac.uk/ba/ba52news.html> (accessed September 2002).

Department of Arts of Africa, Oceania, and the Americas (October 2001) 'Hand prints in African cave' in Heilbrunn Timeline of Art History, The Metropolitan Museum of Art, New York <http:// www.metmuseum.org/toah/hd/sroc/hd_sroc.htm> (accessed June 2010).

—— (October 2004) 'Valdivia Figurines' in Heilbrunn Timeline of Art History, The Metropolitan Museum of Art, New York <http://www.metmuseum.org/toah/hd/vald/hd_vald.htm> (accessed June 2010).

—— (October 2004) Photographs: Figs 1–4 <http://www.metmuseum.org/toah/hd/ngss/hd_ngss. htm>. See also: Kjellgren, Eric and Jennifer Wagelie (2001) 'Prehistoric stone sculpture from New Guinea' <http://www.metmuseum.org/toah/hd/ngss/hd_ngss.htm>.

Department of Asian Art (October 2002) 'Jomon Culture (ca. 10,500–ca. 300 B.C.)' in Heilbrunn Timeline of Art History, The Metropolitan Museum of Art, New York <http://www. metmuseum.org/toah/hd/jomo/hd_jomo.htm> (accessed June 2010). Photographs: Fig. 1a. <http://www.metmuseum.org/toah/works-of-art/1978.346>; Fig. 1b. <http://www. metmuseum.org/toah/works-of-art/1975.268.191>.

—— (October 2004) 'Neolithic Period in China' in Heilbrunn Timeline of Art History, The Metropolitan Museum of Art, New York <http://www.metmuseum.org/toah/hd/cneo/ hd_cneo.htm> (accessed June 2010).

Dexter, Miriam Robbins (1990) Whence the Goddess: A source book. Pergamon Press: Athene Series, New York.

'Devi' (n.d.) *A Dictionary of World Mythology*, Oxford University Press. Retrieved from Answers.com <http://www.answers.com/topic/devi> (accessed August 2010).

Diamond, Jared (1991) *The Rise and Fall of the Third Chimpanzee*. Vintage Books, London.

Dillehay, Tom (2008) 'Profiles in Pleistocene history', in Silverman, Helaine and William H. Isbell (eds) *Handbook of South American Archaeology*, Springer Science and Business Media LLC, New York, pp. 29–44.

—— C. Ramírez, M. Pino, M. B. Collins, J. Rossen, J. D. Pino-Navarro (2008) 'Monte Verde: Seaweed, food, medicine and the peopling of South America', *Science* 320.

Diop, Cheikh Anta (1974) *The African Origin of Civilization: Myth or reality*, trans. Laurence Mercer Cook, Hill Books, UK.

Doniger, Wendy (2009) *The Hindus: An alternative history*. Viking Penguin, England.

Donkoh, Wilhelmina J. (2009) 'Female leadership among the Asante', in Göttner-Abendroth, Heide (ed.) *Societies of Peace: Matriarchies past, present and future*. Inanna Publications and Education Inc., Toronto, Canada, pp. 117–128.

Drew, Julie (1991) 'Women and gender relations in Australian rock art', Bachelor's thesis (unpublished), University of Sydney.

—— (1995) 'Depictions of women and gender in gendered archaeology' in Bahme, J. and W. Beck (eds) *The Second Australian Women in Archaeology Conference*. ANU Publications RSPAS, Canberra, pp. 105–112.

—— and the Wardaman Aboriginal Corporation (2005) *Renewing Women's Business: A documentary* (DVD) Julie Drew and Burbank Production Services, Crow's Nest, NSW.

Drinnon, Dale (n.d.) 'Arte historia' Frontiers of Anthropology <http://www.frontiers-of-anthropology. blogspot.com> (accessed July 2011).

Early Women Masters East and West (n.d.) 'Jomon: Women's Japanese prehistoric Jomon pottery', <http://www.earlywomenmasters.net/masters/jomon/index.html> (accessed 2 July 2011).

Eco, Umberto (1995) *The Search for the Perfect Language*. Blackwell Publishing Ltd, UK.

Ehrenberg, Margaret (1989) *Women in Prehistory*. British Museum Press, London.

Eisler, Riane (1990) *The Chalice and the Blade*. Harper Collins, USA.

Eliade, Mircea (1976) 'Symbols – patterns, transitions and paradises' in Beane, Wendell C. and William G. Doty (eds) *Myths, Rites, Symbols: A Mircea Eliade reader* (Vol. 2). Harper Colophon Books, New York, pp. 341–406.

Encyclopaedia Britannica Online (2012) 'Pygmy', <http://www.britannica.com/EBchecked/topic/ 484571/Pygmy> (accessed 10 August 2012).

Eogan, George (1986) *Knowth and the Passage Tombs of Ireland*. Thames and Hudson, London.

E!Science News (6 October 2006) 'Archaeologist argues world's oldest temples were not temples at all', <http://esciencenews.com/articles/2011/10/06/archaeologist.argues.worlds.oldest.temple> (accessed October 2011).

Estes, Clarissa Pinkola (1992) *Women Who Run with the Wolves: Contacting the power of the wild woman*. Random House, UK.

Evans, Arthur (1936) *The Palace of Minos at Knossos* (Vol. 4). Macmillan and Co., London.

Eyre, John (1845) *Journals of Expeditions of Discovery into Central Australia, and Overland from Adelaide to King George's Sound, in the Years 1840–1*. T. and W. Boone, London.

Fabisch, Gunter (2008) Exotic Jades (photographs) <http://www.exoticjades.com>; <http://www. exoticjades.com/?cat=7&paged=16> (accessed 10 Feb 2013); <http://www.exoticjades. com/?cat=20&paged=3> (accessed 10 Feb 2013); <http://www.exoticjades.com/?cat= 20&paged=3> (accessed 10 Feb 2013).

Fagan, Brian M. (1991a) *Kingdoms of Gold, Kingdoms of Jade: The Americas before Columbus*. Thames and Hudson, London.

—— (1991b) *Ancient North America: The archaeology of a continent*. Thames and Hudson, London.

'Far-East Realm: Here the old Asian goddesses shall dwell again', <http://inanna.virtualave.net/fareast. html> (accessed July 2012).

Farmer, Steve, Richard Sproat and Michael Witzel (n.d.) 'The collapse of the Indus script thesis: The myth of a literate Harappan civilisation', <http://www.safarmer.com/fsw2.pdf> (accessed July 2012).

Feest, Christian F. (1992) *Native Arts of North America*. Thames and Hudson, London.

Feliks, John (1998) 'The impact of fossils on the development of visual representation', *Rock Art Research* 15 (2), Australian Rock Art Research Association (AURA) and International Federation of Rock Art Organisations (FRAO), Archaeological Publications, Melbourne, pp. 109–124. Also at <http://www.personal.umich.au/-feliks/impact-of-fossils/index.html> (accessed September 2011).

—— (2006) 'Musings on the Palaeolithic fan motif', p. 249–266 in Chenna Reddy, Peddarapu (ed.) *Exploring the mind of ancient man*. Research India Press, New Delhi, <http://www.edu/-feliks/musings-on-the-palaeolithic-fan-motif/index.html> (accessed September 2011).

Fesl, Eve M.D. (11 September 1990) 'Koorie women: Our future', The Caroline Chisholm Lecture, LaTrobe University, Melbourne.

—— (c. 1991) Lecture at the Monash Indigenous Centre, Monash University, Melbourne.

Field, Judith, R. Fullagar and Gary Lord (2001) 'A large area archaeological excavation at Cuddie Springs', *Antiquity* No 75, pp. 696–702.

Fiorenza, Elizabeth Schussler (1992) *But She Said: Feminist practices of biblical interpretation*. Beacon Press, Boston.

Firth, Raymond (1940/1967) *The Work of the Gods in Tikopia*. Melbourne University Press, Australia.

Fischman, Josh (April 2005) 'Family Ties: These prehistoric pioneers adopted a new way of life based on co-operation, even caring, and gave rise to later humans from the Flores people to ourselves', *National Geographic*, pp. 16–27.

Flannery, Tim (1994) *The Future Eaters: An ecological history of the Australasian lands and people*. Reed Books, Sydney.

Flood, Josephine (1983) *Archaeology of the Dreamtime: The story of prehistoric Australia and her people*. Harper Collins, Sydney.

—— (1990) *The Riches of Ancient Australia: A journey into prehistory*. University of Queensland Press, Australia.

—— (1995) *Archaeology of the Dreamtime: The story of prehistoric Australia and its people* (revised edition). Angus and Robertson Publications, imprint of Harper Collins, Sydney.

—— (1997) *Rock Art of the Dreamtime*. Harper Collins, Sydney.

—— and Bruno David (1994) 'Traditional systems of encoding meaning in Wardaman rock art, Northern Territory, Australia', *The Artefact*, Pacific Rim Archaeology Vol. 20, The Archaeological and Anthropological Society of Victoria Inc., pp. 6–22.

Ford, Clyde (1999) *The Hero with an African Face: Mythic wisdom of traditional Africa*. Bantam Books, Random House, USA.

Fourcroy, Jean L. (2001) 'The three female sorrows', Raising Daughters Aware, 98/99/200/2001/FGM Information Index Page pp. 1–3, <http://.www.fgm.org/fourcroy.htm> (accessed May 2002).

Fourmile, Henrietta (1989) 'Some background to issues concerning the appropriation of Aboriginal imagery' in *Postmodernism: A consideration of the appropriation of Aboriginal imagery forum papers*. Institute of Modern Art, Brisbane.

Fraser, Alex (July 1998) 'Unfinished business: The historical struggle for equal pay in Australia', in *Trust Women for Ideas* 1 (3) Victorian Women's Trust, Melbourne, Australia, p. 5.

Frymer-Kensky, Tikva (1993) *In the Wake of the Goddesses: Women, culture and the biblical transformation of pagan myth*. Ballantine Books, USA.

Fullagar, R. and J. Field (1997) 'Pleistocene seed-grinding implements from the Australian arid zone' in *Antiquity* 71 (232), UK, pp. 300–307.

Gale, Fay (ed.) (1983) *We Are Bosses Ourselves: The status and role of Aboriginal women today.* Australian Institute of Aboriginal Studies, Canberra.

Gamble, Clive (1995) *Timewalkers: The prehistory of global colonisation.* Penguin Books, USA.

Gammage, Bill (2011) *The Biggest Estate on Earth.* Allen and Unwin, Sydney.

Gardner, Helen, Fred S. Kleiner and Richard G. Tansey (1996) *Gardner's Art Through the Ages* (10th edition). Harcourt Brace College Publications, Fort Worth.

Gatusa, Lamu (2009) 'Matriarchal marriage patterns of the Mosuo people of China' in Göttner-Abendroth, Heide (ed.) *Societies of Peace: Matriarchies past, present and future.* Inanna Publications and Education, Toronto, pp. 240–247.

Genova, Judith (1994) 'Feminist dialectics: Plato and dualism' in Bar On, Bat-Ami (ed.) *Engendering Origins: Critical feminist readings in Plato and Aristotle.* State University of New York Press, Albany, pp. 41–52.

Gero, Joan (1996) 'Archaeological practice and gendered encounters with field data' in Wright, Rita (ed.) *Gender and Archaeology.* University of Pennsylvania Press, Philadelphia, pp. 251–280.

Gertsclacher, Anna and Margit Miosga (eds) (2003) *China for Women: Travel and culture.* Spinifex Press, North Melbourne.

Gibbons, Helen (May 2010) 'Possum skin cloaks: Tradition, continuity, and change', *The Latrobe Journal* 28, State Library of Victoria Foundation, <http://3.slv.vic.gov.au/latrobejournal/issue/latrobe-85/tl-g-t10.html> (accessed December 2012).

Gilbert, Kevin (1983) in Coombs, H.C., M.M. Brandl, W.E. Snowdon *A Certain Heritage for and by Aboriginal Families in Australia.* CRES Monograph 9, Centre for Resources and Environmental Studies, Australian National University, Canberra, p. 35.

Gill, N.S. (2012) 'Ancient/classical history: Nugua', <http://ancienthistory.about.com/od/godsand goddesses/g/061010/Nugua.htm> (accessed July 2012).

—— (n.d.) 'Nugua' (Bat goddess) <http://www.jades.com/wp-content/uploads/2006/12/nuwa_bat jpg> (accessed July 2012).

Gimbutas, Marija

—— (1974) *The Gods and Goddesses of Old Europe, 7,000–3,500 BC.* University of California Press.

—— (1974a) 'An archaeologist's view of PIE in 1975', *Journal of European Studies* 2 (3), pp. 289–307.

—— (1977) 'The first wave of Eurasian pastoralists into Copper Age Europe', *Journal of Indo-European Studies* 5 (4), pp. 277–338.

—— (1980) 'The Kurgan Wave 2 (c. 3,400–3,200 BC) into Europe and the following transformation of culture', *Journal of Indo-European Studies* 8 (3–4), pp. 273–315.

—— (1982) *The Goddesses and Gods of Old Europe (6,500–3,500 BC): Myths and cult images.* University of California Press.

—— (1985) 'Primary and secondary homeland of the Indo-Europeans: Comments on Gamkrelidze-Ivanov articles', *Journal of Indo-European Studies* 13 (1–2), pp. 185–202.

—— (1989) *The Language of the Goddess.* Harper, San Francisco.

—— (1991) *The Civilization of the Goddess.* Harper, San Francisco.

—— (1999/2001) *The Living Goddesses.* University of California Press.

Girling, Richard (2003) 'Looking for Nefertiti' [Joann Fletcher] [Part One] 19–20 July, *The Australian Weekend Magazine.* [Part Two] 26–27 July, *The Australian Weekend Magazine.*

Gleason, Judith (1987) *Oya: In praise of the goddess.* Shambala, Boston and London.

Global Oneness (n.d.) 'Sindh History', <http://www.experiencefestival.com/sindh_-_history> (accessed October, 2010).

Göttner-Abendroth, Heide (2009) 'Notes on the rise and expansion of patriarchy' in Göttner-Abendroth, Heide (ed.) *Societies of Peace: Matriarchies past, present and future*. Inanna Publications and Education, Toronto, pp. 424–436.

—— (ed.) (2009) *Societies of Peace: Matriarchies past, present and future*. Inanna Publications and Education, Toronto.

Goodall, Heather (1992) 'The whole truth and nothing but … Some interactions of Western law, Aboriginal history and community memory', in Attwood, Bain and John Arnold (eds) *Power, Knowledge and Aborigines*. La Trobe University Press in association with the National Centre for Australian Studies, Monash University, A Special Edition of *Journal of Australian Studies*, pp. 104–119.

Goodison, Lucy and Christine Morris (1998) *Ancient Goddesses*. British Museum Press.

Gorman, James (17 December 2012) 'Ancient bones that tell a story of compassion', *New York Times* <http://www.nytimes.com/2012/12/18/science/ancient-bones-that-tell-a-story-of-compassion.html?pagewanted=all> (accessed December 2012).

Grahn, Judy (1993) *Blood, Bread and Roses: How menstruation created the world*. Beacon Press, Boston.

—— (20 March 2001) 'Spiraling Moon' [Interview by Vanessa Tiegs], San Francisco, California, USA.

—— and Vanessa Tiegs (n.d.) 'Spiraling Moon: Judy Grahn Interview' in Spiraling Moon, http://www.spiralingmoon.com/img/interviewdocs/judygrahn.htm> (accessed February 2003).

Grand, P.M. (1967) *Prehistoric Art: Paleolithic painting and sculpture*. New York Graphic Society.

Greenberg, J. Turner and Zegura (1986) 'The Settlement of the Americas: A comparison of linguistic, dental and genetic evidence' in *Current Anthropology* 27 (5).

Griffin, Susan (1989) 'Split culture' in Plant, Judith (ed.) *Healing the Wounds: The promise of eco-feminism*. New Society Publishers, Philadelphia, pp. 7–17.

Griffith, Brian (23 June 2011) 'The goddess realms of prehistoric China', *Archaeology News* <http://archaeologynews.multiply.com/journal/item/882> (accessed 25 July 2012).

—— (2012) *A Galaxy of Immortal Women: The Yin side of Chinese civilisation*. Exterminating Angel Press, USA.

Guillermo, Alice (1995) 'Weaving: Women's art and power', in Kaino, Lorna (ed.) *The Necessity of Craft: Development and women's craft practices in the Asia-Pacific region*. University of Western Australia Press, Nedlands, pp. 35–56.

Guss, David M. (1989) *To Weave and Sing: Art, symbol and narrative in the South American rainforest*. University of California Press, Berkeley.

Hakena, Kris (2008) 'Peace in Bougainville and the work of the Leitana Nehan women's development Agency', War Resisters International <http://www.wri-irg.org/nonviolence/nvse08-en.htm> (accessed September 2010).

Hallam, Sylvia J. (1975) *Fire and Hearth: A study of Aboriginal usage and European usurpation in south-western Australia*. Australian Institute of Aboriginal Studies, Canberra.

Hamilton, Roy W. (ed.) (1994) *Gift of the Cotton Maiden: Textiles of Flores and the Solar Islands*. (Catalogue) Regents of the University of California.

Hare, R.M. (1982) *Plato*. Oxford University Press.

Harrigan, Peter (2008) 'Art rocks in Saudi Arabia' in *Saudi Armco World* Compilation Issue <http://www.saudiaramcoworld.com/issue/200807/art.rocks.in.saudi.arabia-.compilation.htm> (accessed January 2012).

Harris, Paula (8–14 May 1997) 'Old souls: Joan Marler's Realm of the Ancestors' *Sonoma County Independent,* Metroactive Books <http://www.metroactive.com/papers/sonoma/05.08.97/books2-9719.htm> (accessed June 2003).

Harris, Stephen (1990) *Two-way Aboriginal Schooling: Education and cultural survival*. Aboriginal Studies Press, Canberra.

Harrison, Jane Ellen (1904/1980) *Prolegomena to the Study of Greek Religion*. The Merlin Press, UK.

—— (1912/1977) *Themis: A study of the social origins of Greek religion*. The Merlin Press, UK.

—— (1913/1978) *Ancient Art and Ritual*. Moonraker Press, Bradford-on-Avon, Wilts.

—— (1924/1963) *Mythology*. Harcourt Brace and World, Inc., New York.

Harrod, James (1997) 'The Upper Palaeolithic "Double Goddess": "Venus" figurines as sacred female transformation processes in the light of a decipherment of European Upper Palaeolithic language' in Marler, Joan (ed.) *From the Realm of the Ancestors: An anthology in honour of Marija Gimbutas*. Knowledge, Ideas and Trends Inc., USA, pp. 481–497.

Hauptmann, Harald (1988) 'Nevali Cori: Architekur', *Anatolica* 15.

Hawkes, Jacquetta (1968) *Dawn of the Gods*. Chatto and Windus, London.

Hawthorne, Susan (1982) *Women and Power: A feminist reading of the Homeric hymns to Aphrodite and Demeter* (MA [Prelim] thesis). Unpublished.

—— (1994) 'Diotima speaks through the body', in Bar On, Bat-Ami (ed.) *Engendering Origins: Critical feminist readings in Plato and Aristotle*. State University of New York Press, Albany, pp. 83–96.

—— (2002) *Wild Politics: Feminism, globalisation and bio/diversity*. Spinifex Press, North Melbourne.

Hays, Jeffrey (2008a) 'China's earliest cultures 7,000–2,500 BP' <http://www.chinavoc.com/history/yangshao.htm> (accessed 10 September 2010/July 2012)

—— (2008b) 'Yangshao, jade, the Yellow River and China's early cultures' <http://factsanddetails.com/china.php?itemid&2&catid=2&subcatid=1> (accessed July 2012).

Heath, Carolyn (2009) 'Women and power: The Shipibo of the Upper Amazon' in Göttner-Abendroth, Heide (ed.) *Societies of Peace: Matriarchies past, present and future*. Inanna Publications and Education, Toronto, pp. 92–105.

Heilbrunn Timeline of Art History – see Department of Arts of Africa, Oceania, and the Americas; or Department of Asian Art.

Heizer, Robert and Martin Baumhoff (1962) *Prehistoric Art of Nevada and Southern California*. University of California Press.

Hensley, William Iggragruk (November 2011) 'Regenerating the human spirit' Narrm Oration in *Voice* 7 (11), 14 November–11 December, University of Melbourne, p. 8.

Hensperger, Beth (1997) 'Legend of the Loaf' in Marler, Joan (ed.) *From the Realm of the Ancestors: An anthology in honour of Marija Gimbutas*. Knowledge, Ideas and Trends Inc., USA, pp. 524–538.

Herda, Phyllis S. (1995) 'The creation of wealth: Women's craft production in Tonga' in Kaino, Lorna (ed.) *The Necessity of Craft: Development and women's craft practices in the Asia-Pacific region*. University of Western Australia Press, pp. 164–175.

Heritage of Japan (n.d.) Photograph <http://heritageofjapan.files.wordpress.com/2007/07/kayumi-ijiri-figurine.jpg.> (accessed July 2011). Also <http://heritageofjapan.wordpress.com/just-what-was-so-amazing-about-jomon-japan/ways-of-the-jomon-world-2/jomon-crafts-and-what-they-were-for/the-mystery-of-the-clay-dolls/>.

Hersey, Irwin (1991) *Indonesian Primitive Art*. Oxford University Press.

Higham, Charles and Rachanie Thosaret (1998) *Prehistoric Thailand: From early settlement to Sukhothai*. Thames and Hudson, London.

Hinsch, Bret (1995) 'Views of the feminine in early Neo-Confucian thought' in Gertsclacher, Anna and Margit Miosga (eds) *China for Women: Travel and culture*. Spinifex Press, North Melbourne.

Hockings, Paul (n.d.) 'Culture of India', Countries and Their Cultures <http://www.everyculture.com> (accessed October 2010).

Hodder, Ian (December 1998) *Catalhoyuk Newsletter* No. 5 of the Catalhoyuk Research Project (2005) <http://www.catalhoyuk.com/newsletters/05/index.html> (accessed October 2012).

—— (December 2001) *Catalhoyuk Newsletter* No. 8 of the Catalhoyuk Research Project (2005) <http://www.catalhoyuk.com/newsletters/05/index.html> (accessed October 2012).

—— (2002) 'A History of the Catalhoyuk Excavations', Catalhoyuk Research Project, <http://www.catal.arch.cam.ac.uk/visit/historyEN.html> (accessed April 2003).

—— (1 January 2004) 'Women and men at Catalhoyuk' *Scientific American*, <http://www.scientific american.com/article.cfm?id=women-and-men-at-ccedilat> (accessed 2004).

—— (2006) *The Leopard's Tale: Revealing the mysteries of Catalhoyuk*. Thames and Hudson, London.

Hope, G.S., J. Golson and J. Allen (2006) 'Paleoecology and prehistory in New Guinea', *Research Journal of Pacific Studies*, Australian National University, Canberra, <http://www.sciencedirect.com/scienc/articles/pii/50047248483800128> (accessed July 2010).

Horton, David (2000) *The Pure State of Nature: Sacred cows, destructive myths, and the environment*. Allen and Unwin, Australia.

Hoyt, Alia (20 October 2008) 'What was Australia's Stolen Generation?' HowStuffWorks.com <http://history.howstuffworks.com/australia-and-new-zealand-history/stolen-generation.htm> (accessed 9 August 2012).

Hughes, Paul (1987) 'Aboriginal culture and learning styles: A challenge for academics in higher education', Frank Archibald Memorial Lecture Series, University of New England.

Huggins, Jackie (7–18 July 1989) 'Miminis, Kudjeris, Kungas and Tiddas: An Australian Aboriginal women's experience' (Conference Paper), 'Finding Common Grounds' International Indigenous Women's Conference.

Huld, Martin (1997) 'Greek amber', in Marler, Joan (ed.) *From the Realm of the Ancestors: An anthology in honour of Marija Gimbutas*. Knowledge, Ideas and Trends Inc., USA, pp. 135–144.

Ilatjari, Nganyintja (1983) 'Women and land rights: The Pitjantjatjara land claims' in Gale, Fay (ed.) *We Are Bosses Ourselves: The status and role of Aboriginal women today*. Australian Institute of Aboriginal Studies, Canberra, pp. 54–61.

Illinois State Museum (n.d.) 'Woodland' MuseumLink Illinois <http://www.museum.state.il.us/muslink/nat_amer/pre/htmls/woodland.html> (accessed July 2011). Photographs:
Fig. 5 <http://www.museum.state.il.us/muslink/nat_amer/pre/htmls/woodland.html>;
Fig. 6 <http://www.museum.state.il.us/muslink/nat_amer/pre/htmls/m_beliefs.html>;
Fig. 7 <http://www.museum.state.il.us/muslink/nat_amer/pre/htmls/m_beliefs.html>;
Fig. 8 <http://www.museum.state.il.us/muslink/nat_amer/pre/htmls/woodland.html> (accessed 12 February 2013).

Indianetzone (n.d.) 'Warli Paintings' Types of Indian Paintings <http://www.indianetzone.com/2/warli_paintings.htm> (accessed October 2010).

InterSol Inc. (1996–2010) 'The Proto-Indo-European Language Tree' (Diagram), Forty First Edition of the *Global Advisor Newsletter* <http://www.intersolinc.com/newsletters/Language_Tree.htm>.

Jain, Jyotindra (1995) 'Art and artisans: Tribal and folk art in India' in Kaino, Lorna (ed.) *The Necessity of Craft: Development and women's craft practices in the Asia-Pacific region*. University of Western Australia Press, Nedlands, pp. 24–34.

Janson, H.W. (1986) *History of Art*. 3rd edition, Thames and Hudson, London.

Jeffries, Rosalind (1988) 'The image of woman in African cave art' in Van Sertima, Ivan (ed.) *Black Women in Antiquity*, Transaction Books, New Brunswick (USA) and London, pp. 98–121.

Jennings, Karen (1993) 'Muddying the mythological waters: Aboriginality in Australian film', in *Metro* 94 Winter.

Jensen, H. (n.d.) 'Venus of Hohle Fels', Venus-of-Schelklingen.jpg. <http://www.nature.com/nature/videoarchive/prehistoricpinup/image> (accessed January 2011).

Jespersen, Otto (1922) *Language: Its nature, development and origin*. George Allen and Unwin Ltd, London.

Jhanjharpur Today (n.d.) 'Maithili Art Images' *J.W.D.C. Exhibition Catalogue* <http://www.jhanjharpur today.wordpress.com/about/> (accessed October 2010).

Jiayin, Min (1995) 'Introduction' and 'Conclusion' in Jiayin, Min (ed.) *The Chalice and the Blade in Chinese Culture: Gender relations and social models.* China Social Sciences Publishing House, Beijing.

Johnson, Colin (March 1988) 'The growth of Aboriginal literature' in *Social Alternatives* 7 (1) pp. 53–54.

Jones, Rhys (1980) 'Hunters in the Australian coastal savanna' in Harris, D. (ed.) *Human Ecology in Savanna Environments*, pp. 128–9.

Jones, Tim (11 September 2009) 'Flax Fibres Dated to 34,000 Years BP Found at Dzudzuana Cave, Georgia', Anthropology.net <http://anthropology.net/.../flax-fibres-dated-to-34000-years-bp-found-at-dzudzuana-cave-georgia> (accessed October 2010).

Judd, Tony (May 2007) 'Presumed cattle petroglyphs in the Eastern Desert of Egypt: Precursors of classical Egyptian art?' in *Rock Art Research* 24 (1), pp. 65–78.

Kabel, Matthias (14 January 2007) 'Venus of Willendorf' (Photograph), Wikimedia Commons <http://en.wikipedia.org/wiki/File:Venus_of_Willendorf_frontview_retouched_2.jpg>.

Kahukiwa, Robyn (1984) *Wahine Toa: Women of Maori myth. Paintings and Drawings by Robyn Kahukiwa*, (Catalogue). Collins, New Zealand.

Kaino, Lorna (ed.) (1995) *The Necessity of Craft: Development and women's craft practices in the Asia-Pacific region.* University of Western Australia Press.

Kawagoe, Aileen (n.d.) 'Jomon Dogu: The mystery of the broken clay dolls', Heritage of Japan, p. 2 <http://heritageofjapan.wordpress.com/just-what-was-so-amazing-about-jomon-japan/ ways> (accessed July 2011).

Kehoe, Alice Beck (1998) *The Land of Prehistory: A critical history of American archaeology.* Routledge, London.

Kenoyer, J.M. (n.d.) 'Images of Asia: Harappa archaeological research project', <http://www.images ofasia.com/images-of-asia-php> (accessed January 2011).

Kerala Travel Tours (n.d.) 'Mural paintings' <http://www.kerala-travel-tours.com/kerala.../mural_ paintings> (accessed October 2010).

—— (n.d.) 'Religion in Kerala' <http://www.kerala-travel-tours.com> (accessed October 2010).

Kershaw, Peter A. (1993) 'Palynology, biostratigraphy and human impact', *The Artifact* 16, Pacific Rim Archaeology, Vol. 20, No 1997, The Archaeological and Anthropological Society of Victoria, Inc., pp. 12–18.

Kirch, Patrick Vinton (1997) *The Lapita People: Ancestors of the Oceanic World.* Blackwell Publishers, UK.

Kivisild, Toomas (22 May 2007) 'Revealing the prehistoric settlement of Australia by chromosome and mtDNA analysis' in *PNAS (Proceedings of the National Academy of Sciences of the United States)* 104 (21), pp. 8726–8730, <http://www.pnas.org/content/104/21/8726.abstract> (accessed November 2012).

Kjellgren, Eric and Jennifer Wagelie (2001) 'Prehistoric stone sculpture from New Guinea', in Heilbrunn Timeline of Art History, The Metropolitan Museum of Art, New York, <http://www.metmuseum.org/toah/hd/ngss/hd_ngss.htm> (accessed 2004).

Kleinert, Sylvia and Margo Neale (eds) (2001) *The Oxford Companion to Aboriginal Art and Culture*, Oxford University Press, Melbourne.

Knight, C. (1991) *Blood Relations*, Yale University Press, p. 222 in Library Exerpts, Indo-European Culture, <http://www.humanevolution.net/a/indoeuropean.html> (accessed September 2002).

Krappe, Alexander H. (1930/1974) *The Science of Folklore.* 2nd edition, Methuen and Co., London.

379

Kumar, Giriraj (1996) 'Daraki-Chattan: A paleolithic cupule site in India', *Rock Art Research* 13 (1), *Australian Rock Art Research Association (AURA) and International Federation of Rock Art Organisations (FRAO)*, Archaeological Publications, Melbourne, pp. 38–51.

Kvavadze, Eliso, Ofer Bar-Yosef et al (11 September 2009) '30,000-year-old wild flax fibers' (Abstract) in 'Making materials from flax fibres circa 32,000–28,000 BCE' *Science* (325) 5946, 1359, <http://www.physorg.com/news171811682.html> (accessed 9 December 2009).

Lamb, Sydney L. and E. Douglas Mitchell (1991) (eds) *Sprung from Some Common Source: Investigations into the prehistory of languages*. Stanford University, California.

Langton, Marcia (1983) in Coombs, H.C., M.M. Brandl and W.E. Snowdon *A Certain Heritage: For and by Aboriginal families in Australia*. CRES Monograph 9, Centre for Resources and Environmental Studies, Australian National University, Canberra.

—— (1988) 'Medicine Square' in Keen, Ian (ed.) *Being Black: Aboriginal cultures in 'settled' Australia*. Aboriginal Studies Press, for the Australian Institute of Aboriginal Studies, Canberra, pp. 201–225, 202, 205.

—— (1991) 'Feminism: What do Aboriginal women gain?' (Analysis) *Broadside*, National Foundation of Australian Women (Adelaide Conference Report: Appendix 4) Canberra, p. 3.

—— (1993) 'Well I heard it on the radio and I saw it on the television', Australian Film Commission.

Lauter, Estella (1984) 'Steps towards a feminist archetypal theory of myth-making' in Lauter, Estella (ed.) *Women as Mythmakers: Poetry and visual art by 20th century women*. Indiana University Press, Bloomington, pp. 1–20.

Layton, Robert (1992) *Australian Rock Art: A new synthesis*. Cambridge University Press.

Leakey, Richard and Roger Lewin (1992) *Origins Reconsidered: In search of what makes us human*. Abacus Books, UK.

Leakey, Roger (1994) *The Origins of Humankind*. Harper Collins, Phoenix.

Leech, Graeme (23 September 1996) 'Challenge to the origin of Man: Scientists split over rock art find example for evolution', *The Australian*.

—— (30 May 1998) 'Between rock art and a hard place', *The Australian Weekend Magazine*, p. 8.

Lerner, Gerda (1986) *The Creation of Patriarchy*. Oxford University Press.

Leroi-Gourhan, Andre (1968) *The Art of Prehistoric Man in Europe*. Thames and Hudson, London.

Leung, Chee Chee (10 May 2007) 'Aborigines' genesis in Africa', *The Age*, Melbourne.

Lewis, E.D. (1994) 'Sikka Regency' in Hamilton, Roy W. (ed.) *Gift of the Cotton Maiden: Textiles of Flores and the Solar Islands*. (Catalogue) Regents of the University of California.

Lewis-Williams, J.D. and T.A. Dowson (1988) 'The signs of all times: Entoptic phenomena in Upper Paleolithic Art', *Current Anthropology* 29 (2), University of Chicago Press, pp. 201–217.

Lhote, Henri (1959) *The Search for the Tassili Frescoes: The story of the prehistoric rock-paintings of the Sahara*. Hutchinson and Co. Ltd., London.

Liddell, Henry George and Robert Scott (1961) *A Greek-English Lexicon*. Clarenden Press, Oxford.

Liebes, Sidney, Elizabet Sahtouris and Brian Swimme (1998) *A Walk through Time from Stardust to Us: The evolution of life on earth*. John Wiley and Sons, Inc., Australia.

Lin, Chen (8 November 2002) 'Dadiwan relics break archaeology records', State Council Information Office and the China International Publishing Group, Beijing <www.china.org.cn> (accessed 10 September 2010).

Liu, Li (2004) *The Chinese Neolithic: Trajectories to early states*. Cambridge University, p. 24.

Lloyd, Genevieve (1990) 'Augustine and Aquinas' in Loades, Ann (ed.) *Feminist Theology: A reader*. John Knox Press, SPCK, p. 97.

Lo, Lawrence (n.d.) 'Nushu', AncientScripts.com, <http://www.ancientscripts.com/nushu.html>.

Lorblanchet, M. (1977) 'From naturalism to abstraction in European prehistoric art' in Ucko, Peter (ed.) *Form in Indigenous Art: Schematisation in the art of Aboriginal Australia and prehistoric Europe.* Prehistory and Material Culture Series No 13, The Australian Institute of Aboriginal Studies, Canberra, pp. 44–58.

Maddox, Sir John (1977) 'Why can Man speak?' *The Economist*, special edition 'The World in 1998'.

Mahmood, Mahmood (n.d.) 'The lost civilization', <http://www.wondersof Pakistan.org/wiki/Mehrgarh> (accessed January 2011). Also: <http://wondersofpakistan.blogspot.com.au/2009/02/mehrgarh-lost-civilisation_22.html>; <http://wondersofpakistan.blogspot.com.au/2009/03/mehrgarhthe-lost-civilisation-part-iii.html>.

Major, Tania (2010) 'Remembering history: Why has Indigenous policy in this country failed? The federal government must realize that what looks good in Canberra looks very different in Kowanyama or the Kimberley', in 'State of the Nation: Essays on Australia', *The Age*, 28 July, pp. 6–7.

Makilam (2009) 'The central position of women among Berber People of Northern Africa: The four seasons life cycle of a Kabyle woman', in Göttner-Abendroth, Heide (ed.) *Societies of Peace: Matriarchies past, present and future.* Inanna Publications and Education, Toronto, pp. 178–192.

Mallet, Marla (1990) 'A weaver's view of the Çatal Hüyük controversy' <http://www.rugreview.com/orr/or132ma6> (accessed January 2011).

—— (1993) 'The Goddess from Anatolia: An updated view of the Çatal Hüyük controversy' <http://www.rugreview.com/orr/or132ma6> (accessed January 2011).

Mallory, James P. (1989) *In Search of the Indo-Europeans: Language, archaeology and myth.* Thames and Hudson Ltd., London. Library of Excerpts, Indo-European Culture <http://www.humanevolution.net/a/indoeuropean.html> (accessed September 2002).

Mandt, Gro (1997) 'The women of Vingen: Aspects of gender ideology in rock art' in Marler, Joan (ed.) *From the Realm of the Ancestors: An anthology in honour of Marija Gimbutas.* Knowledge, Ideas and Trends Inc., USA, pp. 163–174.

Mann, Barbara Alice (2009) 'They are the soul of the Councils: The Iroquoian model of Woman-Power', Bear Clan of the Ohio Seneca, Iroquois, USA, in Göttner-Abendroth, Heide (ed.) *Societies of Peace: Matriarchies past, present and future.* Inanna Publications and Education, Toronto, pp. 57–69.

Mann, Charles C. (June 2011) 'The birth of religion: The world's first temple' [Klaus Schmidt], *National Geographic*, pp. 34–59.

Marglin, Frederique Apfel and Purna Chandra Mishra (2010) 'Death and regeneration: Brahmin and non-Brahmin narratives' in Dashu, Max 'The Meanings of Goddess' Part 3, p. 10 <http://www.goddess.pages.co.uk/index.php?option=com_content&task=view&id=ltemid=99999999> (accessed April 2010).

Marler, Joan (1997) 'The circle is broken: A brief biography' in Marler, Joan (ed.) *From the Realm of the Ancestors: An anthology in honour of Marija Gimbutas.* Knowledge, Ideas and Trends Inc., USA, pp. 7–25.

—— (1998) 'A Tribute to Marija Gimbutas' in *Sojourn* 2 (2) Summer <http://www.gracemillennium.com/sojourn/summer98/marler.htm> (accessed April 2002).

—— (30 March 2003) 'The myth of universal patriarchy: A critical response to Cynthia Eller's "Myth of Matriarchal Prehistory"', *Awakened Woman e-Magazine*, p. 4 <http://www.awakenedwoman.com/br_myth_matriarchal.html> (accessed June 2003/February 2012.)

—— (31 March 2004) 'A letter to the editor', *Scientific American*, <http://www.universitalledonne.it/english/catal.htm.> (accessed February 2012).

—— (n.d.) 'A Vision for the World: The life and work of Marija Gimbutas' <http://oje.lib.byer.edu/spc/index.php/CCR/article/viewFile/12571/12444> (accessed February 2012).

Marshack, Alexander (1976) 'Some implications of the Paleolithic: Symbolic evidence for the origin of language', *Current Anthropology* 17 (2), University of Chicago Press, pp. 274–281.

—— (1977) 'The meander as a system: The analysis and recognition of iconographic units in upper paleolithic compositions', in Ucko, Peter (ed.) *Form in Indigenous Art: Schematisation in the art of Aboriginal Australia and prehistoric Europe.* Prehistory and Material Culture Series No. 13, The Australian Institute of Aboriginal Studies, Canberra, pp. 286–317.

—— (1991) *The Roots of Civilization: The cognitive beginnings of Man's first art, symbol and notation.* McGraw-Hill, Australia.

—— (1994) 'Symboling and the Middle-Upper Paleolithic transition: A theoretical and methodological critique' of A. Martin Byers in *Current Anthropology* 35 (4), University of Chicago Press, pp. 369–399.

Maxwell, Robyn (2010) *Life, Death and Magic: 2,000 years of South-East Asian ancestral art.* National Gallery of Australia.

Max8899 (26 July 2012) 'Prehistoric Lajja Gauri and the 'M' and 'V' sign', Scribd. (online library) <http://www.scribd.com/doc/68035508/The-prehistoric-goddess-Lajja-Gauri-and-the-M-V-sign> (accessed July 2012).

May, Jeffrey (October 2003) 'George Eogan: Knowth excavations' *Current Archaeology* 188 <http://www.knowth.com/current-archaeology.html> (accessed January 2012).

May, Patricia and Margaret Tuckson (2000) *The Traditional Pottery of Papua New Guinea.* University of Hawai'i Press, Honolulu.

Mayell, Hillary (July, 2001) 'Fall of ancient Peruvian societies linked with El Niño', <http://news.nationalgeographic.com/news/2001/07/0723-elninoperu.htm> (accessed May 2002).

McCafferty, Sharisse and Geoffrey McCafferty (1996) 'Spinning and weaving as female gender identity in Post-Classic Mexico' in Blum, Margot, Janet Berlo and Edward Dwyer (eds) *Textile Traditions of Mesoamerica and the Andes.* University of Texas, Austin, pp. 19–44.

McGaw, Judith (1996) 'Recovering Technology: Why feminine technologies matter' in Wright, Rita (ed.) *Gender and Archaeology.* University of Pennsylvania Press.

(The) Melanesian Way Inc. Papua New Guinea (2007) 'The Importance of Traditional Cultures and Indigenous Practices' <http://tmwpng.wordpress.com/2007/04/23/culture-2/> (accessed August 2010).

Mellaart, James (1961) 'Roots in the soil: The beginning of village and urban life' in Piggott, Stuart *Dawn of Civilization.* Thames and Hudson, London, pp. 41–64.

—— (1965) *Earliest Civilizations of the Near East.* Thames and Hudson, London.

—— (1967) *Çatal Hüyük: A Neolithic Town in Anatolia.* Thames and Hudson, London.

—— (1970) *Excavations at Hacilar.* Edinburgh University Press.

—— (1975) *The Neolithic of the Near East.* Scribner, New York.

—— Udo Hirsch and Belkis Balpinar (1989) *The Goddess from Anatolia* (1–4). Eskenazi, Milan.

Memmott, Paul (2007) *Gunyah, Goondie & Wurley: The Aboriginal architecture of Australia.* University of Queensland Press, Brisbane.

—— and Carroll Go-Sam (2001) 'Living spaces: Aboriginal architecture' in Kleinert, Sylvia and Margot Neale (eds) *The Oxford Companion to Aboriginal Art and Culture.* Oxford University Press, Melbourne.

Metropolitan Museum – see Department of Arts of Africa, Oceania, and the Americas; or Department of Asian Art (Heilbrunn Timeline of Art History).

Michaels, Eric (1987) *For a Cultural Future: Francis Jupurrurla makes TV at Yuendumu* (Monograph), Artspace, Sydney.

Miksic, John (1996) 'The hunting and gathering stage in eastern Indonesia' in Miksic, John (ed.) *Indonesian Heritage Volume 1: Ancient history.* Grolier International Inc. Archipeligo Press, Jakarta.

—— (ed.) (1996) *Indonesian Heritage Volume 1: Ancient history*. Grolier International Inc. Archipeligo Press, Jakarta.

Ministry of Culture P.R. China (2003) 'Dadiwan site', <http://www.chinaculture.org> (accessed 10 September 2010).

Mitchell, Sir Thomas (1839) *Three Expeditions into the Interior of Eastern Australia*. (Vol. 1) Boone, London.

Monroe, M.H. (n.d.) 'Aboriginal shelter' in 'Australia: The land where time began. A biography of the Australian continent', <http://austhrutime.com/aboriginal_shelter.htm> (accessed November 2012).

Moore, Andrew, Gordon Hillman and Anthony Legge (2000) *Villages on the Euphrates: The excavation of Abu Hueyra*. Oxford University Press, London. Also: 'Tell Abu Hureyra', <http://archaeology.about.com/od/althroughadterms/qt/Abu-Hureyra.htm> (accessed July 2011).

Morgan, Robin (1982) *The Anatomy of Freedom: Feminism, physics and global politics*. W.W. Norton, New York.

Morwood, Mike, Thomas Sutikna and Richard Roberts (April 2005) 'World of the Little People. Diminutive hominins make a big evolutionary point: Humans aren't exempt from natural selection' in *National Geographic*, pp. 5–13.

Mukkim, Patricia (2009) 'Khasi matrilineal society: Challenges in the twenty-first century' in Göttner-Abendroth, Heide (ed.) *Societies of Peace: Matriarchies past, present and future*. Inanna Publications and Education, Toronto, pp. 193–204.

Muller, Natalie (13 September 2011) 'Dingoes originated in China 18,000 years ago', *Australian Geographic* <http://www.australiangeographic.com.au/journal/the-dingo-came-to-australia-from-southern-china.htm> (accessed November 2012).

Munn, Nancy (1973) *Walbiri Iconography: Graphic representation and cultural symbolism in a Central Australian society*. Cornell University, Ithaca.

Murphy, Anthony (n.d.) 'Dowth megalithic passage tomb' *Mythical Ireland*. <http://www.knowth.com/dowth.htm> (accessed April 2012).

Murphy, Gabrielle (12 December 2010) 'Lessons from North America' [Manley Begay], *Voice Magazine*, University of Melbourne.

Namono, Catherine (2002) 'Women and Art' (Paper) Women's Worlds 2002 8th International Interdisciplinary Congress, Makerere University, Uganda, <http://www.makerere.ac.ug/womenstudies/full%20papers/namono.html> (accessed July 2003).

Navarrete, Rodrigo (2008) 'The prehistory of Venezuela – Not necessarily an intermediate area' in Silverman, Helaine and William H. Isbell (eds) *The Handbook of South American Archaeology*. Springer Science and Business Media LLC, New York, pp. 429–458.

Neale, Margo (ed.) (2008) *Emily (Utopia: The Genius of Emily Kame Kngwarreye)*, Exhibition Catalogue, National Museum of Australia Press.

Needham, Joseph (1971) 'Science and civilization in China' (Vol. 4, Part 3) in Kehoe, Alice Beck (1998) *The Land of Prehistory: A critical history of American archaeology*. Routledge, London.

Neidjie, Bill (1989) *Story about Feeling*. Keith Taylor (ed.) Magabala Books, Broome, Western Australia.

Nelson, Sarah M. (December 1994) 'The development of complexity in prehistoric northern China', Sino Platonic Papers 63 <http://www.sino-platonic.org/complete/spp063_prehistoric_china> (accessed September 2010).

New World Encyclopedia contributors (6 November 2008) 'Prehistoric Korea', *New World Encyclopedia*, <http:// www.newworldencyclopedia.org/entry/Prehistoric_Korea> (accessed July 2012).

Ngarrinjeri Tendi, Ngarrindjeri Heritage Committee and Ngarrindjeri Native Title Management Committee (2007) *Ngarrindjeri Nation Sea Country Plan: Caring for Ngarrindjeri country and culture*. Ngarrindjeri Land and Progress Committee.

Nielson, Paula I. (2010) 'Origins of the Ainu people of northern Japan: Were they descended from the ancient Jomon people?', <http://suite101.com/articleorigins-of-the-ainu-people-of-northern-japan-a187402> (accessed July 2012).

—— (2010) 'Prehistoric Japan: The Jomon Culture', <http://suite101.com/article/prehistoric-japan-the-jomon-culture-a186416> (accessed 10 February 2013).

Niigata Prefectural Museum of Prehistory (n.d.) 'The Jomon Period in Japan', <http://www.nbz.or.jp/eng/prehistoric.htm> (accessed August 2012).

Nind, Scott (1831) 'Description of the natives of King George's Sound (Swan River Colony) and adjoining country', *Royal Geographical Society Journal* 1, pp. 21–51.

Noble, Vicki (2009) 'Declaration on matriarchal politics' in Göttner-Abendroth, Heide (ed.) *Societies of Peace: Matriarchies past, present and future.* Inanna Publications and Education, Toronto, p. 441.

Nolan, Michael (April 1997) 'Opinion: The myth of soulless women', *First Things* 72, pp. 13–14, *The Journal of Religion and Public Life* <http://www.firstthings.com/ftissues/ft9704/Nolan.htm> (accessed April 2002).

Nzenza-Shand, Sekai (1997) *Songs to an African Sunset: A Zimbabwe story.* Lonely Planet Publications, Australia.

O'Kelly, Michael (1989) *Early Ireland: An introduction to Irish prehistory.* Cambridge University Press.

Okpewho, Isidore (1992) *African Oral Literature: Backgrounds, character and continuity.* Indiana University Press.

Olmert, Meg Daley (28 July 2012) 'The human-animal bond: Made for each other' (Lecture) <http://www.youtube.com/watch?v=xgWL7RcwVdg>.

—— (n.d.) Warrior Canine Connection, <http://warriorcanineconnection.org/>.

Olson, Steve (2003) *Mapping Human History: Genes, race and our common origins.* Mariner Books, USA.

O'Murchu, Diarmuid (2000) *Religion in Exile: A spiritual homecoming.* Crossroad Publishing Company, New York.

O'Neill, Graeme (4 April 1992) 'Evidence of the first settlers 140,000 years ago', *The Age*, Melbourne.

Orenstein, Gloria Feman (1990) *The Reflowering of the Goddess.* Pergamon Press, New York.

O'Sullivan, Muris (1993) *Megalithic Art in Ireland.* Country House, Dublin.

Owen, James (27 January 2012) 'Stonehenge precursor found: Island complex predates famous site', *National Geographic News*, <http://news.nationalgeographic.com/120127-stonehenge-ness-brodgar-scotland-science/> (accessed July 2012).

—— (14 March 2012) 'Cave fossil find: New human species or "nothing extraordinary"', *National Geographic News*, <http://news.nationalgeographic.com/news/2012/03/120314-new-human-species-chinese-p> (accessed March 2012).

Parker, Francis (n.d.) 'IWD in Australia: 70 years and still going strong' in *International Women's Day 1998* National Broadsheet, <http://www.isis.aust.com/iwd/bs98/iwdoz.html> (accessed February 2003).

Parkin, Robert (n.d.) 'Munda – Religion and expressive culture', Countries and Their Cultures <http://www.everyculture.com> (accessed October 2010).

Parrilla, Vanessa (1999) '*Sati*: Virtuous women through self-sacrifice' <http://www.csuchico.edu/~cheinz/syllabi/asstool/spring99/parilla/parr1.html> (accessed May 2002).

Pericot-Garcia, Luis, John Galloway and Andreas Lommel (1967) *Prehistory and Primitive Art.* Thames and Hudson, London.

Perkins, Hetti (2010) *art + soul: a journey into the world of Aboriginal art.* Meigunyah Press, University of Melbourne.

Peterson, Nicolas (1981–1982) *Aboriginal Australia* (Catalogue). National Gallery of Victoria, Art Gallery of Western Australia, Queensland Art Gallery.

Petrie, William (1939) *The Making of Egypt*. Sheldon Press/Macmillan, London/New York.

Petroglyphs.US. (2010) 'Big Petroglyph Canyon', Fig. 2: <http://www.petroglyphs.us/photographs_petroglyphs_big_petroglyph_canyon_california_BP.htm>; Fig 3: (2010a) <http://www.petroglyphs.us/BP04_petroglyph_medicine_bags.jpg>; Fig 4a: (2010b) <http://www.petroglyphs.us/BP05_patterned_body_anthropomorph.jpg>; Fig 4b: (2010c) <http://www.petroglyphs.us/BP06_PBA_petroglyph.jpg> (accessed 12 February 2013).

Phillips, Graham (13 March, 2003) 'Life was not a walkabout for Victoria's Aborigines' [Heather Builth] *The Age*, Melbourne, p. 15.

—— (13 March 2003) 'Secrets of the stones', *Sydney Morning Herald*, <http://www.smh.com.au/articles/2003/03/12/1047431096364.html> (accessed December 2012).

Phillipson, David (1985) *African Archaeology: Cambridge world archaeology*. Cambridge University Press.

Piggot, Stuart (1961) *The Dawn of Civilisation*. Thames and Hudson, London.

Pinker, Steven (1994) *The Language Instinct*. William Morrow and Company Inc., New York.

—— (2012) *The Better Angels of Our Nature: The decline of violence in history and its causes*. Allen Lane, UK.

Plant, Judith (1989) (ed.) *Healing the Wounds: The promise of ecofeminism*. New Society Publishers, Canada.

Plumwood, Val (1993) *Feminism and the Mastery of Nature*. Routledge, London.

—— (1996) 'Environmental ethics and the master subject: A reply to Janis Birkeland' in 'Comment', Environmental Ethics Online, *The Trumpeter* 13 (4) <http://www.cep.unt.edu/Comment/Plumwood.htm> (accessed May 2003).

Polyak, Victor J., Yemane Asmerom, Stephen J. Burns, Matthew S. Lachniet (1 November 2012) 'Climatic backdrop to the terminal Pleistocene extinction of North American mammals' in *Geology*, pp. 1023–1026.

Possehl, Gregory (2006) 'Mehrgarh: Period I, Period II, Period III, craft production in early periods, Preiod Hordeum vulgare, vulgare' <ahref=http://www.jrank.org.history/pages/6295/Mehrgarh> (accessed January 2010).

Price, Christine (1980) 'Clay for the potter' in *Made in the South Pacific*. Bodley Head, England.

Pringle, Heather (2013) 'The First Americans: Humans colonized the New World earlier than previously thought, a revelation that is forcing scientists to rethink long-standing ideas about these trailblazers', *Scientific American* 22 (1), pp. 68–75.

Rashidi, Runoko (1988) 'African goddesses: Mothers of civilisation' in Van Sertima, Ivan (ed.) *Black Women in Antiquity*, Transaction Books, New Brunswick (USA) and London, pp. 72–87.

Raymond, J. Scott (2008) 'The process of sedentism in north-western South America' in Silverman, Helaine and William H. Isbell (eds) *Handbook of South American Archaeology*, pp. 79–120.

Renfrew, Colin (1974) *The Explanation of Culture Change: Models of prehistory*. University of Pittsburgh Press. In Library of Excerpts <http://www.humanevolution.net/humanevolution/a/language.html> (accessed 22 September, 2002).

—— (n.d.) 'Indo-European culture', Library of Excerpts <http://www.humanevolution.net/a/indo-european.html> (accessed April 2003).

—— and Paul Bahn (1991) *Archaeology: Theories, Method and Practice*, Thames and Hudson, London.

Respicio, Norma (2003) *Our Pattern of Islands* (Philippine Textile Exhibition Catalogue), Melbourne pp. 8–24.

Reynolds, Henry (1989) *Dispossession: Black Australia and White invaders*. Allen and Unwin, Sydney.

Rockman Napaljarri, Peggy and Lee Cataldi (trans.) (2011) *Walpiri Dreamings and Histories/Yimikirli: Newly recorded sayings from Aboriginal Elders of Central Australia*. Yale University Press, New Haven.

Roe, David (1992) 'Rock art of North-West Guadalcanal' in McDonald, Jo and Ivan P. Haskovec (eds) *State of the Art: Regional rock art studies in Australia and Melanesia*. Australian Rock Art Research Association (AURA).

Rose, Deborah Bird (1994) 'Flesh and blood and deep colonising' in Joy, Morny and Penelope Magee (eds) *Claiming our Rites: Studies in religion by Australian women scholars.* The Australian Association for the Study of Religions, Special Studies in Religions Number 8, Sydney/ Adelaide, Flinders University, pp. 327–341.

Rosenfeld, Diane (2009) 'Sexual coercion, patriarchal violence and the law' in Muller, Martin and Richard Wrangham (eds) *Evolutionary Perspectives on Sexual Coercion.* Harvard University Press, pp. 410–446.

Ross, Annabel (21–22 December 2012) 'Traditional culture: "It's almost like an autobiography, this cloak". The skins of the father, uncle, aunt and sew on', *Saturday Age Holiday Edition*, p. 24.

Ross, John F. (n.d.) 'First city in the New World? Peru's Caral suggests civilization emerged in the Americas 1,000 years earlier than experts believed' <http://www.smithsonian.si.edu/ smithsonian/issues02/aug02/caral.htm> (accessed October 2002).

Roughsey, Elsie, Paul Memmott and Robyn Horsman (1984) *An Aboriginal Mother Tells of the Old and the New.* McPhee Gribble, Fitzroy.

Rudgley, Richard (1998) *Lost Civilizations of the Stone Age.* Century, USA.

Ruhlen, Merritt (1994) *The Origin of Language: Tracing the evolution of the mother tongue.* John Wiley and Sons, Inc., USA.

Sahtouris, Elizabet (1999a) 'World views from the Pleistocene to Plato' in *Earthdance: Living systems in evolution* <http://www.ratical.org/LifeWeb/Erthdnce/chapter13.htm> (accessed April 2003).

—— (1999b) 'Living systems in evolution' in *New Renaissance e-Magazine* 10 (2) <http://www.ru. org/10-2sahtouris.html> (accessed May 2003).

—— (2000) *Earthdance: Living systems in evolution.* iUniversity Press, San Francisco.

Sanday, Peggy Reeves (1–7 July 1998) 'Matriarchy as a sociocultural form: An old debate in a new light' (paper) 16th Congress of the Indo-Pacific Prehistory Association, Melaka, Malaysia <http:// www.sas.upenn.edu/~psanday/matri.htm> (accessed July 2003).

—— (2002) *Women at the Centre: Life in a modern matriarchy.* Cornell University Press, Ithaca and London.

—— (2009) 'Matriarchal values and world peace: The case of the Minangkabau' in Göttner-Abendroth, Heide (ed.) *Societies of Peace: Matriarchies past, present and future.* Inanna Publications and Education, Toronto, pp. 217–227.

Sandladder (December 2010) 'Introduction to Saudi Arabia rock art and petroglyphs' Article 4, Issue 234 <http://ancient-cultures.info/attachments/File/RR_article_petroglyphs> (accessed January 2012).

Saul, John Ralston (1995/1997) *The Unconscious Civilization.* Penguin Books, USA.

—— (1995) *The Doubters Companion: A dictionary of aggressive common sense.* Penguin Books, USA.

Scham, Sandra (November/December 2008) 'The world's first temple' [Klaus Schmidt] abstracts, *Archaeology* 61 (6) Archaeological Institute of America, <http://www.Archaeology.org/0811/ abstracts/turkey.html> (accessed July 2011).

Schoeffel, Penelope (1995) 'Craft, prestige goods and women's roles in the Pacific Islands' in Kaino, Lorna (ed.) *The Necessity of Craft: Development and women's craft practices in the Asia-Pacific region.* University of Western Australia Press, Nedlands, pp. 1–23.

Schmandt-Besserat, Denise (1992/1996) *How Writing Came About.* University of Texas Press.

—— (2007) *When Writing Met Art: From symbol to story.* University of Texas Press.

'See China': Global Chinese Culture (n.d.) 'Chinese Pyramids – Neolithic Jade', Chung Kwong, <www.seeChina.org.cn/2010/06/26/chinese> (accessed September 2010).

Shanker de Tourreil, Savithri (2009) 'The Nayars of Kerala and matriliny revisited' in Göttner-Abendroth, Heide (ed.) *Societies of Peace: Matriarchies past, present and future.* Inanna Publications and Education, Toronto, pp. 205–216.

Sheil, Christopher (2001) (ed.) *Globalization: Australian impacts.* University of New South Wales, Sydney.

Shelach, Gideon (28 June 2012) 'The earliest known pottery', <http://popular-archaeology.com/issue/june-2012/article/the-earliest-known-pottery> (accessed July 2012).

Shiva, Vandana (1989/2010) *Staying Alive: Women, ecology and development.* Zed Books; Spinifex Press, Melbourne.

—— (1993) *Monocultures of the Mind: Perspectives on biodiversity and biotechnology.* Third World Network, Penang, pp. 50, 56, 58.

Shou, Benjamin (2010) 'Jerf el Ahmar', <http://wki.sjs.org/wiki/index.php/Jerf_el_Ahmar>).

Shyam, Anand and Sanitha Shyam (2009–2010) Tara Books Catalogue 2009–2010 <http://desseinall.wordpress.com/tag/warli-art-greeting-card/#jp-carousel-889>. See also: Tara Books.

Silber, Cathy (1995) 'Women's writing from Hunan' in Gertsclacher, Anna and Margit Miosga (eds) *China for Women: Travel and culture.* Spinifex Press, North Melbourne.

Silverman, Helaine and William H. Isbell (eds) (2008) *Handbook of South American Archaeology.* Springer Science and Business Media LLC, New York.

Simmons, David (1979) *Art of the Pacific.* Oxford University Press.

Singh, G., A.P. Kershaw and R. L. Clark (1981) 'Quaternary vegetation and fire history in Australia' in Gill, A.M., R.H. Groves and I.R. Noble (eds) *Fire and the Australian Biota.* Australian Academy of Science, Canberra, pp. 23–52.

Sisely, Diane (8 March 2002) 'Trying to find a reason to celebrate' *The Age* <http://www.theage.com.au/articles/2002/03/07/1015365728772.htm> (accessed May 2002).

Sittirak, Sinith (1998) *The Daughters of Development: Women in a changing environment.* Spinifex Press, North Melbourne.

Sloan, Christopher (November 2006) 'The origin of childhood: Meet the Dikka baby, a 3-year-old from the dawn of humanity' [Zeresenay Alemseged] *National Geographic,* pp. 48–159.

Smith, Deborah (22 December 2005) 'Feet of clay offer glimpse of life 23,000 years ago', *The Age,* Melbourne.

—— (14 May 2009) 'Busty "Venus" is first human in art' [Interview with Paul Mellars], *The Age,* p. 11.

—— (15 March 2012) 'Scientists stumped by prehistoric human whose face doesn't fit', *The Age,* Melbourne, pp. 1, 6, <http://www.theage.com/au/national/scientists-stumped-by-prehistoric-human-whose-face-doesn't-fit-20120314-1v3m0.html> (accessed March 2012).

Soffer, Olga (April 2000) 'Woven clothing dates back 27,000 years' in Denison, Simon (ed.) *British Archaeology Magazine Report* 52, pp. 2–3, <http://www.britarch.ac.uk/ba/ba52/ba52news.html.> (accessed September 2003).

—— J.M Adovasio and D.C. Hyland (2000) 'The "Venus" figurines: Textiles, basketry, gender and status' in *Current Anthropology* 41 (4), pp. 511–537.

Solis, Ruth Shady (n.d.) 'First city in the New World?' <http://www.smithsonian.si.edu/smithsonian/issues02/aug02/caral.html> (accessed October 2002).

South Asian Women's Forum (19 February 2007) 'Connect' <http://www.sawf.org/> (accessed August 2010).

Spelman, Elizabeth (1994) 'Hairy cobblers and philosopher-queens' in Bar On, Bat-Ami (ed.) (1994) *Engendering Origins: Critical feminist readings in Plato and Aristotle.* State University of New York Press, Albany, pp. 3–24.

Spretnak, Charlene, (1997) 'Beyond the Backlash: An appreciation of the work of Marija Gimbutas' in Marler, Joan (ed.) *From the Realm of the Ancestors: An anthology in honour of Marija Gimbutas.* Knowledge, Ideas and Trends Inc., USA, pp. 399–405.

Stanner, John (1983) in Coombs, H.C., M.M. Brandl and W.E. Snowdon *A Certain Heritage: For and by Aboriginal families in Australia*. CRES Monograph 9, Centre for Resources and Environmental Studies, Australian National University, Canberra, p. 30.

—— (1998) *The Global Ecocrisis*. (Series broadcast) Allen and Unwin, Australia.

Starhawk (1989) *The Spiral Dance: A rebirth of the ancient religion of the Great Goddess*. (10th Anniversary Edition) Harper, San Francisco.

—— (1997) 'Marija Gimbutas's Work and the Question of the Sacred' in Marler, Joan (ed.) *From the Realm of the Ancestors: An anthology in honour of Marija Gimbutas*. Knowledge, Ideas and Trends Inc., USA, pp. 519–523.

—— (2002) *Webs of Power: Notes from the global uprising*. New Society Publishers, USA.

Sternfeld, Eva (1995) 'A Stone Age matriarchy: The Yangshao culture' in Gertsclacher, Anna and Margit Miosga (eds) *China for Women: Travel and Culture*. Spinifex Press, North Melbourne.

Stone, Merlin (1991) *Ancient Mirrors of Womanhood: A treasury of goddess and heroine lore from around the world*. Beacon Press, Boston.

Stuart, Charles (1833) *Two Expeditions into the Interior of Australia* (2 volumes). Smith, Elder, and Co., London.

Sullivan, Agnes (1985) 'Nga Paiaka O Te Maoritanga: The roots of Maori Culture' in Moko Mead, Sidney (ed.) *Te Maoru: Maori art from New Zealand collections*. Heinemann, UK.

Sullivan, Mary Lucille (2007) *Making Sex Work: A failed experiment with legalised prostitution*. Spinifex Press, North Melbourne.

Sunday Age (19 May, 2002) 'EU-hopeful Turkey moves towards religious equality for women', Melbourne, <http://www:age.com.au/breaking news.html> (accessed 19 May 2002).

Suzuki, David (1999) *From Naked Ape to Superspecies: A personal perspective on humanity and the global ecocrisis*. (Series broadcast, 1998) Allen and Unwin, Australia.

Tan, Pamela (1995) 'Women farmers in Qinghai Province' in Gertsclacher, Anna and Margit Miosga (eds) *China for Women: Travel and Culture*. Spinifex Press, North Melbourne, pp. 317–322.

Taonga Maori: A spiritual journey expressed through Maori art (Exhibition Catalogue) (1989) National Museum of New Zealand and the Australian Museum.

Tara Books (2009–2010) 'Catalogue' Gond Art Patterns: *Nurturing Walls – Animal Art by Meena Women*, <http://www.tarabooks.com> (accessed October 2010). See also: Shyam, Anand and Sanitha Shyam (2009–2010) Tara Books Catalogue.

Teillhet, Jehanne (1983) 'The role of women artists in Polynesia and Melanesia', in Mead, S.M. and B. Kernot (eds) *Art and Artists of Oceania*. Pacific Arts Association, USA.

Thadani, Giti (2004) *Moebius Trip: Digressions from India's highways*. Spinifex Press, North Melbourne.

Thakur, Manjula (2010) 'Scene of Child Birth' by Manjula Thakur, Maithili Wall Art. *J.W.D.C. Exhibition Catalogue* <http://www.asianart.com/exhibitions/jwdc/25.html> (accessed October, 2010).

Theobald, Ulrich (2000) 'Prehistoric cultures of China: Paleolithic China', Chinese History – Prehistory <http://chinaknowledge.de/History/Myth/prehistory.event.html> (accessed 2012).

Thomas (pseud.) (December 2010) 'Introduction to Saudi Arabian rock art and petroglyphs', *Sandladder* 234, pp. 30–37, <http://ancient-cultures.info/attachments/File/RR_article_petroglyph> (accessed January, 2012).

Thorpe, Nick (April 2000) 'Origins of war: Mesolithic conflict in Europe' in *British Archaeology* 52, p. 1 <http:www.britarch.ac.uk/ba//ba/52features.html> (accessed September 2002).

Tiegs, Vanessa (20 March 2001) 'Spiraling Moon' [Judy Grahn interview], San Francisco, California, USA.

Too, Lilian (2003) *The Buddha Book: Buddhas, blessings, prayers, and rituals to grant you love, wisdom and healing*. Harper Collins, USA.

Treistman, Judith M. (1972) *The Prehistory of China: An archaeological exploration.* David and Charles Publishers, UK.

Turnbull, David (14 November 2011) 'Other knowledges: Reflections on recent archaeology in South America', Fig. 15: Caral Geoglyph Human Face <http://www.southernperspectives.net/tag/peru> (accessed January 2013).

Twohig, Elizabeth Shee and Margaret Ronayne (1993) 'Prehistory: A present perception' (Introduction) in *Past Perceptions: The prehistoric archaeology of south-west Ireland.* Cork University Press, Ireland.

—— (eds) (1993) *Past Perceptions: The prehistoric archaeology of south-west Ireland.* Cork University Press, Ireland.

Ungurmarr-Bauman, Miriam Rose (January 1998) 'Ngangkurungkurr (Deep Water Sounds)' (Paper) International Liturgy Assembly, Hobart, Diocesan Liturgical Commission.

United Nations Permanent Forum on Indigenous Issues (10–12 May 2004) 'Indigenous women today: At risk and a force for change', Third Session, New York, <http://www.un.org/esa/socdev/pfii/documents/Indigenous_women_UNFII_session_3_pdf> (accessed December 2012).

United Nations Sustainable Development Department (1998) 'Asia's women in agriculture, environment and rural production: China' Report, SDdimensions, Food and Agriculture Organisation of the United Nations <http://www.fao.org/sd/WPdirect/WPre0107.htm> (accessed July 2003.)

Van der Suijs, Marinus (2008) 'Korea's prehistoric past' in *Far East Asian Monthly Business Newspaper* (9), pp. 24–25 <http://www.mythopedia.info/prehistoric-Korea.pdf> (accessed July 2012).

Van Sertima, Ivan (1988) *Black Women in Antiquity.* (Journal of African Civilizations) Transaction Publishers, Piscataway, New Jersey.

Vastokas, Joan (1988) 'Reply' in Lewis Williams, J.D. and T.A. Dowson 'The signs of all times: Entoptic phenomena in Upper Paleolithic art', *Current Anthropology* 29 (2), pp. 229–230.

Vidale, Massimo (2011) *Lady of the Spiked Throne: The power of a lost ritual,* Department of Asian and North African Studies, University of Padua, <http://a.harappa.com/sites/harappa.drupalgardens.com/files/Spiked-Throne.pdf> (accessed June 2012).

Wade, Nicholas (17 March 2010) 'Desert's mystery: Ancient boat people', *The Age,* Melbourne, pp. 1–2.

Walsh, Graham (1994) *Bradshaws: Ancient rock paintings of north west Australia.* Bradshaw Foundation, Geneva.

Warming, Wanda and Michael Gaworski (1981) *The World of Indonesian Textiles.* Kodansha International Ltd., Japan.

Warren, William and Luca Invernizzi Tettoni (1994) *Arts and Crafts of Thailand.* Thames and Hudson, London.

Waters, Michael R., Steven L. Forman, Thomas A. Jennings, Lee C. Nordt, Steven G. Driese, Joshua M. Feinberg, Joshua L. Keene, Jessi Halligan, Anna Lindquist, James Pierson, Charles T. Hallmark, Michael B. Collins, James E. Wiederhold (25 March 2011) 'The Buttermilk Creek complex and the origins of Clovis at the Debra L. Friedkin site, Texas', *Science* 331 (6024), pp. 1,599–1,603. Also at: <http://www.sciencemag.org/content/331/6024/1599.abstract> (accessed January 2013).

Watson, William (1961) 'China: The civilization of a single people' in Piggott, Stuart (ed.) *The Dawn of Civilization: The first world survey of human cultures in early times.* Thames and Hudson, London.

Wendorf, Fred and Roumald Schild (1998) 'Nabta Playa and its role in Northeastern African prehistory' *Journal of Anthropological Archaeology* 17, pp. 97–123, Article no AA980319 <http://faculty.ksu.edu.sa/archaeology/Publications/General/Nabta%20Playa%20Role%in%20Northeastern%20African%20Prehistory.pdf> (accessed July 2012).

Wertz, Richard R. (n.d.) 'Yangshao Culture' Exploring Chinese History, <http://www.ibiblio.org/chinesehistory/contents/02cul/c03s04.html#The Yangshao culture> (accessed September 2010).

Whitaker, Alex (n.d.) 'Stonehenge', Ancient Wisdom, <www.ancient-wisdom.co.uk/englandstonehenge.htm>.

—— (n.d.) 'Chauvet-Pont-d'Arc Cave', Ancient Wisdom <http://www.ancient-wisdom.co.uk/francechauvet.html> (accessed September 2010).

White, Mary (1994) *After the Greening: The browning of Australia*. Kangaroo Press, Australia.

Whiteford, Andrew Hunter (1998) *North American Indian Arts* (A Golden Guide). St Martin's Press, New York.

Wichterich, Christa (2000) *The Globalized Woman: Reports from a future of inequality*. (trans. from German by Patrick Camiller [Globalisierte Frau]), Spinifex Press, North Melbourne.

Wikimedia Commons (18 October 2008) 'Partial tree of Indo-European languages' (Diagram) <http://en.wikipedia.org/wiki/File:IndoEuropeanTree.svg>.

—— (2012) 'Tlapacoya_figurines' Snite Museum of Art, <http://commons.wikimedia.org/wiki/File:4_Tlapacoya_figurines.jpg>; <http://commons.wikimedia.org/wiki/Category:Snite_Museum_of_Art> (accessed February 2013).

—— (2013) 'Sculptures of Ancient India' <http://commons.wikimedia.org/wiki/Category:Sculptures_of_Ancient_India> (accessed February 2013).

Wikipedia contributors (2010) 'Dravidian peoples', *Wikipedia, The Free Encyclopedia*, <http://en.wikipedia.org/w/index.php?title=Dravidian_peoples&oldid=520815011> (accessed August 2010).

—— (2011) 'Cuddie Springs', *Wikipedia, The Free Encyclopedia*, <http://en.wikipedia.org/w/index.php?title=Cuddie_Springs&oldid=474421805> (accessed October 2011).

—— (2011) 'Jōmon period', *Wikipedia, The Free Encyclopedia*, <http://en.wikipedia.org/w/index.php?title=J%C5%8Dmon_period&oldid=513457960> (accessed July 2011)

—— (2012) 'Fremont Culture', *Wikipedia, The Free Encyclopedia*, <http://en.wikipedia.org/wiki/Fremont_culture> (accessed 9 February 2013).

Willett, Frank (1995) *African Art*. Thames and Hudson, London.

Wilson, Allan C., and Rebecca L. Cann (1995) 'The recent African genesis of humans' in *Scientific American* 266 (4), April 1995, pp. 22–27.

Wilton, Alan (8 April 2010) 'Genome-wide SNP and haplotype analysis reveal a rich history underlying dog domestication' in *Nature* 464, pp. 898–902. Also at: *Nature International Weekly Journal of Science*, <http://www.nature.com/nature/journal/v464/n7290/full/nature08837.html> (November 2012).

Witt, Charlotte (2 October 1996) 'How feminism is re-writing the philosophical canon' (lecture) Quinnipac College, <http://www.uh.edu/~cfreelan/SWIP/Witt.htm> (accessed January 2003).

Women's Prehistoric Jomon Pottery, <http://www.earlywomenmasters.net/masters/jomon/index.html.> (accessed July 2011).

World Health Organisation Human Genetics Program (12 February 2003) 'Human genetics', <http://www.who.int/ncd/hgn/overview.html> (accessed September 2003).

Wright, Rita (ed.) (1996) *Gender and Archaeology*. University of Pennsylvania Press.

Wu, Xiaohong, C. Zhang, P. Goldberg, D. Cohen, Y. Pan, T. Arpin and O. Bar-Yosef (June 2012) 'Early pottery at 20,000 years ago in Xianrendong Cave, China', *Science*, 336 (1696-1700). Also: <http://archaeology.about.com/od/xterms/qt/Xianrendong.htm> (accessed July 2012).

Wysinger, Myra (n.d) 'Pre-history Africa and the Badarian Culture' (Extract by Gregory Possehl), <http://www.wysinger.homestead.com/badarians.html> (accessed 20 April 2010/September 2010).

Yarborough, Camille (1988) 'Female style and beauty in Ancient Egypt' in Van Sertima, Ivan (ed.) *Black Women in Antiquity*. Transaction Books, New Brunswick (USA) and London, pp. 89–92.

Zimmer–Tamakoshi, Laura (n.d.) 'Papua New Guinea', Countries and Their Cultures <http://www.everyculture.com> (accessed October 2010).

INDEX

A

accounting systems: innovation by women, 313; Neolithic use, 23, 61, 92; precursor to writing, 61

Ackerman, Kim: Australian Indigenous trade, 259–60

adat philosophy, Indonesia: based on nature, 239–40; centrality of women's roles, 240, 241, 242; inherent equality, 241, 242; integration with Islam, 239, 241, 242; men's roles, 240; threatened by Western power structures, 240, 241, 242; true matriarchal system, 19

African prehistory: agriculture, 163, 164, 165, 166; animal sacrifice, 163; art and religion, 167–8; boats and fishing, 165, 166; buildings, 161, 163, 165; colonisation and dispossession, 175–6; domestication of animals, 161, 164; earliest lifestyles, 161–7; female principle, 168, 170, 177; goddess symbolism, 168–71; matriarchal societies, 172–4, 176; Nile and northern Africa, 164–6, 172–3; peaceful nature, 161, 163, 168; pottery, 163, 164–5, 166; ritual burial, 164, 165–7; rock art, 164, 165, 167, 168; southern Africa, 166–7, 173–4; timeline, 162; trade, 165, 166

agriculture: Africa, 163, 164, 165, 166; Anatolian, 91, 92–3; Australian Indigenous practices, 247–8; Chinese Neolithic, 203, 205, 207, 209; European Neolithic women, 72–6; Ireland, 95; Japan, 219–20; Korea, 216–17; Mesolithic India, 184; Natufian settlements in Turkey, 76–81; Neolithic India, 185, 187–8; Oceania, 267, 274; Papua New Guinea, 267; role in changing status of women, 130–1; Saudi Arabian rock art evidence, 82; South America, 302, 304, 307; Thailand, 227, 229, 231; women's pioneering role, 316–17

Ahmed, Leila: changing status of women, 129–31, 134–6

Ainu people, Japan, 218–19

Allen, Paula Gunn: conflict resolution in North American societies, 295; impact of colonisation on Native American women, 295–6; myth as living tradition, 39; North American spiritual traditions, 292–3, 295; peaceful egalitarian early Americans, 291, 292

Altamira Cave, Spain: age of paintings, 53; bias in early interpretation of art, 16; meander symbols, 50

American prehistory: first arrivals, 285, 288; hunter-gatherers, 285, 288, 290, 301; matrilineal/matriarchal societies, 297, 300–1, 309–10; Mesoamerica, 300–1; North America, 288–300; South America, 301–10; timeline, 286–8

Anatolian prehistory *see* Çatal Hüyük

Andrews, Munya: Pacific navigation, 274, 276; symbolism of the Pleiades across cultures, 49–50, 196, 312

animal and bird imagery *see also* cave art; rock art: Africa, 167–8, 170; Çatal Hüyük, 89–90; Chinese goddesses, 213; Minoan Crete, 106–7; Natufian culture, 76, 78–9; Saudi Arabian rock art, 81–2

animal sacrifice: Africa, 163; early Indo-Europeans, 115, 122, 124; Minoan Crete, 108

Anthony, David: work supporting Maria Gimbutas, 6

Anthony, David and Dorcas Brown: origins of Indo-Europeans, 116, 117

anthropomorphic imagery: Çatal Hüyük, 88, 89, 97, 99; cave and rock art, 53–6; North American, 290; Oceania, 268, 273, 276; Old European cultures, 75, 76, 78; Thailand, 229, 236

art *see* cave art; prehistoric art; rock art; traditional arts

Australian Indigenous culture: age of rock art, 55, 246; circle symbol in women's art, 48; communication systems, 35; cupules, 251, 253; early lifestyle, 257–9; first arrivals, 246–8; impact of colonisation/development, 257, 258–9, 261; importance of 'country,' 243; kinship system, 260–1; Lake Mungo evidence, 248, 250; land management practices, 247–8, 258–8; modern resurgence, 261, 319; non-material culture, 20–1; oral transmission of stories, 35–9, 246; philosophies of nature, 143–54; process of remembering myths, 36–7; rock art styles and motifs, 249–57; snake symbolism, 243, 252, 253, 257; symbolism in rock art, 251–7; timeline, 244–5; trade, 259–60; visual symbols in stories, 38–9; women's and men's business, 243, 253, 257, 263; women's stories overlooked, 37; women's traditional roles, 261–3

Austronesian cultures *see also* Oceania's prehistory: differing impacts in the Pacific, 155; influence in Indonesia, 234, 236

B

Baghor, north-west India, 184

Bahn, Paul: critical of Maria Gimbutas, 9; definition of prehistoric art, 46; lack of Palaeolithic warlike images, 56; Neanderthal burial rituals, 53; processual 'New Archaeology', 17; 'scientific' view of rock art, 44–6

Banning, Ted: Göbekli Tepe settlement, 80–1

Barber, Elizabeth: Indo-European presence in China, 125–8; rules for transmission of myths, 34; women's clothing symbolic of status, 129–30

Baring, Anne and Jules Cashford: arts in Minoan Crete, 108; goddess myths and imagery similar across cultures, 62; Indo-European impact in Crete, 110; peaceful Çatal Hüyük life disrupted by nomadic warriors, 109; women diminished by Indo-European myths, 136–8

barkcloth (tapa) making: Indonesia, 236, 237; Oceania, 272–3, 281; Thailand, 227, 231

Barnes, Gina: Chinese Neolithic villages, 207; Chinese pottery development, 203, 205; Korean prehistory, 216–18; peaceful Chinese Neolithic lifestyle, 210

basket making: Australian Ngarrindjeri people, 314; North American prehistory, 290, 291, 297, 299

Beaker people, 109

Bednarik, Robert: earliest female figurines, 53; early dating of cultural beginnings, 17; evidence of early language, 29–30; evolution and spread of *Homo erectus*, 69–70; interpretation of images, 44; meander symbols, 50; Phosphene theory of art origins, 44–5

Bell, Diane: Australian Indigenous connection to land, 144; Australian Indigenous oral traditions, 36, 37–9; Australian Indigenous social systems, 261–2; Australian Indigenous women's roles in clothing and health care, 71; Australian Indigenous women's weaving, 48

Bhimbetka cave, India: earliest symbolic art, 43, 46, 50, 181

bias: art and culture, 15–18; definition of civilisation, 19–24; definition of matriarchy, 18–19; development of writing, 23–4; identifying in research, 13–25; myth as fiction or truth, 32–9; need to overcome in analysis of prehistory, 312–13; 'new' worlds outside Europe, 24; 'objectivity' and 'subjectivity,' 13–14; persistent image of ignorant savagery, 313; sex and gender roles, 13–15

bilum making: Oceania, 273

bird imagery *see* animal and bird imagery

boat building skills *see also* navigation: African prehistory, 165, 166; Flores Island, Indonesia, 233

Bronze Age *see also* Indo-European culture: Beaker people in Ireland, 109–10; China, 127, 210–12; fierce angular symbolism, 52; Indonesia, 236; Korea, 218; language indicators, 31; negative impact on women, 130, 135; reduced status of goddesses, 62, 141; Thailand, 229–30; warrior culture, 6, 72, 103, 109

Brown, Dorcas *see* Anthony, David and Dorcas Brown

buildings: biased interpretations and misconceptions, 317; Çatal Hüyük, 85–6; Chinese Neolithic cultures, 207, 209, 210; Japanese, 218, 219; Korean, 217; Mesolithic India, 184–5; Neolithic India, 185, 187–8; Sesklo culture, 75–6; South American, 302, 304, 305, 307–8; Thailand, 227, 231; Vinča culture, 75

Builth, Heather: Australian Indigenous eel 'farming,' 258–9

bull/horn symbolism *see also* cow symbolism: African goddess figures, 170; Indo-European religion, 141; Laussel figurine, 61; Minoan religion, 106; Neolithic Anatolia, 89–90

C

Campbell, Joseph: myths as communication, 32–3; sun and moon symbols, 47; support for Maria Gimbutas, 7; symbols indicating cross-cultural beliefs, 43

Capon, Edmond: Chinese pottery styles, 207; matrilineal culture in early China, 209–10

Carter, Susan: matriarchal society in Japan, 220, 222

Cartesian philosophy *see* Descartes, Rene

Cashford, Jules *see* Baring, Anne and Jules Cashford

Çatal Hüyük, Anatolia: accounting/record-keeping systems, 92; agriculture, 91, 92–3; art and sculpture, 86–90; bias in interpretation of culture, 86, 89, 90; buildings, 85–6; clothing, 85; goddess religion, 86–90; matrilineal culture, 17, 19; postprocessual research, 15; ritual burials, 86, 88; status of women, 85; textiles and weaving, 90–1, 92

Cavalli-Sforza, Luigi: work supporting Maria Gimbutas, 6

cave art *see also* Altamira; Lascaux; rock art: bias in early interpretation, 16; Spanish and French, 43–4

caves: symbolism, 141–2; wombs of life, 108

Chakrabarti, Dilip: errors in interpretation of Indian history, 179, 181; Mehrgarh civilisation, 187–8, 190–1; Mesolithic India, 182, 184–5; Palaeolithic India, 182; prominent female principle in India, 179

Chakravarty, Kalyan: meander symbols, 50; North American rock art, 288

Chariot Road: Indo-European access to Africa, 125, 164

Chauvet-Pont-d'Arc cave: goddess figurine, 55

chevron symbols: earliest examples, 51

China: 'great goddess,' 212–13; Bronze Age, 203, 210–12; contact with other cultures, 203; Indo-European influences, 125–8, 203, 210–12; matrilineal traditions, 209–10, 214–15; Neolithic period, 203, 205–10; presence of early humans, 203; secret women's writing, 213–14; traditional minority cultures, 215–16; women's status, 205, 209–10, 213–15, 216

Christ, Carol: gender bias, 14; support for Maria Gimbutas, 7

Christianity: bias towards, 33; impact on indigenous culture, 36, 196, 237; subordination of women, 136

circles as symbols in early art: cycles of life, 48–9; lunar and solar cycles, 46–7; use by Australian Indigenous women, 48

civilisation: bias in definition, 19–21; importance of writing, 21–4

clothing: Çatal Hüyük, 85; development by women, 71; Japanese, 218; Loulan people, West China, 127–8; Maree Clark, making/

wearing of possum-skin cloaks 5,000 BP, Australia, 313; Palaeolithic goddess figurines, 59; symbolic of status, 129–30

Clunies-Ross, Margaret: Australian Indigenous communication systems, 35

colonisation: affecting interpretation of indigenous culture, 36; destruction of African traditional life, 175–6; impact across Oceania, 273, 281, 282, 283–4; impact on traditional India, 198–9; loss of women's knowledge and power, 318–19; philosophical basis in Plato and Descartes, 153–4

colour symbolism: changes from Neolithic to Indo-European symbolism, 141–2; Native American arts, 299

conflict resolution: African matrilineal societies, 174; Australian Indigenous traditions, 56; indigenous communal societies, 116–17; Japanese prehistory, 219, 220; Minangkabau matrilineal society, Indonesia, 240; North American prehistory, 295; traditional Indian societies, 195

Confucius: subordination of women, 213–14

corporatisation: based on *power-over,* 152–3

cow symbolism *see also* bull/horn symbolism: African prehistory, 170; Indian prehistory, 190–1

Crete *see* Minoan Crete

cross symbols: earliest examples and meanings, 51

culture, origins of: bias in early interpretations, 16–17

cupules: Australian Indigenous culture, 251, 253; Indian cave art, 181; North America, 288; Oceania, 273; Saudi Arabian rock art, 82; symbolism, 43, 50, 181

Cycladic female deity figures: grave goods, 106; in Minoan Crete, 58, 105–6; representing stiff white goddess, 64

D

Dames, Michael: bias against 'subjective' research, 14; canons of mythology, 33–4; goddess in landscape, 64–5; support for Maria Gimbutas, 7

Danshilacuo, Hengde (He Mei): Chinese matrilineal traditions, 214, 215

Darwin, Charles: bias in evolutionary theory, 15–16; limitations to theory, 17–18

Dashu, Max: African female deities, 167; Chinese shamanic 'great goddess,' 212–13; definition of 'goddess,' 58; female principle in South

America, 308–9; Indian cow-boat and goddess figurine, 190–1; matrilineal society in Africa, 172–4
dating systems: differing European and Asian terminology, 159
Davidson, Hilda: moon and female deity, 61; study of 'goddess' mythology, 62
dé Ishtar, Zohl: Pacific women's traditions and colonisation, 279, 283–4; snake symbols in Australian Indigenous art, 51–2; transmission of Australian Indigenous women's culture, 38–9
DeMeo, James: alternative theory of rise of patriarchy, 119
Descartes, Rene: dualistic philosophy, 149, 152; influence on scientific/economic rationalism, 153; mechanistic world view, 151–2
Dillehay, Tom: early settlements in South America, 301–2; firestick farming in South America, 317
Diop, Cheikh: peaceful north African societies, 163
division of labour: Confucian influence, 214; contributing to rise of patriarchy, 119; effect on matrilineal society, 197, 214; hunter-gatherer societies in Old Europe, 70–2
domestication of animals: African prehistory, 161, 164; Chinese Neolithic cultures, 205, 207; Mesolithic India, 182; Neolithic India, 185, 187; Thailand's prehistory, 227
Dong Son culture, northern Vietnam: influence in Indonesia, 236–7
Doniger, Wendy: origins of modern India, 191–2
Donkoh, Wilhelmina J.: matrilineal society in Africa, 173–4
Dowson, T.A. *see* Lewis-Williams, J.D. and T.A. Dowson
Dravidian people, India, 192, 195–6

E
economic rationalism *see* scientific and economic rationalism
egg symbols: earliest examples and meanings, 52
Ehrenberg, Margaret: agriculture and women's status, 131; male and female hunter-gatherer roles in Old Europe, 70–2
Enheduanna, Sumerian high priestess and writer, 132, 138, 318
Entoptic/Shamanistic theory, 44–5
Eogan, George: interpretation of Irish Neolithic temple mounds, 94, 95, 96

evolution: Darwinian bias, 15–16; human species, 69–70
eye symbols: earliest examples and meanings, 52

F
Fagan, Brian: critical of Maria Gimbutas, 9; early American hunter-gatherers, 285, 288, 290; role of shamans, 295; warfare in Olmec culture, 300
Feest, Christian: changing lifestyles in early America, 290, 291
Feliks, John: observational theory of art origins, 45
female figurines: African prehistory, 167–71; evolution of female deity, 57–8; goddess figures, 58–64; Indonesia's prehistory, 235, 238; Japanese prehistory, 220–1, 223; male misinterpretation, 56–7; metaphysical meanings, 55, 57–64; Neolithic Europe, 57–8, 61–4; Neolithic India, 186–90; Palaeolithic, 56–7, 58–61; South American prehistory, 303, 304, 306, 308–9; Thailand's prehistory, 228
female principle; bias against, 33, 312; Çatal Hüyük, 110; central to African culture, 164, 168, 170, 177; declining power, 134; European Neolithic cultures, 74; future peace and harmony, 319; goddess culture of Old Europe, 3, 10, 311; implications for status of women, 11; Indian traditions, 67, 179, 188, 191, 193–5; Ireland, 94, 97; Minoan Crete, 102, 103, 111; Oceania, 284; permanence compared to male transience, 293; symbolism, 49–50, 67, 182; Thailand's prehistory, 231; widespread evidence in goddess figurines, 314–15
female symbols in early art see also female figurines: 51–2
Flannery, Tim: agriculture in Papua New Guinea, 267; Australian Indigenous lifestyle suited to environment, 247; climatic conditions influencing human development, 20; Lapita culture, 274
Flood, Josephine: Australian Indigenous art imagery, 253–5, 257; Australian Indigenous origins, 246, 248, 250; firestick farming, Australia, 317; semi-agriculture in Australia 30,000 BP, 316
Flores Island, Indonesia: early evidence of *Homo erectus*, 24, 69, 233; separate human species, *Homo floresiensis*, 233

food provision *see* agriculture; hunter-gatherer societies

Ford, Clyde: female principle central to African culture, 164, 168, 170; loss of African prehistory, 163–4

frog symbolism: Neolithic goddess figures, 63

Frymer-Kensky, Tikva: diminution of goddesses' power and women's status, 134; writing as indicator of women's status, 132

G

Gatusa, Lamu: Chinese matrilineal traditions, 214–15

Gero, Joan: gender bias, 14

Gimbutas, Marija: achievements and legacy, 7–11; analysis of Anatolian culture and religion, 88, 89–90; books by, 3; changing status of women, 129, 131, 139; contribution to understanding of prehistoric women's lives, 311–12; criticism of her views, 8–10, 119–20; Cycladic figurines of death/ regeneration, 106; definition of 'goddess,' 58; great goddess theory, 3–6; interdisciplinary methodology, 3, 9, 10, 17; interpretation of symbols in art, 43, 47, 50, 51–2; Neolithic agriculture, 72; Neolithic and Palaeolithic writing, 21, 23; peaceful nature of Neolithic life, 72, 74; preferred terminology, 18–19, 20, 21; Proto-Indo-European warlike invaders, 115–24; Sesklo culture, 75–6; supported by other scholars, 7–8; symbolism of goddesses' clothing, 59; types of Neolithic goddess figures, 61; Vinča culture, 75; women's religious roles in Neolithic Ireland, 94–5, 97, 99

Göbekli Tepe, Turkey, 78–81

god of the shining sky *see also* sky god (male): early Indo-European, 122

goddess concept: birth-giving, 63; cross-cultural parallels, 62; death and regeneration, 64, 138–9; earth goddess in hunter-gatherer cultures, 72; hearth and home, 63; landscape as embodiment, 64–5; life-creating, 63–4; meaning of 'goddess', 58; modern challenge to Cartesian world view, 153–4; reduced status in Bronze Age warrior societies, 62

goddess figures, African, 168–71

goddess figures, Asian: Japan, 219, 220, 222; Korea, 217; Thailand, 231

goddess figures of Old Europe: clothing symbolism, 59; death/regeneration symbolism, 88, 89–90, 97–8, 106; declining status indicative of women's loss of power, 136–9; findings of Marija Gimbutas, 3–6; male misinterpretation, 4; moon symbolism, 61; Neolithic examples, 61–4; Palaeolithic examples, 53–61; reduced status in warrior societies, 62, 122; role disputed by some critics, 9–10; Sesklo culture, 76; varying forms, 58–9

goddess figures, Indian: destruction by colonisation, 198–9; enduring status, 191, 193–5; images, 186, 190–1; Indo-European impact, 193, 194; origins, 193–4

gods, male *see also* god of the shining sky; sky god (male); sun god; thunder god: appropriation of female symbols, 140–1; early Indo-European, 122, 124; Neolithic types identified by Marija Gimbutas, 67; supplanting goddesses, 138–9

Goodall, Heather: Australian Indigenous process of remembering myths, 36

Goodison, Lucy and Morris, Christine: goddess figures in Minoan Crete, 106, 108

Göttner-Abendroth, Heide: alternative theory of rise of patriarchy, 119–20

grave goods *see also* ritual burial: Africa, 165–6; China, 207, 209, 210, 211–12; Mesolithic India, 184; Neolithic India, 187, 188, 191; Thailand, 227, 229–30

Griffin, Susan: damage caused by economic/ scientific rationalism, 153

Grimm, Jacob and Wilhelm: Eurocentric view of culture, 35–6

H

Harappa, Indian subcontinent, 181, 188–9, 190, 192, 193

Hauptmann, Harald: Nevali Cori settlement, 78

Hawkes, Jacquetta: Neolithic culture in Minoan Crete, 102–9

Hawthorne, Susan: colonial dispossession of women's food rights, 175–6

Heath, Carolyn: matrilineal Shipibo culture, 309–10

Heilbrunn Timeline of Art History: Neolithic Japanese hunter-gatherers, 219; Papua New Guinea stone sculptures, 258; pottery in China, 203; use of jade, 207; Valdivian figures, 303 hierarchic social structures *see also* Indo-European culture: early evidence in India, 185, 188, 190, 191; impact of colonisation, 237, 240; Indonesia's prehistory, 236–7, 240; Thailand's prehistory, 229, 230–1

Higham, Charles *see* Thosaret, Rachanie and Charles Higham

Hodder, Ian: bias in interpretation of Anatolian culture, 86, 89, 90

Homo erectus: capacity for art and language, 27–8; China, 203; early evidence in Flores, 24, 69, 233; evidence throughout India, 179, 181; evolution and spread, 69–70; presence in South-East Asia, 225, 233

Homo floresiensis, 233

Homo habilus: China, 203; evolution, 69; presence in South-East Asia, 225

Homo sapiens: archaic form, 69–70; China, 203; early evidence in India, 179, 181; migration to Australia, 247

Hongshan culture, China, 206, 210, 211

horn symbolism *see* bull/horn symbolism; cow symbolism

horse riding: practised by Proto-Indo-Europeans, 115–16, 117; related to Indo-European invasion, 3, 6

housing *see* buildings

hunter-gatherer societies: America, 285, 288, 290, 301; China, 205; Japan, 218–19; Korea, 216–17; male and female roles in Old Europe, 70–2; Thailand, 225, 227–8

I

India *see* Indian subcontinent

Indian subcontinent: 'development' and traditional arts, 199–202; female principle, 179, 194–5; goddesses throughout history, 193–5; matriarchal societies, 196–8; Mesolithic period, 182, 184–5; Neolithic period, 185–91; origins of modern India, 191–2; Palaeolithic lifestyles, 181–2; religion and nature, 192, 194–5; significant prehistory, 179–81; traditional life today, 195–8; women's roles and status, 182, 185, 188, 190–1, 194–202

Indo-European culture *see also* Bronze Age; Warrior Age: hierarchical and patriarchal nature, 3–6; human and animal sacrifices, 124, 211–12; impact in India, 185, 188, 190, 191, 193; influences in China, 125–8, 203, 210–12; Korean prehistory, 218; Old Europe, 3–6; Thailand's prehistory, 230–1

Indonesia's prehistory: Bronze Age, 236; earliest humans, 233; female figurines, 235, 238; hierarchic social structures, 236–7, 240; matrilineal societies, 239–42; Neolithic period, 234, 236; Palaeolithic period, 233; pottery, 234, 236; ritual burial, 237, 241; timeline, 226; use of symbols, 237, 241–2; weaving styles and motifs, 236, 237, 239, 242

intangible evidence, 27–39 *see also* religion; interpretation by Maria Gimbutas, 27; use in deciphering symbols, 312

Irish prehistory *see* Knowth, Ireland; Newgrange, Ireland

Iron Age: Thailand's prehistory, 230–1

J

jade: use in Neolithic China, 207, 210

Janson, H.W.: definition of art, 44

Japanese prehistory: agriculture, 219–20; buildings, 218, 219; clothing, 218; female figurines, 221, 222; goddesses, 219, 220, 222; pottery, 219–20; timeline, 226; tools, 219; use of symbols, 220, 222; women's status, 218, 220

Jeulmun people, Korea, 216–17

jewellery: Mesolithic India, 184; Neolithic India, 187–8; Thailand's prehistory, 227, 229; worked metal, 74

Jomon people, Japan, 216, 218, 219–20

K

Kehoe, Alice: Asian influences in South America, 300, 304–5; bias against female archaeologists, 15; cultural appropriation, 295–6; 'new archaeology', 17

Khasi people, India, 196–7

Kirch, Patrick: classification of Pacific cultures, 265; Lapita-style pottery in Indonesia and the Pacific, 234, 236, 273–4

Knossos, Crete *see* Minoan Crete

Knowth, Ireland *see also* Newgrange, Ireland: Neolithic circle images, 47; tombs as body of goddess, 64

Korean prehistory: agriculture, 216–17; Bronze Age, 218; buildings, 217; earliest human settlement, 216–17; goddesses, 217; Indo-

European influences, 218; Neolithic period, 217; pottery, 217; ritual burial, 217–18; rock art, 217; timeline, 226; women's status, 217

L
Lady of the Spiked Throne, The, 190–1
Lamarck, Jean-Baptiste: evolutionary theory ignored, 16
language development: Indian subcontinent, 192; prehistoric evidence, 27–30; reasons for change, 31; search for common source, 30–2; transmission of myth, 32–9; unproven theories, 30
Lapita pottery and culture: Indonesia, 234, 236; Pacific Islands, 273–4, 276–7
Lascaux Cave, France: bias in early interpretation of art, 16; evidence of rope, 71
Laussel figurine: moon symbolism, 60, 61; significance overlooked, 57
Lauter, Estella: critique of myth as fiction, 34
leatherwork: North American prehistory, 299–300
Lerner, Gerda: changing status of women in patriarchal societies, 132, 134, 135
Lespugne figurine: description, 58; part of ancient traditions, 57, 60; significance of clothing, 59
Lewis, E.D.: Indonesian matrilineal society, 242
Lewis-Williams, J.D. and T.A. Dowson: Entoptic/Shamanistic theory of art origins, 44–5
lines as symbols, 46
Liu, Li: Chinese Neolithic culture, 207, 209, 210
Loulan people: evidence of Indo-European origins, 125–8

M
Makilam: matrilineal society in Africa, 172–3
male gods *see* gods, male
male images: absent in Palaeolithic culture, 64, 67
Mann, Barbara Alice: matrilineal societies in North America, 297
Maori women's art and traditions, 282–3
Marler, Joan: matrilineal indigenous societies, 18; support for Maria Gimbutas, 8–11
Marshack, Alexander: capabilities of *Homo erectus*, 27; cognitive aspect of prehistoric art, 46; interpretation of meander symbolism, 50; lunar notation, 61; ritual aspect of art, 44

matriarchy *see also* matrilineal/matriarchal societies: alternative terminology, 19; characteristics, 220; Japanese prehistory, 220; variable definition, 18–19
matrilineal/matriarchal societies: absence of male images, 64; Africa, 172–4; China, 214–15; goddess imagery, 64; Indonesia, 239–42; Mesoamerica, 300–1; North America, 297; South America, 309–10; Oceania, 279–80; persistence despite patriarchy and colonisation, 315; traditional India, 196–8
matristic society: characteristics, 18–19
McGaw, Judith: gender bias in research, 14
meander symbols in early art, 50–1
Mehrgarh, north-west India, 181, 184–8, 190, 193
Mellaart, James: analysis of Anatolian culture, 83–93; Natufian culture, 76; Neolithic women's role overlooked, 15, 17
Memmott, Paul: and Carroll Go-Sam, early dwellings in Australia, 317; on Heather Builth and Australian Indigenous housing, 258–9
Mesoamerican prehistory: matrilineal/matriarchal cultures, 299–300; Olmec culture, 300
Mesolithic period: Indian subcontinent, 182–5
metalworking *see also* Bronze Age; Iron Age: Indonesia, 236, 237; Neolithic India, 187, 188; peaceful uses, 74; Thailand, 229–30
Michaels, Eric: Australian Indigenous oral traditions, 36, 37
Minangkabau matrilineal society, Indonesia: concept of *adat*, 239–41; conflict resolution, 240; Islam's role, 241, 242; threatened by Western power structures, 240, 241, 242; visual symbolism, 241
Minoan Crete: art and religion, 104, 105–8; buildings, 103, 105; caves as wombs of life, 108; clothing, 102–3; crafts, 105, 108–9; female principle in figurines, 102, 105–8; importance of women, 102; palace-temples, 103, 105; peaceful egalitarian lifestyle, 103; pottery, 108; snake, bull and axe symbols, 105, 106–8; trade, 108–9
Mohenjo-daro, north-west India, 181, 189, 193
moon symbolism in ancient art: forms and uses, 47; Palaeolithic/Neolithic goddess figures, 61
Morris, Christine *see* Goodison, Lucy and Christine Morris
Mosuo people, China, 214–15

Mukkim, Patricia: matrilineal society in India, 196–7
multidisciplinary research methods: supported by Luigi Cavalli-Sforza, 6; used by Maria Gimbutas, 3, 9, 10
Munda people, India, 192, 195
Munn, Nancy: transmission of Australian Indigenous women's culture, 38–9
myth and folklore: role in changing status of women, 136–40
myths: canons of Northern Hemisphere myth, 33–4; critique of myth as fiction, 32–4; modern definition, 32; rules for transmission, 34; theories on similarities, 35–6; validity as archaeological source, 32

N

Natufian culture: agriculture, 76, 81; art, 76, 77, 78–80, 81; description, 76; housing, 76, 78, 80; peaceful nature, 81; rituals, 78, 80–1; settlements, 78–81; tools, 76, 80, 81; women's activities, 81
navigation: in the Pacific, 274, 276
Nayah people, India, 197–8
Neolithic culture: Çatal Hüyük, Anatolia, 83–93; China, 203, 205–10; cross-cultural similarities and differences, 110–11; ending, 109–10; female principle, 110–11; goddess figures, 61–4; Indian subcontinent, 182–90; Indonesia, 234, 236; Knossos, Crete, 101–9; Korea, 217; Natufian cultures, 76–81; Newgrange and Knowth, Ireland, 93–101; Old Europe, 3–6, 57–8, 61–4, 65, 67; peaceful egalitarian lifestyle, 3–4, 6, 81, 88, 94; role of goddess, 3–4, 6; Saudi Arabian evidence, 81–2; secondary role of male gods, 67; Sesklo culture, 75–6; significance of stone circles, 65; Thailand, 229; trade, 92, 101, 108; Vinča culture, 75
Ness of Brodgar, Orkney Islands, 163
net symbols: earliest examples and meanings, 52
Nevali Cori, Turkey, 78
New Zealand cultures *see* Maori women's art and traditions
Newgrange, Ireland: agriculture, 95; art and religion, 97–101; buildings, 95–7; death/regeneration symbolism, 97–8; first inhabitants, 94–5; goddess forms in temple mounds, 64, 94, 99; macehead – differing

interpretations, 98, 99; Neolithic circle images, 47; pottery, 101; regenerative symbols, 65; temple mounds, 93–4, 96–7
Ngarrindjeri people: female creation principle, 49; oral traditions, 37–8; philosophy and connection to land, 49; rituals of life, 262; women's weaving, 48, 314
Nile valley *see also* African prehistory: art and religion, 167–8, 170; settlements, 164–6
North American prehistory: 'warlike' tribal life, 291, 292, 296; arts, 289, 290, 291, 297, 299, 300; basket making, 290, 291, 297, 299; conflict resolution, 295; hunter-gatherers, 285, 288, 290; impact of colonisation, 292–3, 295–6; pottery, 290, 291, 299; ritual burial, 291; rock art, 289, 300; social structure, 291–2, 297; spiritual traditions, 292–3, 295, 297; use of symbols, 297, 299–300; weaving and textiles, 290; women's status and roles, 290, 291–3, 295, 297
nüshu: women's secret writing, China, 213–14
Nzenza-Shand, Sekai: colonisation destroying African women's traditions, 176

O

O'Kelly, Michael: interpretation of Irish Neolithic temple mounds, 93–4, 96–7, 99, 101
O'Murchu, Diarmuid: support for Maria Gimbutas, 7
O'Sullivan, Muris: interpretation of Irish Neolithic mace-heads, 99
Oceania's prehistory: agriculture, 267, 274; arts, 268–73, 276–7, 280–3; barkcloth (tapa) making, 272–3, 281; boats and navigation, 267, 274–5; classification of original cultures, 265; creation myths, 267, 271, 272–3; female figurines, 270, 275, 278; impact of colonisation, 273, 279, 281, 282, 283–4; matrilineal societies, 279–80; Near Oceania, 265–73; Papua New Guinea, 267–73; pottery, 269, 271–2, 276–7; Remote Oceania, 273–84; timeline, 266; tools, 268, 277; use of symbols, 268–9, 272–3, 276, 281–2; weaving, 273, 277, 281–2, 283; women's status, 271, 280–4
Okpewho, Isidore: impact of colonisation on interpretation of indigenous culture, 36; theories on similarities in myths, 35–6

P

Pacific island cultures *see* Oceania's prehistory

Palaeolithic culture: goddess figures, 55, 58–61; Indian subcontinent, 181–2; Indonesia, 233; Japan, 218–19; Korea, 216–17; lack of warlike images, 56; Lower Palaeolithic figurines, 53; metaphysical features of rock and cave art, 53–6; Old Europe, 3–6, 53–61; Upper Palaeolithic figurines, 56–61

Papua New Guinea: arts, 268–73; barkcloth making, 272–3; *bilum* making, 272–3; creation myths, 267, 271, 272–3; early societies, 267–8; pottery, 269, 271–2

Parthenogenic goddess: Neolithic, 63–4

patriarchal society: loss of women's rights, 120, 122; reasons for development, 119–20

peaceful nature of prehistorical societies: Africa, 161, 163, 168; Chinese Neolithic lifestyle, 210; disrupted in Çatal Hüyük by nomadic warriors, 109; early Americans, 291, 292; lack of Palaeolithic warlike images, 56; Minoan Crete, 103; Natufian culture, 81; non-violent African hunter-gatherers, 161, 164, 166; Thai lifestyles before invasion, 227, 229–30

phallic symbols: Japan, 219–20; Neolithic goddess figures, 62; representing male force, 67; Thailand, 229, 231

Philippine women's art and traditions, 281–2

Phillipson, David: non-violent African hunter-gatherers, 161, 164, 166

philosophies: *see also adat* philosophy; early Indo-European, 145; female-focused, 153–4; Indigenous Australian, 143–4; influenced by Plato, 151–2; modern, 152–3; Platonic, 147–50; pre-Platonic, 143; stages of development, 153–4

Phosphene theory of art origins, 44–5

Pinker, Steven: common source of language, 31–2

Plato's philosophy: based on Indo-European warrior ethos, 147, 149–50; dualistic structure, 147–9; influence on later thinkers, 151–3; subordination of women and nature, 147–50

Pleiades, the: Australian Indigenous beliefs, 49–50; symbolism across cultures, 49–50, 196, 312; traditional Indian meanings, 196

Plumwood, Val: Australian Indigenous philosophies, 143; mechanistic view of nature and women, 152; Platonic subordination of nature and women, 147–50; recent responses to mechanistic world view, 153–4; stages in development of philosophies, 154–5

Polynesian cultures *see* Oceania's prehistory

pottery: Africa, 163, 164–5, 166; China, 203–10; cultural significance of designs, 173, 234, 236; Indonesia, 234, 236; Japan, 219–20; Korea, 217; Lapita style across the Pacific, 234, 236; Mesolithic India, 184–5; Minoan Crete, 108; Neolithic India, 187–8; North America, 290, 291, 299; Pacific islands, 276–7; Papua New Guinea, 269, 271–2; Sesklo culture, 76; South America, 304, 309–10; Thailand, 227, 229, 231; Vinča culture, 75; women's invention, 72, 313

prehistoric art *see also* cave art; rock art: evidence of language development, 29; significance of symbols, 41–6

Pringle, Heather: pre-Clovis people's hide garments, 313–14

processual archaeology: beginnings, 17; limitations, 8–10; reasons for change from peaceful to violent communities, 74

Proto-Indo-Europeans: art, 114; domestication of animals, 115–16, 118; invasion of Europe, 124–5; lifestyle, 115–16; origins and homelands, 117–18; patriarchal society, 116, 118–20, 122; religion, 122, 124; ritual burials, 124; spread to China, 125–8; use of horses, 115–16; warlike tendencies, 116, 118–20; weaving methods, 117, 127–8

R

rainbow symbols: earliest examples and meanings, 51–2

religion: African, 167–71; early Indo-European, 122, 124; gender bias in research, 14–15; impact on Indonesian culture, 236, 241, 242; limited Palaeolithic evidence, 58; Neolithic evidence, 75, 76, 80; overlooked in Palaeolithic culture studies, 56; role in changing status of women, 135–6

Renfrew, Colin: critical of Maria Gimbutas, 8; ignoring indigenous women, 15; influence, 9; 'New Archaeology', 17; variant reasons for end of peaceful Neolithic cultures, 74

ritual burial: Africa, 164, 165–7; Australian Indigenous example, 248; China, 207, 209, 210, 211–12; early Indo-European, 115, 124; Indonesia, 237, 241; Japan, 219, 220; Korea, 217–18; Loulan people in China, 125, 127–8;

Mesolithic India, 184; Neolithic India, 187, 188, 191; North America, 291; South America, 302, 304; Thailand, 227, 229–30
rock art *see also* cave art; prehistoric art: Africa, 164, 165, 167, 168; Australian Indigenous traditions, 37, 246, 249–57; interpretation of symbols, 44–6, 55–6; Korea, 217; metaphysical imagery, 53–6; North America, 289, 300; India, 181–2, 185; Saudi Arabia, 81–2; South America, 307–8
Rose, Deborah Bird: Australian Indigenous spiritual beliefs, 243, 262–3
Roughsey, Elsie: building Indigenous shelters, 317
Rudgley, Richard: biased approach to early writing, 24; early anthropomorphic images, 53
Ruhlen, Merritt: origins of language, 30–1, 32

S

sacrifice rituals: Africa, 163, 167; Çatal Hüyük, 88; Chinese Bronze Age, 211–12; early Indo-European societies, 115, 122, 124; Indian matrilineal society, 197; Minoan Crete, 108
Sahtouris, Elizabet: changing status of women under patriarchy, 134–5; earth goddess in hunter-gatherer cultures, 72; evolution and balance in nature, 145; limitations to Darwinian theory, 16, 17–18; support for Marija Gimbutas, 7–8
Sanday, Peggy: definition of matriarchy, 18; Indonesian matrilineal society, 239–41, 242; Minangkabau matriarchal society, 19
Saudi Arabia: rock art, 81–2
Schmandt-Besserat, Denise: early date of Sumerian writing, 151, 192; Neolithic accounting systems, 23, 61, 92, 126; patriarchal origins of clay tokens, 132
Schmidt, Klaus: Göbekli Tepe settlement, 78, 80
scientific and economic rationalism: control of natural world, 153; roots in Platonic and Cartesian philosophies, 152–3
'scientific' approach to archaeology *see also* processual archaeology: criticism of Marija Gimbutas, 8–10; rock art, 44–6
seafaring: *see also* boat building skills; navigation; as evidence of language development, 29–30
Sesklo culture: location and features, 75–6
Shamanistic theory of art origins *see* Entoptic/Shamanistic theory

shamans: Chinese 'great goddess', 212–13; gendered interpretations of role in early America, 295; indigenous Indian, 195; Korean goddess, 217; male role in cave art, 58; metaphysical role, 56; proposed as creators of early art, 45; reduced power in warlike American societies, 291; rituals linked to goddess myth, 62; role in Native American fighting rituals, 295; trance equated to death in African cave art, 167; wise woman status in China, 128
Shanker de Tourreil, Savithri: matrilineal society in India, 197–8
ship of the dead motif: Indonesia's prehistory, 237, 238
Shiva, Vandana: colonial impact on Indian women's traditions, 198
Shuwaymas, Saudi Arabia, 82
sky god (male) *see also* god of the shining sky: sun as symbol, 47
snake symbols: African goddess figures, 170; Australian Indigenous culture, 243, 252, 253, 257; earliest examples and meanings, 51; Indo-European religion, 141; Minoan religion, 106
Soffer, Olga: evidence of woven textiles, 59, 71
Solis, Ruth: city of Caral, South America, 307–8
South American prehistory: agriculture, 301, 304, 307; Asian influences, 304–5; buildings, 301, 304, 305, 307–8; city of Caral, 307–8; early human activity, 300; female figurines, 303, 304, 306, 308–9; female principle, 308–9; matrilineal Shipibo culture, 309–10; pottery, 304, 309–10; ritual burial, 301, 304; rock art, 307–8; use of symbols, 305, 308, 309–10; weaving and textiles, 305, 309–10
spiral symbols: earliest examples and meanings, 51
Spretnak, Charlene: support for Maria Gimbutas, 7
stamp-seals: Çatal Hüyük, 87, 88, 108; Minoan Crete, 108
Starhawk: appropriation of Native American culture, 296; European invaders' view of wilderness, 144; support for Maria Gimbutas, 7
stars as symbols in early art: the Pleiades, 49–50
status of women: beginning of decline, 131–4; changes in symbolic meanings, 140–2; China, 205, 209–10, 213–15, 216; Japan, 218, 220; Korea, 217; Oceania, 271, 280–4;

Palaeolithic/Neolithic equality, 129–30; role in agriculture, 130–1; role of Indo-European myth and folklore, 136–40; steps to patriarchal 'invisibility,' 134–6; Thailand, 229, 230–1

stiff white goddess: conflicting interpretations, 64

Stone, Merlin: critique of myth as fiction, 33

string *see also bilum*; weaving: apron worn by Palaeolithic goddess figurines, 59, 60; invention and early uses by women, 71–2; crafts in Oceania, 273, 277, 280

Stuart, Charles: 1840s Indigenous women's woven mats, 314

Sullivan, Agnes: Lapita culture and crafts, 277

sun god: Indo-European, 122

symbolism: Africa, 167–71; African goddess figures, 168–70; circles, 46–9; classification as 'male' or 'female,' 43–4; communication of women's ritual knowledge, 318; cross-cultural significance, 43; evidence in prehistoric art, 41–4; Indian goddess figures, 190–1, 193–4; Indonesia, 237, 241–2; Japanese prehistory, 220, 222; lines, 46; meanders, 50–1; North America, 297, 299–300; Oceania, 268–9, 272–3, 276, 281–2; other Palaeolithic symbols, 51–2; role of myth in deciphering, 312; 'scientific' interpretations, 44–6; South America, 305, 308, 309–10; stars, 49–50

T

tapa cloth *see* barkcloth (tapa) making

Tell Abu Hueyra, Syria, 78

Thailand's prehistory: agriculture, 227, 229, 231; Bronze Age, 229–30; buildings, 227, 231; Chinese influences, 229, 230–1; domestication of animals, 227; earliest humans, 225; female figurines, 228; female principle, 231; grave goods, 227, 229–30; hierarchical social structure, 229, 230–1; hunter-gatherer societies, 225, 227–8; Indo-European influences, 230–1; Iron Age, 230–1; jewellery, 227, 229; metalworking, 229–30; Neolithic period, 229; peaceful lifestyle, 229–30; pottery, 227, 229, 231; ritual burial, 227, 229–30; timeline, 226; tools, 225, 227, 231; traditional arts and crafts, 231–2; use of symbols, 229, 231; weapons, 229–31; women's status, 229, 230–1

Thosaret, Rachanie and Charles Higham: peaceful Thai lifestyles before invasion, 227, 229–30; Thailand as gateway to South-East Asia, 225

thunder god: Indo-European, 122

time: traditional societies' views, 48–9

timelines of prehistory: Africa, 162; Americas, 286–8; Australia, 244–5; China, 204, 226; human prehistory, x–xiii; India, 180–1; Indonesia, 226; Japan, 226; Korea, 226; Oceania, 266; Thailand, 226

Tongan women's art and traditions, 281

tools: Chinese Neolithic cultures, 205, 207, 209–10; Japanese prehistory, 219; metal, 74; Neolithic India, 187, 188; Oceania's prehistory, 268, 277; Palaeolithic India, 179, 181–2; Sesklo culture, 75–6; Thailand's prehistory, 225, 227, 231; women's use in Old Europe, 71–2; worked metal, 74

trade: African prehistory, 165, 166; Australian Indigenous culture, 259–60; Neolithic India, 187, 192

traditional arts: Indonesia, 234, 236, 237, 242; Oceania, 268–73, 276–7, 280–3

traditional cultures: Chinese minorities, 215–16; Indian subcontinent, 192, 195; Japanese Ainu, 218–19

triangle symbols: evidence of female principle, 315; female and male meanings, 65, 67, 182; Indian prehistory, 182

U

urbanisation: role in changing women's status, 131–2

V

V-shaped symbols: earliest examples, 51

Valdivian figurines, Ecuador, 298, 303, 304

Vinča culture: duration and features, 75

Vinča script: discovery by Marija Gimbutas, 75; possible meanings, 23

vulva symbols: earliest examples, 51; evidence of female principle, 314–15

W

war: evidence in early Indo-European societies, 118, 125; irrelevance to indigenous societies, 21; possible causes of social violence, 119–20; rare in Neolithic societies, 124–5

Warrior Age: Indo-European beginnings, 124–5

weapons: evidence in early Indo-European
societies, 118, 124; Thailand's prehistory,
229–31

weaving and textiles: Australian Indigenous
women, 48; early evidence of women's
use, 71; indicator of women's status, 130;
Indonesian styles and motifs, 236, 237,
239, 242; Neolithic Anatolian women,
90–1; Neolithic China, 210–11, 213; North
America, 290; Oceania, 273, 277, 281–2,
283; ritual symbolism in Africa, 173; South
America, 305, 309–10;spiritual connections,
237, 242; symbolic of women's roles in
prehistory, 319; Thailand, 229, 231; women
of Old Europe, 59

wheeled vehicles: use by Proto-Indo-Europeans,
116, 118

Willendorf figurine: Alexander Marshack's
interpretation, 57; description, 58

wolves: symbolic of female power and
oppression, 139–40

women's roles *see also* agriculture; pottery;
weaving: inventors and innovators, 313–14;
overlooked in traditional archaeology, 313

writing: Chinese secret women's script, 213–14,
318; earliest examples, 21–2; early Chinese
pictographs, 209; Indian subcontinent, 192;
invented by women, 318; Maria Gimbutas's
discoveries, 23; relevance to civilisation,
23–4; Vinča script, 23, 75

Y
Yangshao culture, China, 209–10

Z
zigzag symbols: earliest examples, 51

www.ingramcontent.com/pod-product-compliance
Lightning Source LLC
Chambersburg PA
CBHW080042280326
41935CB00014B/1758